GEORGE HENRY MORLING

'Our Beloved Principal'

A DEFINITIVE BIOGRAPHY

GREENWOOD PRESS
in association with
The Baptist Historical Society of New South Wales Inc
120 Herring Road, Macquarie Park, 2113 Australia
May, 2014

Cover

The line drawing (front cover) of 'Fairmount', 40 Charlotte Street, Ashfield which was The Baptist Theological College from 1934 to 1961 is by Sydney artist **Douglas Fielden Pratt** (1900-1972). Pratt developed his love for drawing when working as a Jackeroo at Singleton. Later he became a draftsman at the MWS&DB (Water Board) where a colleague encouraged him to develop his drawing and painting skills. He studied at the Royal Art Society's drawing classes and at Sydney Long's Etching School.

His sketches were published as postcards and included such prominent places as the Sydney Town Hall and St. Mary's Cathedral. The cover sketch of "Fairmount" was made somewhere between 1937 when the Ruggles wing was built and the early 1960's when 'Fairmount' was demolished.

GEORGE HENRY MORLING

'Our Beloved Principal'

Baptist Theological College of New South Wales
Australia
1923-1960

A DEFINITIVE BIOGRAPHY
by
Rev ER Rogers

Compiled and Edited by
Dr JM Stanhope

Foreword
Rev Dr K Manley

GREENWOOD PRESS
in association with
The Baptist Historical Society of New South Wales Inc,
120 Herring Road, Macquarie Park, 2113, Australia
May 2014

© **Copyright:**

GREENWOOD PRESS
in association with
The Baptist Historical Society of NSW Inc 2014.

This publication is copyright. Other than for the purposes and subject to the conditions of the Copyright Act no part of it in any form or by any means (electronic, mechanical, micro-copying photocopying or otherwise) may be reproduced, stored in a retrieval system or transmitted without the written permission of the publisher.

**Morling, George Henry, 'Our Beloved Principal' 1923-1960.
ER Rogers.**

ISBN 978-0-9876084-1-3

Prepared for publication by Bruce Thornton

FOREWORD

This comprehensive biography of George Henry Morling, one of the most influential and loved leaders among Baptists in Australia, has been a long time coming. Not that the value and necessity of it were ever doubted! Perhaps the task seemed too daunting as so many, around Australia and overseas, had personal memories of just how much his life, spirituality, and teaching had inspired them.

To be Principal of a Theological College for so many decades, a pastor remembered with deep affection by his congregations, an inspiring preacher at almost innumerable denominational and convention events to say nothing of memorable addresses at scores of weddings and funerals is to leave a legacy that is not easily analysed. Personal friendship and wise counsel endeared Morling to a great many people.

But here, at last, is the biography that so many, for so long, have wanted to read. At the same time, a new generation for whom the name 'Morling' simply means a widely respected Theological College have opportunity to learn about 'the Prof' as successive graduates called him before his retirement as long ago as 1960. Indeed, this book, together with a forthcoming history of the College now named after him, will greatly enhance the celebration of the College's centenary in 2016.

This biography will, however, be welcomed not only by Baptists but by fellow-evangelicals and, indeed, by all who wish to understand more of Australian religious life during the long years of Morling's ministry. Unable to attain the full academic honours for which he was undoubtedly gifted by the often unreasonable demands laid upon him by a denomination that was slow in coming to value the scholar-pastor, his contribution was typical of many from his era. Possibly frustrated by his own circumstances he nonetheless strongly encouraged younger students to pursue the opportunities that had been denied to him. That alone is part of his legacy that needs to be recognized and this writer is not alone in acknowledging a debt to GHM.

Even the casual reader will detect that several people have combined to make this book a reality. Several former students have sought to tell aspects of this story. Rev David Nicholas drafted a biography in the 1960s but for a variety of reasons its publication was delayed until quite recently.[1] Another former student and successor of Morling as Principal, Rev Ron Rogers carefully prepared two lectures on the Principal for the Baptist Historical Society of NSW in 1984. These were the basis of an entry on Morling he prepared for the *Australian Dictionary of Evangelical Biography* (1994)[2] The full text of Rogers' papers together with some of Morling's lectures and addresses were published in 1995.[3] A later Morling College graduate and faculty member, Dr Graeme Chatfield, prepared another dictionary entry in 2003.[4]

But a comprehensive biography was still needed. In a labour of love Rev Bruce Thornton published many of the Bible Studies written by Morling as well as his MA thesis on Francis of Assisi.[5] Apart from booklets and Bible Studies, Morling published only one book, *The Quest for Serenity* (1950*)*. However, there was considerable material available for a biography in church news reports, denominational reports and papers and in articles in *The Australian Baptist*. Of particular value were Morlings intermittent diaries which enrich this account with intimate revelations of a deep and humble spirituality that longed for a richer experience of God.

Special acknowledgements are due to Mrs Joan Whetton and Ms Judy Close who worked closely with Ron Rogers typing his material and, more recently, to Ron Robb and Dr John Stanhope, successive archivists of the NSW Baptist Historical Society. John has reviewed the Rogers' manuscript with great care, checking details and adding new material. Bruce Thornton has again prepared this book for publication. As one of a decreasing number of graduates proud to be numbered among 'Morling's men' I am grateful to all who have made this book possible.

As we recall his distinctive presence - and tell again our own stories of this extraordinary and lovable man of God - we cherish the hope that through this biography successive generations will honour the memory of George Henry Morling and thank God for him.

Ken R Manley

Baptist Theological College of NSW 1958-61
Lecturer in Church History, Morling College 1972-80
Principal, Whitley College, Melbourne, 1986-2000
Distinguished Professor of Church History, Whitley College,
University of Melbourne
Melbourne, February 2014.

---

[1] D Nicholas, *Journeys with God,* (Sydney, Baptist Historical Society of NSW Inc, 2002.)

[2] B Dickey (ed), *The Australian Dictionary of Evangelical Biography* (Sydney: Evangelical History Association, 1994), pp. 267-68.

[3] IB Thornton (ed), *George Henry Morling. The man and his message for today* (by ER Rogers with lectures and addresses by GH Morling) (Forest Lodge: Greenwood Press, 1995).

[4] T Larsen (ed), *Biographical Dictionary of Evangelicals* (Leicester:Inter-varsity Press, 2003), pp. 444-46.

[5] For a list of recent Morling titles see Page xiv

CONTENTS

Foreword iii

Contents vii

About the Author ix

Reflection xi

Introduction 1

1 The Early Years 7

2 Pastoral Preparation and Experience 15

3 Principal at Petersham 37

4 Principal at Granville 63

5 Principal at Ashfield 121

6 Principal Emeritus 331

7 Stirring Eulogy to an Outstanding Baptist 413

8 Selected Tributes 425

9. References 431

10 Select Bibliography 465

11 Appendices 469
      Morling College 471
      Theological Educators 473
      Presidential Address 475

12 Epilogue 489

13 Index 499

Rev Eric Ronald Rogers
1922-2008
student, scholar, writer,
pastor, preacher, Principal
mentor, man of God, friend.

'He being dead yet speaks'

REV ERIC RONALD ROGERS, BA, BD,ThM.

Eric Ronald Rogers (known as Ron) was born in South Australia on 16th June, 1922 the second of three children. Early in his life his mother died, their daughter went to live with an aunty and the two boys remained with their father.

In his early teens the father and the two boys moved to Sydney. Ron attended Sydney Boys' High School where he was dux at the Intermediate Certificate. At High School, scripture teachers Rev John Morley and Mr H.Alec Brown made a marked impression on him. Following the Intermediate Certificate Ron left school to work and study as an Accountant.

When Ron was about 16 his father took the two boys to Waverley Baptist Church where Ron was encouraged to attend Christian Endeavour. During an evening service Ron made an inward response to the gospel and was baptised on 30th June, 1940 by the Pastor Rev Ron Smith.

When Ron was nineteen he was called up for military service. Feeling an inward urge Ron applied to and was accepted by the Baptist Union of New South Wales for training for the ministry. During his College course Ron served as student pastor at Nowra, Port Kembla and Strathfield-Homebush churches. In his final year Ron was senior student and commenced degree studies at Sydney University. later gaining BA and BD degrees. He was encouraged by the Principal, GH Morling with whom he had a warm personal relationship. He regarded him as both a mentor and a model and a strong personal rapport developed.

At the conclusion of College Ron married Nancy McLeod of Black Mountain whom he met at Waverley Church. .

Ron's post College pastorates were at Matraville, Burwood and Epping. His ten year ministry at Epping was characterised by thoughtful and biblical expository preaching and the church grew significantly.

After a three year ministry at Hobart Baptist Tabernacle Ron returned to Sydney to the Baptist Theological College as Lecturer in New Testa-.

ment and Greek where his personal piety, his concern for people and his intellectual gifts soon became apparent

In 1971 Ron was appointed Vice-Principal and in 1974 Principal. Before taking up his appointment he spent an academic year at Ruschlikon Seminary, Switzerland earning a Master of Theology (Th.M.) degree.

Ron was greatly appreciated by Morling College students where his thoughtful lectures, the quality of his life and his personal relationships made a marked impression.

Throughout his ministerial career Ron greatly valued the counsel and advice of Principal Morling and gained much from their friendship and interaction. Rev Dr. Victor Eldridge who served with Ron on the College staff wrote of Ron - 'as his colleague on the staff of Morling College for more than twenty years I am aware of how much the qualities of the life of 'GHM' are reflected in him'.[1] When he retired in 1987 the students presented him with a book of essays entitled 'A Man of God - Essays in honour of Principal Ron Rogers'.

In retirement, Ron continued his work with the Baptist Historical Society of which he was President from 1992 to 2001.

Acknowledging the profound influence of George Henry Morling on the Baptist Union, the churches, students past and present, on the wider Christian community and on his own personal life Ron was passionate about the publication of a substantial volume about 'GHM' so that others could learn from and about him. The resources he garnered have contributed greatly to this book.

Ron died on 8th September 2008. He would be greatly pleased that this biography of 'George Henry Morling - Our Beloved Principal' has finally been published.

---

[1] IBruce Thornton (Ed), George Henry Morling - the man and his message for today, Greenwood Press, 1995. For further information about Rev Eric Ronald Rogers see IBruce Thornton (Ed), Making their Mark, NSW/ACT Baptist Biographies, Greenwood Press, 2012, Pages 244f.

GEORGE HENRY MORLING
A Reflection
Noel Vose

The outstanding gifts and achievements of George Henry Morling (1891-1974) have resulted in a number of attempts to record them in a biography. All have been helpful but incomplete. Since then, further extensive data has become available. Hence this book.

Noel Vose

The following reflection from yet another of his students, attempts to show the importance of detail, by offering one or two examples in which a word or even a date has thrown light upon the complex character of this remarkable man. Here is an example.

It is now 123 years since the birth of George Morling in 1891. It was a very different world. England was the heart of an Empire upon which the sun never set. In London the great Charles H. Spurgeon (1834-1892) still had a few more sermons to preach; writers like Kipling (1865-1936) and R. L. Stevenson (1850-1894) were successfully plying their trade, Queen Victoria (1837-1901) had another ten years to reign.

Victorian England was seriously religious, exemplified by the way the nation treated the Sabbath. On Sunday, England paused for the decorum of worship, prayer, and reading of the Bible. This was the world in which Charles Morling and Annie Hillman grew up. Both were English and confirmed Baptists in the Spurgeonic tradition. Both were deeply devout.

Charles had, at one time, approached Spurgeon with a view to studying at the Pastor's College. Serious health problems, probably Tuberculosis, made this impossible and brought about his immigration to Australia. His fiancée Annie Hillman, later joined him. Married life began in Ashfield New South Wales where their third child, George, was born. According to him, speaking as a mature adult, he "grew up in a loving household". But there is another side to the story: Charles and his wife were English to the core – as was their Sabbath. Household duties were minimal: no cooking was permitted nor was travel on Public Transport allowed (see page 10). Was the account exaggerated? Not at all. I had an English uncle who immigrated to Western Australia and became a

Pastor. He was happily married when I knew him and had a family of two daughters. In the late 1920's I was occasionally permitted to stay with them. Shoes were cleaned on Saturday; no cooking took place on Sunday. Saturday night was bath night in preparation for Sunday clothes.. Loud laughter and noisy behaviour were quietly checked.

These Sabbatarian facts raise an immediate question: What was the effect on young George, if any? In ***The Quest for Serenity*** he comments on his extremely nervous disposition in childhood. In his own words "Beset by debilitating fears" "Nights filled with dread" and a little later in life there were deeply embedded fears of possible spiritual failure. These facts receive no answer in the biography, but they are to be pondered as an important part of the story. This reminds the reader he is dealing with a very gifted, highly sensitive and complex character.

The book offers a multitude of insights to which there are not always answers. For instance, details of his health: What acute pain lies in his throw away line "I suffered with gout for 55 years"

What stories and sacrifices both for the college Principal and his family that they lived for most of his professional life under the same roof as his students - all single, sometimes boisterous, sometimes high spirited without regard for their immediate neighbours. Perhaps I should add a 'mea culpa' in light of the many quiet and thoughtful students from whom I learned much.

An area of prime interest is the Principal's inner life glimpsed occasionally in his diaries. To read them is to want to pray. In them we overhear something of his on-going journey with the triune God whom he loved and served. Many other topics are noted. For example the extraordinary number of committees and secretarial positions the young Principal Morling occupied.

As a final reflection, this comment:

A perceptive author in an essay on Love insists that in its highest form love is not primarily a relationship to a specific person but rather an orientation of character which determines the relationship of a person to the whole world

There, I believe, lies the secret of the greatly loved George Henry Morling.

I join Dr Ken Manley in commending Rev Bruce Thornton for publishing many of George Henry Morling's writings for a new generation for whom Morling is known only as the name of a College.

G Noel Vose
Darlington WA
March 2014.

Noel Vose came from Western Australia to study for the ministry at the Baptist Theological College of NSW (1947-50) of which George Henry Morling was Principal. While at College he earned an LTh Diploma.

Returning to Western Australia he was ordained and served the East Fremantle and Dalkeith churches (1951-58) during which time he gained BA and BEd degrees. From 1959 to 1963 Noel studied overseas at Northern Baptist Seminary and the University of Iowa (USA) gaining ThM and PhD degrees.

With Morling's encouragement and support Noel became the founding Principal of the Baptist Theological College of Western Australia serving from 1963-1990. He was President-General of the Baptist Union of Australia (1975-78) and the only Australian to date to be President of the Baptist World Alliance (1985-90).

Following his denominational service Noel was founding pastor (1991-1998) of the Parkerville (WA) Baptist Church. He now lives 'in retirement' at Darlington WA.

The Baptist Theological College of WA was recently named Vose Seminary in his honour.

BOOKS BY OR ABOUT GH MORLING

IB Thornton *(ed)*, ***George Henry Morling, The Man and his messsage for Today*** (Greenwood Press, 1995)

GH Morling, ***The Quest for Serenity*** (Young and Morling 1951, Second Edition Morling Press, 2002) with questions for discussion.

GH Morling, ***Living with the Holy Spirit*** - studies in the Holy Spirit with questions for discussion (Morling Press 2004)

GH Morling, ***The Franciscan Spirit and other Writings*** - Morlings MA thesis; his studies in Ephesians, Philippians and the will of God. (Baptist Historical Society of NSW BHS 2008).

GH Morling, ***The Upper Room Discourses*** - studies in John 14-17 and the First Epistle of John (BHS 2010)

GH Morling, ***The Incomparable Christ*** - Selected studies in Luke's Gospel, Marks' Gospel, Acts, Colossians, Hebrews and 1 Peter. (BHS 2010)

DR Nicholas, ***Journeys with God.*** A digest of conversations with GHM during his later life.(BHS 2010)

GH Morling, ***The Romance of the Soul***. - brief studies in the Song of Solomon with epilogue by T.Howard Crago (BHS 2010)

GH Morling, ***Jesus and the Life of Prayer*** (BHS 2010)

GH Morling, ***Living in the Will of God,*** - studies in the will of God. (BHS 2010.)

GH Morling, ***The Acts of the Holy Spirit*** - studies in the Acts of the Apostles (BHS 2011)

GH Morling, ***Faith and Works*** - studies in the Epistle of James (BHS 2010)

GH Morling, ***Amos/Hosea*** - studies in the eighth century prophets (BHS 2011)

Books available from Baptist Historical Society of NSW Inc
Website. http://www.baptisthistory.org.au - click on shop.

INTRODUCTION

THE REV GH MORLING, OBE, MA.
'Our Beloved Principal'

INTRODUCTION

In October 1937, the Central Baptist Church was opened and Principal Morling shared in the celebrations. JA Packer, Editor of *The Australian Baptist*, reporting the event, wrote 'Principal Morling is always at his best, and always speaks with conviction and to edification. He is too near as yet to adequately assess his value to the denomination, but all realise at least that he is a great soul, a fervent witness to the Baptist faith, and a flaming evangelist of the Cross of Christ'.[a]

Now some fifty years later[b] we concur with the preliminary estimate and are in a better position to assess the significance of the contribution he made to the Christian cause and to the Baptist denomination in particular. Principal BG Wright said in his memorable and moving eulogy at the funeral service of his predecessor, 'it is the stature of the Principal which makes it so difficult to paint his portrait or delineate his character. My brush is too short, my canvas too small and I am unskilled in mixing such colours. We must measure the sky before we can measure the man'[2,b]

The Baptist movement in Australia has thrust up few outstanding personalities. There have been a Mead in South Australia, a Goble in Victoria and a Tinsley in New South Wales, each of whom has exercised a notable pastoral ministry. Principal Morling spoke of 'three of the greatest Australian Baptists', Silas Mead, Samuel Chapman and Thomas Porter, and said of them, 'Perhaps no Church in our land could boast of men of greater calibre. All were able, in massiveness of personality, in weight of judgment, in the suggestion of reserves of strength. All were difficult fully to know, because there was so much to know'[3] However, it is arguable that in the history of Australian Baptists no one has been more influential or more universally loved than George Henry Morling, 'our beloved Principal'.

---

[a] *The Australian Baptist,* 26 October 1937, Page 4
[b] Rogers wrote this in 1987

For a period of almost forty years,[c] first as Acting Principal, then as Principal of the Theological College, he had a moulding influence on hundreds of students. As they graduated, they went out to exercise ministries not only in NSW but also throughout Australia and around the world. His influence was extended and perpetuated by the many men who followed him into theological teaching.

Moreover, Principal Morling gently steered NSW Baptists through a turbulent time, and all this in a critical period of world history. He came to office in the aftermath of World War 1. For the young, many of the established conventions and certainties of life had been challenged in the cauldron of war and they were open to and looking for change. Australian Baptists began to become aware of literary criticism and its implication for Biblical studies. The effect on theological teachers and students was unsettling. The resignation of Rev Alexander Gordon, MA, the first Principal of the College, and the exodus of many young ministers from Baptist ranks into the ministry of other denominations or into secular callings was in some measure due to the ferment of thought created by the challenge of new ways of looking at the Bible. Into the midst of this came the young pastor, George Morling.

Co-incident with the onset of critical Biblical scholarship there arose among NSW Baptists earnest and sometimes heated discussions about the details of Christ's Second Coming. George Morling took up his leadership role in the midst of eschatological disputes. By keeping aloof from the debates, refusing to take sides and setting himself to the task of patient teaching, he helped the Union move into calmer waters and more productive enterprises. When later the Union was agonising over the ecumenical issue he did not become a protagonist for either side but went steadily about his business of training men for the Master's service in a responsible way.

The one contentious and potentially divisive issue in which he played a leading part had to do with the 'charismatic' movement. Probably he felt drawn into this because of his consuming interest in the doctrine and experience of the Holy Spirit. His counsel was for caution, balance, understanding and tolerance. He did not accept some of the interpretations and emphases of the charismatic movement but he was glad to see a new interest in, and openness to, the Holy Spirit.

---

[c] 1921-1960

His influence was felt through the contribution he made by a fervent advocacy of evangelism and by a theological undergirding of the evangelical efforts that marked the 1920s and 1930s.

Though he was passionately committed to theological education he was not circumscribed in his vision and sympathies. He was pre-eminently a 'churchman' and showed his commitment to the ideal of the Baptist Union by visiting the churches of the State first promoting the Foreign Mission and subsequently the Home Mission. He became in 1929, as a comparatively young man, the President of the Baptist Union of New South Wales. Nevertheless his concern was limited neither to his home State nor to the Baptist denomination. He was a Christian, and an evangelical Christian, and identified himself with the evangelical emphasis, whether in Scripture Union, the Inter-Varsity Evangelical Unions, the Convention Movement or the Evangelical Alliance. He had close friendships with prominent evangelicals of other denominations, especially those of the Sydney Anglican diocese.

He threw himself into the affairs of the Baptist Union of Australia, and regularly ministered through all the State Unions. As a universally respected 'father figure' and man of God, he became in retirement for three years President-General of the Baptist Union of Australia.

In any attempt to name leading personalities of Australian Baptist history George Henry Morling should be accorded a place in the first rank.

THE EARLY YEARS
1891-1912

Charles and Annie Morling

CHAPTER 1 - THE EARLY YEARS

George Henry Morling was born on 21 November 1891, the third child of Charles and Annie Morling (*nee* Hillman).

Charles Ablett Morling grew to manhood an England. He was a Baptist, and as a young man interviewed CH Spurgeon with a view to entering Pastors' College to train for the ministry. However that was not to be. He became consumptive (tuberculous) and on the advice of his doctor came to Australia in the hope that the warmer climate would help him recover his health. The hope was fulfilled. He settled in Sydney and when on 4 June 1882, the Petersham Baptist Church was formed, he was one of the sixteen foundation members. He was later Secretary of the Ashfield Baptist Church, which became the family's home church.

Meanwhile, patiently waiting in England, was Annie Hillman, the girl on whom he had set his heart and his hopes. Orphaned early in childhood, she had grown up in an atmosphere of harsh repression. In God's good providence she came to a saving knowledge of Christ. At the age of 23 Annie was baptized at the Queen's Square Baptist Church in Brighton, England, by Rev JS Geale, one of the earliest graduates of Spurgeon's Pastors' College. At Brighton, she met her husband-to-be when he was stationed there as a colporteur distributing Bibles and Christian literature. Both Charles and Annie stood firmly in the Spurgeonic tradition. This was evident in the firmness of their convictions and the quality of their lives.

The waiting period for them was to be long. It was not until 6 April 1885 that they stood side by side in the hospitable home of Mr and Mrs EG Selwood and were united in marriage by the Petersham pastor, Rev JA Soper, himself another of Spurgeon's men. The chief bridesmaid, Miss Annie Ridge, came from England to accompany and stand beside her friend.[d]

Charles and Annie set up their home and a grocery business on the corner of Arthur and Holden Streets, Ashfield, opposite the site where in less than a year 'a compact little church' stood. When the Morlings were

---

[d] She became Mrs Maundrell, and both she and Mrs Selwood were present at the CA Morling Golden Wedding Anniversary celebration.

married the Ashfield Baptist Church had been in existence for only a matter of months and was holding its meetings in the School of Arts, with Rev F Hibberd, the first of Spurgeon's men to come to Australia, as its pastor.

The newly-weds at once became members at Ashfield and began a notable family association with that church. Charles Morling was at different times Treasurer, Secretary, Sunday School Superintendent, Bible Class leader and Union delegate of the church.

To the home behind the grocer's shop there came first a daughter Ethel, a son William, and then another son, George Henry. In 1894 yet another son, Thomas Ablett, was born, but he did not survive until his first birthday.

Discipline was firm in the home with its Victorian emphasis on proper order and uprightness. Principal Emeritus BG Wright, in the eulogy to which reference has already been made, described the Morling home as "simple, austere, strong in the strict high ethic of the Baptist faith". For George, home life was strict but loving. His childhood was also marked by 'nervousness', fears and a speech impediment, which was precipitated by his hearing a loud cannon shot at a military display the family attended.[4]

Even in a period when Sunday observance ranked high in the scale of Christian piety the sabbatarianism of the Morling home was a matter of comment. No hot meals, not the simplest chores and no travel in public transport were countenanced. However love was not lacking in the home. At the celebration of the Golden Wedding of his parents, George, as reported by Rev W Cleugh Black (yet another Spurgeon's man), 'referred to his parental heritage of gifts and graces, attributing all honour to his beloved parents, who enshrined in their characters and revealed in the ministries of the home, the most exalted ideals of the Christian faith'.[5]

'The majority of speakers', said Cleugh Black in characteristic style, 'alluded to the granitic character and theological mind of the father, and to the winsome nature and Christlike character of the mother, both of whom had come to life's sunset time with the love-light in their eyes undimmed'.

George never forgot the Sunday nights when his mother gathered her family around her and spoke to them of the Lord Jesus and His love.

George began school at Ashfield Public School and, according to schoolboy friend Bert, later Rev Dr AT Whale, joined fully in the rough and tumble of the schoolyard while at the same time excelling in his studies. However, behind this quite normal boyhood there was another aspect of great significance. In a talk given in later days to ministers he said 'I had a disturbed childhood - was a queer little kid. In the setting of a lovely Christian home I was subject to fear'. He traced the severe speech impediment with which he had to battle for so long to this source. And how manfully he battled against it! Mrs Mary McGee, another childhood playmate, remembers him standing before a mirror struggling to do his voice production exercises and making the strangest sounds.

In *The Quest for Serenity*, the book in which he traced his spiritual pilgrimage, he wrote, 'I carried from childhood into riper years a legacy of nervous weakness. In earlier years I was beset with debilitating fears. There were the usual distresses associated with a highly sensitive nature, and there were others beyond the ordinary. I had eerie experiences of going off into nothingness, which filled nights with dread ... The child is father of the man. I emerged into normal physically healthy youth and manhood and tendencies to nervous unbalance remained. Life education for me has meant largely the control and direction of these elements of my inheritance'.

George switched to Croydon Public School and later again to a private college at Ashfield, continuing to show outstanding scholastic ability. As he grew older George added to the usual domestic tasks that of helping to deliver groceries to nearby customers. The delivery boy received from his father threepence a week to bank and halfpenny to spend.

Meanwhile spiritual impressions accumulated and deepened. The influence of a truly Christian home was reinforced by the ministry of the church. In manhood George paid tribute to Mr TH Vaughan, a faithful Sunday School teacher. Speaking in the Burton Street Church at the inaugural meeting of the Young Men's Missionary League, when he was forty years of age, he recalled a boyhood experience at Ashfield. He was reading the hymn, 'The Son of God goes forth to war ... who follows in His train?' when the familiar words suddenly took on new meaning. Life was a battle and that he had to take sides. During the year that he was President of the Baptist Union of NSW he led a convention at the Auburn Church and in the course of it gave a personal testimony. He paid tribute to home experiences but said that it was the awful dread that his life would be a failure that drove him to the Saviour. Sometimes when facing examinations or other tests he would be awakened by a fearful sweat, so afraid was he of failure. Of teenage turbulence or rebelliousness there is no sign in the record. The spiritual dimension of life was never seriously questioned. Under the combined influence of home and church there was a natural response to spiritual reality.

1908
At the age of 17 George confessed Jesus Christ as his Saviour and was baptised under the ministry of Rev WM Cartwright[e]. In 1908 Cartwright became President of the Baptist Union of New South Wales, at thirty the youngest President by far the Union had had. Moreover, he was still single, until 1909.

1909-10
George was received into the membership of the Ashfield Baptist Church on 29 July 1909. In February 1910 when George Morling was eighteen and had just begun to teach and at the same time to undertake studies at Sydney University, the Morling family left the Ashfield Church and became members of Burwood church.[6] Ashfield reported - 'It with much regret we have to refer to the early removal of Mr CA Morling and family to Concord. He has already resigned his position as secretary of the church and as deacon to make room for his successor'.[7] After a warm-hearted tribute the report concluded 'We wish them much happiness in their new home'.

The Concord Church was in process of formation, and Mr CA Morling apparently threw his weight into the new venture. As reported in *The Baptist* of 1 September 1910, there was a stone-laying ceremony at Concord. At the close of the function it was Mr CA Morling who moved the vote of thanks.[8]

Was CA Morling disturbed by the direction Cartwright was taking the Ashfield church? At the end of 1910 Cartwright accepted a call to the

---
[e] Father of Mrs AT (Kath) Iliffe

Baptist Church in the socially needy Melbourne suburb of Fitzroy and the Morlings returned to the Ashfield Church in October 1910.

After matriculating George gained a position as a tutor and junior teacher of general subjects at a Grammar School. By night the young teacher embarked upon studies towards a Bachelor of Arts degree at Sydney University, a course not common among Baptists at that time. There were on the staff at Sydney University a number of outstanding Christian men. Four of them in particular had a profound influence on George Morling, the geologist Sir Edgeworth David, the Shakespearian scholar Professor (later Sir) Mungo MacCallum, the philosopher Sir Francis Anderson and the historian Professor (later Sir) George A Wood. By MacCallum he was introduced to the painstaking study of a literary text and so began to master the principles of exegesis that would make his later teaching so effective. Francis Anderson, the Christian philosopher, laid the basis for the apologetic approach to problems that marked his early ministry. George Wood imbued him with such an interest in history to lead him subsequently to a master's degree in that field of study.

1912

Despite the dark shadow of fear that fell on him from time to time, life for George proceeded fairly smoothly. He had the average young Australian's interest in sport. Cricket he played fairly well but tennis was his preferred sport. In 1912/13 he and George Lusted, later to be his brother-in-law, were members of the doubles team that won the Western Suburbs District Championship. Then he teamed with A Fraser to win what was called the State C Grade Doubles Average.

With the end of his Bachelor of Arts program in sight George Morling found his thoughts becoming increasingly directed towards the possibility of pastoral ministry. His call to the ministry came as a gentle insistent pressure from God and an answering and growing desire on his own part.

PASTORAL PREPARATION AND EXPERIENCE
1913-1922

George Morling

CHAPTER 2 – PASTORAL PREPARATION AND EXPERIENCE

1913

In 'June 1913 (he) commenced work under Home Mission'[9], having applied to the Home Mission Committee of the Union to become a candidate for the ministry. He was 21 and had just had his BA degree conferred. He was accepted. 'His first preaching experience was in a public hall at East Hills, Sydney'.[10] Soon after, he was sent to Tamworth, in country New South Wales, for his pre-ministry experience - 'Mr Morling to Tamworth, Salary £2.5.0 per month and board'.[11] There he encountered great inner turmoil, but emerged from these struggles with a strong assurance of salvation.

When George returned from evening studies at University, his mother would have supper waiting for him in the kitchen. On the night of his acceptance by the Home Mission Committee he found supper laid out in the dining room. 'George', she said, 'you are a minister now'. That attitude entered deeply into George Morling's thinking and led him always to maintain an exalted view of the ministry.

In those days it was customary to put candidates to the proof in a pastoral situation. George was appointed assistant to the incoming pastor of Tamworth, Rev FJ Dunkley, from Longford in Tasmania. They both began on 14 December.

The period of service for the fledgling minister was quite brief and yet eventful. He had preached previously from time to time. Indeed there is a story that his mother went with him to his first preaching engagement in a public hall at East Hills. Afterwards he asked her, 'Did I preach long enough?' He often recalled her answer, 'You preached quite long enough'.

With a continuing speech impediment, preaching was often very difficult. To overcome the problem he would practise his sermons in the empty church on Saturday night or, like Francis of Assisi, would preach them to his horse and any creature that cared to listen as he drove the Church buggy to outstations.

AT Whale wrote many years after that at Tamworth the student pastor received his baptism of fire. It seems likely that the trouble was not from fightings without but from fears within. Inexperienced, he felt the strain of meeting new demands. There was induced in him a mood of dark self-questioning. In *The Quest for Serenity* he shares something of this experience. 'There came a time in young manhood when although I was a sincere and outwardly loyal disciple, doubts and fears assailed me'. He one day cycled down to the Peel River and spent time examining his life before God. He was deeply troubled, for he had come to doubt his standing in Christ. That day, as it seemed to him, Christ came and spoke peace to his disturbed heart. 'The Sun rising from on high soon visited me. I became assured of sonship with God and I have never for a moment wavered in that assurance'. It was a great day in his experience but there would be many other battles to be fought because of a weakened nervous constitution.

1914

His stay in Tamworth was brief. On 27 January 1914, the Home Mission Committee appointed him to Hurlstone Park under the supervision of Rev W Cleugh Black of Dulwich Hill. Cleugh Black had pioneered a circuit of churches including Hurlstone Park and Campsie. His new assistant received £6.10.0 per month.

His ministry at Tamworth was appreciated. On 2 March 1914, there was a farewell meeting for him, presided over by Rev FJ Dunkley, who said that he and the church officers 'were unanimous in their expressions of appreciation of Mr Morling, both as a pastor and as a man. Always diligent alike in his studies and in his ministry, ever ready to do anything for the good of the cause and the exaltation of Jesus Christ. Mr Morling's ministry and fellowship had been truly profitable to all, and his popularity among the young people greatly impressed..By sheer merit he had won his way into all hearts'.

In March he took up his new appointment. He was required to study under the direction of the Education Committee of the NSW Baptist Union. Being a university graduate he was exempted from preparing for the usual preliminary examinations. What was prescribed for him was a study of James Orr's *The Christian View of God and the World*. He was greatly challenged by that book and readily acknowledged his debt to it. He wrote, 'The writer will never forget the combined intellectual and spiritual uplift which he received when, as a student in his first year, he read Professor Orr's masterly book *The Christian View of God and the World*. The challenge to the mind gave a new direction to the spirit'.[12]

Morling threw himself into his work under Cleugh Black but his delicate nervous system protested. He was taught by Rev Thomas R Coleman the deeper things of God, which helped him persevere in training. The life of holiness ("experimental religion' Morling called it) was to become a major theme of his minstry. At the May meeting of the Home Missions Committee the Superintendent, Rev AJ Waldock, reported that 'Mr Morling was laid aside for a month'. Six weeks later at the June meeting he further reported that 'Mr Morling was still unable to preach and recommended that he be retained for visiting only at .£3 per month'. He suffered a nervous breakdown because of intense inner strain as he sought a special experience of the Holy Spirit.

Meanwhile 'under the preaching of Rev T Coleman at Hurlstone Park eight souls were won on May 24th'.[13] This was during the period of George Morling's indisposition and it seems likely that this is how the two men were brought together. 'God brought him into a close friendship with a senior Welsh minister who for him was a true father in God, TR Coleman by name. Mr Coleman[f] had been through the Welsh Revival and had worked with spiritual giants like Prebendary Carlisle, founder of the Church Army, and the Rev Hugh Price Hughes, who inaugurated the Central Methodist Missions. Coleman recounted incidents of a time when the tide of the Spirit was high. Interest in divine possibilities was awakened, instruction in the deep things of God imparted and generous love given. When this dear man was near to 'glory' (some eighteen years later) he sent for his young friend, George Morling, and with face aglow with the light of heaven, laid his hands on his head and in the name of Christ blessed him.[14] At TR Coleman's funeral service the younger man 'in a brief but tenderly expressed address said they remembered that day a very exceptional life. He had a right to speak, as Mr Coleman was his spiritual father in a very real sense. He had taught him the deep things of God'.[15]

George Morling emerged from his breakdown. When war broke out in August, he offered for military service. Apparently he was not accepted and in view of his recent record of health this is not surprising.

With the outbreak of the war tremendous interest was stirred in the second coming of Christ. 'A Simple Confession of Faith' was published on the

----
[f] TR Coleman was a distant relative of Gladys Rees, later to become Mrs GH Morling.

subject.[16] Among the 25 signatories was P (*sic*) H Morling, BA. It is clear from the nature of the 'Confession' that at that time George Morling accepted the Futurist position. In his later ministry, he was reluctant to commit himself to any one theory of the coming.

In September he sat for his examination on Orr's book and, despite his serious setback during the year, was successful, being awarded 93%.

Although his appointment had been to Hurlstone Park he also became responsible for a new work at East Hills. He saw the building of the first East Hills Baptist church. 'Pastor Morling, BA whose genial personality and splendid character have endeared him to the people and whose organising ability was largely responsible for the splendid success of the day'.[17]

Pastor GH Morling, BA of Hurlstone Park, Pastor E Coleman of Blackheath,[g] and Pastor W Wearne of Walla had completed pre-college studies under the NSW Education Committee, and were selected for College in 1915. They would go to Melbourne to study in the Victorian Baptist College under Principal WH Holdsworth.

Rev W Cleugh Black reported Morling's farewell - 'The Baptists of Hurlstone Park and East Hills are in deep mourning, and would, if possible, return to ancient sartorial customs, by wearing sackcloth and ashes on account of the departure for a season of their beloved student-pastor, George Morling, BA, whose sojourn amongst them has been all too short. His ministry has been most fragrant and fruitful, and is a fine prophecy and promise of a happy and helpful ministry to be exercised by him in coming days'.

The article also recorded the gifts and good wishes extended to him by the several churches.[h]

1915
At the College Commencement Service held early in March at the Collins Street Church the speaker was Rev TE Ruth, pastor of the church and denominational gadfly. With his subject, 'A Plea for the Prophet', Ruth

---

[g] Enos Coleman became one of GHM's closest friends, and later his brother-in-law.

[h] JS cannot verify this quotation.

insisted that the great need was prophets in the pulpit, not priests in the sanctuary.

Ruth, regular contributor to *The Australian Baptist*, had some months previously authored an article that stirred up controversy. The title was 'What is the Bible?' and in it he presented what were then 'modern' views of the Bible.

Writing some years later, AT Whale recalled that 'whilst at Melbourne College the future Principal still won merit, but longed for the ministry again, for as he once wrote 'fagging heresies shrivels the soul'.

He did indeed win merit in Melbourne. Considering his speech problems it is a remarkable tribute to his character that he won a prize in what was variously described as elocution and voice production. His academic results were excellent but his ability was nowhere more evident than in the first place he gained in Apologetics. For that course, taken by Professor Rentoul of Ormond (Presbyterian) College, the students of both Presbyterian and Baptist Colleges came together. GH Morling topped all candidates with 83.5%. This aptitude doubtless influenced his subsequent early ministry.

George Morling's basic stance was traditional and strongly conservative. Though he had to come to terms with the ideas of critical scholarship they had little appeal for him. His approach was 'apologetic'; he was concerned to show how 'modern scholarship' could be seen as a defender of the faith. This was a distinct element in his early preaching.

Gilbert Wright said of him, 'He would often speak of the academic successes of his contemporaries, who were especially gifted, but never of himself'.[18]

He was disappointed with his overall training as a preparation for the work he was subsequently to do. AT Whale years later wrote him a letter asking why he did not sooner proceed with his Master of Arts studies. In reply he indicated that Principal Holdsworth held him back from that course. 'I am afraid', he wrote, 'that my theological education was very badly done'. It was subsequently to prove difficult for him to find time and strength to remedy some of the defects of his divided course, part in Melbourne, part in Sydney, and part extramural.

At an inter-state convention in 1912 a decision was taken to set up an

Australian Baptist College within three years and it was envisaged that this would be a development of the Victorian Baptist College. With the period running out the Victorian Union advised the other States that it could not carry out the Federal scheme. It would not be proper to train students from other States without charge, as it had been doing. The NSW Education Committee found itself facing a considerable financial outlay if it were to continue sending students to Melbourne, and reported to the Executive Committee on the proposed establishment of a NSW Baptist College. The Education Committee drew attention to 'correspondence from the Victorian College authorities detailing conditions on which NSW students would be received in future. When the financial implications of the change were spelled out the Executive Committee adopted the report 'without dissent' and took steps to submit a proposal to the forthcoming Assembly. That was on 3 August 1915, and, remarkably, on 23 September the Assembly resolved unanimously on the establishment of the NSW Baptist College. The very next day the Constitution of the College was adopted. As soon as that was done 'Rev CJ Tinsley proposed that the Rev Alex Gordon, MA, be appointed as principal of the College for three years ... to begin 1 February 1916'. The Executive Committee at its meeting on 9 November had before it a letter from Rev Alex Gordon, MA, accepting the offered position of Principal of NSW Baptist College. The whole matter had been concluded in a matter of months.

1916
One outcome of these rapid events was that in 1916 Morling was among the first intake of students at the NSW College. On his return from Melbourne, he was asked to preach at Ashfield.[19]

While studying he also engaged in pastoral ministry at East Hills, and pioneered a work at Bankstown. Morling adopted and propagated the position that both scholarly exactness and practical pastoral engagement were required of those who received God's high calling to ministry.

The Home Mission Committee in its proposed appointments for 1916 listed 'Morling Bankstown, salary £5-0-0 per month'. This was anomalous in that most other students received £6-10-0 per month and he himself had been appointed to Hurlstone Park on that stipend two years previously. The injustice was removed when at its December 1915 meeting the Home Mission Committee made the salaries of all College students uniform.

The Committee approved the appointment of George Morling to 'organise the work in conjunction with East Hills for a period of three months'. So he would be once more associated with Cleugh Black and back on his old stamping ground of East Hills.

Harris Street Church

On Monday 6 March, the first session of the NSW Baptist College began in the Harris Street Baptist Church. The church made space available for the giving of lectures to students who would travel there day by day. For Student-Pastor GH Morling BA, by reason of university studies and his year at the Melbourne College, 1916 was his only year as a student of the NSW College.

Baptist Theological College of NSW 1916
GHM Back Right

Morling was able occasionally to get back to his home church at Ashfield. He had barely started at college and church when it was reported that 'he delivered an excellent address at Ashfield's Sunday School Anniversary'.[20]

On 29 March at a meeting of the college Students' Association, he moved (successfully) that regular weekly prayer meetings should be held, and on 26 April that a weekly devotional meeting be held with outside speakers once a month.[21] On 25 May he urged his colleagues to attend a meeting of theologians. He was also concerned at the inadequacy of ministerial stipends. On 26 June he was elected captain of the college tennis club.

At the end of first term he moved a resolution which expressed 'appreciation of the lectures delivered by the Principal, not only for the ripe and varied scholarship which has marked them, but also because of the fervent spirituality and the intense loyalty to Christ, which has made them an inspiration in the Christian life, and an incentive to faithful work in the high calling of the ministry'. However he moved on 28 July that examination papers be allotted three hours rather than two, a proposal overruled by Principal Gordon.[22]

At the 1916 Assembly George Morling made his first entrance into the denominational sphere when we find him elected as a scrutineer to conduct a ballot. Later the respect and affection in which he was held invested his contributions to Assembly sessions with powerful influence.

Meanwhile work at East Hills and Bankstown was demanding yet encouraging. In the hall at Bankstown it was necessary to remove the reminders of the previous night's party before it was ready for God's people to gather. With the development of the work the young pastor applied to the Executive Committee and was recommended for registration to conduct weddings.[23] Pastoral tasks were expanding.

At the end of the year with College pressure removed, his presence was noted at the induction of Rev L Sale-Harrison to the Ashfield pastorate. He was beginning to be noticed.

For all his enthusiastic pastoral work he had not neglected his studies and when the results of the examinations were issued he had done exceedingly well, especially in Church History (96%) and Theology (95.5%) his major areas. Surprisingly, his poorest result was in New Testament (74%) in the exposition of which he was later to prove so able and inspiring.

When at the Home Mission committee meeting of 12 September the list of projected appointments for 1917 was tabled, GH Morling was designated for Hornsby. However, at the Committee's next meeting on 17 October the Superintendent reported 'some difficulty in effecting the appointments listed in the previous meeting'. Morling was now to stay at Bankstown. His stipend was still to be £6-10-0 per month.

But Bankstown was not to retain its greatly loved young pastor. He left that rapidly growing work in December[24] for his first and only country pastorate. An emergency in a country church circuit at Dungog/Thalaba saw him transferred to that work in 1917. He was to complete his studies 'extra-murally'.

1917
Up north of Newcastle in the rural circuit of Dungog-Thalaba the health of its pastor, WS Cowling, was poor and he needed to be replaced. Dungog had recently experienced revival when 43 conversions were reported and a new church building was about to be opened. Someone

was needed to take over the work and Morling with only some apparently minor requirement to complete for the College was chosen to fill the breach.

He received £13 per month. That greatly increased stipend doubtless had in view that he was soon to be a married man.

The news of the proposed appointment was not greeted by the Dungog-Thalaba Church with unrestrained rejoicing. As indicated in a letter to Rev AJ Waldock the thought of having a minister with a BA was disturbing. Principal Morling used often to tell of a Thalaba man who informed him that every BA he had ever known had gone to hell.

Despite misgivings, George Morling became pastor at Dungog/Thalaba and soon was winning his way into the hearts of the people. Doubtless his acceptance was helped by what happened less than two months after the start of his ministry. On Saturday 28th April, in the Haberfield Baptist Church, he was married to Miss Gladys Rees by her pastor, Rev William Higlett. She would be an integral part of his ministry, providing in their home a place of sanctuary from the demands of others, yet a place of warm hospitality to all. She would also act as his advocate to the College Council when she saw him over-committing himself in ministry to the detriment of his health. Yet she readily accepted that her ministry was to release her husband from the home to exercise his ministry on state, national and international stages. A measure of the regard of his college friends was that each student was levied five shillings to buy the couple a wedding present.[22]

Assisting Mr Higlett was the Rev Enos Coleman who became George Morling's brother-in-law, being married to Ethel Rees. Most likely it was through Enos Coleman who, though somewhat older than George Morling[i], had been a theological student in the same year, that the couple had come to know each other. Rev Horace Cubis, a close College friend, was best man and George's brother, William, was groomsman.

Gladys Rees was born of devout Congregational parents and grew up in South Wales during the period of the Welsh Revival. She responded warmly to the evangelical message. Coming to Australia with her parents at the age of seventeen she became associated with Haberfield Baptist Church. There she was baptised by Rev W Higlett, and up to the time of

---
[i] Enos was born 20 August 1885, and was therefore 6 years older.

her marriage served as a Sunday School teacher.

Among the guests at the wedding were Mr and Mrs Searle and Mr Yates who were described as 'friends from Mr Morling's church at Dungog who had come to honour their pastor and his wife'. So Gladys Morling came as a young and beautiful bride to the people of Dungog-Thalaba and soon won their hearts as she served beside her pastor-husband.

It took some time to win the confidence of some of the Thalaba people. However in the township of Dungog there was a ready, even enthusiastic response to the purposeful stance he took. Reporting the opening of the new church building at Dungog to the September meeting of the Home Mission Committee the Superintendent, supported by the Union President, Rev David Steed, spoke 'concerning the success of Mr Morling's ministry'. Some aspects of the impact of the young pastor on his quiet country charge were spelled out in a published report.[25] 'On his arrival in Dungog and Thalaba the Rev G Morling was instrumental in forming a Ministers' Fraternal. Through this association Dungog has had many united meetings…Under the auspices of this association Sunday January 6, the King's Day of Intercessory Prayer, was the occasion of the largest religious gathering ever seen in Dungog. Over 800 people of all denominations, including Roman Catholics, gathered in the picture theatre, when the ministers led the people by prayer, praise and exhortation right up to God's throne, and a glorious hour and a half passed quickly by. There was no special feature … only the glorious presence of the Holy Ghost. During the week following special intercessory prayer meetings were held in the Presbyterian, Methodist and Baptist Churches, when record weeknight attendance and interest was manifested. People outside the church as well as in are discussing the necessity of 'Bringing Back the King' into the heart of the nations before it is possible to win in the present world-wide struggle, and the question is not, Whose side is God on? But who is on God's side? We are praying that much honour to our King Jesus will result from these united meetings'.

When towards the end of 1917 the Home Mission Committee had before it the list of proposed appointments there appeared Dungog-Thalaba, Morling £14-0-0. Meanwhile, he had completed whatever was required of him by the Education Committee, and at the December meeting of the Executive Committee the recommendation was accepted that he, along with several others, be granted full ministerial status, to be ordained at Bathurst.[26]

The Executive Committee had to deal with two letters concerning GH Morling's ordination. One was from the man himself expressing the desire of the church that his ordination be held at Dungog. That reveals a bond between the people and pastor. The Executive Committee was unmoved by the plea but made the suggestion that 'an Induction Service in Dungog would be fitting'.

The other letter was from his home church, Ashfield 'desiring opportunity to convey a greeting at the ordination service in respect of GH Morling'. This was refused as being impracticable and inappropriate.[27]

1918
The Ordination Service was duly held on 12 February at Bathurst, with Principal Gordon giving the address, on 'The Honourable Calling'.[28]

'Rev GH Morling, BA' was soon again in Sydney, amongst those who received their College diplomas at the College Commencement Service in Petersham Church on 14 March.[29]

At the April meeting of the Home Mission Committee 'The Superintendent reported having preached at Thalaba and Dungog churches on the previous Sunday. The work throughout the district was in a good state. The Church has succeeded in clearing off the remaining debt of £130 on the building. The deacons were prepared to urge the church to increase the assessment (the amount it was willing to send to the Home Mission) with the view of increasing Mr Morling's stipend to £17 per month'.

The increase would certainly have been welcome because the family circle was about to be extended by the advent of baby Dorothy - a true gift of God. She was born in May.

However, when the committee met on 21 May there was a letter from Dungog accepting and one from Thalaba rejecting an increase in their assessment. Nonetheless the committee raised the pastor's salary to £17 per month from 1 May and by the next meeting on 18 June Thalaba had yielded to the Superintendent's gentle persuasion and agreed to increase their contribution.

It said something of George Morling's community acceptance when 400 attended the Anzac Memorial Service at which he was the preacher.

A very significant happening in the life of the Dungog Church was the baptism of Mr F Burton. Prior to the formation of the church, though not himself a baptised believer, he kept the Baptist services going. In the church which his money and counsel had helped to build, he was baptised by George Morling. How much that tells us of the winsomeness and effectiveness of the young pastor.

Probably because of the impending 'happy event' GH Morling did not attend the Half-Yearly Assembly Meetings in 1918. As a result he was not received as an accredited minister of the Union along with those who were ordained with him. The minutes of the Annual Assembly indicate that on 26 September 'The Rev GH Morling, BA, was received into the Union, status having been previously granted'.

During the Assembly he was called on at short notice to fill a gap in the Home Mission Conference. He rose to the occasion splendidly and stirred the Assembly. In humorous vein he boasted about the babies, especially his own first-born, and about the butter of Thalaba which had recently gained second prize against world competition in London. Then, more seriously, he drew attention to the Baptists of Thalaba, speaking particularly of some he designated 'giants'. 'In Thalaba', he said, 'sixty years ago there was hardly a Christian, now there is hardly one person who is not'. He attributed this largely to several outstanding men who had served Christ there. 'The men there', he said, 'read their Bibles; it is about the only book they can read. They cannot read the newspaper but, as by a miracle, they can read the Bible'.

Years later, in 1962, he went back to preach at Thalaba and started his address, 'It is no ordinary experience for me to stand in this pulpit on the occasion of a baptismal service and with people both of Thalaba and Dungog ... present. I saw the erection of this church. I preached the first sermons. I conducted the first baptismal service - that was some 45 years ago. Holy memories crowd in upon me'. No wonder, for his had been a most significant ministry among them.

Despite the success that had attended his ministry, the Home Mission Committee at its November meeting decided to appoint Morling to Hornsby-Pymble, still at £17 per month. Seemingly it was policy not to leave a man more than a couple of years in a church. In September members of the Annual Assembly noted with approval a speech by the young minister. He was transferred back to a city pastorate to commence early in 1919. During his final service at Dungog/Thalaba he baptised 14 people, evidence of his effectiveness as a preacher and evangelist. Consequently, *The Australian Baptist*[30], under the heading 'Farewell at Dungog', carried the following report:

'On Sunday, 22 December, after morning service eight candidates from Thalaba were baptised, and on Sunday, 29 December, three from Thalaba and three from Dungog. On 29 December Pastor Morling gave his farewell address and spoke to a crowded congregation. The communion service that followed will be remembered. By special request Mr Morling preached at Big Creek (our fifth Sunday outpost) on Friday afternoon last ... and was presented with a purse of sovereigns. On Saturday Thalaba's picnic was a great success ... a cheque was given with all good wishes. Dungog's farewell was on Monday night, December 30, when a musical program and addresses from representatives of the churches (were given). There was a large and representative audience. Mr Morling was given a cheque, Mrs Morling a piece of plate and Baby Morling a silver cup. They left on Tuesday by mid-day train for Hornsby'.

1919
On taking up his appointment at Hornsby/Pymble in 1919 he made two innovations, the systematic exposition of books of the Bible and public lectures defending Christian faith in a public hall.

There was scarcely time for George and Gladys Morling to catch their breath. They arrived at the Hornsby manse, got unpacked and just a week after leaving Dungog, Hornsby had a 'Tea and Public meeting' to welcome them. It was a kind of homecoming. Rev W Cleugh Black, an old friend and now President-Elect (Vice-president) of the Union, chaired the function. 'Mr Morling' he said, 'was a man among men. He was held in the highest esteem by the denomination. His was a loving and sympathetic nature and he felt assured that he would be a great success in his holy ... calling'. His father was there and participating in the service by reading the Scriptures.

In his response Morling said that he was 'much touched with all the kind things said ... He would continue, as he did in Dungog, to preach the simple gospel in all its fullness'. He did that and more, for it was at Hornsby-Pymble that he began the practice of systematically expounding books of the Bible. He did this both on Sunday mornings and Wednesday evenings and the people welcomed the practice enthusiastically.

There had been a Baptist work in Hornsby since 1903 and such men as W Cleugh Black, L Sale Harrison and the New Zealand firebrand, Donovan Mitchell, had laboured there. When George Morling came to the pastorate the area in and around Hornsby was experiencing a post-war expansion and he was eager to exploit the possibilities for Christian outreach.

A few days after the Hornsby welcome there was another at Pymble chaired by Rev David Steed, a friend of the Morling seniors and pastor of North Sydney Baptist Church.

In the membership and on the diaconate was Rev S Hotston, who had exercised a notable pioneering ministry in the New England area. He left in March to resume country ministry. In farewelling him, George Morling said that 'he had found him a great help in many ways, and he prayed that God would bless him even more abundantly in his future endeavours'.

The return of George Morling to Sydney was welcomed by more than the Hornsby-Pymble people. At the College Commencement Service in March it was stated that the College staff consisted of Principal A Gordon, Rev WH Bain, Rev GH Morling and Rev S Sharp. So the College lost no time in securing his services to teach Church History. When later in March Mr William Buckingham provided a launch picnic for the College it was George Morling along with College student AC Fox who led the vote of thanks.

Early in his ministry, however, he was hampered by the deadly influenza pandemic that was sweeping the world. Death visited many homes and Baptists had no special exemption. The authorities restricted public gatherings but small gatherings were held at the manse and its door was always open for hospitality.

The account of a memorial service for Mrs Ivy Long in Hornsby Church in May 1919 said 'The service was fruitful in spiritual decisions'. The pastor had the fire of evangelism in his bones and would not miss an opportunity to press the claims of Christ.

Plans were on hand for developing the work and, despite the restrictions, the President of the Union, Rev AJ Waldock, attended a function at Hornsby early in April to launch a fund for a new building. George Morling outlined plans for fund raising and during the evening the quite considerable sum of £70 was promised. Mr Charles Morling was present and was the first to respond to his son's appeal with a cheque for £10. Pymble was also on the move and in May a site was purchased for a church building.

By June the pandemic had abated and restrictions on public gatherings were lifted. Hornsby reported signs of 'renewed activity in our church'. About this time his parents moved to Auburn and conducted a grocery shop on the corner of Cumberland Road and Phillip Street[31].

1919 saw George Morling moving into the denominational life of the Union. At the Annual Assembly he featured prominently in the College Council session. However, he also spoke in the Home Mission session arresting attention by presenting the work at Hornsby in the form of a parable; he led in devotions which provided 'just the right atmosphere for the Communion Service', and he was elected to the newly constituted Evangelistic and Propaganda Committee. He was to remain on it and be active in its affairs for a number of years. Evangelism was very close to his heart. Dr Basil Brown expressed the opinion that it was association with those who were members of this Committee that brought him to prominence in the Union.

When the proposed appointments for 1920 came before the Home Mission Committee in October GH Morling was designated for Pymble and JF Christian was to go to Hornsby. The work was to be divided. Clearly GH Morling and the Home Mission Superintendent had felt the challenge of the new work and its possibilities. It is equally probable that some of the influential Baptists then settling in Pymble saw in George Morling the minister they wanted to lead them. They had not reckoned with the fighting spirit of the Hornsby people

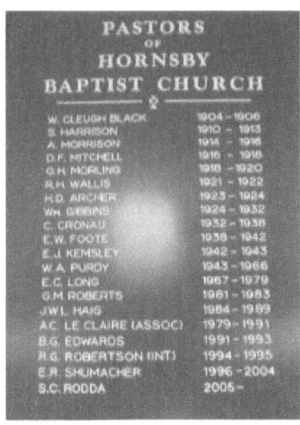

Hornsby Honour Roll

who saw their splendid young pastor being taken from them. At the November meeting of the Home Mission Committee the Superintendent presented a petition from Hornsby asking that Rev GH Morling be allowed to remain as minister there. Bankstown showed a like loyalty by writing to ask the Committee to receive a deputation against Pastor Christian's removal.

In the discussion that followed, the Superintendent, Chairman and others 'protested against the leakage of information from Committee meetings'. However, the leakage prevented a *fait accompli* and two churches were kept happy. Morling was to continue pastoring both Hornsby and Pymble with Pastor CJ Rixon as his assistant principally responsible for the Pymble end of the work.

1920
At the April meeting of the Home Mission Committee there was a letter expressing gratitude from Hornsby and also plans for building extensions. There was also to be another extension - in April the Morling family was extended by the arrival of another daughter, Elaine. Things were on the move at the church and the pastor was in the thick of them, in spite of increasing extra-pastoral commitments. Early in 1920 the Northern District Baptist Association was formed and Rev GH Morling was its first Secretary.

On 24-26 May the Evangelistic and Propaganda Committee held its first Convention at the Stanmore church. Morling 'organised the meetings admirably and the result was a splendid success exceeding the most sanguine expectations'. The speakers included Dr GR Cairns of America, in Australia to conduct missions as arranged by the Committee, Enos Coleman, Stephen Sharp and Sale Harrison. 'Rev GH Morling, as he gave the concluding address on the pre-eminence of Christ, with great spiritual power and insight, brought each and all up to a high level of Christian living and service'.[32]

When in August Pymble celebrated its third anniversary the preachers were the pastor's closest friends, Enos Coleman and Horace Cubis, both of whom, within a few years, were to leave the Baptist ministry. In the course of several years almost all of his associates would seek other avenues of service.

At this stage of George Morling's ministry nothing was more distinctive than his intense evangelistic zeal. In the preaching of this naturally nervous servant of Christ there was an almost aggressive element. In early August he had Dr Cairns conduct a mission at Hornsby. He followed it up with messages aimed at arresting the attention of the community. Adopting the role of an apologist he carried his campaign into the enemy's territory. Hiring the Masonic Hall for Sunday nights he advertised himself to preach on such subjects as 'Christianity, An Unanswerable Argument', 'Christianity and Roman Catholicism: a Plea for Positive Protestantism', and 'Christianity and Spiritualism'.[33]

Meanwhile his lecturing continued at the College. The Principal's Report to the 1920 Assembly directed attention to the Union's deep indebtedness to him for lecturing in Church History and for acting as an examiner.[34] In the College Council Report there was reference to a College Dinner to stimulate interest in the College and Rev GH Morling BA featured prominently. The Assembly again elected George Morling to the Evangelistic and Propaganda Committee and, for the first time, to the College Council.[35] His course was becoming more and more entwined with the Theological College for at the meeting of its Council after the Assembly he was elected Secretary.

However all this was overshadowed by a sensational development - Principal Alexander Gordon submitted a letter of resignation which, in spite of urgent approaches, he declined to withdraw.[36] With the resignation to take effect from the end of the year heavy responsibility fell on one who was both lecturer and secretary.

It was moved that an approach be made to the United Faculty, the body responsible for training Presbyterian, Methodist and Congregational ministerial candidates, asking it to undertake the training of Baptist students until such time as a Principal was found[37], but it was decided instead to continue their training by means of a panel of Baptist lecturers. The panel appointed comprised S Sharp (Theology), W Higlett (Homiletics), WH Bain, BA (Greek grammar, Greek Testament and English), GA Craike (Bible Introduction), L Sale Harrison (Modern Heresies) and GH Morling, BA (Church History and Baptist Principles). Much of the organising of the program fell on George Morling.

He was much in demand to speak at Sunday School anniversaries. If the subjects on which he spoke at the Sunday School anniversary services of his own church in 1920 are any guide his attraction lay more in what he might say to the parents than to the children. The morning subject was 'Christ in the Home' and the evening 'Christ's Estimate of the Child'. Rather heady stuff but the zealous pastor would not miss an opportunity to get a message across to some he might not often have in his services. The Pymble wing of the pastorate was growing and in December, with the pastor presiding, a stone was laid for the erection of its first church building.

When the list of suggested appointments for 1921 came before the Home Mission Committee it was seen that Pymble's hope had only been deferred for a year. Rev GH Morling, BA, was to be their pastor and theirs alone. With the prospect of a new church building they were anxious to exploit the possibilities for expansion.

Hornsby was disappointed to lose its pastor and the financial support of the Pymble people. Having gained its cherished objective Pymble could afford to be magnanimous and offered financial assistance to Hornsby, the child supporting the parent.

1921
Probably because Pymble had not yet secured a manse, the Morlings were living with Gladys' parents at Hurlstone Park. Accommodation must have been crowded and public transport to Pymble a problem but at least Harris Street Church, where George had an increased lecture load, was on the way. Early in the year, he was elected President of the Northern Suburbs District Baptist Association.

At the Half-Yearly Assembly early in April he presented his first report on behalf of the College Council.

In June his first son Gordon was born[j]. Meanwhile he was pushing himself to the limit. With growing family responsibilities, college lecturing, Committee work, and District Association Presidency he yet made time to be a concerned, faithful and effective pastor. At Pymble's fourth anniversary on 10 July, the Immediate Past-President of the Union, W Cleugh Black, preached in the morning and he at night. The annual report showed that membership had nearly doubled and though that made only 34, it is significant that eleven had been added by baptism, four by visitation and only one by transfer.[38]

----
[j] George Gordon Rees Morling was born 21 June 1921.

In August at the Annual Meeting he was again elected President of the Northern Suburbs District Baptist Association. His Presidential Address was on 'Aggressive Christianity' and it was described as being of 'an impressive character'.[39] As President he was involved in a range of activities, leading rallies, chairing ministerial farewells and welcomes as, for example, that of Rev JD Mill at Chatswood when he proved to be 'an efficient and able chairman'.

September 21 was an eventful day for the Pymble pastor. At the Annual Assembly he presented the Report of the College Council. Immediately Rev Archibald Jolly, then comparatively young, moved, and Rev AJ Waldock seconded, that Rev GH Morling, BA, be appointed Acting Principal for twelve months on a full-time basis.[40] The motion was carried despite the opposition of some who deemed him too young, and it was left to the incoming College Council to decide the matter of remuneration. There was no Principal's Report but all the panel (including GH Morling as lecturer in Church History and Baptist Principles) gave verbal reports of the academic aspect of College life.

In the afternoon session of the same day, GHM sought from Assembly an interpretation of his appointment as Acting Principal and it was indicated that he would be required to devote his whole time to the Principalship of the College.[41]

By prior arrangement the report of these momentous proceedings was written by the man most concerned in them. The day had dealt with Trust Funds, the College and Foreign Missions. In somewhat playful mood, Morling wrote, 'The lover of alliteration would say that things monetary, mental and missionary were discussed'.[42]

Two days later he was again elected to the College Council and to the Evangelistic and Propaganda Committee. The same day a letter from him came before Assembly advising his acceptance of appointment as Acting-Principal of the College. He was then only 29 years of age and those who thought he was too young consoled themselves with the thought that it was merely a stopgap appointment. Assembly received the notification gladly and decided that the appointment should date from 1 January 1922.[43]

When on 18 October the Home Mission Committee met, the Acting-Principal was present by invitation and on the motion of the

Superintendent was associated with the Committee for the year. He was then at once elected to the Appointments Committee. On the list of proposed appointments that came before the Committee that night his name stood against Pymble, but he would be there only till year's end.
It was through his pastorate at Pymble that GH Morling became a close friend of Mr and Mrs AS White. Before the year was out he made, in their company and as their guest, a holiday trip to New Zealand. It was the first of several overseas journeys that he would undertake. Among his papers that he left was a little book with comments made day by day during the New Zealand holiday. Everything was seen as grist for the preacher's mill; everything furnished points for preaching.

Towards the end of the year a letter in *The Australian Baptist* showed another facet of George Morling. A correspondent had written to the denominational paper urging that something be done to provide a Sunday School lesson book on 'Baptist Principles and Teaching'. Mr HJ Morton took up the issue and suggested that while there were men capable of preparing such lessons they were not 'willing to contribute'. That really stirred the usually restrained pastor and teacher for he saw it as a slight on the ministry. He wrote this letter:

'Dear Sir, Mr Morton's letter reflects seriously on the industry and loyalty of the Baptist ministry of New South Wales. His rebuke is merited if no one could be found to prepare special lessons on Baptist principles for use in Sunday Schools. But Mr Morton cannot know all the facts. At the beginning of the year the Sunday School Department requested me to undertake this task. I willingly consented and they were supplied with a manuscript of four lessons, which still remains in their possession. However no use has been made of it because, I understand, the expense of printing was prohibitive. Our ministry therefore, stands exonerated'.[44] Having made his point he proceeded to stress the need to propagate distinctive Baptist principles.

The man who thus sprang to the defence of the ministry, though he could not have envisaged it at the moment, was about to embark on a task that would occupy him for almost forty years, the task of training men for what he held to be life's highest vocation, the ministry. He had taken the first step that would lead to him being almost universally regarded among Australian Baptists as 'Our Beloved Principal'.

PRINCIPAL AT PETERSHAM
1922- 1926

PETERSHAM BAPTIST CHURCH

CHAPTER 3 – PRINCIPAL AT PETERSHAM

1922

George Henry Morling became the Acting-Principal of the NSW Baptist College on 1 January 1922. Although the College session would not begin until 7 March there lay before him the dual daunting tasks of organising the year's program and of preparation for his heavy lecturing responsibility.

On 7 January he participated in the opening of Hornsby church's building as 'Principal GH Morling BA (Baptist College'[45], and on 14 January he assisted at the wedding of Briton Wilson and Elizabeth Rees at the Hurlstone Park church.[46] [k] On 30 January Pymble Church farewelled the popular preacher/pastor whose ministry though short had proved so effective.[47]

At that time and for many years after the College was responsible for meeting all its own expenses. Consequently during the entire fortnight before lectures began its Acting-Principal was in the Newcastle district promoting the College and seeking financial support.[48] Part of the promotion took the form of a week-long evangelistic campaign at the Islington Church. In this George Morling was assisted by his friend Enos Coleman.

On the eve of his departure for Newcastle the Home Mission Committee had a letter before it from Rev HA Cubis resigning from both his appointment to the Drummoyne Baptist Church and from the Baptist ministry 'feeling' as he wrote, 'that he had lost the enthusiasm which accompanies a divine call'. This was doubtless a bitter disappointment for George Morling as he faced his new responsibility. Horace Cubis, a man of considerable ability, had been his best man and was a close friend. He had recently gained a Bachelor of Arts degree with distinction. The only recorded clue to what lay behind his resignation is provided by something he wrote in an article on 'The Primitive Jewish Church'.[49] He concluded the article - 'of those early Christians it can be said with truth, as it can never be said of their modern descendants, that their

---

[k] Elizabeth Rees was sister to Gladys Morling.

souls were not strangled with doctrinal or 'politic' 'red-tape". Cubis was one of many of Morling's contemporaries who left the Baptist ministry. Also, Rev AC Fox took an appointment as lecturer in philosophy at the University of Perth.[50] An editorial comment reflected some of the disquiet that was being felt. 'The question might well arise, do we train students to become ministers or university lecturers? Has the denomination no reasonable claim on their services?' It would become clear that George Morling was in no doubt as to the purpose of the College. It was to train men for the Christian ministry as exercised in Baptist churches and on Baptist mission fields.

From the beginning the Acting-Principal received encouragement and support. The denominational paper reported.[51] 'The College commemoration, to mark the opening of the new term, was without precedent for the size of the gathering and the enthusiasm manifested. It must have appealed to the College Council and particularly to the new Acting-Principal as a happy augury for the new term'. The Chairman of the College Council, Rev W Higlett, saw it as 'evidence that a new interest in the College had been aroused'.

The 1922 session had begun in the vastly improved facilities of the Petersham Church. The Secretary of the College Council Rev RS Pickup said that 'under the new conditions they wanted the students to feel that the whole denomination was behind them and interested in them'. It was a promising start and in the course of what amounted to a policy speech George Morling sought to allay any suspicions and to ground the College in the confidence of the churches. 'The College', he declared, 'stands for the Bible as the inspired and authoritative word of God'. However he went on to say, 'Because it is a denominational College it cannot stand officially for any particular theory of interpretation but just because it is a denominational College it must stand officially for the divinity of the Bible'.

His teaching program was daunting, especially for one with limited experience to call upon. His responsibility covered Theology, Church History, Baptist Principles, Old Testament Exegesis, Psychology and English/Greek grammar. He was to be assisted by Rev WH Bain BA (New Testament Greek - 1 Corinthians), Rev GA Craike (Outlines of New Testament Books) and Rev W Higlett (Pastoral Theology and practical sermon work). There were twelve students preparing for ministry, six attending College, and six 'in the field' doing pre-college studies.

At once he was in demand as a special speaker. In late March, he preached at the 85th Anniversary of the Bathurst Street Church. A report of the occasion[52] ran, 'Sunday was a day when all felt the Holy Spirit was brooding over the meetings ... Rev GH Morling, BA, left us with a great message, 'Jesus Christ, the same yesterday, today and forever". How often subsequently he would preach on that text, never in the same way, and always with freshness.

A few days later at the Good Friday Rally of the Cumberland District Baptist Association he spoke on the Second Coming. One of the reasons for the resignation of Principal Gordon was that he found himself out of step with influential persons in the Baptist Union over his views of the Second Advent. It may be that the Cumberland Association was giving the Acting-Principal a chance to nail his colours to the mast. The report of the Rally said that his 'practical address on the 'Lord's Second Coming' was greatly valued.[53] That was faint praise. What was rather looked for was speculative embellishments of the subject. Editorial comment in *The Australian Christian World*[54] suggested that this was the case. Though a letter to the Editor initiated by the Executive Committee of the Baptist Union denied the suggestion, the suspicion lingers that it was a consideration. This view is supported by a letter that Rev John G Ridley, ardent advocate of the Second Advent theme, wrote to Principal Morling on the occasion of his retirement. In it he said, 'I remember so well when you came into your office and how we hoped for a change of policy following the previous Principal. Our hopes were wonderfully fulfilled'.

The Acting-Principal at the Half-Yearly Assembly of the Union moved 'a hearty vote of thanks .. to the Harris Street Church for their generous help to the College program for some years past'.[55]

Early in June he returned to Pymble to share in a 'complimentary social' to Mr AJ Harvey, forced by ill health to resign as Treasurer. Through the advocacy of George Morling he was admitted to studies at the College.[56] Indeed his health sufficiently improved for him to undertake a country pastorate and to return to complete his studies at the College before his untimely death.

A significant issue was Biblical criticism. In December 1919, an American, Dr Henry, preaching in the Ashfield Church on 'A Mutilated Bible', had warned against the dangers of higher criticism. Now 'The

College authorities have invited Professor Wilkin, MA DD, of the Baptist College of Victoria, to deliver a course of lectures to the students on Biblical criticism'.[57] George Morling felt his need of help to enable his students to come to terms with the new ferment of thought that was moving through Biblical studies. It was not an easy time for the young Acting-Principal.

Towards the end of second term he did some preaching at Eastwood for Rev Archibald Jolly who had nominated him for his position.[58] The two men were of very different temperament and personality but there was a bond of mutual respect between them and a shared evangelistic zeal. Moreover they had begun their preparation for the ministry the same year.

George Morling was appointed as a NSW delegate to the Third Baptist Congress in Melbourne and played a prominent part in proceedings. On the fourth day Rev Donovan F Mitchell gave a paper, 'Baptists and Their Belief about the Spiritual Condition of the Young Child'. It was characteristic of GH Morling's evangelistic concern that 'while expressing his appreciation of the paper (he) emphasised the supernatural side of child conversion - the fact of regeneration'. He himself 'read a paper to the Congress, 'The Distinctive Message and Mission of the Baptists in the New Era''. In it the historian, the Baptist and the passionate evangelist were much in evidence. It fell to him also to write the published report of the eighth day of the Congress. Anyone who reads it would need no convincing that he was much in sympathy with the theme of the day, 'Evangelism and Foreign Missions'.

Soon after the Congress, came the NSW Assembly Meetings and the Acting-Principal was in the thick of things. It was indicative of the place he was coming to hold in the Union that he was the one called on to express the thanks of the Assembly to Mr George Searle for his Presidential address. Moreover, he preached at the Ordination Service. George Morling also presided over a conference on the better equipment of Sunday School teachers. After stressing the urgent need for teachers to be trained he outlined a three-year course of study comprising ten weeks each year. Rev Enos Coleman would give lectures on child psychology in its relation to teaching and he on the Scripture witness to Baptist Principles. The Assembly adopted the suggestion and entrusted its implementation to him and the Examination Board.

Assembly took a decision that imposed a vastly greater task upon him. In presenting the Report of the College Council its Secretary, Rev RS Pickup, referred to the appointment of George Morling as Acting-Principal and added, 'The work of the College, under his wise and able leadership, has confirmed the hopes of the hopeful and allayed the fears of the careful'.[59] The Acting-Principal then gave his Report on the College and expressed thanks to those who had entered into a 'holy conspiracy' to make his exacting task as easy as possible. 'The staff of tutors', he wrote, 'have kept before them the ideal of a Biblical expository and evangelistic ministry, and have adapted their teaching to this high end'.[60]

How he felt about the College is revealed in the conclusion to his report which ran 'The internal life of the College is happy and spiritual. The prayer meeting is a source of blessing. My experience of the College work this year has resulted in these impressions:

(1) Our present system of training men needs considerable alteration. We badly need a residential college. This would be fairer to the men themselves, who are badly overworked. It would also provide them with the benefit of a College life, which could be regulated by our highest ideals.

(2) It is very possible that the College could play a much larger part in our denominational life, and make a distinctive contribution to our progress - if we had a proper centre.

(3) My third impression is that our people believe in the College and are heartily behind it. We have splendid men for College, who are worthy of our best. I believe they will receive it'.

As soon as the Report was adopted Rev RS Pickup rose and moved a recommendation on behalf of the College Council that Rev GH Morling, BA, be appointed Principal of the College for twelve months. The record of the meeting says that 'after some considerable discussion the Assembly resolved (with one dissenting vote) that the Rev GH Morling, BA, be appointed Principal for three years'. The salary was fixed at £350 a year.[61] He remained in that position until his retirement in December 1960. His early years as Principal were marked by periods of frenetic ministry and total incapacity due to ill health.

Of his appointment, it was said[62], 'Mr Morling is a young man for such an important position, but the Assembly showed its confidence in him by a practically unanimous vote'. His comparative youthfulness was a matter of concern to some. Rev JH Baker wrote at the time of Principal Morling's retirement in 1960, 'I remember, George, when you were appointed Principal of the College. There were some who questioned the wisdom of it, because you were so young. After your appointment you assured the Assembly that you would grow out of that fault ... You have kept your word'.

One consequence of the appointment was that the new Principal became an *ex officio* member of the Annual Assembly, the Council, the Executive, Home Missionary, Foreign Missionary, Sunday School and Christian Endeavour Committees. He had no great love of committee meetings, though minutes clearly indicate the growing part he was playing in denominational life. More often than not he was absent from the Executive Committee due to the pressure of College commitments and additional teaching tasks.

Having been confirmed in his position as Principal, George Morling took steps to secure a family home. He negotiated the purchase of 'Apsley', 178 Holden Street, Canterbury. It was the Morling home until the family moved to Granville in 1926.

Despite the demands of his new role Morling involved himself with local churches. Towards the end of the year we find him giving a lecture on 'Our Baptist Ancestors' to the Auburn Church Young Men's Social and Debating Club with a collection for the College. They invited him to return and speak on the life of CH Spurgeon. He also participated in the opening of a new church at Bexley[63], and preaching at one of the services, preaching at Sunday School Anniversaries at Pymble[64], Hornsby[64] and Drummoyne, speaking just before Christmas at Haberfield's Young People's Society of Christian Endeavour[65] and a little later to the Granville Men's Morning meeting with the proceeds of an offering going to the desperately needy College Library Fund.

1923
The cautious approach of Morling and the NSW Baptist Executive to the question of Biblical criticism prompted a letter from Rev T McDougall objecting to a supposed ban against modern criticism being considered at the College. McDougall was on leave of absence from

NSW but was negotiating admission to the Presbyterian ministry.[66]

George Morling was now seeking to work towards a Master of Arts degree at Sydney University. The first entry of a diary, spasmodically kept, is dated Sunday, 4 March 1923, and reads, 'This week important - the week previous to preliminary examination for MA degree. I want to know experimentally the peace of God. I have to prepare also an address for MMM at Hurlstone Park and Teachers' Helps for lesson on Baptism. I hope to make both a blessing. Very much helped by Isaiah 35:4, 'Say ye to them that are of a fearful heart, 'Be strong, fear not''. Two days later this entry appears, 'Learnt yesterday that my range of reading has been insufficient to allow me to take the examinations - two papers being prescribed - a keen disappointment. This year must be arranged better so as study shall be more systematic. I need greater mental discipline and control'.

The next entry in the diary is dated Monday, 12 March: 'Today make a new commencement at systematic study. Every day must make some contribution to my desire to be a Bible student, a man of prayer, a soul winner, a student'.

That the previous week had been a severe trial is obvious from the further notation, 'Enos (Coleman) preached well yesterday on 'God is faithful'. He was faithful last week. I have not been confounded'. By the end of the week (Sunday 18 March) he was able to consider 'A much better week. God has restored my soul and given me a capacity for more concentrated study'. That evening he was to preach at Eastwood for his friend Archibald Jolly who 'had broken down'. He felt that this was 'a special opportunity' probably because of the experience he had been passing through, and counselled himself, 'Remember

(1) To speak in the love and with the authority of Jesus Christ
(2) To be happy and express my own individuality,
(3) To preach for some to live the victorious life (my subject)'.

By Friday 23 March, he was able to note, 'The first College week over. Very good on whole. The men seem a splendid lot. Individual attention in some cases. I must seek God's help in giving personal assistance to remedy faults and develop Christian character'.

The week had brought encouraging news on GHM's study program.

'My essay received a good place', he wrote, 'unexpectedly good'. This was probably a major essay on Francis of Assisi entitled 'The Franciscan Spirit'. In a letter to Morling, Professor GA Wood wrote 'I .was especially impressed by the ability of your essay on St Francis which for a short essay was most admirable'. The 'short essay' ran to almost a hundred pages. The one so praised was quick to acknowledge God in his success. 'As I definitely asked Divine guidance in this matter', he wrote, 'I must likewise definitely thank Him'. The diary entry continues, 'Also able to take examination at my own time. God has indeed 'saved' me'.

The danger of non-attendance at a meeting was demonstrated at the Executive Committee of 3 April. In his absence it was decided that Principal Morling represent the Union at Joseph Hunter's ordination in Newcastle and read the Scriptures at the ordination of Pastors Swan and Gibbins.[67]

For the 1923 College session there were again six students in residence. Three others were pursuing preliminary studies in country churches. The Principal lost a valuable lecturer with the departure of Rev WH Bain BA for Western Australia. This meant that he had to take up Greek New Testament, lecturing on the Greek text of Romans. In addition he took English Bible Exegesis in both Old Testament and New, Greek Grammar, Church History, English and Voice Production. He was assisted by Rev Stephen Sharp who took over theology for the year, and, as previously, by Rev GA Craike and Rev W Higlett. However he also conducted correspondence courses for men in the country and with Enos Coleman ran a course for Sunday School teachers.

The College Commencement Service was held at Stanmore on 10 April. 'The College Council is to be congratulated on the position the institution holds in the esteem of Baptists of New South Wales. There is universal agreement that this position is very largely due to the work of the Principal, Rev GH Morling BA. The commencement service must have made his heart glad with hope. This is no small task for a young man, but the denomination by that gathering paid to Mr Morling the finest tribute possible - that of appreciation of his scholarly attainments and his spiritual enthusiasm'.[68]

Not until May did another entry appeared in his diary. It said simply 'The examination over satisfactorily. Even in the arrangements the guidance of God was manifest. Professor Wood's suggestion about taking the Puritan revolution instead of Renaissance also under God's control'. He was moving steadily towards an advanced degree.

For several years his health had caused no great problems but the strain of his duties as Principal, denominational responsibilities and his inability or reluctance to say 'no' to the many requests for his services were beginning to take their toll on his naturally delicate nervous system. In August he was unable because of sickness to take the Undercliffe Church Anniversary. However this was but a passing indisposition because we find him shortly after welcoming WS Cowling to the pastorate of Hurlstone Park[69] and a little later again sharing in the Annual Assembly. In contrast with the previous Assembly, he took no part aside from presenting his Report.

In that Report, his first as Principal, he wrote, 'Perhaps there is little in the work of a theological college which immediately strikes the imagination, yet it would be hard to exaggerate the importance of that work. As a literal fact, the salvation of countless people depends upon the wisdom and faithfulness with which the college studies are directed. I may be permitted, therefore, to say, although with a profound sense of personal shortcoming, that it has been our aim to make the lecturer's desk a pulpit, and the classroom a sanctuary, and the college life a holy fellowship'.

'It has been realised, too, that ours is a College which has been instituted to train men for the Baptist ministry. It has been, and will be increasingly, our purpose to provide a course of study, and to create an atmosphere that will ensure, as far as lies in our power, the production of men who will proclaim our Baptist principles with intelligent and earnest conviction'.

'As one reviews the work of the year the need of patience is keenly felt. For myself I regard the College more as a splendid possibility rather than as an accomplished fact. We have no apology to make for our present achievements, but much remains to be done before there can be entire satisfaction. A residential college, an extensive library, better facilities for practical training in evangelistic and pastoral work must be among our objectives for the future. But we are strong in hope and in courage. The work is arduous and exacting, yet rich in inspiration and reward. We shall see the day when the Baptist Union of NSW will have a college of which it will be proud'.[70]

With what earnestness he pursued his goal may be seen in several diary entries towards the end of the year, the last he was to record for almost five years.

'Nov 10. After return from a week spent at Merewether, see clearly -

(1) That prayer life must be more systematic - helped by RF Horton's *The Open Secret* - this will enable me to attain ambition to be a man whom the students will follow. I must be a soul-winning preacher to be an ideal principal.

(2) That special preparation for the MA degree shall again be a constant matter of prayer. Help already received'.

He then outlined a prayer program for the coming week and noted two preaching commitments for which he needed immediate guidance.
'Sunday, Nov 18. Today have asked for and received special grace for the work of the MA degree which I hope to attempt in March, and to which 1 can now apply myself, College work being over. Two texts given – 'Thou wilt keep him in perfect peace *etc*' and 'I can do all things through Christ who strengthens me'. Resolve (1) To seek Divine Presence in study. (2) To begin and end the day with spiritual rather than with intellectual ambitions. (3) To keep prominent the greater ideal of life by definite acts of witnessing'.

'Saturday, Nov. 24. God has been very good this week. I have had much assistance in study - restfulness and power of application. The outline of the thesis is coming well'.

Things however, were not to work out just as George Morling hoped and prayed. At the College Council a few days later on 29 November it was reported that Stephen Sharp would be unable to lecture in theology next year and it was decided that the Principal should take over the subject.[71] The Council spoke of him 'rearranging other subjects' but from the 1924 program it is clear that theology was an extra load for him. His only helpers would be GA Craike and W Higlett taking their usual subjects, with Mr H Thomas taking a weekly class in elocution. Despite his study program he was constantly busy in the churches even in the holiday period, a Sunday School Anniversary at Haberfield[72], a Church Anniversary at Hornsby and the next Sunday a baptismal service in the same church because the pastor was ill[73].

1924

Morling's workload in the wider Baptist community was extensive. At times he acted as Moderator for the Blackheath Church. The strain was telling increasingly and the following years would be marked by repeated health problems. The College Council meeting of 24 January reported that Principal Morling was undergoing treatment in hospital and was not well enough to attend Council Meeting. The Secretary was instructed to write to him expressing the sympathy of the members and urging him not to overtax himself with preaching engagements during the coming term.[74] It was reported, 'Principal Morling of the NSW Baptist College is, we regret to state, under doctoral orders to cancel all engagements for a month at least. He has been in a nursing home under medical observation during the week'.[75] A week later there was good news, 'The friends of Rev GH Morling BA will be glad to learn that he is improving in health, having left the hospital and gone to the Mountains for rest. Mr Morling's medical adviser, however, has forbidden him to go on with his work for the MA degree, which he had hoped to take in March. This is a keen disappointment for his studies were almost complete'.[76] This report seems to have contained the first reference in any official record of his personal study program. Six weeks later he was said to have recovered from his indisposition and, slightly incongruously, that the doctor was pleased with his progress.[77] He resumed work for his MA. The relationship between health and spirituality became an increasingly important theme in his personal life and later in his public teaching ministry.

The 1924 Session started with seven students attending lectures and four doing work by correspondence. On 14 April the Baptist College of NSW Annual Tea and Meeting was held and GH Morling was present. Rev GA Craike, President of the College Council 'paid a high tribute to the Principal. The work of the College was not to make parsons but to further equip men who had been called of God to preach the Gospel of His grace. In doing this, Mr Morling was proving eminently successful'. Rev AL Leeder, Secretary of the Council, wrote, 'Principal Morling was greeted with loud applause. It was evident he became conscious of an inspiration to go forward as he was assured of the love and esteem of the large gathering of warm-hearted friends. He spoke of the confidence with which he faced the future. Moule's translation (Phil 4:13) 'I am strong for anything in Him who makes me able' had been a great help and the work of training men for the ministry, being a divine work, he was sure of the favour of God. He had faith in the men who were in training. They had made sacrifices. The unction of the Holy One was upon them. They had received the call from God and were being trained not only to become efficient ministers, but Baptist ministers. He desired they should be real 'hard-shelled' Baptists'.[78]

There was no explicit reference to the experience he had suffered. He was quickly back into stride and on 1 April was found representing the College and the Ministers' Fraternal at the farewell of Rev Archibald Jolly, at Eastwood.[79]

At the end of first term he reported to the College Council good progress at the College and in what looks like the origin of a slightly different characteristic phrase declared of the term 'It had been his happiest'[80]. Churches were asked not to 'be too exacting on him in seeking his services'.[81] With fine disregard of this advice we find him in June taking the services at Leichhardt[82] while his friend, AT Whale, was in hospital for surgery [1]. Also in June he was found arranging for an applicant, Rowland Newport, to preach in the Hurlstone Park Church, going along to hear him and reporting back to the Council[83].

On 8 June he preached at the first Anniversary of the Chullora church. The Home Mission Superintendent, Dr AJ Waldock, reported the service[84] and doubtless had a twinkle in his eye as he wrote, 'The evening service was conducted by Principal Morling BA, who preached to a large congregation. 'It was the finest discourse ever delivered in the building' said all and sundry, and this unqualified testimony left some of us wondering, who at odd times had reproduced our best sermons before that critical audience of expert sermon-tasters. It was a delight to everyone to have the Principal, and the influence of that evening will never pass away'.

He attended the Executive Committee on 3 June, and arising out of the tendered resignation of Dr AJ Waldock as Home Mission Superintendent, was appointed to a sub-committee 'to deal with the resignation and questions arising therefrom.[85] One of those questions was to be the re-organisation of Union work. By 8 July the sub-committee had come up with a plan for the radical reorganisation of Union work which never

---

[1] Rogers writes 'Eastwood' but AT Whale was pastor at Leichhardt. RN Whale was secretary of the Eastwood church, according to the BUNSW 1923-24 Year Book.

became a reality. Morling had no further part in this for the record states, 'Bro EJ Phillips to take the place of Bro Morling'.[86] No reason was given. Then in July AT Whale, having recovered, assisted the Principal at a Memorial Service for Mr AJ Ellis at Eastwood.[87] On 26 July he shared in a convention at Burwood on 'The Holy Spirit in Relation to the Individual'.[88]

Morling had resumed his study program and completed his MA degree. The College President 'in the name of the Council very heartily congratulated him upon securing this academic distinction which not only enshrouded him with honours but brought dignity and prestige to the College'[89], though the degree would not be conferred until the end of May 1925.

In a letter dated 20 August, 1924. Prof GA Wood wrote, 'I have read the two papers. They show a thorough knowledge of the books, and a thorough understanding of the period, and historical ability so good that, had you been able, as an undergraduate, to work your way in good health through the whole historical course, you would, in my opinion have won a First Class ... I think that, in the circumstances, you are wise to be content with a Pass MA. But I wish to emphasise the fact that ... it is a Pass Degree given to a man of very good Honours ability'.'

In his report to the Annual Assembly, the Principal wrote, 'The work of training men for the ministry of Jesus Christ is such a responsible task, and failure in it is fraught with such far-reaching consequences, that one can never contemplate it without fear of personal shortcomings and prayer for necessary wisdom and grace. For the same reason one cannot view the labours of the past year with any feeling of complacency. And yet it may fairly be said that the year has witnessed a distinct advance. The position of the College is far from being wholly satisfactory, but some measure of satisfaction may rightly be entertained. It is hard to specify causes for this increased assurance. For one thing, I suppose I myself, with more experience and better health, am walking with surer steps in the work of teaching. And then there is evident among the students a much keener College spirit. They have been interested not only in their studies, but in the College itself. There is an awakening *esprit de corps* which must be regarded as a very healthy sign of progress. Most important of all, from the atmosphere of the classes and from numerous incidental happenings, one has the strengthening consciousness that the blessing of God is resting upon the College and that the hand of God is leading onward' ... 'The success of our service for Jesus Christ depends in a large measure upon the efficiency of the ministry. The source of supply for the ministry is the College, and it behoves us to invest our very best in the training of students. Perhaps the time is not yet ripe for any large financial enterprise in order to place the work on a satisfactory basis, but that time must come, and it is hoped that it will come shortly'.[90]

The Council's Report was also forward looking. 'The hope is that the day is not far distant when the Baptist Union of NSW will have a residential College'.[91] With the College barely paying its way, and depending on the generosity of a few friends to supply a few desks for the students and a few books for the library, that seemed a fairly remote prospect. This is confirmed by a discussion that took place concerning the Principal's stipend. Assembly resolved that the College Council confer with the Finance Committee on the possibility of raising the stipend from £350 to £400 and report to the Half-Yearly Assembly.[92]
Assembly resolved 'that the Executive take into serious consideration the reasons for so many of our ministers passing over to other denominations and report'.[93] One who in the course of the year had entered the Presbyterian ministry was Rev Enos Coleman, one of George Morling's closest friends. His letter of resignation had given 'no reason for his action' and was deemed 'hardly courteous to the Denomination'. It was with the denomination that he was disenchanted for he assured his people at Grafton that his resignation had nothing to do with them. At the time there was general unrest among the younger ministers. Six former Baptist ministers were seeking admission to the Presbyterian Church of Australia.[94] 'Members of the churches ... were becoming very dissatisfied at having to support the Baptist College when men trained there were leaving to go to other denominations'.[95] There ensued correspondence discussing the issue. Defence of the College and its Principal was not lacking but it must have been deeply disturbing for George Morling even though the men concerned had not been trained under him. At the very time that the letters were appearing he was giving a course of addresses to young people on the subject 'My Life' He was challenging young people to consider what they were going to do with their lives.

Something happened that must have been a great encouragement to him. 'Following upon the College break-up for the Christmas vacation the students and their young ladies gave a surprise party to Principal and Mrs Morling ... Before taking their leave they presented the Principal with a loose-leafed Bible. There can be no doubt of the affection of the College students for the Principal. There were those who shook their heads doubtfully when the Assembly appointed Mr Morling to this responsible office, but only on account of his comparative youth. Time alone could alter that disability, if such it really was, but from every other point of judgment Mr Morling has earned for himself many good degrees, apart from the distinction he recently won at the Sydney University, and throughout the denomination generally he has deserved golden opinions'.[96]

It must also have been a source of satisfaction to him on 19 November to preach at the Induction of one of his students, Rev W Gibbins, to one of his own former pastorates, Hornsby.[97]

On 25 November a joint meeting of the College Council and the Home Mission Society was held.[98] It fell to Principal Morling to introduce the business for consideration. There were two main matters. One arose out of the fact that with a shortage of men after the war some of the applicants who were being sent to serve a pre-college year as pastors in country churches were not proving satisfactory. The outcome of the discussion was that the Principal organised a preachers' class that was held fortnightly in his home to give intending applicants more adequate preparation. The other matter was a concern about easing the preaching pressure on students in College. There was a suggestion that they should take only one evening service regularly in their own church and preach on a rotating basis in other student churches in the morning. Nothing came of this discussion.

On 30 December the College Council appointed representatives to confer with the Finance Committee about the Assembly resolution that consideration be given to the raising of the Principal's salary to £400.[99] The increase did not happen until the 1925 Annual Assembly.

1925
The College began its tenth year, having survived some earlier uncertainty, and was well established. However there was still a degree of sensitivity concerning its status. One of its students, LH Shakespeare, was preparing for service with the Australian Baptist Mission. It was possible for him to do some desirable hospital training in Melbourne. With this in mind the ABM applied for him to complete his course in the Victorian College. The application was declined because 'it would be

creating a precedent, which at the present stage of the history of our College is very undesirable' and 'it would be a reflection upon the (New South Wales) college'.[100] NSW Baptists were proud of their Principal and jealous for the honour of their College.

Early in 1925 the correspondence columns of *The Australian Baptist* were enlivened by a presentation of differing views of the Second Coming of Christ. George Morling, a man of peace and of wisdom, stood aloof from the debate, as did the theological teachers in the other States. Had he taken sides his influence would in the long run have been diminished. Possibly College training was in the back of his mind when he told the West Ryde Sunday School scholars at their Anniversary, 'God is getting something ready for you, if you only get ready for it'.

Blackheath was a favourite place for George Morling and he was probably taking a holiday there when he is reported as preaching in February at the Blackheath Church Anniversary.

From the flurry of his reported activities in the churches it might have appeared that his health was much improved in the early months of the year. During the whole month of March he preached at Eastwood. The church's gift of *The Life of Bishop Moule* would have delighted him but it may be wondered how much use he made of a leather-bound copy of *Redemption Songs*.

On 22 March, 'College Sunday' was observed as students preached in a number of the churches. On 23 March the opening ceremony of the College year was held in the Auburn church building and attracted a large attendance. This was seen as an evidence of 'the love and esteem' in which the Principal was held. In his remarks he said, 'The College should be the spiritual home of the student as well as an institution for the expansion of the intellect. They were resolved to keep the spiritual fires burning. In all studies the sovereignty of Jesus Christ was the central thought and to Him should pre-eminence be given'.[101]

Despite all his activity Morling was working under difficulties. He reported to the College Council 'that his medical advisers had ordered the extraction of his teeth'. The Council was sympathetic and told him to 'take off any time necessary'.[102] It seems likely that the proposed treatment was intended to alleviate the gout that troubled him on and off for most of his life. Speaking in 1971 on the topic of 'The Holy Spirit and Health' he stated that he had suffered from gout for 55 years. That would mean that the affliction had been with him from the mid 1920s.

He indicated that a Hebrew class had been introduced and that he was taking it.[103] That was a deliberately self-inflicted wound for he had done no Hebrew previously. However there was method in his seeming madness. He was concerned 'to offer a first-class Biblical Course'. Moreover if he were to earn the Bachelor of Divinity degree it was necessary for him to master Hebrew and 'the best way to learn a subject is to teach it'. To his already heavy lecturing load he added a tutorial in the Comparative Study of Religion for the benefit of a single missionary candidate, LH Shakespeare.

Having enjoyed his ministry Eastwood had him back a few days later on 5 April to preach at Rev A Driver's Induction.[104]

When the Executive Committee met on 7 April he was reported to have declined a request to give a paper at the Fourth Baptist Congress in Adelaide. His place as a delegate was assigned to another.[105]

Principal reported to the College Council on 12 May that he had started a Students' Preparatory Class in his home and that six young men were attending.[106] On 27 May at the University of Sydney Commemoration the degree of Master of Arts was conferred on George Henry Morling, his thesis topic being Francis of Assisi.[107] It was a happy day for it marked publicly the successful completion of a venture carried through under great difficulties. Already, he was thinking of further qualifying himself for his teaching task but the future was to prove frustrating.

Hornsby people had not forgotten their former pastor and when on 20 June their enlarged building was opened he was there taking part in proceedings.[108]

Stephen Sharp invited Morling to speak at the Burwood Christian Endeavour Anniversary on 12 July. The report gives insight into his approach to youth, 'Mr Morling quickly succeeded in establishing a very cordial connection with his juvenile audience who followed first the Scripture and comments dealing with Caleb and his whole-hearted allegiance to the Lord and, later, the address on 'Life', with very close interest. Notwithstanding the disparity in the ages of his audience, and the difficulty of addressing them all intelligently, the Principal got his message home, and all were made to feel the importance of life and to glimpse something of its tremendous possibilities for good and evil. At the close a number signified their desire to follow Caleb's example who 'wholly followed the Lord his God' and we anticipate several applications for baptism - wisely stressed by the speaker - as the result. Others who, for the first time, had been brought face to face with the responsibility of publicly confessing Christ as their Saviour were individually dealt with by the teachers'. It was observed that there was an 'absence of all undue pressure'.[109] The evangelistic flame was burning brightly.

It was a unanimous decision of the College Council at its meeting on 28 July to recommend to the Assembly that Rev GH Morling MA, be reappointed as Principal for a further three years at a salary of £400 paid from 1 August[110]. The earnest evangelical was also the convinced Baptist. On the day that the Council made its decision George Morling was speaking at a rally arranged by the Evangelistic and Propaganda Committee for 'propaganda purposes'. His subject was 'Baptism, its Spiritual Significance'. In the report of the rally[111] there was also a reference to a pamphlet written by the Principal entitled, 'Believers' Baptism - A Privilege and a Duty'.

In August a fourth child and second son, William, was born to George and Gladys Morling.

Stephen Sharp had to enter hospital for surgery and who better to help in the pulpit than George Morling.[112] Then a great old man of God, Rev C Pickering, died and the same ever available leader was at Newcastle Tabernacle conducting a memorial Service and giving a splendid tribute.[113]

Once again it was Assembly time and his reappointment came up for consideration. The College Council's recommendation that he be reappointed Principal of the Baptist College for a further term of three years at a salary of £400 per annum from 1 August was approved.[114]

The Principal's Report to Assembly concluded 'let me express my profound sense of privilege at being appointed to this important task. It is an honour to be associated with young men of vision and consecration and ability such as our students undoubtedly possess, and I covet your prayers that their College studies may not only furnish their minds, but may also beautify their spirits and quicken their zeal for Christ and His

Kingdom'.[115]

The Assembly however did give temporary encouragement to the newly reappointed, heavily burdened Principal. It agreed to a proposal that suitable assistance be sought for the Principal and that the Executive Committee should have power to act, though no action was taken. This matter came before the College Council on 27 October. A subcommittee, including the Principal, was appointed to confer with the Home Mission Committee to see if a suitable person could be found. Such a person would give half his time to a church and half to the College. There must have been high hopes for it was decided to defer the appointment of tutors and someone to supervise extramural studies.[116]

The next meeting of the Council decided to ask the Home Mission Committee whether, in the event of Council appointing 'an assistant professor', it could find a position for him in a Home Mission station and find half the suggested stipend of £350 *per annum*.[117] But the proposal was still-born, probably due to two other important factors, the diverting of attention to the possibility of establishing a residential college and the desperate straits of College finances.

The end of the College session brought no cessation of activity for its Principal. Morling preached at the opening of a new manse at Bankstown with his old 'boss', Rev W Cleugh Black, presiding over the occasion. He spoke at Concord's Sunday School Anniversary[118] and gave the charge at the ordination of LH Shakespeare at Dulwich Hill.[119] Speaking to the outgoing missionary on the subject 'Taking Heed to the Ministry' he stressed four needs, an absolute abandonment to the life task, an overwhelming confidence in your message, a passionate ambition for spiritual attainment, and an experimental knowledge of the Holy Spirit. He wrote two articles for a series in *The Australian Baptist* on 'Christian Ideals'. The first to appear[120] was on the Holy Spirit. In it was the germ not only of the address he would give a few years later as President of the NSW Baptist Union but also of the teaching on the Holy Spirit which would mark all his ministry. 'The Deceitfulness of Riches' was the title of the second article[121], in which he reveals the former pastor setting out principles of Christian giving but even more prominently the ardent Baptist 'propagandist' as the following quotation shows - 'It is most regrettable that Australian Baptists are not adequately fulfilling their great mission in this new continent. We have not impressed our principles of spiritual democracy upon the life of the country in any effective way.

Despite our magnificent history and our present world standing, in Australia we are a weak people who do not count much in the affairs either of Church or State. And, strange to say, many seem not only content with this position, but actually proud of it, vaguely thinking that it is a necessary lowliness for the Master's sake. But humiliation is not humility, and this false modesty means that our precious Baptist faith is not being propagated in any proper way. Australia will never respect our principles until she respects us for our comparative denominational strength and influence. Therefore we must rally to the task, ministers and laymen alike. Ministers must pour in the abundant spiritual wealth which is available according to the riches in glory by Christ Jesus, and laymen, though they too have this high privilege, must supply monetary wealth for the lack of which the work of Christ languishes'.

He gave a valedictory address to the recently ordained missionary Rev LH Shakespeare in the course of a social evening at Petersham Church to mark the end of the College year.[122] The Principal preached at Chullora, an outstation of Burwood, and conducting the first baptism in their building on 20 December.[123]

A few days later on 30 December he was on the high seas in the SS Centaur bound for India with Mr AS White.[119] The international aspects of Principal Morling's career began when he visited the mission fields of Bengal. This initiated a long association with the missionary enterprise in that country and the support of overseas mission.

This travel comes as somewhat of a surprise because there was no intimation of it in the records of either the College Council or the Executive Committee. However the Council's Annual Report comments, 'Through the kindly thought and generosity of Mr Alf White of Pymble, the Principal was privileged to pay a visit to India during the annual vacation, and the knowledge thus gained, of our work in the Foreign Field, will be of the greatest value to him in his collegiate work'.[124]

1926
The trip did not go precisely as planned. Writing from Derby where the ship had put in he explained, 'When Mr White and I left Sydney on December 30, our arrangements were to go to India via Java and the Malay States. We had reckoned on being in Java on January 12. It is now January 17 and we are still ploughing our way through the deep blue tropical seas at the top of the West Australian coast'. They hadn't

been informed that their vessel would call in at all major ports up the coast. The delay meant the curtailing of plans to tour Java, Singapore and Burma. This was annoying but he proceeded to reflect on 'comforting compensations', such as 'instruction in the difficult art of patience', 'a greater measure of rest' and 'an unparalleled opportunity for observing human nature'. He was inspired to these reflections by recalling the experience of Matthew Henry, of commentary fame. Waylaid by robbers who took his money he dismounted his horse and 'set out under fourteen heads the lessons to be learned from such an experience'.[125]

The travellers reached Calcutta on 6 February[126] and spent some time in Carey's country 'visiting his church and the college he established at Serampore. There followed a tour of Australian Baptist Mission stations at Serajgunge, Mymensingh, Biri Siri, Comilla, Rajbari and Faridpur'. At Mymensingh he preached through an interpreter to a Bengali audience in the market place. It was a new experience for him. A series of articles in *The Australian Baptist* presented aspects of these visits. Of particular interest was an experience in Comilla. In his own words 'Mr Barry (Rev Walter Barry) has had much success in his approach to the university college students of Comilla, of whom there are 1200. Moreover, he occupies an official position on the college staff as professor of English Bible. In this influential capacity he is able to commend Christ to a section of Indian society which will mould the nation's future life'.

'That Mr Barry is making Christ attractive was amply demonstrated on the Sunday evening. He had announced me to lecture on 'Some Essentials of Nation Building'. To my astonishment and somewhat to my embarrassment, the mission hall was thronged with these educated men, even the doorways and approaches being packed, while scores could not get admission. The Principal of the University College and members of his professional staff were present'.

'My address took the form of an examination of the Western Renaissance in the 15th and 16th centuries, and an application of its principles and lessons to the Indian Renaissance of the present day. The fact that the European Renaissance found its most abiding expression in the Reformation gave the opportunity of a directly religious exposition, and I discussed frankly the impossibility of the Indian Renaissance being rich and fruitful in national development without the recognition of Jesus Christ, because only He can give the unity, inspiration and purity which

India lacks. The Hindu and Mohammedan listeners took no offence. The Principal even gave a public expression of thanks and invited me to address the students at the College on similar lines the next day'.[127]

George Morling had displayed a peculiar affinity with Indians which in later years would produce an enthusiastic acceptance of his ministry by them.

In his absence events significant for the College were taking place in New South Wales. At the Executive Committee of 9 February there was advice of an offer by Mr Luke Bullock of Wellington to convey to the Union a large house in Granville. The suggestion was that it should be used as a secondary school or a residential college. There was a stipulation that the Union pay Mr Bullock £3 per week during his lifetime. The offer was much appreciated but it was decided that Mr Bullock be interviewed[128] because some thought the house 'too small and too dear' for the purpose. However, a week later a joint meeting of the Executive Committee and the College Council agreed that the building and site were large enough for a residential college. The decision of the meeting was 'that there is a unanimous desire to accept the generous offer of Mr Bullock but it hesitates to make a final decision owing to the absence of the College Principal, who was due to return on 14 March'. The deal was to be closed if he was satisfied.[129] But when the College Council met on 18 March the Granville property was discussed and there was no unanimity about its suitability.[130]

About this time a college dinner was held at which it was reported that 'the Rev GH Morling is essentially a cultured gentleman, who has captured the love, not only of his students, but of the whole Baptist constituency'[131] He did not get back to Sydney until 29 March, the day of the College Commencement Service at which he was the preacher. At least in those days there was no jet-lag to cope with but there was the problem of getting one's 'land-legs'. He had boarded the Oronsay with AS White at Colombo and so there was point in the comment, 'His address, which was not only most interesting and inspiring, was full of spicy breezes blown soft from Ceylon's isle'. In the new Dulwich Hill Church 'every available space ... was occupied'. It was a happy home-coming.

The Principal, on his inspection of the Granville property, had misgivings. He did not attend the Half-Yearly Assembly at the Newcastle Tabernacle in April. However, a letter from him was read expressing appreciation of Mr Bullock's offer and doubts about the property. The matter was referred back to the Executive Committee.[132]

By the time the Committee met on 20 April GH Morling had thought again and, though not present, sent a suggestion that the Morling family and four students reside at the Granville property until a more satisfactory one could be acquired. Two days later the College Council decided to recommend to the Union that Luke Bullock's offer be accepted.[133] It seemed that the deal was practically sealed when on 27 April a joint Executive Committee and College Council meeting agreed to accept the offer and to make additions to the building. Hope was expressed that occupancy might be achieved by June.[134]

Apparently, however, Luke Bullock had some slight hesitancy about closing the deal. In an article to which reference will be made a little later, the President of the College Council wrote, '... the response (to Luke Bullock's offer) was not rapid and reluctantly the doors of opportunity were closed but not bolted. Then came the realisation that the refusal of such a timely offer would be an almost irreparable loss and that a residential college would be for another generation but the baseless fabric of a dream'. Principal Morling reported to the College Council on 13 May that he had interviewed the donor. Luke Bullock was anxious that the property be used by the College and agreed to hand it over to the Union in return for the payment of £3 per week during the joint lifetime of himself and his wife. This was a variation of the earlier offer but the Council decided to make the counter proposal that a ceiling of £1600 be put on the total payment that would be made.[135]

When the Executive Committee met on 18 May it endorsed the Council's suggestion. Although Luke Bullock was so unwell that he had not been informed of the counter proposal, the Executive, on the advice and urging of his pastor, Rev James Hunter, decided to go ahead in faith that he would accept it. 'It was agreed to recommend the College Council to occupy the premises as from 1 June on a rental basis until the terms were settled and the transfer effected'.[136]

About this time two things took the Principal back to Petersham, the church of which his father had been a foundation member. Petersham celebrated its 44th anniversary and 'Principal Morling who presided with his customary grace and charm' was one of the speakers. Sir Hugh

Dixson, a successful businessman and prominent denominational leader had died while on board ship bound for Ceylon. His body was brought back to Sydney and George Morling was one of those sharing in the funeral service at Petersham.[137]

Returning to the property matter the Executive's faith was evidently justified for, although the minutes neither of the Executive Committee nor of the College Council make any reference to Luke Bullock's acceptance of the revised proposal, there was an 'Official Opening of the New Residential College' on Saturday, 10 July.

In preparation for that function Rev W Cleugh Black wrote 'An Appeal on Behalf of the Residential College at Granville'[138] and was a characteristic Cleugh Black utterance as the following excerpts show.
'We thank God for this forward movement long overdue, without which we could never build up a great denomination, for a strong evangelical college, with a keen and aggressive evangelistic policy will produce men of sanity and sanctity, men like the ancient Greeks, who will build as giants and finish like jewellers'.

'We believe the number of folk in our churches who prate about the needlessness of education is quite negligible, though there are some misguided souls who regard all theological colleges as synagogues of Satan, and the Principal a kind of ministerial Mephistopheles. From such we expect no financial support, but the vast majority who are otherwise minded, who believe that education is essential and that, in this age of unbelief and apostasy, our young warriors should go to the age-long fight fortified by all the armaments from the arsenal of sanctified scholarship, these surely must support this new venture or else belie their beliefs'.

'The College motto, 'The utmost for the Highest' and its ideal of saintliness allied to scholarship are both exemplified by the Principal and his ministry among men will be all the more effective because they will all live and learn under one roof'.

PRINCIPAL AT GRANVILLE
1926-1934

Granville College, 'Taringa', The Avenue, Granville
1926-1934

'Taringa' was designed by Sir Edmund Blacket and built in 1884 as a residence for the builder William Thackray. It was sold in 1887 to a Mr Ritchie. Later it was acquired by Mr and Mrs Luke Bullock of Wellington who made it available to the Baptist Union of NSW for a Theological College in 1926.

CHAPTER 4 – PRINCIPAL AT GRANVILLE

At the opening the President of the Union, Rev FJ Dunkley, under whom George Morling had served as a probationary student at Tamworth, presided. 'He felt that the denomination had started on a new era in securing a residential college, which it was hoped would hold their students closer together than had been possible hitherto'.[139] Greater *esprit de corps* might prevent or at least lessen defections from the ranks. That may be what he was hinting at. Rev W Cleugh Black, President of the College Council gave an address in which he said that 'their next objective would be a cluster of professors to relieve their over-burdened Principal'. Morling offered the Dedicatory Prayer and doubtless longed for the day, already somewhat deferred, when assistance would be more than token. A new chapter had opened in the history of the Baptist College and of its new resident Principal. There was progress but there would also be problems.

An immediate adverse consequence of the move to Granville was the resignation of Rev J Baillie as tutor in Greek Grammar. It would now be too far to travel from Mortdale. His letter of resignation came before the Council on 17 June. It was then decided that in a re-arrangement of tutorial staff Rev W Cleugh Black be asked to take a subject.[140] Apparently he declined and it was left to the Principal to take up the slack.

At a meeting of the Granville Church on 4 August the transfers of membership of Rev GH and Mrs Morling were received from the Hurlstone Park Church. Principal Morling was rushed into service, for at a special meeting of the church on 10 August he was elected chairman. The business before the meeting was the resignation of the pastor, Rev EH Swan. The Principal said that evidently Mr Swan was suffering great mental strain. Moreover since he had only been in the Union eight years he was not entitled to any benefit from the Superannuation Fund. So he suggested that the deacons go as a body to the pastor and ask him to take a holiday and then return to the pastorate. Meanwhile he himself was willing to take charge of religious instruction at the public school. His wise and generous action enabled the pastor to continue until the following May when his resignation was received with regret.

On the denominational scene interest was focusing on the inaugural meetings of the Baptist Union of Australia held in the Burton Street

Tabernacle starting on 25 August. George Morling was appointed one of the official NSW delegates to these meetings, in which he took an active but not a leading part.[141]

In an article promoting the inauguration it was said[142], 'At the Foreign Mission Conference a voice new to this platform will be heard. And it is a very gracious, appealing voice. Principal GH Morling, MA, fresh from a flying visit to our field of missionary service, will tell of some of our 'Problems and Possibilities in Bengal'. This scholarly young leader accepted a most generous offer from a Sydney layman to put his theories of Indian missionary life to the test of experience. The result should be of vast profit to our work'. That optimistic prediction was fulfilled even though the subject as reported became 'The Missionary Situation in India'.

Probably his major contribution was the support role he played in the establishing of the Federal Board of Education. Ultimately nothing came of the amendment he successfully moved to have the practicality of a uniform exit examination for all the Baptist theological colleges investigated. However he was responsible for the introduction of a Federal extramural course that operated with some degree of success for about forty years.[143]

Two days after the inaugural meetings began, the wife of Rev Stephen Sharp, who was to have been one of the major speakers, died. George Morling took part in the graveside service at the funeral of the wife of his friend. Over the years he-was frequently called on to share in such services and he always brought a special touch to them.

At the Annual Assembly the Principal's Report had as its main emphasis the move to Granville.[144] 'The elevation to residential status', he told the delegates, 'has quite changed the College life and my own position as Principal. The common life in a college makes for efficiency in several ways. The atmosphere necessarily encourages more concentrated study; but beyond that there is much more opportunity for the impact of personality upon personality, and for the cultivation of worthy ministerial character. College discipline, too, is a great aid in the formation of proper, regular and punctual habits. The added *esprit de corps* is also of incalculable benefit'.

Time would show there were also some disadvantages in living at such close quarters. However for the present there was a sense of euphoria. The College had its own premises for the first time and the seventeen men who in one category or another were preparing for full ministerial status probably constituted a record enrolment. The Report concluded,

'We cannot but feel thankful for the College year. There has been a most manifest Divine leading. Already a long-dreamed-of advance has been made, and we enter the future with hope and confidence'.

The Assembly was notified that arising out of the establishment of the Baptist Union of Australia Principal Morling had been appointed a member of the Educational Board.[145]

The Ministers' Fraternal was asked to draw up an order of service for ordinations.[146] It fell to George Morling to present the report of the Fraternal's Committee. One matter that was felt to be especially noteworthy was that 'The Ministers' Fraternal, after exhaustive discussion, decided, with but three dissentients, to recommend the Scriptural practice of the laying on of hands, safeguarded by a carefully worded statement'. There was great concern to allay any fear that a sacerdotal element was being smuggled in. Another recommendation was that an Ordaining Council of five persons be set up to determine the fitness of candidates for ordination by the Union. Morling was elected to the first council. All members of the first council were ordained men.[147]

However George Morling's interest was not confined to the ordained ministry. During the latter part of the year, in response to a request by the Lay Preachers' Society, he conducted evening preaching classes open to all who cared to attend.

As the College year drew to a close there was by now the customary break-up. Reflecting on the year the Principal 'declared that the residential college had altered the whole complexion of College life for the students'. One of them, graduating student CT Smith, in giving his opinion of the College, said 'Our College is worthy of the name Baptist. The martyr spirit still survives in the lives of our men ... Their lives are backed up with a real experience, and their preaching vibrates with spiritual passion for the souls of men. Besides all this they are a happy lot of fellows'. An eventful year appropriately concluded when Rev Stephen Sharp 'spoke right to the heart of the young men'.[148]

As in the December of the previous year Principal Morling preached in the little church at Chullora and officiated at a baptism.[149] At the death-knell of the year on 30 December he preached at the ordination of Pastor FT Smith in the Hurlstone Park church.[150] It was the first such service arranged by the Ordination Council, all members of which participated in it.

1927
When the Executive Committee of the Union met on 27 January 1927, there was an apology from Principal Morling who was on holiday. In his absence a matter was raised concerning the Ordaining Council, which had recommended that the ordination of HT Johnston be deferred for twelve months. Mr Johnston had completed a year in College and had then been granted an extra-mural course which had dragged on for years. Also before the Executive was a letter from Mr Johnston outlining his pastoral experience and one from the secretary of the Temora Church enclosing a petition signed by 66 residents of Mimosa and one signed by 14 at Temora asking for a reconsideration of the Ordaining Council's decision. It was reported that Principal Morling had spoken by telephone to the Temora secretary and was now not averse to the ordination proceeding. The Executive decided to refer the matter back to the Ordaining Council which was rapped on the knuckles for communicating its decision to Mr Johnston before the Executive had considered it.[151] The Council withdrew its objection and at its February meeting the Executive decided that Mr Johnston should be ordained.[152] When Rev Harry Johnston died in 1961 Principal Morling took the funeral. Mrs Johnston wrote thanking him and declaring that it would have been her husband's wish 'for his beloved Principal to take the service'.

A report of a dinner to mark the beginning of the College year said, 'It was a fine gathering, and testified that the College had the warm admiration and sympathetic co-operation of the whole denomination'. That may have been a slightly over-optimistic verdict for Stanmore stalwart Mr William White, who provided the dinner, indicated some misgivings. Mr White was a very forthright gentleman. Speaking of Principal Morling's Hornsby/Pymble ministry AT Whale said, 'For a time he wore his collar in 'reverse gear', but after Mr White had made an appeal to the ministers 'not to put a barrier between themselves and the pew', he discarded the celestial circlet'. 'He was', Mr White confessed, 'surprised when asked to give the dinner as, in some respects, he was not a College enthusiast. He, however, had every confidence in their beloved Principal, and believed the men were being trained under him along the right lines. He was one of those who regarded education as it related to the training of ministerial students as like electricity, a very good thing if properly controlled, but dangerous if it got out of control'. Despite his misgivings he professed himself proud of the College, proud of the men the College was turning out and proud of the Principal'.[153]

In this latter sentiment he was not alone for it was further reported 'At the College dinner it was good to hear past and present students testifying to the great esteem in which the Principal held. The Rev GH Morling is essentially a cultured gentleman, who has captured the love, not only of the students, but of the whole Baptist constituency. He is a scholar who knows how to make the appeal to the emotions as well as to the intellect. He is loved by his students and is popular as a preacher'. It was a good start to the year.

The Principal's standing in the denomination was still further enhanced by his action in vigorously promoting the cause of the Baptist Foreign Mission. He went with Rev FJ Dunkley on a fund raising visit to the churches in the north of the state.[154] In his visit to India with Mr AS White, 'The Principal travelled with seeing eyes and enquiring mind, and he has a good story to tell'.

That he told the story well is shown by results. The comparatively new church at Armidale was first visited and gave £100. In the afternoon of the same day the mother church at Black Mountain 'responded generously' as did the churches at Tamworth, Dungog, Thalaba, Stroud, Islington, Mayfield and Newcastle. The account concluded, 'The target of £2000 set by the Foreign Mission Committee this year will assuredly be smashed'.[155]

The northern visit was followed by others to the south and to the west of the State.[156] Enormous interest was stimulated by the Principal's 'splendid Foreign Mission lecture'. At the next Assembly meetings 'the action of the College Principal and Home Mission Superintendent in supporting wholeheartedly the appeal for Foreign Missions in May last was applauded. It has drawn the various departments closer together'. In a quotation cited in *The Australian Baptist*[157] concerning the Foreign Mission Appeal Rev JC Martin wrote, 'Perhaps the outstanding fact related to the success of New South Wales. With one big effort they lifted up the contributions for Foreign Missions at least fourfold and aimed at £2000. They gained their objective. How? By releasing the Home Mission Superintendent and the College Principal to lead a united co-operative effort'.

It is not surprising that the thought of the denomination turned to its young Principal as and outstanding leader and that approaches were soon being made to him to become President of the Union.

On 18 May Rev EH Swan concluded his tenure of the Granville pastorate.[158] This situation set some people thinking how it might be exploited to help the hard-pressed Principal.

One of the responsibilities of the Advisory and Credentials Committee of the Baptist Union was to assist churches in making pastoral settlements. At its meeting early in May the idea was floated of finding a successor for Mr Swan who could also assist in the work of the College. It was further suggested to the Committee that the Principal might be appointed Moderator of the Church while such a pastor was sought. Rev WP Phillips, pastor at Carlton, was at once approached and, though not encouraging hope of a positive response, promised to consider the matter. At a Special Meeting of the Granville church on 11 May George Morling was appointed its Moderator. He told the members that at this time of crisis there was much need for prayer for guidance in the choice of a new minister. He therefore called the church to devote the month of June to special prayer. While the church prayed others planned.

A special deacons' meeting was called on 23 May to enable Rev W Cleugh Black to put a proposal to the deacons. It was that Granville should be the College Church with Principal as its pastor. According to the minutes of the meeting Mr Black, as a member of the College Council and of the Advisory Board of the Baptist Union, said that the suggestion had the support of the Secretary of the Union and of the College Council. In the latter respect he was either misreported or the wish was father to the thought. Mr Black said that the College Council would have to engage another 'Professor' and he suggested that the Church engage a 'visiting sister' to do visitation.

The deacons unanimously approved the scheme but it was not to work out precisely as planned.

The College Council met on 7 June. A proposal that Principal Morling be appointed pastor of the Granville church was turned down. Instead the Council decided to seek the co-operation of the Church with the College in the choice of a minister.[159]

When the Advisory and Credentials Committee met on 9 June Rev Phillips advised that he would allow his name to be brought before the Granville church. Rev Cleugh Black had then to tell the Committee that thinking that Rev WP Phillips had declined the approach he had suggested that Granville be made a College church with the Principal as pastor with another to assist him in the work. In view of this the Principal had resigned as Moderator and Cleugh Black was acting in that capacity. Nothing abashed the latter proposed to the Committee that the name of Mr John Deane, BA, a Latin teacher at Burwood Intermediate High School, be considered as a possible pastor for Granville. Deane was in fact contemplating entering the ministry. Nevertheless the Committee decided to submit the name Rev WP Phillips to the church but, if he declined a call, Mr Deane would be mentioned. Cleugh Black was directed 'to confer with Principal Morling as to each step'.

Mr John H. Deane, BA.

He met with Granville deacons on 14 June and presented a letter from the Advisory Board recommending that Rev WP Phillips be approached concerning the pastorate. After explaining the situation concerning Mr Phillips he had further indicated that Principal Morling could not accept the responsibilities of the pastorate.

Apparently Mr Phillips was now reluctant to allow his name to be put before the church and Mr Deane must have shown some interest for the deacons agreed, on Mr Black's suggestion, to recommend that Mr Deane be called as Student Pastor.

So another special meeting the Granville church was held on 22 June. Acting as Moderator in place of the Principal, Rev W Cleugh Black outlined a scheme to the church. As already indicated it came with the recommendation of the deacons and resulted in unanimous agreement to the following motion: 'That in compliance with the request of the College Council communicated through the Advisory Board of the Baptist Union this church is willing to call to the pastorate one who can aid in the teaching ministry of the College and accordingly extends a hearty invitation to Mr John H Deane, BA, to assume as student pastor the pastoral oversight of the church on the understanding that he will seek to become at the earliest opportunity a fully accredited minister of the NSW Baptist Union and that whilst he is thus ministering as a tutor and preparing for ordination this church cordially requisitions the services of the College Principal the Rev GH Morling, MA, as Moderator and requests him in return for Mr Deane's services to the College to assist in the preaching ministry of the church, the extent of such participation to be mutually agreed upon by Mr Deane, Mr Morling and the deacons of the church'.

It was further agreed to grant the Principal an honorarium. The College Council and the Advisory Board were to be advised of the decisions made.

The College Council met on 5 July. The Granville property was in a poor state of repair and, in particular, was affected by dampness. A letter from AC Maynard expressing, on behalf of the students, appreciation of the Council's offer of £10 towards the construction of a tennis court. However some money had been raised at a College fete and so the students asked that the promised £10 'be expended on necessary repairs to the College property, especially on the Matron's room'. Work was subsequently done on the property from time to time but it was at the best 'stop-gap' and living conditions were far from ideal.

Rev Stephen Sharp, of whose church at Burwood Deane was a member, moved and Rev WP Phillips himself seconded 'that the College Council sanction the appointment of the Principal of the College as the Moderator of the Granville church until such time as Mr Deane receive ordination and that we sanction the Principal receiving an honorarium if the Church desires to give one'.[160] Thanks were also expressed to the Granville Church for its co-operation in the call of a pastor. But Morling told the deacons he would not accept an honorarium[161], and that any contribution they wished to make should be made to the College.

He met with the Granville deacons on 12 July. He was in the chair and thanked them for the honour conferred on him in appointing him Moderator. The officers for their part declared that they had every confidence in him as Moderator and left him free to act for the church as he deemed fit. He put them to the test at once by declaring that he would like to use Baptist hymnals in the services. At the same time he offered to give a lantern lecture on his travels to and through India to fund the purchase of the hymnals.

When the members of the church met on 3 August he wisely spelled out his relationship to the church. He wanted to help the church in every way he could but the College must have his first thought. On the other hand he said that when Mr Deane came his church work must not suffer by what he does for the College. At that same meeting the resignation from the diaconate of Mr Charles Gray was received. Mr Gray was to enter College as a candidate for the ministry.

Soon the College Council had a letter from Pastor JH Deane seeking permission to study theology and to proceed to ordination. He was accepted and granted a modified course.[162] Help for the hard-pressed Principal was on the horizon. But for the immediate future his workload was increased. His involvement in the work of the Granville Church was more than a token offering. For example, Granville sponsored what was called the Merrylands Mission. In October he suggested that a series of special meetings for young people be held there and that appeals be made for conversion and baptism. Also he suggested that the deacons meet occasionally to consider the spiritual condition of the Church and its auxiliaries. He and the pastor were also given permission to advertise the church meetings for the coming month.

When the deacons met on 2 November the Moderator and Pastor set before them work they wanted to start in the near future. The list included the resumption of the men's morning meeting, the holding of a monthly young people's service and the starting of open air work. They wanted invitation cards for visitors to the church and a box at the door for prayer requests. The Principal suggested that all meetings from 5 to 10 December be suspended in order to support a Bible Conference at the church.

That was not all. The Moderator and Pastor told the deacons that they believed that the names of all Sunday School officers should be submitted to the deacons for approval. The Principal suggested that enquiries be made of other Sunday Schools to discover how they appointed their officers. The new brooms were sweeping clean and perhaps stirring up a little dust.

The Principal's Report for the 1927 Annual Assembly showed that College work had been proceeding smoothly and effectively. Academic work was most satisfactory. However, the report went 'ministerial training has to do also with inspiration and atmosphere, and such things cannot be tabulated. One can only say that with greater experience has come a greater sense of responsibility and, one hopes, a greater degree of efficiency in this most important work for Christ and His Church'.[163] Apart from some continuing help by Rev GA Craike and Rev W Higlett it appears that he had done all the lecturing. He particularly noted that his Old Testament Introduction included 'an examination of modern criticism'. However reluctantly, he was finding it necessary to face this challenge.

In a concluding paragraph he wrote, 'We have made something of an innovation this year in that two of the important subjects have been studied by the tutorial rather than the lecture method. In Bible Introduction and Church History students have been supplied with a type-written copy of my notes. This has allowed much more time for explanation and discussion and is more in line with modern scientific methods'. Many of his students will testify that this theory did not always work out in practice. The Principal was by nature too much a preacher and lecturer to encourage very much in the way of discussion.

At a denominational thanksgiving service held during the Assembly the Principal was one of the speakers. The account of the occasion[164] spoke of the infectiousness of the 'boyish enthusiasm' of his address, the keynote of which was, 'Let the redeemed of the Lord say so'.

On 12 October the Morling family circle was completed by the birth of Trevor Rees. George and Gladys Morling had much reason for thankfulness but also added reason for concern. There were now five children and the whole family was crowded into exceedingly limited quarters. Two bedrooms sufficed for the children. The college lecture room adjoined and hence it was necessary to keep the children as quiet as possible. It was not an easy situation. As the children grew an open verandah was used as a bedroom. Although it was exposed to the weather college finances were such that it was quite some time before a canvas blind was provided to keep out the rain.

In 1927 John Ridden of Cessnock entered College. Writing many years later to Principal Morling he said, 'I think too of the patience and courage of Mrs Morling, trying to raise a young family in cramped conditions with nowhere for the children to play without incurring the wrath of certain students because a childish foot had left its marks on a wet tennis court or some valuable sermon notes had disappeared into the bath-heater. If they hadn't been so dry they might not have burned so easily'. Under such difficult circumstances it is a wonder that the Principal was able to maintain his program. Happily with all the children playing around him he was able to lose himself in a book and keep on with his work. There was even a story, perhaps apocryphal, of him walking about the tennis court reading a book while holding baby Trevor upside down.

At the November meeting of the Union Executive he was again appointed Convenor of the Ordaining Council.[165]

Late in the year George Morling was touched by deep sadness occasioned by the death of one of his students, Arthur J Harvey, almost on the eve of his ordination. Over the years 'our beloved Principal' paid many splendid tributes to departed friends and colleagues. It is hard to believe that any of them was as moving as that to Arthur Harvey.[166] It began, 'For some years my life has been bound in the bundle of life with that of Arthur Harvey. I have been his pastor, his College Principal, his fellow minister in the Gospel and, in all relationships his intimate friend. And having known him this well, I declare that his was a magnificent life'. Having outlined his friend's heroic struggle against ill-health and his dedication to Christ he concluded, 'To the last he fought for life, for he thought that his work was not finished. His one thought was of his return to active service. Even in delirium he spoke of plans for a new church and of how he could win sheaves for the Master. But God touched him and he slept for his splendid course was finished'.

'To him that overcometh will I grant to sit with Me on My throne, even as I also overcame and am set down with My Father on His throne. Arthur Harvey overcame in the strength of the Lord; now he shares the throne. This week he was to have been ordained. The ordination has been replaced by coronation'.

1928

When the 1928 College session began Mr and Mrs JH Burnet hosted a College Subscribers' Dinner attended by about three hundred guests. Mr Burnet called for support to the College and to Principal who was giving his best to the work. For his part the Principal sought 'to set forth the ideals for which the College stood. These were, education specifically for the ministry, and for the Baptist ministry, for their students had to become Baptist ministers. It stood also for the Word of God and the winning of souls ... The need today was for a fresh and manly ministry. It needed to be attractive, non-sanctimonious and to appeal to the man in the street. May we be preserved from turning out men who are merely parsons! The College must stand for a ministry achievement. We must do something for Jesus Chrisy'.[167]

Some of the ramifications of the Church/college relationship were made apparent in two meetings in March. At a Granville members' meeting on 14 March the pastor said that he would not be able to visit as much as formerly because of College claims. He spoke of the Church's association with the College and the uphill fight the College had with the denomination. As a mark of appreciation of the College he suggested that the Church give the whole of one Sunday's offerings to the College. If the Pastor supported the College the Moderator supported the Church. Presiding at the deacons' meeting on 26 March he suggested that during Loyalty Month members and friends be appealed to for promises to pay off the manse debt over the next twenty months. In the light of subsequent events it may be noted that Deacon Terry seconded the motion giving the Moderator and Pastor authority to proceed along the lines suggested. At the same meeting Principal Morling's continuing evangelistic concern was apparent. Announcing that the first meeting of the reconstituted Men's Morning Meeting was to be held (rather inappropriately one might think) on Mothers' Day he declared that it must have 'the definite aim of winning souls'.

An item of special business introduced by him was to be a great concern to him for some months. It concerned an attempt by Mr Coleman, a Granville member, to bring about a reconciliation between the Merrylands Baptist Mission which owed allegiance to the Granville Church and the Merrylands Baptist Church which was related to the Parramatta Baptist Church. Apparently false reports about Mr Coleman's actions were circulated. These led to misunderstandings and strained relations. The matter dragged on for six months and was a great concern to the Principal as Moderator of the Church.

At the May meeting of the Granville deacons the main matter was the 'Coleman Affair'. However another item was also to have a considerable effect on the Church. The need for a new organ was raised. The organist, Mr Overton Jnr, knew of a good one for £85.10.0 and he would be willing to finance with no repayments for two years. The offer was accepted on the condition that no appeal for funds was made until the manse debt was extinguished. The meeting placed on record approval of the successful conduct of the work of the Church by the Moderator and Pastor.

About this time, Rev CJ Tinsley, then President of the Union, was 'instrumental in establishing a chair of Evangelism at the College'[168], and was 'the chief lecturer'.[169] Morling earnestly desired his students to be able preachers of the Gospel.

On 6 May Rev WM Cartwright, a man who exemplified the Principal's ideal of ministry, died. At a Service of Remembrance in the Petersham Church Principal Morling was the speaker. 'It is fitting' he said, 'that I should pay a personal tribute to his life and ministry. Mr Cartwright was the pastor of my boyhood and youth … In my most impressionable years he inspired me with a living example of robust, dignified, genial Christian manhood … It was he who brought me to the point of spiritual decision culminating in my baptism and membership of the church … Then he was genuinely interested in my unfolding life. A constant visitor in our home, he advised and encouraged me to set a high ideal and patiently work to attain it. He was a friend as well as a minister'.[170]

George Morling soon suffered a loss of a different kind, for the Executive Committee received the resignation of Rev Ralph Maidment who was applying for the Presbyterian ministry.[171] Ralph Maidment had shared with him a year in the Victorian College and the first year of the NSW College, graduating with him. The ranks of his contemporaries still in the Baptist ministry were thinning.

During 1928 the Principal began to encourage students to prepare for the Licentiate of Theology (LTh) of the Melbourne College of Divinity. The College Council decided to make enquiries of denominational trust funds concerning the payment of examination fees, and some help was forthcoming.[172]

Morling's abilities as Bible teacher were brought to prominence among Baptists in 1928-1930 through a series of Bible teaching tours associated with the Presidential Years of Rev CJ Tinsley and himself.[173] Tinsley arranged for the Home Mission Superintendent and the Principal of the College to accompany him on a Presidential visit to the south-west of the State for the purpose of conducting a Bible Conference at Leeton.[174] Rev JH Baker commented 'This conference has also revealed to us that the Baptist College of NSW has as the Principal a man of God who has a rich spiritual experience. Rev GH Morling has excelled in a much-needed ministry of today, that of Bible exposition. When it was suggested that he should give Bible readings each afternoon, there was a little uncertainty as to the success of such gatherings. However, it was decided to commence on the Monday afternoon (Surely that was a venture) and the attendance was gratifying. The Bible reading was a veritable feast, which accounted for the attendance being doubled on the following day. Principal Morling has served his Lord, whom he delights to exalt, in a special manner by his visit to Leeton. The crowning service came on Sunday night, the last night of the conference, when there were seven decisions, and also some splendid cases of re-consecration'.[175]

George Morling, after a gap of more than four years, began a series of diary entries related to his daily devotions.

16 July. 'Remembering the blessing of the Leeton Bible Convention and the personal call for prayer pray for renewal of determination to pray more'.

There followed the cryptic note: 'Request concerning (1) College housekeeping. (2) Granville Church'. There were problems in respect of both of these. On 18 July, he wrote, 'Thank God for answer to prayer in regard to Miss Diffey', he was referring to his request concerning College housekeeping. The Council had decided to employ a resident housekeeper and so, it was hoped, resolve a number of problems in the domestic life of the College [m].

This seemingly minor matter was an encouragement to him and he wrote on 20 July, 'prayer to be delivered from weakening of desire to pray especially in view of the answer to prayer regarding Miss Diffey'. Arising out of his time of devotion there came a statement of conviction, 'Felt that more prayer would make my life even a world-wide power'.

The brief notation on 23 July, 'Prayer to be strengthened in resolution to be a man of prayer, to let the College stand for Christ, the Word of God and the winning of souls' had a sequel the following day. Then he wrote, 'Thank God for encouragement last night at Thanksgiving Service at Burton Street, for Mr Hercus's tribute. Later for success of College team at Inter-College Debate. Then for opportunity to confess Christ at supper. This is an answer to yesterday's prayer. The Heavenly Father a mission for the College'.

---

[m] Miss Diffey was not the first housekeeper/matron. Mrs Edwards 17 June 1926-3 May 1927 and Miss Hayman 13 May 1027-31 July 1928 preceded her.

On Saturday, 28 July, he recorded 'A good week. Have to thank God for financial disappointment'. Apparently there was some error in the housekeeping accounts and he felt this called for prayer for a new method of handling them. An answer to so mundane a request might 'be laid hold of as an earnest of answer to the spiritual' (requests).

With Sunday services looming he noted 'I have prayed for the spirit of expectancy for definite blessing tomorrow'. There followed on Monday this acknowledgement, 'I have to thank God for definite blessing yesterday as I prayed. Dave Stevenson waited after the service and at Concord at night there was power. Then there was a definite answer yesterday in regard to Glad'.

'Miss Diffey, the housekeeper' arrived and prompted the note on Tuesday, 31 July, 'pray that her advent may be in accordance with previous prayer and that every detail of her commencement may be overruled by the Heavenly Father'. By week's end he was acknowledging his assurance that her coming was indeed an answer to prayer. On that Saturday morning he listed under 'Petitions' (1) about extra-mural men (2) about Newcastle and Bible readings (3) about Presidency.

He was concerned for men pursuing ministerial studies out in the country and for the effectiveness of the ministry he was soon to exercise at Newcastle but the third matter exercised him most deeply. He had been approached to allow himself to be nominated as Vice-President at the forthcoming Assembly. To accept would impose great burdens and strains but would open large doors of opportunities for service and leadership in the wider denominational sphere.

On the evening of 5 August he was to preach at Granville and wrote that morning, 'Feel the great responsibility and much of anticipation that the Saviour will be present. Again pray for definite power - above mere influence'. These personal notations provide an intimate glimpse of the growth of a true man of prayer.

An event which reflected both denominational pride in, and defensiveness of, the College, was the winning by Baptist students of the inter-collegiate Pierce Memorial Shield for debating. A columnist remarked, 'There has been in some quarters a covert inclination to sneer at the 'learning' of the students of the Baptist Theological College'.[176] He clearly implied that the success of the students showed that the stigma and the sneer were alike unwarranted. The College and its Principal could hold their heads high.

The Principal and the President of the Union, as reported the following week, teamed up again to entertain at a dinner the recently formed Baptist Varsity Gospel Team. Their purpose was to commend and encourage the team in its preaching of the gospel and in its stand against the encroachments of 'modernistic teachings' among undergraduates at Sydney University. Principal Morling who, it was said, was 'showing a genuine interest', undertook to give Bible studies for the benefit of the team.

On Sunday 19 August, he confided to his diary a significant conviction, 'The visit of the extra-mural men has been a blessing. The special days of devotion has shown that there must be a very strong stand taken for doctrinal-experimental truth. I believe that God is calling me to this distinctive work both in College and church'. That conviction he never renounced. He saw that orthodoxy could be merely truth on ice. What was needed was truth on fire.

George Morling really came of age as a denominational leader when at the 1928 Annual Assembly of the NSW Baptist Union he was elected Vice-President[177] and was re-appointed as Principal for a further three years with an increase of £50 in his stipend.[178] A section of his Principal's Report to the Assembly gives further glimpses of the man and his ideals.[179]

'With the presentation of this report 1 complete seven years of service in the College. The years, I hope, have not been without achievement. Our College has set before itself the deliberate ideal of combining spiritual efficiency with educational efficiency. There is evidence that the combination has been effective in moulding students who are commending themselves to the churches. The maintenance of a fervent spiritual life in the College has not in any way meant the lowering of the intellectual standard. We can claim that the work done in the NSW Baptist College well bears comparison with the work done in any other Theological College. The speaking ability of the men is shown by their meeting in and winning the final of the Inter-college debate. But if the years have brought partial achievement they have brought more the vision of possibility. I am convinced that our College can have a very great and a very wide ministry for Jesus Christ'.

'As I observe the religious situation 1 am impressed with the need of sending out a steady stream of ministers full of zeal for Jesus Christ and with ability to present His claims to the multitude. The Baptist witness is as much needed these days as ever it was. We are in the right way of meeting this need. Fortunately a record number of students are applying - and men of the right stamp. In fact, we shall very soon be obliged to consider a scheme of College extension'.

'And, further, the College has this year had a ministry among lay preachers, and in previous years among Sunday School teachers. I have ambitions to extend this ministry, so that all branches of the Union shall benefit by its College. And, then, the Bible Conference work is big with possibility. I have a dream to make the College a centre for State-wide activity in respect to the teaching of the great doctrines of the Word of God, and especially of distinctively Baptist doctrine. Such a ministry also is needed'. '1 hope and I intend by God's grace that the future years will bring out such advance'.

A few days before the Assembly he had returned from a visit to Culcairn where his friend Enos Coleman had been ministering. He wrote in his diary on Saturday, 14 September, 'Two special matters to commit definitely to God: (1) the Dinner at Assembly meetings; concerning Vice-Presidency, my re-appointment and the matter of a new College (2) Granville Church - especially matter relating to Mr Coleman [n] and Mr Terry. These matters I commend now to the Heavenly Father, believing that He already is working'.

The transfer of Mr Coleman along with his wife and daughter to the Parramatta Church had been agreed by the deacons on 12 August so any issue relating to him should have been settled. What the matter concerning him and Mr Terry was does not appear in the official records. Clearly, however, it was causing George Morling some anxiety. Several subsequent diary entries concern significant events during the Assembly and the Principal's response to them.

'Wednesday, 18 September – 'Praise God for splendid start to the Assembly and for record year. Pray that guidance may be given about College in view of reported gift of Mr Bullock. Pray about finance affairs that Mr Ardill may not be wounded'.

----

[n] This Mr Coleman was not Rev Enos.

'Thursday, 19 - Prayer about Mr Ardill certainly answered. Pray today that College affairs may glorify Jesus Christ first. I do not know what Mr Bullock will do or what will be done about the rent. I put the two affairs in God's hands'.

'Friday, 20 - The Lord answered wonderfully yesterday. Mr. Bullock gave the College and my salary was raised. The atmosphere in which all was done was beautiful. Thank God. Pray about ordination of Messrs Haughan and Martin today and for other business'.

On the Wednesday following the Assembly he wrote: 'The Lord was good last week. I must pray for much grace that my new opportunity of service as Vice-President may be met with increased spiritual life'.

'The Lord, too, has shown me that I must take more care of my health. This means withdrawing somewhat from Granville. There is difficulty in the church and I do not want to let Mr Deane down. I must pray about this'.

The next week on 2 October, in the last entry for almost a year, he wrote, 'The Lord must be sought concerning Granville. The difficulty will be faced at the deacons' meeting tonight. I have to thank Him for growing rest about the church'. Later in the day he wrote, 'I have to thank God already for answering prayer in giving Mr Deane blessing this morning in the prayer meeting (probably of the College) from the words, 'I am meek and lowly in heart''.

The only item in the minutes of that deacons' meeting that might relate to the diary entry had to do with him becoming Vice-President of the Union. Because of this, he explained, his work at the Church would have to be curtailed. However, the Church would not suffer as Pastor Deane's duties at the College would be lessened to give him more time at the Church.

In the same meeting he suggested that a special series of evangelistic services be held in November and that the Church try to get Mr Amos the Singing Evangelist, to conduct the meetings. He stressed the importance of preparation by prayer and so asked that the deacons and ministers have a special prayer meeting on 11 October.

The minutes of Council meeting of 6 November record an apology from the Principal because of illness and a motion that he 'be relieved from paying rent of College premises from 1 November, 1928 to opening of College 1929'. The trouble was probably one of the recurrent bouts of gout that from time to time put him out of action and made it desirable for him to get away from College to recuperate.[180]

At the end of the College year there was introduced, on the suggestion of the Students' Association, a Speech Day held on 1 December, in the college grounds.[181] It was highly successful with 300 attending. Rev Henry Clark in his opening prayer gave special thanks to God for the Principal's recovery from ill-health.

Though dogged by health problems he was resilient. The account of the Speech Day stated that he 'gave his report of the year's work at the College with characteristic ability and diction'.[182] It had been an 'exceptionally profitable one in the cause of Jesus Christ' with a record number of students, seven of whom sat for LTh diploma of the Melbourne College of Divinity. He hoped that the College would not only train men to use books but would enable them to think for themselves.

1929

The Principal's respite from the pressures of his college program did not solve his health problem. 'The Council decided that in order to fully recapture his health the Principal be instructed not to take any preaching appointments for at least three months'.[183] At the College Commencement Service it was mentioned with regret that his health was 'far from what might be desired'.[184] However he was present at the function when Rev CJ Tinsley, the Chairman, said 'The Principal was gaining in the confidence of the churches and the love of the people. He combines education and spirituality to a very fine degree. The expressed appreciation of the students as they leave the College is the highest tribute that could be paid to Principal Morling'.

The Union Executive appointed Principal Morling, in his absence, to represent NSW on the Education Committee at the meetings of the Baptist Union of Australia to be held at Melbourne in August.[185] He was also to be asked to speak on 'The Responsibility of the Baptized Life to the Church', but indicated that he would not accept the speaking opportunity and he 'desired to be relieved from attending' because of 'his need to conserve his strength'.[186] With his Presidential year approaching that was but prudent. In this same connection the College Council in August agreed to release him from lecturing in second term because of Presidential responsibilities. He was to arrange for Rev JH Deane to carry on the college work. This somewhat undermined the assurance he had earlier given to the Granville deacons and perhaps created some tensions in the church.

For some time it had been recognised that the College had outgrown the Granville property and the College Council had schemes for a new college. At its last meeting before the Union Assembly meetings it was left with the Principal to place the scheme before Assembly and he was authorised to use his Presidential year to awaken a sense of College needs.[187]

At the Assembly with his ever so proud parents in the congregation George Morling was duly inducted as the President of the Baptist Union of New South Wales. The subject of his Presidential address was 'The Church's Heritage of Power'.[188] It was an attractive and impassioned setting forth of what was to be most distinctive in the thinking and teaching of that ardent servant of God. It represented the mature conviction of a deeply devout man. All his subsequent teaching on the Holy Spirit was in large part an amplification of that address. Rev William Higlett, Secretary of the Union, wrote to the new President, 'After the experiences of the past week, it seems almost superfluous to write anything to you, yet I have pleasure in conveying to you the most cordial thanks of the Union for your Presidential Address. It was the prominent feature in what proved a wonderful Assembly and while your chief satisfaction will be that you were God's messenger to us, yet it is well to be assured that the Union appreciates most highly the important and inspiring message you delivered'.

His old friend, AT Whale, commented 'The denomination might well be proud of its new President, who not only brings academic attainment to his office, but also a consecrated manhood, and a lowly heart'. He went on to say, 'Favourite attitudes of the President are 'arms akimbo', arms full length, with hands clenched, and hand extended, sometimes tapping a point with his finger on the Bible'.[189] Those who are at all familiar with Principal Morling's pulpit mannerisms may be surprised to find no reference to the bringing together of the finger-tips, a frequently repeated action executed with unerring accuracy. Perhaps it was a later development.

Appropriately the Assembly featured a College Day. The Executive Committee recorded at its next meeting that in his report the Principal 'paid glowing tributes to ... every one connected with the College with the exception of himself'. He mentioned that all seven men who sat for the examinations of the Melbourne College of Divinity had been successful. It was also pleasing that the library was growing.

Nevertheless, despite academic successes and growth, there was still sensitivity about the status of the College. The minutes of the Assembly confirm this, recording the following: 'The President of the College Council, Rev CJ Tinsley, drew the attention of the Assembly to a statement which appeared in 'the Baptist' which was not very complimentary to our College and our Principal. Mr Tinsley moved 'that the College Council be empowered to prepare a resolution to be submitted to the Assembly this afternoon which will counteract these remarks referred to in 'the Baptist' which would convey a wrong impression regarding our Principal and the College'.[190]

The motion was a reaction to a plea by Dr FJ Wilkin of the Victorian College in *The Australian Baptist*[191] for the consideration of a Federal Theological College for Australia. One of the suggested advantages of such a College would be a raising of the efficiency of ministerial training. This is what caused alarm in the loyal. It had the effect of provoking a statement of the esteem in which the Principal President was held. The relevant minute reads, 'On the motion of Rev CJ Tinsley, seconded by Rev W Cleugh Black, it was resolved 'that in view of the reported utterance of Dr FJ Wilkin concerning the professional standard of the respective State Colleges this Assembly is convinced that Dr Wilkin did not desire to reflect upon the academic achievements or administrative abilities of his professional brethren when he spoke about the desirability of securing for a central College tutors of great experience and world renown but, lest his utterance be accepted as such a reflection upon the present College Principals in general and our own worthy Principal, this Assembly places on record its recognition of the high scholastic attainments of the Rev GH Morling, MA, and its gratification that since his appointment as Principal of the College he has manifested qualities of leadership that have heightened the prestige of the College, his students having excelled in nearly all competitive tests with distinguished Colleges of other Denominations and furthermore, under his efficient administration a type of graduate has been produced who will not only be loyal to our denominational principles but who will also carry on the great evangelistic traditions, and stand for the College ideals, education and evangelism'. It was a huge and reassuring vote of confidence in the Principal as he faced the pressures of his Presidential year.

Earlier in the Assembly he had urged upon the delegates the necessity of a larger College in the near future. His wish to present this need during his visit to the churches had then been approved by the Assembly. The vote of confidence in him must have greatly encouraged him to press strongly the need for a new College.

When George Morling became President the Depression was beginning to be felt and already the Newcastle coalfields were seriously affected. Unemployment was widespread. Among his earliest visits as President were two successive weekends spent in the Newcastle and Hunter district seeking to encourage the churches.

On 19 October Rev GA Craike, pastor of Petersham Church, died under tragic circumstances. His death was a great loss to the denomination and especially to the college and its Principal. He had been a good friend, a loyal supporter and a valued colleague in the lecturing program of the College for a number of years.[192, o]

George Morling continued as moderator of the Granville Church during his Presidential year. In that capacity he chaired both a deacons' and a members' meeting on 30 October. A motion came before the deacons that a recommendation go to the Church that the Pastor's stipend be increased by £1 per week retrospective to 1 October. It was passed but not before the defeat of an amendment moved by Mr Terry that there be no increase until the Church debt was paid off.

At the Special Church meeting that followed Mr Terry again opposed the recommendation urging no increase until Church and organ debts were liquidated. Six of the 24 members present supported him but the motion was passed. It had been agreed when Mr Deane was called that his stipend of £5 per week would be reviewed if the financial situation improved.

----
[o] Craike suffered a 'sudden illness' which had commenced two months earlier, and which led to 'mental troubles' for which he was admitted to Broughton Hall, a voluntary psychiatric hospital. He died there soon after 'a marked change'. GHM presided at funeral services at Petersham church and Rookwood Cemetery on 21 October.

There was an aftermath. Several months later Mr Terry resigned from the diaconate and shortly after Mr and Mrs Terry and seven others transferred to the Merrylands Church.[193]

Rev FJ Dunkley wrote concerning the President[194], 'The first of the series of special meetings in connection with the district associations has been held at Auburn. The President, who is nothing if not original, has determined that, instead of visiting each church separately, he will conduct conventions in connection with the associations. The meetings, which will last for three or four days, will be held both afternoon and night and will be on a special theme. The President has it in his heart to popularise Bible readings in our churches. At Auburn, which was made the centre for the Cumberland Association, Mr Morling, from the first eight chapters of Hebrews, served out strong meat for three consecutive nights and on the fourth night there was a gathering in of results. On each night Mr Morling was followed by another minister whose special theme was 'The Holy Spirit''. The report indicated an enthusiastic response by large congregations to the venture. The reporter was clearly dubious about similar success in country areas where the churches were more scattered.

Another comment on the same page is illuminating. It confirms the suspicion that the Principal was not as abstracted as he sometimes appeared to be. In commenting on the ways in which students facing examinations occasionally relieved their tensions the reporter said, 'The Principal indulges in many a quiet little chuckle over some things that his professional astuteness prevents him from officially noticing'. Rev McDonald gave a glimpse of another facet of the Principal's character when he recounted an experience from about this same time.

He wrote, 'One thing I, and I alone, can tell of the Principal and his students. In the early days of the Baptist Union of Australia a 'Board of Education' was appointed to try and develop a standard for our Theological Colleges. The Board was located in Melbourne, and was composed of Principal Holdsworth, Dr Wilkin and myself. One of the first official engagements I undertook was to visit the NSW College. It was the occasion for a preaching service, one of the young men having the task of preaching for criticism. I thought that the address was a good one, well delivered, and was surprised when the Principal gave him scathing criticism. When we were at lunch I expressed my feeling that the criticism was too harsh, but changed my view when the Principal snatched a book from the shelf, opened it where it contained a sermon by a London preacher, and said, 'Look at that; I will not stand for dishonesty - he took that sermon and delivered it as his own, and I will not allow that!'. That reveals the man, and the teacher, whom we honour'. In a gesture of support the College Council resolved, on the motion of Dr EL Watson, 'that we express our sincere thanks to Principal for the excellent way in which he is carrying out his duties as President of the Union'.[195]

With the end of the College year came the now customary Speech Day. Because of the hundreds that attended it was held on the College tennis court under the blazing sun.[196] Principal Morling spoke - 'Let us then hold before ourselves this vision which for me has become brighter and more clearly defined during this year. We desire that this college shall be a centre of strong, reasoned, vibrant, effective evangelicalism; that it shall stand unashamedly and aggressively for the Gospel of Jesus Christ; that it shall be both a bulwark of defence and a school of propagation for the Word of God; that it shall have a bold witness for the distinctive principles of the Baptists. We purpose that from this College shall go forth men throughout NSW and Australia and even throughout the world, who shall stand forth and with the ringing confidence of personal experience, the commendation of a holy life, and the added advantage of an efficient education, declare the evangel of the Cross for the salvation of souls'.

He indicated that despite a deep sense of inadequacy and imperfection motivated by the very loftiness and solemnity of the task there were some causes for satisfaction, the loyalty of students to College ideals, their hard work in their studies and churches, the growth of team spirit, the rising passion for foreign missions, a greater ministry among the churches, a thriving lay-preachers' class and requests for Bible conferences. He concluded by saying, 'And now I crave your patience to hear a word about the future. At the Annual Assembly I showed that in a short time these Granville premises would be outgrown. I did not then know how soon the prophecy would be realised. This year seven men have lived in College, while six others have been in attendance. Next March we are being asked to accommodate another seven men in residence while, for the year after, already four men are awaiting entrance, with only one man leaving. All this is very healthy for the denomination but it is very embarrassing for us. It simply means that the Baptist Union of NSW is advancing so rapidly that it requires much larger

College premises. This afternoon, in accordance with the resolution of the Assembly, I remind you of this situation, and ask you very definitely that you, the friends of the College, will join us in prayer that we may have Divine guidance at this juncture. Hitherto the Lord has led us and we have known that He has led us. If it is His will to lead us out into a larger place and into larger service, He will make the way plain once again'.

With the depression deepening it would be more than three years before the Lord made the way forward plain and there would be continuing frustrations and problems.

The chairman, Rev CJ Tinsley 'thanked God for Principal Morling's restored health, and expressed the wish of all that he might be long spared to carry on the work they appreciated so much'. That prayer was certainly nswered and it would appear that in the main George Morling's health from about that time gave much less concern.

The NSW President addressed 'A new year message' to the Baptists of Australia.[197] 1929 had been a good year for them. 'There are tides of the Spirit and reports from all the States encourage the belief that a time of refreshing from the Presence of the Lord is coming upon us ... As we approach the portals of 1930 shall we not reverently kneel before God and ask for a fresh anointing from the Holy One, so that with clearer vision and sterner determination, we may gird ourselves anew for the service of Christ?'

George Morling was well aware that from some points of view the times were not propitious. 'These lines', he wrote 'are penned from the Maitland coalfields in New South Wales. It is a time of industrial strife. Suspicion, hatred, violence are abroad. One feels perhaps as never before, that there is something wrong at the very heart of things; that a political adjustment, necessary and desirable as it is, can only be at the best a sorry patching, that the world urgently needs Jesus Christ, because He alone can transform life at its centre'.

On 19 December he addressed the Preachers' Society on 'the Holy Spirit in the life of a preacher of the gospel'.[198] The same day Fred Whale, fifteen-year-old son of Mr RN Whale, died following a road accident. GHM attended the funeral in his capacity as President.[199]

There was probably a distinct autobiographical element when a little later he wrote, 'It may well be that the close of 1929 finds us depleted of spiritual energy. We know what our task is and we have bravely given ourselves to it. But the reserves of strength have given out and we face the new year with slender resources, yes, and the soul may have received in the battle of life a wound which still gives pain. Yet all is well. Thank God for the provision for tired and wounded lives. We can always reckon on the anointing with fresh oil'.

1930
Significantly this entry appears in the Principal's diary on 22 January, 1930. 'This is Mr Deane's ordination day. I am to speak tonight and desire to prepare myself for the solemn meeting and seek for a fresh anointing in view of the Orange meetings next week'. The ordination service, at which Pastor WG Doull was also a candidate, was held in the Granville Church.[200] Included in the service was the presentation of a 'testimonial' to John Deane by the Principal on behalf of the church. With the ordination of John Deane the Principal ceased to be the Moderator on the Granville church. The church meeting on 5 February decided to present him with a clock in recognition of his services. The Orange meetings to which reference was made comprised a Bible Conference with the theme of 'The Holy Spirit' arranged by the Western Baptist Association. This was part of the Principal's Presidential emphasis.[201]

Growing out of his earlier pastorate at Pymble he had a close relationship with Mr and Mrs FW Winn and their family. On 8 February, Thirza, the eldest daughter, was married to Mr Horace Parsons in the Pymble Church. The former pastor found time in the midst of Presidential duties to attend the wedding and to take over as the master of ceremonies at the reception.[202] It may have been the same day that he participated in the opening of the Waverley Church's new school hall and manse, bringing a message to the people. Though he concentrated his energies on the Bible conferences numerous other demands were constantly made on him.

When fellow-member of the Granville Church, Mr Archie F Patten, a comparatively young man, died in February, George Morling spoke at the funeral service on 24 February.[203]

Meanwhile, he was conducting Bible conferences in various places including Sydney suburbs, the northern coalfields, western districts and the Blue Mountains[204], including Blackheath at Easter time.[205]

The 1930 College Commencement was held in the Petersham Church on 4 March.[206] It was reported that, judged by the speeches some of them made, Principal Morling was 'as beloved by his students as was Arnold of Rugby'.[207] The Principal said that seven years earlier he was considered to be too young to be Principal - that was not his fault but he had lived it down. He paid a warm tribute to the late Rev GA Craike who had given such splendid tutorial help to the College. His mantle had now fallen on Rev JH Deane, BA.

The new College session saw several additions to the staff of visiting lecturers. This meant that the Principal was able to concentrate on a narrower range of subjects with consequent greater effectiveness in teaching. It also meant that the gaps caused by Presidential visits to churches could be more easily filled. The next Bible convention, also with the theme of the Holy Spirit, was at Blackheath over the Easter weekend.

On 14 March he suffered a further loss when Rev John Baillie, much loved young pastor of Mortdale, died. John Baillie was a greatly gifted and attractive man. Principal Morling's tribute at his funeral service[208] was altogether worthy of so splendid a servant of Christ. He had a remarkable ability to strike the right note on such occasions. Within the next few days he presided over Marrickville's 44th Anniversary Public Meeting.[209] He spoke at a public welcome to Petersham's new pastor, Rev Joshua Robertson MA on 17 March.[210]

On 22 March, as President of the BUNSW, GHM set a stone and gave an address at the foundation ceremony of the Croydon Baptist Church.[211] At the beginning of April the Half-Yearly Assembly of the Baptist Union was held in Wellington. Two aspects of the meetings were especially close to the President's heart. There was a lengthy discussion on the training of ministers. His main contribution to the session was to assert that the men in College were being trained for the ministry. They will be given as much culture as they can absorb, the overruling principle being that their whole training must be consistent with a passion for souls.

The other significant element was a series of addresses and discussions, spread over two days, on the theme of 'Spiritual Culture'. The President himself made the major contribution in an address on 'The Culture of the Soul'.[212] 'At the evening session the President of the Union delivered his Presidential address, his theme being 'The Culture of the Soul'. He was not indifferent to the present prevailing troubles, nor did he think that the Church had nothing to do with social matters. He reminded his audience of the fact that Lloyd George, in the early days of the Great War, when almost overwhelmed by the magnitude of the task which devolved upon him said, 'I cannot go on; I must lay down the task'. Dr. Robertson Nicol prayed with him and sent him back. The man of God helped the man of affairs. If we are to be qualified to deal effectually with the varied conditions which come before us, we should be as efficient spiritually as is possible'.

'In a logical address, the President dealt with the foundation and upbuilding of the spiritual life. For physical health we must observe natural laws. Regular, suitable nourishment is as essential to spiritual growth as it is to physical growth. The law of cleansing is equally necessary in the development of either. The need of a suitable 'atmosphere' was emphasised. If the mind is filled with useless and harmful literature and other equally damaging things there cannot be growth. The law of exercise must be observed. The natural man cannot develop without exercise of the muscles and limbs. Left unused, they would speedily become atrophied and useless. In like manner our spiritual nature required exercise. If we want to grow we must work'.
The President closed with an impassioned appeal for real consecration which would not only affect our own lives, but would render us a greater power for good to others. God's willingness to bestow blessings upon us is unbounded. Our willingness to accept the blessings requires cultivation.

A beautiful feature in the afternoon was that Rev and Mrs Hunter, during the time devoted to 'Consecration in the Home'; took the opportunity of publicly dedicating their infant daughter.

He conducted on 12 April a convention at Auburn. There was 'instruction and inspiration' in the whole series of meetings but what made the greatest impression was the Principal's personal testimony. In a most candid way he traced the stages of his spiritual pilgrimage up to the present when 'he testified to a better knowledge of the Holy Spirit and His work, and stated that he had lately emphasised in his preaching and teaching the doctrine of the Holy Spirit'. The report of this testimony[213] concluded, 'The speaker's concluding consecration was expressed in the following words '0 God, take all there is of me that I may enjoy all there is of thee'. The testimony struck almost all the notes that were distinctive of George Morling's teaching.

At the meeting of the Executive Committee on 29 April he spoke of the response to the meetings held and planned for Bible study. He commented that there seemed to be a hunger for plain teaching of the Word of God.[214] On 28 May he spoke at the Newcastle and District Association annual conference, then spent ten days in the area speaking at several churches.[215] Subsequent events confirmed this. A paragraph in *The Australian Baptist* [216] ran, 'The Bible conferences being conducted by the President of the Union are demonstrating that our people are hungry for definite Bible teaching. Crowded congregations gather to listen to what would have been a year or two ago designated heavy stuff. On one occasion recently a congregation more than taxed the accommodation of the church assembled to hear a sermon on 'Baptist Principles'. Bibles were freely used and the speaker's references closely followed. That it was a profitable hour was demonstrated at the close of the service when half a dozen people applied for baptism'.

In these conferences the President often enlisted the help of other teachers. For example, a notable Bible Convention was held in June at Stanmore. The principal speakers were Rev Dr FW Boreham, Rev WD Jackson of Collins Street Church Melbourne, and Rev JH Deane, pastor of Granville Church and College lecturer.[217] However, Rev FJ Dunkley commented[218], 'The President has piloted the meetings throughout, but, on the three afternoons preceding Mr Deane's expositions, he gave in his own tender and simple style some readings and expositions from the First Epistle of John ... Those who heard Mr Morling will know that his expositions, although not of great length, were of cameo distinctness. The afternoon meetings alone were worth the conference'. As many as 600 attended a single meeting and many made open responses.

At its meeting on 9 July the Granville Church showed its regard for the Principal by appointing him an Elder of the Church.

During his year as President his friend from boyhood, AT (Bert) Whale began under his supervision an extra-mural course of studies leading to ordination. The first book that he listed for his friend to study was

Nunn's *Elements of New Testament Greek*. That for Bert Whale was the start of a life-long love affair with the Greek New Testament. It is possible that he had some slight knowledge of Greek before this, for some months earlier he had written an article about the incoming President under the Greek *nom-de-plume Tokeetos* - the whale. However one might hazard a guess that Cleugh Black who was Bert Whale's pastor at Hornsby had given him the name and he probably knew little other Greek. Certainly he was set to study at a beginner level. However, he went on to gain considerable proficiency in the language. At his death his friend George gave the tribute. In it he spoke of Bert Whale, knowing that death was near, seeking permission to go home from hospital. Then he went on to say, 'For two weeks with mental powers unimpaired, he read his beloved Greek New Testament up to the end - and in radiant peace, he prepared for the end'.

But to return to 1930. On the financial front the situation became increasingly grim. The College was not insulated against the effects of the Depression. The College Council declined repeated requests from the students for radiators to be allowed in their rooms. However, help was offered in treating any draughts and a fire was promised for the lecture room. When the council is found seeking to raise an overdraft 'to tide us over the lean period' the reason for such stringent economy is explained.

With the Principal's Presidential year running out, the College Council at its August meeting sustained a motion proposed by Rev CJ Tinsley 'that the Principal be allowed six month's vacation, dating from October to the end of March to study for his BD degree. And as the Principal intends to rent a cottage at the seaside he be released from rent at College during that period'. In expressing appreciation for the Council's action George Morling said that his objective in taking his BD degree was for the greater efficiency of the College.[219]

At the Annual Assembly the Union Secretary, Rev William Higlett, paid tribute to the retiring President's 'memorable' year of office, drawing attention particularly to the influence of the Bible Conferences. There followed, however, the comment concerning the President, 'Occasionally he has overworked his strengths but, with his College duties, he has accomplished what is little short of wonderful. He is a man 'greatly beloved' and his ministry has done much to enrich the life of our churches'.[220]

Despite some domestic problems the reports of the Council and the Principal to the Annual Assembly revealed much cause for thankfulness. The Secretary, Rev A Butler, wrote, 'The Principal has had a very strenuous year. His dual task as Principal of the College and as President of the Union, has added greatly to his responsibilities. Nevertheless, he has put his best into his work, with the result that both the College and the Union have had a record year'. For his part the Principal reported, 'My energies during this year necessarily have been divided between the activities of the College and the wider interests of the denomination. While there has been some loss in concentration the year's experience has been valuable. The College has been brought into closer touch with the churches and, on the other hand, one has been able to see more clearly the actual needs of the churches and the corresponding qualifications which the young minister should have in order to meet these needs. Then, also, the succession of Bible Conferences has given me a still greater love for the Holy Scriptures and a greater desire to send forth men from the College who can expound its treasures. The inner life of the College has never been quite so buoyant and harmonious. The students have conspired to make the year easy for me'.[221] The Morling family moved for some months to Collaroy, living near to dear friends and relations, Rev and Mrs Enos Coleman, Mr Coleman being the minister of the local Presbyterian Church.

This, however, was not to prove an uninterrupted period of study. The records show that he attended the College Council meetings and appeared to be involved in the ongoing affairs of the College. There is however no report of a College Speech Day in 1930. If there were none this may have been due to the Principal's absence but it is perhaps more likely that it was overshadowed by other events. On 6 December, Pastor JH Ridden, the first student to do his entire course at the Granville residential college, was ordained in the Auburn Church. The preacher was the Principal. 'Some', he said, 'spend all their lifetime polishing and sharpening their weapons for the war, but never reach the actual firing line, or use their weapons in active service'. The thrust of his message was that for the ordinand the time of preparation was over and the call to the front line was imperative.[222]

Just over a week later George Morling spoke at the funeral of his first graduate to be called to higher service, Rev RE Newport.[223] Rowland Newport had been out of College for only one year and his death deeply affected George Morling. Year by year at the Communion Service which closed the College session he would speak of Rowland Newport, as also of AJ Harvey another former student who had died, and spoke of them with deep regard and affection. Of Newport, 'only 27 at the time of his death' Principal Morling said, 'He was the most earnest prayer I have known. To hear him pray was to be right at the foot of the throne, for there Mr Newport dwelt'.[224]

1931
Morling spoke again at the memorial service for Rowland Newport at Leichhardt church on 25 January.[225] With the retirement of Rev Stephen Sharp early in the year the Principal lost another valued colleague. At the public farewell on 28 January in the Burwood church[226] Principal Morling said, 'Mr Sharp's ministry had exercised a wider influence than he himself could have any idea of. The college students were his debtors. He had inspired not only their affection but their reverence'. At the end of January he suffered a loss in the death of TH Vaughan. At the funeral service in the Concord church Rev GH Morling, according to *The Australian Baptist*, 'paid a never-to-be-forgotten tribute to the influence of Mr Vaughan when he was a boy in his Sunday School class at Ashfield'.[227]

To judge from limited written records the main feature of the College year was the near desperate financial position. At the February meeting of the Council there was an application by WM Callan to enter College paying his own fees. He took this action because, for lack of funds, Home Mission could find no opening for him. In the same meeting it was moved by the Principal and seconded by the Home Mission Superintendent 'That in view of the large number of students in College and the financial stringency of the times all goods as far as possible be purchased in bulk. Also that economy be considered in the menu'.[228]

According to the College Secretary's annual report, 'He returned to the college in March, greatly benefited by the rest'. His time at Collaroy was termed a 'well-earned vacation'.[229] Taken along with the fact that Principal Morling did not achieve the Bachelor of Divinity degree, it suggests that his health was not equal to the demands of consistent study on top of his strenuous Presidential year.

The new College session started with a total enrolment of 25 with 16 of them living on the Granville property. Seven new students constituted a record. The speaker at the College Commencement Service in the Dulwich Hill church was Rev Joshua Robertson, MA, the recently inducted pastor of the Petersham church[230]. His address was characteristic of him, a blending of passionate evangelism and social concern, something not altogether common at that time. A few days later the Principal was again associated with Joshua Robertson in the unveiling of a memorial to the former Petersham pastor, the late Rev GA Craike. George Morling 'spoke of his personal interest in Petersham church, of which his father was a foundation member …' The subject on his 'most inspiring address' was 'Fellowship' for he felt that this was especially characteristic of Petersham church.

The May meeting of the College council faced the consequences of the closing of the State Savings Bank in which its funds were deposited. The Treasurer was to open an account with another bank[231]. From the annual accounts it would appear that the College had tied up in the Savings Bank the princely sum of £43.0.0. In one of only two diary entries for 1931 he outlined a morning of prayer spent in the Granville Church on 27 May. He was free because the students were taking examinations. In earlier prayer that morning he had been given the verse from Psalm 103:5 'Thy youth is renewed'. He commented that that was 'a good verse after the experience of last Wednesday'[p]. After outlining the elements of his time of prayer, including thanksgiving for freedom of mind from the stress of years, he wrote 'I think I should record the experience which I have had during this past week although it is not easy to set it down. As the dealings of God with other men have helped me so 1 should not withhold relating this when occasion seems to demand'.

'My life has been burdensome, especially during the last months. I have never lived easily and the strain of mind and spirit has always been great. As I have grown into the knowledge of the deeper things of God I have been ashamed that there has not been complete rest within and I have earnestly prayed for it. Last week I was greatly distressed - quite unnecessarily so - about insurance matters which had become complicated through the bank suspending payment. I committed this to God but no rest came. I went to the church and deliberately cried to God for deliverance from this burden of mind. No answer came. On Saturday night I found a book in the Granville library, into which Gladys and I had gone unexpectedly, on 'Outwitting our Nerves'. This gave me much enlightenment about mental control and fatigue. I believe

---

[p] What happened on 19 May 1931? Sources do not tell.

God directed me to the book - but the discovery was only one link in a whole chain of Divine directions. On Wednesday when a letter about insurance came I was again deeply disturbed. I went to God and then something happened. God gave me strength there and then to face such distresses. I rose knowing all was well. The strain had gone and the day was filled with resoluteness and energy. There was no ecstatic thrill although the wonder of it brought glimpses of adoration because it meant the mental difficulties of long years had passed away. I had strength to face interviews the next day. I even welcomed difficulties and the week has been filled with physical and mental health'.

That was an important milestone in his quest for serenity.

GHM assisted at the marriage of John and Ruby Ridden at Auburn church on 13 June[232], and on 11 July was one of a panel of speakers at a 'marriage reunion' service held as part of the Haberfield church's 60th anniversary.[233]

At the July Council meeting it was agreed, in light of the reduction of student salaries by 12.5-20%, to reduce board to 22/6 a week. The Home Mission Superintendent moved 'that the housekeeping allowance be restricted to 10/- a week for each man and that the President of the College Council be asked to interview the Matron, and point out the absolute necessity for the strictest economy in the College menu. So grave was the situation that it was decided to call a special meeting, on 28 July, of the Council to consider the financial position of the College.[234]

On 28 July the Treasurer uttered dire warnings concerning the ensuing year. Offer of the tutors and Secretary of the Council to refund their honoraria and accept only out of pocket expenses was accepted with 'deepest gratitude to the brethren for the sacrifice made'. The desperate character of affairs may be gauged from the motion 'that the whole responsibility of the students' telephone be borne by the students themselves and that they be asked to refund to the College Treasurer the amount of £3.3.11 being rental paid in advance'.[235]

By October the Council was considering an overdraft by lodging the College deeds with their bank.[236] The College Council at this time appointed Principal Morling along with Rev Joshua Robertson and Rev W Cleugh Black to advise on the possibility of publishing suitable literature for the spiritual education of new converts. Nothing seems to have come of the decision.

There is evidence of student unrest - Student Secretary AH Orr wrote a letter to the Council asking that board paid by students be shown as a separate figure in the annual accounts. Sensing that there was more behind the letter than appeared on the surface the Council set up a subcommittee to investigate 'the domestic problem'.[237] The subcommittee, made up of Rev J Robertson, Mr CA White and Mr PV Turk, did its work so quickly that at the December meeting of the Council a thoroughgoing reorganisation of domestic arrangements was proposed and largely adopted. It appears that the Matron, Miss Diffey, exercised some measure of authority in the domestic life of the College. She was to be replaced by a non-resident woman who would 'prepare meals for the students under the supervision of the Ladies Committee and the Principal. Such a lady to have no authority'.[238, q] The action grew out of a concern that the Matron exercised too much influence.

Nothing is recorded of the effect of all this on the Principal but it doubtless took its toll. His absence from the July, September and November meetings of the College Council was unexplained. However in the November meeting it was 'resolved to give a rebate of five weeks rent to Principal owing to his forced absence from College for a month'. It seems likely that it was necessary for him to get away for his health's sake but no explanation was given in the records.

About this time, the Principal was growing vegetables. With a wife and five children to support he was feeling the financial pinch and took to following the horses which were common enough in Granville streets at that time. Someone observing this activity wrote to the Secretary of the Baptist Union complaining that it was undignified for the Principal of the Baptist College to collect horse manure from the street. The Union, it appears, ignored the complaint.

At the end of the year five men, completely trained in the residential college, graduated and were ordained. One of them, Rev FG Smith, was to be, as the Principal said, 'our first representative in China'.[239]

1932
As 1932 began the general outlook was grim. The country was gripped by depression and the Baptist Union of NSW was by no means immune

---

[q] Although the records are not specific, it seems that Miss Diffey received her holiday entitlements and was replaced by Mrs Fitton about April 1932.

from its effects. The Home Mission Superintendent explained that the Home Mission was unable to accept any new men because of the failure of successive Home Mission appeals. Moreover only two out of four men who had served a preparatory year in the country would be able to come to College. It appeared that College numbers would be down but as it turned out there were no vacant desks because three men were permitted to begin studies at their own expense in the hope that opportunities for service would eventually become available.

Evangelist J Ridley, as he was then called, appeared before the College Council and offered on behalf of members of his family entirely to support one of these men. 'Principal Morling moved a hearty vote of appreciation of the fellowship practical and sympathetic enjoyed with the Evangelist'.[240] Through the years there was a strong bond between these two men, the preacher and the Principal.

At this time the College Council designated a small room for Principal's use. At last he had a place where he might work with some hope of reduced interruptions. The same Council meeting gave him permission to preach at Blackheath during March. Clearly the members were concerned about his health and were anxious that he did not over-commit himself.

He was 'unavoidably detained elsewhere' when on 25 February Pastor CG Orford was ordained in the Granville Church. It is natural to suspect a health problem. It would have taken a major obstacle to keep the Principal from an ordination service. In the service the ordinand paid tribute to the Principal.[241]

The opening function of the College year was held on 15 March in the Stanmore Church.[242] The emphasis of Principal Morling's address was on 'the doctrinal basis and the evangelistic outlook of the training received by the students'.

Notwithstanding the gloom of the depression and the uncertainty of the Principal's health 1932 was a good year for him. At the end of first term he reported to the College Council that 'he thought the spiritual tone this year exceeded all previous years'.[243]

At the Council's meeting on 5 July there were applications from two men and the following minute was recorded, 'The Principal explained that these young men were training at Mr B Barnett's college and considered that inadequate and desired the more efficient training of our College'ʳ. Later in the meeting he reported 'that perfect satisfaction prevailed among the students, and that from a purely domestic point of view the year so far had been wonderful, delightful and perfectly peaceful'.[244] The same euphoria was reflected in the Principal's annual report when he wrote, 'We have to notice the College spirit, the subtle but very real atmosphere which finally decides success or failure. Here we speak with confident pride. The College has never been more healthy and friendly and enthusiastic and the life more thoroughly enjoyable. The men have prayed well, studied well, played well, and, as a consequence, have preached well'.

An entry in his diary dated 21 July, 1932, reads 'The year has been good in every way. The alteration in the domestic arrangements of the College has made life easier ... My health has definitely improved. It is a humbling joy to know that lives have been blessed through my ministry'. After thanksgiving the entry went on to petition: 'I desire to bring definitely before the Heavenly Father the matter of my BD examination. It seems right to go on with it now if God gives me continued strength. I want to consult Him about this'.

The Principal told his Council on 6 September that he had been invited again to fill the pulpit at Blackheath during the long vacation. What did they think about that? The Council agreed provided he did not feel that 'It would react detrimentally on his health'. There was a continuing solicitude for him. Rev CJ Tinsley, 'President of the Council spoke feelingly on the widening avenues of usefulness the Principal was having, mentioning the invitation extended to Mr Morling by the Victorian Union to their next Assembly'.[245]

In the College session of the Annual Assembly he had spoken strongly in support of the students explaining that, contrary to the opinion of some people, they did not receive free board and lodging. 'He had', he said, 'deepest sympathy for the students, some of whom were suffering hardship on account of their magnanimous acceptance of the reduction of their small allowances'.[246]

ʳ Rev Benson Barnett's college evolved into the Sydney Missionary and Bible College.

In his annual report the Secretary of the College Council, Rev JH Deane, amplified that theme, 'The report would be incomplete if it did not pay simple tribute to the faithful ministry of the man whom you have made Principal. The Council assures you of its perfect confidence in him, and testifies to the efficiency of his service. We rejoice that his health has been better this year than for many years past. With pride and satisfaction we notice his ever-widening circle of influence on the whole Christian community, not only of this State, but of the Commonwealth'.[247]

The death of Rev TR Coleman in October was an especially great personal loss for the Principal. Mr Coleman was the father of his close friend, former fellow-student and brother-in-law Rev Enos Coleman. But there was a closer bond to which reference was made earlier in this chronicle. At the funeral George Morling spoke of TR Coleman as in a very real sense his spiritual father since he had taught him deep things of God. 'I have walked and talked with him' he said, 'I loved him and he loved me'.[248]

At the Council meeting of 6 December 'The Principal in accordance with the College regulations and the request of the Council at its last meeting produced a written report on each student. The report was comprehensive. Summarising he said, (1) There was much to be pleased about the year's work and that we had no need to be ashamed of our men. (2) The standard of intellectual capacity was somewhat reduced by several of the first year men'.[249] However this situation was somewhat retrieved when at the College Speech Day[250], the Principal declared 'our men this year have maintained more strongly than ever the fundamental doctrines of the faith, together with a warm evangelical note. These factors are the foundations of our growth'. As a result of the sacrifice of the students and the strenuous efforts of the Ladies' Committee the College finished the year without debt. Being in such a happy financial position, the College Council 'Resolved to allow Principal to purchase for the college library books needed for next year's work with a limit of expenditure of £10'. Things were looking up.

At the end of 1932 Principal Morling spoke at the Upwey Convention (Victoria), apparently for the first time. From 1932 he was a frequent platform speaker at significant Bible Conferences in Australia: Upwey (later Belgrave Heights, at least ten times), Katoomba in New South Wales, and from 1937 at Auckland in New Zealand. His association with Bible Conferences continued until 1967. He was described 'as a most significant figure in the (Katoomba) Convention from 1930 to 1960 where he occasionally served as chairman … He served as a Council member from 1932 to 1955'.[251]

The Principal was becoming more and more enthroned in the esteem and affection of the denomination. When he rose to speak at the College Speech Day he was greeted by prolonged applause - 'He is beloved of every student; his Christianity is rich and wholesome; his piety is blended with his scholarship, each as genuine as the other'.[250]

1933

The opening of another year brought little sign that the financial situation was reaching a turning point. The Home Mission was able to accept few applicants and several sought College training without payment of fees or at their own expense.

Under these circumstances a motion of appreciation to the Principal by the College Council is most understandable. He had preached at Blackheath for three months and had voluntarily given half his preaching fees to College funds.

Meanwhile he was making a contribution of a different kind to his fellow-Baptists. In the early part of the year two articles by him appeared in *The Australian Baptist*, 'The Spiritual Significance of Baptism'[252], and an Easter message, 'The Likeness of His Resurrection'.[253]

With the esteem in which he was held by his students it was natural that he would exercise a great influence over them. Rev FJ Dunkley recalled that it used to be said that there were as many young Spurgeons about as there were students in his College. He felt that something similar would take place in almost any college. He then went on to say, 'It is certainly correct so far as our own students in New South Wales are concerned. Principal Morling is much beloved by his students, and his carefulness in the pronunciation of his syllables is unconsciously copied by those with whom he is in daily contact'. The students, as the writer went on to say, were even copying their Principal in arranging convention-style meetings over two or three days. Dunkley concluded, 'The sincerest form of flattery is imitation, and the Principal may comfort his heart with this practical intimation of the love of his students'.[254]

On 26 July, almost exactly a year after he had confided to his diary his half-formed resolve to press on with preparation for BD examinations, he made another entry suggesting that that purpose was to be abandoned. He wrote, 'It seems that God is setting my life in the course of more concentrated College work on the one hand and of a public ministry for the deepening of spiritual life on the other. 1 feel 1 should cultivate a greater and quieter intimacy with the Heavenly Father'.

What prompted this sense of a changed direction is not stated but whatever it was it appears to have been quite decisive. Although he continued to feel that a further degree would have enhanced the standing of the College and there was from time to time a stirring of desire to pursue further studies it seems unlikely that he set himself seriously to the task. Too many other calls were made on him.

On 29 July he conducted the funeral services for Mrs Lillian Nunn at Manly Baptist Church and the graveside. She was the only daughter of Principal's dear friends, Rev and Mrs EG Hockey of the Manly Church. She was married to Mr Frank Nunn. The Principal paid a glowing and moving tribute to the deceased.[255]

A few days later on 3 August there was a further diary notation, 'The weekend has been very helpful and my soul has been uplifted. I realise how little there is in me of reality and sincerity'. That last comment is to be understood as the self-deprecatory comment of a spiritually sensitive man. The entry continued, 'Lillian Nunn's death was very moving and the funeral service was rich in inspiration. The College prayer from 6 to 10 on Friday evening was much used in drawing us nearer to God. Then Sunday's services at Stanmore and Burton Street added their share of spiritual stimulus. Now I feel that the Holy Spirit wants to show me a greater degree of intimacy with Christ. This thought is much in my mind'.

George Morling was a man who gave himself in friendship. One of his close friends was Willie Cleugh Black. In August this popular preacher-pastor of Auburn and denominational leader suffered a break-down in health.[256] This had greatly concerned his friend. Worse was to follow. Cleugh Black's mother, a remarkable woman, had a heart attack just before the Assembly meetings and died. Family friend, George Morling, found himself ministering in the graveside funeral service.[257] He also participated in the funeral of Mrs Owen Jones of Concord.[258]

In his absence from the September Council meeting, there was discussion of the poor condition of his residence. As an outcome it was decided to recommend 'to the Assembly that the rental be reduced by £26 per annum and that the whole question of the residence and the present College property be remitted to the incoming Council'. The Council unanimously resolved, and the Annual Assembly agreed, to appoint Rev JH Deane, BA BD, as a paid part-time lecturer. Mr. Deane, to the Council's considerable satisfaction, had recently added a Bachelor of Divinity to his Arts degree.[259]

At the Assembly meetings GHM took a leading role. Of his contribution to the Great Thanksgiving Service which climaxed Foreign Mission Day it was said that he 'was in great form and his address was a magnificent utterance'.[260] He addressed the Ladies' Zenana Missionary Society on the subject of 'Spiritual Idealism in Missions'. 'It was', the report said, 'a masterly message, given in the Principal's own arresting way, and spoken right to the hearts of the hearers'.[261] In his report as Principal he indicated the encouraging achievements, academic and otherwise, of the year and assured delegates 'that good foundations were being laid for an ever-expanding ministry of the Word. One has an increasing sense of responsibility in the holy business of training men for our Baptist ministry which surely is divinely called to a special ministry in these days when many trumpets are giving an uncertain note'. This comment was without doubt prompted by the 'Angus Case' which was then agitating Presbyterian circles and, indeed, the wider church, regarding the controversial teaching of Dr Samuel Angus, Principal of the St Andrew's Presbyterian Divinity Hall in Sydney University. Rev WL Jarvis at Bathurst Street and Rev JJ Weller at Ashfield inveighed against the Presbyterian professor.

As convenor of the Ordination Council, George Morling doubtless had much to do with having the Ordination Service included in the Assembly program for the first time. In the service 'the beloved Principal of the College' indicated the steps leading to ordination. FJ Dunkley described the service as 'perhaps the most impressive of all the ordination services that we have ever seen, in connection with our own denomination'.[262] The Principal's influence could be seen in this.

The Home Mission aimed 'to launch the greatest appeal in its history' and it chose Principal Morling for the task. 'Home Mission Day came to a 'grand climax' in a meeting that overflowed the Burton Street Church.

'The Principal of the College was asked to launch the November Home Mission Appeal. Mr Morling said at the outset that he hoped he was in good form, as he was about to launch 'the greatest Home Mission Appeal in history'. The Principal was in excellent form, and it will not be his fault if the results are not beyond all expectation'.[263] The comment may be added that although the response did not resolve the serious financial crisis faced by the Home Mission, more was given by churches than ever before. This was offset by reason of the fact that generous personal givers of former years had passed from the scene, namely Sir Hugh Dixson and Mr William Buckingham. It was an indication of greatly improved health that the Principal was able to throw himself so wholeheartedly into the life of the Union. Apparently he felt able also to accept appointment as Vice-President of the NSW Christian Endeavour Union. At the Annual Convention in October he was the speaker at the Inspirational Rally.

It was with regret that the Granville Church on 27 September accepted the resignation of its Pastor, Rev JH Deane. He had responded to a call from the Blackheath Church.[264] However, he continued as Secretary of the College Council and as assistant to the Principal. One consequence of John Deane's resignation was that George Morling was again appointed Moderator of the Granville church. Happily it was a short-lived responsibility for on 12 December he preached at the induction of Rev CG Orford to the pastorate.

On its first meeting the newly elected College Council authorised the Principal to make any necessary arrangements for the College program during his absence overseas.[265] On 9 October 'The Council inspected the premises noting that the flooring was damp and reeking and observing that the walls in a number of instances bear the marks of water - in some places both ceiling and walls were dark with mildew. During the meeting a heavy downpour of rain occurred and a pool of water soon collected in the main hall'. No firm decision was reached about action but it was agreed 'that a big change was inevitable and must be made soon'.[266]

Further evidence that he was a prophet honoured even in his own country was shown by the fact that he was the speaker at the Public meeting of Granville's Church Anniversary on 11 October.

In his regular column Rev FJ Dunkley advised that the Principal of the College would leave 'on a much-needed holiday' early in the new college year. He added, 'He has the opportunity of visiting England and will also, before return, visit America. He will avail himself of the privileges that occur of seeing the work in other colleges in the lands to which he is going. He expects to be away from Australia for six months, or a little more. We congratulate the Principal on being able to take this holiday which will so greatly augment his experience. It will also give him the rest of mind and body that he so much needs. The long sea voyages in themselves will be very beneficial'.[267] Mr and Mrs AS White were to travel to London with their daughter, Dorothy, who was to take up a scholarship at the Royal College of Music. They had invited the Principal to accompany them and then, after time in England, to return to Australia by way of America.

Gladys Morling

It was an opportunity for which George Morling would always be grateful though it must have imposed greater burdens on his wife, Gladys, as she shouldered the care of her growing family. And, as it turned out, there would also be during this time many anxious discussions and a major decision concerning the future location of the College and the family home. Since the Principal's rent was remitted during his absence it appears that the family did not occupy the Granville residence. During at least some of the time they lived with the Hockey family in Croydon.

The College Council, at its November meeting, from which he was absent because of illness, was told that all the details of the lecturing program had been arranged. As intended John Deane would take up most of the slack.[268]

In the closing months of the year seven entries in the form of prayers are found in the Principal's diary. This unusual activity was prompted by the provision of the tour. They represent a spiritual exercise on the part of the diarist and are hereunder presented in full.

October 18, 1933
My Heavenly Father,
I must believe that Thou art at work in my life and in the affairs

surrounding my life, seeing that Thou has inspired Mr White to arrange this trip abroad for me. I worship and adore Thee, Thou Kind Father. I ask Thee to arrange every detail of the plans, especially as which countries I shall visit so that the experience may best minister to my life in relation to Thy Kingdom. I ask this the name of Jesus Christ whom I serve, as Saviour and Lord. Amen.

October 26, 1933
Heavenly Father,
I feel not only a sense of pleasure when I think about the tour of next year - but also a sense of responsibility. Partly lest I should not derive as much educative value and spiritual profit from the experience as I should and partly lest I should not minister on Thy behalf to those with whom I travel and those whom I shall meet. So in accordance with Psalm 37 I desire to delight myself in Thee and then to commit my way unto Thee. Then I believe Thou wilt bring to pass the desires of my heart. So teach me rest in Thee and wait patiently for Thee. Through Jesus Christ my Lord. Amen.

October 27, 1933
Heavenly Father,
I fear that my type of holiness is not very attractive. It is serious without being buoyant. It has on it the spirit of heaviness but does not clothe my life with the garment of praise. Teach me something of spiritual joyousness, something of that which breathes through the words 'Whom having not seen ye love, whom though now ye see Him not yet believing ye rejoice with joy unspeakable and full of glory'. I feel that the secret of this is a certain clearness and vividness in seeing Christ. I do not think that I have yet seen Christ as I ought to see Him. I still long for such an experience. Grant it me, I beseech Thee, that Christ may be glorified in my life. Amen.

November 9, 1933
My Heavenly Father,
I desire to submit to Thy judgment in all things and now I ask that the arrangements for my family may be under Thy kind direction. Please give special leading about Dorothy and Elaine's schooling next year so that in each case there may be the most effective help given for their whole life development. Let my wife be without anxiety in all her responsibilities. For the Saviour's sake.

November 10, 1933
My Heavenly Father,
I ask Thee for this grace that when I commence my tour I may have heart full of love for Thee, great sense of Thy care and favour and a heart full of love for others. Take all resentment from me. Let me learn too, that worry is a sin because it calls into doubt Thy constant care over Thy children. So fill me with quietness and love for Jesus' sake.

November 19, 1933
Heavenly Father,
It is a feature of my life that I seem to pass by the simplest things without having properly understood them. Teach me again concerning faith that the blessings of God are received only by being believed for; that the order is not Thy work then my faith, but my faith and then my work. Strengthen my faith, give me always a sense of happy anticipation in Thy response. For Christ's sake. Amen.

December 4, 1933
My Heavenly Father,
It does appear that my work would be more effective if my physical health were more robust. I ask that my tour may minister to my physical reserves. Yet teach me Paul's experience that finally Thy grace is sufficient for me. For Jesus' sake.

These prayers afford revealing glimpses of one who aspired to be a man after God's own heart.

The matter of moving the college was taken up again in the December meeting where it became clear that the mind of the Council was to seek new premises[269]. With the College year drawing to a close the annual Communion service was held in the Granville Church. We read [270], 'Speaking at the Lord's Supper, the Principal reminded the students of the increasing breadth and beauty of the fellowship. The fellowship of the College included not only the resident students, but tutors and men who were now engaged in the full ministry. It even extended to India and China, where graduates of the College now serve their Lord and Master. Even more, the fellowship included the late Revs AJ Harvey and RE Newport, who had passed to their reward and are now with Christ'. In later years there would be grieving references to a few unspecified past students who for one reason or another had failed to fulfil their ministry. Such times were unforgettable experiences for College students.

1934

A conversation with Dr Graham Scroggie at the Katoomba Convention of 1934 brought Principal Morling a vital new insight, being 'that the life of faith includes the deliberate offering of the body to God, with the expected outcome of improved health and greater effectiveness in service'. He later noted as a consequence of that bodily surrender of himself to God 'a continuance of health which makes spiritual rest easier and deeper'. Having been 'entertained by the NSW College Council on December 21, warmly felicitated upon their impending tour and bidden a prosperous voyage and happy return', on Saturday 6 January, 1934, Principal Morling, along with the Whites, sailed from Sydney on the 'Orama'.

At the beginning of the 1934 College session student-pastor Max Howard wrote[271], 'There is a conscious incompleteness about the opening of the College this year. The much-loved person of the Principal is missed. Obviously it was already hard to think of the College apart from the Principal who had so definitely shaped it. And it was becoming hard think of the NSW Baptist ministry apart from the College Principal for more and more Morling men were ministering the churches'. A paragraph in the denominational paper[272] noted that 'on the Northern line alone there are at least nine ministers who have passed through our own College in recent years'.

There appears to be little surviving record of the more than five months spent touring in the Holy Land, England and America. During the period one brief item from the Principal appeared.[273] 1934 was the centenary of the birth of CH Spurgeon. George Morling wrote a commendatory note on *The Treasury of the New Testament*, a publication that brought together 600 of Spurgeon's sermons. In it he said, 'The Spurgeon Centenary has awakened renewed enthusiasm for the great preacher. It is impossible to estimate the value of the legacy which he passed to this generation ... And Spurgeon has not lost his appeal. This note is being written from London. It is significant that the man who has outlasted every London preacher, and who still commands the greatest congregation in this world centre, should have deliberately designed his ministry on that of Spurgeon. I refer to Dr. Dinsdale Young, of the Methodist Central Hall, who regularly addresses a congregation of some 3000 people'. The rest of the article made clear the regard that the Principal had for the great Baptist preacher.

A pleasing aspect of his time in England was that it enabled him to visit relatives of his mother and learn from them of the esteem in which she was held and of the consistent and uncompromising character of her Christian life.

It was apparently while on his way back to Australia that he committed to writing for no one's sake but his own a deeply personal response to his travel experience. For the glimpse it gives of the spiritual intensity of the man reproduced in full.

'I must believe that this interlude in my life has been divinely planned. This thought has been strengthened by the numerous Divine cares which have been shown me. I want then to listen to the voice of God as He has spoken to me in quiet times of prayer and in the numerous happenings of the journey'.

'I know that God spoke to me early in the voyage on the 'Orama' telling me that in my inner life there was too much strain and that seeking must be balanced by enjoyment of that which is already possessed of the life in Christ'. 'The words 'I sat down under His shadow with great delight and His fruit was sweet to my taste" come to me as an experience to be cultivated'.

'In reading CT Andrews' book *Christ in the Silence* I was arrested by the phrase 'the rest of steadfast purpose' and later by the insistence for the necessity of discipline in the life. He speaks of the need of discipline gained in prolonged seasons of prayer. I gather Andrews does not know fully the secret of abiding in Christ and the possibility of avoiding a fluctuating life; but I do believe that there needs to be discipline to maintain the life of restful abiding and for myself, the maintenance of a controlled mind'.

'This was put into practice at Taligha by the Sea of Galilee where four days of quiet - almost a retirement - were spent. How the Enemy tried to defeat that purpose! Everything seemed to be in rebellion against those days spent thus - everything without and within - all sorts of arguments came to resist the idea. My own inner nature was in league with the Enemy. But the days were spent - there was little of ecstasy but the discipline resulted in fellowship and permanent enrichment'.

'There came also some light about the mood of prayer. The soul should not assume a heaviness, a wrongful solemnity which makes prayer burdensome. Instead there should be a reverent naturalness, 'His soul shall dwell at ease', and a certain happy anticipation'.

'Three facts stand out vividly as the result of that prayer: (1) That the Lord Jesus may be very real. (2) That He is very mighty. The events associated with the lake indicate that. (3) His mighty works are performed on the principle of faith. This is a patent fact of the sacred record and such faith comes only through prayer. 'This kind goeth not forth but by prayer and fasting'.

'Later on the way back to Cairo I realised that Christ's presence was not confined to Galilee or any sacred place. I found Him in my room in Port Said'.

'Having been made to understand this, I was shown in subsequent days that the Holy Spirit had given me a vision of truth and that I must be true to that vision. Surely now I see some things as clearly as I will ever see them. I must be strong in my attitude and in my witness because it is a trust from God to have such a vision'.

'During the busy days in England I did not receive any new Divine word. Yet the same thought concerning spiritual vision was being impressed upon me. In America the conversation with Mr Wishart in New York seemed another message from God. This leader of the Oxford Group Movement spoke of masks behind which we hide - the sinner behind his blatancy and seeming carelessness - the believer behind his piety. He emphasised the helpfulness of frank confession of inward states before an intimate – in his case with Helen, his wife. I think that my life would be healthier if I had grace to speak freely about my own inner life. The discord and repression would thus be eliminated. I have read and I know it to be true that nothing conduces so much to tiredness as resentment and bitterness and annoyance, and nothing ministers so much to strength as happiness and liberty within. This is a much desired objective'.

'I have said that nothing of particular value came to me in England. A lasting impression however was made by the perfection of the paintings in Windsor Castle. Such ideally finished paintings as those by Van Dyke and Rubens made me realise how much pride should put into my own work'.

'Since speaking with Dr Fleming there has been a keenly renewed desire for my studies. I must believe that God has set my way in these intellectual directions. Yet I cannot afford to lose any spiritual tone. This fact of tone has been much in my mind. I have found it to be rare. Mr Black has thought that I should lead a quiet meditative life. I would like do this and stand definitely for a spiritual culture, informed, strong and even aggressive as far as my temperament and strength allow'.

'My home going I desire to make an act of faith. I have really prayed about my home in connection with the College. It seems that there is a possibility of a new College in Ashfield. This appears be an answer to my prayers. I must place this also by faith in God's hands'.

With the return of the Principal imminent, plans were made to welcome him. The College Council arranged a denominational welcome on 18 May at the College. There were several speeches interspersed with singing. Then, 'on rising to speak the Principal received a great ovation which demonstrated the love in which he is held by the whole denomination'.[274] Student-Pastor Max Howard's note in the same issue read, 'We are most happy to have our beloved Principal with us again after his extensive tour. We are praying that his reserves of strength thus accumulated will not too easily be drained during the remainder of the year's toil'.

Principal Morling scarcely had time to get his land legs before he was ushered into a round of extra-curricular activities. On the King's Birthday holiday, 4 June, he was one of the featured speakers at a Back to the Bible Convention at Burwood. The Convention was but one aspect of the conservative response to the perceived teaching of Dr Angus. At the same time a series of meetings addressed by the Scottish Baptist preacher, Dr Graham Scroggie, was being held in the Scots Church Assembly Hall. The purpose of the meetings was to give a positive presentation of Biblical truths believed to be put in question by the teaching of Dr Angus. On the last Saturday of the series George Morling was associated with him as the first speaker in the afternoon service.[275]

With his fourth term as Principal drawing to a close the College Council resolved on 5 June to recommend his reappointment as Principal.[276] Three months later the Council gave some thought to the Principal's remuneration. First it decided that an amount of £17 already paid by Principal be considered as sufficient rental for the year just ended. He had, of course, been away for a considerable period. Then it decided to recommend that his salary on reappointment be £400 *per annum* rent free.[277]

On 24 and 25 June Hurlstone Park Church had its 21st Anniversary and George Morling, who had been its pastor twenty years earlier, was invited to share in the festivities. Mrs RH Lawrenson had made an elaborate cake with 21 candles. 'Rev W Cleugh Black had the honour of lighting the candles, being the founder of the work. Principal GH Morling, MA, blew them out, while our own pastor (Rev FT Smith) cut the cake which was then distributed to all present'.[278] The Principal was the speaker. It was a relaxed occasion and he shared experiences of his world tour, highlighting famous churches and noted preachers. Much might be read into his reported remark that he realised that 'God uses men of all types in His work'.

It had been his stated purpose 'to work all the material he had gathered into two or three lectures, which, as opportunity offered, would be given to the churches'. There is little evidence that this happened. Apart from Hurlstone Park he seems only to have given travel talks to his own church at Granville, and, as a fund raising exercise, at the Home Necessities Fair organised by the NSW Baptist Home Mission Auxiliary.

In all probability there were other more pressing interests at the time, the Spurgeon Centenary, the 'Angus Case', Church of Christ and Baptist dialogue and, from a more directly personal angle, all the excitement and work of a move to new College premises.

During the Principal's absence overseas the College Council had taken steps to give effect to its resolution of 7 December 1933, to investigate the possibility of acquiring new premises for the College. At the February meeting the suggestion of Rev SA McDonald that the Lewisham area be considered was taken up. By May a property 'Fairmount' in Charlotte Street, Ashfield, had been selected as ideally suitable. A month later, with the Principal by then returned, the Council recommended to the Executive of the Union that the property be purchased. With the blessing of the Executive on the purchase, the Council meeting of 3 July wrestled with the financial details of the transaction.[279]

The figure to be found was £4400. There were no available funds. The ordinary account of the College was already overdrawn by £240. Rev

JH Deane outlined in a pamphlet entitled 'What God Hath Wrought'[280] the series of providences whereby the purchase became possible. Of those providences one may be mentioned as having a link with the Principal. AS White, as treasurer of Denominational Trust Funds was entitled to attend College Council meetings. He was present on 3 July when the financial hurdle was being faced. The minutes record that 'while this proposition was being discussed Mr White made a donation of £600 towards the purchase'. At a committee meeting at which difficulties were being discussed and the sum of £600 was mentioned for additions and repairs, a member said quietly, 'You need not bother about that £600; I will give it ... So the College was laid under still greater obligation to one to whom it already owed much, and whose personal friendship has meant an incalculable enrichment to the Principal'.

A series of diary entries the Principal give some insight into his involvement in decisions that were being made.

June 30
'My home coming has been beautiful. Certainly prayer is never wasted. In respect to the new College there has been providence after providence. Now this afternoon I meet Alf (AS White) to talk about alterations and additions. In these things I desire to glorify God. I can do this by always keeping first calm, then sweet and then, as I intend to preach at Maroubra tomorrow morning, leaving it all quietly with God.

I pray definitely (1) that the right thing may be done so that there will be an atmosphere of contentment in the College (2) that Alf's interest may be retained and unity among the brethren maintained'.

July 3
'The College matter seems to be progressing very happily. God brought a happy ending to my fears on Saturday. We have a half-day of prayer today specially to ask God to give definite guidance about the College Council meeting this afternoon. We want happy unanimity about the disposal of land and alterations'. 'If ye ask ... I will do'.

July 4
'All is well thus far even though there is a little delay. Yesterday's prayer has made me desire that those coming in contact with the new College, and especially Alf, may receive spiritual blessing. I should pray that this were true of my contact with denominational leaders and others. Let me have this point of view'.

July 9
'The alterations have been arranged beautifully. Last week was a good week. I really feel that I have received something these days ... Christ has become my 'Life' in a new way. My fears and anxieties have been disappearing. My preaching (on Sunday) at Maroubra was blessed. Today I have felt Christ's presence. It did me good seeing Mrs Eaton whose face in the presence of impending death was radiant. Tomorrow there are conferences with Home Mission leaders. I want to spread His new life – to love all with whom I come into contact. I shall pray that I may have a new view of the possible influence of a Christ possessed life'.

July 17
'The outstanding Divine inspiration last week was the kindness and generosity of the Ogdens. The Heavenly Father is still working on our behalf'.

In the diary entry of 17 July there were two other matters of considerable interest: 'On Sunday too, Dorothy expressed the desire for baptism. I have long prayed that there might be a real work of the Spirit in the lives of the children. I have prayed this morning that I may have a spiritual ministry in the denomination. I dislike committee work but surely through prayer I may have a ministry to the brethren. I can use unfavourable circumstances as a ministry for Christ'. Clearly the diarist left some things unsaid.

Before the diary fell silent for more than seven months there was one more entry on 13 August: 'There can be no doubt that I have had a new experience of prayer during these weeks. Certain things stand out in memory, apart from actual answers which have been too remarkable to be mere coincidences and which have covered every part of my increased praying'.

'Prayer brought a greatly increased sense of satisfaction with Christ who meets my deepest instincts'.

'It has resulted in a far richer love especially towards those who have caused irritation. Also my prayer has given both rest and courage in face of responsibility. There will be more revealed concerning this I feel sure'.

'One particular thing stands out – I have felt that I have actually been praying directly to God - there has hitherto been some vagueness about this. It has now been as though the Holy Spirit has shown me Christ and thus Christ, the minister of the heavenly sanctuary, has conducted me to the Father, so that there has been a faint approximation to the naturalness of Christ's address in John 17'.

The purchase of the Ashfield property would mean a change of location in the course of the College year.[281] All the attendant problems naturally occupied a large part of Principal's time and thought, and so left little opportunity for developing the proposed lectures on his overseas experiences.

Meanwhile he was still involved the life of the Granville Church. When Gideon Patten, who had become his good friend, died in July he conducted 'a solemn but sweet and impressive memorial service for him'.[282] The link of the Patten family with the College and its Principal was to prove enduring.

On 25 August he spoke at the opening of a new school building at Chatswood where his friend Rev JD Mill was the pastor.[283] In subsequent years several Chatswood men, including the pastor's son Doug, entered the College. And there was never a more loyal 'Principal's man' than Doug Mill.

With the move to Ashfield, links with Granville were loosened. On 29 August there was a special night to farewell the Principal and his family. Principal gave a talk on his overseas tour and presentations were made. This was followed by their membership transfer to the Ashfield church in May 1935.[284]

The death on 19 September of Luke Bullock, generous giver of the Granville property, severed a link with a most important stage of the College and its Principal's history. It marked the end of a significant chapter of development.

At about the same time a link with earlier times was strengthened. In a letter dated 14 August George Morling wrote to Mrs Cartwright, widow of his former pastor, saying, in part, 'It is not easy to make a proper reply to your letter. The generous gift in itself is one of those divine surprises which have been such a token of God's approval of our advance.

But in addition your letter stirred my heart strangely because of the awakening of sacred memories which revolve around your husband's strong and gracious ministry'. On 4 September the College Council had a letter before it from Mrs Cartwright offering £50 to be applied initially to the purchase of the Ashfield property but ultimately to be earmarked for library purchases.[277] One is tempted to suspect a suggestion by the Principal but, in any case, Mrs Cartwright was a woman who knew the value of books and how desperately the expanding College was starved for them.

A few days later he was off to Brisbane to be the guest speaker at the Queensland Assembly. At the Foreign Mission rally his address 'The Spirit of Missions' was described as a 'magnificent statement' driven home by 'the passion of the preacher'. Drawing upon experiences in his world tour when he had visited the pyramids in Egypt and the Grand Canyon and the Niagara Falls in America he addressed the Home Mission meeting on 'The Tonic of Big Things'. He had not been thrilled 'by the gigantic proportions of the pyramids' for they were 'memorials to colossal conceit'. They pale in significance in comparison with the little brass tablet commemorating the work of the missionary Temple Gardiner in Cairo. 'Behind one monument one saw pride, but behind the other was sacrifice".[285]

Of particular interest was his contribution to the ministers' School of Theology on 14 September. 'Any doubts as to whether the address by Principal Morling, MA, would be interesting or not were quickly driven away as Mr Morling launched into his subject, 'The Modern Accent in Christian Experience". What he had to say was in line with the whole series of books that at that time was appearing under the general title of The Library of Constructive Theology and as emphasising the role of experience[285]. However the Principal brought his own characteristic insight to the subject. 'The central authority in religion' was 'Christ made real to us in His Word by the Holy Spirit and confirmed in experience'. It seems clear that the experiential element loomed large in his thinking. This was in keeping with his own spiritual quest.

Later he wrote in his diary, 'I have been to Brisbane in September when God gave blessing. There was the distinct message in the train about going in the spirit of humility'. Seemingly he attributed the blessing to this message. There follows in the diary an interesting comment, 'During the absence a rumour was spread about my death. Surely an occasion for deep thought about the significance of life'.

The 1934 Assembly unanimously re-elected George Morling as Principal for a further three years.[286] He began his report to the Assembly with some comments on his latest overseas experience: 'This report is somewhat special, because it covers a year in which I had the great privilege of a world tour. Such an experience has been of incalculable benefit not only in respect to physical health, but also in respect to one's work in the College. Opportunity was afforded to visit theological institutions in England and in America and much interesting and valuable information was gathered. One realises that a college like ours must slowly build up its own ideals and method to suit the particular purpose for which it was called into being. But such visits as have been made, minister to one's efficiency and, above all, develop enthusiasm and wideness of outlook. In some things one frankly criticised other institutions, in other things one admired and sought to imitate'.[287]

At the Assembly Ordination Service on 28 September nine men were ordained. A tenth was prevented by sickness but it was a record number of ordinands for NSW Baptists. Of the nine, eight had trained under the Principal and the other was a close friend, Evangelist John Ridley. They composed a remarkable group who have offered conspicuous service for Christ. Max Howard, Malcolm McCullough, Harry Orr, Alan Prior, Frank Starr, Ern Watson, Hilton White and Arthur Wilkins. One might feel fulfilled just to have shared in the training of one such group but there were hundreds of others.[288] Next day the Principal assisted at the wedding of Rev Arthur Wilkins at Auburn.[289]

George and Gladys Morling

PRINCIPAL AT ASHFIELD
1934-1960

Ashfield College, 'Fairmount,' 40 Charlotte Street, Ashfield.
1934-1961

'Fairmount' was the family home of Mr Hunter McPherson and his wife Ada from 1902-1933. Hunter McPherson was Chairman of Directors of Thomas McPherson, Hardware Merchants of Kent Street, Sydney and the Port Jackson and Manly Steamship Company. Their son, Major Thomas Roy McPherson was killed in action at Hill 60 in August, 1916. 'No known grave'. After Hunter McPherson's death in 1932 the property was acquired by the Baptist Union of New South Wales for the Theological College

CHAPTER 5 – PRINCIPAL AT ASHFIELD

On 29 September and as part of the Assembly meetings the new college at Ashfield was officially opened. 'Fairmount' was an 'imposing' property and it was hailed as adequate for all future development of the College. Indeed part of it was sold to help finance its purchase. Repairs and considerable alterations had been made to adapt the property to its new purpose but it was acknowledged that until extensions could be made living conditions would be far from ideal.[288] This was true not only for the students but also for the Morling family. However the cramped conditions were endurable when there was the prospect of improvement in the near future.[290]

The significance of the new college for its Principal is indicated by an entry in his diary: 'The building must stand as a monument to the love and faithfulness of the Heavenly Father. It would be sin for me not to venture in His name and not to trust implicitly. In a real sense this is a house of prayer for me. It has been provided by God and surely He dwells here'.

14 October was a special day for George and Gladys Morling. All the family was at Granville Church which was celebrating its 46th anniversary. Principal was the preacher, his subject being, 'Jesus Christ, the same'. In the service he paid tribute to the fact that the church, Sunday School and Christian Endeavour societies, had accomplished much in the spiritual training of his children. He had good reason to be grateful for in the service he baptised his elder daughter, Dorothy.[291]

With the aim of providing linen for the new College, a garden party was held on 16 October at 'Elim' the home of Mr and Mrs JA Young. The Principal spoke to the gathering chiefly about the aims of the College. 'He said that an age when education is so widespread it is necessary to have a highly trained ministry to meet the intellectual and spiritual needs of the people. He pleaded for a deep devotion and an evangelical fervour joined to a wide spiritual scholarship'.[292] This gathering may be seen as a precursor to the 'Fellowship of the College' which within six months was formed with Mr JA Young as its President.

An indication that the depression was lifting was to be seen in revived building activity. On successive weekends in October Principal Morling was at the opening of new church buildings in the pastorates of two of his students, on 20 October at Kogarah with Norm Reeve as pastor and on 27 October at Earlwood with Eric Marks as pastor. Characteristically he was ardently promoting the Home Mission Appeal.[293]

At Croydon Church, under Rev Charles Gray, the Home Mission month of November was given over to evangelistic outreach into the community with a most encouraging response. On the final Sunday of the month Principal Morling challenged the church to a more real consecration to Christ. It was described as a time 'of deep heart-searching ... when Christians looked within'.[294] Increasingly the Principal would exercise such a ministry.

Progress was in the air and this was the note struck by the Principal at the first College Speech Day at Ashfield as the following extensive extract shows.[295]

'Principal Morling said it was with thankfulness and pride that he was able to present his report in their new college. The year had been a remarkable one in the history of their theological college and of his own life. They had no expectation when they met at Granville last December, that they should be meeting under these much happier conditions. There had been many Divine surprises. Their heavenly Father had been very gracious. The altered location and the more spacious building and grounds, together with the manifest Divine blessing, had opened up a new vision in respect to their college work. They had prayed that their new college would make possible a bigger and better contribution to the work of the Kingdom. They anticipated more efficient work in the actual training of men for the Baptist ministry. They realised that Baptists are taking an increasingly effective part in the life of this State. They needed a ministry not only zealous and loyal but sufficiently educated to meet the demands of the rising Australian generation. Also there were signs that the college will have a part to play in the training of men for the Baptist ministry of other States. There had surely been a Divine purpose in this important year's development.

'It is our desire further', continued the Principal, 'to have something of a public Bible ministry. This lecture-hall, we trust, will be availed of by people who desire help in the understanding of the sacred scriptures'.
Rev A Butler, President of the Union, traced the past ten years of the College and said that the Baptist Union owed the College (and the Home Mission Committee) a great debt. Of the Principal he said, 'No man was more loved throughout the State than the Principal. They loved the spirit of the Principal. It was not always the gifts or ability, but the Spirit, that made the man'.

With a growing reputation as a convention speaker, Christmas 1934 found him speaking at the Katoomba Christian Convention. The overseas guest speaker was Dr Graham Scroggie. A conversation with the distinguished Scottish Baptist had a deep and lasting effect on the Principal's life and thought, as will be presently noted [s].

The link with the Granville Church was but gradually broken. In part this was because of the affection that Principal had for its pastor, Rev CG Orford. Towards the close of the year the church had a 'Blessing Box Social' which was in fact a surprise social for the pastor and his wife. The Principal who was the master of ceremonies spoke with warm appreciation of Mr Orford's ministry during the past year. Then, on behalf of members and friends, he presented the pastor with 'some longed-for volumes. As a token of their esteem and regard'. Mrs Morling made a presentation to the 'lady of the manse'.[296] There was a happy family fellowship at Granville. It was a great sorrow to the Principal that within a few years Mr Orford was out of ministry.

1935

Another church that featured prominently in the Morling family was Blackheath. Principal's parents, Mr and Mrs CA Morling, had lived there for some years. Moreover Principal's assistant, Rev John Deane, had become the pastor at Blackheath. Understandably the Morlings frequently took holidays there and Principal was called on to preach. On the unlikely date of 20 January, 1935, Blackheath had its Sunday School Anniversary and at night 'he gave a message which must have touched the hearts of many'.[296]

At that time the NSW Baptist Union was vigorously conducting a well organised Discipleship Campaign. On l9 February a Day of Conference was held. At night Principal Morling spoke to a gathering of ministers and deacons commending the plan to them and urging their fullest cc-operation.[297] It was a scheme that enlisted his sympathy and wholehearted support. As part of his contribution to the campaign he wrote an article for widespread distribution, 'Questions About Baptists Answered'[298] which revealed George Morling the convinced Baptist.

However at this very time convictions of a different kind were

---

[s] There are no extant College Council minutes from November 1934 till June 1956. College Executive Committee minutes are missing from 1930 to 1939.

crystallising in his thinking. They were of a deeply personal kind and represented a spiritual crisis and turning point in his life and ministry. 4 March 1935, was a day of great significance for George Morling. It was a Monday, so, although College had been in session for almost a week, there were no lectures. Clearly he was spending part at least of the day in spiritual reflection and soul-searching. In his diary, which had seen no entry for some months, he wrote, 'My health at Christmas time was very unsatisfactory. A talk with Dr Graham Scroggie after my address at Katoomba Convention on 'The Life of Faith' concerning his own experience has led me to include this in the life of faith also. The cold water treatment which already has done me much good seems to be directly connected with that. There has also been an absence of strain about the financial and other needs of the College. I am wonderfully well and I have reason to expect unprecedented health. This will make possible a concentration on my studies and possibly on writing which before has been impossible. I must be full of gratitude for this'.

Several things in that entry need explanation, but happily the main matter is clarified by the Principal himself in his book, *The Quest for Serenity* where he writes, 'During his fruitful ministry in Australia Dr Graham Scroggie told me of an impressive incident in his life. At one stage he had violent attacks of nausea before preaching. He was advised by an eminent medical authority to abandon the work to which he was sure God had called him. In his distress he consulted his friend Dr Harry Guinness who asked searchingly whether he had ever obeyed the counsel of Romans 12:1 to present our bodies a living sacrifice to God. 'Yes, in a general way,' he answered the other. 'Do it in a specific, deliberate way,' suggested his saintly friend. 'I went alone with God,' said Dr Scroggie, 'and allowed to Him search my life. It was revealed to me that I had been cherishing a secret purpose of building up a reputation. I made confession and resolved that, henceforth I would preach only to the glory of God. From that day the nausea ceased'.

'The conclusion to be drawn is that the life of faith includes the offering of the body to God with the expected outcome of improved health and greater effectiveness in service'.

On a separate page in the diary is this solemn undertaking.

'The Presentation of My Body to God
Believing that I should live the life of faith and that it should comprehend every part of my life, in accordance with Romans 12:1 I present my body a spiritual sacrifice to God'.

'I believe that the Holy Spirit indwells my body which is thus a temple of the Holy Ghost. Thus I have the resurrection life of the Lord Jesus flowing through my life.'

'I shall endeavour to pass my days and do my work calmly, in happy dependence on my Heavenly Father Who is all wise and all loving and I shall joyfully expect to have sufficient strength to do the work which He has set out for me.

GH Morling
March 4th, 1935'.

With the first college week behind him he recorded on the Friday,

'There has certainly been in these days a more restful sense of the Presence the Lord Jesus. The life of faith has been lived to some little degree.

I shall have to realise that my trust is no less real because there is no strain; that the Heavenly Father works just the same though I do not worry. Deliberate asking and happy expectation and resting in the Lord are rather the way of faith'.

At that time the College depended for its main financial support on an appeal made each year in March. The Principal who had often felt the strain of this arrangement now in faith made a definite request to God in regard to the appeal. Later he was able to note 'a gracious intervention of God regard the appeal'.

Meanwhile the demands made on him did not diminish. When under the notable ministry of Pastor Robert Leghorn a new church building was opened at Hurstville on 16 March, Principal Morling was the speaker and took as his theme 'Christian Service in the Church'.[299] Two days later he was back at his former pastorate of Hurlstone Park, speaking at the Fifth Anniversary of the Senior Girls' Missionary Union. He shared the thoughts that had filled his mind as he stood by the Lake of Galilee during his recent visit to Palestine.[300]

As had been foreshadowed he used the fine lecture room of the new college to launch The NSW College Bible School on 21 March. The preliminary announcement in the denominational paper[301] said, 'The

Principal proposes to give a series of Thursday evening lectures entitled 'Portraits of the Divine Worker' which will comprise studies in the Gospel of Mark'. That series spanned two terms and later in the year he lectured on the Epistle to the Colossians. On the day the School began, its teacher wrote, 'Yesterday there was the promise of all the chairs needed for the Bible School which commences tonight. This is surely a token that God will bless this teaching. This has been a dream of mine. I am praying that it will be a real service for the Lord Jesus'. Perhaps the movement will spread. The sense of rest remains. I need a deeper humility and love - surely elements of a quiet spirit. My attitude must be right towards those who are annoying. I have to thank God for a continuance of health which makes spiritual rest easier and deeper'.

The Bible School proved both popular and useful for a number of years, until the Second World War forced its cessation.

Another venture initiated just a few days later was full of promise but unhappily was comparatively short-lived. On 26 March the Fellowship of the Baptist College of NSW had its first meeting in the College lecture room and agreed upon its constitution. Its first President was Mr JA Young and its Secretary, Mr AT Iliffe. Its object was to enlist interest in and support for the College and to promote fellowship among College supporters. It was hoped to have appointed in every church a person or persons who would provide a two-way link between the College and the church. By the time the College was reporting its activities to the Assembly the Fellowship could boast between 70 and 80 members. At its second meeting in July Principal Morling gave a significant address on 'The Bible and Modern Scholarship'[302]; George Morling the apologist re-emerged. He entered the lists as the defender of the faith and was not reluctant to call Karl Barth to his support.

Meanwhile *The Australian Baptist*[5] had shown two aspects of George Morling, the close family man and the far-sighted denominational leader. It reported the Golden Wedding celebration of Mr and Mrs CA Morling. The function was held at the College on 6 April. Reporting the occasion Rev W Cleugh Black wrote, 'The honoured President of the Baptist Union (Rev A Butler) presided as butler at the banquetting board, and, like his predecessor in the palace of the Pharaoh, toasted the king's health and then in his inimitable way held aloft the golden chalice of congratulation'. Among others who supported the toast was the Principal who spoke as a representative of the family. Rev John Deane, pastor of the couple, led family worship and in closing prayed that they might be spared 'to be a benediction for many years to come'. The prayer was to be denied. The purple passage with which Cleugh Black concluded his report hinted at a more realistic view. Reluctantly the denominational representatives and family friends left the beautifully decorated banqueting-room, which, unlike Belshazzar's hall, had no visible handwriting on the wall, but, to mystical eyes luminous with faith and memory, there seemed written in golden letters not a witness of judgment but a message of mercy epitomising, in the language of the Psalmist, fifty golden years of devoted life and service. 'Surely goodness and mercy have followed us all the days of our lives and we will dwell in the house of the Lord for ever'.

George Morling, the denominational leader, was prominent in the report of the Half-Yearly Assembly held at Auburn on 10 April.[303] It was said concerning him that he spoke on behalf of Home Mission interests. He said that Foreign Mission interest had its root in the Home Missionary spirit. It was this Home Mission spirit in the first English Baptists that later blazed out into Foreign Mission service in William Carey. His visit to Nazareth had made him realise that Jesus had been in His day challenged by a world view to the North, South, East and West, and yet He left that to become a Home Missionary. There were special considerations, international, economic and theological, which called for the development of the missionary spirit. He concluded by commending the Home Missionaries, with whom 'he had been bound in the bundle of life' as being well worthy of prayerful and material support.

Principal Morling's mother was taken ill soon after the excitement of the Golden Wedding Anniversary. 'We are sorry to learn that Mrs Morling (wife of Pastor CA Morling) is ill in the Katoomba Hospital. She was very ill for some weeks with a bad cough, and the strain broke again a rib that was fractured three years ago. This was followed by a stroke, which seriously affected her heart'.[304] A month later her condition was not improved and she was by then a patient in a private hospital in Croydon.[305] Pastor Morling was staying with his son at the College so as to be near her. Just a few days later she died[306] [†] and was interred at Rookwood Cemetery after a service in the Ashfield Church conducted by Rev A Butler with Rev Stephen Sharp giving the tribute.[307] At the

---

[†] On 27 July.

graveside the service was taken by Rev John Deane, her pastor. This was the first break in the Principal's immediate family. As a result CA Morling made his home with his son and daughter-in-law. Accommodation was taxed to the limit.

When the Newtown Church celebrated its Diamond Jubilee, the President of the Union presided at the Public Meeting on 9 July and Principal Morling was the speaker giving 'a beautiful message on 'Fellowship".[308]

The church at Bexley had begun about the same time that George Morling went to assist FJ Dunkley at Tamworth. At its 'Coming of Age' one of his men, Rev AH Orr was its pastor. The celebrations included an extended Discipleship Campaign and a brief evangelistic mission by Evangelist Jarvis, and came to a climax in a special week-end of meetings. As was by this time almost inevitable the Principal was one of the featured speakers.[309]

On 4-6 August the City Tabernacle, Brisbane, celebrated its 80th Anniversary and the Sydney Principal was the guest speaker. Apparently with the family growing up it was possible for his wife to accompany him. It was a visit that made a deep and lasting impression. He was certainly worked hard. He spoke three times on the Sunday, preaching morning and evening and speaking at a children's and young people's service in the afternoon. His morning subject was 'A tribute to the past and challenge for the present' based on Joshua 1:1-2, 'Moses, my servant is dead – now therefore arise – go'. *The Australian Baptist*[310] gave a summary of the address. 'Remember. the work of God goes unceasingly on, the rulership of the ages is vested in Jesus; because Moses was dead, advance became possible. In the year that King Uzziah died, Isaiah saw the Lord. It was expedient that Jesus should go away that the Comforter might come'. Here was expressed the same thought as in Paul's phrase, 'being baptised for the dead'. Joshua baptised for the dead Moses, Isaiah enlightened and commissioned for the dead king. The Holy Spirit is the abiding witness of the crucified Christ - continuity, conditioning, companionship, a threefold endowment'. At night the service was broadcast over 4QG and the subject was 'Re-digging the well' the text being Genesis 26:18. The outline of this address reveals some of the preacher's deepest convictions.

'In an arresting sermon in which Mr Morling spoke with great liberty, he reminded his hearers that there were three wells dug by their Baptist forefathers that must be redigged today (1) an acute and vivid consciousness of the sovereignty of Jesus Christ, founded on their acceptance of the Bible as the Word of God, and backed a steadfast determination to secure consistent recognition of Christ's personal, direct and undelegated authority over the souls of men. (2) A clear conception of the Church as a holy fellowship, based on the principle of a regenerated church membership, walking in the ways of the Lord and availing itself fully of the means of grace that the church provided for their edification and sustenance. (3) An intense belief in the reality of Christ's salvation by His death on the Cross, arousing in them a burning passion for the souls of men, whom Jesus came to seek and to save, and who gave His church the great commission 'Go ye into all the world and preach the Gospel to every creature".

In the afternoon session Principal Morling spoke to the young people about Caleb whom he called, 'an Old Testament Baptist, who wholly followed the Lord'.

Monday found him relaxing with his fellow-ministers. One of them, Rev SM Potter, wrote 'The presence of Principal GH Morling, MA, in our midst is greatly enjoyed by the ministers. On Monday he joined us at Indooroopilly at a game of tennis. He can tell a good yarn, enjoy a good game, as he can preach a good sermon. His laughter is contagious, and thoughts can't run in gloomy channels while he is around. He radiates happy fellowship and is a tonic in any company. We should like to see him looking better in health. We fear he is burning the candle too liberally, and require to 'douse the gleam' more frequently'. That pen portrait will bring instant recognition on the part of his ministerial colleagues.

In the evening he was present and spoke at a gathering of the members and friends of the Mothers' Meeting. His text was Mark 2:1, 'It was noised abroad Jesus was home again'. The reporter summed up his message most succinctly, 'Jesus still comes home, and when He does, something happens'.

The climax and highlight of his visit came the following evening when in the presence of representatives of other denominations and under the chairmanship of the Governor of the State Sir Leslie Orme Wilson, a great company of Baptists assembled to celebrate the Anniversary. The Chairman claimed to be well acquainted with Baptist work and history.

In particular, having served for some time in India, he knew of the remarkable work of Dr William Carey. The report of the guest speaker's contribution deserves be quoted for it too will bring a flash of familiarity to those who often heard the speaker, and a revealing glimpse of some cherished convictions.

Principal Morling, as a prelude his address, touched upon the good fortune of all the States in the character of the representatives who represented the best traditions of the old aristocracy. Principal Morling excelled himself in a magnificent address on 'Fellowship'. Fellowship comprehensive and unifying transcends differences of all kinds, leaps national boundaries, and penetrates into the far away past. It is characterised by high principles, strong purposes and glowing passions.

'Mr Morling illuminated his address with beautiful and arresting illustrations; one of old Bishop Westcott, which specially befitted the occasion. He had held service on a cold wintry day in old Durham Cathedral and when he returned, his daughter, knowing that few would have assembled in such bleak weather, enquired as to the congregation. 'Why' said the old Bishop, 'it was crowded'. 'Crowded, father, why you astonish me!' 'Why, my dear, it was full of the spirits of the great past, and I held communion with them and with God'. It is not fanciful, but a glorious truth that the past great dead are not lost to us. So these past 80 years are crowded with those who walked in the light of high principle, strong purpose and glowing passion.

It was a memorable visit made even more significant by the fact that in the course of it the Brisbane Tabernacle extended a call to Rev A Butler, Principal's close friend and President of the Baptist Union of New South Wales, to become its pastor, a call subsequently accepted.

Early in September the Triennial Assembly Meetings of the Baptist Union of Australia were held in Sydney. The theme of the Assembly was 'Things most surely believed among us'. Most appropriately the subject assigned to Principal Morling was 'The Doctrine of the Holy Spirit'. His address began by relating the Holy Spirit to the Godhead and then presented the Spirit as the Spirit of truth, of holiness and of power.[311] Among Australian Baptists he was coming to have a monopoly on public utterances concerning the Holy Spirit, and this remained true throughout his life.

The Assembly of the NSW Union followed without intermission. His annual report made several observations concerning the life of the College. The work of the College was 'a spirit of life as well as a curriculum of studies. We hope that due regard is paid in our college to this aspect of things'. 'One feels more keenly than ever that the future of our Baptist churches is intimately bound up with the efficiency, both intellectual and spiritual, of our College, so that the sense of responsibility is very considerable. Reference must be made to the new college building because the atmosphere of the college life is partly dependent on the external setting. We can be justly proud of our college home - of its dignity and spaciousness. We believe that the time is not far distant when a wing containing individual rooms for students will be erected and so complete the scheme'.[312]

Despite the move to Ashfield the Granville connection persisted. On 13 October the Principal was the speaker at Granville's 47th Anniversary.[313]

At the celebration of Ashfield church's Jubilee on 5 October, Morling was the special speaker[314] - 'The jubilee sermon was delivered by Principal GH Morling, MA. It was an inspiring meditation on Joshua 1:2 - 'Moses, my servant, is dead; now therefore arise, go over Jordan, thou and all this people, unto the land which I do give to them'. Mr Morling, as an old Ashfield Sunday School boy, spoke of the precious memories he held of boyhood associations, particularly of former pastors - Frederick Hibberd, Samuel Harrison and William Montague Cartwright. 'Our fellowship', he said, 'is threefold: with God, with one another, and to supplement these two, the church is peopled with holy memories and tender recollections of saintly men and women who have served God here".

'His text Mr Morling separated into three divisions (1) continuity of God's work. 'Moses, my servant, is dead'. The final verses of Deuteronomy dealt with the passing of that great leader, but after his decease, the work of God was still to be done. In spite of man's death it continued, and no man was indispensable. One succeeded another, the instruments were changed, but the Master's hand was unchanged. The grand old pioneers have passed on, but God was still at work in the Church. (2) Commissioning of a new leader and generation. 'Now, therefore, arise, go over this Jordan, thou'. A challenge was culled from the record of the past. Paul spoke of 'they which are baptized for the dead, commissioned to continue the work of the departed. Isaiah was baptized for dead Uzziah; Saul (afterwards Paul) for Stephen, whose martyrdom he had witnessed. From the record of those splendid souls now departed, the present members were challenged and commissioned that the Lord's work might yet be done. God called men in the days of Isaiah, Amos and Obadiah. He was calling today. (3) Companionship. Joshua's stupendous task called for God's help, and he was reassured with the promise of the Lord's presence. He was always with His servants. Paul wrote of his appearance before Nero, 'No man stood with me ... notwithstanding the Lord stood with me, and strengthened me'. To the apostle, the most real figure at the tribunal was not the pompous Caesar, but Christ strengthening him; and the most humble men and women might live every day in the presence of the Lord. His own promise was 'Lo, I am with you always, even to the end of the age'. They should commence their jubilee services with this thought – 'We thank God for the past, we are thankful for our own privilege to serve in the present, and we trust God for the power of His presence in the future'. This service was broadcast from National Station 2BL.

Though he had used the same text shortly before at Brisbane the treatment each time was quite different and adapted to the particular situation. This was characteristic of Principal's preaching. Even though he preached frequently from the same text he was always fresh and arresting.

The last week of October was a week of farewells. On 28 October Principal Morling was present at Concord's farewell to its pastor, Rev A Butler as he left for Brisbane. He offered the final prayer commending his friend to God and seeking His blessing on the challenging ministry in the Brisbane Tabernacle[315]. The next night he chaired the farewell of former mentor and present friend, Rev W Cleugh Black. After a most significant ministry at Auburn, Cleugh Black was leaving to succeed FJ Dunkley as Home Mission Superintendent.[316]

In the published report of the College Break-up held 14 December[317], there was special reference to Principal's wife. The Ladies' House Committee presented to her 'a beautiful basket of flowers expressive of their affection and esteem'. There followed the comment, 'From the remarks of the exit students, later in the afternoon, one could see that Mrs Morling, in her quiet way, materially contributes to the effectiveness of the college by her motherly concern for the welfare of the students'.

The Principal reflected the current Angus controversy when he stated that the policy of the College was 'one of sound evangelical teaching as opposed to modern theological conceptions'. There was gratification in Principal's reminder that during the past six years the College had won the debating competition four times and been second on the other two occasions. Looking to the year ahead he indicated that the College appeal in March would be inaugurated by a week's Bible Campaign in the Ashfield Church. Clearly the depression had lifted for the Home Mission Committee had advised that fifteen new students would enter College in the new year. This would spur the resolve to build a new wing to the College for student accommodation. Meanwhile some students would have to live out.

Rev W Cleugh Black was present in his new capacity as Home Mission Superintendent and brought a greeting. President of the Council, Rev CJ Tinsley, gave him three minutes but according to the report he took fifteen treating the company to 'an avalanche of alliterative aphorisms'. It must have been a long afternoon because there were speeches by Mr JA Young, President of the College Fellowship, and the exit students followed by an address by the President of the Union, Rev A Driver, making a plea for a spirit of revival the churches.

In connection with the prize giving, Principal made the suggestion that prizes might be associated with individual donors, thus beginning the practice that has prevailed ever since. By the time the Vice-principal, Rev JH Deane, had moved a comprehensive vote of thanks to all those who in whatever way had helped the College during the year, afternoon tea must have been most welcome. However the gathering was a fitting climax to a significant year in the life of the College and its Principal.

The end of the session brought some respite but the request for his services scarcely slackened. It was now a rare year that he was not a speaker at Katoomba and/or Upwey conventions. He ended the year by preaching at Ashfield's Watch Night Service on Isaiah 52.12.[318] Throughout the year there had been few Sundays when he was not speaking at anniversaries of one kind or another, welcomes, farewells and special occasions.

1936
Dulwich Hill church was awaiting the arrival of Rev EJ Rogers, so the Principal helped out there.[319] Then the Morling family went to Blackheath for a holiday. So we find the Principal bringing a greeting to the church

as it celebrated its anniversary. He seized the opportunity to thank the church for its valuable contribution to the College.[320] There were two main elements in that contribution. For several years it had happily acquiesced in its pastor, Rev JH Deane, maintaining a lecturing ministry as Vice-principal and serving as Secretary of the College Council. Then Mr GW Ruggles, an honoured member of the church, was both Treasurer of the College and the Commissioner leading the fund-raising campaign for the new College.

The Principal's expression of appreciation was timely for within a short time the Blackheath Church was bereft of its pastor. Morling spoke at Blackheath's farewell to John Deane, as he left to become the pastor of the Haberfield Church.[321] A few days later, reversal of roles, he spoke at Haberfield's welcome to his colleague.[322] There was a deep bond of mutual respect between these two greatly gifted men who with their contrasting personalities wonderfully complemented each other.

The same week Principal Morling presided at the welcome of one of his students, Albin Betteridge, to the church at Gladesville.

Bathurst Street Church, soon to change its location and become the Central Baptist Church in George Street, celebrated its centenary early in March and the Principal was one of those sharing in the occasion.

The start of the 1936 college session was introduced by a College Convention in the Ashfield Church lasting 9-12 March[323], the last meeting coinciding with the College Commencement Service. It was an ambitious project with students early in the afternoon and evening sessions preaching from favourite texts and between sessions holding open air meetings. The Vice-principal in the afternoon meetings gave expository messages on the Epistle the Hebrews under the title 'The Rest of the Soul' according to one report, and on 'The Secret of the Life of Victory' according to another. At the evening sessions Principal Morling spoke on the following themes, 'Can a Modern Man Accept the Bible?', 'Salvation and Atonement', 'Salvation and the Future', and 'Salvation and Sacrament'.[324] Rev Robert Goodman, very much a preacher of the period, reduced the subjects treated by 'our much loved Principal', to "The Bible, The Blood, The Beatific Vision, the Baptistry', thus almost anticipating the shibboleths of a later time. The same reporter wrote, 'A crescendo of interest and power characterised the gatherings until, on the last night, the building was crowded' to hear 'one of the finest utterances ever made by Principal Morling'. Of the whole series he said, 'The preaching was great. With clear exegetical statement and apt illustration, the Principal held his audiences to the last minute ... There was a blissful absence of appearing to be wise, and of useless mental speculation. The note of certainty was heard ringing continually. We believed. We were glad. We felt the strength of God'. That enthusiastic response was echoed by Rev AT Whale who said of the final address on 'Salvation and Sacrament', 'It was a stirring discourse combining scholarly exegesis and textual analysis, with the glowing fervour which characterises all Mr Morling's utterances'. His son AA Whale (Bert Jnr) and ten others were new incoming students. Theirs was a most inspiring commencement but it must have left the principal participant rather drained.

However with a new vitality he plunged enthusiastically into the year's work and found particular encouragement in the evening Bible School. Soon he was recording in his diary, 'The Bible School is a constant inspiration. There is a much improved spirit in the College'.

In between the claims of the College, the Bible School, denominational commitments and the constant call for his services as a special speaker he made time to review a number of books for *The Australian Baptist*. It is of some interest that among those reviewed in 1936 was one by Karl Barth (*Credo*). In a brief review he paid tribute to a valuable influence that Barth was exercising on theological thought. Indeed, in his review of *Man and Revelation* by G Dehn he wrote, 'Something more than the cold, barren theology of modernistic schools was found necessary to meet the exacting demands of life. So Karl Barth was thrust up under Divine Providence with his message of sovereign grace ... The massive thinking of Barth has won, at least, the respect of scholars of all schools and has won large acceptance among the younger generation'. This is not to suggest that the Principal was Barthian but he was able to recognise the importance of Barth's contribution.

On l5 April Mr GW Ruggles, a very good friend of the College and its Principal, died suddenly. Though a member of the Blackheath Church the funeral service was held at Stanmore. It was appropriate that the Principal presided and the Vice-principal, his former pastor, gave the address[325]. The same pattern prevailed when a few days later a memorial service was held in the Blackheath Church.[326] Perhaps because he had lacked the opportunity for it, George Ruggles valued education the more highly and served the College sacrificially. It was fitting that the extensions to the College property were named the 'Ruggles Wing'.

More and more the Principal was involved in the lives of students and former students. Although Rev Ern Watson had done most of his training as an external student he held the Principal in high regard. So when he left Mortdale to go to the Unley Park Church in South Australia[327] the Principal spoke words of farewell. Subsequently this association led to an extended ministry for him in South Australia and in other States as well.

In 1936 Mr EH Jenkins was President-General of the Baptist Union of Australia. Being 'a man of figures' Jenkins had been stirred by the Commonwealth census figures that showed negligible Baptist growth. He wanted Baptists to face 'the challenge of statistics' and proposed an intensive enlistment campaign during the month of July. In connection with this an article by Principal Morling 'The Call to Advance' appeared in *The Australian Baptist.*[328] It began in racy style, 'The President-General, full of the zeal of his office, is leading a team of writers who will bring under repeated notice the challenge of the Commonwealth statistics to Australian Baptists. The present writer is first wicket down in the team, although the President has not yet completed his innings. He will probably finish up with some big hitting'. The article suggested that current complacency needed to be shattered, that the temptation to evade the challenge must be resisted, that the challenge must be faced by individual churches and that the revelation of comparative failure must not be allowed to lead to a defeatist spirit. He concluded - 'A literary critic has advanced the opinion that the most suggestive line in our literature is Browning's terse sentence, 'A little more, and how much it is. A little less, and what miles away'. It would appear as though many of our churches, with many splendid features, yet fail because of 'a little less'. May Enlistment month bring from the great Head of the Church, Source of Life and Supreme Director, that 'little more' of devotion, of energy, of vital flame of compelling power which will mean victory in the name of Christ'.

The first diary entry for fifteen months was on 17 June. In part it reads, 'I write now to lay definitely two things before God. (1) The spiritual condition of Will (his brother) who was removed to Western Suburbs Hospital on Friday last. (2) The matter of the DD offered by the Central University, Indiana. May God direct in this or in some other direction. Whatever happens may all be so ordered that my best life may develop and Christ may have still more pre-eminence.

This latter offer was refused, but the previously expressed desire for Christ's still greater pre-eminence in his life was granted. Clearly he had considerable doubts about Central University for he added, 'I ask the Father to open some worthy university door for a degree to be used for His glory'.

The diary then fell silent for more than six years.

On King's Birthday, 29 June, the College held a Convention in the Mosman Church. The theme was 'The Holy Spirit' with the Principal taking the closing address.[329]

In *The Australian Baptist*[330] there was an article under the heading 'Principal Morling's Bible School'. Doubtless the reason for the article was the fact that after a brief recess the School was to resume on l0 September. However the article has so much to say about the Principal that it merits extensive quotation.

'Mr Morling combines, very happily, the role of exegete and that of homilist, or of the professor and the preacher. He could never be satisfied to be a mere exponent of the letter of Scripture; indeed, at times, the preacher gets the upper hand of the professor, and those who take notes forget for the time their pencils and notebooks and fasten their eyes on the speaker, as he carries their thoughts into regions remote from all mere verbal criticism or exposition'.

'In the best sense of the term, Mr Morling is a mystic - of the evangelical type, who never loses sight of the great objective truths of revelation. Dr Maclaren, in his famous address from the chair of the Baptist Union of Great Britain and Ireland, on 'Evangelical Mysticism', remarked that there is a danger, not that the preacher should draw the Cross too large, but the Dove too small. Principal Morling preserves carefully the balance and equipoise of these complementary aspects of truth, and never over-emphasises one doctrine to the detriment of another'.

'Probably he would demur to any precise theological classification, for while, in essentials, he is a Fundamentalist, he is not blind to the contribution which some of the best thinkers of the Modernist School have made to our knowledge of the Scriptures. His lectures are frequently enriched by quotations from his favourite authors, interspersed at rare intervals with some illuminating anecdote or touch of humour of which 'saving grace' he is by no means devoid'.

'But dominant throughout is emphatically the spiritual and prophetic note, with its stress on the supernatural character of Christianity, together with its imperious summons to a holy life; not the cloistered type of holiness which shrinks from contact with the world, but rather the festive and victorious type, which overcomes the world and rejoices in whatever things therein are pure, lovely and of good report'.

'It is doubtless this combination of qualities which has made the Principal a welcome speaker on platforms modelled on the famous Keswick lines, as well as a most acceptable preacher in pulpits, both inside and outside the Baptist denomination, and which moreover has won the confidence of the churches in our College'.

Rev LJ Gomm had accepted a call to come from Western Australia to be the pastor of the Newcastle Tabernacle. The Induction Service was on 13 September and Principal Morling travelled to Newcastle to give the charge to the congregation.[331] On the following day and running through to 18 September the Ministers' Retreat was held at Port Hacking, the first for eleven years. The Principal hurried back to it for he was the main speaker. The Retreat was advertised as part of the Annual Assembly Meetings.

Immediately after the Retreat the Assembly embraced the opening of the Central Baptist Church on Saturday, 19 September. In this too the Principal was involved. After the week-end the Assembly Meetings proper began and the Principal came up for re-election. Rev CJ Tinsley, President of the College Council, injected a rather relaxed note into proceedings when he addressed the Assembly in an artificially alliterative manner.[332] 'I count it a privilege', he said, 'to have the pleasure of proposing the re-appointment of the Principal of the College. He is not only a professor with a pleasing personality, but a preacher ever welcome in pulpit or on platform because of his principles and passion'. Rev AT Whale showed his pleasure in the Assembly's response to the motion[333]. In his report on the Assembly he wrote, 'In appointing Rev GH Morling, MA, to the office of Principal for a further term of three years the denomination paid itself a compliment. I should have appointed him Principal for the term of his natural life, or at least *sine die*. All trust that this triennial term will be a blessed trinity in the midst of years'.

Commenting on the fact that the Principal had been in office for sixteen years he said, 'He is still as warmhearted as ever, a keen theological professor, with the merry heart of a boy'. And with reference to the Bible School, 'What a blessing the Thursday evening college lectures have been'. "No doubt,' he concluded, 'the 'Prof' is the hero of the students. He is the personification of the College motto *Summa Supremo*. NSW Baptists are proud of their College, and prouder still of its Principal'. It may be remarked that the sixteen years, to which reference was made by the Principal himself' was either a miscalculation or, as is less likely, included just one year of the period when he was a part-time lecturer.

Rev JH Deane, in his report to the Assembly as Secretary of the College Council, spoke of the Thursday night Bible School as having been the Principal's dream for years. Of the School he said, 'The Principal is perhaps heard here at his best, and at the task dearest to his heart. Fresh, eager, intense, clothed with spiritual grace and the dew of the Spirit on his brow, he unveils the Lord Jesus Christ to the hungry hearts of men and women. Amidst the prevailing modernism of the day it is exhilarating to find Christ so proclaimed by one in whom modernism in all its forms finds an unflinching and unsparing opponent'.[334] Many would not have thought of him in these terms but there was always that element in him.

It was a different facet of the man that he himself revealed in his report. He recalled that in his inaugural address many years before he had 'expressed the hope then as I was leaving the regular pastoral ministry that I would not shrivel into a mere theological professor. With all humility, let me declare myself, after these years of experience of life and of added knowledge, a simple lover of the Lord Jesus, firm and convinced believer in the Word of God, a proud herald of the Gospel of Grace'.

After that declaration he outlined briefly what had been achieved, a College property of which NSW Baptists might be justly proud, and a succession of men, trained in the College, exercising ever widening spheres of influence 'known for their uncompromising loyalty to Christ and devotion to the great things that cannot be shaken'.

Despite all this 'there is', he wrote, 'a sense of failure which, at times, is almost oppressive. Would that the teaching were more efficient, the inspiration of example stronger and more contagious, the administration wiser'. From what may be known of George Morling there was no playing to the gallery in those words. They represented the baring of his soul. 'If the Lord shall grant another sixteen years of service, may they be filled more abundantly with the fruits of devotion which will be reproduced in the lives of those who will be called in the coming years to the high and holy ministry of the Word'.[335]

Affirmed and encouraged by the Union meetings he resumed his only partly interrupted tasks. The weeks ahead were eventful.

On 14 October his elder brother, William, died at the age of 48. In his early days he had been a member of Ashfield Church. Later he drifted out of church connection and, as has been noted, his brother, George, was concerned for his spiritual well-being. The Ashfield pastor, Rev Robert Goodman, conducted the funeral, assisted by Rev Stephen Sharp and Rev John Deane. The report of the service indicated that towards the close of his life 'his enquiries were always solicitous of 'The Tabernacle".[336] Because he was not well enough attend the Principal had to be satisfied to send an affectionate message. Out of respect for their Principal most of the College students attended.

The Principal's illness was probably the recurrent gout and must have responded quickly to treatment for it appears probable that a few days later he visited Haberfield, home church of his wife and pastorate of his Vice-Principal, to speak at the Sunday School Anniversary. The next week he maintained a tradition when once more he spoke at Granville's Church Anniversary, its forty-eighth.[337] Shortly after there was a retreat for thirty home missionaries at the Port Hacking Baptist Camp and he was one of the lecturers.[338]

With the coming of December there were separate functions to mark the winding up for the year, first of the Bible School and then the College. The Bible School held its annual celebration on 10 December in the College lecture hall.[339] In appreciation of his teaching ministry the Principal was given 'a handsome travelling bag and toilet'. Rev Stephen Sharp, who made the presentation, said, 'While no Christian preacher, or minister, cared anything for mere compliments, the assurance that one's labour had really done something to build up the faith and enrich the character of one's fellows, was never unwelcome, and the testimonies to which their honoured guest had listened must have conveyed such assurance to him'.

Two days later there was what was called the College Breaking- up and the lecture hall overflowed. The report of the function[339] noted that 'Principal Morling was in his happiest mood for more reasons than that a well-earned vacation was in sight'. After the rigours of the year it would be understandable if that prospect paid a large part in inducing his mood. He said that the one word that best described the year was 'happy' and he itemised the elements that justified that assessment. The imminent building extensions and a splendid group of students. 'They were happy too', he said, 'in the administration of the college; happy in the Vice-Principal and the Council; happy in their new treasurer, Mr RE Walker, a lawyer and, what was not too common in these days, an honest lawyer'.

A happy aspect of the evening was the dedication of a communion table and chairs given by the Principal's father as a memorial to his late wife.

In paying a tribute and presenting a gold watch to Rev JH Deane who, as secretary of the College Council, had been largely responsible for making possible 'the splendid additions to the college building' the Principal testified, 'Mr Deane seems be a man who knows everything, and can get everything done. He supplements me in a wonderful way. He is strong where I am weak'. There is no doubt that the two men made an excellent team.

During the function Rev CJ Tinsley set the foundation stone for the new students' wing of the College. Memorial tablets were also unveiled to Mr and Mrs Luke Bullock, the donors of the Granville building, and to Mr GW Ruggles the late commissioner for the Ashfield property. The foundation stone and the two tablets were subsequently moved to the Eastwood campus.

The close of the College session did not bring for long the luxury of relaxation. Two days before Christmas the Principal was involved in an ordination service and not long after he was off to Victoria to share in the Upwey Convention. However, although this ministry was physically taxing it brought him great stimulus and satisfaction.

1937
His first message to the Convention was entitled 'The Call to Advance' and was based on Deuteronomy 2:6. It began, 'Beloved friends, it is inevitable that there should be some sense of strangeness and trepidation as I stand here for the first address at this Convention - but far more real than that is the sense of fellowship'. That fellowship meant a great deal to him.

Having shared himself with the Convention crowds he was at last able to get away to Blackheath, a mountain resort that for him was a place of renewal. Not that he got away altogether for it was recorded that there were five other Baptist ministers holidaying at Blackheath and yet another five at Katoomba.

He wrote a paper on the Lord's Supper, intended to help young people prepare for the forthcoming Sunday School examinations. The Editor of *The Australian Baptist* felt that it would be useful for a wider circle and so published it.[340] This article presented the Supper as commemoration, a participation and a proclamation. Of particular interest is his treatment of participation.

'Here we enter into one of the deep and blessed mysteries of the Christian faith. Let be remembered that there are things which remain meaningless to the unaided reason which are full of light for the believing mind because they are spiritually discerned. Just how do we partake of Christ in the Lord's Supper? The answer of the Roman Catholic Church is that through the prayer of the priest the material bread and wine are transformed into the actual body and blood of Christ ... We cannot accept such a belief. Such power is not given to man. And spiritual blessing is not conveyed by such mechanical means. Yet we may partake of Christ and we are strongly encouraged to do so at the Lord's Table. Let these things be carefully observed and reverently pondered, and the mystery will yield treasure. This first! Christ is not present in the bread and the wine but He is really present at His Table. The young Christian should deliberately cultivate the sense of Christ's presence, and nowhere will so much help be given as at the Communion. Then remember that the Lord thus really present is the Host at the Supper, and such a Host! At our tables we give food and drink to our guests, this Divine Host gives Himself – 'This is My body', 'This is My blood'. He says so. Therefore, as you sit at the Communion table, understand that Christ Who gave Himself for us on the Cross is still giving Himself to us in constant renewals of love and with constant renewals of the blessings of grace. Can you not see then that when the needy trusting heart responds in active love and receptive faith, there is a warm, vital laying hold of Christ, and even more, a real loving union with Him which may truly be called a participation in His body and His blood? It will make the Lord's Supper a very real experience if you remember that the Lord Who died for you is now offering Himself to you for the fulfilment of whatever need you may have. He is active in His love. Be active in your faith'.

The celebration of the Lord's Supper was tremendously important for Principal Morling. In line with the emphasis of Calvin he held a position somewhere between the materialistic view of the Roman Church and the merely symbolic view held by some of his fellow Baptists.

There was a flurry of activity when the College Session began in 1937 and the Principal was in the midst of it all. On 23 February the students began assembling though it was five more days before the new students' wing was completed. Only two days later on 2 March in the Stanmore Church, the College Tea and Commencement Service was held. Rev LJ Gomm came from Newcastle to speak and to give spur to the annual appeal for funds to keep the College operating. On Saturday, 6 March, the Ruggles Wing was officially opened and dedicated with the Union President, Rev RS Pickup, the speaker. Reporting at the next Assembly the Principal commented, 'With the completion of our College building the formative stage of our history comes to a close. It has taken us 21 years to bring us to this point. These years have been full of changes through which the unchanging Lord has patiently led us, so that we have been in turn chastened by failure and encouraged by progress, and always enriched by the fellowship of this essential service.' The final event was the Opening Session of Principal's public Bible School on Thursday, 11 March.[341]

The weekend before the students returned found him fully occupied. On 21 February he preached at the 25th anniversary of Rev WP Phillips' notable ministry at Carlton.[342] He spoke at the dedication of Granville's additional property on 20 March.[343]

On Saturday 3 April, he was at Liverpool for the opening of the new building of the recently reconstituted Church. One of his students, SMF Brook, was pastor of the Church. His former boss and close friend, Rev W Cleugh Black, unveiled the plaque at the official opening. He preached at the evening service.[344] These incessant demands upon his services indicated that with considerably less than half his long term service behind him George Morling had already become something of a Baptist institution. If there was a denominational function or a major church happening in which he was not in some way involved it is natural now to suspect a significant reason. Such constant extra-curricular activity made practically impossible the cherished hope of higher studies.

In this connection a significant event of the year was a fortnight in July spent in South Australia at the Unley Park Church conducting 'A Bible School of Experimental Religion' as a prelude to the church anniversary.[345] The School was intended for those 'ambitious to enlarge their knowledge and their experience of the higher things of the spiritual life' and took up such topics as Illimitable Salvation, The Believer's Sense of Power, The Wonder of the Divine Indwelling, Christ and Human Personality. The church responded enthusiastically with large congregations attending.

He returned from South Australia in time to preach 'a rousing message based on Genesis 26:18' at the opening of the Wollongong Baptist Church on 7 August.[346] He had used the theme of 'Re-digging the Wells' earlier at Brisbane and perhaps elsewhere, but every time the Principal preached on a previously employed theme he thoroughly reworked the sermon and made it appropriate for the particular situation. This was what kept his preaching fresh and vital though there were subjects that were preached frequently.

Somehow he found time for involvement in his local church which was once more Ashfield. With the pastor, Rev Robert Goodman, seriously ill in the first part of the year, it fell to the Principal to find preachers for the church and to assist the church in other ways.[347] There was a close bond between the Principal and his pastor. Later the pastor's son Colin married the Principal's daughter, Dorothy. A further involvement in the life of the Ashfield Church came later in the year when the new Church building was opened. Indeed it was a family affair. Principal's father, Mr CA Morling, a life-deacon of the church, officially opened the door of the church and when the crowd had assembled inside his son welcomed them.[348]

George Morling was certainly 'a man for all seasons' and for all groups. In the space of a few weeks in the second half of the year he spoke at a great variety of anniversaries; the Men's' Morning Meeting at Mortdale on 26 July[349], the Ladies Zenana Society on 31 August (JH Deane being indisposed)[350], and Dulwich Hill Church's 35th[351] and Parramatta's 86th anniversaries.

He has been quoted as saying, 'I like a good funeral'. There was nothing morbid in that. It seems rather that he responded to a situation in which the realities of the Christian faith and the confidence of its hope were positively faced and asserted. Probably this is why he came to be much in demand to participate in funeral services. He brought a special touch to them. He shared in the funeral service of Mr W Ardill, former President of the Baptist Union.[352]

The two men who had at one time teamed at Granville, the Principal of the College and the pastor of the Church, now the Vice-Principal, teamed in a special effort at a rally of the Ryde-Hornsby District Baptist Association. In the afternoon John Deane spoke on 'The Person and Work of the Holy Spirit' and at night George Morling on 'The Power of the Spirit'. Quite deliberately the College was seeking to extend its ministry in the life of the denomination. In 1937 three Student Conventions were held, at Croydon, Bankstown and Bexley. The pattern was for the Principal to give the concluding major address. He was unable to do this at Bankstown because of illness. On the whole, however, it would seem that he was maintaining better health and so felt able to spread his wings a little.

The Australian Baptist[353] carried an article by him entitled, 'How Study and Devotion Combine to Make a Good Minister'. No occasion or reason for the article was given but it seems to have been addressed to a specific situation. From the content it might be concluded that it was originally addressed to a joint meeting of the Ministerial Applicants' Committee and a group of students facing their College course. At all events it is a fine statement of the desirable balance between diligent study and devout spirituality in the life of the minister. The concluding paragraph carried the serious message, 'Therefore, let the minister of Jesus remember that success or failure depends on the way he uses his study. He will use it aright when it is for him both his work room and his prayer room'. The Principal had a great dread of failed ministries. Another of his ruling convictions concerning the ministry found fresh statement in his Report presented to the Annual Assembly that year. 'It has been our aim', he wrote,' to ensure that every man coming to us shall enter into a College life and undertake a course of study which will normally lead to a ministry not only evangelical in a general way, but positively evangelistic - and that, combined with a proper culture which will commend Christ to this highly educated age. Whatever the deficiencies in our men, as a sheer matter of fact they do win souls. Most of them do much better in the practical work of the ministry that in formal studies; they are better preachers than students. This is a more desirable state of affairs than that the academic should predominate, but we could desire that there were more men capable of higher studies who could widen the range of our Baptist appeal. Education and Evangelism are a mighty combination'.[354]

The great event of the denominational year was the opening of the Central Baptist Church at its new location in George Street. The opening was attended by special meetings that, in an ambitious, highly publicised promotion, went on from 9 to 22 October. Greetings were received from Baptist leaders around the world and guest speakers were gathered from near and far. On the Day of Dedication the Principal offered the dedicatory prayer.[355] On Loyalty Night in the second week of celebrations he spoke on 'Baptists and Loyalty to the Message of Baptism'. Mr JA Packer wrote 'Principal Morling is always at his best, and always speaks with conviction and to edification. He is too near to us yet to adequately assess his value to the denomination but all realise at least that he is a great soul, a fervent witness to the Baptist faith and a flaming evangelist of the cross of Christ'.[356] 'Listener' quoted Morling thus - 'The human heart in all ages is much the same, and only Jesus Christ can supply its longing and quiet its restlessness'.[357]

On 30 October he participated in the funeral of Mr Richard J Ball, a Baptist layman who was designated 'Father' of the NSW Legislative Assembly'.[358] On 9 November he was the speaker at the Senior Girls Missionary Union NSW AGM at Central Baptist.[359] When Mr RE Burns, who had been his fellow-member of the Granville Church, died on 26 November his friend, the Principal, gave the tribute.[360]

There was a delightful touch when on 2 December the Principal's Bible School had its last session for the year on 2 December.[361] In appreciation of his ministry to them the class members presented him with an easy chair. They must have been prescient for he needed that chair almost immediately. The report of the College Speech Day on 11 December noted with regret that the Principal had injured a leg in a fall and so was not able to be present. Clearly it was not a major injury because under medical care he was sufficiently recovered to sail for New Zealand in the 'Awatea'.[362]

1938
The purpose of the voyage was to give a series of addresses at the New Year Christian Convention in Auckland. Subsequently he made a number of other visits to 'the land of the long white cloud' to share his distinctive teaching ministry.

On his return from New Zealand the Morling family went for their now customary vacation at Blackheath. The pulpit was vacant so Principal was appointed moderator and had his usual busman's holiday taking the services for several weekd.[363] In his annual report the church secretary, Mr FP Thompson, wrote 'To our beloved moderator, Rev Principal GH Morling, MA, we owe everything for his advice, his choice ministry, his brotherliness and gracious assistance, which is ever evidenced in time of need. We are blessed beyond measure that he continues to spend his vacations in the Mountains'. Even so he broke that vacation to go down to Sydney to speak on 22 February at the public meeting of Central Baptist's 102nd Anniversary. His address on 'Fellowship' was described as 'inspirational in the highest and truest sense of the word'.[364]

The College Commencement Service in 1938 was held in Central Church on Monday, 7 March. Much was made of the fact that it represented the 21st birthday of the College[u]. Preceding the service there was a Birthday Tea with a cake said to be 'the last word in the confectioner's art' presented by Mr William White. The visiting speaker was Rev James Mursell, pastor of the Brisbane Baptist Tabernacle and formerly of London. An honoured guest was Mr GP Barbour, MA, former secretary of the NSW Education Committee out of which the Theological College developed.[365] Principal Morling who had begun his training under the Committee was one of those who paid tribute to Mr Barbour.

On 10 March he addressed the Baptist Women's Home Mission Auxiliary on life in the College and taking part in College commencement activities. Principal's pastor, Rev Robert Goodman, was in declining health and so an increasing burden of pastoral involvement devolved on George Morling.[366] This may well account for his non-involvement in the funeral of Mrs CG Orford, wife of Principal's former student, his pastor at Granville and College lecturer. Although some seven or eight ministers shared in the service, Principal was not one of them. However he wrote the tribute to the deceased.[367] Something of his regard for her is seen in the following extract from that tribute, 'Mrs Orford occupied a worthy place among those select ladies who preside over the destinies of our manses. She was a truly womanly woman, tasteful and efficient whose home was a sanctuary and whose service in it a ministry unto her Lord.

----

[u] It was actually the 22nd anniversary. College commenced tuition on 6 March 1916.

Those of us who shared the inner circle of her friendship know how deeply she influenced the life of her husband. She was his great encourager in all that was best. She was his helper in the study as well as in the work of visiting. Furthermore she was wise in counsel and a steady helper in prayer ... For long months she suffered bravely, retaining brightness of faith and warmth of devotion. Such women are the glory of the Church and the true witness of Divine grace'.

Unbeknown to the Principal this 'ideal' marriage was under great stress and before the year was out the man for whom he held high hopes had resigned from the ministry. This was to be a continual source of grief to him.

On 13 March he spoke at the fifth anniversary of the East Chatswood Church, and on 25 March he spoke at the ninth anniversary of the Canberra Church.[368] Early in April a 'Pageant of Baptist History' was presented in the Sydney Town Hall. The seventh scene, for which the script was written by Mr RE Walker, the College Treasurer, was entitled 'The School of the Baptists'. Students enacted the history of the NSW Baptist College and, of necessity, gave prominence to Principal Morling.[369]

During 30 May to 11 June Principal shared in an Evangelistic Mission in the Central Baptist Church organised by the Sydney City Mission.[370] In the afternoons there were 'Bible Readings' and this was his special field. There followed the King's Birthday Students' Convention at Kogarah Central and he preached the concluding address.[371] He then gave 'a searching and inspiring message' at the opening of the Gladesville Baptist Church building on 25 June.[372] Next day he was involved in a special children's service at Ashfield. His father who had started the Sunday School 53 years before opened the service with prayer and he offered the closing prayer. It was also noted that his daughter, Dorothy, was one of the teachers.[373]

The College Secretary's Report to the NSW Assembly contained two matters relating especially to the Principal. Dealing with the College's responsibility to the seventeen young men in training he wrote, 'The prayer life has been maintained, and, in the spiritual direction of the men's lives, the Principal's capacity and faithfulness are unrivalled'. Few students who trained under Principal Morling would dissent from that verdict. The other item concerned Principal's weekly Bible School.

Over 200 were enrolled in the School with an average attendance of 85. A printed *précis* of the lecture was being circulated to 250. Noting that 'practically all Protestant denominations' were represented John Deane commented, 'There is not the least hint that only the Baptists hold and teach the truth but it is plain that, through the esteemed Principal, the denomination has a large ministry among others who hunger for the bread we break'.[374]

In his Report the Principal began - 'The life and work of a Theological College may seem to change little from year to year, and yet there are subtle differences which make our service for Christ a thing of perpetual interest; and then we always hope that every year marks an advance in efficiency'. He spoke of the College as a home, a spiritual fellowship and an institution of learning. Of the first aspect he wrote, 'The College gives not only comforts but opportunities for courtesies and comradeship' and perhaps necessary corrections which are at the root of character development'. The last point probably referred to the give and take, the rough and tumble of community living. What he said under the second and third headings is here reproduced because of the insight it gives into the Principal himself and his approach to the task.

'Our College is also a spiritual fellowship. Here are men differing greatly in educational standards, in temperament, in Christian experience and in many other ways, but after apostolic example these men are really of one heart and one soul; in the highest sense of the word they are together. Here, then is the incalculable benefit of that mystic fellowship which lies at the heart of our Christian faith. Here are possibilities of vision and of inspiration unobtainable apart from College life. One writes with the lingering benediction upon the spirit of a recent half-night of prayer with the men. At such a happy, searching, stimulating time at the end of term, fellowship ascends to the heights'.

'And our College is an institution of learning. All our energies converge upon the high purpose of instructing men in those sacred things which enable the preacher of the Gospel to reach the men of his age. It is not an easy task and we of the College Staff feel the responsibility greatly. We have frankly to face the position that some excellent men, obviously called of the Holy Spirit to the ministry of the Word, have little capacity for scholarship. These men cannot be rejected, but they should show their sincerity by added industry and a determination serve the Saviour in their studies to the best of their ability, more especially in their mastery of the Holy Scriptures. Others on our College roll combine spiritual gift with intellectual ability of no mean order. Three at least are setting themselves to definite work for a university degree'.

'From the purely scholastic point of view our system, by which College students are also Home Ministers in charge of churches, may be open to criticism, nevertheless, we defend it strongly. It means that during the years of concentrated study our men are in touch with the needs of men and women and are saved from many of the dangers incidental to academic work. Our men are winning souls while they are pursuing their studies'.[375]

The Principal's involvement in the Ashfield Church was illustrated by the report[376] of the death of John Ison, a devout young man aged 20, on 29 November. In the absence of Rev Robert Goodman through illness he became a pastor to the young man and, in particular, remained by his side for hours as he was dying. At John's request he read the great promises of Scripture to him until 'he entered into his rest'. It also fell to him to conduct the funeral service, a service in which he emphasised the triumphant victory of the young man's faith.

He was present at the College Break-up on 10 December when he 'indicated that the year had been very happy and successful, even venturing (the opinion) that the standard of spiritual life and accomplishment was higher than before'. Interestingly of the four graduating students only one, Basil Brown, was present. The other three had already departed to their spheres of service, Alan Williams to Murwillumbah, Harold Evans to Taree and Cyril Moore to India. Basil Brown, as the last of his tribe, paid fitting tribute the Principal and Vice-Principal.[377]

On Sunday, 18 December, at the Ashfield Church Principal Morling was the preacher at the morning service. It must have been a great encouragement to him when at its conclusion he baptised five young men and at the immediately following Communion Service received three of them into membership.[378]

Over the Christmas-New Year period, the Principal made time to give a series of addresses on Abraham, Isaac and Jacob at the Katoomba Christian Convention.[379]

1939

In January Rev Goodman announced his resignation from the Ashfield pastorate on the grounds of his continued ill health.[380] With true Christian graciousness the church refused at least for the time being to accept the resignation.[381] The Principal was preoccupied not only with Ashfield but also with Blackheath. At the annual meeting of that church[382] the secretary said, 'We cannot close our report without recording our indebtedness to our moderator. Principal GH Morling, MA, has been to us guide, philosopher and friend in every phase of our responsibility. Covering the last three years since the removal of Rev JH Deane we have had to lean on our moderator rather heavily'. The Secretary indicated that it was cause for thankfulness that during this pastorless period the work had prospered. Clearly he was contrasting this situation with the warning which, he said, the moderator had given at the opening of the new church building ten years previously: 'If we neglect deliberately and seriously to exalt Christ we are out of line with the divine method of operation, and we fail'.

On 20 February the Principal and Vice-Principal were further linked when the former was the speaker at the public meeting of the Haberfield Church's 26th Anniversary.[383] There was a deep mutual regard.

Another whom the Principal held in high esteem and affection was Rev EG Hockey of the Manly Church. After forty-seven years in the Christian ministry, the last nineteen of which had been at Manly, he was retiring.[381] At a special function on 25 February a large and representative company came together to wish him well. One of many speakers, Principal Morling spoke warmly of his friend as a Christian gentleman.

Meanwhile at Ashfield he was undertaking much of the pulpit work himself. In the morning services he was doing what few others could manage, a series of addresses on the Song of Solomon. The emphasis in the evenings was on the preaching of the gospel. There is record of Adjutant Duck Chong of the Salvation Army preaching at one of the evening services in February and leading into an 'after meeting' in which responses to the gospel were sought. 'It was good see the Principal of our College and a Salvation Army officer side by side seeking to lead souls to Christ'.[384]

The persistent ill health of several ministers, including Robert Goodman, was causing concern. Consequently a meeting at the George Street headquarters of the Union for definite intercessory prayer was called for Friday, 3 March. The Principal was charged with the conduct of the meeting.[385] There could have been no better choice, for the role of the ministry of prayer in healing was increasingly challenging his thinking and practice. Later in his ministry this would be a frequently emphasized element.

Opportunities for wider influence were continuing to present themselves. The Principal was appointed a part-time lecturer in Church History for the Board of Divinity Studies at Sydney University.[386] The Executive Committee of the Union, when officially advised, passed a resolution on 23 May 'recording the honour conferred and congratulating the Principal'.[387] In his Annual Report the Secretary of the College Council, in recording the satisfaction of the Council over the appointment, pointed out that it was honorary.[388]

The Principal in his Report indicated the significance of an expanding ministry among tertiary students. 'This year marks the inclusion of our College in the life of Sydney University. For some years we have had a ministry among University students through the medium of the Evangelical Union. In May I had the privilege of conducting a house party at Austinmer attended by some 40 men and women students. At the end of this year I have been asked to speak at a conference in Adelaide for students drawn from all the Australian Universities. This directly spiritual approach to the life of students is fruitful beyond computation. In addition to this we shall now have an honorary lectureship in Ecclesiastical History. We appreciate the widening range of influence'.[389]

Judging only from activities of which there is a record he drove himself with almost frenetic energy in 1939 yet apparently maintained good health. With College already in session March 8 and 9 found him in Bathurst as one of the speakers at the Western Baptist Association Half-Yearly Meetings.[390]

The College Commencement Service was held in Central Baptist Church on 14 March with Morling introducing new students and Rev John Deane giving the address. The President of the College Council, Rev CJ Tinsley, in pressing the claims of the College for support, said that '(1) It was the largest Baptist College in Australia, and probably in the Southern Hemisphere. (2) It had one of the ablest tutorial staffs of any college anywhere. (3) It had one of the strongest evangelical platforms of any college in the world, being based wholly and solely upon the Word of

God. (4) Its spiritual atmosphere is without superior. (5) Its influence is spreading by the merit and type of its graduates throughout the whole Commonwealth of Australia'.[391]

On 23 March Principal's Public Bible School recommenced with a crowded lecture room. This occupied not only his Thursday evenings but hours every week in preparation of the lessons and the printed notes, in handling of queries and general administration.

The Ashfield connection involved him on 27 March when he chaired the public meetings of the Sunday School Anniversary.[392] Between April and August he was virtually pastor of the Ashfield Church.

Then for the next two days there were the Half-Yearly Assembly Meetings at North Sydney. The emphasis was on the 'Forward Movement' and the Principal addressed the final session on 'The Secret of Progress'. The message was an exposition of one of his favourite texts, 'For the love of Christ constraineth us' (2 Cor 5:14). It was reported that 'Mr Morling was both tender and trenchant'.[393]

The Principal featured in his familiar role as special occasion preacher addressing the public meeting of the Concord Church Anniversary on 2 April.[394]

On 12 April Rev Robert Goodman, whose health had been so long a cause for concern, 'took a turn for the worse'. Anxious days followed and on 17 April Robert Goodman died.[395] The Principal lost an honoured pastor and dear friend. In the denominational funeral he took a prominent part, in particular conducting the graveside service.[396] At the Ashfield Church a Service of Remembrance was held the following Sunday, 23 April. Principal Morling both led the service and preached, his subject being 'He being dead, yet speaketh'. It was a confirmation of the subject when an appeal was made at the conclusion of the address and 'quite a number indicated their desire to live a more consecrated life, and two precious souls expressed their desire to accept Christ as their Saviour'[397].

From 2 May to 6 May he was the main speaker at the Ministers' Retreat at Blackheath. The published account of the Retreat said that the chairman, Rev SA McDonald, 'having stated the purpose of the 'retreat' subsided into an easy chair, there to listen with his brethren to the masterful exposition of the Epistle to the Hebrews by Principal Rev GH Morling.

MA, lovingly termed 'the Prof'.[398] He had become the denominational guru.

A NSW delegation was about to leave for the Baptist World Alliance congress in Atlanta, USA, when on 10 May at a farewell function GH Morling was one of those who expressed the good wishes of their fellow Baptists for a profitable and enjoyable tour.[399]

It was announced[400] that he had been appointed moderator of the Ashfield Church, which, in effect, he had been for some months past. Fortunately in that *de facto* capacity he had arranged for Mr Roy Gordon and Mr Wal Guildford, who worked together as the Sydney Evangelistic Crusade, to take most of the Ashfield services in May.[401] He also arranged for several visiting preachers for June, for he had some previous commitments.

For the ninth year in succession the students had a King's Birthday Convention. It was held at Parramatta on 12 June. Following the firmly established tradition the Principal was the final speaker. The next weekend 17 and 18 June, along with the Home Mission Superintendent, Rev W Cleugh Black and a party of students, he shared in a series of special services at Stroud and Dungog. Mr FE Andrews and Mr HF Jeskie, two prominent laymen, provided transport and in other ways helped in the venture.[402] For the Principal it was a sentimental journey to a former pastorate. The report in *The Australian Baptist*[403] declared it 'the best convention we have ever had'.

During the month the newly appointed moderator conducted two baptismal services at which five young women were the candidates. The morning service of 25 June recalled vividly his pastoral ministry to John (Jack) Ison for in it he unveiled a memorial tablet to the young man who that day would have been 21 years old.[404] A fortnight later in the morning service he performed another unveiling. This time it was an enlarged portrait of the late pastor, Robert Goodman, presented by his widow and family. In the evening, although Rev Walter Barry was the preacher, the Principal conducted the baptism of yet another young woman.[405]

On 15 July he organised at the College a day of special prayer. It was a prelude to a month of mission at the Ashfield Church to be led by Evangelist EW (Ern) Brainwood.[406]

In the morning of 23 July, he shared in the Silver Jubilee celebrations of the Bexley Church, preaching on 'Jesus Christ, the same yesterday, today and forever'. It was back to Ashfield to take part in the mission service at night. At the conclusion of the service he baptised two young women. In response to an appeal a number came forward indicating a desire to be baptised. Few things could have given the evangelistically earnest trainer of ministers more satisfaction than the response he was seeing in his own church and through a ministry in which he was personally involved at a deep level.

Another of his deeply felt convictions surfaced in an article that he contributed to *The Australian Baptist*[407], 'The Faith of Some Australian Baptist Fathers'. In it he presented stories of the inner life of three of the greatest of Australian Baptists - Silas Mead of Flinders Street Church Adelaide; Samuel Chapman of Collins Street Melbourne; and Thomas Porter, best remembered for his ministry at Petersham New South Wales. 'The common denominator in these stories was an experience of holiness by faith and a consequent preaching of that emphasis'. The article went on to present the origin and teaching of the Keswick Convention Movement. George Morling had been involved in such teaching for some years and the article was probably intended to commend it to the general Baptist constituency.

In his involvement in the Convention Movement he demonstrated his kinship with those who held similar convictions regardless of their denominational affiliation. There were Baptists who criticised him for the breadth of his sympathies shown in his fellowship across denominational boundaries. In particular there were some who looked askance at the number of Anglicans who were included in his circle of friends. He certainly valued such friendships but they did not make him any the less a convinced Baptist. It was George Morling, the Baptist, who was to the fore on 29 July when he was the speaker at the Granville Church on the occasion of the unveiling of a newly installed open baptistry[408]. Prior to this Granville, like many other Baptist churches, had its baptistry hidden under the floor, to be revealed only when called into use. He spoke of 'an open baptistry, from an open Bible, with an open heart, giving an open testimony, bearing an open invitation'.[409]

On 2 August as the moderator of the Ashfield Church he chaired a meeting that confirmed a decision to appoint Rev Walter Barry as acting minister of the church for six months.[410] That must have brought a great sense of relief to the heavily burdened Principal. When on 26 August there was a social evening to welcome Rev and Mrs W Barry no-one would have more gladly extended a welcoming hand than the now superfluous moderator. To express appreciation of what he had done in that capacity the church presented him with a pen and pencil set.[411]

Next morning he inducted his friend, Walter Barry, into the pastorate, preaching on the call of Moses. In the service he unveiled a memorial tablet to Mr and Mrs T Hedges, both of whom had recently died after long association with the church.[412]

Morling was now comnmencing a new series of Bible School lectures on 'Men and Movements in the Old Testament'.[413] In September the Second World War broke out. Early optimism about its outcome was soon shattered. The years ahead brought great concern to the Principal and the College but the vital work of training men for Christ's service proceeded without major disruption.

Rev Archibald Jolly, his friend of student days and College Council member, was pastoring the Auburn church with great effectiveness. On Sunday 10 September, the pastor and the Principal were together again when the latter preached at Auburn's 51st anniversary. His message to the church was based on Revelation 2:4, 'I have somewhat against you, because you have left your first love'.[414] It was a reminder of the priority of love in the life of the church.

At the 1939 Assembly George Morling gave an address on 'The Authenticity and Authority of the Scriptures'[415] and came up for re-appointment. It was reported that 'the Assembly, with great enthusiasm, decided to reappoint Principal GH Morling, MA, for a further term of three years'. His election was greeted with sustained applause – 'The delegates rose to their feet and accorded the Principal prolonged applause'[416]. The College Secretary said in his Report to the Assembly, 'The Council feels increasingly the blessing of God's gift in Principal Morling, who not only stands always on the tiptoe of mental effort, but ever reaches out in spiritual longing for the development of the future ministry'.[417]

The opening paragraph of the Principal's own report was an enunciation of his ideal for pastoral preparation - 'We are acutely conscious that theological learning is not always consistent with religious effectiveness.

The Church has ever with it the danger of pride of reason, the intolerance of the intellect which is just as great as the intolerance of ignorance, and the coldness of heart, which absorption in books only too readily begets. We humbly hope that our realisation of the danger is a safeguard against it. We at least sincerely endeavour to ensure that men who undertake our course shall have reverent love for the Word of God increased, and not lessened; desire for the salvation of souls intensified, and not weakened, and helpful contact with the world of men encouraged, and not compromised. We really aim to provide an atmosphere of warmth and enthusiasm for our students. On the part of the men the response has been gratifying. In five of our Australian States, as well as in Eastern Bengal, our NSW graduates are exercising powerful ministries'.[418]

Though no longer moderator, there was continuing ministerial involvement for George Morling, the loyal member, in the Ashfield Church. When the wife of ex-President of the Baptist Union, Mr EJ Phillips, died he shared in the funeral service in the Ashfield Church on 23 October. That weekend, Rev Alexander Hodge, the outstanding pastor of the Auckland Baptist Tabernacle, preached at Ashfield. In the same service, apparently in the absence of Walter Barry, the Principal baptised four candidates, three married women and a young man.[419]

Always a staunch denominationalist he gave his utmost support to every aspect of the Union's work. On 26 October the Foreign Mission held a farewell meeting for Neville Andersen. He was to proceed to East Bengal at the end of November, as soon as his LTh examinations were over and he had been ordained. The Mission therefore had the farewell early so that he could have an uninterrupted preparation for his final encounter with the Melbourne College of Divinity examiners. His Principal said, 'We are all conscious of a thrill of pride because one of our own is going to India. The College is proud to see Neville Andersen going out, and so is the whole denomination'.[420] In support of the Home Mission Society he commended its November Appeal.[421]

A fortnight before there had appeared an important announcement.[422] It read: 'In our next issue we shall introduce for the benefit of our readers an entirely new feature. It is our intention to conduct, through our columns, an Australian Baptist Bible School [v]. The leader of the School will be Principal GH Morling, MA… We shall publish (each week) notes

---

[v] Note the distinction to be made between the Thursday night live Bible School and the written studies constituting this Bible School.

which though necessarily condensed, will be sufficiently thorough and suggestive to become the basis for serious Bible study'.

The School, which began the following week with the first of a series of studies on the Epistle to the Hebrews[423], was to continue for some ten years and to become a source of spiritual enrichment to a great number of readers. Although the school to some extent drew upon studies given at the Principal's Public Bible School at the College it yet entailed a considerable amount of additional work. In particular there was the preparation or adaptation of notes for publication and although, as he explained, he was not able to conduct a large personal correspondence with those who used the notes of the Bible School 'there were inevitable demands made on his time by enquirers'. The Australian Baptist Bible School was one of the Principal's most significant ministries. Subsequent to his death some of the material was repeated in *The Australian Baptist* for the benefit of a later generation of readers.

From the beginning he sought to build up a relationship with those in whose interest the work was undertaken. At the beginning of one of the early studies he wrote[424], 'I am very anxious to get in touch with those readers who have, in spirit, become members of 'Our Bible School' ... I have been delighted and humbled by the reports that have come through regarding the session just closed. Will every reader regard this lesson as written to him, or her, personally, and thus enter into that atmosphere of intimacy that will make you in very truth a member of our Bible School'. That kind of approach helps explain the popularity and long continuance of this feature in the paper.

When the Public Bible School broke up for 1939 on 2 November tributes were paid to the loved and honoured teacher and, as a token of appreciation, a Master of Arts gown and hood were given to him.[425] It is a reflection of that fact that the School attracted scholars from many denominations that the speaker for the final night was the Principal of Moore College, Canon TC Hammond, MA.

The College Speech Day was held on 9 December. The Principal spoke in warmest terms of the students, prompting the reporter to say that 'all his geese were swans and he never lets them down in public'.[426] It was expected that he would find some reason to declare that the particular year 'was the best year yet'. Some took it as statement of absolute unqualified truth. The man himself has been quoted by Rev David

Nicholas as saying, 'It has been a constant plea that I've thought all my ducks were swans and every new intake of students was superior to the previous one. I chose to believe in my students. For the most part they didn't let me down. For the failures I still pray and deeply desire that I could have done more to help them'.[427]

Somehow in the midst of many demands he made time to get up to Blackheath to preside at a farewell function to Evangelist J Cumming who had had an interim ministry there for fifteen months.[428] He also officiated at the wedding of one of the graduates, LM Thompson, pastor of Bankstown.[429]

The end of the academic year merely meant that GH Morling could turn his attention more specifically to other commitments. Foremost among these were speaking engagements at the Katoomba and Upwey Conventions. Perhaps because of the unremitting labours of the year his old enemy gout was playing up. Indeed it was so bad that he had to cancel his commitment to the Katoomba Convention at the last moment. There was great disappointment and a telegram was sent to him expressing the very real sympathy of the Convention.[430] Apparently he improved at least slightly for he travelled to Upwey in Victoria. A report of the convention said, 'Mr Morling had arrived from NSW in somewhat poor health; suffering from a swollen foot (seemingly there was some reticence about calling it gout), which became worse, so that he sometimes had difficulty in mounting the platform. Although urged to rest and let others take his place on the program, he firmly declined the kind offer and manfully fulfilled his share of the ministry by delivering, in a strong voice, all seven addresses allotted to him. The four morning Bible studies on Abraham, Isaac and Jacob had had a trial run the previous year at Katoomba but had been reworked and adapted.

1940
He was back in Sydney conducting a wedding at East Chatswood on 6 January.[431] As noted earlier he was committed to speak at a conference of the Inter-varsity Fellowship in Adelaide early in the year but there is no record him fulfilling the commitment. What is sure is that he would have done so if had been at all possible.

Early in January there were two events that deeply touched the Principal. AA Whale, son of his friend AT Whale, having completed his College course found himself unsettled concerning his call and resigned just prior to ordination.[432] Then Rev Dr FJ Wilkin, one time his teacher in

Melbourne and later his friend, died. Though an old man his mind was still keen and his passing was a great loss to the Baptist cause and his friends.[433]

When the new College session began on 12 February there were, despite the war, nine new students welcomed, apart from some doing work while pastoring country churches.

The Principal was one of the speakers at the Western District Baptist Association Half-Yearly Meetings then in process at Lithgow[434], but no report of his address survives.

In the early part of the year the Principal participated in a number of funerals. On 6 March Mrs N Claughton, a young woman, died in childbirth. She had been Edna Winn, daughter of Mr and Mrs FW Winn.[435] A report of the funeral said, 'The Principal of the College (Rev GH Morling, MA) spoke beautiful words of healing and comfort. He was pastor of the church (Pymble) when Mrs Claughton was but a little girl. He had had the joy of baptising her and of instructing her in the meaning of church membership. He had witnessed her service for Christ with extreme pleasure and satisfaction, and gave thanks to God for the radiant beauty of the character of her Master reflected in her charming personality'.[436]

The funeral service of the great Stanmore Baptist stalwart and denominational leader, Mr William White, took place on 20 March.[437] Once more the responsibility of the address fell to the Principal. In a 'beautiful tribute' he outlined Mr White's eminent success in the world of commerce and industry and his outstanding leadership in the church. 'But William White was not remembered so much because of what he had done, but because of what he was' – a man of love, faith, prayer and generosity. One consequence of William White's death was that some of the massively elegant furniture in his home found itself in the College dining room. It was at about the same time that the leadlight window incorporating the College crest was installed in the same room. That window is now featured in the GH Morling Chapel at Eastwood.

In the following week he gave a graveside eulogy at the funeral of Mr M Hubbard who died on 28 March. Mr Hubbard who in retirement lived at Manly was not a prominent Baptist but he had played a significant part in pioneering Baptist work in Leeton.

When on 4 April Mr JH Burnet died the Principal lost another close friend and the denomination another distinguished leader.[438] Like William White he had been a President of the NSW Baptist Union. Among the many capacities in which he served was that of Treasurer of the College Council for a number of years. It was probably inevitable that the Principal should offer the memorial tribute to one who had not only taken a friendly interest in him from his earliest ministerial days but also in the College and in its students. In the Petersham days before the College was residential the students would gather on a Monday morning at the Burnet home for tennis and morning tea. Mr Burnet, a prominent business man, was one of God's gentlemen and his death was a personal loss to George Morling.

All the time, however, other activities went on, the College program, the Bible School and ministry in the churches. He was, for example, involved as special speaker at the opening of new Baptist buildings. On 9 March Hurstville opened a new Sunday School building and extensions to the church.[439] The subject on that occasion was 'The Power of the Church', a sermon on the Holy Spirit. From 9 to 12 March the Bankstown Church celebrated its Silver Jubilee. At the Reunion Tea George Morling, as its first pastor, brought 'words of reminiscence and encouragement for the future'. When on 16 March Yaralla (Concord West) opened its church building he preached on 'Christ and the Church'.

The College Commencement Service was held in the Central Church on 12 March with Commissioner Dalziel of the Salvation Army as the speaker.[440] In connection with the service the fifth issue of the College Chronicle appeared. In it the Principal had an article on 'Leadership in the Church'. The church, its true nature, its purpose and the way to secure its highest interests, continually concerned him.

Somehow he made time to participate in the Baptist Union Half-Yearly Assembly at Goulburn on 2 and 3 April. Apart from bringing an encouraging report on the College[441] he was the chief speaker at a conference on 'Baptists and the Bible'. The following extracts are taken from what was described as 'Principal's magnificent address'.

'Russian Communism which is defiantly atheistic, and German Nazism which is blatantly materialistic, may seek to suppress Biblical Baptist fellowships but persecution has even brought a blessing, not a curse, to the church. Baptists are emphatically loyalists in respect to the Bible, believing and declaring it to be God's authentic word to man'.

'Historically the Baptist movement in Europe came as the crown of the Protestant Reformation and that mighty revival brought into the clear light of day principles of the Christian faith which had long been obscured. It had accomplished this by placing the open Bible before men and women. Baptists, they proudly and confidently claimed, carried to their logical conclusion the principles of that Biblical Reformation'.

During 22-24 April he participated in the NSW ministers' retreat. His addresses on Ephesians (as reported by Rev AA Whale) 'soared into the heavenlies, leading us ever upward to the throne of God', and he did his share of domestic duties, as he 'swept out the corners'.[442]

On 27 April there was a Students' Convention at Yaralla Baptist when he spoke on 'Christ and Worry', a topic especially relevant in war time. The next day he spoke at Regent's Park Church Anniversary.[443]

With Rev FT Smith of Hurlstone Park away on chaplaincy duties during May the Principal's assistance was enlisted for the Sunday morning services[444]. And when on 30 May the Strathfield-Homebush Church was formed he shared in the service.[445]

Early in June five men from the Victorian Baptist College visited the Sydney College and the Principal welcomed and hosted them.[446] For some years visits between the Colleges took place and helped to foster fellowship.

In the same month he spoke to the NSW Women's Home Mission Auxiliary on the need for repose in the Christian life in days of strife and anxiety. This was what seems to have been a rare recognition of the global conflict that was raging at the time. The message was based on Christ's delay after hearing of the serious illness of Lazarus. 'The best living is not done in a hurry. Christ', he said, 'was never hurried'.[447]

Before the month was out, the Principal experienced a deep personal grief when his father Mr CA Morling died. Since the death of his wife he had lived with his family at Ashfield. At the funeral service the tribute was given by George's dear friend and brother-in-law, Rev Enos Coleman. A fine appreciation of the deceased by Rev John Deane appeared in *The Australian Baptist*.[448]

In that same issue of the paper the Principal replied to its South Australian correspondent, Rev H Estcourt Hughes, who had taken him to task over a couple of minor inaccuracies in the notes for the Australian Baptist Bible School for 11 June.[449] He acknowledged the mistakes, pointing out that the notes were written under great pressure for his public Bible School and had not been revised for publication.[450] The wonder is how he managed, with minimal secretarial assistance, to prepare them at all.

On 7 July he spoke on the Educational Session on Station 2CH and 'his address was full of profit'.[451] An indication that continuance of the war was creating problems was the decision that Principal's weekly public Bible School classes were henceforth to be monthly. The announcement added 'Principal Morling, MA, has very graciously consented to take the lectures in spite of the demands upon his time and energy'.[452]

In early August we find him preaching at the Church Anniversary of Mortdale, the church of which the College Treasurer, Mr RE Walker, was a member.[453]

Year by year, in the Report he presented to the Assembly, the Principal was not content merely to list facts and statistics. He used the opportunity to share his thoughts and feelings concerning the College, its program and its purpose. 1940 was no exception as the following extract shows.[454]

'One's sense of responsibility in directing the work of our Theological College does not grow less with the passing of the years. Humanly speaking, the success of the church depends upon the efficiency of its ministry and, in turn, the quality of the ministry is bound up with the faithfulness of the work of the institution which trains the students. Such a consideration is calculated to weigh one down. Who is sufficient for these things? One can only cast one's self in humble dependence on the all-sufficient God, recognising that all the spiritual resources available for the winning of souls are also at our disposal in informing the minds and moulding the lives of men who will plead with souls for Christ'.

'We desire to record that it is our convinced opinion that there should be some modification of the system under which our college students, throughout their whole course, are also Home Missionaries in charge of churches. Our men have not enough time for uninterrupted study and, from the Home Mission angle, churches need something more than the services which can be rendered by immature and inexperienced men, however warm their zeal and commendable their lives. A move is on foot to release first year students from pastoral duties. We hope that financial arrangements which will make this possible will soon be consummated. At present our men have too many interests. We fear that they have not enough leisure to achieve that mastery in the Word of God and that deep fellowship with Christ which every minister should attain'.

At the conclusion of the College Reports the President of its Council, Rev CJ Tinsley, moved and Rev W Cleugh Black seconded the following addendum, 'The College Council desires to place on record its unqualified appreciation of the services of the Principal, Secretary and Treasurer. Each has, in his own sphere, rendered outstanding service to the College and we feel that we are particularly blessed in having men of such ability and grace in control of the affairs of the college. Their loyalty to the great doctrines of grace, their deep spiritual life and their fine administrative gifts have helped to make the College more and more one of the most influential in the Commonwealth'.[455] It needs hardly to be said that the motion was carried.

On the last day of the Assembly, 24 September, the man who seconded the motion, Rev W Cleugh Black, Home Work Superintendent and dear friend of the Principal, died after a sudden illness. The funeral service was largely in the hands of fellow graduates of Spurgeon's College but the Principal shared in it.[456]

It was a happy occasion when on 5 October he shared in a very different service. On that day, in the 'Baptist College Chapel' he officiated at the wedding of his niece, Joyce Lusted, and Wallace Blatch of Yeoval.[457] Both were members of Strathfield-Homebush Church which then had no building of its own.

The 104th Anniversary of the Central Church coincided with the 3rd Anniversary of the opening of its new church building and was celebrated on 13 October. Principal Morling was preacher at the morning service.[458]

The next Sunday found him at Bowral where the previous day a new school hall had been opened. His sermon on 'Suffer the little children to come unto me and forbid them not' was directed to the occasion. He urged 'those associated with the church to make church life attractive to the young'. He spoke against the background of statistics showing a great decline in the numbers of children attending Sunday School in Great Britain. He said 'The task of the Sunday School teacher was to show Jesus Christ to the children - once they see Him, they will want to come to Him'.[459]

On 17 October Rev W Bell, MA, Principal of the Queensland Baptist College died. Of this older colleague in the task of theological education Principal Morling said, 'He was so genuinely good, so entirely free of affectation, so saturated with the Spirit of Christ that one always felt blessed in his presence. He will be greatly missed'.[460]

Always keenly interested in his graduates 'the beloved Principal' attended and brought a greeting at Waverley Church's welcome on 2 December to Rev AC Maynard[461], one of the first men to train at Granville. Bert Maynard's return to the city meant for the Principal the acquisition of an able church historian as a visiting lecturer.

The Ordination Service was held on 10 December in the Central Church when Principal Morling presented the three graduating students to Mr RE Walker, BEc, LL.B, President of the Union and Treasurer of the College Council.[462]

Four days later there was the Speech Day at the College. In his report delivered in his 'usual happy and homely vein' the Principal indicated that the enlarged College was already too small. In presenting and unveiling a portrait of his late father, Rev W. Cleugh Black, his son Arthur spoke of him in terms of love and reverence.[463] In addition to the portrait there was the announcement of an annual memorial prize to be awarded to a graduating student judged worthy of it.

At 8am the next day, 15 December, in the Central Church the Principal was the preacher at a Baptist Men's Communion Service.[464]

1941
He and Mrs. Morling were said, early in January, to be on holidays 'somewhere in New South Wales'.[465] Nevertheless, he was back in Sydney on 11 January to conduct the wedding of recently graduated and ordained student, Rev E Clive Smith to Miss Edna Andrews, daughter of Mr and Mrs FE Andrews. The bride was the sister of another recently ordained student, Rev EF (Ern) Andrews[466] who was soon to be accepted as a missionary by the Sudan United Mission.

Student weddings were not uncommon at this time of the year and presently he was sharing at North Sydney Church in that of Pastor Ern Milson and Miss C Taylor.

With the resignation of Rev William Lamb, whose health was failing, from Burton Street Church GH Morling was one of those who provided pulpit ministry. At a service in February he baptised three candidates and, to his great delight, two others responded to his appeal to trust in Christ.[467]

At West Ryde's 17th Anniversary he preached the latest revised version of a favourite sermon on 'Fellowship' based on 1 John 1. The sermon was most appropriate to the situation.

The College Commencement Service was again held in Central Baptist Church. At the preceding College Tea Mr RH Lawrenson shot scenes for a movie film 'The Making of a Minister' which proved very effective in promoting the College. The film, scarcely in mint condition, is in the archives of the NSW Baptist Historical Society. The Principal was not the star but he appears in it. The speaker at the service was Rev Hugh Paton, much loved evangelical minister of St Stephen's Presbyterian Church. He was a friend of George Morling who warmly welcomed and introduced him to the crowded congregation of College supporters. Six new single students entered College in 1941 bringing the total in residence to a record 21.[468] Two married men would be attending lectures and several others would be pursuing extramural studies. Of the six new single men two, Alan Tinsley and Doug Mill, were sons of ministerial colleagues of the Principal.

Now well into its second year the war was going overwhelmingly against the Allied Powers. British cities were being blasted and Britain had its back to the wall. King George VI issued a call to a day of special prayer.[469] The NSW Baptist response was centred on a series of prayer sessions in Central Baptist Church on Sunday, 23 March. Principal Morling, as one of the fathers of the denomination, led one of the sessions in his specially telling way.

On 25 and 26 March the Half-Yearly Assembly Meetings took place at Dulwich Hill. In the course of his verbal report on the College the Principal said, 'I have spent twenty years in the College. At first I thought I knew something; I do not think so now'.[470] Despite personal misgivings others were sure not only that he knew a great deal but that he was a great man. Dee Why was another pastorless church and it too looked to Principal Morling. On 30 March he preached there and conducted 'an inspiring and impressive baptismal service' in which he baptised seven believers.[471] At its conclusion three others came forward seeking baptism. This was a great encouragement to one whose evangelistic zeal was unabated after 20 years out of pastoral work.

During the next week his Bible School conducted at the College recommenced for the year on a monthly basis and again proved most popular.[472] Many were asking for the Principal's notes to be once more printed in the denominational paper.[473] They had ceased being published at the end of 1940 perhaps because the writer of them needed a rest from the pressure of their preparation.

The Principal's Blackheath connection was to the fore when on 26 April in the Central Church he joined Miss Betty Evelyn Thompson, only daughter of his Blackheath friends, Mr and Mrs FP Thompson, in marriage to Flying Officer Maurice A Nettle, BSc, DipEd, of Armidale.[474] With men leaving for active service special arrangements had often to be made for marriages to be solemnised at fairly short notice. Only a few days later the wedding could have been celebrated in Blackheath for Principal was there to conduct yet again Bible studies each morning at the Ministers' Retreat from 28 April to 2 May.[475] The Retreat was voted 'the best yet'.

The Granville Church granted its pastor, Rev JD Mill, three months leave of absence to fulfil an engagement with the church at Lismore. In his absence a special campaign was to be conducted at Granville under the direction of Principal Morling, honoured former member the church.[474] That responsibility didn't noticeably affect other activities on his part. Thoughts of Granville were much with him when in the following week Mrs Bullock of Wellington who with her husband, Luke, had given the Granville church property' died. She died in the city and a funeral service was held in the Central Church with the Principal participating.[476]

The war intruded in a more direct way into the Morling family with the announcement towards the end of May that Mrs Morling's nephew, Kenneth Rees, had been killed in action in Greece.[477]

Lugarno's first anniversary in its new building was celebrated in mid May and the Principal appropriately preached on the Church as the

Temple of God, the Body of Christ and the Bride of Christ. It was another of his familiar themes.

On 8 June 'the beloved Principal of our College' travelled all the way to West Maitland to preach at the anniversary of the Young People's Society of Christian Endeavour.[478] Rev Basil Brown was the pastor there and that was doubtless part of the reason for him making the trip. He took a continuing interest in his graduates.

The death of Jabez A Packer occurred on 21 June.[479] His friend, George Morling, shared in the funeral service, offering prayer for the bereaved family. In the same week another friend and former College secretary, Rev AL Leeder, suffered the loss of his wife. Morling spoke at her funeral.[480]

The month of July brought a renewal of earlier associations. As George Morling was growing up in the Ashfield Church the organist was Mr GS Potter. His ministry in music was greatly appreciated and when in retirement he moved to Katoomba his memory was kept fresh by the pipe organ which was installed through his personal efforts. At Katoomba he almost immediately became organist and had by the beginning of July completed fifty years of service. The two churches decided jointly to honour him by the presentation of a dining room clock. The Principal went to Katoomba, preached and made the presentation. The following week Mr. Potter was brought back to Ashfield to be honoured.[481]

On 13 July Pymble church celebrated its 25th Anniversary, and as its first pastor he had been invited back to preach.

On 19 July Ashfield opened the Robert Goodman Memorial Hall.[482] At the opening, as a church member, George Morling gave 'an eloquent tribute' to his friend and former pastor. The next day he preached at the morning service and through the week that followed shared in a Convention at the church.

When the Baptist Union of Australia Triennial Assembly meetings were held in Brisbane at the end of August the Principal was not among the delegates.

As noted earlier there had been requests for the Australian Baptist Bible School to be resumed by the publishing of Principal's notes. At last on 2 September they were granted when a series of studies on The Song of

Solomon began.[483]

At the 1941 Assembly Rev FT Smith became the first man who had studied under Principal Morling to occupy the Presidential chair. The opening paragraph of the Principal's Report to the Assembly said, 'With the passing of the years, the sense of privilege which we have in training men who have been separated by the Holy Spirit for the work of preaching Christ grows more and more; and, with the sense of privilege, the accompanying sense of responsibility. We pray that the College may be worthy of this holy task'.[484]

He was then just about midway through his long term as Principal. He proceeded to say that 'the real life and ministry of the college ... must be seen in the ministries of our men who are serving throughout Australia as well as in India and China and are building up what we hope is a distinctive tradition of a positive, warm heralding of the message of the Cross'. That hope was realised.

During the Assembly there was an ordination service at which the Principal presented the sole candidate, Pastor Ern Milson.[485]

The 53rd Anniversary of the Auburn Church on 28 September brought together again two men who had started out at the same time, the pastor, Archibald Jolly, and the Principal, George Morling. The latter preached at the morning service.[486]

On Saturday, 4 October, he was again in that vicinity when at the Granville Church he shared in the wedding of Margery Watts and Kenneth Angeleri. He spoke on behalf of the bride's parents at the reception.[487]

His sermon at Dee Why's l0th anniversary on 9 November was one which in ever varying forms he preached on numerous occasions, 'The Unchanging Christ', based on Hebrews 13:8.[488]

A family announcement told of the engagement of his daughter Dorothy to Sergeant Colin Goodman, son of the late Rev R Goodman.[489] He was ever welcome at his previous pastorates as was again evident when on 6 December he was the speaker at the opening of Bankstown's enlarged church.[490]

On 9 December, in the Central Church, the graduating students, J

Drakeford, E Agerakis and E Wykes, were ordained.[491] There was for the Principal a further association with Auburn pastor, Archibald Jolly, for he was the preacher.

At the College Speech Day on 13 December the newly ordained graduates gave farewell messages paying tribute to the Principal and to the College.

1942
At the beginning of the year the Morling family went as usual to their cottage at Blackheath for on 12 January the Principal chaired the public meeting of the Sunday School Anniversary there.[492]

References in available sources to Principal Morling's activities in early 1942 are limited. It may be that this reflects the actual situation for there is evidence that at least in the first half of the year his health was a problem, which may explain the delay in publishing his 'Bible School' series until February.[493]

By 1942 the fact of the war was entering deeply into the Australian consciousness. It was by this time clear that the outcome was uncertain and that the struggle would be long and hard. In most places the Allied forces were in retreat. Even Australia's remoteness was no longer thought to render it inviolable. Darwin had suffered major attacks and enemy shells had fallen, while Sydney harbour had been penetrated by midget submarines. In the course of the year great numbers of children were evacuated from Sydney and other coastal cities. There were for a period Baptist hostels for evacuated children at Narrabri West[494] and Quirindi.

College resumed the first week of March and on 10 March the Commencement Service took place in the Central Church. Rev E Clatworthy, recently returned from India, was the speaker. At the preceding tea Mr RH Lawrenson screened the movie film he had been making of College life.[495]

Within a few days the Executive Committee of the Union was deciding to send a letter of sympathy to the Principal who was ill in hospital 'assuring [him] of prayer for his speedy restoration to wonted health'.[496] Just one week later on 24 March the Half-Yearly meetings of the Union at Islington noted his absence due to illness and sent greetings to him.[497] Soon after, *The Australian Baptist* rather optimistically reported that his health was much improved and he had returned from Blackheath in hope of resuming his duties.[498] It was in fact some weeks before this happened.

Doubtless he did his best to be present at the Ashfield Church when on 26 April Rev Walter Barry baptised 'Master Billy Morling'.[499] The Principal's second son was then sixteen.

The first indication of returning health was his invitation to intending students of tutorial classes to meet him on 21 May.[500] Then he resumed duties at College.[501] He preached at Strathfield-Homebush's 2nd Anniversary on 31st May.[502]

Over the King's Birthday weekend, a well-planned Student Convention with the theme 'Light in the Darkness' was held at North Auburn. The Principal filled his accustomed role as the concluding speaker. His subject was 'The House Management of the Ages' based on Ephesians 1:10.

He spoke at Bexley's 28th Anniversary on 19 July taking as his subject 'Ye shall receive power'.[503] He attended Pymble's farewell to Rev AT Whale and welcome to Rev CT Bryant on 15 August[504], and was among those present when Rev E Clatworthy, one of his men, was welcomed at Ashfield, his home church, on 5 September.[505] He preached the following day at Kingsgrove's 67th Anniversary.[506]

The NSW Assembly which opened on 14 September found him considerably involved. At the Assembly another of his men and close colleague, Vice-principal JH Deane, BA, BD was elected Vice-President of the Union.[507] Incidentally, at the South Australian Assembly yet another of his former students, Rev EH Watson, became President of that Union.[508]

The report of John Deane's election in *The Australian Baptist*[509] said, 'His present ministry at Haberfield commenced in 1936, since which year Mr Deane has also been vice-principal and secretary of the NSW Theological College, the marked progress of which during recent years has been largely due to his fervour and zeal'. Without question he had done much to promote the College but it could be argued that the comment overstated the case. Perhaps the editor himself thought so for in the next edition of the paper in reporting the election of Principal Morling he corrected the balance when he wrote, 'Rev GH Morling, MA, who was reappointed Principal of the Theological College for a further three years at the recent Assembly Meetings of the Baptist Union of NSW will complete 21 years in that office during the ensuing year.

Apart from the outstanding service he rendered the denomination during that period as College Principal Mr Morling has made a great contribution to the Church and the Kingdom of God by his expository addresses at conventions and missions in various States of the Commonwealth. His 'Bible School' column in *The Australian Baptist* is also greatly valued by a great section of our readers'.[510]

Although there is no mention of it in the Minutes the Assembly marked the completion of his 21 years of service by authorising the College Council to make a presentation to him of £100.

The evening sessions of the Assembly were designated 'A Campaign for Christian Conquest' with the subtitle, 'Accepting the Challenge of Christ in the World Crisis'. The second night, Wednesday 16 September, was Christian Workers' Night and the Principal was the speaker, addressing the subject, 'The Challenge of Christ and the Source of Spiritual Power'.[511] It was a subject made to measure for him.

The Principal's report to the Assembly began with an interesting comment. 'The work of the College has inevitably been affected by the war conditions. Mental disturbance does not conduce to the results in the realm of studies. On the other hand the spiritual challenge of the times is an excellent stimulus to high endeavour for Christ, and we hope that the tone of the College has risen as a consequence. We believe that this is so. There is real cause for satisfaction in the devotion of the students to their high calling'.[512]

Never a great committee man George Morling was probably less than excited when at its meeting of 20 October, the Executive Committee elected him to the Pensions and Annuity Committee.[513]

For several months the Evangelistic and Propaganda Committee had been sponsoring a weekly series over Station 2UW called 'Talks for the Times'. On 25 October the series came to a climax when Principal GH Morling gave the final talk 'What must I do to become a Christian?' He was wisely chosen for such a commitment.[514]

On 5 November, 1942, denominational stalwart and dear friend of the Principal, Mr FP Thompson, was honoured on his 75th birthday by the Blackheath Church whose secretary, most of the time since he came from Waverley, he had been. In an official capacity George Morling gladly travelled to Blackheath to express 'the felicitations of the whole denomination'.⁵¹⁵ The discharge of this happy responsibility meant that he had to send a letter of apology to Mortdale's welcome to Rev SM Bryson the same night. Two days later he was celebrating an even more venerable birthday when he spoke on 'Church Fellowship' at a conference after the Tea Meeting of Parramatta Church's 91st Anniversary.⁵¹⁶ He was kept on the move for the next weekend he conducted Anniversary Services at Goulburn.⁵¹⁷

Sometime in November he was moved by something he had read to make another entry in a diary. 'There has been during the last couple of years a growing knowledge of the self-life which, I am sure, lies at the root of my troubles physical as well as spiritual. It has surprised me to know that inner tension has been due to the persistent attempt to 'bolster up one's own self, which has involved much strain. The philosopher Yoritomo has enlightening words about fears or timidity. 'One form of timidity', he says, 'springs from an exaggerated self- esteem and the fear of not appearing sufficiently brilliant".ʷ

'The loss or weakening of the will power is the principal cause of attacks of timidity. At the root they spring from vanity and egotism: then there is the lack of energy to put into operation remedial measures. Energy is the highest goal of all things and the world belongs to the energetic'.

'There are many ways of curing stammering but the best way is by exercising a firm will supported by energy. Energetic action does more than any treatment. We can, if we will, get rid of the stammer'.

'Audacity when it does not degenerate into boastfulness is a great virtue marching ahead of the cortege led of energy. It is the exclusive attribute of the strong requiring energy but especially will power'.

It may be concluded that the foregoing are extracts from, or summaries of, the writings of Yoritomo. However GHM adds this note, 'These qualities of energy and strength of will can be supplied only by Christ through the Holy Spirit in answer to believing prayer'.

The whole entry reveals a spiritually sensitive, somewhat introspective

---

ʷ Yoritomo Tashi was a Japanese philosopher whose work 'Common Sense How to Exercise It" was published in English in 1916 – JS Google man, seeking earnestly to be his best for God and not satisfied with his current level of attainment. Most would be content with much less but not George Morling who on the next page of his diary lays bear his questing, aspiring and believing heart – 'I must be filled with the Holy Spirit; I cannot lead without His fullness. I may be filled; the promise is for me. I would be filled; that is the point reached. I shall be filled. If I entrust myself to Jesus, He cannot disappoint me. It is His very nature; it is His work in heaven. It is His delight to give souls the Holy Spirit'. Reading that, we may feel that we have unveiled the deepest secret of his life and that we are treading on holy ground.

The theme of the recent Assembly was taken up in other centres. At Burwood, from 21 November to 9 December there was 'A Campaign for Christian Conquest'. Included in the Campaign was a Young People's Rally and, significantly, the chosen speaker was the Principal. Doubtless it was reckoned that he should know a good deal about young people both as a family man and as a teacher of mainly young men.

On 3 December in the Central Baptist Church there was a conference between members of the Churches of Christ Preachers' Fraternal and of the Baptist Ministers' Fraternal.[518] The conference was initiated by the Churches of Christ Fraternal in order to discuss certain areas of agreement and disagreement between the two bodies. Principal AR Main, MA, spoke for the Churches of Christ and Principal Morling for the Baptists. A pamphlet giving the substance of the latter's address is in the archives of the Baptist Historical Society of New South Wales. It is concise, gracious in tone yet forthright in the statement of issues. The conference probably provided a clearer understanding of how the two bodies saw their respective positions but didn't serve to bring them nearer to each other. It may be said, however, that Principal Morling proved a worthy denominational spokesman on theological issues.

On 6 December he preached at Wollongong church.[519]

The College Speech Day or Break-up was held at the College on 12 December. There was a slight shadow over proceedings because two of the graduating students had each failed by a narrow margin in one subject. On the previous evening, despite the support of the Principal for their ordination, the Executive had decided that a precedent should not be established. Consequently the Ordination Service, planned and announced for 15 December with a US Army Chaplain as speaker, had been postponed.[520] At least the decision meant that the Principal had a few extra days to prepare his addresses for the Katoomba Convention just after Christmas[519] but it may have taken almost as long for his wounds to heal. The series of Bible readings on which he had to work were on John 14-16, an area that never ceased to demand his interest and exposition.

His time of preparation was not without interruption for on 19 December he officiated at the wedding of another of his students, Rev RK (Keith) Redman to Miss N Wright.[521] Moreover there was the continuing necessity of preparing for publication his Bible studies that appeared week by week in *The Australian Baptist*. By the end of 1942 the current series on the Acts of the Apostles had reached Number 47.

1943
Christmas with the family, the Katoomba Convention and then he was off to the Newcastle area. One of his responsibilities there was to preach at the Maitland Road Islington Church on 10 January, as its pastor, Rev W Gibbins, was on vacation.[522] Duty done he was able to retire to Blackheath, his mountain retreat. Even so, as almost invariably he was the preacher on 14 February at Blackheath's Anniversary.[523]

When College resumed on 22 February he spoke 'at his inimitable best'.[524] He had completed 21 years as full-time Principal of the College. The College was enormously and justifiably proud of its Principal. March was recognised in the Union as College month. In an advertisement for College month it was asserted: 'In supporting the College you are supporting the College in its Divine mission'.[525] Prompted by the Principal having attained his 'majority' the President of the College Council, Rev CJ Tinsley, wrote a tribute which in part read, 'he has displayed ability, tact and a quality of character that has placed the College in an impregnable position and given it an outstanding prestige … he deservedly retains the growing confidence and esteem of the denomination'.[526]

The leaflet issued by the College Council to promote College month featured the Principal. It included the following – 'March is College Month and this year completes the 21st Anniversary of the appointment of the Rev GH Morling, MA as Principal of our NSW Baptist Theological College'.

'We are certain that every Baptist and many friends of other denominations will be anxious to give tangible expression (to their appreciation of him and join with ours, their commendation of the person and work of our Principal'.

'This you can do by supporting to the full the work of the College, through which our Principal serves such a large constituency'.

'The College Council feels that the magnificent work performed by the Principal over this period of 21 years merits some signal recognition and at the College Commencement exercises to be held in the Central Church, Sydney on 16 March, the College President, Rev CJ Tinsley, will present to the the Principal £100 as a mark of esteem and affection from the Baptists of New South Wales'.

It was a significant gift being a quarter of the annual salary which he had been receiving for most of his period of service. The man so honoured was the preacher for the service and so was able not only to reflect on the past but to share his dreams for the future despite the prevailing war clouds which even that night had forced the cancellation of the customary College Tea.

In *The Australian Baptist* he began a new series of Bible studies on Our Lord's Discourses in the Upper Room[527], following his 57-part series on 'The Acts of the Apostles'. These were a considerable expansion of the topics he had taken a little earlier at the Katoomba Convention. Possibly there was no part of the Scriptures more frequently or more helpfully expounded by Principal Morling than John 14-16.

Early in 1943 special evangelistic missions were being conducted in many churches. In preparation for a mission to be conducted by Rev WL Jarvis the Principal preached in the Lithgow Church on 21 March.[528] He was glad to have some part in evangelistic activity.

The Half-Yearly Meetings of the Union were held at the Central Church on 6-7 April with the theme 'The Challenge of the Crisis'. On 7 April GHM spoke on 'The Challenge of the Crisis at Home'. There was, at that time, public controversy about the place, if any, of religion in education. Professor John Anderson of Sydney University had claimed that education and religion were incompatible, the latter being a denial of the former. In his address the Principal said, 'We have been stirred by the utterance of Professor John Anderson, who confesses himself an atheist. We are living in an atmosphere that discourages belief in God. The Church must take a strong attitude to this situation, live its life courageously and proclaim its message with passion'. He proceeded to say that the world had become so self-sufficient that it felt no need of

God. The business of the Church was to break down confidence in the false gods that man had made for himself. The seriousness of the situation could be seen in the terrible collapse of morality.[529]

In the evening the Ordination Service deferred from December was held with Principal Morling presenting Pastors J Godwin, N Horn, G Parish and K Redman to the President of the Union for ordination.

At the next meeting of the Executive Committee on 20 April there was criticism of the College students for their non-attendance at the Foreign Mission meeting of the Half-Yearly Assembly. In their defence the Principal stated that they were attending Christian Endeavour meetings in their churches and if required to attend Assembly should be so directed by the Home Mission Superintendent.[530] He was jealous for the good standing of his students. Later in the year in his Report to the Assembly there was this significant paragraph.[531]

'An outstanding feature of the year has been the outbreak of added missionary zeal in the College. Mr Lincolne has given a most informative series of reviews of the world situation in respect to missions at our early Tuesday morning prayer meeting, which is always devoted to prayer for foreign missions. Challenges brought by the Rev FA Marsh and the Rev W Barry also had an effect. All the men were moved carefully to examine their lives in the light of the will of God, and four felt the clear call to volunteer for service in India'.

On Monday, 12 April, he was the speaker at the public meeting of Concord's 23rd Anniversary.[532]

The end of first term at College in May gave him opportunity to travel to the Newcastle area to share in a 'Spiritual Campaign'.[533] He spoke on the early part of Romans 6 and it was reported that 'ex-students present had never heard the Principal speak with such liberty and power'. The report added, 'This message awakened many souls'.[534]

From the north he went south to Woonona, preaching there on 23 May. For the Principal term breaks presented an opportunity for ministry in the churches, especially those outside the metropolitan area.

On 28 May a death occurred that would involve the Principal in various ways. It was the death of Mr JM Crawford, MBE, the President of the

Baptist Union. Mr Crawford, a distinguished engineer, was a deacon at Pymble, as he had been when Principal Morling was the pastor there. In a tribute[535] to him the Principal recalled the trepidation he had felt when first he had become pastor at Pymble. He wrote, 'He (Mr Crawford) had recently ... come to live in Pymble. I was young then and I expect that I was a little nervous about his presence in my congregation, but his entire friendliness soon dispelled all fears'. It was at Pymble that the Principal first began to expound the Scriptures systematically. He acknowledged that it was this man's enthusiasm for the Scriptures that had led to this practice.

A consequence of his friend's death was that John Deane became at once the Acting-President of the Baptist Union. Therefore, the Vice-Principal's activities at the College had to be curtailed and it was largely left to the Principal to stand in the breach. This meant that he had to limit his availability for ministry outside the College.

It was therefore somewhat unrealistic on the part of the Executive Committee at its meeting on 29 June to appoint the Principal on a committee to draw up a public statement on the Baptist view of post-war problems.[536] If the other members of the Committee were as preoccupied as he was it is not surprising that the statement never saw the light of day, despite an Executive decision on 20 July that it be ready for the next Assembly.[537] The matter was revived at the Executive meeting of 20 February, 1945, with the Principal appointed as convenor[538] but events took a different course.

On 26 June 1943, the Principal, in the absence of Rev FT Smith on chaplaincy duties, conducted the wedding of a Brisbane girl and a Newcastle naval officer at Hurlstone Park.[539]

Two Church Anniversaries at which he spoke were reported in July. On 11 July his address at Bexley's 29th was 'A restful heart in a time of war' based on Matthew 11:28-30.[540] His sermon at Hurstville's 13th on 25 July was on Daniel 3:17-18, a passage that calls for costly refusal to compromise one's convictions.[541]

Next we find him addressing the Ministers' Fraternal Meeting on 3 August, taking as his topic, 'Recent Theological Thought'. The Barthian School received special mention.[542] On 17 August, having completed his 22-part series on the Upper Room discourses, he commenced a series of articles on 'The Abiding Life'.[543] He spoke at Auburn's 55th Church Anniversary on 5 September.[544]

At the Annual Assembly later in the month Rev JH Deane, BA BD, Vice-Principal of the College, Secretary of its Council and pastor of the Haberfield Church was formally inducted as President of the Union, a role he had already been fulfilling for some months. For the year ahead he continued to be greatly missed at the college, especially by the Principal. One of the students, Ian Emmett, was virtually acting-pastor of the Haberfield Church but, although some little additional help was found for the College lecturing program, an increased burden was borne by the Principal.

The theme, chosen by the President, for the Assembly was 'Christ's Program for His Church – A Quest for the Souls of Men'. He invited several men to promote his emphasis. On Thursday, 24 September, Principal Morling was the speaker.[545] His address made such an impression that the Assembly recorded appreciation and instructed the Evangelistic Committee have the address printed along with other suitable literature bearing on the President's theme.

The Principal in his Report to the Assembly, having noted the difficulty of tabulating the results of work done at the College, said, 'The incalculable element of inspiration and insight is the final test of success. We of the teaching staff feel that this has been one of our best years'.[531] In another way it was a good year for the Principal for his ministry was expanded. The last paragraph of his Report was definitely understated when it read, 'It may be of interest to report that, as a member of the honorary teaching staff of the Faculty of Divinity, I am giving a series of lectures in Ecclesiastical History at the University of Sydney'. The denomination was very pleased to have its Principal recognised in this way.

As GHM completed 21 years as Principal, Rev CJ Tinsley wrote – 'Called to the principalship at a comparatively youthful age, and at a time of peculiar difficulty, he has displayed ability, tact and a quality of character that has placed the college in an impregnable position and given it an outstanding prestige'.[546]

On 2 October in the Burwood Church he officiated at a wedding that had special significance for him. The bride, Constance Marjorie, was the daughter of his friend AT (Bert) Whale and the bridegroom, Albert Dube, was one of his students released from the College for military service.[547]

An ordination service that was later seen to be of more than ordinary significance for the Principal was conducted on 9 November. One of those whom he presented for ordination was Rev BG Wright[548] who subsequently served with him as Vice-principal of the College and still later himself became Principal.

It was back to Dee Why on 14 November to preach once more at its Church Anniversary. On 20 November he assisted in the wedding at Ashfield Church of graduating student, Pastor Doug Ison, to Gwen Burniston.[549] They would be proceeding to Eastern Bengal and in a departure from established practice they were being allowed to marry before the prescribed period of service on the field.

On 23 November Rev HG Hercus of the Drummoyne Church died suddenly[550] and, as so often happened, it fell to the Principal to give the tribute in the church and to conduct the service at the crematorium.[551]

Another ordination service was held on 25 November[552,x] with the Principal presenting Pastor Doug Ison to the President.[553]

On 11 December there was the College Break-up function. Of those graduating one in particular, Pastor EG Gibson, LTh, was subsequently very greatly involved in theological education, and was for some time both in a part-time and in a full-time capacity a colleague of the Principal in his teaching task.

1944
Baptist stalwart, Rev JD Mill, died on 23 January, 1944, and a funeral service was held in the Central Church. 'A moving address was given by Principal GH Morling'.[554]

For the third time in four months he was involved an ordination service when on 8 February he presented four candidates who had graduated in December for ordination.[555] Such services were a source of satisfaction for him as he saw in them the fruit and proof of the special ministry to which he had been called. On the day of the ordination *The Australian Baptist* [556] expressed sympathy to Principal and Mrs Morling because

---
[x] Rogers states that the ordination took place on 7 December.

their son, William, had been injured in an aeroplane accident. Bill was an enlisted member of the Air Force. He was out of action for several months.

It should cause no surprise that when Blackheath held its 55th Anniversary on 13 February its long time friend and counselor, George Morling, was speaker.[557] Soon it was back from Blackheath to Ashfield for students came into residence on 21 February.[555]

Then was announced an engagement of more than ordinary interest to George Morling, of Jean, daughter of his friends, Mr and Mrs AS White, to Lieutenant Clive Rice, grandson of his spiritual mentor, the late Rev TR Coleman.[558]

Early March found him preaching at the Harvest festival of Hurlstone Park[559] where as a young man he had been helped by TR Coleman.

Rev WH Wingfield the second Home Mission Superintendent died after a comparatively brief illness on 1 May. For many years he had been the children's Uncle John in *The Australian Baptist* and he was universally loved. His death was the more keenly felt because at 58 he was thought to have some years of significant service ahead of him. As expected the Principal participated in the service.[560]

With a residential Ministers' Retreat in abeyance it was decided in 1944 to hold a non-residential 'School of Theology' during 15-17 May with all day sessions at three churches, Ashfield, Central and Stanmore. The Principal spoke on 'Trends in Modern Theology'. He contrasted the stress in Schleiermacher on the immanence of God with that on the transcendence of God in Barth.[561] But it was no mere exercise in abstract theology. Reporting the session Rev FA Hoad said, 'One felt like kneeling down and worshipping'.

When, soon after, George Morling preached at the Anniversary of his home church, Ashfield, his subject was 'The Baptist Witness in the Modern World'[562]. On 23 May he began a new series of lessons on 'The Australian Bible School' on John 16.[563]

June was a good month for the Morling family. 'L/Cpl Gordon Morling, AIF, is home on leave after two years active service in New Guinea. His brother LAC Bill Morling, RAAF, who was seriously injured in an aircraft accident in February last, has fully recovered and has resumed duty and is flying again'.[564] Soon after Gordon Morling and Joyce McKay announced their engagement to be married. However the end of the month brought sadness with the death of Mrs Rees, Mrs Morling's mother.[565]

During AH Orr's pastorate at Bexley a special link had been established with the Principal and 25 July found him once more at Bexley, preaching at its 30th Anniversary.

Deep sorrow descended on the denomination, the College and especially on the Principal through the death by drowning in Eastern Bengal of missionary graduate, Rev Cyril Moore, his wife Edna, and Victorian missionary Rev Ron Potter.[566] Men who had been called to missionary service had a special place in the interest and prayers of their Principal. Cyril Moore, as the first of his students to die while in missionary service, henceforth became a part of the College tradition and was remembered in a special way at least as long as George Morling was Principal. A communion set given in his memory to the College by Bengali Christians often gave rise to the retelling of his story.

At the 1944 Assembly the retiring President, Rev JH Deane, as Secretary of the College Council, presented his Annual Report. In it he mentioned the re-arrangement of tutorial work made necessary by his Presidential duties. Then he added, 'These rearrangements, however, could not relieve the Principal of greatly added responsibility and work. The Council recognises the value of the contribution the Principal thus made to the denomination by assuming the major part of the Vice-Principal's lectures, etc. It is consistent with his every action in the College work, and we are grateful to our Heavenly Father that sufficient strength was given for the task'.[567]

The Assembly instructed the officers of the College Council to draw up a suitable addendum expressing appreciation of additional burdens borne by the Principal. This was not done because later in Assembly a motion was sustained that no addenda be added to reports.[568]

In the Principal's own Report he noted a decline in numbers of students because the war effort was claiming more men for military service. Another significant note was that several recent graduates were pursuing studies with London University. The three he listed, Gilbert Wright,

Basil Brown and Ted Gibson, all subsequently played major roles in Baptist theological education in Australia.[569]

On 7 November he began a study series in 'The Australian Bible School on 2 Samuel.[570]

Answering the challenge of broken ranks Rev and Mrs E Clatworthy of the Ashfield Church volunteered to return to India for further service. At their farewell on 13 November George Morling, one of their church members, welcomed the President, Mr FH Farrer, and other visitors to the function and later in the proceedings made, on behalf the church, a presentation to the pastor and his wife.[571]

In a reversal of roles he was at the Blackheath Church on 22 November to preside at the welcome extended to Rev and Mrs JB Wilson.[572] The mountain church regarded him almost as an honorary member.

There was a touch of drama on 9 December, the night of the College Break-up.[573] There had been an announcement to the churches that there would be an ordination service on 12 December. Most unfortunately one of the students due to be ordained had failed one of his final examinations. A special meeting of the Executive Committee of the Union to see what could be done was convened at the College early on the evening of the Break-up. With the matter still unresolved the Principal and the President the College had to leave the special meeting to attend the Break-up function in the College lecture room. Understandably the customary high spirits of such an occasion were slightly subdued. The Executive, standing on principle, finally decided that the unsuccessful student could not be ordained until he had satisfactorily tackled a supplementary examination. On 12 December when the Principal presented five men for ordination, Rev E Clatworthy, on the eve of his departure for India, was the preacher.

1945
A slight breathing space. a little time for the family and then once more he was off to the Katoomba Convention to share his convictions about the possibility of victorious living in and through Christ.[574]

So much was he a regular contributor to Blackheath's Anniversary that when he was absent from their 56th on 11 and 12 February they put on record, 'We greatly missed the presence of our old friend and helper,

Principal GH Morling, MA, who was engaged in Sydney by other engagements'.[575] There is no report of what he did on the Sunday but Saturday 11 February, he was at the wedding of Miss Joy Lindstrom and Rev Allan Tinsley.[576] They were both the children of dear friends of the Principal and themselves enjoyed over the years an increasingly close bond of affection with him. In later years their home in the Adelaide hills was a haven to which from time to time he resorted. At the reception he proposed the toast to the bride and bridegroom.

On 3 March in Wesley Chapel, Sydney, he conducted the wedding of Miss Esma Lindstrom, cousin of Joy, and Rev JG Leigh Wedge.[577] His ties with the Lindstrom family were close and strong.

Making much of its 'coming of age' the West Ryde church had him preaching at their 21st Anniversary on 10 March. His sermon was on the unchanging Christ, Hebrews 13:8. There been some suggestion that the College training course should be more intensive. At the Executive Committee on 20 March he outlined the entire College course and his report was 'received with satisfaction'.[578]

On 27 March there was an ordination service at which the student who had caused such heart burning a few months before was ordained. The Principal not only presented the candidate but also preached the ordination sermon.

He was also in action at Sans Souci's Easter Convention, speaking at the afternoon session on Good Friday.[579]

There was an interesting development when at the Executive Committee on 17 April two recommendations were received from the College Council. The first was that the Principal's salary be increased to £450 *per annum* 'plus the present emoluments of office', whatever they may have been. He was also to retain preaching fees. The other was more daring. It was that Rev JH Deane, the Vice-Principal, be invited to join the College staff full-time also on £450.[580]

The war touched the Principal and the College family with sorrow when the death of GR Saville was announced.[581] Gordon Saville had suspended his College course to join the Air Force. His death occurred when two Lancaster bombers collided over Germany.

On 4 May there was for the Principal a further sorrow, occasioned by the death of Mrs RN Whale of Eastwood, a sister-in-law of AT Whale. George Morling assisted in the church service giving the tribute to one whom he described as 'one of God's choice saints'. He also conducted the service at the graveside.

It was with great relief and thankfulness that the news was received that on 7 May Germany had surrendered unconditionally. Victory had been secured in Europe but war in the Pacific theatre still dragged on for some months and thousands of lives were lost.

The last week of May witnessed the revival after a lapse of four years of the Ministers' Retreat at Blackheath. Once more the Principal was pressed into service. He presented two studies of which a report by John E White said, 'The first was an enquiry into the mystery of the Holy Spirit and the Godhead; the second was concerned with the Holy Spirit and human personality. They were highlight addresses, satisfying for the faith they proclaimed, and the recognition of the need for a 1945 expression of it. The Principal has an easy method of presentation that is appreciated when a deep subject is being considered'.[582]

With the war entering its final phase the Social Questions Committee of the Baptist Union arranged a 'Church and State' Conference in Central Church on 9 June. In the afternoon session Principal Morling addressed the Conference on 'The Baptist Attitude to the Social Order'.[583] On 19 June his published studies on 2 Samuel were succeeded by a series on Colossians.[584]

He reported to the Executive Committee on 17 July concerning steps being taken to issue a book on the Baptist attitude to post-war problems.[585] It was more than two years since that matter had first been raised. However even this belated response was to be still-born. At the 21 August meeting of the Executive a change of plans was advised. The proposal now was that a series of conferences be arranged with major contributions being reported in *The Australian Baptist* and later issued in pamphlet form.[586]

At the 1944 Assembly Rev Frank Robinson had been elected Vice-President of the Union. At the end of July, less than three months before he assumed the office of President his wife died. A memorial service for her was held at the Concord Church on 2 August. At the graveside the Principal 'paid a tender tribute' to her.[587] The links with the Robinsons went back to the days when Gladys Morling (then Rees) was in their church at Haberfield.

When the Baptist Union of Australia Board Meetings were held in Melbourne at the end of August GHM represented NSW[588] on the Educational Board.

Returning to Sydney *post haste* he inducted Rev Eric Wykes to the East Chatswood pastorate on the morning of 2 September. In the evening he preached on the Holy Spirit at the 43rd Anniversary of the Dulwich Hill church. He made the point that it is only through the church that the Holy Spirit can have an impact on the world.[589]

Over those few hectic days he would already have known of the announcement[590] that his colleague, John Deane, had accepted an invitation to become the Principal of what was then known as the New Zealand Bible Training Institute (now The Bible College of New Zealand). On 4 September his series on Colossians was succeeded by a series on Mark's gospel.[591] It must have been a rather concerned and pre-occupied man who set off from Sydney about a week later to be the speaker at the Assembly Meetings of the Baptist Union of Queensland.[592] He certainly didn't spare himself, but even that is not the whole story. A letter written to the Principal many years later by Miss EW Evans of Lismore fills in but one of the many gaps in the public record. She wrote, 'I thought you might be interested in a note I have in my Five Year Diary. 'September 15, 1945, We had a wonderful day when Principal Morling of the Baptist College, Sydney, addressed three gatherings at the Lismore Baptist Church. He spoke on 'How men saw Jesus', 'How men see Jesus today' (a study in the Holy Spirit) and 'How men will see Jesus'". On the way, on 16 September he preached at Casino in the morning and at Murwillumbah at night.[593]

Meanwhile in NSW the Assembly confirmed its confidence in the Principal by enthusiastically electing him for a further three years.[594] John Deane, in his last report as Secretary of the College Council, wrote, 'The Council is unceasingly thankful for the spiritual leadership, as well as the teaching qualifications of the Rev Principal GH Morling, MA, now in his 23rd year as Principal. The profound influence of personal leadership is one of the most obvious facts of human life. To have a spiritual personality, alert to every new phase of thought, and yet utterly loyal to the ancient faith of the New Testament and, withal, fervently aglow with a passion for the winning of the lost to Christ, is a matter profound thankfulness, and such is Principal Morling'. The man so lauded returned from Queensland in time for the last day of Assembly and the ordination service.[595]

On 25 October Mrs AM Selwood died, aged 93. It was in her home that Mr CA Morling resided when he came to Australia seeking recovery of health.[596] Moreover, it was there that he was married to Miss Annie Hillman by the Petersham pastor.

At the end of November the Newcastle ministers had a four-day spiritual retreat. To conduct it they called on the one than whom there was no more helpful director and preacher, the Principal.[597]

College Graduation, as it was now called, was held on 4 December in the Ashfield Church. Associated with it was a farewell to the Vice-Principal as he was about leave for New Zealand. Principal Morling spoke 'of our loss in Mr Deane's departure and emphasised the sincerity, the power and the fruitfulness of his ministry as pastor and as Vice-Principal and Secretary of the College. In spite of all his splendid work we should miss Mr Deane most as a man of God'. He then read a minute of appreciation passed by the College Council.[598]

The beloved Principal was much in demand for student weddings. On 15 December he officiated at that of recently graduated Senior Student Charles Lockyer and Dorothy Paisley.[599]

With the passing of yet another year with its many predictable aspects it may be appropriate to acknowledge that, as with many others, the main ministry of the Principal had long since settled if not into a rut yet into a quite definite routine. Towards the end of February College started and settled into a regular succession of three terms each concluding with examinations and followed by a term break during which the Principal marked papers, attended to administration and tried to catch up with other tasks awaiting attention. The third term was regularly punctuated by the Baptist Assembly Meetings. During the long vacation the routine had come to include convention ministry and a holiday at Blackheath. There were, as has been obvious, numerous intrusions into and additions to this routine and it is these that perhaps have called most for notice. It is well, however, to remember that it was by faithful and capable application to the unspectacular routine of the duties of Principalship that his greatest contribution was made.

1946
Morling sent an apology to Rev and Mrs James Hunter's farewell at Burwood.[600] He felt a special debt of gratitude to James Hunter for his part in helping to secure the Granville property for the College. It is not unlikely that early in the new year he was recovering from the toll of the previous year's activities. Never robust his health continued to be a source of concern.

Stanmore's farewell to Rev CJ Tinsley on 31 January celebrated his long and notable ministry. 'Principal Morling was at his best in paying a tribute on behalf of the BU.[601] On Sunday, 3 February, he was at Stanmore to induct Rev NF Reeve into the pastorate.[602] A week later he was again in Sydney to induct Rev AH Orr, Tinsley's former associate at Stanmore, into the pastorate of his own church at Ashfield.[603] This would have brought both joy and relief to him, for he had been acting as Ashfield's moderator in its pastoral interregnum. With these matters effectively and happily dealt with he was back at Blackheath the next day to chair the public meeting of its Church Anniversary.[604]

On 26 February College resumed and in the evening at the Central Church he presented the previous year's graduates to the President for ordination.[605]

On 3 March Rev Allan Tinsley began ministry at Campsie and it was the Principal who, with ever strengthening bonds, inducted him.[606]

Several times during the course of the year he was specially associated with his good friend, Rev RS (Bob) Pickup. The first was when the latter was the preacher at the College Commencement in Central Church on 12 March. At that service it was reported that a record number of forty students would be associated with the College that year. Clearly help needed to be found for the Principal.

The Christian Workers' Training College was an ambitious venture launched by the Central Church to provide worthwhile evening courses to meet the need of those not able to study full-time. Principal Morling was listed as one of the lecturers and when the first session was held on 25 March he gave the special address.[607]

On 30 March the Dulwich Hill Church had a welcome home to Rev RS (Chaplain) Pickup and other members of the forces already discharged. GHM was present and was thanked for conducting many church services in the pastors' absence.[608] So that was yet another way in which the Principal kept himself occupied.

Concord, Church of the Union President, Rev Frank Robinson, had its anniversary on 7 April, and George Morling preached for his old friend.[609] A week later he presided at the welcome to Waverley of his young friend, Rev EG Gibson.[610] He took the opportunity to congratulate the church in securing the services of such an able young man.

The next week witnessed the death of two elderly women for whom the Principal had a high regard. Mrs Nancy Jane Coleman, widow of the late Rev TR Coleman, died[611], and it was merciful that Herbert, their invalid son, had died just a few months earlier. A service for Mrs Coleman was held at Islington and then another at Ashfield presided over by the Principal before interment at Northern Suburbs Cemetery.[612]

On 22 April Mrs. Walter Barry died.[612] The following Sunday at Concord West Church George Morling conducted a memorial service.[613] A report of the service said that in paying a tribute to her he referred to outstanding characteristics of her life which he said centred on the words radiance, serenity, refinement and motherliness. Those were qualities highly prized by the Principal.

With first term drawing to a close Principal Morling left for Brisbane on 6 May to give lectures at the Queensland College for a fortnight.[614] It was part of an exchange arrangement, with Principal Warriner visiting the Sydney College[615] as did also a number of students from the Victorian College. As might have been expected the Queensland ministers seized the opportunity to have the Sydney Principal speak at their Sandgate Retreat. A report said in part, 'Our students and ministers will ever be under a deep obligation to Principal Morling for the valuable lectures which he delivered at the Ministers' Retreat and College. We shall ever carry with us their influence, teaching and inspiration. We hope that some day Mr Morling will be led to publish his lectures on the Epistle to the Hebrews. They will be a magnificent contribution to expository literature'.[615]

Another elect lady with whom the Principal had been associated died a little later. Mrs JH Burnet, a most gracious woman, had been a good friend to the College, as had been her husband.[616]

On 27 September, his series on Mark's gospel completed, he began a series on the Holy Spirit.[617]

1 September found the Principal back at Dulwich Hill Church for its 44th Anniversary, bringing a message on 'Witnessing'. Dulwich Hill had been the mother-church of Hurlstone Park where the young George Morling had served under Rev W Cleugh Black. To the latter church he returned on 17 September to speak at the public meeting of its Anniversary.[618]

Next day the Assembly Meetings began. The outgoing President, Rev Frank Robinson, and the incoming President, Mr FW Winn, being both friends of George Morling, it was not surprising that he and another mutual friend, Rev CJ Tinsley, expressed their appreciation to them.[619]

Rev F Starr, the new Secretary of the College Council, drew attention to the peculiar difficulties the College had experienced with the resignation of Rev JH Deane and the record number of students caused by post-war conditions. 'Bulk of the work' he wrote, 'has fallen on the Principal" On the human side he has carried us through the year and we give thanks God for his consecrated scholarship and his ability to teach men the word of God'.[620]

It was with some realisation of the need to look to the future that the Assembly adopted a motion moved by Rev Dr AJ Waldock 'instructing the incoming Council to take into consideration arranging for suitable students to take a university course with a view eventually to strengthen the College tutorial staff'.[621]

24 September 24 was a significant day for the Principal. His and Gladys' second son, Bill (William Charles), announced his engagement to Miss Marcia Rofe.[622] At the evening session of the Assembly he spoke on 'Divine Conditions of Spiritual Guidance'.[623] The denomination was bracing itself for post-war expansion. Tragically in the early evening of that day Mrs AJ Waldock fell down the steps of Central Church and died a few hours later.[624]

With Student Pastor W Schubert preparing to leave as soon as possible for India Principal presented him for ordination at a service in Central Church on 8 October, and on 31 October spoke briefly at the farewell to outgoing missionaries.[625] Few things more moved him than the thought of any of his men proceeding to missionary service.

On 15 October he began a new series of published studies on the book of Amos.⁶²⁶

Not all aspects of student affairs were satisfying. The Secretary of the Union reported to the Executive on 19 November that he had received a complaint that the students had put a cricket ball through a neighbour's window. It was the Principal who had to deal with the complaint and make peace with the neighbour.

In October-November the North Sydney Church was celebrating its Jubilee. In the midst of the celebrations, under tragic circumstances, its pastor Rev RB Fraser died. Principal Morling shared in the funeral service on 6 November.⁶²⁷ It could not have been easy to go back to the church on 12 November to speak at the public meeting of the Jubilee but he always was enabled to rise to the special situation.

Under happier circumstances he inducted one of his men, Rev Ron Smith, into the Earlwood pastorate on 24 November.⁶²⁸

He visited Leeton to participate in the formation of a Southwestern Baptist Association, beginning with a civic reception on Wednesday 13 November. Among the Principal's papers were the notes of an address 'On Living Restfully' with the notation, 'Address at Women's Meeting, Leeton, November, 1946'. This meeting took place on 14 November. He also spoke on Saturday 16 November and twice at Sunday services next day.⁶²⁹ At least one of his addresses was on 'The Ministry of Suffering'. How he found time travel there and fulfil what was probably a number of commitments must be a matter of wonder but somehow he did.

On 3 December ʸ at the Graduation Service in the Ashfield Church the curtain fell on what for the Principal was a most exacting yet richly rewarding year.

The concern that continued to be felt concerning the Principal's health emerged in a College Council meeting held earlier on the evening of the Graduation Service. The Western Australian Union had written concerning the possibility of an extended visit of Principal Morling to that state in 1947. The Council agreed that he might spend one month (22 May to 22 June) there. The Secretary's letter laid down a proviso,

---
ʸ Or 5th December according to announcement TAB 26 November 1946
Page 4

'The Council were unanimous in imposing one condition in view of the Principal's health and the long journey by train, that he travel by air both ways'.

1947
On 14 January, his Amos studies completed, he began publishing a series on 'Jesus and the life of prayer'.[630]

This was a year with more than usual travelling for the Principal. He spent January in Victoria as guest preacher at the Kew Church. [631-632]. This, presumably, was after speaking at the Upwey Convention. These commitments completed, he returned to his holiday retreat at Blackheath. His good friends there not only had him preach at the Church Anniversary on 9 February but preside at the public meeting the next night.[633]

The students gathered at College on 25 February. Some concern was expressed that in the previous year four had resigned from training. Principal expressed the hope that they would be better laymen for the time spent in training. At Executive Committee level the Applicants' Committee was counselled to be increasingly careful in its choice of candidates.[631] When the record number of students in College and the post-war settling down into final roles is taken into account, the concern about the resignations was probably excessive. Of the 32 students in 1947 19 were married men. Nine of these were doing extramural courses. In addition three women were day students at College preparing for missionary service.

On the evening that College resumed, an ordination service for the students who had recently graduated was held in Central Church with Rev John G Ridley the preacher.[634] Of the six candidates that Principal presented for ordination five were married men. This was in marked contrast to previous years when most men were single.

At the College Commencement Service on 11 March a well-known Sydney Anglican, Dr Paul White, was the speaker.[635] He was a close friend of the Principal.

In preaching at Croydon's 21st Anniversary on 16 March he shared one of his controlling convictions. The report of the service said that he 'spoke on Romans 6, showing that the victorious life is a reality only in Christ'.[636] He sought to realise that life and wanted others to know of its possibility.

The Half-Yearly Meetings of the Union took place at Ashfield Church on 25 and 26 March with the theme 'Our Achievements and Aims'. Being so close Principal was able to attend. He 'gave a fine resume of the past and present activities of the Theological College and expressed his belief that we need have no fear of the future of our churches while we have young men of the calibre of our present College students'. The report of his address concluded, 'Principal Morling emphasised that the College stood for an educated, expository evangelism'[637].

When Rev Albin Betteridge, who had been trained in NSW but ordained in South Australia, returned to NSW to become the pastor of Pennant Hills Church the Principal presided at his welcome on 12 April.[638] On 15 April he began publishing 'Studies in the Prophecy of Hosea'.[639]

On 16 April he was one of the Union's representatives at a conference with members of two independent fellowships in Greenacre.[640] The conference was amicable but it took ten years for the 'missions' to join the Baptist Union as the Greenacre Baptist Church.[641]

Slightly earlier than originally planned, he left for Western Australia on 18 April.[642] The stated purpose was 'to conduct an intensive spiritual and teaching campaign in connection with the Ministers' Fraternal. Western Australian Baptists then had no theological college but two of their candidates were studying in the NSW College. One of them, GN (Noel) Vose, eventually became the first Principal of Western Australia's College, and subsequently President of the Baptist World Alliance. The other, Albert Kroenert, became a pioneer missionary in New Guinea.

Principal Morling was in the West for slightly more than a month and numerous meetings were scheduled. On 28 April in the Perth Central Church (Museum Street) he preached at the ordination of two men, LP Perkins and MA Wells. 'The Principal's choice address', it was reported, 'was based on three questions asked by and of Moses, Who am I? What is Thy name? What is that in thine hand'?[643]

To enable him to meet informally as many of the men as possible the YMCA dining room was booked on 16 May and 44 men from the metropolitan churches attended. He spoke to them on 'The Modern Man and the Bible'.[644]

On 22 May the Great Southern Branch of the Men's Association arranged a meeting at Boddington. It was greatly appreciated that although he had had a crowded week he travelled there and addressed the men on the Lord's Return.

The closing days of his visit were given over to a Teaching Mission in Perth. The topics in some of the earlier sessions were a bit daunting to many local Baptists. The attendances were described as fair. However the reporter went on to say, 'Those who attended were amply repaid as the preacher dealt with great affirmatives of the faith. During the series the following questions were answered, 'Is it reasonable to believe in God?' 'Does modern science refute religion?' 'Was Jesus Christ a religious genius or God Incarnate?' 'Is religion too mystical for the man of business?' 'Can broken lives be made over again?'

On the closing night, which was directed to Baptist youth, he spoke on 'The Faith of Baptists' and the church was crowded.

In reporting his home-coming, it was mentioned that in the West he had given 37 addresses.[645] He was appointed a delegate to the Triennial Assembly Meetings of the Baptist Union of Australia to be held in Adelaide at the end of August.[646]

Soon after his resumption of duties tragedy struck the College family. Student Pastor HV Sales, an extramural student at Millthorpe, was electrocuted on 17 June while seeking to help one of the church members.[647] 'We record, with sorrow,' Principal said in his Report, 'the passing of one of our most promising married students …' Doubtless he felt the death even more keenly because of links he had both with the Sales family and the Mill family. Mrs Jean Sales was daughter of Rev JD Mill.

On the following Sunday, he preached at a Memorial and Thanksgiving Service almost certainly at the Granville Church in which Herb Sales had grown up and from which he had entered the ministry. The Principal, deeply sharing the sorrow of the stricken mourners, said, 'In a time such as this we need, not reasons that will satisfy the questioning mind, but grace that will heal the sorely wounded heart and impart courage to go on living. We need not answers to problems but God, God Himself, the God and Father of our Lord Jesus Christ'.

Having sensitively indicated the grounds on which thanksgiving could be offered to God even in such an experience he turned his hearers' 'thoughts in another direction'. 'We are', he said, 'poor creatures of the earth, earthy unless such an event as this overwhelms us with sense the mystery, the ultimate meaning, of life - also of the greater responsibilities bound up with our possession of life. And there is this to say to one another, our brother's sudden, unexpected home-going has meaning for us. I suggest to you that that meaning is set forth in a phrase used by the Apostle Paul 'Baptised for the dead' (1 Cor 15:29). He interpreted those words to mean 'baptised to replace the dead' and then asked, 'Does there not come to us tonight a challenge along those lines?' He presented the challenge of the broken rank, of the seemingly unfulfilled life and of the Advancing Kingdom.

The very day of the death, Central Church began a Baptist Youth Week entitled 'Never a dull moment'. For what was styled the Finale on 21 June the Principal was the featured speaker. Two days later at the same place he chaired the public meeting marking the opening of the second term of the Christian Workers' Training College.[648]

Having helped to bridge the missionary gap in East Bengal Rev E Clatworthy accepted a call to the North Sydney Baptist Church. His Principal and former church member inducted him into the pastoral charge on 6 July.

The following Sunday he preached yet again at Bexley for the morning service of their 33rd Anniversary. Someone of their number wrote, 'In common with other churches of the Union we look forward to a visit from the Principal of our College, and as one listens to this learned and devout servant of God one realises how fortunate we are that such a man should guide and train our future ministers'.[649] The sermon that morning was on one of his most loved texts, 1 Peter 1:8. In the evening he was 'Back to Pymble'. Preaching at their 30th Anniversary he 'recalled with helpful recollection his days of the pastorship of the church'.

Early in the week the news broke of the sudden death on 15 July of Rev Albert Butler, pastor of the Brisbane Tabernacle.[650] On 17 July Principal Morling was flown to Brisbane to conduct the funeral of his dear friend.[651] Few ministers in Queensland were held in such high regard and so the Tabernacle was packed to capacity, not only with Baptists but with leaders and representatives of other Protestant Churches and Christian organisations. Both in that service and at the graveside service in the Toowong Cemetery he lifted the people to such a sense of God's presence that standing around the grave under a cloudless sky they sang the Doxology.[652]

Following the funeral he remained in Brisbane to take the services on Sunday, 20 July. The morning service, broadcast over 4QR, was a Service of Thanksgiving in memory of their late beloved pastor. With the recent vivid reminder of human frailty and uncertainty he preached on Jesus Christ, the Eternal Contemporary, from one of his favourite texts, Hebrews 13:7-8. The evening service had been planned as the Annual Service of the Australian Nurses Christian Movement. He spoke on 'Jesus Christ and the Art of Healing'.[652]

Then it was back to College to try to make up lost time and to meet deadlines for regular commitments.

On 3 August he inducted Rev Basil Brown, BD, to the Arncliffe pastorate.[653] He was one that the Principal could envisage taking a greater part in the College teaching program. The following Sunday he preached at Yagoona's 4th Anniversary.[654] The student-pastor there was David Stewart. He was a brilliant young man and Principal had great hopes for his future, hopes that were realised.

At the end of the month he attended the Triennial Assembly Meetings of the Baptist Union of Australia in Adelaide. In particular he contributed the session given over to the Educational Board.[655] The Assembly decided to call Australian Baptists to an ambitious venture to secure a Christian social order. The venture was called the 'Christian Commonwealth Crusade'.

In the NSW Assembly Meetings he shared in the Presidential Induction of Rev W Gibbins, commending him to God in prayer.[656] One matter that he dwelt on in his Report to the Assembly had to do with students, past and present, taking what he called 'higher studies'. He was clearly concerned that there should be men well qualified to assist him in teaching and also to perpetuate his ideal for the College in the future. Probably he had in mind a resolution of the previous year's Assembly when he wrote, 'Two students of promise are being encouraged to take higher studies'.[657] The General Secretary of the Union in referring to that previous resolution said that no student had come within its terms but he too made reference to two College students being given special treatment.[658] There was a consciousness abroad that the Principal could not carry his present load indefinitely. However it was still some little time before a replacement was found for John Deane.

The Principal presented a report of the Adelaide Educational Board session to NSW Assembly, which approved and wholeheartedly supported the Christian Commonwealth Crusade that had been mooted at the Triennial Meetings in Adelaide. It then appointed three NSW delegates to a Crusade Council and the Principal was one of them.[659]

It was a happy function when on 29 September a farewell social was given to Rev Walter Barry on his retirement. Principal was one of the honoured guests who shared in the evening.[660]

Central Church might almost be thought to be getting a lien on the Principal for he was again there on 9 October to preach at their 11th Anniversary.[661] Something the same might be said of Pymble because three days later he inducted Rev Gray Parker to its pastorate.[662]

It was but a comparatively slight addition to his responsibilities when he was elected Chairman of the Applicants' Committee, a Committee, be it remembered, recently charged to exercise increasing care in its choice of candidates for the ministry.[663]

Principal Morling began a new series of 'Studies in the Epistle of James' for the Australian Baptist Bible School on 11 November and the Editor took opportunity to express the appreciation of many readers for his regular contribution to their study of the Bible.[664]

On Sunday, 16 November, he preached at both services of the Bowral Church which, the previous day, had opened a new school hall.[665] In the afternoon he travelled to Tahmoor to speak at its second Anniversary.

It had been a most demanding year and one believes that it must have been with a sense of deep thankfulness that the beloved Principal attended the College Graduation Service at the Ashfield Church on 8 December.[666] He ought to have been ready to fall in a heap but, considering his health problems, he had remarkable resilience.

Saturday, 13 December, found him at Central Church solemnizing the marriage of Student-pastor FP (Fred) McMaster and Miss Dorothy Lee.[667] and also at Hornsby Church performing the same service for Student-pastor HK (Keith) Watson and Miss Una Hazel.

At year's end he was involved in an unusual ceremony. Growing out of

Rev CJ Tinsley's attendance at and chairmanship of the Baptist World Alliance Congress at Copenhagen the Berkeley Baptist Divinity School decided to recognise his long and distinguished service to the Baptist movement in Australia by conferring on him the degree of Doctor of Divinity *honoris causa*.[668] With Dr Sandford Fleming, the President of Berkeley Baptist Divinity School, visiting the country of his birth it was decided that while in Sydney he should take opportunity to confer the degree at an appropriate ceremony. So it was that on 30 December a large and representative congregation of Baptists gathered in the Central Church summoned for the purpose of honouring Rev CJ Tinsley.[669] Of the Principal's part in the ceremony the report in *The Australian Baptist*[670] said, 'Presenting Mr Tinsley to Dr Sandford Fleming, Principal GH Morling, MA, in an eloquent address, paid tribute to the Rev CJ Tinsley, and referred to him as a product of Divine grace; as one who had a true love for the souls of men and women; and as one who, influenced by the Spurgeon tradition, had fostered that tradition in his own far-reaching ministry'.

Over the Christmas/New Year period he was a speaker at the Upwey Christian Convention.[671]

1948
On Saturday, 10 January 1948, he was present at the opening of Blackheath's new manse. A presentation was made to him 'as a past-Moderator of the church over many years'. The reporter of the occasion mentioned that he had also given the address and had officially opened the manse. Then, carried away, he added, 'both the pastor (Rev JB Wilson) and he (the Principal) went two-and-two on a pattern that had the same logical conclusions as Noah laid down when he took full possession of the Ark'.[672] When the Principal read that in *The Australian Baptist* it must have taken all his exegetical skill to determine its intended meaning. One of Principal's sermons, 'Grace for Instant Need' on the text Hebrews 4:16, bears the notation 'Blackheath, January, 1948'. It is just possible that it was the address given at the opening but it seems more likely, from its nature, that he also preached on at least one other occasion at Blackheath that month.

Over the next week or so Principal's family received honourable mention. It was reported that Gordon Morling had been appointed secretary of Ashfield's Young People's Society of Christian Endeavour.[673] One week later[674,] Mr Trevor Morling was congratulated on completing the requirements for the Bachelor of Arts degree of the Sydney University. Australian Baptists were putting an enormous amount of united effort into the Christian Commonwealth Crusade. Great things were expected from it. For three days from 3 February representatives of all the States met in Melbourne. Principal Morling, who was the chairman of the NSW committee, was one of three who represented the State, the others being Rev Archibald Jolly and Rev Wilfred Jarvis.[675]

Probably he was not well when he went to Melbourne, for the report of the Blackheath Church Anniversary on 8 and 9 February in *The Australian Baptist* said, 'The public meeting was held on the Monday night following and, to our intense delight, our beloved Principal, Rev GH Morling, MA, was so far improved in health that he was able to occupy the chair. We were also glad that there was no observable diminution of his hilarity – out of a rich store house of good things for a chairman to remember, he enjoys the telling of them equally with his listeners, so much that one and all are attacked by his infectious humour and are made as happy as a batch of sand-pipers'.[676] However awkwardly that may have been expressed it did emphasise an aspect of the Principal's personality that might escape general notice.

He returned to Sydney a few days earlier than otherwise he would have done, because Mrs HJ Morton, while on holiday in the Blue Mountains, died suddenly. The funeral service was held in the Petersham Church on 21 February and George Morling paid tribute to one he called 'a life-long friend'.[677]

On 24 February when an ordination service was held in the Central Church the Principal presented eight candidates. The church was filled to capacity.[678]

A few days later on 28 February Pastor FW Evans of Manildra died'.[679] In the course of a warm-hearted tribute to a man whom he described as 'the embodiment of Christian courtesy, of helpfulness and of loyalty to the highest and best' the Principal said, 'On several occasions Mrs Morling and I were guests in the Manildra manse. The graciousness and affectionateness of the hospitality stands out as a precious memory. Ever since, the godly pastor and his wife have been in the inner circle of our friends. Such simple-hearted, hard-working, saintly people are Christ's most effective witnesses and the veritable salt of the earth'.[680] Apart from its revelation of a wonderfully warm relationship the interest in the tribute is the evidence it affords of unrecorded activities on the

Principal's part and of Mrs Morling sharing in his country visits.

At the College Commencement Service in the Central Church on 9 March fourteen freshmen were welcomed and handed over to the Principal for training.[678]

Central's Christian Workers' Training College began its second year with an Opening Convocation on 15 March. Principal Morling, who had been appointed President of the College, presented Diplomas and Certificates of Merit to successful students from the previous year.[681] He threw the full weight of his support behind this lay training scheme. He was elected President of the Intervarsity Fellowship for the whole of Australia, with the hope that he might be able to visit all the universities; and he was congratulated on the honour conferred on him.[682]

The Principal left on 20 March by flying boat for New Zealand where he was the guest speaker at the Easter camps of the Baptist Union[682] and fulfilled other commitments. He was in New Zealand all told for a fortnight, returning on 4 April with a most encouraging account of his visit.[683]

Maroubra was the venue for the Half-Yearly Assembly on 6 April. The Principal had returned in time to take a leading part in a conference on the Christian Commonwealth Crusade and was appointed Chairman of the Crusade Council.[684] His growing recognition in interdenominational circles was confirmed when on 15 April he was the speaker at the Annual Meeting of the Malayan Evangelical Mission.

The NSW Baptist Ministers' School of Theology was held at Mt Victoria from 19 to 23 April. Principal AJ Grigg, MA BD, of the Victorian College, was the greatly appreciated guest speaker. However there could hardly be a School without our beloved Principal taking part. It was said that he 'brought the week's feast of good things to a fitting close, as, on Thursday evening, we met around the Table of the Lord's Remembrance'.[685]

Back in Sydney on 25 April he took both services for the Petersham Church whose pastor, Rev Allan Brooke, was away with a young people's camp.[686] He prepared the way for Principal TC Warriner, MA BD, of Brisbane, who the following week was the preacher at Petersham's 66th Church Anniversary. On an unspecified Sunday in April he somehow managed preach at Hurlstone Park. His sermon topic was 'Grace for Instant Need'. He was mentioned as one who during the absence of Chatswood's pastor, Rev DC Harper, for the previous three months had supplied the pulpit.[687]

May for Australian Baptists was by long standing tradition Foreign Mission Month. The Annual Day of Prayer was set down for 4 May in Central Church. It was in keeping with Principal Morling's strong commitment to the cause of missions that he conducted one of the sessions.[688] On 21 May he spoke at the same place but to a very different gathering, a meeting of the Ministers' Wives Union.[689] From time to time he addressed similar gatherings and always with great acceptance. The next day a Teaching Mission arranged by the students and staff of the College began at Earlwood Baptist Church. According to a report the mission got off to a good start with the Principal delivering two excellent teaching sermons. In the morning he spoke on the Holy Spirit and in the evening on the Second Coming of Christ. He was the speaker again on Wednesday night.[690] It was term vacation at College but the Principal wouldn't be allowed to get too rusty.

On 25 May he began a series of 'Studies in the Song of Solomon'.[691] As a general rule reports of his activities decrease for a couple of months once June comes along. Two possible reasons for this suggest themselves. It is a time of the year when few special functions are held in most churches. Moreover it is a time when the teaching program settles into a steady gait and lecturers seek to push ahead in order to cover course prescriptions.

He wrote a letter to express the gratification of Australian Baptists that an Australian, Dr Sandford Fleming, had been elected President of the Northern Baptist Convention in USA.[692] Dr Fleming's most recent visit to his homeland would still have been fresh in the minds of many Baptists.

July had in fairly recent times come to be recognised as Youth Month. With the promotion of the Christian Commonwealth Crusade being heavily emphasised, the theme of 'The Christian Commonwealth Crusade Challenges Youth' was chosen for two meetings in Sydney on 2 and 3 July. The speaker for the Saturday night rally was the Principal.[693] Although he was by then well into his sixth decade he gave, it was reported, an inspiring message. Despite his senior status he was still able to get across to young people. This ability was further demonstrated during July, for the Stanmore Church which was having 'a month of missions, had him speak at two Christian Endeavour Campfire Meetings'.[694] On both occasions he spoke to the young people on the Holy Spirit. At this time he was much concerned with young people for on the manuscript of a study 'Resources for Heroic Living' prepared for an Australian Baptist Youth Conference to be held in 1949 is the notation, 'Date prepared - 20 July, 1948'. On 20 July he began a series of 'Studies in the Psalms'.[695]

Part of the report of proceedings of the Annual Assembly of the Baptist Union of NSW on Monday, 20 September, ran, 'The period dealing with the Theological College suffered by the absence of the Principal, Rev GH Morling, MA, who was unable to attend because of an infirmity in one of his pedal supports'.[696] Being interpreted that doubtless means that he was suffering from an attack of gout. The Assembly resolved to send him a message of sympathy. However, whatever may or may be true of others he was one good man who couldn't be kept down. Quoting further from the report of proceedings we learn, 'On Friday the evening session on the Crusade was a fitting climax to a great series ... the speaker was Principal Morling, MA, Chairman of the State Crusade Council, who left his sick room to speak on 'The Crusade's Inner Life'. It was a striking and searching word'.[697]

In his Report which he was not able to present personally to the Assembly he noted as remarkable that there were fourteen first year students in College, coming not only from NSW but also from England, Western Australia and Tasmania. He pointed out that several of the men were turning their eyes towards service in non-Christian lands and that a woman student would that year complete her training with a view to service in India. That was pleasing to him and he didn't hide his pleasure on another score, writing, ' ... we are happy to report that the Rev Basil Brown, who, in addition to his London degree, has now acquired the Honours BD of the Melbourne College of Divinity, has been appointed to the lecturing staff'.[698] That was only as a visiting lecturer but it afforded some relief to the Principal.

During the Assembly on 24 September, exactly one year from the death of Mrs Waldock, Mrs AL Leeder died.[699] The funeral was on 27 September at Central Church, then proceeding to Gore Hill Cemetery, where her first husband, Rev W Cleugh Black, was buried. Yet again the Principal was called on to voice the thoughts of all. The account of the funeral service was that he 'paid a tender and touching tribute to the one who had gone to her rest. The Principal spoke of the queenly yet simple grace that was characteristic of Mrs Leeder, and of the choice memories he had of by-gone days which he spent in her home'. That would have been when he was at Hurlstone Park under the supervision of Cleugh Black, pastor of the Dulwich Hill circuit of churches.

After the Assembly, Principal had the pleasure on 29 and 30 September of a visit by Dr. Gordon Palmer, President of Eastern Baptist Theological Seminary, Philadelphia.[700-701] Dr Palmer gave several lectures to the students.

Early in October Rev and Mrs Ern Andrews were returning to Africa for service with the Sudan United Mission. Principal Morling preached the valedictory sermon at a meeting on 4 October.[700]

The rest of the year appears to have been taken up with the routine of lecturing, preparing his Baptist School lesson, marking examinations and attending to administration.

It would doubtless not have been unwelcome that College Graduation, which was again held in the Ashfield Church, was slightly earlier than in previous years being on 2 December.[702] At the November and again at the December meeting of the Executive Committee the issue was raised as to what action the College Council was taking to secure assistance for the over-taxed Principal. To its credit the Executive Committee continued pressing for action although it was some months before anything concrete could be announced.

The Christmas/New Year period found him once more at the Upwey Convention leading studies on the Holy Spirit.[z]

1949

On 4 January there appeared the first of his 'Expositions in Luke's Gospel'.[703]

Rev Stephen Sharp, a man of rare spiritual quality, of outstanding gifts, of striking physical attractiveness and of impressive refinement of taste and manner, died on 3 January, 1949. Though at 88 he had outlived most, if not all, of his contemporaries a large and representative congregation gathered in Central Church on 4 January to pay their respects to a choice servant of Jesus Christ. Principal Morling was one of those who took part in the service.[704]

---

[z] He is not listed in the Convention advertisement although nine speakers are listed. TAB 14 December 1948 Page 5

A few days later he travelled to Brisbane to preside as Commonwealth President over meetings of the Intervarsity Fellowship. There was time for the usual break at Blackheath and then it was back to College in time for the gathering of the students on 22 February.[705]

It was a happy occasion when on Sunday, 27 February, he conducted a dedication service for Alan Douglas Orr, son of his pastor, Rev AH Orr and wife Lois.

There was action a-plenty for the Principal in the next few weeks. On 1 March the College Commencement Service was held in the Central Church with British Baptist, Rev TM Bamber, the preacher.[705] Nine new students were welcomed. That was encouraging but was offset by the disclosure of a serious situation so far as the College finances were concerned. It was probably partly because of this fact that the very next day the Principal and the Home Mission Superintendent, Rev EF Heather, left to visit the churches at Orange, Molong, Parkes, Dubbo and Wellington in the interests of the College and also the Christian Commonwealth Crusade.[706]

By 7 March he was back in Sydney to chair the Annual Convocation of the Christian Workers' Training College.[707] An ordination service was held the next day and he presented three graduates to the President. One of them, David Stewart, he would dearly have liked to see preparing for a ministry in theological education but he was almost equally pleased to see him committed to missionary service in China. Invited to be the speaker at the public meeting of Marrickville's 62nd Anniversary on 16 March his subject was 'The Magnificence of the Church'.[708] From 13 to 21 March West Ryde was celebrating its Silver Jubilee. At the Praise and Thanksgiving Service that concluded the celebrations he was the chosen speaker.[709]

On 22 March *The Australian Baptist* carried an advertisement announcing the opening of a book and stationery business by Messrs Leslie Young and William Morling.[710] The business was comparatively short-lived but was to be the publisher of a book, *The Quest for Serenity*, that enshrined many of the Principal's deepest insights and convictions.

Campsie's Anniversary was observed on 10 April and he was the guest preacher. During Holy Week on 13 April Petersham presented Stainer's Oratorio *The Crucifixion*. Being pastorless, the church invited the Principal to bring a brief message before the musical presentation.[711]

At the February and March meetings of the Executive Committee of the Union the College Council was not able to report any positive action or recommendation for giving assistance to the Principal.[712] However, at the meeting of 19 April the College Council reported that although it was still unable to make any recommendation about a permanent assistant for the Principal it 'had decided to appoint a Lady Secretary as a first step toward the ultimate aim of appointing a full-time and qualified Vice-Principal'.[713] That report might have raised a number of questions, as, for example, how such an appointment might be seen as a first step towards the provision of a Vice-Principal. On the contrary, it might have been thought that, by creating financial problems, such an appointment might only further defer the appointment of a Vice-Principal. However, assured that something positive was being done, the Executive apparently raised no questions. At this meeting the Executive, for its part, added to the Principal's burdens by appointing him to a sub-committee 'to consider the objects, aims and workings of the World Council of Churches' and of the Australian section of that organisation.[714] This was to enable the Baptist Union of NSW to decide whether it should recommend that the Baptist Union of Australia affiliate with the World Council of Churches.

On the very day of the Executive meeting Mrs ID Ruggles, widow of

Mr G Ruggles, died.[715] With her husband, she had been good and generous friends of the College and the Principal. It had already been arranged that the Principal would conduct the funeral service in the Blackheath Church. The Executive asked him to represent the Union at the service and to express its sympathy to the relatives. It was arranged that Rev Frank Starr would drive him to Blackheath by car and so make things much easier for him. It may not be widely known that Principal never had a driver's licence and was often dependent on public transport. Some of the students did attempt to teach the Principal to drive but it proved to be a hazardous and nerve wracking experience.

Shortly after this he began a fresh brief series of entries in one of his prayer diaries. The series was prefaced by a statement about his relation to his work at the College.

'This is my special service for Christ. To this work I am sent in the will of God even as Paul was to his. I must realise that the work is God's before it is mine, that the Lord Jesus is Head of the Church, that the Holy Spirit is the Administrator, and that the Church and its ministry have unspeakable need'.

On one page there is a list of those for whom prayer should be made and on the opposite page a series of personal entries. Clearly they were triggered by contemplation of the possibility of setting down something of his own spiritual pilgrimage in a book. The first entry, dated 24 April. demonstrates this. 'Definite prayer that I might have grace for the writing of the book *The Rest of Faith* [aa]. I ask for rest in order to write about rest. Today, I have seen that it can only come as a gift of the Spirit. Therefore I must quietly depend on him for inner quietude of spirit'.
'I am asking the Holy Spirit to let the peace of God guard my heart and my mind in Christ according to Phil 4:6'.

'The basis of the peace is the holy union with the Lord Jesus. I have been able to rest more happily in Christ'.

'I have to thank God (1) For the definite urge to write the book (2) For the financial backing (3) For light about the outline, after last night's burden (4) For the extension of time'.

[aa] Seemingly the tentative title of the book eventually published as *The Quest for Serenity*

'I make request for the Holy Spirit's aid in writing the book'.

25 April 'If there is to be rest there must be restful joy in the Lord Jesus. George Muller began each day sure that he was happy in the Lord. This is one aspect of union with Christ in which peace that garrisons the heart and mind is rooted'.

26 April 'I see today that there must be <u>real labour</u> to enter into rest. Not dreamy wishing or weak sentiment but <u>strong purpose</u> and <u>deliberate cultivation</u>. I am seeking to realise my union with Christ, which is the basis of peace, in a new way. I have put it this way, I live in the heart of the Lord Jesus. He lives in my heart'.

27 April 'Today I have the heartening thought that the Lord Jesus is Himself interested in this new determination to live restfully. There is energy lost in exhaustive aspiring which takes no practical form. There is an aspect of prayer which is healthy routine. I must pray without thinking about time and without expecting elation of soul'.

In the next few entries the thought of the writing of the book is still there but another element has entered. On 9 May he went to Victoria to preach at the Victorian Baptist Union's Half-Yearly Assembly and then went on to Tasmania for special ministry.[716] This then is reflected in the following entries.

2 May 'This week I seek for strength to work on steadily without inner strain or excitement. As also to continue last week's emphasis - dependence upon the Spirit, living in the heart of Jesus, the remembrance that the Lord Jesus is interested in the developing of my life. I want this to be a week of quiet preparation for next week. Good words from Ps 62 this morning. 'The rock of my strength is in God. Power (strength) belongeth unto God. My expectation is from Him".

3 May 'Again rejoice that I am able to go on praying and working without worrying about feelings. Another good word from Ps 63. 'Because Thou hast been my help, therefore in the shadow of Thy wings I will rejoice".

4 May 'Tired today, but able to do a good day's work. Fresh tonight so able to pray well after tea for book and trips to Victoria and Tasmania. I have been able to depend upon the Holy Spirit for powers of concentration in contemplating Christ and resting in Him'.

6 May 'Although I am tired this morning I am thankful for an excellent week in which the outline of *The Rest of Faith* has been completed.

Now I seek for complete rest of heart as I finally prepare to go to Victoria and Tasmania. For this too I must quietly, deliberately wait upon the Spirit and carefully exalt the Lord Jesus, forgetting about reputation'.

8 May 'Sunday. Some gout. Quite obvious that there is much more yet to learn about relaxation and rest. Some uncontrolled thoughts in preaching this morning. Prayer for the possibility of travel tomorrow'.

Where he preached on the Sunday is not recorded but his prayer concerning travel was answered and he was able to travel to Kerang in Victoria for the Half-Yearly meetings. Rev KA Smith reported 'Special interest centred in the visit of Principal GH Morling, MA, Sydney, as the guest speaker: and the Principal fully justified the high hopes of those responsible for the invitation. His three addresses provided a fine example of 'truth through personality', and combining elements of graciousness, directness and spiritual fervour, made a deep impression on his hearers'.[717]

At the meetings the Christian Commonwealth Crusade was commended to the delegates. Principal's friend, Rev LJ Gomm, then Chairman of the Victorian Department of Evangelism, emphasised the Crusade as a mission through the churches to the community. 'Principal Morling', it was reported, 'followed with a searching and challenging address, urging that the Crusade should not be just 'another organised adventure', and calling for recognition of 'our complete dependence on God for success'.[718] Two sentences of the Principal that particularly struck the reporter, and will awaken an echo in many who sat under his teaching, were, 'We can't abandon the Christian faith and keep the Christian morality', and 'The curse of the Church to-day is spiritual mediocrity'.[718]

The meetings over, he journeyed at once to Launceston and during 14-18 May took a series of meetings in connection with the 65th Anniversary of what was then known as the Launceston Tabernacle. One of his men, Rev Hilton White, was the pastor and another, Rev Clive Smith, was pastor at Burnie, where he then conducted several special meetings.[718]

Although he had arranged the College teaching program so that visiting lecturers filled in for him, and also for his time away to overlap part of the first term vacation, he faced increased demands on his return, plus the necessity to push ahead with his book.

Under the heading 'Australian Baptist Colleges and the Crusade' *The*

Australian Baptist[719] featured contributions by Principals Grigg (Victoria), Warriner (Queensland) and Morling. The last-named made a definite personal statement, 'I mean to invest my interest and energy in the Christian Commonwealth Crusade, and urge others to do the same'. His actions had already backed his words. For him evangelism was not a peripheral aspect of the Church's life. It was an essential element.

On 6 June he wrote in his diary. 'I am endeavouring to learn to write restfully. I shall write for thirty minutes now, then for five minutes rest in Christ'.

Rev FH Starr had succeeded John Deane as Secretary of the College Council and was also sharing in the College lecturing work. It was an added joy therefore for the Principal on 12 June to induct his colleague into the pastorate of the Petersham Church.[720] Doubtless it was good to have him in such proximity to the College.

Principal's commitment to the Christian Commonwealth Crusade received further confirmation when on 19 June he helped to launch a special campaign by the Mosman Church. He and the Director of the CCC, Rev WL Jarvis, preached at special services to inaugurate a week of visitation and evangelism, concluding with preaching services by Evangelist John Ridley.[721]

The matter of assistance for the Principal was raised again at the Executive Committee meeting of 21 June. The Secretary of the College Council reported that the Council proposed to build a new house for the Principal on the College tennis court in order to make room in the College for a deputy.[722]

At the next meeting of the Executive on 19 July the Principal, on behalf of the College Council, requested that the educational standard for entrance into the College be raised from the Intermediate to Leaving Certificate. Notice of motion for a change to the rule was given and at the August meeting of the Executive the change was adopted.[723]

A decision was taken at the July meeting to appoint some of the members of the World Council of Churches Investigation Subcommittee as a Commission charged with the responsibility of preparing cases for and against affiliation with the World Council of Churches as a basis for discussion and decision. The Principal with four others comprised the

Commission.[724] This involved a good deal of time and work.

The Theological Students Fellowship (which drew its membership from the various theological colleges) held a meeting on 22 July. Principal Morling addressed the students on his favourite subject, 'The Holy Spirit'.

On 24 July the Blacktown Church celebrated its 20th Anniversary. Recalling that Principal Morling had preached at the first service in the church at its formation the church invited him to speak at this significant milestone.[725]

On 15 September, Principal Morling gave a 'valedictory address' at the farewell to missionaries departing for China.[726] Rev David Stewart and twelve other new workers and two experienced missionaries were leaving for China for service with the China Inland Mission. He must often have reflected on the occasion when within a few months many of the outgoing missionaries, including David Stewart, were imprisoned by the Communist government which had taken over China.

In September, Rev BG Wright, BA, BD, was appointed Vice-Principal of the College.[727] In the years ahead he gave enormous support to the Principal, in particular by relieving him of administrative and financial concerns. In the College Session of the Baptist Union Assembly the following week the appointment of Gilbert Wright as the Vice-Principal 'was received by the Assembly with gratitude to God and appreciation of the man of God's choosing'. The report commenced, 'There will be a sense of relief in the knowledge

Gilbert Wright

that this assistance been provided for Principal Morling who has carried a heavy responsibility for many years'.[728] The assistance was certainly needed for, as the Principal told the Assembly in his Report,[729] there were 41 students attending College and another three pursuing extramural studies. He confided 'One feels that the denomination at large does not realise the urgent need in the College for adjustment to a situation which has now become really acute. I desire to bring to the Assembly in as strong a way as possible the concern being felt in respect to these matters. It should be known that a large part of our teaching work is being carried on in practically an honorary capacity by men who occupy busy pastorates and whose work deserves the greatest praise'.

'I myself desire to pay tribute to these my loyal College colleagues'. He then indicated that in addition to tutorial assistance a considerable sum of money was needed to extend the already overcrowded accommodation facilities.

Rev EG Gibson, BA LTh, was one who had been for some years 'a most valuable tutor'. His help was lost during the year by reason of his appointment as Principal of the Perth Bible Institute. The Principal was comforted by the thought of the contribution that he would be able to make in Western Australia and he added the gracious note, 'We shall follow his career with affectionate interest'. That career proved a significant one in Australian Baptist theological education and in interdenominational Bible College leadership.

In the opening paragraph of his Report he had opened his heart to his fellow Baptists, 'As one sits down to compose the report of the year's work one is confronted more definitely than ever with the fact that the service which the Theological College renders to the Kingdom of Christ is of such importance that failure in it has most serious consequences. It is not claimed that the service of our college is as faithful and efficient as it might be. One confesses deficiencies and limitations with the expressed hope, however, that there is something at least which has the approval of the divine Head of the Church. With thankfulness it is added that we are not without signs of the presence of God'.

That his own efforts were not without effect was emphasised by Rev FH Starr in his final Report as Secretary of the College Council when he wrote 'Principal's Report outlines the course of training for the year, but to the academic work must be added the personal influence of our honoured Principal. Council is indeed thankful that the Principal has such deep and real interest in each man as a man and seeks not only to impart knowledge but to mould and develop character and spiritual experience'.[730]

The Secretary reported that during the year under review Miss Ivy Wright was appointed to assist the Principal with the secretarial and administrative work. As long as he remained she proved invaluable to him.

In September, 1949, under the editorship of GN (Noel) Vose and MC (Mel) Williams the first issue of *Summa Supremo*, the journal of the NSW Baptist Theological College Students' Association, appeared.[731] Principal Morling provided a foreword in which he pronounced his blessing on 'this journal which is the child of men whom I love and esteem' and commended it to 'our Baptist people'. Rev LM Thompson, then State Evangelist for the NSW Baptist Union, wrote 'after three years of wandering around NSW observing the ministry of our graduates I think our College should be called 'The College of the Holy Ghost' for this is the emphasis of our beloved Principal, Rev GH Morling, MA'.

Under the heading 'Around the College' various matters were touched upon. One of them concerned a new role occupied that year by the Senior Student. However, in an incidental way it gives significant information concerning the Principal. It reads, 'For over twenty years the Principal has led the 7.30am College prayer meeting on Tuesdays and Wednesdays, but when he was forced, under medical orders, to curtail his daily activities, the Senior Student was given the responsibility of leading these meetings'.

This aspect of the Principal's ministry in the devotional life of the College, not only in the early morning prayer meetings but in family worship at the evening meal table, in chapel services and especially in communion services, calls for special mention. For many it was the most spiritually significant aspect of College life. The comment indicates the difficulty under which so much of the Principal's service was offered. Like Paul, he had his thorn in the flesh, yet he too found God's strength revealed through his weakness. Apparently in 1949 his thorny problem of gout was more than usually troublesome.

On 11 October Principal Morling completed his published series of studies on Luke's gospel.[732] 'Rev Principal GH Morling, MA, who has for ten years been the contributor of' our Bible School has felt it necessary to retire from this position… Surely no one has contributed more than he to the life and work of our Baptist churches in Australia'.[733] Amid all the pressures of his various responsibilities it had been a magnificently sustained and costly effort. Years later some of the studies were given a second airing in the columns of *The Australian Baptist* and another generation was enabled to profit by them.

Towards the end of October Dr AT and Mrs Whale visited the Morlings. Whether because of George Morling's approaching birthday or merely because of their long friendship, Bert Whale gave him, among other things, a copy of a commentary by J Armitage Robinson on the *Epistle to the Ephesians*. Surprisingly he had not possessed a copy and the gift was to him as if he had suddenly received a handsome legacy. In writing to his friend a week later he described it as solid gold and in another letter three weeks later on 24 November he wrote, 'I use Armitage Robinson extensively. It is of great value'. It would always be a special treasure to him.

By virtue of his office the Principal was a member of the Advisory and Credentials Committee and the Applicants' Committee, serving as Chairman of the latter.[734] These positions were no sinecure and sometimes made considerable demands on his time and nervous energy. With his finely strung constitution George Morling often found these demands very trying but he never flinched from seeking to meet them.

By contrast it would have been almost pure pleasure on 10 November to speak to the NSW Women's Home Mission Auxiliary on the subject, 'What I owe to Home Missions'.[735] He always felt a debt arising from his early experiences as a home missionary and was ever eager to do what he could to discharge it.

The College year moved again inexorably to its close through the hectic attempt to complete lecture programs, the setting and marking of examinations and setting of the administrative house of the College in order. There was considerable satisfaction for the Principal when at the Graduation Service in the Ashfield Church on 1 December[736] he was able to assure Rev E Clatworthy, the President of the Union and speaker for the night, that no less than nine men had satisfactorily completed all the requirements of their College course.

Now he was able for a little while at least to give less divided attention to the writing of his book. Moreover he could face the coming year in the knowledge that he would be supported by an enthusiastic and able lieutenant.

1950

His small book *Quest for Serenity*, published in 1950, brought together his mature reflections on the person and work of the Holy Spirit, and the life of holiness, including some comments on health and healing.

If his reported activities for the first half of the year were rather less than usual it may well have been because the writing of his book made considerable inroads into any time he had outside his College program.

This preoccupation, however, did not preclude his presence from a function at Central Church on 10 January, 1950 when Rev JH Deane was entertained at afternoon tea by some of the Union officers and fellow ministers. John Deane had come back to Australia for some convention ministry and former friends seized the opportunity to renew fellowship.[737] Principal Morling was the chosen speaker for the occasion.

Six days later he was again at Central to attend the funeral of Professor AJA Waldock, only son of Dr AJ Waldock, then pastor of Canberra Baptist Church.[738]

Towards the end of their customary break at Blackheath there was good news for the Morling family. Under heading 'Brilliant Young Baptist' *The Australian Baptist*[739] announced that Mr Trevor Morling had secured first place in the third year law examinations and had been awarded the Pitt-Corbett Prize for International Law and the Harris Scholarship.

Back in Sydney for the new College session Principal Morling was soon off again to Central Church for the ordination service when he had the pleasure of presenting seven men to the President of the Union.[740] He was there yet again on 2 March as President of the Christian Workers' Training College to chair its Annual Convocation and to present diplomas and certificates of merit to successful students.[741]

The official opening of the Theological College year in 1950 took the form of a Youth Night on Saturday, 4 March, and a Bible Conference on 6 and 7 March.[742] Each night of the conference there was a public tea at the College followed by a film and Bible expositions taken by the Principal. His Commencement Address was on 'The Passion for Christ', his text being 2 Corinthians 5:14.

He was more than ever anxious that it should be a spiritually profitable year. If this was to be it must start with himself. In his prayer diary we find him setting out a 'Morning of Faith' with which to begin each day. 'I know that I cannot manage my life either within or without with my own resources. I am sure likewise that with Christ living within me through the Holy Spirit, invited, recognised, trusted and obeyed, every thought can be brought into captivity, every detail of this day's activities property managed, every situation confidently met - and my whole life be happy, restful and strong, filled with the perfect love that casts out fear : so that if I meet the Lord Jesus today I shall have confidence and not be ashamed before Him'.

'Deliberately, definitely I surrender the control of my inner life to the strong Son of God - as also the management of my outward affairs'.

'I trust Thee to do the mighty work within, of cleansing, empowering, enriching'.

'I leave all with Thee and refuse to take anything back into my own care'.

'As all these are acts of will I ask to be strengthened with might by Thy Spirit in the inner man'.

He followed this up with two sentences. The first was a quotation from Streeter (Canon BH Streeter?) connected with the word <u>trust</u>, which he had underlined. 'With Jesus, prayer is not so much petition as uttered trust'. The second seems to have been an admonition to himself, 'Live in an atmosphere of trust so that becomes natural to trust'.

Then he listed three matters for 'definite prayer'. These stood apart from daily prayer lists. They were 'That there may be a greater work grace in the hearts of students. That there may be less friction with the housekeeping. That the College finances may be maintained'.

While there was doubtless a background to each of these petitions they were in themselves natural concerns at the beginning of a College year.

Probably, as an encouragement to himself in his praying, he added the following propositions:
I have no rights as a sinner – all is of grace.
I have no rights as a servant - I remain an unprofitable servant.
But I have rights as a child.

He finished this extended entry with a further comment, 'Observe God's hand in the <u>natural</u> developments of life. He answers prayer in this way'.

For each day, Monday to Friday, he listed items for prayer. For example on Monday he prayed particularly for Dorothy, his older daughter, for the fourth year men, listed by their names, for the Housekeeping staff and Committee, for graduates serving in India (four of them) and then for personal matters. Among matters listed under the last-mentioned were 'Thanks for accession of strength' and prayer for 'The definite anointing for the book', that is for the writing of *The Quest for Serenity*. On each of the five days some special thought was set out:

Monday - 'Make prayer definite: expect God to answer for Jesus' sake thank Him afterwards'.
Tuesday – 'Our part is to trust: God's part is to work. If ye pray I will do'.
Wednesday –'In Thee, do I put my trust' Psalm 31.
Thursday – 'If God is to do the work, we must make careful adjustment to Him'.
Friday – 'The tears began to flow whenever Spurgeon heard the Lord exalted'.

On Saturday he reviewed in prayer the College week, asserting again his absolute dependence upon God the Holy Spirit as the Divine Administrator. Perhaps because of some experience in the week in which he wrote the note he admonished himself, 'Rest after a certain point of helplessness has been reached'. That may have referred to his book which he did not find easy to write. He proposed each Sunday in the time of prayer to consider what new aspects of truth may have come to him during the week. While there were certain constants in his practice of prayer the pattern was changed from time to time. His prayer never fell into a formalised stereotype.

There was a happy function at the College on 16 March. The Directors of the Australian Baptist Publishing House in appreciation of the Australian Baptist Bible School which he had conducted for ten years presented him with a standard reading lamp. In replying he said that the work in connection with the Bible School had brought him much satisfaction over the years through the knowledge that the Bible studies had been widely read and much used.[743]

It was announced that on 17 March the Principal, along with the Vice-President of the Union and the Home Mission Superintendent, would leave for a tour of the churches of the Northern Rivers in the interests of the College, March being the month in which the College appealed for funds. Something prevented the Principal from joining the party until the final meeting and his place was taken by Rev Basil Brown.[744] It may well have been the necessity of pressing on with *The Quest for Serenity* that caused him to curtail his involvement. There certainly were deadlines that the Principal was anxious to meet. A concentrated effort may have brought his task at least within sight of the end.

At all events he allowed himself the luxury of a night off on 13 April to represent the College at a welcome home extended by the Petersham Church to much loved missionary, Miss Flo Harris.[745]

Shortly after there was a report of him speaking at the Anniversary of the Regents Park Church.[746]

The Special Assembly concerning the World Council of Churches was held on 30 May. As a member of the Commission preparing the cases for and against Baptist affiliation the Principal would have had a further reason for preoccupation in the earlier part of the year. The Assembly decided not to affiliate and Principal Morling was listed as one supporting that position. The Special Assembly placed on record its thanks to the Commission for the splendid service rendered to the denomination.[747]

Then the Principal completed the writing of his book, *The Quest for Serenity,* and it was published.[748] It was a tremendous relief to him that his venture had reached this stage. The following diary entry of 10 July indicates that, but also shows that there was still room for concern and that this had to be met by prayer. 'There has been very special grace given in respect to the completion of the book *The Quest for Serenity*. There has been rest amid conflict. But for the help of God the book would never have been finished. During the last week definite fear brought incapacity to think clearly. The co-operation of Noel Vose was a provision of God. If the book succeeds it will be an indication that God wants me to write more. In any case now that the thought is with me I want to do my work a great deal better in preaching and in lecturing. I must maintain greater intimacy with God and rest more in Him. There must be direct dealing with God - this in regard to the acceptance and sale of the book and about further writing'.

One would like to know the significance of the final brief note, 'Especial prayer about John's reaction'[bb].

[bb] Does he refer to John Deane?

He need have had no concern about the sale of the book for it sold out quickly and was subsequently republished by Eerdmans[749,cc] in America and again by Word Books with an introduction and marginal notes by Ruth Graham.

The Executive Committee Meeting of 20 June appointed him an official NSW delegate to the Triennial Assembly Meetings of the Baptist Union of Australia[750] held in Sydney at the end of August and the beginning of September.

From this point reports of extracurricular activities began to increase. On 15 July he preached at Lidcombe's 16th Anniversary when 'seats had to be placed in the aisle' and the next day inducted Rev Eric Wykes into the Bexley pastorate with the church filled to capacity.[751]

At the Executive Committee meeting on 18 July the Secretary reported on the Baptist World Alliance Congress[752] to be held at Cleveland USA. Probably George Morling had hoped also to attend the Congress for on 27 July he wrote, 'The disappointment about the World Alliance is of God. I do believe the Father wants me to live quietly with Him and for Him and be a blessing in this College'. That entry suggests that he had contemplated some involvement in the Baptist World Alliance. If so it was not to be and he acquiesced in the closing of the door. When, a few days later on 2 August, he wrote, 'I must keep constantly before me that I am responsible to Christ for each one of these students', and appended a quotation from CE Raven, 'Remember that Jesus worked with a handful of men', he appeared to be accepting his Divine calling as a trainer of comparatively small numbers of men. At the same time he drew comfort from the consideration that trained and dedicated minorities can exercise enormous influence, as was demonstrated by Christ's apostles.

A brief review that he had written of HH Rowley's *The Biblical Doctrine of Election* appeared in *The Australian Baptist*.[753] The book was based on lectures that Dr Rowley had given at Spurgeon's College in London. The main thesis of the book is that in the Bible election is for service and may be forfeited by unfaithfulness. Principal Morling commended much in the book but commented that he didn't think the book was in the tradition of the Spurgeonic doctrine of Divine Sovereignty. In that opinion he was most probably right.

[cc] First published in 1952, republished again by Word in 1989.

It was doubtless a reminder to him of the passage of time when in August he spoke at Pymble's 33rd Anniversary[754] and recalled his association with that church in its earliest days. Also in August he travelled to Grafton to be the guest preacher at the 75th Anniversary of the church. On the Saturday night he spoke in relaxed fashion on 'World Travel Impressions and Reflections' and then preached at both Sunday services.[755]

In 1950 the Assembly Meetings of the BUNSW were arranged around the Triennial Assembly Meetings of the Baptist Union of Australia, and occupied 28 and 29 August and 7 and 8 September. Principal Morling's first involvement in the NSW Assembly was to move the election of Rev NF Reeve as Vice-President of the Union. Mr Reeve was duly elected.[756]

When in the College Council session he presented to the Assembly his Principal's Report[757] there could be no doubting the absolute conviction of his opening sentences: 'The most important event of the year in the internal work of the College has been the appointment of the Rev BG Wright, BA, BD, to the Vice-Principalship. Mr Wright began his new duties at the beginning of the year. I report with great thankfulness that already the Vice-Principal has made his presence felt in no unmistakable way. The administrative work of the College has gained immeasurably by his outstanding ability'. Principal proceeded to pay tribute to those who shared in the teaching responsibilities and then highlighted the emphasis that was being placed on more practical aspects of pastoral preparation.

In seconding the reception and adoption of the Principal's Report Rev AT Whale 'paid a warm tribute to the Principal and referred to his thirty years of splendid service ... in the College'.[758] Among interstate visitors present because of the Triennial Meetings were Rev Ray Farrer, President of the Victorian Baptist College and Principal AJ Grigg of the same College. Grigg spoke to Principal's report in terms of warmest congratulations.[759]

On the final day of the NSW Assembly, 8 September, the Service of Remembrance, which recognised Baptists who had died during the year, was held. In his characteristically helpful and moving way Principal Morling lifted the Assembly above the consciousness of loss to a realisation of the unbroken fellowship that exists for Christians in Christ.

Meanwhile at the Triennial Meetings on 4 September he addressed the delegates who had assembled from all over Australia on 'The Supremacy of Christ'. According to a report of the occasion it was 'a splendid utterance. He traced the history and stressed the importance of the Lordship of Christ in the development of the Baptist denomination and in the experience of individual Baptists. He asked whether this priceless heritage was being prized as it deserved to be so by Australian Baptists. He pleaded for a more definite loyalty to the Lord of Lords'. It was regretted that because of deferred business it was not possible for a conference on the theme to follow.[760]

The Australian Baptist[761], published during the overlapping Assemblies, carried a warm appreciative review of his book *The Quest for Serenity*. It commenced, 'This book from the pen of the Principal of the Baptist Theological College of NSW is not massive theologically. It is a book of devotion, the strength of which lies in its choice presentation of the life in Christ. Those who know the writer well will see at once the book is himself in miniature; a cameo of his own Christlikeness'. It concluded, 'We commend the publication and hope that it will prove to be only the first of such good things from one whose words and work are highly regarded among us'. Unhappily, despite the best of intentions, much urging from friends and admirers and not a little preliminary work on his own part, no major work would see the light of day. Years later Bert Whale wrote, 'My dear George, thank you for inscribing the 'Quest'. It is a fine book, an intimate sketch, baring your soul for others to scrutinise. A brave thing to do'. Many have been grateful that he dared to do it.

Rev BG Wright wrote, 'Since the day we heard that the publishers were handling a MS for a book by the Principal we have looked forward to reading it. Our expectations as to its choice message have been more than fulfilled ... we have a book written with a pen dipped in the stream of life's experiences. By exploring his own heart the writer explores ours and, with delicate touch, expresses what have often been, for us, vague and undefined experiences, hopes and fears'.[762] Rev JH Deane wrote, 'I look back with affection and joy to my connection with and share in the training of the NSW Baptist ministry, and especially do I look back with joy on the long, unbroken, unruffled and affectionate fellowship with Principal Morling'[763] Both were remarkable men and the mutual esteem and affection between them was rare indeed and said much for the spiritual quality of them both.

During the NSW Assembly it was resolved that the incoming Executive Committee should set up at its first meeting a Baptist Efficiency Commission. It was to investigate the economic position of members of the ministry, the conditions under which the ministry was related to the churches, any changes necessary to increase the efficiency of Baptist churches, and any matters of doctrine or polity which might need to be re-examined in the light of the present needs of our work. There was to be a report to the next Assembly[764]. At the Executive Meeting on 19 September the Principal was one of those appointed to the Commission.[765] Subsequently it became The Faith and Life Commission and its original charter was somewhat changed. Principal Morling was not greatly involved in what became a major reorganisation of the NSW Baptist Union. His main interests ran in other directions.

It was much more to his bent, for instance, that he should be found the following week sharing with Home Mission Superintendent Heather, Vice-Principal Wright and Rev Basil Brown in a three day College Students' Convention at Bowral.[766]

At the Executive Committee Meeting on 17 October a letter which affected him considerably came up for consideration. It was from the College Council informing the Executive that he had been invited to speak at the Commonwealth and Empire Baptist Congress to be held London the following June and also afterwards to a conference of Principals of Baptist Colleges. The College Council approved his acceptance of the invitation and was willing to grant him six months leave of absence on full salary in order for him to attend the Congress. The Executive Committee, for its part, congratulated the Principal on the invitation and resolved to inform the College Council that permission for leave of absence would be willingly granted. It was further resolved to ask the College Council to arrange all details in connection with the Principal's visit to the Congress and report to the next meeting.[767]

There was another matter of personal interest to the Principal at the October meeting. It was agreed to affix the Union seal to a contract for the erection of a residence for him and his family.[768] When completed this would mean that for the first time since he became Principal the Morling family would have their own separate dwelling even if it was still in the College grounds.

On 24 and 25 October he conducted special mid-week meetings at

Armidale in the New England district.[769] Then, early in November he visited Adelaide to conduct a Teaching Mission in the Flinders Street Church from 5 to 9 November and to preach on Sundays, 5, 12 and 19.[770] To make the most of his visit it was arranged for him to attend a Ministers and Wives Picnic, to speak at a Rally of Baptist Youth and an Inspirational Rally organised by the Department of Evangelism, taking his Triennial Assembly theme, 'The Supremacy of Christ'.

In order to assist the Principal in the heavy expense of going to the Congress, estimated to be about 250, the Executive Committee decided to ask the College Council to raise the amount by private subscription through the graduates of the College and other members of the denomination[771]. When it became known that Principal had been invited to go to America after the Congress, the College Council and the Executive Committee agreed to extend his leave of absence. As things turned out there was a change of plans and he did not go on to America.

In the latter part of 1950 feelings ran high within the Union over accusations made against a man who was proceeding to ordinatiob.[772] Naturally Principal was involved in many of the interviews and discussions. It was probably this situation that is reflected in the brief note in his prayer diary, 'Pray definitely for harmony in the Union - for the repression of evil passions'. This was followed by another note of a much different kind yet almost certainly written at the same time, 'There is no doubt that God has called me anew to a life of humility, of dependence, of prayer - all in a natural happy way.

It was a mark of the place he occupied in the esteem of the general evangelical community that in December he went to Melbourne at the invitation of the Melbourne Bible Institute to give the address at its Graduation Ceremony. As he began the College year calling his own students to have 'a passion for Christ' so he concluded it on the same note as he addressed the Melbourne students.

1951
Early in 1951 the results of the Sydney University Law Examinations were published and congratulations were again in order for Principal's youngest son, Trevor, on having gained First Class Honours.[773]

In *The Australian Baptist*[774] there was a report of the ordination in Perth of Rev GN (Noel) Vose. He had trained in the NSW College and as

Senior Student in 1950 had given invaluable support to Principal Morling. There was a bond of mutual esteem between them and Principal had great expectations of his promising young friend. Acting on advice the Western Australian Union allowed and encouraged the newly ordained minister to pursue university studies. He became the 'Morling' of Western Australian Baptists.

About a week later in Sydney Principal Morling presented six men for ordination[775] and was also responsible for bringing the charge to the ordinands. It was with the nature of the ministry very much mind that he wrote an article, 'Our Theological Colleges'.[776] the first of a series of annual articles relating to ministerial training that he contributed to the denominational paper in connection with College month which was celebrated in March.

When he spoke at the opening of a new school hall at Earlwood on 24 February the subject of his most moving address was 'Is Christ at home ... in your heart'.[777] In his preaching he always aimed to move his hearers and provoke a response to the truth that he proclaimed.

Though a deeply convinced Baptist he rejoiced in fellowship across denominational boundaries. A further token of this was seen when at the College Commencement Service on 6 March his friend, fellow convention speaker and theological teacher, Canon Marcus Loane, was the guest preacher.[775]

His early association with the Whale family in the Ashfield Church was recalled when on 17 March in the same church he officiated at the wedding of Patricia Anne Whale, daughter of Mr RN Whale and the late Mrs Whale to Jack Raymond Haigh.[778]

At the Executive Committee Meeting on 20 March it was reported that Mrs. Morling would accompany the Principal to the Commonwealth and Empire Baptist Congress in London.[779] This must have represented a venture of faith because at the previous Executive Meeting the amount that had been received towards Principal's travelling expenses was a princely £39-0-4. However, a letter dated 22 March put a whole new complexion on the situation. It was to Mrs Morling and read,

Dear Gladys,
When I took your husband away from you on overseas tours on those several occasions in the past, I always felt a bit mean because this meant leaving you at home without his company.

When I heard that George had been invited to go overseas and that steps were being taken to make it practicable for him to do so, I concluded that he would be leaving you behind. I then thought that I would make up for some of my past meanness by offering to pay your fare so that you could go with him.

Then when I learned that you were going with him in any case, it rather knocked the bottom out of my little plan. However, having heard the story as to how you are having a bit of a scrape to make the trip to the best advantage, I decided that it would be worth while carrying out my original intention and so I am forwarding herewith a cheque for £300, which I hope will pay your return fare and perhaps a bit over for extras required on the voyage.
I trust you both have a really good time.
With best wishes, Yours faithfully,
 Alfred S. White.
There was a PS to the letter speaking of a hat that 'was left behind after you went home last night'. It would not be hard to guess whose hat was. The typical absent minded professor, Principal Morling, tended leave a trail of things behind him. AS White's letter was a treasured memento and as such was the token of a grateful heart.

Since Mrs Morling was going to London the Executive Committee decided to appoint her an official representative of the Union, so enabling her to be more than just a visitor to the Congress. Meanwhile Principal was working hard to fit in as much lecturing as he could before leaving for England. He spoke at Central's Good Friday Convention and was involved the Half-Yearly Assembly at Parramatta.

On 13 April the College Council and the Executive Committee held a dinner at the College to farewell the Principal and Mrs Morling. A cheque for £350 was presented to them towards their expenses[780].

At the Executive Committee Meeting on 17 April a former President of the Union, Mr EJ Phillips, drew attention to the absence of College students from the Half-Yearly Meetings.[781] Doubtless it was a commendable desire to have ministerial students identified with and informed about the activities of the Union that prompted the observation. However, as often as not the Half-Yearly Meetings were held in the country when it would have been impracticable for the students to attend. In 1951, though they were at Parramatta, it was understandable that the Principal would be anxious to avoid any interruption to the College program because he was seeking to cover as much ground as he could before leaving for England. The Executive Committee resolved, 'That the College Council request the Principal to make arrangements for the students to attend major denominational gatherings where practicable as a part of their education'. Ever since the College has had a student rule to that effect.

To bid Principal and Mrs Morling Godspeed a rally was held at Central Church on 19 April. Principal had 'to sing for his supper' for he addressed the rally on 'A Baptist Declaration of Faith'[782] Later in the year the address was published at the request of the Federal Board of Evangelism[783].

The SS Otranto sailed from Sydney on 21 April. Accompanying the Principal and Mrs Morling in the Baptist party were Rev Allan and Mrs Joy Tinsley, a young couple who through the years continued to be especially close to the Principal.

George and Gladys both made a record of their overseas trip, indeed Mrs Morling had two brief accounts of the main events of the journey. Much of Principal Morling's record is missing. This is unfortunate for what there is, is quite detailed.

They were entertained by friends in Melbourne, Adelaide and Perth. In Perth Rev Noel Vose showed them the sights and looked after them. They were met at Colombo by the Principal of the Carey Grammar School and spent the day with him and family. In the city the sight of 'burnt out' lepers particularly distressed them. Of Port Said Mrs Morling wrote, 'We were not very welcome. We were warned not to take a camera (ashore) or we would likely end up in jail'. In the other diary she wrote, 'Told to behave ourselves, which we did'. It is hard to imagine them doing otherwise. On the twelve hour journey through the Suez Canal they were tremendously impressed by the magnitude of the engineering feat that constructed it. Aden they found be a dirty, dusty place, it raining there only once in seven years. A note in the diary says, 'I'm sure they never wash'. Mrs Morling had been looking forward to some cheap shopping in Aden so was disappointed to find that the ship arrived there on a Sunday. She recorded candidly, 'I didn't get over it for days'. There was a stop at Gibraltar and then on to England.

Sunday 27 May was the last day of their voyage. It was a clear calm day and the captain sailed the Otranto in close to the coast. Principal wrote,

'Against the green of the fields and the blue of the sky the chalk cliffs appeared very white. The white cliffs of Dover were very white indeed'. They anchored in the Thames overnight and in the morning proceeded to Tilbury Docks. The Baptist Port Chaplain, 'a very cultured and friendly man', came on board and welcomed them on behalf of the Baptist Union. With his help they were speedily through Customs and on their way to the home of Rev SG and Mrs Morris, 'delightful people of almost incredible kindness'. That was the start of a deep friendship that was to grow only stronger despite the distance between England and Australia. The Morlings had been conveyed to the Finchley home of their hosts in a Daimler car made available by the head of the West Australian Government Insurance office. Principal wrote, 'In the Morris home refinement, fun and spirituality mingle beautifully. Mr Morris (on our arrival) at once declared that their home and the whole street was raised several degrees in the English social scale by the presence of the aristocratic Daimler'.

It was down to business at once. Mrs Morling went off to Wales to visit relatives while the Principal travelled to Southampton to speak at the Southern Baptist Association Meetings. He had two assignments. With Rev WD Jackson, formerly of Collins Street Baptist Church, Melbourne, as chairman, he spoke of the interests of the British Baptist Spiritual Advance Campaign. Then, by request, he told the story of the recently commenced Australian Baptist New Guinea Mission. After a very full day he returned the 100 miles to London that night. The next day he was off to Romney to preach the Annual Sermon at the Middlesex Baptist Association Meetings. Mercifully the next couple of days were comparatively free so that he was able to attend to private business matters and to preparation for the Congress which was to start on 4 June. He also had some opportunity to try to master the complexity of the London transport system with its 270 stations, most of them underground. He felt that eventually he became almost an expert in getting from place to place. Writing later he increased his estimated stations to 350.

On Saturday he travelled south again, this time to the ancient city of Winchester to preach on the Sunday at the Anniversary Services of the Baptist Church. The Principal delighted in all the historic associations and reminders of Winchester, King Alfred's Wessex capital, and wrote at some length about them to the family. Of the Sunday Services he wrote '… it was easy to preach. I find no fault with the responsiveness of English people'. After the evening service he returned to London for the Congress was to start the next day, Monday, 4 June.

Rev Sydney G Morris wrote an article on the Commonwealth Congress stressing particularly the contribution made by Australian Baptists. He referred to several individuals and then continued, 'Naturally, the name outstanding is that of Principal Morling whom, together with his wife, we have been so pleased to welcome. Your folk will have heard his voice during the Empire broadcast from Spurgeon's Tabernacle, where he sounded the deep evangelical note in an address which was a fitting complement to that of Dr Gordon Jones, of Calgary, Canada. This whole broadcast made a deep impression and put our Denomination on the map as never before. The Principal has been a notable figure on the various historical tours, he has delivered uplifting addresses to our associations and churches and his fine personality has been a means of grace to all. We are glad that the visit of this gifted and gracious servant of God will extend to many months and we are grateful to the College for sparing him'.[784]

Principal Morling addressed the Congress on the subject 'What the Baptist Church does' and it gave a resume of the address. 'In this clear, thoughtful and instructive address, which gripped the attention of all, Principal Morling had raised several questions which called for discussion'.[785]

During the Congress the Morlings were entertained by Mr and Mrs CT Le Quesne, distinguished English Baptists. At the time Mr Le Quesne was an eminent King's Counsel and an acting judge. Principal's own comments are full of interest. He wrote, 'Merely to keep on seeing things and places begins to pale, but worthwhile people are another matter. The Congress Committee (arranging hospitality) were rather scared about the Le Quesnes - so we heard later - and thought the Morlings might at least be respectable and safe. It was an experience to be with them'. After describing the huge home and the background and accomplishments the family he added – 'altogether a rather formidable set-up! However we had a thoroughly good time with the Le Quesnes. We have found that it is not easy to get inside the characteristic English reserve but once one has been really admitted to friendship, the warmth one receives is almost embarrassing'.[786] The friendship then formed was kept in good repair through the years and correspondence was maintained. The letters of Mrs. Le Quesne, who was a daughter of Sir Charles Gould, a famous surgeon, show that she was widely read in theology and took a most lively interest in all aspects of church life, including the ecumenical movement. The Principal provided an insight into the lifestyle of his hosts when he commented that Mr Le Quesne, on arriving home late to dinner was surprised to find that grace had been said in English instead of the customary Latin.

Overall he was disappointed with the Congress. He confessed that his 'own response to such series of meetings has rather waned during the years'. Though there was a high average quality of preaching there was no outstanding personality or great preacher. On the Sunday of the Congress he preached in Bloomsbury Chapel, the leading London Baptist Church 'on the practice of the Baptist Church'.[787] About this time he published a paper on 'A Baptist Declaration of Faith'.[788]

Following Congress there was a series of tours to places of historic and ecclesiastical interest and he revelled in these. His accounts of tours of London and Canterbury have survived but unfortunately the report of the rest of his activities has been lost. However Mrs Morling gave at least an indication of their main movements. During various periods in London they visited all the popular tourist sites and saw all the 'Royals' including 'little Prince Charles' enjoying himself. At Cambridge University a nephew of Mrs Morling showed them around. Oxford University was also visited and there Peter Young of the Petersham Church entertained them.[787] They journeyed to Scotland, not only the brave, but the beautiful, as they found it to be. Edinburgh was greatly enjoyed. In Glasgow the Principal preached in the City Church where Rev WD Jackson's brother was the pastor. Returning to Wales another cousin drove them about a thousand miles through Devon, Somerset and Cornwall in all their autumn beauty.

In his absence the NSW Assembly appointed him for yet another three years as Principal.[789] He had already been at the College for thirty years.

Once more in London they were in time to see four doctors entering Buckingham Palace. Soon bulletins were being posted indicating that the much loved George VI was gravely ill. At Australia House they met a graduate of the Ashfield College, Mr Robert Pitt, then established as a professional photographer in London. In the next few days they went to Albert Hall to attend a missionary pageant presented by a thousand young people. A tour chartered by the Baptist Union took them again to Canterbury and then successively to Bunyan's, Carey's and Dickens' country.

There followed a tour of the Continent. Acting on the advice of the minister where they were staying (probably Sydney Morris) Principal adopted clerical dress and was apparently taken to be a bishop. Apparently it did prove helpful but after a day or so he discarded it. They travelled through the lovely Kent countryside and down to Devon[dd] where their coach embarked on the ferry to Ostend, Belgium. In Germany they saw beauty, devastation, poverty and unsmiling women. The war was still a vivid, painful memory. There were, of course, visits to historic sites including some associated with

Martin Luther. Though funds were limited Principal bought a cuckoo clock in Germany. Switzerland, Mrs Morling found too beautiful to describe, the shops of Zurich too expensive even to enter and the food superb. In Italy their tour took them to Venice, which though fascinating 'didn't smell too nice'. The next day they were in Genoa where the extremes of wealth and poverty struck them. Then it was on San Remo, through Padua and Mantua, Mentone, Monte Carlo and Nice ('the most beautiful sea-side resort I have ever seen'). They travelled to Paris by the winding roads of Napoleon's Route through the French Alps and with rather frayed nerves reached Paris. Some time was spent seeing the sights of the French capital which they found lovely and ugly, most interesting and most wicked.

With time running out they stayed only briefly in London and went on to Wales to take their leave of Mrs Morling's relatives. For their last few weeks in London they were hosted again by the Le Quesnes. Through the good offices of Judge Le Quesne they were able to get tickets to attend the House of Commons on 19 November, sit in the Distinguished Strangers' Gallery and hear Anthony Eden speak. It was also at this time that they went to hear Sir Malcolm Sargent conduct a choir of a thousand voices and 'London's best orchestra' in Handel's 'Messiah'.

Though details are not available it is clear that during much of his time in Britain Principal Morling was kept busy. In his Report to the NSW Baptist Union Assembly in September Vice-Principal Wright wrote of the Principal, 'Thus far a large number of appointments have been

---

[dd] I think Rogers means Dover. JS-

fulfilled, with full preaching engagements each Sunday, College Graduation services and four or five engagements each week. The Principal speaks of 'a busy and a profitable time', of 'responsive English congregations fundamentally like our Australian people' and of warm fellowship extended to them. Also of much helpful knowledge gained in his contacts which should make a real contribution to our needs in New South Wales'.[790].

In his own Report written from overseas Principal Morling spoke of attending graduation ceremonies at Spurgeon's and Regents Park Colleges and of arrangements for him to visit and speak at all the Colleges after the summer vacation.[791] In the students' magazine[792], he contributed an article, 'A Tour of the British Baptist Colleges'. In it he told of visits to Bangor in North Wales where he was greeted 'by one of the kindliest of Welsh scholars, Principal William Hughes', to Manchester and its Principal, Kenneth D Dykes, to Rawdon where its Principal, Dr Marshall, was fighting a losing battle to keep the College going, to the Ladies' Missionary College in Birmingham with its principal, Rev Gwynneth Hubble, to Bristol, the oldest of all Baptist Colleges with its Principal, Dr Arthur Deakin, 'among the greatest theological teachers in Great Britain', and to Cardiff, where it was possible only to make a brief call on its Principal, Rev Edward Roberts.

In Birmingham he had preached for Rev AJ Barnard, an Australian who was then the Principal-designate of the South African Baptist Theological College. The family came from Tasmania and the father (Rev A) and two brothers (Rev CV and Rev LR) at various times pastored churches in New South Wales.

In his last week-end in Britain he returned to Regents Park College at Oxford, meeting the theological students on Friday night, speaking to the John Bunyan Society on Saturday night and preaching on Sunday at the 298th anniversary services of the Baptist University Church. Rev Frank Morton of London wrote 'The Principal's visit to Britain has justified the high hopes of those of us who knew him and the impact he would have upon our British Baptist Constituency. He made a favourable impression wherever he went, and his graciousness has endeared him to our people'.[793]

The Morlings left England on 21 November on the Oronsay, the first available booking. The homeward journey was 'a lovely trip' 'in a luxurious ship'. They touched at Gibraltar, Naples (where they visited

Mt Vesuvius and Pompeii), Aden, Colombo, Perth, Adelaide, Melbourne and 'then dear old Sydney' with the thrill of reunion with children and grandchildren. They arrived home on Christmas Eve, to a fine residence whose construction had been completed while they were away. Architectural work on the home was by one of his students, Doug Vaughan, and the building by a good friend from the Haberfield Church, Tom Lumb.

Principals Residence

1952
Sometime early in 1952 he wrote in his diary, 'In preparation for these last ten years of ministry, perhaps ten, I pray for the capacity to have control and composure to pray and read in relaxed yet attentive continuity'. And, perhaps a day or two later, 'I am instructed to take the Holy Spirit into partnership with me in this work of the College, as a preparation for His taking me into partnership with Him'.

After so long away it was natural that many would be anxious to hear what 'our beloved Principal' had been doing. On 5 February he spoke at the Ministers' Fraternal Meeting and gave a report of his experiences. Two days later the members of the Executive Committee and the College Council, on the invitation of Principal and Mrs Morling, met to inspect their new residence. The President of the Union expressed a 'welcome home' to the hosts and GHM 'gave a most interesting account of his experiences in England and on the Continent'.[794]

Consequent upon the resignation of Rev WL Jarvis, the Central Church invited Rev James McClendon, a young American from Texas, to fulfil an interim pastorate[795] while he was in Australia working on a thesis. The Principal inducted him into the pastorate on 2 March. Two days later he was back at Central for the College Tea and Commencement Service at which he was the preacher. He reported a record student enrolment with sixteen new students commencing courses.[796] Having become both Principal and President of the Christian Workers' Training College, by reason of Mr Jarvis' resignation, he was once more at Central on 7 March to chair the Convocation of the College.[797]

On 15 March the Theological College had a Visitors' Day when the Principal's residence was officially opened and made available for inspection.[798]

The front page of *The Australian Baptist*[799] carried an article by the Principal, 'The Holy Spirit and the Believer'. Prepared for what was known as New Life Week it represented an admirable condensation of his main teaching on the subject.

A letter written by Mr S Emery[800] contained a tribute to the Principal. It recalled that when the Woollahra Church was formed in 1892 there was only one Baptist student in New South Wales, D Davis and, by arrangement, he was attending Camden, the College of the Congregational Union. The writer went to say 'This little review brings out in contrast the wonderful position today, and calls to mind the progress and development of the College especially under the inspiring leadership of Principal Morling, who, we hope and pray, may be spared for many years to come to continue his fine work'.

At this time the earnest propagation of the distinctive tenets of the Pentecostalist movement was disturbing many Baptist members so at Executive Committee meetings on 22 April and 13 May he was asked to prepare a tract dealing with the 'error of the Pentecostalists'.[801]

One of Principal Morling's former students, Rev PJ Hayes, was the pastor of the Footscray Baptist Church in Victoria. When, on their way to London the Morlings had a brief stay in Melbourne, Phil Hayes and his wife had met them and looked after them. Early in June Mrs (Hilda) Hayes died suddenly and the funeral was held on 7 June.[802] There was no time for the Principal to attend but he made a special visit to Melbourne to conduct a Memorial Service in the Footscray Church on 15 June. He was reported as being 'a true son of consolation' to his bereaved friend.[803]

In the same month he was the speaker at Granville's celebration of the first anniversary of Rev C Victor Barnard's ministry, at Chatswood's Second Coming Convention taking 'Fellowship and Hope' as his subject[804],[ee], and at Hurlstone Park's Church Aid when he gave a talk on his trip overseas.[805]

[ee] The event happened on 22 June.

On his way from England to become the pastor of the Auckland Baptist Tabernacle, Rev John Pritchard along with Mrs Pritchard and their four children spent some days at the end of June and beginning of July in Sydney.[806] Principal Morling made them most welcome and had Mr Pritchard take some lectures at the College. After arriving in New Zealand the Pritchards sent him Geldenhuy's recently published commentary on Luke's Gospel as 'a token of grateful appreciation of happy fellowship and many kindnesses'. As markings and comments indicate the Principal worked his way carefully through it. John Pritchard subsequently became a lecturer at the New Zealand Bible College and like the Principal a much-sought convention speaker.

On l3 July the Principal once more shared in Bexley's anniversary, this time the 38th.[807] At the Executive Committee on 22 July, his tract on Pentecostalism was received and it was decided to ask the Department of Evangelism to have it printed and circulated.[808] It also appeared in two instalments of *The Australian Baptist.*[809] In the last week of July he was in Victoria giving lectures to the students of the Baptist Theological College[810]. Within a few days of that visit it was announced that Rev BS Brown, BD, had been appointed a professor at the Victorian Baptist College.[811] Principal Morling was sorry to lose his services but was delighted to see another of his men perpetuating his ministry of theological education.

Another of his men, Rev NF Reeve, was nearing the end of his Presidential year and at the Executive Committee of 19 August, he expressed on behalf of that Committee thanks to the President for the happy and efficient manner in which he had conducted the meetings of the Committee during his year of office.[812]

From Sunday, 31 August, to Sunday, 7 September, Dulwich Hill engaged in Jubilee Celebrations. The Principal was Guest Preacher at all services. On the Tuesday night there was a Great Baptist Rally and on Wednesday a Service of Dedication and Fellowship. The 50th Anniversary was especially featured on the final Sunday. According to a report it provided 'the splendid climax to the series of services. The morning service brought a fine congregation who listened with rapt attention to Principal's message on 'The Cloud of Witnesses'.. Then came the final service in the evening. The church was again full...Mr Morling reached the heights and the depths of spiritual insight and power as he spoke of 'The Name that Binds the Ages'".[813]

The following weekend he was at the Maitland Road Islington Church for its 66th Anniversary and the church 'was blessed by his ministry'[814]. Shortly after this he fitted in a visit to East Chatswood where Rev John Howes was the pastor to share in the dedication of a new manse. He is said to have 'delivered an interesting address on the ministry in the home'.[815]

Then it was Assembly time again. A report at the College Session began, 'Obviously refreshed by his recent visit to Great Britain and his wide contacts with Baptist leaders and theologians in the Homeland Principal GH Morling expressed his confidence that, assisted by a splendid team of tutors, the future is full of promise'. One of that team was Basil Brown and the Principal moved a motion of appreciation and congratulation to him on his appointment to the Victorian College.[816] In his own Report he said, among other things, 'It is fitting that I should express appreciation of the Principal's new residence which Mrs Morling and I found ready for occupancy upon our return from abroad'.

'In respect to the experience gained in Great Britain I have little to add beyond what I wrote in the *College Chronicle* last March. The British Colleges have a stronger academic emphasis than we have but our practical training is much more thorough. Observation abroad has confirmed our thought to give more place in our course to students' own research. This year we have prescribed many more essays which will replace term examinations'.

'Another change has been the organising of additional classes for instruction in preaching and general ministerial practice. No less than five classes each week, all under my own direction, are conducted for this purpose. A proper balance is being preserved between the cultural and the practical. Within the cultural sphere we still give pride of place to the exegetical study of the Word of God'.[817]

He was the chosen speaker for the Assembly Pastoral Session and 'was at his rich, masterly best'. 'His subject', said a report, 'was 'The Wider Religious Outlook' and was a survey of the scene in England as he had seen it during his recent extended visit. Principal Morling has a rare ability to absorb and interpret impressions. His presentation of the British churches, their religious and the Baptist traditions, was vivid. It gripped, hushed and moved profoundly the large audience of ministers'. He was described by the reporter as 'our scholarly and aesthetic friend' and each of those words is deserving of emphasis and exemplification.[818]

On the last day of the Assembly as its 'crowning glory' there was an Ordination Service at which the Principal presented three candidates.[819]

He was to have chaired Stanmore's farewell on 27 September to Rev NF Reeve who on the completion of his Presidency concluded his Stanmore ministry. He was prevented by doctor's orders and had to be content to send a greeting. In a few days it was apparent that the College was being swept by 'an epidemic of measles' the Principal being one of the victims.[820] It was placed in quarantine until 8 October.

It was not possible, however, to keep the Principal out of action for long for as soon as the quarantine was lifted he was off to the Northern Tablelands.[821] He went back to Tamworth, the first church in which he served under the Home Mission Society as a candidate for the ministry, to preach at its 62nd Anniversary[822], in the second week of October.[823] He preached in the little Black Mountain Church, mother church of the whole area, on Wednesday 15 October. On Friday 17 October and at the evening service on Sunday, he preached at Glen Innes in connection with its 22nd Anniversary.[824] Saturday 18 October found him speaking at a function in Armidale to mark the eighth year of Rev John Owen's ministry there. Next morning he preached in the Armidale Church and the service was broadcast.[825]

In his absence from the Executive Committee on 14 October it had been reported that Rev John Ridley, prominent Baptist evangelist and dear friend of the Principal, had come under the influence of 'Pentecostal' teaching.[826] The Executive, at its adjourned meeting on 21 October, wisely appointed George Morling to the committee formed to confer with John Ridley.[827] It may well be significant that *The Australian Baptist*[828] mentioned that the Principal's booklet on Pentecostalism had been forwarded to all churches. Also worthy of note is the fact that in the previous week's denominational paper it was reported that he had been appointed Chairman of the Advisory Committee, a committee which along with other matters, dealt with sensitive issues involving both churches and ministers. So he was deeply and painfully concerned in the whole affair.

On 1 November he spoke at the opening of Gosford Baptist Church building.[829] He reported to the November Executive meeting that Ridley had stated that he did not accept the position that only those who had spoken in tongues were baptised in the Holy Spirit.[830] However in the interval between that assurance and the Executive meeting John Ridley had openly identified himself with Pentecostal meetings being held in Sydney. So the committee was asked to see him again. Because many Baptist members were being disturbed by reports and rumours it was decided to draw up a statement on the situation to be published in *The Australian Baptist*. The Principal was one of those charged with the responsibility of framing the statement.[831]

It was back to Pymble on Sunday 23 November, to preach in its newly extended church building.[832] He had been the first preacher in the building when it was originally opened more than 30 years before. Three days later he was the speaker at Chatswood's Anniversary Public Meeting.

On 4 December the record-breaking College session concluded with what was that year described as the College Commemoration Service.[833] But this meant but slight respite for the Principal. There was scarcely time to clear his desk before he was off to be one of the speakers at the 35th Annual Convention at Belgrave Heights (previously the Upwey Convention) in Victoria.[834] It ran from 24 December to 4 January.

1953
This was to be a busy but fairly uneventful year. On 11 January he presided and preached at the induction of another of his men, Rev A Neville Horn, to the Stanmore pastorate.[835]

Sometime during February he was the speaker at the Western District Baptist Association meetings. It is possible that he fitted this in while taking his usual vacation at Blackheath.

Single students went into residence on 24 February, as most probably did the Principal. There was a week to settle in and get everything in order before the married students joined them and lectures began.[836]

A front page article in *'The Australian Baptist'* by the Principal, intended to give emphasis to March as College Month, was entitled 'Our Theological College ideals'.[837] It is a fine article, worthy of being quoted at length. However, one extract must suffice. Writing of the responsibility that theological colleges have to their students he said 'We can immerse them in an atmosphere in which the impulse, which thrust them forth in their high calling will be conserved, so that spiritual passion will keep pace with growing enlightenment ... To provide a setting of spiritual dynamism is part of our responsibility. Again it is our business to encourage in every way the acquisition of that quality of mind and spirit which we call culture. Necessarily a college must educate, but education which stops at the giving of multitudinous facts is insufficient'.

'In my undergraduate days an eminent lawyer told us at a University Commemoration function that many of us were nothing but educated asses. 'That is' he added, 'if you are educated'. Culture rather than education is the desideratum. Culture is education which ripens into humility and wisdom and understanding sympathy. It is the fruit of long years of learning and living, but it should begin in College days'. The article is notable also for its recognition of the need for greater emphasis on practical preparation for ministry. He referred to what was being done in American seminaries but drew attention to their large staffs of full-time teachers, concluding, 'We Australians envy and do our best with lesser resources, but with clear vision and purpose'.

Scarcely had College lectures began than, on 9 March, a College Bible Class, conducted by the Principal and open to all, was commenced. It was followed by a Local Preachers Instruction Class which was taken by the Vice-Principal. Every Monday night found about 60 visitors to the College for these classes.[838]

It had become clear that the College was rapidly outgrowing the capacity of its current site. On 14 March a College Garden Party and Sale of Work was held, its object being to augment a College Rebuilding Fund.

At that time large numbers of young people met monthly at Central church for Baptist Youth Crusade Rallies. The March Rally was designated 'Kollege Kapers' and with students participating was judged to be highly successful. 'The climax of the evening came when Principal Morling showed his capacity to adapt himself to a situation and spoke on 'Donkeys'. With characteristic skill the Principal brought his message to a high water mark in the challenge to dedication, surrender and service'.[839]

The Executive Committee meeting of 17 March had before it a statement concerning Pentecostalism drawn up by the Principal, Rev WL Jarvis and Rev Dr CJ Tinsley. The issue was still lively and there was continuing anxiety concerning the situation of the greatly respected evangelist, Rev JG Ridley, whose accreditation as a Baptist minister was withdrawn.[840]

Rather later than usual the College Commencement Service was held in Central Church on 24 March with Rev Dr Sandford Fleming, the Australian born President of the Berkeley Baptist Divinity School as the speaker.[841]

Principal Morling was not given to writing letters to *The Australian Baptist* but he broke his usual reticence by his response to an Easter presentation by the Baptist Choral Society. A letter in most appreciative terms appeared over his name.[842] It revealed the aesthetic side of his personality. He was deeply moved by the presentation of truth in beautiful form. The same issue of *The Australian Baptist* had an account of the opening of a new church at Pennant Hills and of the Principal's share in proceedings.[843]

At that time it was the practice in Baptist churches to designate the week leading up to Whitsunday as New Life Week. It was a week of spiritual emphasis. In 1953 Principal Morling's contribution was to prepare suggested sermon outlines for the services that began and ended New Life Week, 17 and 24 May.[844] At the College, he was also conducting a regular Monday night Bible class for the public.[845]

The coronation of Queen Elizabeth II took place on 2 June. The NSW Baptist Union held a denominational Coronation Service in Central Baptist on 1 June. The address given by the Principal was described as worthy of the historic occasion.[846] On the Coronation Day a 'Special United Gathering' was held in the Manly Church with the Principal again charged with the responsibility of preaching.[847] It was a wise choice of speaker for not only did George Morling rise to the challenge of this special occasion but he was a Britisher and a royalist to his bootstraps.

On 23 June, consequent upon certain assurances received by the Executive Committee, and much to the Principal's relief and thankfulness, Rev JG Ridley was reinstated to the list of accredited Baptist ministers. At the same meeting Principal Morling was again appointed the NSW representative on the Federal Educational Board.[848]

In close succession three men with whom he had been associated in various ways died. There was a report in *The Australian Baptist* of the death of Rev Roy H Wallis[849], who had been a member and subsequently Secretary of the Hornsby Church when the Principal had been its pastor. Later he trained under Principal Morling and entered the Baptist ministry.

On 24 July Rev Walter Barry, who had been Principal's pastor at Ashfield and a close friend, after some months of distressing decline also died[850]. In the midst of a splendid survey of Walter Barry's life and ministry there were deeply personal notes by George Morling.[851] He wrote for example, 'He was one of the few men whose spoken word had power to thrill me. Memories still abide of missionary addresses which I heard in my boyhood which roused me to excited response. In more recent years Mr Barry was my pastor ... He still possessed the power to inspire me. Always his expository preaching satisfied me. Sometimes my minister's genuine eloquence thrilled me. Of course such a capacity had its explanation in a spirit that burned ... With reverent reserve I pay tribute to my friend as having, to a rare degree, inner fires of spiritual passion constantly fed by meditation and secret prayer. Sometimes he would come and pray with me. One knew then that the light that was in him shone so brightly because it first of all burned in him'. In Walter Barry George Morling had found a kindred spirit. 'His mind was refined. He kept company with the noble minds of the ages. There was a choiceness in his spirit. He knew Christ so well and had served Him so faithfully that heaven was in him long before he was in heaven'. At the Executive Committee meeting of 18 August Walter Barry's death was recorded.[852] At the same meeting there was a report of the resignation of Rev FA Hoad, who was entering the Presbyterian ministry, the first man trained under Principal Morling to do so.[853]

It was only about a week later that Principal lost another friend with the death of Mr A Wykes of the Ashfield Church. Mr Wykes was the father of Rev Eric Wykes[854] and it was reported that during the latter's training in the College his father endeared himself to the Principal by his willingness to serve in any capacity to further the work of the College. The Principal shared in the funeral service and, in particular, spoke at the graveside.[855]

Remarkably, since he often seemed to live on another plane, he never lost his ability to communicate with young people. So it is not really surprising that when in August Wentworthville opened a Youth Centre he was one of the speakers who shared over the special weekend.[856]

Surprisingly he does not appear to have returned often to his early Hornsby pastorate. However, on 12 September he was back there for the unveiling of the foundation stone of a new church building.[857]

Rev RG Schaefer, a recent graduate of the College and due soon to leave for missionary service in East Pakistan, was the pastor at Undercliffe. On 20 September the Principal was the guest preacher at the 46th Anniversary of the Church.[858] Doubtless he saw in the young missionary-designate some continuation of the ministry of his recently deceased friend, Walter Barry.

The Principal's Report at the 1953 Assembly was interesting for its indication of his involvement in the practical aspects of training. He wrote, 'Since the appointment of Rev BG Wright as Vice-Principal the general policy has been for me to take as much practical work as possible. That has meant a considerable strengthening of this section of our teaching'. After referring to preaching classes and regular courses in Pastoral Theology he went on to say, 'Further, for the last two years I myself have directed a course in Evangelism with the help of visiting lecturers who are directly engaged in evangelistic work'.[859] Evangelism was always close to his heart.

The Ordination Service which concluded the Assembly was notable for the record number of clever ordinands whom the Principal was able to present. His pastor, Rev AH Orr, was the preacher.[860]

With the influx of visitors over the Six-Hour Weekend early in October, the Ettalong Church arranged special services and the Principal preached to overflow congregations.[861]

Sources of information for activities in the last months of 1953 are limited. No copies of *The Australian Baptist* for November and December are preserved among denominational records. The Executive Committee on 17 November appointed him to a committee charged with the implementation of 'The Home Work Scheme' which on the recommendation of the Faith and Life Commission was to replace the Home Missionary Society.[862] At Campsie Church on 22 November he chaired a farewell to his young friends Rev and Mrs AS Tinsley, as they left for Unley Park in South Australia.[863] At the end of the month accompanied by Mrs Morling he travelled to Armidale to share in the opening and dedication of a new school hall and to preach at both Sunday services on 29 November.[864]

1954
After the vacation period there was a brief flurry of activity on the part of the Principal. Early in February he inducted Rev Frank Gallagher at Campsie.[865] On 6 February he was again at Hornsby, this time to be the preacher at the opening on its new church building.[866]

The 1954 College session began on 23 February. The settling in period concluded with a College Month Prayer Meeting on Friday, 26 February.[867] The time had yet to come when the main financial support of the College was derived from the Baptist Union Co-operative Budget. It was still necessary for the College to promote itself and to raise its own funds. During March the Principal, Vice-Principal and students visited churches to keep the claims of the College for support in prayer and finance before their members. This was seen not merely as a fund raising activity but as a spiritual exercise when the challenge of preparation for christian service was presented. It was appropriate that it should be undergirded by prayer.

The first issue of *The Australian Baptist* in March, as in the previous year, gave prominence to an article by Principal Morling.[868] The banner heading was 'Theological Colleges Make Their Appeal', but the article was addressed to theological students rather than the general constituency. It breathed his concern for the men in training. He reminded them that entrance into College put them in a position of trust as custodians of the principles and ideals of our ministry. He wrote, 'That is what we expect of the theological student – a humble heart, a teachable spirit, a robust sincerity, a steady determination to justify the faith that is reposed in him'. The suspicion that these words may reflect some disappointment that the Principal had experienced is strengthened by his following words. 'An English minister recalled that, in his student days, he was reading in the College Library when, not observing his presence, the venerable Principal Henderson slowly entered reading a letter that was obviously causing him distress. Looking up he saw the student and exclaimed almost fiercely, 'Will you let me down, too?', Doubtless another concrete situation was in his mind's eye as he made his second point that it is possible for genuine men to lose heart. Under the burden of studies, sermon preparation, pastoral problems and their own disappointed aspirations even the best of men may sink in despondency. The remedy is in part to be found in the clarifying and purifying of motives. Their devotion must not be offered on the altar of self-esteem and self-seeking, not even on the altar souls. The ground of their consecration must not finally be devotion to souls but devotion to Jesus Christ. His further reminder to students was 'that unless some things are learned in the days of preparation for the ministry it is at least most unlikely that they will be acquired in the days when the burden and heat of the full ministry oppress'. In particular he urged them to give themselves to the ministry of the Word and of prayer. 'Let the ideal', he wrote, 'be cherished and practised in the more secluded years of College training. These precious years will never recur, but they may be used to establish life-long attitudes and habits'. He concluded with a personal touch, 'When I was a young minister, Dr Thomas Porter, then an aged and venerable father-in-God, came to me after a service and said with deep affection: 'God bless you. How I thank God that young men are being raised up to take the place of the older generation''.

Principal Morling was speaking his heart's concern for the young men entering upon training. Several such men were officially received at the College Commencement Service on 9 March in the Central Church, when the pastor, Rev EH Watson, was the preacher.[869,ff] A total enrolment for the session of 45 students constituted a new record.

The previous weekend Principal Morling had been in Newcastle keeping the ministry of the College before the coalfields churches. On the following Sunday (14 March) he preached at West Ryde's 30th Anniversary.[870]

However, his unsparing labours took their toll on his health and brought a halt to all activity including his greatly enjoyed College Bible School. More than a month later *The Australian Baptist* carried the note[871], 'We deeply sympathise with Principal GH Morling on his prolonged indisposition and assure him of the prayers of all for a speedy recovery'. A week later the Half-Yearly Meetings, held at Goulburn, sent greetings to the Principal who was absent on account of illness but making progress.[872] Three weeks later there was the further note, 'We are pleased to report that Principal GH Morling is now making good progress and is convalescing at Collaroy'.[873]

Nevertheless it was still some time before he was back in action. On 3 August he spoke to the Ministers' Fraternal on 'The Meaning of Ordination', and on 27 August he shared in a farewell function to Rev John Drakeford as he prepared to leave for post-graduate studies at Southwestern Baptist Seminary at Fort Worth, Texas.[874]

At the Assembly Meetings his appointment as Principal for a further three years was unanimous and enthusiastic. In the College Session Dr CJ Tinsley reminded the Assembly that the Principal had served the

---

[ff] Rogers says 'ten men' but only eight are named. A ninth is listed in TAB 24th March 1954 Page 7

College for 34 years with an ever-growing influence.[875]

Whatever changes those years had brought there was change in George Morling's perception of the College's function. In his Report he noted certain changes, but asserted, '... it is important to record that our College policy of providing a ministerial training course designed to ensure an evangelical, expository and soul-winning ministry persists, and indeed, is set before us with increasing clarity and purpose'.[876]

On the first weekend in October Principal Morling, long a good friend and trusted counsellor of the Epping church, preached at the opening of its new church building. Proceedings had been under way for two hours before the time came for the address. 'The Principal rose to the occasion, of course, and triumphed over the difficulties'.[877]

The following Monday, 4 October, was the Six-Hour Day holiday. The Burton Street Baptist Church held a 'Revival and Second Coming Convention'. Principal Morling was one of the speakers and was advertised 'to defend the Doctrine of the Second Coming in the light of the recent statement 'that the doctrine of the literal return of Christ is of the devil and assists the devil to lull the church to sleep".[878]

In subsequent weeks he preached at South Carlton's 24th Anniversary.[879] shared in a teaching mission on the Holy Spirit at Cronulla[880], inducted Rev Albert Dube at Dulwich Hill,[881] and was guest speaker at Lakemba's Church Anniversary and opening of its new manse 13-14 November.[882]

At the College Graduation Service at Ashfield on 2 December he had the satisfaction of seeing four more men leave the College equipped to serve Christ in the Baptist ministry.[883] A few days later in the Petersham Church he was able to present them for ordination in a service at which the Welsh Evangelist, Rev Ivor Powell, preached.[884]

There was a touch of sadness for the Principal at year's end when Mr CT Le Quesne, QC, died. He wrote[885], 'I pay tribute to one truly distinguished and truly devoted. At the time of the Empire and Commonwealth Congress in London Mrs Morling and I were entertained by Mr and Mrs Le Quesne in their spacious Hampstead home and were admitted into an enriching family friendship which still remains to satisfy and stimulate. Mr Le Quesne was a great Englishman. In him the standards and loyalty of the English gentleman had notable expression. A scholar with a range that extended beyond his own special field of law, he added to his knowledge the quiet dignity, the inner refinement, the ripe wisdom of culture'. He went on to speak of his friend as the kindliest of men, a man with a faith humble and warm and a convinced Baptist. It might be said that his former host and friend epitomised his ideal of the Christian layman.

As so often in the past, he was again one of the featured speakers at the annual convention at Belgrave Heights over the Christmas and the New Year period.[886]

1955
Then presently he was back to the beloved Blackheath to relax, to read and to reflect. Even so there was the now almost inevitable preaching at the local church anniversary, the 66th. His addresses were thoroughly enjoyed.

With the regularity of the recurring seasons the 1955 College session began[887] and in due course the Principal's article appeared in *The Australian Baptist*.[888] Its subject was Ministerial Training. It began with a reminder of the importance that Baptists, in the course of their history, had placed on adequate preparation for ministry yet warned that it must not be assumed that a theological college can make a minister. The ministry belongs to the whole church and if some have a special function within that ministry it is because God has gifted and called them. The role of the Holy Spirit in 'making a minister' must be recognised. In concluding, the Principal took one of his hobby horses for a brief canter, writing 'It is not unnecessary in this consideration of the ministry and the training for it to confirm our thought concerning ultimate loyalties. Baptists, we remind ourselves, are not in the Catholic sacramentarian tradition but in the Evangelical preaching tradition. In a lecture given some three years ago in London by a specialist in church architecture, illuminating information was given that in two-thirds of the so-called non-conformist church buildings erected in recent years the communion table occupies the place of honour in the centre with the pulpit at the side. In many instances the arrangement has no ulterior significance but the overall picture is disquieting. It does indicate, what other facts confirm, that the preaching of the Word is yielding place of priority to the observance of the sacrament. Let Baptists never be caught up in that dangerous trend. We belong to the Gospel tradition. Therefore let us give preaching its rightful place'.

That tailpiece created a slight flurry of literary activity. In a letter to the Editor[889], one correspondent took the Principal mildly to task for laying 'undue stress on preaching as though it were an end in itself and reducing the observance of the memorial feast to a minor position'. A week later another correspondent rallied to his support.[890] Then the Editor, in whose church a side pulpit had recently been installed, entered the lists against his friend the Principal.[891] The following week a further letter appeared rejecting the importance of architectural features in churches.[892] Sad to relate there was no manifest response to other more positive aspects of the Principal's article.

The Commencement Service at Central Church on 8 March[893] saw eleven new students presented to the Principal for training, an encouraging indication both of God's working and of the confidence enjoyed by the College and its Principal on the part of the churches.

While the College work was his principal preoccupation, absorbing most of his time, thought and strength, he maintained constant ministry in the churches. He was, for example, the preacher at Cabramatta's 39th Anniversary in March. On 3 April he presided and preached at the induction of Rev John Owen to the Granville pastorate.[894] From 17 to 24 April at a series of meetings at Auburn he expounded aspects of the Person and Work of the Holy Spirit. 'We give thanks to our Heavenly Father', it was reported, 'for having such an eminent and beloved teacher of the Word in our midst'.[895] On 1 May in the morning he preached at Mosman in connection with the inauguration of a pipe organ[896] and in the evening at Concord's 35th Anniversary.[897] The next weekend he was at Maitland for a 'Deeper Life Convention'. His theme was again the Holy Spirit and the topics included one that was to become increasingly important to him, 'The Holy Spirit and Physical Health'.[898]

In *The Australian Baptist*[899] there was an account of the funeral of Mrs EJ Marshall of Blackheath. She had lived the last 45 of her 87 at Blackheath and so was well known to the Principal who 'paid an affectionate tribute' to her.

At the meeting of the Eastern Suburbs District Baptist Association on 14 May, the speaker was reported to be 'our beloved Principal of our Theological College, Rev GH Morling, who gave us a scholarly deep spiritual message from the second chapter of Acts on the Holy Spirit'.[900]

Rev Dr CJ and Mrs Tinsley celebrated their Golden Wedding on 18 May at a family gathering. George Morling, almost one of the family, represented the Baptist Union at the function.[901]

The record of such things is fragmentary and haphazard but is sufficient to show that he had a constant ministry to the churches. He was the speaker at Wollongong's 23rd anniversary[902], on 19 June he was preaching at Burton Street Church.[903]

From 1 to 10 August the Brisbane Baptist Tabernacle celebrated its Centenary. Principal Morling, who had served the church so well in the past, was the guest preacher for the series of meetings.[904] He was also the speaker at the Queensland Union Centenary Assembly.[905] He highlighted 'the heritage of the past' but in the concluding services reminded his hearers of Jesus Christ, the Eternal Contemporary.

He returned home just in time to speak 'words of comfort, consolation and courage' at the funeral of an old Granville friend, Mr J Thomas.[906]

At the 1954 Assembly The Faith and Life Commission had submitted recommendations concerning ministerial training. With only slight modifications by the Assembly these had been accepted. They concerned two areas. One had to do with the relation of students to work in the churches during their training. The other was directed to the training program itself. It had been resolved 'that the College give greater emphasis to courses in practical evangelism, pastoral training, social studies that concern the relationship of the minister to the community, Baptist history, doctrine and polity'.[907]

In his Annual Report to the 1955 Assembly[908] the Principal indicated initiatives already and enthusiastically undertaken in response to the Assembly's directions. It was a turning point for NSW Baptists in ministerial training. But Principal's Report also foreshadowed the shape of greater changes to come. Rev AH Orr had visited America and brought back information concerning the directions that theological education was taking in Baptist seminaries there. The Principal used this as a springboard to comment, 'With the expansion of the College of recent years, an expansion which seems to have come almost suddenly, we all feel that the review should be made of our whole College life, teaching and organisation. The expansion in itself is a sign of the blessing of God. We remember that our evangelical emphasis has commended itself in such a way that the type of ministry for which we stand is acceptable in an increasing way right throughout Australia. We are determined to maintain this emphasis and at the same time to have our eyes wide open to every suggestion that will increase efficiency'.

The College was poised for its next phase of development. Principal Morling brought it to the threshold of a new era but handed over to another at that point.

Though the action was unusual it was an expression of concern for and appreciation of the Principal when the College Council sponsored a notice of motion which gave him a rise in salary.[909] The action triggered a review of all denominational stipends.

Right after the Assembly he left Sydney to be the chief speaker at the Southern Highlands Christian Convention over the Six-Hour Day weekend, 30 September to 3 October. In October he preached at Jubilee celebrations at both Arncliffe[910] and Woonona[911] and was involved on 29 October in a stone setting ceremony for Croydon's Youth Centre.[912]

In November there was a Jubilee of a different kind. The Principal's friend, Rev Frank Robinson of Concord, had been in pastoral ministry for 50 years. Principal and Mrs Morling hosted a function to honour him.[913]

At the College Graduation and Prize Giving in Ashfield Church on 1 December no less than thirteen men were graduated and went out into the Baptist ministry. Though the rain poured down in torrents the church was crowded. It was a great encouragement to the Principal and a cause for deep thankfulness.

On Christmas morning he preached 'a truly inspiring message' in the Katoomba Baptist Church and conducted a dedication service for Pastor and Mrs John Coard as they presented their infant son before the Lord.[914]

1956
College resumed on 21 February but in the first week single students were merely settling in.[915] However with lectures beginning in a couple of days the Principal preached at both services of the North Canberra Church on 26 February.[916]

With students of all the theological colleges assembling for the 1956 session the NSW Principal wrote an article 'What is a Baptist Minister?.[917] It dealt with 'the inwardness of the Baptist view of the Ministry'. Some of the notes sounded in the article are so characteristic of our beloved Principal that they merit quotation for their own sake. Any who studied under the Principal will recognise them as old and familiar friends.[918]

'Dr James Denney used to say that it is impossible for any man to convey the impression at one and the same time that he himself is clever and Jesus Christ is great'.

'The noble Alexander Whyte, as Moderator of the Church of Scotland, poured out his heart to ministers and students of his day in these burning words – prayer and work. All great and true and eminently successful ministers from Paul's day downward bear the same testimony – prayer and work ... Let us pray and work, my brethren, in what remains to us of our time on earth, with all our might'.

'He supported his plea by a quotation from Quintilian – 'We shroud our indolence under the pretext of a difficulty' and concluded, 'Oh, no! We cannot look seriously in one another's faces and say it is want of time. It is want of intention. It is want of determination. It is want of method. It is want of conscience. It is want of heart. It is want of anything and everything but time'.

As a balancing corrective to the foregoing he urged the necessity of the saving grace of a sense of humour and proceeded, 'How many dark, unlovely things, such as morbidness and misunderstanding and suspicion disappear under the benign influence of healthy laughter'. He quoted Dr JH Jowett as saying, 'I wonder how many of us so thoroughly believe in God that we can laugh in His name'.

The final point in his article was that in our conception of the ministry there should be some element of apostolic fire, some manifestation of 'the Spirit's calm excess'. 'The typically Baptist preacher should never come under the condemnation of being (1) faultily faultless, (2) icily regular, (3) splendidly null'.

On Saturday, 3 March, the 80th birthday of Dr CJ Tinsley was celebrated at Stanmore.[919] As if to make up for the comparatively quiet way he had concluded his great ministry at Stanmore this was a great occasion with the church overflowing. The chosen speakers were evangelist, John Ridley, and theological college principal, George Morling. The latter emphasised his friendly influence and guidance in the development of the NSW Baptist Theological College. At that time Dr Tinsley was still President of the College Council.

Mrs Morling had not, through the years, taken a prominent place in public meetings so it is interesting that it was announced that during March she would be available to speak at Ladies' Fellowships.[920] She too was to have a part in the forward thrust of the College.

The College Commencement in Central Church on 6 March[921] was somewhat overshadowed by the celebration of the College President Tinsley's birthday a few days previously. It marked the College's 40th Anniversary and the beginning of Principal's 35th year of leadership.

A correspondence in the *London Times* sparked by the visit of Dr Billy Graham to Cambridge University brought out the Christian apologist in the Principal. In an article titled 'The Evangelical Faith and Scholarship'[922] he staunchly defended an 'evangelical' view of revelation and contended for 'our responsibility to preach the New Testament gospel of justification by faith'.

On 27 March he was the preacher at a Valedictory Service for Rev and Mrs John Burton as they left to work among Aborigines in Central Australia.[923]

The next day, there was the first of a series of entries in a new diary. As written for himself alone it is interesting because it shows him responding to a problem that was very much his own.

'March 28 - A person quoted in the Life of Faith: 'I want something more than His blessed keeping power. My soul cries out with intense longing to be brought nearer into His holy Presence. If there is such a thing as a manifestation of Himself which would consume the dross in our souls it would be almost better than pardon was at first: but <u>faith stands abashed</u>'. I respond. The comment follows that there must be entire and continual dependence upon Christ and the Holy Spirit must not be grieved through (1) lack of surrender or (2) want of faith. One must be factual about these conditions'.

That he is counselling himself is apparent from what he goes on write. 'What does such surrender involve in regard to the present threatened schism? I conclude, a committal to the Holy Spirit of the matter: then deliberate maintained, believing prayer. This must be the creation of the Spirit. Thus condition (2) is also met'.

The reference to a threatened schism was probably to a church which, as will be later indicated, had complaints against the College. There may well have been a suggestion that other churches would also be influenced to withdraw from the Baptist Union. Clearly the Principal was deeply concerned.

An entry, undated but before 3 April, touched on another issue. It reads, 'Self-consciousness is a potent cause of loss of peace and joy. It is an integral part of the self-life. Flesh is that which refers everything to oneself. The interest in God and in others is the only cure. It just does not matter about one's feeling states, one's reputation, one's rebuffs, lack of recognition, etc'.

Whether anything specific lay behind those observations it is not possible to say. Certainly the next entry on 3 April is quite general in nature containing several ideas related to health.

'Strong concentration and then normal relaxation appears to be a good rule. The human will can then cooperate most effectively with the Divine Will. Consistent with this is a certain ease in the spiritual life. Labour must result in an habitual strainlessness which is restful and joyous. 'His soul shall dwell at ease'. Disease is dis-ease. The (mind and spirit) transfers its tensions to the body. It is not so much what sort of germ the fellah has but what sort of fellah the germ has'.

During the month he gave an 'inspiring address' on the Holy Spirit at Eastwood[924] and on 29 April he inducted Rev VN Willis, lately come from England, to the Cronulla pastorate.[925] Possibly it was also in April that he shared in a China Inland Mission prayer conference. His experience is reflected in yet another diary note. 'There seems to be three levels in prayer. The mystery of speaking to a God who dwells in the light unapproachable is ever present. Hebrews with its doctrine of the Holiest of all emphasises that. Then there is the matter-of-factness of telling the Lord one by one the things that are in our hearts. The China Inland Mission prayer conference at Gilbulla exemplified this.

'Then there is the intimately personal communion - of which 'the Communion of the Holy Ghost' speaks. The simple speech with Christ - even aloud - and imagining Him speaking to us is most helpful. There comes the restful consciousness that one has asked the Father for something, for example about John Thompson, and that He has the matter in hand. The above is proof of the growing inwardness of faith. The psychologist insists upon divisions in the life in terms of the Superego and the Id. Peace is harmony. The final harmony is achieved when the Divine through one's personal abandonment is one with the human spirit. Then there are no vocal minorities'.

At its meeting on 5 June the College Council decided to invite Mr JA Thompson of Melbourne to become 'a third tutor' on the College staff. As the above note suggests the Principal had been making this a specific matter of prayer. His restful confidence was justified when later in the year the invitation was accepted.

Two further unrelated observations appear in his diary at about this time. (1) 'One rises in anger against manifestations of the poison which self injects into the life, for example jealousy of the blessing of God in the ministry of another. However, that rising of anger is an encouraging mark of the Holy Spirit's Presence and work'. It would be interesting to know what gave rise to that comment but what is more important is its disclosure of spiritual sensitivity.

(2) Of quite a different mood is the other note, 'It is most restful to realise that we may lead a life pleasing to the Father'. To this, he added a quotation, 'God is easy to please but hard to satisfy'.

Near the beginning of his Principalship George Morling spoke to the Central Cumberland District Baptist Association on the subject of 'The Second Coming' and received rather muted response. In 1956, probably about this time, he addressed the Association's Annual Rally on the same subject. Unfortunately the response is not recorded.

On 9 May he 'delivered an inspiring address' at the Fellowship Rally of the Jubilee Annual Meetings of the Newcastle and Northern Districts Baptist Association.[926]

Then, it being the first term vacation of College, he was off to Canberra Church where from 13 to 20 May he conducted special services. A report on his visit said, 'The teaching mission conducted by Principal GH Morling was a unique experience in the history of our church ... All the services, both on Sunday and the week nights were well attended, and many people sought personal help in private interviews with the Principal. Our people have been helped and inspired by the masterful manner in which the Principal dealt with his subjects and encouraged by our fellowship with him, and were conscious of the presence of the Holy Spirit among us'.[926] It can be confidently suggested that no-one was more encouraged than the Principal himself for he longed to help others spiritually. One of his addresses was on 'Spiritual healing'. Evidently someone took it down in shorthand and sent him a typed copy of it. It is of especial interest because the subject held an increasing place in his thinking in subsequent years. It exemplified the balance that he often insisted must mark the presentation of Biblical truth. He began with an acknowledgement of the health problems that had troubled him through the years and then stated that he had never been as healthy as he was then. It was against this background that he made three assertions.

(1) Undoubtedly there is a ministry of healing within the Christian scheme of things.
(2) This fact does not justify the claim that God has undertaken to heal every case of sickness.
(3) There is an intimate connection between the life of the Spirit, our spirit, and physical health.

He was appointed to go to the Triennial Assembly Meetings of the Baptist Union of Australia in Hobart as NSW representative on the Education Board.[927] In the same issue it was noted that Dr John Drakeford, one of Morling's men, had been appointed Associate Professor of Psychology and Counselling at the Southwestern Baptist Seminary in Fort Worth, Texas.[928]

By what CS Lewis called 'the law of undulation' our 'highs' are often followed by 'lows'. Principal Morling was having a 'low' when he wrote on 23 June, 'There has been sensitiveness this week and the return of fears'. From time to time throughout his whole life these irrational fears plagued him. Now he wrote, 'The way out is threefold. Living with God's glory only in mind, which rules out the desire to please man. Then, as above (referring to an earlier entry in his diary), the personal relation of love to the Father must be maintained. Finally, it is good to be absorbed in work. This means in terms of Tersteegen: The true Christian life to which I find myself called by the mercy of God demands <u>a disciplined companionship</u> and <u>inner life with Him</u>. There must be added to the mystic(al) the evangelical; riches of grace to the riches of glory. The passiveness of contemplation must lead to strong activity within and without. Faith is active as well as sinking into God. We must do something about each successive situation'.

In connection with a commitment to speak at the Triennial Assembly an American preacher, Dr Oscar Johnson, visited the several Australian States. This is the background to the entry, 'Dr Oscar Johnson's visit has shown the need for more boldness in the service of Christ. *Parresia* always. Remember Mrs Johnson and the milkman'.

Ever concerned about his responsability to witness for Christ he was challenged by an account of Mrs Johnson's witness to her milkman. So he turned it into a prayer, 'Let me not fail Thee, O Lord Jesus, when Thou dost require me to speak, and let me be stronger in my appeal to the College men'.

On 30 June Rev EG Hockey 'The Grand Old Man' of the NSW Baptist ministry died. There appeared a 'choice *In Memoriam*' written by Principal GH Morling.[929] It was a warmly glowing tribute to one, whom the writer regarded with boundless affection and admiration.

In light of his later deep interest in the subject of healing, his diary entry of 11 July is interesting, 'Mary's (probably Mary Kramer who had given him some secretarial assistance) willingness to accept pain is inspiring. I remember her view about healing not sometimes being the best thing for us'.

The entry then reverts to a subject that had been touched on earlier. 'Faith as 'sinking into God' and allowing Him to come to us must always be balanced by 'faith as action'. We must ourselves come into the picture - God works all things <u>with</u> those who love Him'. We must first let God come to us but immediately take action with Him.

'The Kierkegaard doctrine of <u>inwardness</u> as the only reality has helped. This means abandoning the spectator attitude, coming into some concrete situation and committing ourselves. JG Mackay's experience recorded in the first chapter of '*God's Order*' illustrates this'. 'We can be spectators in reading books of devotion and even in prayer'.

He was referring to the well-known distinction that Mackay made between those who survey the road of life from a balcony in detached objectivity and those who see and experience it as committed travellers on that road.

Five days later, doubtless growing of introspection, he had two further notes. 'There is a <u>self-regarding</u> spiritual culture which is a spurious form of holiness'. He appended a quotation from Theodore Monod, 'In Christ: through the Spirit: <u>for the glory of God</u>. All else is nothing'. And then, 'it remains true - when faith begins anxiety ends, when anxiety begins faith ends'.

The nature of faith continued to preoccupy him and so on 21 July he wrote, 'I find in respect to the 'reckoning' of faith that (1) It must be very quiet – 'the sinking into God'. (2) It must be positive as well as negative. Being 'alive unto God' means alive to the Presence - as being 'alive unto the beauty of a sunny morning: alive in warm response to Him who comes to me: above all, alive to receive the communication of God's own life in Christ. There is also the 'aliveness' of 2 Cor 5.15'.

Clearly Principal attended a prayer meeting (perhaps for ministers) at Stanmore church on 31 July for next day he wrote, 'Helpful prayer at Stanmore yesterday makes one long for (1) power in reaching men for Christ - Neville Horn has been much blessed in these contacts, (2) power to impress myself more on the College students for Christ's sake'.

On 5 August one of his men, Rev Harry J Rowe, began his ministry at Central Church and it was the beloved Principal who inducted him.[930] It was the beginning of a significant ministry.

A diary entry of 9 August indicates experience of another kind of devotional method. He wrote, 'There is considerable help in placing oneself among the band of disciples in the days of Christ's flesh and assessing what one would or should have done in that setting. One can then transport oneself into the present setting of the exalted Christ who gives the enablement of the Holy Spirit'.

Sunday 12 August was a busy day because he was the preacher at Gladesville's Silver Jubilee in the morning[931] and at Carlton's Diamond Jubilee in the evening, where his subject was 'Christ never changes.[932] That day he wrote, 'Stanley Jones advocates a quiet receptivity instead of an anxious activity'.

He also made the general observation, 'In the death of self as a (matter of) practical living one must take the position that in respect to all matters involving self interest one does not deserve, one does not expect, one does not want; The Father will take care of such things as we need'.

In a further admonition to himself he wrote some days later, 'The deliberate determination to commit and then to trust and then the continuous practice of it will tend to create the habit of trusting in everything'.

John Thompson

The meeting of the College Council on 11 September had before it a letter from John Thompson signifying his acceptance of the invitation to join the College staff.[933] Advice of his acceptance must have arrived some days earlier for the Principal wrote on 5 September, 'A new era should begin in the history of the College. For myself I feel an urge to ask the Father for the spiritual gift of 'helps' and 'governments' - the 'ability to render loving service' and 'powers of organisation'. The former he certainly already possessed; it is doubtful whether the other was ever bestowed on him but, providentially, he was ably supported by those who had been given it in abundance.

The NSW Assembly meetings, held 13-21 September, were, as for several years past, dominated by the report and recommendations of the Faith and Life Commission which was carrying through a major restructuring of the Union. Principal Morling was a member of the Commission. He took some part in its presentation, seconding the acceptance of its statement on ordination, in whose preparation he had made a major contribution.[934]

In his Report he emphasised three points. One was the addition of a third staff member as from the end of the current year. A second was that the enlargement of College facilities was under serious review and the third related to steps that had been taken to enhance the practical/pastoral aspect of training.[935]

Arising out of the College session a motion seconded by the Principal requested the Executive of the Union to call the people of the churches to a prolonged period of prayer so that the needed but seemingly impossible extension of the College property might become possible'[936].

Subsequently the Executive appointed 28 November as the day for special prayer[937]. Though it required several years before its full implementation the new era was beginning to dawn.

On 3 November he dedicated the new manse of Central Baptist Church. The house was located at Roseville.[938]

A special meeting of the College Council held on 19 November was of considerable significance. On the motion of the Principal (following up a resolution of the Annual Assembly[939]) it resolved unanimously to recommend to the Union 'that the educational function of the College be enlarged'. This in time led to the establishment of the NSW Baptist Bible College and the introduction of new courses of study. It was envisaged that courses would be provided for deaconesses, directors of religious education, full-time church office secretaries, ministers' wives and students' fiancées. Principal Morling supported by Vice-Principal Wright moved that decision on the details be deferred until the next meeting but the Council had a mind to brook no delay. It was decided to plan for the introduction of all the suggested courses.

The other momentous decision of the meeting was to 'endeavour to seek a new and larger site for the Theological College in order to make provision for (the) new training function'. On this too the Principal was a little more cautious and put forward the amendment 'that the possibility of securing a new and large site be explored'. This also was unsuccessful. Indeed the Council decided to launch an appeal for £25,000 in order to finance the expansion.[940]

In an atmosphere of excited expectancy Graduation and Prize Giving was held on 22 November, with eleven students graduating.[941] Reporting the occasion Dr EH Watson, General Secretary of the Union, wrote, 'NSW has every reason to be proud of its Theological College... The exit students, in giving their testimony, emphasized again and again the contribution that life in the College has made to their spiritual experience. Principal Morling has done a magnificent piece of work over the years and we thank God for his leadership in both the scholastic and spiritual realms'.

Again the Principal was an advertised speaker at the Katoomba Christian Convention.[942]

1957
The feeling that the College was approaching a new era in its history was heightened when on 4 January, 1957, Mr JA Thompson, MA, MSc, BD, BEd, formerly Director of the Australian Institute of Archaeology, arrived from Melbourne to become the third lecturer on the staff of the College. In the evening a delighted Principal hosted a welcome to John Thompson and his wife, Marion.[943]

The next day he accompanied the President of the Union, Mr JC Mackay, to the Maitland Road Islington Church, to share in the public welcome to Rev EV Marks.[943] That same day the wife of his former student, Rev HE Evans, died. At the funeral service 'Principal GH Morling paid a beautiful tribute to Mrs Evans as a 'Minister's Wife'.[944]

His sensitive soul searching was again evident in two diary entries toward the end of the month. On 22 January he wrote 'The vacation is advanced midway. The usual inner fears, quite unreasonable in character have come. It is clearer to me that fears and worries are due to self-centredness. These positions come out of the thinking of these months.

1. That I should fix (my) thoughts on God Himself. There is constant danger that devotion might be self-regarding and minister to self-consciousness rather than to God-consciousness.
2. That inner strength follows in the wake of warm intimacy with Jesus Christ. I may try to live in a doctrine rather than in personal relations with Christ.
3. The matter of personal relations with the Holy Spirit is prominently before me. It seems to me that relations with the other members of the Godhead fail unless I have personal relations with the Holy Spirit. I must (i) abandon my inner life to Him as a whole, (ii) commit individual matters to Him, (iii) remember that He has at His disposal all the mighty powers of the Cross and Resurrection for the conquest of inbred sin and 'its grim reality', (iv) quietly, confidently trust Him for inner life and outward events'.

In similar vein, he wrote on Sunday, 27 January; 'I find that in any approach to God or in any correction of my inward state my first business is to give myself over to the Holy Spirit - else I am using self power instead of God's. If I seek to abide in Christ it is the I, the Me, the Mine that seeks to do it. The first step must be the humble adoring use of the Holy Spirit. So with Christ; the I is too weak to engender trust'.

Towards the end of January Dr WL Jarvis, a greatly honoured veteran evangelist and pastor left for an extensive preaching tour in the United States of America. His friend, George Morling, shared in the denominational farewell that he was given.[945]

Then on 4 February a day of prayer for metropolitan ministers was held at Dee Why. The Principal was the speaker.[946] In a letter dated 5 February he wrote to Rev John Ridley about a course in evangelism that he was trying to establish. He outlined what he proposed and requested his friend 'to help us in such a course'. Not wishing to place an undue burden on the frail evangelist he asked him to take one lecture a month. In closing he assured his friend that he was constantly in his affectionate prayerful thought'.

Later in the month he was not at Blàckheath to farewell Rev FG Smith from the pastorate but on 20 February he inducted him to his own former church at Pymble.[947]

The College Council met on 5 March and decided to purchase at least ten acres in the Parramatta-Blacktown area 'for a new College campus'. The Executive of the Union was to be informed of this decision. The very next day an advertisement appeared with the heading 'College Site Wanted'.[948] At a special meeting of the Council on 27 March Principal Morling moved 'that we recommend to the Executive of the Union that we proceed to purchase 'a block of land about a mile from Liverpool Station". However at yet another meeting of the Council on 9 April there was advice from the Executive that 'the approval of the Assembly would have to be sought before the purchase of the new site is made'.

In an article Principal Morling described the growth that was taking place in the Baptist Theological Colleges of Australia.[949] He spoke of Christ's training of the twelve disciples and then concluded, 'We may not make an artificial parallel of the ministry of a theological college and the ministry of the Son of God; but we may hold before ourselves the way of Jesus with His disciples as containing ideals which one may cherish. And there are times in a theological college when this same Lord is very near. I complete this article having first come from an inaugural College Communion Service and I know ... Pray God that from our college men may go forth to be convinced, forthright, devoted, enthusiastic heralds of the King'.

An old Blackheath friend, Mr FP Thompson, died on 9 March, and so often in such circumstances he was the one who brought comfort and inspiration at the funeral service.[950]

At the College Tea and Commencement at Central on 12 March, a more recent friend and colleague, Mr JA Thompson, was the speaker.[951] It was observed that the attendance was disappointing[952] but that scarcely diminished a growing sense of optimism concerning the future development of the College.

However, the sky was not entirely cloud-free
Two years previously for reasons not made fully public an incoming student had his course suspended by the Baptist Union Executive Committee for failure to attend on the opening day of College. The previous year, the same student had accused two ministers of doctrinal errors. On 23 February 1954 the Executive Committee informed the accused ministers that their replies were satisfactory. On 5 April 1954, the Applicants' Committtee advised the Executive Committee to withdraw the incoming students approval to enter College. But the Executive rejected this advice and, on 20 April 1954, approved the student for enrolment. On 23 May 1955, the student was suspended for twelve months by the College Council for 'failure to report at College on the date of commencement'.[953]

This sparked a running exchange between the church from which he came and the Executive Committee. This was not without distress to the Principal. The matter came to a head when the church announced a meeting at which charges would be brought against, among others, the Theological College.[954] At that meeting, held on 6 April 1957, a motion was presented that the church withdraw from the Baptist Union because of its alleged failure 'to rebuke modernism among our pastors' - 38% of those present voted not to remain in the Baptist Union; the motion was lost.[955]

When the Executive met on 21 May it appointed the President, General Secretary and Principal to investigate the matters which were of concern to the church and report back.[956] Morling reported that he had counseled a pastor accused of false teaching, and 'there did not appear to be grounds for strong action to be taken at this stage'.[957] However, in October, the pastor resigned from his church and from the Baptist ministry and took up secular employment.[958]

The whole episode must have been deeply hurtful to one as sensitive as George Morling. However, through it all he had the support of the Executive Committee which, in a letter to the church 'regarded the charges against the College and its Lecturers without justification'. The resignation of the pastor, one of the most able men who had trained under him from his church and the Baptist ministry saddened Morling. For several months the Principal sxought to counsel and help this man. He had flown some hundreds of miles to see him. When he spoke to him of 'the distress of heart and mind he was causing among our Baptist people' he was no doubt in part reflecting his own feelings. He had returned from the visit with a measure of hope but a subsequent letter to his young friend brought no reply. How the letter of resignation would have wounded and grieved him.

Life goes on
Early in April the Hurlstone Park Church had a 'Variety Mission'. On Wednesday 5 April the Principal was the teacher/preacher.[959] Always in demand at Epping he preached at its Church Anniversary in April. At the end of the month Chatswood Baptist held a series of convention meetings and who better to speak at them than 'our beloved Principal'.[960]

No sooner was the Chatswood commitment discharged than he and Vice-Principal Wright left for special meetings at Taree the first weekend in May[961] and doubtless at other northern centres.

Mr EJ Phillips, who had been President of the Baptist Union in 1928-29, died on 12 May. The Principal conducted the funeral in Central Church and 'paid a glowing and worthy tribute to the departed'.[962] There was no one quite like him for a funeral.

During July he was again much in demand as a church anniversary speaker. With new staff member John Thompson, and a team of students he preached at Stanmore's 56th Anniversary on 10 July.[963] He spoke on 13 July at the weekend-long celebrations of the reception of the Greenacre Gospel Mission, founded in 1929, into the Baptist Union as the Greenacre Baptist Church.[964] He preached at Leichhardt's on 21 July[965] and at Herne Bay's (now Riverwood) on 28 July.[966]

On the recommendation of its Executive, the College Council at its meeting of 6 August agreed unanimously to nominate the Principal for reappointment at the forthcoming Assembly. He was already approaching

66 years of age but it was thought that his health was sufficiently good to enable him to serve for another term.

When it was opened at the end of August the Punchbowl War Memorial Church was the pride of the denomination. Principal Morling was one of the speakers in a series of Commemorative Services.[967]

The 1957 Assembly Meetings were again largely preoccupied with the reconstruction of denominational organisation and life as recommended by the Faith and Life Commission. Moreover: there was a visiting preacher, Rev JH Deane, who returned from self-imposed exile in the land of the long white cloud to encourage NSW Baptists to 'Extend Faith's Frontiers Together'. Hence George Morling played no great part in the Assembly. He was 'declared elected' as Principal[968]; he had the satisfaction of presenting eleven candidates for ordination[969]; he prayed the 'prayer of dedication' as graduate Norris Brook was set aside for work at Cobar[970]; he joined in the congratulations extended to his friend Dr CJ Tinsley as he retired after 29 years as President of the College Council[971]; and was gladdened when the Assembly with great enthusiasm adopted a plan for the development and enlargement of the College program and for the obtaining of a new campus containing at least ten acres.[972]

A visit to preach at the 27th Anniversary of the South Carlton church on 13 October is recorded[973] but it is the only report of preaching during a period of about three months. On 16 November Mrs Ethel Mill, widow of the Rev JD Mill, died. George Morling conducted the funeral service in the Ashfield church and at the Northern Suburbs Cemetery. 'Principal Morling, in his beautiful tribute, said that Mrs Mill was 'in the noble tradition of womanly sanctification'. The combination of strength and beauty was truly to be seen in her Christlike character ... Mr Morling spoke of the beauty of gentleness. 'Mrs Mill was gentle and therefore so refined, and also so influential. The beauty of the Lord - love and holiness - was upon her. She had speech that ministered grace. Every remembrance of her is sweet'.[974]

He was again in the Ashfield Church a few days later on 21 November when he presented his colleague, Mr JA Thompson, for ordination and preached the charge to the newly ordained minister.[975]

In the same church a Students' Association Convention was held 25-29

November.[976] It included, on 28 November, the Graduation Service which attracted what was reckoned to be the largest ever attendance. The Principal was in high spirits. He told the gathering, 'I have never been as satisfied with things both inside and outside the College as I am now'.[977] A report of the occasion ran in part, 'The ministry of the College had been unmeasurably strengthened by the coming of Vice-Principal BG Wright eight years ago, and now a further advance of the same kind has taken place with the appointment of Rev John Thompson to the staff during the current year'.

Related to the wider plans for the College was the resolution made and the action now being taken to extend the scope of training and move to a more adequate site. 'We intend to provide training for young people who desire to prepare for the mission fields, or to serve Christ at home', the Principal said, addressing the many young people in the congregation. 'A subcommittee is examining prospective sites for the new College Campus. This project is estimated to cost at least a quarter of a million pounds. I expect that has taken your breath away', the Principal said, 'so it is a good time to sit down'.

He was obviously excited by the prospect of the new era that the College was entering.

The following night the Students' Convention came to a climax with the Principal as the preacher. He was nowhere more at home than in the atmosphere of a Convention meeting with its emphasis on a biblical doctrine of experienced holiness.

He was, therefore, happy when year's end found him once more one of the featured speakers at the Annual Convention at Belgrave Heights.[978]

1958

Back in 1951 George and Gladys Morling had been hosted by the Le Quesnes, eminent British Baptists, at their London home. In response to their Christmas greeting Mrs Le Quesne, by this time widowed, wrote at some length to them. They had kept the friendship in good repair, as was the case with a wide range of friends. 'I expect', Mrs Le Quesne commented, 'you still enjoy your home in the Blue Mountains'. They certainly did. Though they returned to it year after year they never tired of it or of the restful beauty of the mountains. However with Mrs

Morling's health declining the pattern was presently broken.

It may have been in part that for the same reason George Morling became less involved in activities outside the College. There is evidence, however, that he was seeking to devote more time to writing and had in mind the possibility of having another book published. His colleagues, Gilbert Wright and John Thompson, were increasingly exercising preaching and teaching roles in the churches.

On l March he presented a special candidate for ordination at a service held in the Punchbowl Church.[979,gg] As he had done on several previous occasions he preached at West Ryde's Anniversary on 9 March.[980] With the College Commencement Service, again at Central Church, on 11 March his 39th session as head of the College was officially under way.[981] He attended Epping's Silver Anniversary Reunion Dinner on 18 April but merely 'extended felicitations'.[982]

Much to his disappointment the Executive Committee Meeting of 18 March had before it a letter from one of Principal's men notifying his resignation from his church as he was entering secular employment and intended withdrawing from the ministry.[983,hh] The Principal and Home Work Superintendent had been appointed to interview him. At the meeting of 22 April they reported themselves satisfied with the reasons for the resignation.[984] However Principal Morling had such an exalted view of the ministerial role that every relinquishment of it disturbed him.

A sequel to the 'Quest'?
In a letter from Dr Leon Morris written on 4 April it is revealed that the Principal had been working on another book. It was probably to be a development of the theme of Christian serenity, a sequel to his *The Quest for Serenity*. The letter indicated that Dr Morris was returning a manuscript under separate cover. Of it he wrote:

'As I have re-read it and pondered it and prayed about it, I find I like it just as much as 1 did on a first hasty perusal. Indeed, I like it so much that I have changed my mind somewhat. I think that a short book along those lines has something to be said for it. You are conveying a good deal in a short space and I think that a Pathway book like this would be immensely valuable. When you were here I was wondering whether it might not be better to expand this into a much longer book. I would

---
[gg] The candidate was Pastor DM Cameron
[hh] The minister was Rev GS Tanner.

now think it advisable to complete it much on the present scale... There would be nothing to stop you going ahead on a longer work, perhaps with a more devotional flavour, afterwards. The one could lead into the other. I shall be very interested to hear what you decide'.

A further letter from Dr Leon Morris dated 3 May thanked him for his two letters, 'the first regarding your writing and the second inviting me to speak to your students in August'. The tenor of the first letter is indicated by Dr Morris' reply, 'I am glad that you are happy both to do the Pathway Book and then go on to something larger'.

In a letter to Dr Morris on 17 July he wrote, 'The present situation about my manuscript is this. I have completed in writing two more chapters and another chapter has been outlined in considerable detail. I have talked the thing out with John Thompson and it would seem to be a wise policy to let him see the manuscript at this end before it is sent on you. I am not finding the more precise task of writing easy, but I feel that the greater exactness needed for it is a very good discipline... I do want the work to be worthy so that it will be of some real service'.

In reply, Dr Morris expressed pleasure that the book was progressing and the wish that it might be speedily completed. That called forth another letter on 25 July saying, among other things, 'I trust I am not worrying you unduly about the slow progress of my manuscript but there have been real difficulties about limitation of time and strength and typing facilities, but I am working on steadily and by the time you come across I expect that the whole thing will be ready for your inspection and suggestions, after which there will be a fortnight's vacation in which revision can be made. I do hope that I shall be able to bring the thing to a conclusion very soon'.

Most unhappily that did not happen. As will become increasingly apparent George Morling was passing through trying experiences, the nature of which can only be surmised. There was unrest among many of the younger ministers and some of the most able were leaving the Baptist ministry. Almost inevitably the College would become a target for criticism and, if so, he would feel it keenly. Great changes were taking place in the structure and future direction of the College. While for the most part he welcomed these there were many adjustments to be made and at his stage of life that would not be easy. Probably the most important factor, however, was his increasing concern for his dear wife's failing health. This greatly preoccupied him.

Whether for these or other reasons, he was not able to bring the book to completion. More than a year later on 7 September, 1959, Dr Morris was to write, 'I am very sorry to hear of your continuing difficulties. I do not wonder that in the midst of them you have found it more than difficult to do any writing. It would be extraordinary had it been otherwise. As things are, I do not think we should ask you to forego the Pathway assignment ... I am very sure that I would like to see a book from you appear in this series. So I think the right thing is for you to go ahead as you are able. Please do not let the thought weigh you down. I would be very sorry indeed to add to your troubles. Just go on as you have opportunity and do not think of there being any target date. I think that if you work steadily at it, it should not be such a tremendously long time before you finish it. After all you have done quite a lot of work on it already'.

Despite these assurances and encouragements the book was not completed and the manuscript has not survived.

More preaching commitments
The first notice of his activity for several months was that Principal Morling preached at Wentworthville Church's 34th Anniversary[985].

On 28 June EW Watts, who during 1926-55 had been Secretary of the Granville Church, died. At his funeral the Principal, a long standing friend, said that Mr Watts was at home in three spheres; in the family circle, in the church fellowship and in the Lord's presence. 'We shall ever remember a quiet thoughtful large-hearted man, whose godly influence has been a large factor in the lives of many'.[986]

His old church at Pymble had not forgotten him and so on 13 July he preached at its 41st Anniversary.[987]

He was not present at the College Council on 12 August when, under the heading 'Plan of Advancement' a major reorganisation of the life of the College after an American model was put forward for later consideration. Among other things it envisaged the appointment of a President of the College to be the executive head of the College with a Principal or Dean to be responsible for the academic program. A discussion of the total scheme was deferred from meeting to meeting until after about eighteen months it was decided to take no further action 'at this stage'.

Central Church had him occupying its pulpit on 31 August.[988] On 6 September he officiated at the wedding of Rev JR Godwin at Hamilton.[989]

Able, because of his age, to be elected only for twelve months at a time, he was endorsed enthusiastically by Assembly as continuing his Principalship.[990] He was absent from Assembly, as guest speaker at Queensland Baptist Assembly.[991] His report noted that changes were taking place so that, for example, fourth year men might seek approval to marry. This was seen as part of a worldwide trend and, contrary to earlier thinking, was even seen to be distinctly beneficial for the study program of men. Speaking of the plans for advancement to be presented to the Assembly by the Council Secretary he wrote, 'We await the inauguration of the ambitious scheme with a degree of proper excitement. As the cords are lengthened we shall need to strengthen our stakes. We feel that the greater range of activities will entrench us still more deeply in the interest and prayers of the Church, which under Christ, we serve'.[992]

On 4 November he 'as a life-long friend 'spoke kindly at the funeral of Mrs ML Davis (*nee* Whale)'.[993]

The stakes were considerably strengthened when Rev AH Orr, who had been appointed Honorary Administrator of the College[994], promoted and directed a daring venture styled 'C' Day, held 17 November.[995] At the College Council on 25 November he was able to report that £22,000 had been given or promised. At this meeting the Council decided to purchase the present Herring Road site of the College (for £24,850). The minutes of the same meeting refer to Principal's new residence at Pennant Hills then in course of construction.

As the College session concluded great changes were in the air and confidence was running high. The Principal shared in the ordination of Rev George Dickman (a missionary bound for New Guinea) on 13 December in the Ashfield Church.[996]

1959
At an earlier time Principal's father had been the lay pastor of the Leura Church. The building was destroyed by bushfires and, perhaps unwisely, rebuilt.[997] It was fitting, however, that on its reopening Sunday the Principal should have been the morning preacher.

FW Winn, Pymble stalwart and former President of the Baptist Union, died on 11 January.[998] At the funeral service on 13 January George Morling, who had been his pastor and colleague, said, in paying tribute to him, 'the character of Mr Winn could well be summarised around the words, 'Loyalty', 'Sincerity' and 'Devotion'.[999]

Blackheath was yet once more the Morlings' vacation retreat. The Principal had again been appointed the Moderator of the church and on 25 February he chaired the Annual Church Business Meeting.[1000]

Soon, with exciting events waiting in the wings, another College session began and he was caught up in the regular pattern of College life. At the Commencement Service in Central on 10 March Rev John Morley, MA, one of the most able men to train under the Principal, was the preacher. He 'paid a graceful tribute to his Alma Mater and to its Principal then, and now, Rev GH Morling'. With the opening of its doors to others besides ministerial candidates, twenty men and women were welcomed to begin their various courses. A report of the Principal's remarks ran, 'Principal GH Morling drew attention to the great amount of prayer and planning that had led to this new occasion. Never, in all his long association with the College, had he known so much prayer and interest on the part of so many people, he said. 'There are key people from our churches already enrolled in all the new courses of training', the Principal stated. 'Already one young lady has enrolled for next year'.[1001]

'The Principal said that he believed that the Billy Graham Crusade (about to be held in Sydney) would thrust up many more young people who would want to prepare themselves for service for Jesus Christ'. 'One evidence of the blessing of God on the new program was that the site for the new College had now been secured and paid for'.

At the Chester Hill Church Anniversary on 22 March he preached a sermon that over the years helped many of his hearers[1002], 'How can we touch Jesus?'

Two days later at the College Council he mentioned the 'disorganisation' of College routine caused by the Billy Graham Crusade. Subsequently it was decided to end the first term early because of the demands made on students in the counselling and following-up of converts.[1003] A decision was also taken to sell the Ashfield property to the Social Service Department of the Presbyterian Church of NSW for £40,000. Of more directly personal interest was the indication that Principal and Mrs Morling had moved from the Ashfield premises to their own home in Pennant Hills[1004]. The President of the Council, Mr RE Walker, said that this 'marked an historical occasion in the life of the College. For more than 30 years the Principal had lived within the life of the College, often under very restricted accommodation conditions, and had carried the burden of administration for so long'. The Council expressed pleasure that the Principal now had the opportunity in the later years of his ministry of living privately while still continuing his work as Principal.

At this time Mrs Morling was beginning to encounter serious health problems. 'There was a gradual process of hardening of the arteries of the brain'[1005]. Elaine, who alone of the family was still living with her parents, held a responsible position and could not easily meet emergencies. It was, therefore, great relief and comfort that Dorothy and her husband Colin Goodman would now be neighbours and be available to help.

On 5 May George Searl, another ex-president of the Baptist Union, died. When, as a young minister, George Morling went to Dungog, he met his senior namesake and they become life-long friends. Mr Searl was living in Singleton when he died and the Principal conducted the funeral[1006] in the Singleton Methodist Church, there being no Baptist work in the area. On 23 May he spoke at the ordination of Rev IF Kilvert in North Canberra[1007].

A copy of a letter that the Principal wrote on 17 June has survived and is of such significance as showing both his influence and farsightedness that the main part of it should be noticed. It was addressed to Rev Tom Binks who had graduated only in 1956 and was serving in Western Australia.

'My dear Tom - Now that the Billy Graham Crusade is over we are returning to the normal routine of life. It has been in my mind for some time to write to you about one or two matters. First of all I want to say how interested I am in your appointment as Union Secretary ... Your attainment of such status is very pleasing to me and I want to say so in no ordinary way. You will have an opportunity of leadership of no ordinary kind and for it you will need much grace. However, the source of grace is well known to you ... Then I wanted to communicate with you about your prospective College. Both Mr Vose and Dr Gibson have been across here and had consultations. Mr Vose in particular came definitely to ask advice about the appointment of the first Principal. He had certain suggestions from the Subcommittee appointed by the Union. I have given long and careful thought to the matter. I went through all the names that were listed and came to the conclusion that none of them can be (seriously) considered. Some are not available and some in my opinion are not wholly suitable for a position which will so largely determine the future of Baptist work in your State. At the same time it has become a strong conviction with me that the Rev Noel Vose is the obvious man to be appointed the first Principal of the West Australian Baptist College. He knows the local situation through and through. He loves WA and is loved by your Baptist people. He has not only adequate intellectual and educational equipment but is also going overseas to gain new experience and culture. His comparative youth is a great advantage in my thinking because there will be many adaptations to make. The establishment of your College will be a very exacting task which an older man would perhaps find too exacting. Anyhow I thought I should write to you about the matter'.

Principal Morling went on to suggest that, though Western Australia would have to wait for Noel Vose to return from overseas study, Western Australia could continue to send men to NSW 'for the next year or two'. He drew his letter to a close with a diplomatic disclaimer, 'I know that I have no right to intervene in this matter but I know your situation so well and I know also the qualifications of possible appointees so well and I have such warm interest in you all that I do not think that a letter like this would be resented'.

It wasn't, and subsequently Noel Vose became Western Australian Baptists' George Morling. An article by Rev AC Maynard, one of the first men trained under Principal Morling, was prompted by the opening of the GH Morling Chapel of the NSW College and was entitled 'Morling's Men and the Western Australian Baptist College'[1008]. It began, 'When the story of the Western Australian Baptist Union is written, one chapter could be well called 'Morling's Men''. After outlining the contribution to Baptist theological education in WA by four Morling trained men, Foote, Ridden, Maynard and Gibson, it continued:

'GN Vose, destined to become first college principal, was the fifth 'Morling's Man'. West Australian by birth, he was sent to NSW to train under Principal Morling. Returning to the West, he became a member of the ministerial training board in 1956 and was chairman during 1958-59. When the committee of investigation concerning a Principal made its enquiries, Principal GH Morling wrote a strong letter recommending that Mr Vose should be considered for the position. This suggestion was enthusiastically accepted, and the 1959 Baptist Union Assembly appointed Mr Vose as Principal-Elect. Upon his return from studies in the United States, Dr GN Vose became Principal in 1963. He became Chairman of the College Council, and led the college forward to the opening of a esidential college in 1967. His Principalship was a tremendous force in Baptist life in the West'.

The article also noted the contribution made to the life of the college by Tom Binks, Michael Dennis and Keith Wilson, all of them 'Morling's Men' and the last-named Gladys Morling's nephew.

E.G. (Ted) Gibson

A meeting of the NSW College Council on 30 June decided to invite Dr EG Gibson, then Principal of the Perth Bible Institute, to join its staff as from 1 February 1960, with special responsibility for the new courses that had been introduced. Acceptance of the invitation was announced[1009], and was officially reported at the Council's meeting on 23 July. Just one week earlier Principal Morling wrote, 'My dear Ted, I had meant to write at once concerning your appointment. The matter of an additional member of our staff has been prayed and thought about for a long time. I have no doubt that the invitation and your acceptance of it are of God. I am very concerned, not only about the academic standard of the College, but even more about the evangelical tone of it. Our invitation to you had both these factors behind it. For myself, too, I need scarcely say there is also the satisfaction that we shall have one who lives warmly in our hearts. I confess to deep satisfaction concerning the whole matter'.

The end of the letter has its own special interest, 'We shall look forward to next year with keen anticipation. We are engaged on working out some details concerning it. It has become obvious that if I continue I shall have to do less teaching than I am doing now. The general idea seems to be that I should be something of the nature of a Principal-pastor and confine myself to Theology'.

His long period of service was starting to wind down but the next eighteen months would not see him unduly slackening pace.

That he had preached at Ryde Memorial Church and inducted its new deacons into office was noted but references to his preaching ministry in this period were few and far between.

At the College Council on 18 September the Principal was not present. It was reported that 'he was nominating for the Principalship for a further twelve months, but had indicated that while after that period he would still be prepared have a share in some lecturing program, because of increasing years and home circumstances he would be no longer able to occupy the position as Principal'. The minute adds 'The announcement was noted by Council members with regret that the years thus bring their changes'.

The Annual Assembly took notice of Principal's intention when it appointed him as Principal for a further year. The following report appeared[1010]

Assembly Recognises Principal Morling

Rev GH Morling will conclude his service as Principal of the Baptist Theological College of NSW next year. He will then have served as Principal for 40 years. The Annual Assembly of the Baptist Union NSW resolved 'That this Assembly, recognising that Rev GH Morling has now entered the final year of his long term as Principal of the Theological College, gives authority to the Executive Committee to commission a portrait in oils for hanging in the College'.

The cost of the portrait was to be met by individual subscription. Subsequently Mr Joshua Smith, a prominent Sydney artist, was commissioned to carry out the work.

On 4 October the Principal was able to relinquish his role of Moderator when he inducted Rev JR Godwin as Pastor of the Blackheath Church[1011]. An old acquaintance was renewed on 18 October as he shared in the opening of what he described as Granville's 'thrilling' new hall.

In a significant outreach the Principal led a team of six, made up of the College staff and Council members, to the Newcastle district on 13 November. There in the Hamilton Church they met 60 young people drawn from the coalfield's churches. Ministers of the District Association brought together those who had shown an interest in preparing for Christian service and were seeking guidance. Principal Morling's part was to indicate how the will of God can be discovered for one's life. Similar meetings had been held in Sydney. The College was expanding its operation[1012].

In the short term this expansion was helped by a letter that came before the College Council on 24 November. It was from the Union Secretary indicating that the company[ii] which owned the Sydney Bible Training Institute (SBTI) property in Strathfield had asked the Union to take control of it. The meeting decided to advise the Executive Committee that the College Council was willing to operate the SBTI under its auspices. Initially the women students of the Baptist College would be housed there and classes open to the public would be conducted on selected nights.

Nine men graduated at the service held in Ashfield Church on 26 November. It was noted that they were soon to be scattered 'to the ends of the earth', New Guinea, Africa, Western Australia and various country towns including Cobar and Broken Hill. Thus the Principal's influence spread. In his review of the year's work he said that he was thrilled to see the men grappling in their examination papers with the great evangelical themes. He was gratified that on the eve of his retirement he could sense that in the present student body there were leaders for the future and in the teaching staff there were men who would preserve the tradition of the College[1013].

The following evening 27 November, in the Ashfield Church, the Principal shared with Rev AH (Harry) Orr in the wedding of one of the graduands when Bruce Thornton married Velma Donaldson younger daughter of Rev and Mrs AC Donaldson. Mr Donaldson was one of the Principal's first students when classes were held in the Harris Street Church.

George and Gladys Morling 1959

[ii] The New South Wales Stewards' Company incorporated in 1942.

A letter written by one of his 'men' just two days later is of interest not only because of its testimony to the tradition that George Morling had established and the regard in which he was held but also for its hints of painful problems that might not otherwise have been suspected. The Principal had written the previous month to this graduate of much earlier years, though there is little to indicate why. The reply came addressed to 'My Dear Friend'. After a warm acknowledgement of the Principal's letter it went on, 'It is from your inspiration - and I hope that this is more than immature hero-worship - that my poor ministry has derived such impetus as it has done. You will never know just how <u>very</u> much some of us fellows looked up to you (and still do). Yes, there has been suffering indeed; some kinds that God alone is aware of, besides ourselves, the frustrations, disappointments and heartbreaks caused often by those we trusted most. In the case of my own experience, I would say that I <u>did</u> know a little of what you yourself have been through - enough to break lesser spirits than those of yourself and your dear wife. Some of us had been given discernment we could not ever voice, and prayed for you the more because of it. It is not too much to say that ... you as Principal have deftly moulded a pattern of spiritual culture which, unknowingly, has been adopted (without acknowledgement - much of it) into that pattern of upsurge which lifted our Eastern Churches to such efforts between 1936 and 1956. Still <u>much</u> is lacking. But once again I must acknowledge, on my part, the unmistakeable 'Morling touch' which has given NSW a place unique in the history of Australian Baptist evangelism … Once again, thank you with all my heart for the priceless tradition of utterly dependable and devotional and scientific scholarship with which you set us fellows up upon the track. Our only shame is that we do not make better use of it all. If, like me, you feel that gratitude is wealth, your westering sun will be all gold just now - aglow with tributes from grateful and unstinting men whose lives you have enriched'.

Almost as heart-warming was a letter written about a week later by one of the men who had just graduated. It was in the first place an outpouring of gratitude for all that Principal's ministry in the College had meant to him. The writer then proceeded to set an agenda for Principal Morling's retirement. 'It is my humble opinion, Principal, that, as you face the time when you shall retire from the position as Principal of the College, you ought to give a great deal of time to writing'. What he had mind was that Principal's teaching on the Holy Spirit and on the work of Christ, for example, should be made available for a wider circle.

However, he was most concerned that he should write a really worthwhile book on Believers' Baptism. 'I believe', he wrote, 'a large book written by a truly great scholar should come from the Baptists on this issue. And in my opinion you are the only man who can do this'.

The Principal doubtless had a more modest view of his own abilities than did his deeply grateful student but he too cherished the hope that he might be able to have a wider ministry through writing. Unhappily many factors would conspire largely to frustrate his desire.

However, there were encouragements. With Christmas approaching Rev Phil Hayes, then at the Caringbah Church, wrote:

'Dear Principal and Mrs Morling,
You have had a long, happy pilgrimage together and I pray that 1960 will be the greatest year of them all, and during the Christmas season may the Lord Jesus be wonderfully precious. I may not see much of you next year, as we leave on our long tour to Rio. It's wonderful to think that the no-hopers of the College are the two appointed by the Baptist Union of Australia to conduct the tour and be Australia's official delegates. Well, Principal, I hope this gives you a little satisfaction to know your labour and patience has not been hopeless'.

Death cast a shadow over the end of the year. On 8 December Mrs C Constable, wife of the Blackheath secretary, died and the Principal, who for so long had been involved in the life of the Blackheath church, shared in the funeral service.

Away in New Zealand on 21 December Blackheath's former pastor and Principal's dear friend and former colleague, John Deane, was killed when apparently he suffered a blackout at the wheel of his car. He was about to leave for Australia to speak at the Belgrave Heights Convention. A daughter and grandson died instantly, his wife was seriously injured while another grandchild escaped without injury.

1960

A Memorial Service was held in the Central Church on 6 January. Principal Morling was the occasional speaker. John Deane was a man of rare quality and his friend's warm and insightful tribute was worthy of him. The account of the service[1014] included a summary of it. Some extracts from that summary reveal its character.

'It was simple truth to say that we loved and revered John Deane. In the presence of God we testify that we were enriched by him and we are thankful to God that he came our way ... John Deane was a remarkable man, truly distinguished in character and service. There were harmonised in his unique personality complementary qualities not commonly seen in combination'.

In some detail Principal Morling presented two aspects of the contrasted qualities of his friend (1) He was strong - but warm and kindly. (2) He was a mystic - but a man of affairs.

So began one of the most crowded and official years of the Principal's busy life.It must be said, however, that colleagues and the College Council sought to ease his load. On the basis of a recommendation in the Tutors' Committee Report the College Council on 2 February determined the following program for him;

(1) To take evening classes at SBTI.
(2) To take evening classes and interviews for theological and non-theological students at both Ashfield and Strathfield.
(3) As compensation his lectures on Tuesday and Thursday not to start until mid-morning.
(4) If possible, Friday to be free for counseling and interviews.

Doubtless he was grateful for the consideration shown to him but he could not but be aware that the reins he had held so long and so well had now slipped from his grasp and he was to some extent a pillion rider. The Tutors' Committee and his good friend, the Administrator, Rev AH Orr, were now in effective control of the day-to-day activities of the College.

The evening public classes of the SBTI began on 25 February[1015]. Principal Morling began a series of studies on the Epistle to the Ephesians, perhaps his best-loved book of the Bible.

One of Principal's men, Rev Basil Brown, was on the MV Fairsea returning from England. On 27 February he wrote to his former teacher giving details of his experiences while travelling. What prompted the letter was indicated in its opening paragraph, 'Before leaving London I paid a visit one Sunday to Westminster Chapel and afterwards went to the vestry to meet Dr Martyn Lloyd Jones. On learning that I was from the Baptist College in Victoria he immediately asked after you. He remembered conversations he had with you when you were in London'. That had been almost ten years previously.

During that visit to London George and Gladys Morling had deeply impressed many and made lasting friends. Two of the latter were a prominent senior Baptist minister, Rev Sydney Morris and his wife Winifred. For some years Sydney Morris wrote a regular column, 'Our London Letter', for *The Australian Baptist*. He and George Morling kept up a correspondence through the years. Some of the letters from England have survived and reveal a very warm relationship. Back in August 1958, Sydney Morris, who would have been ten to fifteen years older than his friend, had written:

'My dear George, ... We are delighted to receive yours of July 10 with all the family news. Do give our love to Gladys and tell her there is still a place in our hearts and a welcome in our home if, and when, she can bring you over ... Now good-bye George. Our warm love to you. Of our many visitors none left such a lasting impression as your dear self. Always affectionately ...'.

A letter dated 20 January 1960 was headed 'Our very dear George'. It was in response to a letter written just before Christmas, full of frank, friendly talk. He said of his contributions to *The Australian Baptist*, 'I enjoy writing and while avoiding being provocative yet I do try to slip in a para here and there in order to try to stimulate thought. So far Prior (Rev AC, the Editor) has given me freedom'.

After news and comments on the British Baptist scene he finished with a paragraph which he knew would have disturbed many Australian Baptists. He had spoken of 'unhealthy rivalry between the Baptist Union and the Baptist Missionary Society in Britain' and then added, 'Church Union generally is a difficult problem but there is a growingly better spirit. Will it shock you when I predict that some closer working must come about, considering the forces alive in the world. The strength of Islam and other religions and the mass of anti-Christian Communism. It seems to me that - long after we have gone - there will come about a twofold unity (1) that of all Evangelicals in all the Churches and (2) that of the Sacerdotals - for want of a better name, then - again at a much more distant date - a Unity of all the Church, Western, Eastern – and each church seeing more clearly its own imperfections and seeing also what other churches can contribute. Through <u>such</u> a Church Jesus shall Reign'.

Then playfully, 'Now come over by air plane and rebuke me on the spot. Very much love'.

Dated 25 February there came a letter from another friend made on the occasion of the London visit, Mrs FEE Le Quesne. It came in response to a letter from the Principal telling of a visit of Mrs Le Quesne's son, Laurence, to the Morling family. Laurence was in Australia doing a three year stint of teaching at the University of Tasmania and had made a trip to Sydney. Subsequently he too had written to his mother and made reference to Gladys Morling. Mrs Le Quesne commented, 'You have my deepest sympathy. I remember her gracious and sweet personality vividly, which makes all the harder to picture the change. I am sure that you are right to retire, and I hope a quieter life will help your own health and in a new way bring you inward peace and happiness in the deep things of life'.

After a full account of the family and church affairs the letter concluded, 'With very affectionate greetings to you both. Yours gratefully'.

And that was not the only letter that George Morling had written. On 31 March Sydney Morris wrote, 'Our very dear George, We both were greatly touched by your kindness in writing so early and so fully *re* our beloved Tinsley. We were able to picture the scene at the remarkable funeral, and since your letter came in Allan and Joyce (*sic*) have called on us bringing photos of the service. What wonderful times are these! ... My heart is sad at the loss of so valued a friend. By frequent correspondence I have learned to know and to love him. Next to your dear self he meant more to us than anyone else in Australia. I too sensed a mellowing and a broadening of his outlook so that he was able to put up with even my heresies'.

'I sometimes wonder that Prior prints all I write though I do try not to be unduly provocative. Our hearts go out to you, dear man. You have a heavy load and while in our prayers together we try to bear your burden yet the fact remains that every man must bear his own burden largely alone - sustained by God's unfailing love and grace. We do so wish that when College duties cease you may be able to come over for a few weeks. Winifred and I would be just delighted for you once more to sit in our room and look out on a little London garden, already showing signs of spring ... My impulse now is to comment on the working of your own mind as revealed in your two recent letters. I must not just now but will write again, DV, later'.

There followed a response to comments by George Morling on the Roman Catholic Church and some remarks on books, and then, 'Now give our love to Mrs Morling and believe me Winifred – not Mrs Morris please – joins me in deep and warm affection for your dear self. As ever'.

That closing note was echoed in a further letter of 20 April:

'George, our very dear friend, a lovely spring day. Our little garden sparkles in the sunshine and everywhere, for eyes that can see, are signs that the Lord God still walks in His garden. How lovely it would be were you here!'

Plans to holiday in Switzerland had had to be abandoned because Mrs Morris was still suffering the effects of a motor accident some time previously. 'So, we shall take some short day trips to the countryside and spend a quiet delightful time - in each other's company - and what better? I must add, however. that it would be better, were you here! We eagerly scan *The Australian Baptist* for every reference to you. All the pages on Evolution [jj] - which I never read - are as nothing as compared with a brief para of news *re* your dear self ... Winifred unites in warm love both to your dear self and to Mrs Morling. Please tell her that she is also often in our prayerful thought - and so is her dear husband - in his many and varied duties! Tell Mrs Morling that she can make the crossing to London in a few days and that her room will be ready here for her ... Much love, as ever'. It was a rare and beautiful friendship.

Writing on 8 March Rev DC Mill, newly appointed by the Ministers' Fraternal as organiser of a function to honour the Principal and Mrs Morling, informed them of the desire of the ministers and their wives to express affection for them. He then asked the Principal if he would please reserve the evening of Tuesday, 13 September, for the occasion.

On the evening of 8 March the College Commencement Service was

----

[jj] A series in TAB at the same time by Dr WA Criswell, pastor of First Baptist Church, Dallas, Texas, USA.

held as ever in the Central Church[1016]. For George Morling it was a year of closing doors. This was his last Commencement as Principal. There was no looking back, however. The presence of Dr EG Gibson, the new fourth member of staff, represented the developments that were taking place, as did the large intake of new students. Appropriately Dr Gibson gave the address.

There was a further development when on 16 March a Ministers' Wives Course was commenced. The series began with a Communion Service conducted by the Principal[1017].

With the death of Dr CJ Tinsley on 18 March Australian Baptists lost one of their most outstanding leaders[1018] and the Principal, a close friend. At the funeral service in the overflowing Stanmore Church, the oration was given by Rev JG Ridley[1019] but George Morling also added greatly to the impressiveness of the occasion. Son, Rev Allan Tinsley, and his wife, Joy, were overseas. Allan wrote to the Principal, 'From all accounts we have received the funeral service must have been most fitting and very triumphant, and for that, I gather, you were largely responsible. May the gracious Lord reward you indeed for your love and kindness. Your letter will be retained with its valued insight into the last hours of Dad's life'.

The winds of change were certainly blowing at the College. At the College Council on 11 April Rev JA Thompson was granted leave of absence to pursue research studies at Cambridge University[1020]. He would leave in August and be away for three years, returning with the degree of Doctor of Philosophy. The Principal was delighted that his colleague should have this opportunity, the more so because he remembered his own frustrated desire to do higher studies.

Perhaps he was too much of a pastor to his men to have had time to concentrate on academic scholarship. Rev Malcolm McCullough had been one of his earlier students and was now pastor of a Victorian church. Hearing that his son had been married the Principal wrote expressing his pleasure and extending good wishes. A reply, dated 19 April, said, 'My dear Principal, Your kindness in writing is much appreciated; such a gesture of interest and regard deserved an earlier answer'.

After family and personal news the letter concluded, 'The years have passed and soon your retirement will be effective. Basil (Brown) and I plan to be at any official function which will mark the time. We would delight to do you honour. Your ministry has been magnificent; we rejoice in our opportunity of having shared the blessing. The years are closing in upon us, and about us is the glow and glory of the gloaming. Those of us coming a little way behind are well sited to fully appreciate how wonderfully it rests upon you'.

There was a postscript. 'Should Mrs Morling's health allow her to recall me please convey my sincere regards, and to other members of the family who might remember me. Trevor's success is pleasing to us all'.

On 17 April 1960, GHM was a speaker at a Second Coming Convention at Petersham Baptist Church[1021.] *The Australian Baptist* carried a brief article by the Principal on 'The Theology of Giving'[1022].

In keeping with the College's new emphasis on training men and women for various ministries a Missionary Convention was held on 30 April at the Strathfield property (Wynola). The Principal, assisted by Dr Gibson, organised the Convention. He also chaired its final session[1023].

The Quest for Serenity was still in demand. He had autographed a copy for 'his old friend' Dr AT (Bert) Whale, and sent it to him. On 4 May he wrote, 'My dear Bert, Thank you for your kind letter about *The Quest for Serenity*. I am thankful if the little book has had a ministry. I fear that there is so much strain and stress in these modern days that we all need the 'peaceable habitations, the sure dwelling places, the quiet resting places' which are promised us. You find, with me, that old age with all its disabilities has its rich compensations. One deals more directly with God Himself and finds, in so doing, relief from one's own deficiencies and failures. One learns something of what it is to delight oneself in the Lord, to rejoice in Christ. So we go as led on by the Good Shepherd until we dwell in the house of the Lord forever. Yours as warmly as ever, George'.

After a break of more than three years, on 21 May George Morling turned again to his diary. The first entry indicates a reason for the resumption. He wrote, 'Distressed about withdrawal of men from the ministry. Inspired with the need of waiting only upon God (Ps 62), with taking hold of a situation (Is 63:12?), with taking hold of God's strength (Is 27:5), with the need of pestering myself to take hold of God (Is 64:7). So the Daily Light, 2 Cor 12:9f'[1024].

For a variety of reasons in 1959 and 1960 nine men left the ranks of accredited Baptist ministers and for some of them in particular Principal Morling had entertained great expectations. An article by Mr FE Peffer suggested that the fault lay with the training of ministers[1025]. Morling's students replied thus – 'We regret that such an article ... should appear in the final year of Principal Morling's ministry ... we desire to express our real appreciation of the work done on our behalf by the Principal and his staff'[1026].

Having broken the ice he made several further entries in his diary.
22 May. 'Have been directed to Ps 73:23 ff. 'I am continually with Thee ... whom have I in heaven but Thee?' Evelyn Underhill says this is the highest expression of mysticism in the Psalms'.

23 May. 'I still feel the need of more active participation in the spiritual life whose source is always Christ. There must be energy - not the energy of the self - not the energy of the self with Divine assistance - but the energy of the personality wholly possessed by (God) because surrendered to the Holy Spirit. I feel, in particular, the need of effort of this kind in mental control, that concentrating first 'on the Holy Spirit' as the Revealer of the Lord Jesus I should steadily contemplate Christ in accordance with 2 Cor 3:17-18. This was Henry Drummond's special text.
There is a glory of the blessed life.
There is a glory of the sacrificial death
There is a glory of the risen, ascended life
There is a glory of the Coming.

The contemplation of each in turn and in detail within each needs mental effort and brings transformation into the same image'.
24 May. 'Today I have to keep on in spite of physical and mental tiredness. Paul must have done this. 'In weariness oft'. There is a time
1. To practise a scriptural quietness. As Thomas Chalmers and Hudson Taylor. 'Not too tired to trust'.
2. To be careful not to let go in purpose .
3. To learn that when we are weak then we are strong because of felt dependence on Christ. So 2 Cor 12. Blaiklock in his *Acts* thinks Paul's thorn was malaria that made him physically tired'.
26 May. 'I am impressed with 'that' in the words 'that the power of Christ may rest upon me' - the reference is to the Shekinah in the Tent of Meeting. 'The power' is the glory of the indwelling Christ'.

30 May. 'In the Daily Light reading (apparently the evening of 7 September) the fact of God being mindful and visiting us in our insignificance is a Divine message. 'I am poor and needy yet the Lord thinketh on me' Ps 40:17.

A further indication that in the midst of his own burdens and responsibilities he made time to minister to others in their troubles came in a letter dated 26 May. It was from Mr AC Joyce, CBE, Commonwealth Auditor General and former President of the NSW Baptist Union.

'Dear Mr. Morling, I do appreciate your kindness in writing to me at this time of sorrow. I found your kindly message very comforting, and I tender to you my heartfelt thanks. We do miss our loved one very sorely, but I thank God for His goodness in giving her to me for over 50 years. She was certainly one of God's good women ... I thank you for your kindly gesture of friendship. Life would be very poor indeed without human friendship and I agree with you that we have too little time to cultivate these friendships which mean so much to us ... I am sorry to hear that Mrs Morling is not in good health and it will be a comfort to you both to know that if and when you retire from active work in the College you will be able to devote more time to her in her declining years. We all thank God for the wonderful gracious ministry you have exercised in the College and throughout our Denomination. You have indeed earned a rest but I am sure that you will continue to serve the Denomination for a long time to come'.

A letter from the Overseas Christian Fellowship written on 28 May served as a reminder of a wider ministry exercised by Principal Morling. It thanked him for giving so freely of his time to have fellowship with them. 'We have received a tremendous spiritual challenge from your message on 'the witness of the Holy Spirit' and have obtained a fuller understanding from the Word of God'. It was a tribute to him that the letter invited him to join them in the fellowship whenever he was free to do so.

Rev DF Crowhurst commenced a ministry at Lakemba Church on 5 June and the greatly loved Principal was there to induct him[1027]. Later in that week on 11 June he had his first sitting for Joshua Smith as he began his first sketches preparatory to painting a portrait of the Principal[1028]. There were many such sittings before the work was finished.

Subsequently in speaking of contemplation as an element of spiritual culture he insisted on the necessity of a prolonged gazing at God if He was to be spiritually perceived with any degree of truth. In illustrating this necessity he recalled the frequency with which Joshua Smith would lift his eyes from his work to look at him. Then one day he said somewhat surprisingly, 'I have seen you for the first time, this morning'. He had glimpsed some aspect of his subject that provided a key to a portrait of him that was more than a mere likeness. As a result he scrapped the work that had taken untold hours and began again but this time with conviction and confidence.

The College Council of 28 June had before it a letter from the Secretary of the Union advising that the Executive approved of a Testimonial Fund for Principal Morling and that it felt that the College Graduation Service in 1960 would offer the best opportunity for the presentation of this testimonial. Accepting this, the Council decided that the service should be held in the Central Church rather than at Ashfield, the date should be 26 November and that the Principal should be the speaker instead of the then customary speeches by all the graduating students. Because of illness the Principal was not present at that meeting.

Informed of this the Students' Association wrote to both the Executive Committee of the Union and the College Council asking for the arrangements to be reconsidered. The students' view in relation to Principal's farewell was that a combined function 'may well appear a lack of courtesy to Principal Morling, who, after 40 years of fine service, is surely worthy of a public farewell in which the whole program is devoted that end'.

As a result of these representations the Executive Committee decided to have a separate function for the Testimonial, and advice of this was received by the College Council at its meeting on 26 July. The date was at first set on 26 November, two days after the Graduation. Later, on the recommendation of the College Council, it was changed to 2 December[1029].

Starting at the end of June and running through July several entries appear in the Principal's diary.
27 June - 'In weariness I must wait for the coming of the Lord Jesus. I am never too tired to wait expectantly for His coming. Ps 116:7. 'Return unto thy rest' helpful'.

28 June – 'The practical and the mystical associated. 'He that hath my commandments and keepeth them ... I will (love him and) manifest (myself) unto him'. John 14:21'.

2 July – 'It occurred to me this morning with the sun shining that one should not always be 'religious' in prayer but come to God in a bright, natural manner. Surely this pleases Him who is the God of nature'.

11 July – 'I see that one may consider the impersonal doctrine or hymn more than the Divine Person. One may think of 'abiding' more than (of) Him in whom we abide, about 'resting' more than 'in Thee' who is the centre of rest'.

18 July - These have been days of weariness. The thought came last night that if Christ comes to us in the Spirit then life in the spirit should be as restful and intimate and warm as was life for the disciples with Christ. Compare the 'with' and 'in' of John 14:17'.

24 July – 'What I have learned of the Christian life seems to be summed up thus, as I have lived in it this past week:

1. God comes to me before I come to Him. It is He who enables my response.
2. This means that He desires to help me more than I desire to be helped.
3. This Divine approach is through the Holy Spirit - within.
4. The Divine help is given in Christ with whom the Holy Spirit unites me.
5. I must act fully with the Holy Spirit as He works in me and through me'.

25 July (should be 27?) – 'To the foregoing must be added the necessity of <u>trust</u> in everything. Last night as the College Council drew to a close the need for a much higher spiritual ambition with which to enter the new phase of my life next year became evident'.

The Principal preached at Blacktown Church 31st anniversary on 24 July.[1030] a letter from Grace and Owen Thomas, friends of earlier days, expressed disappointment that they were not able to be present because of the latter's ill-health. They had heard, they wrote, of the times of blessing at the service. There was also an expression of concern about Mrs Morling's health.

He preached on 7 August at the Anniversary of the Riverwood Church[1031] where one of his students was pastor and at Mortdale's 55th Anniversary on 14 August.[1032] Mr RE Walker, President of the College Council, was a member of the Mortdale Church and its pastor, Rev JC Campbell was also a member of the College Council and would subsequently be its President and for a period its Acting-Principal. George Morling had a special affinity with both of these men.

In between these preaching engagements he presided on 9 August at an informal function at College to farewell Rev JA Thompson as he left with Mrs Thompson for overseas. Speaking in what was described as 'his inimitable style' he indicated how much the College would gain from the advanced studies that Mr Thompson would do at Cambridge.[1033] It may be commented that many of Principal's students didn't find his style at all inimitable. In fact some were almost perfect mimics of it.

In *The Australian Baptist*[1034] there was a brief article by Principal Morling, 'The Call to College Training'. His starting point was an earnest remark made to Frances Ridley Havergal as girl by an aunt, 'Frances, God is getting something ready for you if you will get ready for it'. In the light of the new opportunities for specialized training offered by the College he challenged young people to get ready for what God had in mind for them.

On 26 August, Rev John G Ridley, who had written a biography of the late Dr CJ Tinsley, wrote, 'My dear George, Thank you, indeed, for your kind and gracious foreword for 'CJ Tinsley of Stanmore'. I appreciate your fellowship in this service for the glory of God and in memory of our dear old friend. As ever you have written with grace and unction'.

The writer went on to express appreciation of the Principal's life and service. 'What a wonderful record of royal service you can look back upon. I thank God for your holy influence upon my own life and your heavenly imprint upon the ministry of the Baptist Union of New South Wales. Even beyond that you have touched the pulse of the Christian Church in Australia by your wide Convention witness'.

During August he attended a staff conference of Baptist theological teachers in Melbourne. He reported to the College Council on 30 August the trend towards a requirement of matriculation for entry to ministerial training and also on an emphasis that was being placed on postgraduate work. At the same meeting it was decided to invite Rev NP Andersen to become Secretary of the Council from the Assembly Meetings and Dean of the College from the beginning of 1961. The old order was yielding place to new.

Change, however needful, is often painful and the Principal was finding it so. This is seen in a brief resumption of diary entries at this time.

1 September – 'In these difficult days there must be positive action rising above tiredness to abide in Christ - all fears and resentments and the like have their source in the self-life which in faith and surrender must be put under the Blood. Strength and peace come from the Blessed Union'.

2 September – 'There has been distress about College affairs - the new buildings - utilitarian rather than architecturally creative; the dispute about the Principalship. *Daily Light* for the day helps. 'The trying of your faith worketh patience'".

3rd September – 'A good text: 'He maketh me to lie down ...' also I 'Rest in the Lord'. (Both passages are from *Daily Light* for the day.) The life of simple faith. The College Principalship - prayer that bitterness may be eliminated'.

It was not an easy time for George Morling. Whatever thoughts he had about his successor he did not commit them to writing. In a letter from America dated 5 September Rev Noel Vose, Principal-Elect of the Western Australian College wrote, 'We await the outcome of the NSW Assembly with no little trepidation'. After indicating his preference for a successor to Principal Morling he proceeded to say, 'I'm sure he is the man to guide the College through these next few difficult years'. Possibly he was reflecting the Principal's own thoughts. Two candidates were nominated for Principal – Dr EG Gibson and Dr E Roberts-Thomson, the latter being elected by Assembly on 15 September.[1035]

Earlier in the letter Noel Vose had written, 'By the time this letter reaches you, your long span of years as Principal of the NSW College will be almost at an end. But not your work: you have many sons. And I do hope that the freedom from administrative cares will enable you to spend more time in writing. We look forward to your work on the Holy Spirit with keenest anticipation; as well as something more along the line of your first book'. In that hope many shared but it was not to be fulfilled.

His sister Ethel wrote to him from Queensland on 7 September. After passing on family news she spoke of his situation – 'It is getting near the end of the year and I know how weary you get at that time. And when I think at the end of the year you retire as Principal of the College I feel quite sad because I know it is going to be a big break for you. But you and I know God does our planning, and when one door closes for us another opens, and that is what it will be for you. George, we don't often see each other but believe me I don't forget you in my prayers: and I am so proud that a brother of mine was able to do such a mighty service for God over all these years, and I know whatever is ahead for you the help will be there for you to carry you through'. There was an almost prophetic element in what she wrote. Other doors opened and help was wonderfully given, though the way was often hard almost beyond endurance.

On 9-11 September the Principal participated in the opening of new buildings at Pymble. The local State Member of Parliament, Mr Stuart Fraser, said the new structure was an 'adornment of the Pacific Highway'. It was more than that, the Principal said, it was also a witnesss.[1036] His hope was that the very building would commend Jesus Christ to travellers on the Highway. GHM opened the new Sunday School hall.

An old friend that he met at Pymble wrote to him on 12 September, 'Dear George - My pleasure of meeting and talking with you on Saturday was marred by the last few words you said to me. It made me quite sad to know of your wife's condition. I will remember you always in my prayers. Thank you for the very beautiful and helpful book you wrote. I treasure it'.

All the special occasions associated with his approaching retirement were shadowed by his wife's declining health.

'MINISTERS HONOUR PRINCIPAL MORLING'

was a heading in *The Australian Baptist*.[1037] The Editor's report of the event is splendid and is here reproduced in full:

> A gathering unique in the history of Baptists of NSW was held in the Memorial Hall, Hurlstone Park, on Tuesday, September 13, when 206 ministers and wives met to salute and felicitate Rev GH Morling on the eve of his retirement from the position of Principal of the Baptist Theological College of New South Wales. The occasion was organised by the Ministers' Fraternal and presided over by its President, Rev Ron Rogers. Other recognitions on a denominational level will take place later.
>
> **FORTY YEARS**
> Principal Morling, who will retire at the end of 1960, will then

have concluded 40 years as Principal of the College. Almost all of the ministers present were men who had graduated during the term of the Principal's leadership..

Two men, Rev M McCullough and Rev Clive Smith, came from Melbourne to attend the function. Graduates in all States of the Commonwealth and on the Australian Baptist Mission Fields in India, Pakistan and New Guinea sent greetings and written tributes. Rev FT Smith wrote on behalf of the Queensland graduates; Rev TJ Cardwell for those in South Australia; Rev Tom Binks for the West Australians; Rev Murray Ling from Tasmania.

For the missionary graduates, Rev Doug Ison sent a message from India-Pakistan and Rev Ken Osborne from New Guinea.

Dr WL Jarvis cabled from Arizona, USA.

The function commenced with a banquet at 6.30 pm. It was planned to conclude at 9 pm but with so many preachers making speeches, the program got riotously out of hand and concluded at 11 pm.

CONTEMPORARIES
Rev VJ White had been chosen to speak on behalf of the Principal's contemporaries. Of these, he said, only the Principal and he remained in the NSW Baptist ministry. He recalled the chain of the Principal's influence stretching down to that moment.

FOR THE 'TWENTIES'
Rev E Clatworthy was the spokesman for the first group of students to be trained under Mr Morling's Principalship. In a characteristic speech in which ebullient humour and deep appreciation and spiritual conviction mingled not incongruously, Mr Clatworthy recalled incidents both humorous and holy. Principal had not changed in 40 years, he said. There were still the same mannerisms; he still told the same jokes - every class of students had laughed at them. He still took the same pride in his students. Every class was still 'the best year we have ever had'.

The popularity of the Principal had not waned. He was still held in the highest esteem and affection by the whole denomination and his influence radiated beyond the Baptist fellowship and beyond Australia.

Mr Clatworthy concluded by affirming that Principal's purpose had not changed. He repeated a statement of the policy of the College made by the guest, early in his career: 'To teach and encourage men to preach Christ passionately and convincingly because they have an invincible faith in Him'.

FROM THE 'THIRTIES'

For the men of the 'thirties' Rev AH Orr was the voice. After naming some of the men who sat under the Principal's teaching and influence during 1930-33 Mr Orr recalled that these were the difficult years of the terrible economic depression when it seemed that there would not be money enough to keep all men in College and the students imposed upon themselves a reduction in stipends from £10 to £8 per month.

He also reminded the gathering that they were the days when the beloved late Rev John Deane as Vice-Principal stood beside Principal Morling in the development of the College.

Mr Orr brought warm responsive comments from the audience when he spoke of the Principal's 'other-worldliness'. He always had about him and on him that which spoke of the presence of God, the speaker said. There were times when, like Moses and for the same reason, the Principal's face shone.

Mr Orr thought that perhaps the dominant characteristic of the influence of their guest in the lives of his students was that, 'a man of the Book' himself, he had imparted to them all a lifelong determination to pursue expository preaching.

Allied to this in influence was his undeviating purpose to draw his students out into lives of deep personal devotion to Jesus Christ.

THE 'FORTIES'

It was given to Rev Doug Mill to speak for the men of the 'forties'. From his beautifully concise tribute these points may be taken. Principal Morling was a friend. He was a friend to every student and to the wives and families of graduates. Mrs Morling shared this ministry fragrantly.

Principal Morling was the greatest preacher he had ever heard. Of all the preachers he had listened to, whether Australians or visitors to this country, no one was Principal's peer in proclaiming and imparting the deep teachings of scripture, Mr Mill said.

While he will always be significant for what he has said and what he has taught it will be finally for what he has been that Principal will be remembered and loved, he concluded.

AND THE 'FIFTIES
For the graduates of the 'fifties' Rev Gilbert McArthur was the representative. He stressed that the men who had profited from the experience and the teaching of the Principal in the latter years of his work underlined and reiterated all that had been said by those who had spoken for the earlier periods.

He epitomised the spiritual leadership and intellectual insight of the guest by quoting a statement by Principal which had remained with him from College days: 'May all your heightened experiences come from deeper insights into truth'.

THE PRINCIPAL'S WIFE
Mrs CH Gray, wife of the President of the Baptist Union, made a choice speech directed particularly toward Mrs Morling, to whom she presented a tasteful basket of flowers.

Mrs Gray reminded the company of the more than usual sacrifices made by Mrs Morling in mothering 'the largest family of any Baptist minister's wife' for she had been a mother to all the students.

The duty of supporting her husband in his work and of bringing up her family on College premises were mammoth tasks, Mrs Gray said. Mrs Morling had earned and deserved the admiration and love of all present.

The President supported his wife's remarks. He also said that no name stood as high in the thought of the Baptists of NSW as that of Principal Morling. 'Your ministry will never come to an end', he assured the Principal'.

On behalf of the company the President then presented a canteen of cutlery and a cheque for £100 to the honoured and beloved guests.

'GRATITUDE, HUMILITY, HAPPINESS'
Deeply moved but also abundantly assured in the love surrounding them, Principal Morling replied for Mrs Morling and himself.

He summarised his emotions as he came to the end of this part of his life work as gratitude to God, deep humility, happiness.

His life had not been easy, he said, but it had been a chain of the mercies of God. He affirmed that deep truths for which his teaching had become known had arisen from his own need. He needed the doctrine of the Holy Spirit; he needed the truth of the soul's union with Christ. He said that, near the end of his life, Harriet Auber's

words were increasingly true of his experience –
'And every virtue we possess, and every victory won, and every thought of holiness are His alone'.

He stood before them at this time of his life as a man happy in Jesus Christ, he said. At the end of the years he believed even more firmly in the guidance of a sovereign God. He was happy in the fellowship of the Baptist people.

The Principal thanked speakers for their recognition of Mrs Morling and laid his tribute at her feet also. He quoted words spoken by Mrs Morling to a close friend early in their ministry: 'I knew when I married George that he would put his work first - and so he should'.

He concluded by telling of a Professor at Harvard who had come to the end of his teaching and was speaking to his last class when a robin alighted on the window sill of the lecture room. 'Excuse me, gentlemen, I have an appointment with spring', the Professor said, and walked out of the room.

'Please God my life is not finished', said the Principal, I too have an appointment with spring'.

He will also have an abiding appointment in the hearts of hundreds of his students and of thousands in the churches who have shared in his life and ministry.

'MY CUP RUNNETH OVER'

Rev John Ridley drew the company to the Mercy Seat in family worship based on Psalm 23 and stressing 'Thou anointest my head with oil, my cup runneth over'.

The size of the gathering, the duration of the program and the depth of feeling, wealth of fellowship and unashamed confession of love for the guests, were a cameo of the life and work of this holy man of God who has passed our way.

Dozens of letters and greetings flooded in for the occasion. The following extracts from a few of them are an impressive witness to the place that the Principal held in the hearts of his fellows.

From Rev Robert Pickup, a patient in the Concord Repatriation Hospital – 'It is a pleasure and honour to join with you this evening in an expression of the appreciation and high regard in which we hold the Principal of our College; a regard shared by men of all denominations and throughout Australia. Some of us remember the Assembly 40 years ago when, with some trepidation, the Rev George Morling, as a young man, was appointed Principal of the Theological College of New South Wales; and not as a goodly number of older and wiser? men would have liked in appointing him for a short period, but for an indefinite period of time [kk]. The passage of time has proved him an outstanding leader among the preachers and teachers of his day, and his ministry amongst a great number of young men passing through the College has confirmed this. Many men in all walks of life and belonging to all generations will join me in saying 'Thank God for George Morling".

From Rev Wilfred Jarvis, missioning in Phoenix, Arizona – 'As is well known by most of the brethren, he came into the office of Principal at one of the most critical periods in the history not only of the College but also of the Baptist Union. His was no easy task, and through the years since then he has had more than one man's share of burdens and problems in his devoted service for Christ and the denomination he loves'.

From Rev Basil Brown of the Victorian Baptist College – 'There can be little doubt that Principal has made a deeper mark on Australian Baptist life and service than any other man. The long list of graduates of the NSW College, which includes the names of missionary statesmen and distinguished denominational leaders in Australia and overseas, bears witness to the effectiveness of his service... All of us continually thank God for his influence upon our lives, and know that we are more deeply committed to the cause of our Master because of his ministry to us and his personal influence'.

It was indeed George Morling's year. It was announced[1029] that the Executive Committee had arranged a Testimonial Gathering for him on 2 December on which occasion Joshua Smith's portrait of him would be unveiled.

On 15 September, the Assembly of the Baptist Union of NSW elected him as the Ministerial Vice-president of the Union for the next three years.[1038] A report commented, 'The Assembly is fortunate in thus retaining the Principal's experience and wisdom in the high counsels of the denomination'.[1039] It would have been pleasing to him that his friend RE Walker was reappointed as Lay Vice-president.

His report to the Assembly was the last of a long series. After a detailed presentation of the teaching program he added 'All these studies are

---

[kk] In fact three years.

subordinate to the high purpose of the ministry of the Word and the winning of souls. The College is firmly grounded in the evangelical tradition'.

In presenting his first report as Administrator of the College, Rev AH (Harry) Orr paid tribute the Principal's 40 years of service. He said '… as his work as Principal will draw to a close before the presentation of the next annual report, we record at this stage our gratitude to God for a service unique, inspiring and effective in the training of men for the ministry. Throughout Australia the eyes of graduates are turned this way, watching with deep appreciation the crowning events of his Principalship. The love and prayers of Australian Baptists are his at this time. Both men and churches who have known his leadership and training are permanently enriched in the things of God'.[1040]

At the ordination service at which he presented his last group of ordinands the preacher was one the first graduates to do all his training under him, Rev FT Smith.[1041]

Early in the Assembly Rev Dr E Roberts-Thomson, MA DD, then Principal of the New Zealand College, was elected to succeed him as Principal of the NSW College. Dr. Roberts-Thomson wrote to him on 24 September. 'Dear Principal Morling, It was good of you (to) write as you did regarding our appointment to succeed you at the College in Sydney. I appreciate more than I can tell the assurance of your confidence in the decision of the Assembly'.

Edward Roberts-Thomson

The letter concluded with the prayer that God would richly bless him in the closing months of his 'great ministry'.

Two letters dated 26 September were testimonies to his varied ministry. One was from Mr BA King, Secretary of the NSW Union expressing the Assembly's appreciation of the midday devotional he had conducted. 'We felt indeed that on that day you gave us your best. The time spent was a rich spiritual feast; light was given on many choice portions of scripture and the presence of the Spirit of God was evident to all'.

The other letter was from the Eerdmans Publishing Company in America.

About eleven years earlier the company had re-published his book *The Quest for Serenity*. It forwarded to him a collection of reviews from a number of journals and papers. Coming to him when they did they must have been a great encouragement to him for they were uniformly positive and appreciative as the following extracts show:

'I have read many devotional books but think that this one is a gem. ... We would recommend this to our ministers'.

'This is a choice book that leads the reader into the understanding and experience of a life of serenity ... His book shows deep spiritual insight and reflects the spirit of one who has learned to live what he writes'.

'A part of the value of the book lies in its revelation of a man's own soul ... This is a book for every restless person to read in these days. Here is what few of us have and all of us need'.

'In the tremendous amount of 'peace of mind' literature today, it is refreshing to find a book that gets to the real secret of peace. There is an adequate answer, and it is clearly portrayed here. It is a choice contribution to a vast library in the field. The author speaks with the scholarship of a trained mind which has been strangely warmed by the glow of a deep spiritual life'.

'This book is written in a poetic style, it seems to me, and yet keeps its thoughts from drifting away from Biblical and true doctrinal moorings. How changed many a distraught life would be if people would absorb the principles found herein'.

'Into the book he has brought mature experience as a Christian and great interpretive quality'.

'The content of this book, which may be easily read at one brief sitting, bears remembering for a lifetime. In its field, this little book with its simple style direct approach and evangelical tone nears being a classic-in-miniature'.

'Defining carefully what he means by serenity, he states in beautiful language how he found the adjustment to life's burdens by leaving it all quietly to God and living restfully with Him. A most thoughtful spiritual study'.

'This is a book that will do the reader good'.

'The author speaks from the richness of his trained mind and with a deep understanding of the human heart and of Christian needs. He writes as one who has faced this problem of serenity in his own life and knows whereof he speaks'.

'If any one desires to read something which ranks with the very best of the mystical output of the ages, a small book that is as good as Brother Lawrence's *The Practice of the Presence of God* and Abraham Kuyter's *To Be Near Unto God*, then let him buy, or give away at Christmas time this attractively published little volume. It is an inexpensive little work. But it is worth being read and re-read many times. Its price is above rubies'.

'The chapters are short but packed with wise counsel from one who obviously has made his own quest and arrived triumphantly at the goal'. That final comment was in part true but George Morling, a man athirst for God, would continue to aspire after a deeper serenity'.

Principal Mervyn Himbury wrote on 27 September thanking him for his kind remarks about an article the Victorian Principal was about to have published in *The Australian Baptist*. He added, 'It was good to read the way that NSW Baptists showed their appreciation of the way you have served our denomination there, and indeed throughout the Commonwealth'.

A month later Rev Sam McKittrick, Secretary of the Victorian College, wrote sending the greetings of the College Council and Staff on the occasion of his retirement. The letter said that he had earned the esteem and gratitude of his brethren in all the other states and especially in Victoria. His influence had extended far beyond New South Wales. For many years Principal Morling had been closely associated with the Blackheath Church serving for various periods as Moderator and preaching there frequently. On 2 October, in recognition of his contribution, the church unveiled a portrait of him to be hung in the vestry.[1042]

The Australian Baptist announced the appointment of Rev NP Andersen, another of the Principal's men, as Dean and Honorary Secretary of the College.[1043] This was yet another evidence of changes that were taking place.

Neville Andersen

On 21 October Open House was held at the College for young people considering the possibility of training.[1044] Near to the end of his own long association with the College the Principal led the staff in challenging young people to come to College to prepare themselves for Christian service.

On 1 November, Rev Gilbert McArthur, Secretary of the Baptist Ministers' Fraternal wrote to the Principal. Having finalised accounts for the graduates' farewell the letter was primarily to send a cheque for £10 as an addition to the presentation made to him However, he added, 'We do lovingly remember you at this time, Sir, being very much aware of the difficult period through which your dear wife is passing. May the 'joy of the Lord' which joy you have shared so fully with so many of us, be your own personal 'strong consolation' at this time. With deep affection ...'

In NSW Baptist circles about this time there was some disturbance because of a vigorous promotion of the special emphases of 'Pentecostalism'. By request Principal Morling wrote an article on the matter. It appeared in two instalments.[1045] Subsequently the article was printed as a pamphlet and distributed to the churches.

If he was to be inactive after his retirement it would be by his own choice for already on 10 November there was a letter from Rev RN Ham, Secretary of the Victorian Baptist Ministers' Fraternal, inviting him to give three addresses at their Annual Retreat in the following April. Another letter, dated 23 November, came from Principal EC Burleigh writing for the Educational Board of the Baptist Union of Australia, asking him to write an article for *The Australian Baptist* on the subject of Post-graduate studies. The letter concluded, 'Under the magic of your pen this can become quite a thrilling story for our ministers'.

Among the numerous letters relative to his retirement there were others that showed that with all the concerns that preoccupied him the Principal made time to minister to others. In particular there came letters from the wife of a former student, from an ex-student whose wife had been ill, and from an aged fellow minister.

'Dear Principal, 'said the first, 'How did you know that I was in need of such a letter as you sent to me?' The second, 'My dear Principal, Thank you so much for your letter of a few days ago. It was kind of you to write as you did, and we deeply appreciate both your prayerful remembrance and personal interest'. The third, 'Your most gracious letter has just arrived. I am deeply moved that you should take the trouble to write and in such gracious and loving expressions. I thank you very sincerely'.

Yet other letters indicated the Principal's involvement in affairs outside the College. Some had to do with mundane matters such as one from the President of the Union, Mr Stan Squire, about the working environment of the Union's staff in Church House. Seemingly, he was on a committee to look into the matter.

Of a very different kind was a letter revealing the Principal's missionary interest. Retired missionary, Miss Helen Cousin, wrote, 'Thank you sincerely for your letter received a week or two ago. I only wish I were more worthy of the thoughts expressed in your letter. Mr Dube has told us of the gift from yourself and Elaine (GHM's daughter) for the Birisiri Hospital. It humbles me to think of your doing this'. The letter expressed thanks for his 'wonderful service' and indicated that he would be taking a retreat for missionaries the following week.

Sometime in the crowded days of November he conducted the funeral of Mrs Vera Wallace. It took him back to the early days of his ministry. In his address and tribute he said, 'I knew Vera Wallace for some 45 years. As Vera Mogensen I knew her in her teens. She lived then in Raymond Terrace and attended the Dungog Baptist Church of which I was pastor. I had the privilege of baptising her and receiving her into the Church of Jesus Christ. I remember so clearly the girl Vera Mogensen of those days. She was vital, glowing with health. She was uninhibited, spontaneously expressive and especially so in warm affectionateness. And there was genuine spiritual quality. Yesterday I preached on I Peter 1:8 ('Whom having not seen you love, in whom, though now you see him not, yet believing you rejoice with the joy unspeakable and full of glory') and I said that there should be a radiance in the life of the Christian. There was a touch of that radiance in the girl Vera Mogensen'.

He concluded his address with a tender appeal 'You will miss your sister and your mother. You are an affectionate family and you will feel this loss sorely. You need God in an hour such as this. Your loved one has gone home but I remember that you even here can go home too. God is our home. Go home to him through Jesus Christ whose blessed offer is, as Saviour, to take us home to God'.

The Special Diploma Courses had their Graduation on 19 November and the Principal brought them a word of greeting.[1046] In a card that accompanied a presentation to him 'the students at Wynola' wrote, 'This gift is an expression of our appreciation for the contribution you have made to our lives. Thank you, Principal, for the inspiration of your life'.

The next day he preached in the morning at Central Baptist.[1047] However, on the following day there was an apology from him at the College Council Meeting. It would have been his final meeting with the Council but the minutes are silent as to the reason for his absence and, indeed, there is no mention of him in them except for the apology.

His final Graduation Service was on 24 November in the Ashfield Church. It was to his satisfaction to see eleven men graduate, two of whom subsequently served on the College faculty, Dr Victor Eldridge and Dr Darcy Taplin. Part of a report on the occasion ran[1048], 'Claiming that they were the 'best year ever to graduate from the College' one graduand drew attention to the fact that Principal GH Morling was graduating with them. The Principal concludes his forty year term as head of the College with the end of this session. Stating that he was 'not leaving a sinking ship' the Principal referred to the fact that 'there are currently more than 50 men in College training for the ministry'.

The student magazine *Summa Supremo*[1049] was a tribute to Principal GH Morling, MA, to whom it was dedicated as 'pastor to pastors, the friend of God, guide to the denomination'. The dedication (page 1) offered an explanation of the cover designed by student, David Nicholas. 'The symbolism of our cover reaches after elements in the ministry of Principal GH Morling which have made it effective and enduring. **The Bible**, symbolic of his expository emphasis, lies open under his glasses at **Romans**, one of the storehouses of great truths which his evangelical ardour loved to study with care and proclaim with authority. **The light** streaming in is reminiscent of the fact that there was more than intellectual acuteness in his exposition; there was light from above; there was in his work and life the presence of the Holy Spirit. The **hands raised in prayer** speak of the mystic in his soul which led him into spiritual deeps where his personality, aesthetic and sensitive, found profound rest. But no symbols could show how richly and warmly these elements were bound together in the person of this lovable man of God, nor how he gathered up in himself the lofty challenge of SUMMA SUPREMO – 'The Utmost for the Highest".

The Principal himself contributed the first article under the heading 'These Forty Years'. From it (pages 3-5) the following extracts are taken.

'It occurs to me first to affirm that there has been a Divine Dimension in the ordering of my life. One does not speak lightly of the Sovereign Will of God. The problems involved in such a belief are not inconsiderable, but for me it is inevitable. Looking back, I am confident that there has been a Beckoning Hand at certain points of departure, often a Restraining Hand where else there had been danger, and always a Presence Who could be consulted'.

'The life of a ministerial training college is exacting both for the students and even more for the staff. The demands of this high calling are tremendous and, though grace abounds, difficulties inherent in human nature are many. But mine has been a happy life in which there have been rich rewards. Teaching is ever satisfying work and when the teaching has its centre in the Book of God and has its outreach into the researches and thoughts of the noblest and saintliest minds of the ages the satisfaction is rich indeed'.

'And these sacred studies have been pursued within the fellowship of theological students. Not an unmixed blessing, the cynical might insist! But I have believed in and loved the successive generations of students. I have been chaffed for fondly believing that all my geese are swans, but I have preferred to have it so even though the hurt has been the deeper when, sometimes, a man has failed to fulfil his promise. But, thank God, how many have proved worthy of confidence and have even exceeded expectations. And, be it said, it is not alone or mainly in the ministries of those who have achieved positions of public distinction that one has joy; it is much more in the ministries of many who serve Christ so faithfully in comparative obscurity'.

'It seems natural to say something about the policy of these 40 years. I came to the work of the College from pastoral experience in which, brief as it was, I had discovered beyond any doubt, that the great evangelical doctrines 'spoke to my condition' as George Fox used to say, and spoke also to the condition of my people. Coming also to the New Testament from university studies in the text of Shakespeare, I found with enthusiasm and delight what treasure is yielded by a minute examination of the text of Scripture. There it was that I came to present to my people in a patient, exegetical way the sublime truths of such books as the Epistles to the Philippians and to the Ephesians.

'This naturally became the pattern for my College teaching. Perhaps I could best describe the tradition which I have sought to establish as <u>an evangelicalism positive, forthright and balanced</u>. <u>Positive</u> it should be because in its essence the Christian faith is not a quest for truth with uncertain results, but a revelation of truth authoritative and sure. And <u>forthright</u> it should be in proclamation if it is positive in content. Dr JA Hutton once said that for him the most suggestive passages in English literature were Browning's words, 'A little more, and how much it is, A little less, and what miles away''.

I have often quoted these lines in respect to preaching. Such forthrightness cannot be other than evangelistic. Most certainly also there must be <u>balance,</u> because truth with its parts out of balance becomes all too often heretical caricature'.

'There will be new leadership. The College will have a new location and new buildings. Another era opens. I have confidence that the values of the past will be conserved with more effective adjustment to new generations living in a changing world'.

The magazine contained splendid tributes from several friends and colleagues, old friend Rev RS (Bob) Pickup, College Council President, Mr RE Walker, College Lecturer, Dr EG Gibson, Chairman of the NSW Graduates' Fellowship of IVF, Dr. John Hercus and General Director of the Overseas Missionary Fellowship, Mr J Oswald Sanders. The Editor of *The Australian Baptist*, Rev AC Prior, wrote a finely crafted article in which he summarised 'Forty Years of Achievement'. Student James C Wilson put his tribute in the form of a poem while students Allan Jennaway, Randolph Leckie, Ken Manley, Keith Bennett, John Brooks, Frank Willis, John Giles and Victor Eldridge offered discussion of Baptism 'as part of our tribute to the Principal'.

Of the two editorials one by Senior Student John Strugnell addressed itself to the changes consequent upon the Principal's retirement, while student Editor, John Brooks, commented briefly on the thoughts behind the issue of the magazine. He wrote, 'In compiling this edition of *Summa Supremo* to be issued upon the retirement of our Principal we have felt ourselves to be under a great burden of responsibility. It is not possible in a few short pages to estimate a man's life - and to praise a great man ineptly is to do him dishonour. What has encouraged us is the knowledge that the magazine will go to those who already know and love this man. Out of their own experience they will amend what we have said poorly and share the thrill where something has been said aright…'

'Mention has been made only scarcely of Mrs Morling, whose loyal and wise support of her husband has been an essential part of his ministry. She will know that, nonetheless, her work is remembered, for those who know the Principal well know how much he speaks of her and has leaned on her down the years. It can truly be said that in honouring the Principal, we honour also the lovely Christian lady who stood with him in his high office'.

The editorial concluded with the expression of the hope that 'there might arise in material form a more fitting tribute to the Principal in a College Chapel on the Marsfield site'. It was felt that this would be a fitting expression of the lifelong aim of the Principal "to plant worship and devotion deep in the heart of learning".

Through the final months of 1960 a steady stream of letters reached the Principal from former students wishing to express their gratitude for all that he had meant to them and wishing him well for his retirement. These comments are culled from them:

'I look back with a good deal of joy and satisfaction … to the years at Granville when the foundations were laid for my subsequent ministry'.

'I shall always carry with me the influence of those formative days spent under your influence (at Ashfield) and teaching. Although I have seldom been called a 'Morlingite' I have always replied that that was the highest Baptist compliment anyone could pay me!!'

'I owe you (under God) the working knowledge of the Holy Spirit and His office, which has been the greatest single feature in my own devotional life and of my teaching in the ministry. I do not hesitate in saying that I believe you are the greatest exponent of this invaluable teaching in Australia'.

'I would like you to know how much I have appreciated your influence in my life all through these years ... you have been both a blessing and an inspiration and I would like to thank you most sincerely for all this ... nothing can ever rob me of the memory of College days and of your fellowship and leadership'.

'It may interest you to know that in this State of Queensland men whom you have influenced through the NSW College are taking the lead and showing the way in the life of the denomination. ... God has used you and you have been willing. Thank you for the holy example. May we who have been trained in the evangelical exposition of the Scriptures be granted grace and wisdom to follow in so great a tradition'.

'1 am indebted to you Principal for your patience and forbearance with me during College days, as well as for the encouragement over the years during my ministry. I feel honoured to be one of your early students and will never be ashamed to be associated with the Word of Truth you so faithfully proclaimed'.

From one who trained with him – 'I could not add to the great sum of worthy tributes paid to your gracious self. However, I would like to send you a few lines to express my sincere appreciation of your wonderful ministry. I am afraid that it was not my lot to reach to any degree of scholastic attainment nevertheless I have always been inspired and instructed by your words, your leadership and your life. I praise God that my path was crossed by such a one as GH Morling'.

'From one who had left the ministry under a cloud but with whom the Principal had maintained contact – 'Often as some aspect of life comes to the fore some saying of yours comes into my mind as a pronouncement upon it. I think of Amos and Hosea, of Philippians and John and those old time lectures. Thank you for them. I do thank God upon 'every remembrance of you' and I pray that an abiding sense of the 'Presence' shall go with you'.

One who was somewhat his senior, a retired minister, expressed 'very sincere appreciation' of his service during the past 40 years and went on to say, 'It has been a rich spiritual experience to mark the steady development of the College from humble beginnings to its present honoured place of strength and influence'.

Rev John Garrett, Principal of Camden College (the Congregational Theological College), in writing to add his greetings and tribute said, 'As your former student I send my affection and gratitude'. He had studied under Principal Morling at Sydney University.

A graduating student - 'This letter is to simply say a very big thank you for your kindness, interest, guidance, understanding and Christian love which have been afforded to me during my College course'.

A country church wrote, 'We feel that every Baptist and every Christian owes you a tremendous debt for the faithful way in which you have carried out your ministry as Principal of the NSW Baptist Theological College'.

A letter from Rev JA Thompson at Cambridge dated 20 November is of interest because it mentions that the Principal had been ill and expresses the hope that he may be feeling better. Another letter from England, dated just one day later, was from Rev EF Kevan, Principal of the London Bible College. It was to acknowledge advice sent by Principal Morling about one of his men but also conveyed 'prayerful good wishes' as he laid down his responsibilities as Principal.

Mrs Joan White had been invited to sing at the function to farewell the Principal. Because of a family commitment she had to decline but wrote, 'I feel very honoured at being asked to sing, and having always been a great admirer of yours, nothing would have pleased me more than taking part in this important occasion ... I wish I could be present to add my word of appreciation of the wonderful help you have been to me over the years, and to pay you honour. I will never forget your kindness in coming to see me when I first came to Sydney after Weeks[ll] died'.

The 40 years of special ministry came to a climax in the Denominational Farewell extended to the Principal in the Central Baptist Church on Friday, 2 December. Numerous greetings were sent to be passed on to the one being honoured and these came not only from NSW Baptists. Representative of the wider Baptist constituency was one that came from Principal TC Warriner of the Queensland Baptist College:

'On the occasion of the Public Meeting to honour Principal GH Morling please convey the warmest greetings of this College to him. By his

---

[ll] Her husband Dr Weeks White.

scholarship, the depth of his spiritual experience, his consecration to Christ and his great gifts as a speaker and preacher he has made an outstanding contribution to the Baptist communion in Australia, by imparting knowledge, training and spiritual inspiration to a long succession of students who have proclaimed the glorious evangel throughout Australia and in distant parts. I personally greatly value his friendship and appreciate the kindness which he has shown to me'.

Mr Colin K Beecroft, General Secretary of Scripture Union, was one who spoke for the wider Christian circle:

'Principal Morling has been a valued Vice-President of the Mission for many years and we have greatly appreciated not only his interest in our work but also all that he has stood for in the Christian Community. It is therefore a great pleasure indeed to add our word of acknowledgement of all that God has done through him in his teaching ministry. We have looked to Principal Morling as one who has been a master of the exposition of the Scriptures. Many of us have been greatly blessed through this ministry and we feel sure that as a result of this contribution and all he has stood for there will be many others in the regular ministry and in Christian work generally who will seek to follow his example with God's enabling'.

On behalf of the Intervarsity Fellowship of Evangelical Unions Mr Ian Burnard expressed 'its gratitude to God for Principal Morling's association with this body. The Principal was a frequent speaker at its conferences and at Sydney University and was one of its valued Vice-Presidents'.

In *The Australian Baptist* the occasion was reported[1050] under the heading:

Principal Morling Farewelled
Valedictory Meeting at Central Church Sydney

A drenching wet night could not dampen the ardour or repress the affection of Baptists of NSW who thronged the Central Baptist Church, Sydney, on Friday, December 2, to honour and felicitate Rev Principal GH Morling on his retirement from the office of Principal of the Baptist Theological College of NSW after having served the denomination in this way for 40 years.

This was the last of a series of farewell gatherings. Previously the ministers of the denomination had recognised the Principal and this was followed by a valedictory given by the Theological College. This concluding recognition was the official gesture of the whole of the Baptist Union of New South Wales. The President, Mr SC Squire, was in the chair and he was supported by representatives of our own Church and the wider Christian fellowship.

TRIBUTES
Speakers were: Rev ER Rogers, representing the Baptist Ministers' Fraternal; Rev Professor BS Brown, speaking for graduates; Mr RE Walker, President of the College; The Venerable Archdeacon RB Robinson, representing the evangelical community of the Commonwealth; and Rev BG Wright, who voiced the thoughts of the College Staff.

Several tributes referred to the expository ministry exercised by the Principal. He had been like the spire of a cathedral, pointing men's thoughts heavenward. One recalled this statement: 'Why do people want to run off to Keswick when we have Principal Morling in Australia?'

His preaching ministry in the Churches was extolled. Peter Taylor Forsyth's words were applied: 'You must live with people to know their problems and you must live with God to solve them'.

The congregation heard such phrases as: 'Scholar and theologian', 'Evangelical mystic' applied to the guest of the evening.

PORTRAIT UNVEILED
A feature of the meeting was the unveiling of the portrait in oils for which the well known artist Joshua Smith had been commissioned. It was unveiled by the President. The portrait, which depicts the Principal with the open Word of God in his hand, captures and presents the deep sympathy and tender spiritual concern which his intimates have seen so often on his face. This masterpiece will hang in the new College at Marsfield.

A further recognition of the service of the Principal was in the form of a cheque for £810 handed to him by the President.

Rising to reply the Principal was greeted by a sustained ovation. He graciously averred that he was not worthy of what had been said. It night be true, he said, but it was not all the truth. His speech, a combination of a statement of faith and of a homely 'thank you' is one that defies summary, His emphasis was thanksgiving. He was a thankful man; he thanked God for what he had done in his life.

The tribute of Vice-Principal BG Wright deserves more than a mere mention. He made these points.

1. 'Our Principal has been a scholar and a theologian of the highest order. In this sphere of scholarship head and heart knowledge have been finely balanced. If anything, heart has had precedence over head. He has always been aware of the world of critical scholarship and, often with penetrating insight, has seen its weaknesses and changing fashions. Few men have read so widely and with such discrimination. Perhaps it was because of his wide reading and deep reflection that he concentrated his effort on and gave first priority to a carefully informed devotional emphasis. His choice has greatly enriched his students and the whole denomination. Some years ago the Principal of a College in another State. a highly degreed man with a reputation as a scholar, visited Sydney. I said to Principal, 'There is no doubt that you could have had a doctorate and all the degrees of X but you may also have had a college like his with five students ... He has nourished his soul on the mystics, the Quakers, the Puritans, the great theologians like Handley CG Moule, Peter T Forsyth, HR Macintosh, BF Westcott, RW Dale, J Denney and many others of the same calibre - men in whose lives massive intellect, devotional fervour, evangelical passion and mystical insight were almost perfectly blended. Perhaps the best description for the Principal would be to call him an Evangelical Mystic. Christ might have said of George Morling, 'He has chosen the better part and it shall not be taken from him''.

2. He has been a fine Principal and a splendid lecturer. We have had no recluse for a Principal, writing abstract theses in a sound-proof room. We have had a spiritual leader and teacher and lecturer who stood in the mid-stream of the life of the College and of the denomination. There have been no jarring notes between the Principal and the faculty. Every man has counted it a privilege to be in his presence and work with him. He has been the Prince of Conversationalists and Storytellers - with the most infectious laugh in Christendom...

His conversation is always on a high level - about great topics, great men, great preaching, great services and so on. In all his conversation there has been an absence of sarcasm, of jealousy. He has been an Israelite in whom is no guile .

And what a mastery of English prose is his. That sensitivity for just the right word to convey the exact meaning, the vivid description or the throbbing emotion.

A dominant feature of the College life has been the Principal as leader of morning devotions. Perhaps it was here that we saw him at his best. a true pathologist of the soul with spiritual insight, glow and power. His messages were nothing less than logic on fire. And often, his face shone without him being aware of it.

3. The Principal has been a Friend and a Father to the students. Peter Taylor Forsyth has said, 'You must live with people to know their problems and live with God in order to solve them'. Principal lived with his students and with God. No minister ever left the ministry without bringing him sorrow of heart and soul travail in prayer.

Through all the years he has constantly called the College community to extended periods of prayer, to pray for the problems and burdens of his students or their churches, homes and personal lives. He made their sorrow his own and then bore them up to God in ceaseless intercession. In conclusion I want to say of the Principal that he magnified Christ and so Christ has magnified him.

Something of Principal's response may be indicated by the following partial reconstruction of it.

'Mr President, my brethren, my friends all, I would be insensitive indeed if I were not deeply moved by your kind reception and by the generous - the embarrassingly even bewilderingly generous - things which you have said tonight. 'Grace seems to outgrace itself', said Spurgeon on one occasion. Grace certainly seems to have outgraced itself in making possible such honour as you have shown an unworthy man tonight. I am grateful to you and in my inmost heart I give glory to God. <u>I am grateful</u> (He expanded on this) and <u>I am sensible</u>'.

'I am quite aware that there is more to be said about me than has been said tonight. Even if what you said was the truth it was not the whole truth. You know more about me than you have said. There have been judicious omissions and silences'.

'And I know more than you know. 'It is our last conceit that we know ourselves' said Oswald Chambers. How readily we lie to ourselves. But we do find ourselves out. I know more about myself than you know - and the knowledge is disturbing. And He whose eyes are a fire knows more than I know'.

'So I am sensible and put your tribute in proper perspective'. 'Grateful, sensible <u>and aspiring'</u>.

'For what days and years remain I should seek to be worthy of what you think me to be'.

'In that regard let me make some reference to the painting of this portrait. It has been an instructive experience for me to observe how a master of his art goes about his work. There was first of all the mechanics of art. Yet the mechanics never spoiled the beauty of artistry. Then there was repeated looking. On average Joshua Smith looked at me every five seconds. So on a conservative estimate over the whole period of the painting he looked at me 60,000 times. There came a moment of insight when he felt he 'saw' me for the first time. Then followed the patient endeavour for the painting,, as he put it, 'to give back to me what I have seen''.

'That is all very instructive for the reproduction of Jesus Christ in our lives. There must be the constant looking to Him. St Therese cried to her friends who didn't share her vision of Christ. 'If only you would look'. 'There is a new dimension when we look at Christ', writes a modern French mystic. We need to look at Christ until we 'see' Him.

'Then there must be the patient process of reproduction'.

'And there was something else that encouraged me. The portrait 'came up' in the last stages. Suddenly it took form and definition and the artist's purpose' became clear'.

'So there is still hope for me to 'come up' for something of the likeness of Christ to appear in me, and for that I must and do aspire'.

'Well, a span of 40 years of life and service comes to a close. In reviewing these 40 years I find it in my heart to say some things about my faith, my personal relations and my ministry in the College'.

'**My Faith** - For 40 years I have been a teacher and for 46 years I have been a preacher. What I have taught and preached has come out of the whole experience of life. My faith has had to be won - and not without cost. Mine has been a nature not easy to satisfy. As a child I was a queer little fellow subject to dark fears and with intense longings. I thought there was no-one quite like me'.

'If ever one needed the peace which is harmony with God and harmony within oneself that one was the queer little fellow named George Morling. That peace came progressively through a deepening apprehension of Christ who promised to 'give us His peace''.

'I can mark the stages of that apprehension.

1. Through the nurture of a truly Christian home and the influence of Godly ministers and Sunday School teachers I became a follower of Christ quite early.

2. After graduation from the University as an evening student - I taught school during the day - a quiet but strong urge took me into training for the ministry. In my first student pastorate at Tamworth doubts arouse about my acceptance with God. I faced the haunting question in the light of the New Testament. I remember so vividly the moment when light came. I had the faith of assurance. I knew I was accepted the Beloved. I have never doubted my standing with God in Christ since.

3. There were still inner needs to be satisfied, a vacuum to be filled. It became filled by Him who satisfies the longing soul. I came to have deeper insights. I learned of the 'Emmanuel knot of Union' - the mystical union of love between Christ and His redeemed. I learned experimentally that the soul joined thus to Christ is blessed with all spiritual blessings and abides in Christ. I learned also that reciprocally Christ dwells in the heart by faith. My soul leapt towards these glorious truths.

4. Parallel with this insight came a fuller understanding of the Holy

Spirit, the Promise of the Father, the Divine Consumation in salvation, the 'Beyond Who is within', the Comforter.

5. Still greater enrichment came when I took hold of the teaching of the Epistle to the Hebrews that Jesus Christ is the Apostle and High Priest of our confession who on the basis of the New Covenant sealed by His blood takes us into the Holiest of all to live in the Presence.

6. Faith, for me, has found its completion in John's adoring words, 'Unto Him that loves us and loosed us from our sins by His blood, and has made us kings and priests unto God and His Father; to Him be glory and dominion for ever and ever'.

7. To this confession of faith I add this. In these last years I have loved to take all these massive truths into the Godhead and to contemplate God
    - as God in all the mystery and majesty of His Eternal Being, God in the full range of His ineffable Tri-unity:
    - as Father - not fate
    - as Son - Who came out of the Godhead to be, live and die, so that now He bears that best dear name of Saviour
    - as Holy Spirit - God Himself in His final self-giving <u>within</u>.

These precious things have been the precipitate in the crucible of my life experience and have been the joyous burden of my teaching and preaching. If there has been any virtue in them it is because I have sought to tell of these Divine things. In this at least I have been Spurgeonic. The secret of his mighty ministry was that he set before his hearers the great doctrines of grace. I remember how impressed I was as a youth in reading a Christmas sermon of Spurgeon. His text was Isaiah's word about the Feast of Fat Things that God would make for all people. The treatment was to set before his people an elaborate Christmas dinner of many courses, each one representing some great aspect of truth. In my own humble way I have sought to do that and it has paid dividends. There has been response'.

<u>'Let me now say something about personal relations over these forty years.</u>
1. A most fruitful conception has entered deeply into modern theology and philosophy. It was pioneered by a Jewish philosopher, Martin Buber, and is known as the 'I-Thou' relation. The 'I-Thou' relation

stands in contrast to the 'I-It' relation. In the latter the I stands over against the It and is aware of it. The It is entirely passive in the relation; the knowledge of it is wholly objective.

But in the 'I-Thou' relation, while the I and the Thou remain independent and both remain as individuals there is a meeting - the meeting is the significant thing and neither remains unchanged. Knowledge is reciprocal and personal. And it is on the personal level in our dealings with other people that we encounter God.

2. The 'I-Thou' relation of a meeting that changes and transforms the participant is, I say, a fruitful conception.

3. Over these 40 years I have had life-enriching meetings in which I have encountered God.

   3.1. Let me speak meaningfully and reverently - it is no matter for light and cheap reference - of one meeting. As a student I met, in an 'I-Thou' relation, a girl with a peaches and cream complexion and with choice qualities of character. She became wife and mother of my home. During 44 years the 'I-Thou' relation - the meeting has become ever more meaningful. I thank God for a home and a home circle in which there is <u>love</u> and <u>devotion</u> and <u>thoughtfulness</u> and <u>peace</u>.

   3.2. My sphere of life and ministry has been within the Baptist Union of New South Wales. Throughout these 40 years there have been meetings, a succession of 'I Thou' relations through which I have encountered God.

   We Baptists could tell Buber about one illustration of his 'I-Thou' principle of which he knew nothing. I refer to our conception of the church as the gathered community with Christ in the midst. It has come to me with great force during these days how closely I am bound with you NSW Baptists in the bundle of life. We have met, <u>really met</u>, in a transforming way.

   3.2.1. We have met really in the lecture room - through the medium of sacred study. I have met some great souls there. I shall ever cherish the memory of times of prayer and of College Communion Services. They were sacred seasons. There have been changes and many of you encountered God.

3.2.2. We have met in the sanctuary of God as I have preached in the churches. And there too I have been changed and, please God, some of you have been too. Let me stress my conviction of the importance of preaching.

3.2.3. There have been meetings in the wider field of the household of faith. In that wider field I have met such men as Archdeacon Robinson - and so many more. I believe in Church Unity, not in the Church Unity that can be imposed mechanically from top levels but in the Church Unity that is among those who, living in the Spirit, are already one in Christ Jesus.

3.2.4. I have had meetings with those in the immediate Presence. I take literally the words of Hebrews 12:22f. 'Ye are come to the spirits of just men made perfect'. I am fond of the story of Bishop Westcott who assured his daughters that on a dreary morning when the worshippers were few the Cathedral at Durham was full of the saints of all ages. I have met not in a spiritualistic but in a high spiritual way those in the immediate Presence. I owe a great deal to the great spiritual masters of the ages, and they are part of the communion of saints'.

'Three things only I desire to say specifically about these 40 years in respect to the College - and without elaboration.

This first. I trust that I have helped to create an educational consciousness in respect to the ministry. NSW Baptists have passed beyond the stage of believing that uninformed zeal suffices for the ministry of Christ.
And this. I am sure that the Theological College is now firmly established. Establishment, in any realm, takes time and patience. I think that firm foundations have been laid so that a greater superstructure can now be erected.

Also this. I think I can say that a distinctive tradition has been created. I have enunciated it as a positive, forthright, balanced, evangelical tradition'.

'I expressed the hope in committee as I was about to leave the College that two things would be kept in mind; that the tradition would be maintained, and that it would be maintained at a increasingly high level of culture'.

'I believe that my hope will be realised and that under its new leadership and in its new location the College will move forward to yet more significant service for Christ'.

In concluding he made two points. He had found the notes of his inaugural speech when first he had assumed responsibility in the College. He was happy to think that the ideals espoused and the hopes expressed in that speech had been in measure realised. Over the years, he said in the second place, he had found comfort in a sermon by Percy Ainsworth on Luke's account of the miraculous haul of fishes. Ainsworth made the point that if we have, like the disciples, faithfully toiled it is no disgrace if we have taken nothing. George Morling said that he wished that 'the boat were more filled' but whatever effectiveness his service had had was due entirely to the grace of God.

The tributes and expressions of appreciation that continued to arrive in succeeding weeks made it manifest that his labour had not been in vain.

The Ministers' Fraternal met at Manly on 5 December. One of the matters decided was that the Fraternal would make itself responsible for an annual College prize as a memorial to the ministry of their beloved Principal.

On 9 December he addressed his 'dear friends' in a brief letter. He pleaded the impossibility of acknowledging individually those who directly or indirectly had contributed to the generous presentation made to him at what to him was a memorable occasion. He asked all to be assured of his appreciation and concluded, 'You will readily understand that I have conflicting emotions as I lay down the exacting task appointed to me 40 years ago, but predominant is a sense of gratitude to God and to you, my dear friends of our beloved Denomination, who have shown me such affection and honour'.

His teaching responsibility was an end but the closing days of the year witnessed his continued involvement in activities related to the College and his ministry in the churches.

The Saturday following his farewell he conducted the wedding service of recent graduate, David Nicholas. A couple wrote thanking him for his 'patient counselling and valued advice'. A letter from a former student spoke of his kindness and interest in him and expressed a desire to be worthy of it. He had been passing through a difficult time. Another of his men acknowledged with pleasure a letter from the Principal who had remembered him in his being laid aside for three months. The same writer expressed deep sympathy with the Principal in the strain he was experiencing. A minister, not one of his men, wrote thanking him for his gracious greetings and word of interest. The man was waiting for an opportunity for service to open for him.

When on 17 December he chaired the farewell that the Stanmore Church extended to its pastor, Rev AN Horn, one of his men, it was at once the final closing of the door of his College ministry and the token of a ministry in the churches and beyond them that he would continue to exercise for another almost fourteen years[1051].

At last at the end of an emotionally and physically exhausting year he was able to leave for a desperately needed holiday. The Trevor Morlings had taken a flat at Collaroy and the Morling seniors had one adjacently. Unhappily the holiday had to be interrupted because of Gladys Morling's health. It was better for her to be in the familiar surroundings of the Pennant Hills home with daughters Dorothy and Elaine at hand.

Along with all the reasons there were for a sense of fulfilment and satisfaction the Principal had the sadness of seeing his dear partner gradually failing in health. Retirement at least meant that he could be more with her and offer her support and assurance.

The day following the Public Farewell an elderly woman wrote to express appreciation and encouragement. She quoted words given her when she had to give up helping in the church kitchen,

> *'I laid it down in silence, this work of mine,*
> *and took what had been sent me - A resting time.*
> *The Master's Voice had called me, to rest apart,*
> *'Apart with Jesus only' echoed my heart'.*

The Principal's major ministry had come to a deeply satisfying and heart-warming conclusion and he may well have hoped 'to rest apart'. But it was soon apparent that his service for Christ was far from finished. Other doors of opportunity were already opening for him. However his service would be offered in a context of severe trial and sorrow. Despite or perhaps because of this the final chapter of his life was in many ways the most inspiring.

1961

Retirement came none too soon for 'our beloved Principal'. Mrs Morling's health was steadily failing and he was thus able to spend more time with her.

However, though the public record is largely silent as to other activities on his part there is evidence in letters and other records that he continued to exercise a ministry outside the home.

On 9 January he wrote to Bert (AT) Whale. Apparently his friend had been puzzled by some of the information on the program of the public farewell to the Principal, who wrote, 'The mystery of my birth date is resolved in this way. For some unknown reason my birthday during my childhood was celebrated wrongly on Nov 14. Then the correct date, the 21st, was discovered'.[mm] 'You are right about the graduation. It was at 20 although the degree was not conferred until May when I was 21. It was Principal Holdsworth who held back the MA studies. I am afraid that my theological education was very badly done. I began the MA studies when I was Principal of the College'.

He told his friend that he didn't think it worth doing anything to correct the misinformation.

How he proposed to face the new chapter of his life is indicated in a diary entry on 16 January. 'I am determined to live for God in my present difficult home circumstances. Perhaps these months are a preparation for a more mature ministry in our churches and among ministers'. 'I shall make the Holy Spirit my teacher and seek what He has to show me about the life in Christ'. 'I know that inner strength is a primary necessity and the Holy Spirit can give this'.

A letter from Sydney Morris, dated 24 January, reveals the remarkable affinity between the two men and also a rare quality of spirit that they shared.

'My very dear George, No, I do not think you would prefer this room you know so well this morning. Truly a bright warm coal fire burns in the grate but our little Atlantic island is dull and misty and a cold wind sweeps it. At 11am I am writing by artificial light. Ah, but out in our London garden the Lord God is busily at work and the tune of the singing

---

[mm] The official program was incorrect.

birds is at hand; and His victory is assured - in nature as in grace. I am not preparing a sermon, but you draw all this out of me - even though you like myself are now an 'Emeritus"!

'What a grand send-off you had and what a lovely illustration it was you used of the bird flying into the roof - suggesting you had an appointment with the spring. I have already used it - even as l have a dozen times your parable of 'Dr Little [nn].

'Your portrait, as reproduced in *The Australian Baptist*, is excellent. Now, your life-work continues in the generations of men you have trained ... I liked your article on the Holy Spirit, as reproduced in the *Baptist*, especially the conclusion up to which it led ... You are very busy - and can thank God for so many open doors. Your place in Australian Baptist life is unique - a veritable Father in God - honoured and beloved by all ... We both would be delighted to see you again, beloved, the way for you is decided otherwise. Do give warm love to dear Gladys - together with a suitable message - bless her!! ... So we keep on - and never was my faith firmer in the ultimate triumph of God and our Saviour Christ'.

'Once again, friend beloved, all grace be yours for your public life and your domestic problems. God bless you this and every day. Our united affection'.

On 29 January he spoke at the induction service of Rev EG Wykes to the Hurlstone Park pastorate.[1052]

George Morling had enough continuing commitments to keep him occupied and to help him through his wife's sad decline. In the absence of a report it seems likely that he didn't feel able to travel to Victoria to speak, as arranged, to the Baptist Ministers' Retreat. However, since his successor, Principal E Roberts-Thomson, was not able to take up his duties until the end of first term he lectured on theology in the interregnum. He also continued to share in the teaching program of the 'Special Diploma Courses' (Bible College). Moreover, he took part in the course for the wives and fiancées of ministers and theological students.

He gave eight lectures at Strathfield Baptist Church in February[1053], and four in a lay preachers' class at Central Baptist Church in March[1054]. On 5 March he inducted Pastor G Waugh as first minister of the North Epping BC[1055]. He chaired the meeting to dedicate the 'Glad Tidings' gospel

---

[nn] A favourite children's talk given by the Principal

launch ministry on the Hawkesbury River. This meeting was held on 18 March at Epping church.[1056]

GHM sent an apology[1057] and did not attend the Special Assembly held 24 March to consider approving the participation of the Baptist Union of Australia in the World Council of Churches, a proposal rejected by a vote of 74 for and 365 against.

On 4 May he presided over the funeral service for Rev Dr AJ Waldock at the Mosman church.[1058]

On 7 May he participated in a farewell to Dr EG Gibson, leaving the NSW Baptist College to become Principal of Adelaide Bible Institute[1059]. On 8 May he gave the address at the funeral of Mrs E McDonald at Chatswood church[1060]. His successor Dr Roberts-Thomson was welcomed to the college on 30 May at Ashfield church[1061]; at which Dr Roberts-Thomson 'referred to the wonderful influence of Principal GH Morling and declared that his was an influence that the denomination could not afford to lose'.[1062]

During the school vacation at the end of first term he was the speaker at the Inter-School Christian Fellowship Counselors' Conference. In thanking him the Conference Secretary wrote, 'Thank you for expounding the deep truths of God with such clarity; thank you for choosing a subject of such relevance to our lives and purpose and work; thank you for showing us Christ's joy and peace in your words and in your life. I'm sure I am not alone in saying that you have set for me, at least, a new richness in Bible study not previously glimpsed. For this we are and will long be grateful. Our prayers go out for your wife and yourself'.

On 5 June he delivered the charge to Rev JH Brooks on the occasion of his ordination at Strathfield-Homebush church.[1063]

Seemingly the Executive of the College Council had raised the question with the Finance Committee of the Baptist Union whether Principal Morling was entitled to any payment for long service leave. A letter from the Committee came before the College Council at its June meeting. It stated that any entitlement had been met by leave when he travelled overseas in 1934 and 1951.

While there is little record at this time of his regular preaching activity in the churches it would seem to have continued. On 17 July the Secretary of the Mosman Church wrote, 'I have had occasion today to speak with some of our Church people at different times and their spontaneous expressions of appreciation of your ministry to us over the past two Sundays, together with my own feelings, prompt me to write to you on behalf of the Church saying how grateful we are for the privilege of participating in worship of our God and Saviour at such a level of exaltation and exultation'.

He proceeded to say that the whole congregation felt purified and had a new awareness of the Holy Spirit. So strong was the response of the people to the messages delivered that they wished a permanent record of them.

Over the weekend 22 and 23 July the Principal gave a series of addresses on the Holy Spirit at a house party of the Economics section of Evangelical Union. The Secretary, John Connor, wrote, '… we were all brought into a fuller realisation of the nature and place of the Holy Spirit in the Godhead. More than this we came to realise the tremendous practical applications of these glorious facts. We left the house party rejoicing in the wonder and beauty of our God'.

Principal Morling attended the rather dull July meeting of the College Council. His attendance would have been as Vice-President of the Union and does not appear to have been repeated. Possibly he paid courtesy visits to other committees and councils also.

In July one of his early students, Rev HT Johnston, died after a long illness[1064],[oo], and he took the funeral service. Mrs Johnston wrote to thank him for his 'wonderful help at the Chapel Service'. It would have been her husband's wish, she said, 'for his beloved Principal to take the service'.

He contributed an appreciation of British Baptist Rev Sydney G Morris, whose diamond jubilee of ordination was celebrated.[1065] He published an obituary of Mr William Ferguson, a Baptist layman, businessman and 'generous giver to … The Baptist Theological College of NSW ', so presumably had conducted the funeral.[1066]

[oo] Johnston was a student pastor at Marrar in 1922 and had country pastorates until 1948

There was encouragement for George Morling when in August Dr James F Sellars, pastor of a Baptist church in North Carolina wrote, 'Thank you a million times for your wonderful little book, *The Quest for Serenity*. I shall always be grateful to you for it. It has been such a tremendous blessing to us. In fact it is the most helpful and blessed book we have ever read. Next to our Bible we prize it above books'.

For his own part he continued to exercise a ministry of encouragement. One of his men had been out of pastoral service because of ill-health. Eventually he was able to return to the pastorate and towards the end of August wrote to the Principal, 'It was a great encouragement to receive your letter of fellowship and love in our Lord'.

The writer went on to speak of the help and encouragement that his brother had recently experienced through Principal's ministry in the Narraweena Church. Then he added, 'We do pray for you in your needs at home and in your occasional ministry, and thank God for the profound influence you had upon me in my College days, leading me to greater love for Christ and experimental living in the Holy Spirit'. So the encourager was himself encouraged.

A few days later on 28 August a member of the Haberfield Church wrote thanking him for his ministry there – 'We have truly enjoyed a month of good times and learned to love our Lord more. But you left the best wine till last night. What a beautiful service. None present could fail to benefit ... Hearing of your own Beloved being so near to the Kingdom we revered you more than ever'.

It was in the Haberfield Church that the Morlings had been married. The above letter probably arrived the day Gladys Morling died on 31 August. The day before her death he wrote to Sydney and Winifred Morris and an answer came dated 4 September. 'Our very dear George, Your letter of August 30 came on this morning and I hasten first to acknowledge. We expected such news as you record. You know how almost constantly you are in our loving thoughts and prayers, both Gladys and yourself. Your spirit is that of a man filled with Christ's own Spirit. But for that fact we should have to say you are <u>wonderful</u>. Even so, your soaring faith and quiet courage thrill us and we thank God. Beneath all this we sense your heart-throb and two hearts here beat in loving unison'.

'It is indeed a matter of thanksgiving that our Father so often grants a

period when our dear ones in extremis know not either their own condition or the poignant grief of their dear ones who can only look on - in seeming helplessness'.

'1 say no more - at this present, but to thank you for thinking of us in this your 'hour' and to send the needless assurance that you are both more than ever in our hearts. May God's great blessing continue upon and within you. Always affectionately, Sydney and Winifred'.

In his diary on 31 August George Morling wrote, 'Gladys died at 12.55pm at Bethel. I had prayed that the heavenly Father would be kind to her - and He was. There were several 'small' providences. The tender care of the nursing staff, especially Matron Holland and Sister Saville. The sedation on going to Bethel and during the ten days of her stay. The rapidity of the physical decline. My presence for the fifteen minutes before she died. For all I do thank the Heavenly Father'.

An obituary appeared.[1067]

'WITH CHRIST
MRS GLADYS MORLING

On Thursday, August 31, at 'Bethel' surrounded by loving Christian nurses, and her husband by her side, Mrs Gladys Morling passed Home to be with the Lord. Born of devout Congregational parents, Mrs Morling's early setting was in the valleys of South Wales in the days of the Welsh revival. Her mind and heart were well stored with the memories of that great awakening. She would recall the meetings of Evan Roberts, the singing of groups of miners on their way to work, and later, the preaching of outstanding Welshmen such as Campbell Morgan and Elvet Lewis, to hear whom men would willingly forego a half day's pay'.

'To that warm evangelical faith she responded whole-heartedly. She came to Australia with her family at the age of seventeen. She was baptized in the Haberfield Baptist Church and served as a Sunday School teacher up to the time of her marriage to the young minister who later became Principal GH Morling, MA. The marriage service was conducted by the Rev William Higlett'.

'In the pastoral years prior to the time of his Principalship, and during his wonderful and strenuous ministry of 40 years in that office, Mrs Morling gave to her husband the blessing of a happy and contented home. The measure of her greatness was the measure of her self-effacement. She contributed richly to the Principal's ministry by her willing acceptance of a restrictive home life and the somewhat primitive accommodation which was all the College could offer in the earlier days of development. He was able to visit far and wide, preaching the Gospel and exercising his expository ministry because Mrs Morling was willing to make her boundaries the four walls of their College home'.

'Successive generations of students recall the kindness and hospitality of Mrs Morling, and many hundreds of people from all walks of life have enjoyed the fellowship of her home. She had the capacity for friendship and had a sweetness of character that established abiding friendships. She was a genuine lover of little children and her children and grand-children were her delight'.

'A large number of people, representing many denominations and walks of life, gathered in the Ashfield Church for the funeral service. The pastor, Rev Harry Orr, presided, the President of the Baptist Union of New South Wales, Mr SC Squire, read the Scriptures, and the President of the Baptist Ministers' Fraternal, Rev ER Rogers, offered prayer'.

'Following an address by the pastor, Vice-Principal Wright, colleague of Principal Morling for so many years, brought the service to a close in prayer. The cortege moved to the Lawn Cemetery in Northern Suburbs where the Rev AL Leeder shared in that final ministry'.

'Around the homes of Principal and his sons and daughters will ever rest the afterglow of her godly blessing and hallowing their homes through all the years to be'.

For some days the bereaved husband resorted to his diary and found relief in committing some of his thoughts and experiences to it.

1 September 'Gladys was buried today. There was a sense of spiritual elation after the pain of the oncoming of death was put away. I am able to concentrate on the glorified spirit of my wife'.

2 September 'The sense of spiritual exaltation continues. It helps to think of Gladys now spiritually nearer me than before since there is heavenly knowledge. 1 can conceive of her being in closer fellowship than before.

3 September 'Sunday. The thought of Gladys knowing and praying for me is very real'.

4 September 'Monday. Some of the distress returned. 1 see that the spiritual stimulus of Gladys's home-going must be continuous, closer abiding in Christ. For these years that remain - if there be years - spiritual truths that I have learned must be strenuously practised'.

5 September 'Tuesday. At Manly and Collaroy with Dorothy's family and Elaine [pp], Enos [qq] deplored the lack of a spiritual message in younger preachers'.

6 September 'Wednesday. Reading Rufus Jones's *Social Law in the Spiritual World*'.

7 September 'Thursday. In evening felt too tired to pray - the night before had a frightening nightmare. But through the Holy Spirit was able to have a sense of nearness to Christ'.

8 September 'Friday. Have been humbled by the confidence of people such as Joan White and Myrtle Pickup in me. The more of such confidence the greater should be my humility. It is what God thinks about me that matters'.

9 September 'Saturday. Family unanimous about going overseas. How thankful I should be to the Heavenly Father for such love and helpfulness. Must pray that the trip will be to His glory'.

12 September 'Tuesday. A degree to recovery from tiredness. Impressed deeply with the Divine element in the spiritual life. One should think of the whole of what <u>God</u> is doing in us and through us. The one Great Cornerstone is God'.

17 September 'Preaching at Castle Hill. Feel the urge to seek more definitely the changing of lives in my teaching missions - both for Christians in sanctification and sinners in salvation. Remember Wilbur Chapman's words about definiteness'.

18 September 'Yesterday the plan to go abroad was changed. Clearly this is in the will of God who has other plans for my life. One matter is the opportunity to have a disciplined day after all the disturbances of the past'.

[pp] His two daughters
[qq] Rev Enos Coleman

Through this whole period the letters that jammed the mailbox were eloquent of the love and esteem in which the Principal and his late beloved partner were held. 'Mrs GH Morling – a tribute by Mrs A Bamford' was published.[1068]

In responding to a letter from the son of his old friend, Bert Whale, George Morling wrote, 'Yours is one of the choicest of hundreds of letters and one of the few that I shall keep. It moved me deeply and greatly helped. You have a beautiful spirit, Bert, as well as an eloquent pen. God is very real just now'.

From the letters that were kept the picture emerges of two greatly loved people and of the difficulties they had faced together. 'My recollections of life at the College with Mrs M and you are tinged with chromatic hues – they will never fade. Those four years remain forever as the highlight of my life - chiefly because of you and your dear wife and our beloved late friend John H Deane'.

'It was only after we returned that we heard that your dear partner had gone on ahead. It was sad that she had journeyed back into the past much sooner than most people but now she has completed that journey and is back with God'.

'I am one of that large company so deeply indebted to you. Possibly I more so than others, as I needed so much encouragement which was so lavishly bestowed, to get me started on my way. And I, too, gratefully acknowledge my indebtedness to the one who was your partner for so long and who made so large a contribution to your ministry. Mrs Morling was always so gracious to me when I was raw from the country and so painfully conscious of my limitations'.

'We give thanks to God that a beautiful and fragrant life now finds its consummation in the very presence of the Saviour... We thank Him, too, for your example of 'patient endurance' through long years of trial, which has been an inspiration to many of us'.

'(My husband) is also interred at the Northern Suburbs Lawn Cemetery so when I pay my frequent visits to that, to me, hallowed spot I shall not forget a tiny posy for Mrs Morling whom I dearly loved'.

'... as time goes on you will forget ... her condition of recent years and your mind will cherish memories of your earlier life together and of the great joy and happiness you experienced. I shall always think of Gladys Morling - as I first knew her - how she cared for you and thought for you - and how your ministry in your various pastorates and in the College would have been so much poorer had she not been at your side'.

'We fell in love with Mrs Morling when we first met her when holidaying at Blackheath and will always cherish the picnics we enjoyed together in those days with our young families. And, although we haven't seen much of her down the years, Mrs Morling had that rare quality of complete friendliness which took no count of time, so that whenever we met, it was always as if we had seen each other the day before. Then, too, her constant thought of others always endeared her to us. I remember when the manse was opened at Ashfield we arrived late and all the seats were taken. Mrs Morling saw us from her seat on the platform, and, somehow or other, produced a chair from somewhere, and handed it down to us. Only a small thing, perhaps, but so typical of her consideration for others and so much appreciated'.

'(We) have fond memories of Mrs Morling's friendliness. Certainly her ill health of recent times would have been largely the result of her exacting life she had to live at the College. Let me say what an inspiration you have been to me and others of us who have a deep affection for you, and esteem you highly as we have seen you translate into experience your favourite doctrine of the soul's union with Christ, during your very difficult period of sorrow and trial'.

'You have been a tower of strength to me and to many others, and now know our Heavenly Father will uphold and comfort you...'

'We've just heard with saddened hearts yet with gratitude for having relieved the agony of Mrs Morling's going home' If I can be half as sweet and faithful as your dear partner I shall do well. Every memory lingers of Mrs Morling quietly standing by. In stillness and quietness was her strength. Her presence in 'The Ridge' enriched so many of my earlier years because Christ was always there'.

'It was not our privilege to have known Mrs Morling well but we have frequently heard testimony of her character and companionship in all the life of the College through the years'.

'Once again we thank God for your ministry to us. Without your love and friendship and guidance we wouldn't be in the ministry now'.

'How wonderfully joyous your dear one must be now after nine years or so of cloud and confusion. Her Saviour and Heaven will give her the perfection of beauty and clarity of mind and fulfilment which dear Gladys Morling sought all her life. I remember her eyes always lighted with pleasure when she saw lovely colours, good pictures and art, nice clothes and homes - a true Welsh characteristic. I can see her sweet smile now and the look of pleasure in her eyes the last time I saw her - this year - when you brought her to see me. The colour and brightness of this flat pleased her. She made friends with the right kind of people and cultivated the graces of life - I remember these things especially about her. There was another true Welsh characteristic in her - she would fight for all that was true and godly and right and express herself forcibly about them, often bringing people to think her way. Yet her spirit was always sweet and she never made enemies. She has passed many of her gifts on to her children. Her voice was fascinating - and never lost the attractive Welsh accent....'

'I am delighted that I have had the opportunity of meeting Mrs Morling, especially as her background was so similar to mine in that, not only were we of the same nation, but from the same area of the municipality. You have often been in our prayers as we have remembered the burden which you have so lovingly carried in the past years'.

'My Gwladys and I always admired her for her quiet, friendly and kindly disposition'.

'Somewhere at the foundations of my life where influences still prevail I admit to a deep sense of loss since your life and the fellowship of your family has stood as the bulwark against complete failure. There has always been the image of your regard and affection at those critical times in my life - since to fail you would be tantamount to failing Him completely ...'

'We appreciated Mrs Morling's warmth and evident interest in our highest welfare down the years ... There is awaiting for you across the land the opportunity to minister Christ to thousands. I read again recently your volume - *The Secret of Serenity* - with great profit'.

'My memories of Mrs Morling are filled with appreciation for her attitude and encouragement to me as a callow student, and for her ministry to her family'.

When later in September the Annual Assembly of the NSW Baptist Union convened it had before it an enthusiastic recommendation from the Executive Committee 'that in recognition of his contribution to the life and work of our Denomination Rev GH Morling, MA, be accorded the title of 'Principal Emeritus'". The recommendation was unanimously and enthusiastically adopted[1069].

His contribution to the denomination was indicated, though briefly, in two minutes of appreciation that came before the Assembly. One was from the Executive Committee:

'The Assembly of 1922 appointed Rev GH Morling Principal of the Baptist Theological College of New South Wales. It was a God-directed appointment, as the following 38 years gave proof. December 31, 1960 saw the official termination of that appointment but not of its results or the ministry of the revered and honoured appointee. In a special edition of *Summa Supremo,* at a testimonial dinner given by graduates of the College and other ministers of the denomination, and at a denominational function, opportunity was taken to pay tribute to GH Morling to whom, by formal resolution, has been accorded the title of Principal Emeritus, to which might appropriately be added the appellation '*Cum Laude*'. The Principal Emeritus has become widely known as a well informed theologian who has also a deep interest in church history and biblical exposition. It is difficult to say whether his influence in the denomination has been greater as a teacher or as a Pastor among the students committed to his care. During his long term as Principal the College expanded in numerical enrolment and in influence. Today almost all pastorates in NSW are occupied by ministers who graduated from the College during his term of office, in which period he lectured at some time or other in every subject in the curriculum. This tribute calls attention also to the fact that over these years Rev GH Morling's ministry has been in demand among evangelicals of all denominations and in all States of Australia. This ministry, it is hoped, will be available for many years in even wider influence now that he is freed from the responsibility of lectures and administration. As a denomination we give thanks to God for George Henry Morling and for the unique service he has performed in our midst'.

The other was from the College Council:

'At the close of the year in which the Rev GH Morling, MA, retired as Principal of the College, the Council wishes to record its heartfelt appreciation of one who, in so many ways, came to represent the College to our Churches. He came to the College in the first few years of its life - at a time of crisis - and saw it through many a problem and through all the stages of growth that have marked its history so far. To the residential quarters at Granville, and then to Ashfield where the developments at Charlotte Street were marked by a continual expansion which all added to the burdens so cheerfully shouldered. The years of the depression and the war all added to the difficulties which were borne by one who had a constant battle with ill health. During his Principalship the College grew from nine students to its present 74, from a full time staff of one to a staff of four. A constant stream of men have joined the ministry at home and abroad during this period. The commencement of the new non-ministerial courses and the decision to move to Eastwood have brought a fitting finale to a ministry rarely equalled and never excelled among the Baptists of New South Wales. The College records its thanks for the privilege of having GH Morling as its Principal for so long and thanks God for his emphasis which always pointed men and women to Christ, teaching was firmly Bible centred and his example of faithful service so humbly rendered'.

During October two close friends of George Morling died, Rev AL Leeder[1070] and Rev RS Pickup.[1071] It fell to him to write tributes to his older brother ministers for inclusion in *The Australian Baptist*. They were two outstanding men and the tributes were worthy of them as the introductory paragraph of each of them will show:

'With the passing of the Rev AL Leeder at the age of 81, one of the few remaining links with the middle period of Australian Baptist history has been removed. Of the period AL Leeder was no mean representative. Physically he was a striking figure; sturdy in frame, erect in bearing, handsome, well-groomed, he was a man to attract attention. Moreover, in his character he was of impressive stature. He won honour by his transparent goodness'.

'Those of us who were closest to RS Pickup had for him an admiration reserved for the very choicest characters. One of his own ideal men was Professor Henry Drummond. Concerning him his close friend Dr John

Watson wrote: 'One did not realise how commonplace and collarless other men were till they stood side by side with Drummond ... It was as if the prince of one's imagination had dropped in among common folk. He reduced us all to peasantry'. In some degree such elevation belonged to RS Pickup. 'He is the best man I have ever met', said a Roman Catholic friend of him'.

Among his varied activities in the latter part of the year was a retreat he conducted for former students at Evans Head from 13 to 17 November. They expressed their appreciation for his 'strengthening and stimulating ministry'.

He continued to lecture for the Special Diploma students at 'Wynola' and attended a somewhat light-hearted function at the end of their year. One of the students wrote to him a few days later, 'I am indeed grateful for the privilege that has been mine: that of sitting and hearing yourself and other members of the staff, opening unto us the Scriptures. However, it wasn't just what you said that was so impressive, but the way you said it (sincerely and with conviction) and even more so the way you live it'.

Because of ill-health he was unable to attend the Graduation celebrations of the College.

On 7 December at the Stanmore Church his good friends Dr and Mrs AT Whale celebrated their Golden Wedding.[1072] He sent a gift and in the accompanying note expressed gratitude to the Heavenly Father for their friendship. He had known them through the entire period of their marriage and even before.

Christmas Day brought its reminder of the loss he had so lately suffered. There was a further touch of sadness for on that day his colleague Principal AJ Grigg of the Victorian Baptist College died.[1073]

PRINCIPAL EMERITUS

*George Henry Morling
a portrait by Joshua Smith*

CHAPTER 6 – PRINCIPAL EMERITUS

1962
It was as well that the holiday season gave him a brief respite for 1962 made great demands upon him. It proved to be a busy and eventful year.

One of his early preaching appointments was at Lakemba where he earned the thanks of the people by opening up to them the subject of the 'Holy Spirit and the Trinity'.

It was probably the first week-end of February when he travelled to Islington to preside at the church's welcome to Rev HK Watson and on the Sunday morning to induct him into the pastorate.[1074]

Although it would be many months before it was official Basil Brown, one of his men teaching in the Victorian College, had heard a whisper that moves were afoot in NSW to nominate George Morling as the President-General of the Baptist Union of Australia later in the year. He wrote on 4 February, 'I believe that your presence in the office at this juncture would be providential. Some of us are deeply concerned for the unity of our Australian Baptist work at this time. Our one-ness has been strained at a period when a united witness is vital. You command the love and respect of all, so your leadership would undoubtedly draw brethren in the various States more closely together, so furthering the Kingdom of God. I trust that you may be able to accede to the desires of your colleagues in New South Wales. You may be interested to know that those Victorians who are closely associated with the Australian Baptist Union, with whom I have been in conversation about the leadership of the Union in general, have responded most cordially to any tentative mention of your name. I am certain that you would have the whole-hearted endorsement of Victoria. I really enjoyed the brief time with you at Christmas. You are always in our prayers'.

At the time there was a deep and strongly held difference of opinion in Australian Baptist ranks over possible Baptist affiliation with the World Council of Churches and/or the Australian Council of Churches. There was genuine concern that this could lead to open division.

Another of the Morling men, Rev Tom Binks, was then General Secretary of the Baptist Union of Western Australia. A letter to the Principal dated

5 February invited him to be the principal guest speaker for Assembly from 2 to l0 October. The Union was to commence its own Theological College in 1963 and it was felt that Principal Morling's presence in the West for the Assembly would be of special significance since he had done so much to encourage the project and had suggested the thought of Rev Noel Vose as the Principal for the College.[1075]

The Australian Baptist[1076] carried a report about conversations between the Churches of Christ of NSW and the NSW Baptist Union of Churches. George Morling was one of the signatories to a combined statement included in the report. He had been a leading figure in these and similar talks through the years. On 6 March, he spoke at the ordination of Rev JA Blankley (formerly a Church of Christ minister) at Ingleburn.[1077]

On l0 March the Baptist Theological College on the Eastwood site was officially opened by Rev FA Marsh, the President-General of the Baptist Union of Australia. Principal DM Himbury of the Victorian College was the occasional preacher. Principal-Emeritus Morling took no part in proceedings but doubtless took great satisfaction in seeing the fruit of his earnest efforts over the years in the spacious new campus and its enlarged facilities.

It was announced[1078] that Principal-Emeritus GH Morling was to leave Sydney on 17 April to speak at an Easter Convention in the Boroko Baptist Church, Port Moresby, and then to visit and minister at mission stations at Baiyer River, Kompiam, Lapolama, Netherlands New Guinea (now Irian Jaya) and Telefolmin, in that order. He was to return to Sydney on the 'Malekula' on 7 June.

On 17 March Rev RK (Keith) Redman, pastor of the Boroko Church, wrote outlining the six sessions the Principal was to take in Port Moresby. He added the comments, 'We sense a spirit of anticipation in the air and much prayer is going up that the Lord will give us a gracious visitation of power and blessing'.

The Secretary of the Auburn Church in a letter dated 20 March thanked him for his ministry there during the past month. He had given a series of addresses on the deeper Christian life[1079] and many had indicated their personal response to the teaching. One of them wrote to him, 'May I thank you for your kindness in passing on to me your book *The Quest for Serenity*. One will always be grateful to God for the privilege of hearing your message. Whilst you were speaking I forgot completely the 'Principal' and was lost entirely in the message; surely there can be no greater ambition for any preacher. Your book will be a constant reminder of that memorable series which led us to such tremendous heights. I am delighted to read your assurance that there is 'Something Better' than a life of constant strivings, unfulfilled aspirations which make up so many Christian lives. I had resigned myself to a second best experience being unable to explain to others just what I was seeking for fear of being considered too introspective. I had found that my experience as a Christian was far from satisfying. I am so grateful that you describe so ably these feelings and that I am far from alone in this experience. Whether I can attain to this experience I do not know - but I am quite sure that believing that there is something better I will not be satisfied with anything less. Thank you for 'putting me on the right track', and for showing me the possibilities for the Christian life'. The writer of that letter was clearly kindred in spirit to George Morling.

Coming events were casting their shadows before them. It would appear that Rev Malcolm McCullough had invited him to take a week of meetings at the Ringwood East Church when he came to Melbourne for the Baptist Union of Australia Triennial Assembly meetings. In his reply he must have indicated certain time constraints and also the possibility that he might be nominated as President-General. On 29 March Malcolm McCullough wrote, 'We have at last made the necessary arrangements and are happy in the pleasant prospect of your coming. The SS Anniversary has been postponed and the all clear given for an unbroken week ... So please say that you can come! We would, of course, be very honoured to welcome the President-General of the Baptist Union of Australian! Please accept the nomination. I could not imagine the honour more fittingly bestowed or honourably adorned ... It would give your old graduates a very deep pleasure and, in the proper sense, pride to have you elevated to the office, disinclined though you are toward such matters'.

The news was spreading and two days later Rev Allan Tinsley wrote from Adelaide, 'From this part of the country, both personally and officially, may I urge you to accept nomination. No one more richly and rightly deserves the honour. No one could give a more constructive lead in our church life just at this moment'.

Another two days later Rev Tom Binks, General Secretary of the Western

Australian Baptist Union, added his endorsement: 'I am taking this opportunity to say, both personally and on behalf of the WA Baptists how much we hope you will accept nomination. We feel strongly that you would be able to give wise and sound leadership that would be acceptable and appreciated by Baptists throughout the Commonwealth'.

The following day Rev Arthur Wilkins, pastor of the influential Kew Baptist Church in Melbourne, urged his former Principal to accept the nomination. It was clear that there would be universal support for him as President-General.

Over the weekend, 31 March and 1 April, he took special services at Springwood and it is evident from a letter that he was a source of enrichment to the people.

As the time for him to leave for Papua New Guinea drew near there came assurances of prayerful interest and support for his demanding program. A married woman who had been a student in the special Diploma (Bible College) Course saw the wonderful trip as a reward for faithful service. However, others were more realistic. Rev JD Williams, General Secretary of the Australian Baptist Missionary Society, wrote on 5 April, 'Our Board Executive has learned with a great deal of pleasure of your projected visit to our mission fields in New Guinea. Over the years during which you have been in charge of the training of our ministers we have been very grateful for the unfeigned and practical interest that you have taken on this side of Baptist work. Your journey to New Guinea is but a confirmation of the gracious contribution you have made to Baptist missionary work throughout your long and fruitful service as Principal of the NSW College. The Board Executive have asked me to assure you of their prayers that your visit to New Guinea may bring great blessing to our missionaries. Their work is a difficult and lonely work which subjects them to difficulties and tensions unknown at home. We feel sure that your ministry will make them aware of the great spiritual resources they have in the living Lord of the Church and in that way enable them to continue in their work, conscious of the presence of God'.

In somewhat similar vein Rev J Howard Kitchen, Chairman of the ABMS Board, wrote to him and added, 'I still remember with gratitude the addresses you gave from John's Gospel the last time you were at Belgrave Heights (Convention) and am more thankful than I can say to think that this same ministry will now be extended to our missionaries, many of whom are your old students'.

One of his former students, Rev Ken Callan, then serving in Principal's early Dungog-Thalaba pastorate wrote assuring him of prayerful interest and sharing his own sense of burden, 'Having spoken to some of the fellows who are home on furlough, I feel concerned that there is a need and your going is very much God-directed. I think that there is a difficulty in experiencing the constancy of abiding, and for confident trust in a Heavenly Father. Knowing a little of New Guinea and a lot about my own weakness and deficiencies and how God has blessed through the simple trust of letting Him work in and through me (I am still a long way down the ladder) the life of faith in God as my loving Heavenly Father, my heart is burdened for them'. There was a postscript – 'Am looking forward to July'. Principal Morling had accepted an invitation to take some special services at Dungog-Thalaba.

A few days before he left for New Guinea, on 10 April, there was a farewell service at Northbridge Church for Rev Doug and Mrs Rosemary (daughter of Gladys' sister Elizabeth) Vaughan as they returned to missionary service in New Guinea. Opportunity was taken at the same meeting to bid the Principal Godspeed.[1080]

If evidence was needed that he could exercise a continuing ministry of great effectiveness it was supplied by his seven weeks in New Guinea. *The Australian Baptist*[1081] carried the following interim report:

'GH MORLING IN NEW GUINEA

Blessing has attended the meetings addressed by Principal Emeritus, Rev GH Morling, who is at present visiting the mission stations in New Guinea. The following comments of his visit to the Baiyer River indicate the missionaries appreciation for the Convention conducted by the Principal.

From Mr and Mrs Arthur Paterson: 'For our Annual Convention and Conference, Rev GH Morling, former Principal of the NSW Baptist Theological College, gave us eight addresses in nine days as well as devotional talks before each day's business began. What he gave was exactly what we needed - we all felt blessed as he told us the way to a quieter and calm inner life and how to make the most of prayer times. The first result was a Conference conducted in a quiet, calm atmosphere with no clashing wills and no discordant notes! In fact it was a most helpful Conference both in matter under discussion and the manner in which it was discussed'.

'From Miss Ruth Marks: 'Well, the Principal has been and gone. He certainly helped to prepare the way for one of the best conferences I have attended. The spirit of fellowship was terrific. You will not hear anything but praise for the way in which he seemed able to help us, each one personally. We all thoroughly enjoyed his ministry on Ephesians, and I think that the appreciation in Conference minutes hardly expresses our appreciation. I think we were dumb-struck and couldn't find enough of the right words to use to express our thanks"'.

'Principal Morling has since visited the Lapolama and the Kompiam Stations in the Sau Valley and West Papua [π] where he attended the first baptisms at Tiom in the North Baliem Valley. Before returning home he will visit Telefolmin and pay another visit to Boroko, Port Moresby. He is due back in Sydney on June 5'.

'The NSW Missionary Council is arranging a welcome home to Principal Morling, details of which will be published in the next issue of *The Australian Baptist*'.

The Minute of Appreciation to which the report made reference read 'Field Council wishes to record its heartfelt appreciation for the visit of Rev GH Morling who gave himself and ministered very acceptably in convention and discussion groups. His wealth of practical experience, theological perspicuity and rare ability to accommodate to primitive culture, contributed at the time when the first Dani churches are being established, will play a vital part in the spiritual development of these people'.

As planned he arrived back in Sydney on 5 June 'well but tired'. There was a welcome home at North Sydney Church on 22 June [1082] and he was able to give an account of his experiences and impressions.

Rev JD Williams wrote to him on 26 June thanking him for material he had written on his visit to New Guinea. The Australian Baptist Missionary Society published it under the title 'Impressions of New Guinea' by Principal GH Morling.

[π] Now Irian Jaya province of Indonesia.

Shortly after his return another of the NSW Baptist stalwarts, Rev Percy Goodman, died on 16 June.[1083] The funeral was held in the Hurlstone Park Church on 18 June. It was almost inevitable that George Morling should be called to give the tribute, part of which ran, 'Rev Percy Goodman was a minister of Jesus Christ of whom it could be said without any reservation that he magnified his office. He possessed in rare degree the grace of humility. He effaced himself that Christ might be exalted. There was in him the stability and dependability of the truly strong man. An outstanding pastor of souls he had the nature that went out in sympathy and helpfulness to all sorts and conditions of people. He gave himself utterly to others for Christ's sake'.[1084]

In June he preached for three Sundays at Merrylands.[1085]

Early in July Dr Peter and Mrs Burchett were to return to the CJ Tinsley Medical Centre in the Baiyer River area.[1086] A denominational farewell was given to them at the Parramatta Church on 3 July. Under the heading 'GH Morling Tells the New Guinea Story' *The Australian Baptist*[1087] presented a *précis* of his address at the meeting. He gave a factual account of the actual conditions under which the people live, effectively stripping away any falsely romantic ideas of missionary service. But then he stirred the congregation with an account of what God had done and was doing in the highlands of New Guinea. He claimed that as a result of his visit to that needy field he would never be the same again. It was decided that he should be asked to speak at other regional meetings that would be arranged.

Within a week or so he was off on a preaching visit to some of the churches in the north of the State, beginning with the long anticipated sentimental journey back to his early pastorate of Dungog-Thalaba.[1088] A report of his visit summed it up briefly – 'From 15 to 22 July we were blessed with the gracious ministry of Rev GH Morling. These meetings took the form of a Holiness Convention. Our churches combined for the two Sunday evenings, the first of which was a baptismal service'.[1089]

That was indeed a remarkable service for eighteen were received into membership. It meant a great deal to their former pastor and he made this clear as he said: "It is no ordinary experience for me to stand in this pulpit on the occasion of a baptismal service and with people both of Thalaba and Dungog, perhaps of other places present'.

'I saw the erection of this church. I preached the first sermons. I conducted the first baptismal service - that was 45 years ago. Holy memories crowd in upon me. In the circumstances, at this time of reminiscence, I feel the urge not to preach a formal sermon but to speak about my spiritual pilgrimage'.

'Let me tell you more particularly what the Lord Jesus has come to mean to me - now that I am 70 years of age. In a word <u>Real</u>'.

The points of his address were that Jesus meant
1. Rest from the sense of guilt – 'As a boy I knew the terror of the law - then in Christ I knew the calm of sins forgiven'.
2. Rest from the fear of failure. The fear of failure had almost obsessed him.
3. Rest from inner disharmony.

It was an account of his 'quest for serenity'.

There is no complete record of the other churches he visited but he was with another of his men, Rev Reg Pope, at Lismore, taking a teaching mission from 3 to 5 August and preaching at the 49th Anniversary of the church, and with yet another, Rev Merv Hammond, at Casino[1090] and with yet one more, Rev Jim Cox, for a week of meetings from 15 August at Maclean.

Then on the first weekend in September he was at Millthorpe with Rev David Nicholas telling the story of his New Guinea visit.[1091]

He was appointed a delegate of the BUNSW to the Triennial Assembly of the Baptist Union of Australia.[1092] Unofficially it had been taken for granted that he would be nominated for the position of the President-General of the Baptist Union of Australia. The Executive Committee of the Baptist Union of NSW made the nomination official by a decision at its August meeting.[1093] At the Triennial Assembly meetings of the Baptist Union of Australia in Melbourne on 5 September, Rev George Henry Morling, MA, was elected President-General for a three year term, the fourth NSW man to have that honour. Rev LJ Gomm, then pastor of Flinders Street Church, Adelaide, wrote to him, 'The sustained acclamation with which the news was received was really heart-warming'. The report in *The Australian Baptist*[1094] had no fear of contradiction when it declared 'his appointment will be acclaimed by all'.

Its confidence was confirmed by the messages of congratulations that he received in the weeks that followed. Individual churches and unions assured him of their delight at his appointment and of their prayerful support. Among the individuals was Rev Stanley Dickson, one of his fellow-students of Harris Street days, living then in retirement at Belmont on Lake Macquarie.

The Baptist Union of Victoria Assembly Meetings overlapped the Triennial meetings. So it happened that his first official function as President-General was to give the ordination charge to five Victorian ordinands. In his address he emphasised some of the tensions that confront every minister. He must achieve a balance between pastoral responsibility and the rest of faith, a sense of authority and a spirit of humility, 'apostolic madness' and 'apostolic discipline'.

After the address Rev John Morley, the Victorian President and one of Principal Morling's men, made an appeal and four young people responded 'for full-time service'. Subsequently the General Secretary of the Union wrote thanking him for what he described as 'a very notable service'.[1095]

Immediately following the Assembly meetings, from 9 to 16 September, the Principal conducted an 'Inner Mission' at the Ringwood East Baptist Church. The pastor of the church, Rev Malcolm McCullough, in a letter to his people concerning the details of the 'mission' spoke of the President-General as 'the beloved 'Prof''. It was the title commonly used by students in the College right through the years. In all, he took nine meetings at Ringwood East. It was a good introduction to the demanding years ahead.

Back in Sydney he officiated at the opening of the new building at the Clemton Park Church on 22 September. He declared the church open and preached.[1096] Next he shared in the Assembly Meetings of the NSW Union. In particular on 26 September he spoke at the Missionary Rally, telling the story of the birth of the church in the North Baliem Valley of West New Guinea.[1097] He had witnessed some of the first baptisms in a church which was soon to experience a baptism of blood and enter some of its number in the roll of martyrs.

Almost at once he flew to Perth as the guest preacher at the Assembly meetings of the Baptist Union of Western Australia. His first responsibility was to speak at the College night on 8 October. It was reported that it was 'particularly appropriate that the President-General, Principal-Emeritus GH Morling of the NSW Baptist Theological College, should be our guest speaker when the need and enormity of instituting our own Theological College was placed before the Assembly'.[1098]

He had in fact been quietly influential in his advice and suggestions to the Western Australia committee that was working to establish the College.

Once more it was his joy to speak at the ordination service and also at a men's dinner. On Sunday, 7 October, he preached at the Bedford Park Church[1099] where Rev A (Bert) Maynard, one of his earlier students, was the pastor. Bert Maynard had taken a prominent part in working towards a Western Australian College.

Rev Tom Binks, yet another of his men and General Secretary of the WA Union wrote on 16 October saying, in part, '… many expressed the feeling that this last Assembly was the 'best ever'. This was in no small way due to your godly ministry of the Word and your gracious warm-heartedness which were an inspiration to many of our people. Several commented that now they can understand why ex-NSW students always speak so highly of their Principal'.

On 3 November he was in Melbourne to speak at the Melbourne Bible Institute graduation service. For some reason at that time the continuing ministry of the great missionary to China, Hudson Taylor, was being remembered. He chose to speak on 'What I owe to Hudson Taylor', and began by saying, 'In the life of the Spirit there is 'a law of triangularity'. That is to say, God does not normally come to us in a direct vertical way but through another illumined soul who 'speaks to our condition''. Hudson Taylor was one who had been used by God to speak to him as a young minister. 'Hudson Taylor', he said, 'came into my life at a time when I was earnestly and somewhat painfully seeking for a more satisfying and effective spiritual life'. One of the hearers that day wrote to him, 'you spoke of 'triangular blessing' and this was certainly experienced for God spoke to me through your message'.

The following day the Principal was the speaker at a meeting arranged by the China Inland Mission.

On 18 November the Eastwood Baptist Church had a Day of Thanksgiving when a new gallery in the church building was dedicated. The President-General, an old friend of the church and a father in Christ to its pastor, Rev Doug Mill, preached at the service of thanksgiving.[1100] On the morning of the same day he was the speaker at Chatswood's Church Anniversary. Around the same time he was a leading advocate for the Baptist Union of Australia World Relief appeal.[1101]

Within the space of a few days he received two letters on the official stationery of the Governor-General of Australia. The first, dated 21 November, was from the Aide-de-Camp acknowledging a letter of sympathy written by the President-General on behalf of Australian Baptists. The other was marked <u>Personal and Confidential</u>. It was from the Official Secretary to the Administrator and read in part, 'I have the honour to inform you that Her Majesty The Queen would be graciously pleased to appoint you an Officer of the Most Excellent Order of the British Empire and I am therefore directed by His Excellency the Administrator to ask you to telegraph me whether this honour would be acceptable to you'.

It was and the required telegram was duly sent saying simply, 'Gratefully Accept'.

Two items in *The Australian Baptist* concerned George Morling. Rev Sydney Morris in his 'London Letter' congratulated his dear friend on his appointment as President-General and the Union on having such a President.[1102] There was also a brief exegetical treatment of John 3:5 by the Principal-Emeritus. It was designed to help some of his fellow-Baptists who were having trouble with the verse.[1103] Subsequently, several others contributed their interpretations to a lively discussion.

The days were fully occupied for he had a demanding program ahead of him. Christmas came and he was at home in West Pennant Hills until after Christmas dinner. In the afternoon he was taken to Collaroy where his close friend Enos Coleman lived and members of the family were holidaying. Then it was off to Katoomba where he was one of the featured speakers on 26 and 27 December at the Christian Convention.[1104] Always thirsting for complete uniformity to Christ he took as his subjects, 'The Antecedents of Holiness', and 'Holiness is by Faith'. He preached out of a rich experience but to no one more than himself.

George Gordon Rees Morling
25 June 1922 -3 March 2008

On 27 December he had lunch with his friends the Lindstroms at Blackheath and then spent the night with son Gordon and his wife Joyce at Springwood.

Next morning at 11am he flew out of Sydney to visit mission stations and to speak at conferences in Singapore, India and Pakistan.[1105]

Arriving in Singapore late in the afternoon he was met by the local Director of the China Inland Mission and entertained at the Mission's headquarters.

In the evening he spoke at their Friday Evening Fellowship. Saturday was busy; in the morning, a tour of the city, in the afternoon a visit with Dr Alan Cole (then at Trinity United Church College) and in the evening, an address at a young men's barbecue social. Sunday was busier for he spoke four times, 7.30am and 9.30am at the Presbyterian Church, 5pm to an evangelical group on the will of God and in the evening at the China Inland Mission fellowship. Monday morning he again addressed the China Inland Mission people who were having a day of prayer.

In the afternoon he caught a plane to Calcutta and was met there by Rev Walter Corlette, pastor of Carey Baptist Church, and entertained warmly at his manse. That night there was a Watch-Night Service and in a crowded church the Australian visitor was the speaker. In a letter home he commented, 'New Year's eve was a bit disturbing ... At the turn of the year loud explosive fireworks went off. The noise disturbed the crows which abound here everywhere and they set up a harsh protesting that went on for a couple of hours'.

1963
New Year's Day was Sunday[ss] and he was the guest preacher at the 154th Anniversary of the Carey Church. He noted in a travel diary, 'The Metropolitan Bishop of India, Burma and Ceylon was present. I felt very much at home. Mr Corlette has preserved the warm evangelical tradition'. 'In a letter next day he wrote, 'I feel the tour has opened well and promises to be without strain. I am speaking easily'.

[ss] New Year's Day was a Tuesday. Perhaps this service was a special event, or happened later in January.

Back in Australia when the Queen's New Year Honours list was released the name of George Henry Morling was among those honoured as an Officer of the Most Excellent Order of the British Empire.[1106] Though it was some time before he received them numerous messages of congratulations arrived at the Pennant Hills home. Apart from the customary telegrams from the Prime Minister, the State Governor and the Premier, messages flowed in from Baptist Unions, Boards, Committees and churches and from his wide range of friends and admirers.

O.B.E

In acknowledging an official cable of congratulations he subsequently wrote, 'I appreciate your congratulations. I owe much to the fellowship of my Baptist brethren and I would like to think that in honouring me Her Majesty is honouring you all'.[1107]

The Queen would be visiting Sydney in March and an investiture would be held at Government House. George Morling had to decline an invitation to attend it. This meant, however, that during his visit to England he was invested with the honour at Buckingham Palace.

Sydney Morris's London Letter in *The Australian Baptist*[1108] included this item – 'The news ... that ex-Principal Morling has been made an OBE for his services to Theology gives widespread pleasure to our Baptist folk in Britain as well as to thousands in Australia and elsewhere'.

This was a final salute from George Morling's dear friend for before he reached England his friend was dead. Meanwhile he was some months in India and East Pakistan.

After the early burst of sustained activity it appears that he was given further speaking engagements for the next few days. He even comments that he went to a badminton match on Wednesday night.

On Thursday Mr Corlette accompanied him to Lucknow for the Annual Conference of the Evangelical Alliance of India. He was the special speaker and was associated with Rev Subodh Sahu. In a letter home he wrote, ' ... about 300 missionaries and Indian pastors from all over India have attended. This is the first purpose of my coming and there will not be anything as important. There will be small pastors' conferences after this'.

The meetings were held at the Martiniere College – 'a great building more like a military academy with battlements'. He shared a room with Subodh. It was at the top of 39 stone stairs; it measured 50' by 30' and had 'a great domed ceiling quite 30 feet high covered with representations of Greek mythology in gold and ivory'. Despite its grand scale it was comfortless and toilet and washing facilities were none too good. Fortunately on Thursday Mr Corlette arranged for an American missionary couple to take him into their home and look after him.

He took two series of addresses, one on John in the mornings and the other in the evenings on The Life of Devotion. There was a most encouraging response to his ministry.

While in Lucknow he visited the residency famous for the Sepoy mutiny and associated with General Havelock. He also picked up a 'tummy wog' but soon responded to treatment. A letter to his daughter Dorothy concluded, 'They are not working me too hard'.

After almost a week there he moved on to New Delhi and again was entertained by American missionaries. Until the weekend he had a chance to relax and visit some of the famous tourist sites, Agra (in an air-conditioned train) with the Taj Mahal and the great red fort. On Sunday he preached at the Free Church (alternately Methodist and Baptist) in the morning. It was in its Baptist phase with a keen evangelical minister and the church was full. In the evening he was at a new Methodist Church pastored by an American evangelical Quaker. He described it as a small but warm service.

His diary reflects the concern that was then abroad because of the Chinese-Indian border dispute. Mrs Banderanaike of Ceylon was even then in New Delhi consulting with Mr Nehru in reference to it. In a tour of the official buildings of the capital he was aware of tension and of rising patriotic fervour.

In Hyderabad he was looked after by Australian missionaries (Mr and Mrs S Skillicorn). He also spent some time with two Anglican missionaries, Mr Jack Dain, later to be Bishop Dain of Sydney, and Rev Laurie Pullen of Sydney. They were less than impressed with the Church of South India which had embraced a number of denominations. A new bird, it was said, had appeared in South India, The Great Swallow. It had the power to reduce all that it swallowed to 'the lowest common denominator'.

By contrast the Principal was taken to 'Hebron', the centre of a movement led by an Indian Christian Bahkt Singh. He wrote, 'I saw the end of a service which had lasted 5-1/2 hours. People had come in from miles away. The faces of the women, so strong and shining, deeply impressed. Some had been cast out of their homes and had been given shelter. Frequent days of prayer and fasting are held. He has 300 preaching places in South India. Unhappily he has only condemnation for missionaries of the church. He himself is warm and strong. He came to one of my meetings and at tea at 'Hebron' prayed appreciatively for me'.

On Monday 21 January, he travelled on to Poona via Bombay and was given hospitality at the Poona and Indian Village Mission home. At no great distance from Poona was Nasrapur where the Mission had a Spiritual Life centre. There he conducted a Pastors' Retreat, leading studies on Ephesians and giving practical talks, through an interpreter. The Retreat ended on 30 January with a Communion Service.

The next day he was taken to the Western Ghats, the chain of mountains that runs down the western side of India. It was an eventful day with sight-seeing, visits to Christian institutions, vehicle breakdown and unexpected hospitality in an Indian village home. The party did not get back to Poona till late that night.

Some of the records of the following weeks are missing and others are lacking in detail. However, until early in March he conducted a series of Retreats and Conferences for Pastors and Christian workers (largely missionaries).

11-17 February at Palidhi, a village in Madhya Pradesh.
19-24 February at Balingir in Orissa.
26 February to 2 March at Ballasore.

At the last-named he took on successive days the themes of Fellowship, The Will of God, The Soul's Union with Christ, The Holy Spirit and The Church. These were probably the areas of preaching on which he concentrated in all the Retreats.

For much of March he visited a number of the mission stations of the Australian Baptist Missionary Society in East Pakistan. The political situation was tense, some missionary activity (for example bazaar preaching) was curtailed and by and large the morale of the missionaries was low. Some felt that external factors and the demands of routine and administrative tasks kept them from doing adequately the work for which they had been trained and for which they had come to the field. The visit of the President-General was just what they needed.

An article headed 'President-General in E Pakistan' appeared in *The Australian Baptist*[1109] - 'The President-General, Rev GH Morling, OBE, MA, has stirred congregations of nationals and missionaries in East Pakistan and India as he has addressed them on the great facts of the Christian faith. Rev Henry West of Birisiri said, 'The meetings took us back many years in the history of the Christian Church here. Principal Morling linked us with the spirits of just men made perfect as he spoke vividly and vitally of the work of devotion of the Nalls, the Lanyons and the Whites, to mention only a few. On Friday morning he gave another stirring address to the students and staff of the Training Institute. He spoke of the presentation of truth through personality, the material was weighty and solid, but this is the Principal's greatness - he takes the matters of truth and grace, practical service and righteousness, and interprets them in simple, forthright terms. Though his words needed translation, his enthusiasm and vitality bore directly on each hearer. This time with the President-General was blessed indeed'.

At Birisiri he again met leading Garo Christian, Bilu Babu. Principal Morling remembered that more than 36 years previously during his first visit to 'the Indian field' Bilu Babu had acted as interpreter at his meeting at Birisiri. The Garo leader had forgotten that fact but the score was even because the Australian visitor had forgotten meeting Bilu Babu when he had visited Sydney[1110].

Nearby at Joyramkura he unveiled a plaque at the site of a mission hospital. 'This hospital in Joyramkura', he said at the unveiling, 'would open up new vistas of opportunity for the service of Christ in Pakistan'[1110].

The Australian Baptist[1109] also reported that the Executive of the Baptist Union of Australia 'decided to ask the Rev GH Morling, while in Moscow, to sound out our Russian brethren on the proposed visit of Russian Baptists to Australia'[1111]. It would appear that his plans were changed for there is no record of him visiting the Soviet Union.

On 30 March away in London his dear friend Sydney Morris died. He was in his ninetieth year. When he had celebrated 60 years in the ministry George Morling said of him, 'There would be few to dispute the judgment that Sydney Morris is the best loved Baptist in Great Britain'. In a brief comment on his friend's death he wrote[1112], 'Sydney Morris was very much of a personality. In him were blended robust strength, mature wisdom, understanding tolerance, deep conviction, whimsical humour - every quality beautified by a love for his fellows that one has rarely seen equalled. His warm humility found all manner of practical expressions'.

That same day Elaine Morling left Sydney by air to join her father at Mt Hermon School, Darjeeling. She then accompanied him for the remainder of his overseas tour.[1113]

Having completed his visit to East Pakistan Principal Morling had moved on to Mt Hermon where one of his former students, Rev David Stewart, was the Principal.[1114] Despite his age and a somewhat 'old world' approach to life he had a remarkable ability to get across to young people. At Mt Hermon he shared his insights into Scripture with students and staff and endeared himself to all.

On 4 April, Easter Sunday, he deeply impressed all as he preached on 'The Gladness of the resurrection'.

Precise details of his activities during the next three months are not available. Very likely he and Elaine moved on to England fairly soon after Easter. At some stage visits were paid to relatives of the Morling family in England and to those of the Coleman family (the late Mrs Morling's family) in Wales. There were also visits to English friends including Mrs Le Quesne and family and Mrs Winifred Morris. Notes indicate that he also went to see officers of the Baptist Union of Great Britain and Ireland. He also spent time with three former students then in Great Britain. One was Mr Robert Pitt who after pastoral work in Australia and Canada was in business in London as a professional photographer. Another, Rev Arthur Cundall, was also in London lecturing in Old Testament at the London Bible College. He and Elaine were entertained by the Cundalls for several periods. The third was Rev Ken Manley. He was pursuing further studies at Bristol University with which the Bristol Baptist College was associated.

Meanwhile back in Australia on 19 June yet another of his men, Rev GN Vose, was installed as the first Principal of the Western Australian Baptist Theological College.[1115] At the service acknowledgment was made of the part played by Principal Morling in bringing that 'Great

Day' to fulfilment.

A letter to The Reverend George H Morling, OBE, from the Secretary of the Central Chancery of the Orders of Knighthood advised that an Investiture would be held at Buckingham Palace on Tuesday, 16 July, and requested his attendance. Needless to say he complied and with his essential 'Britishness' it meant much to him to be invested with his honour by the Queen in Buckingham Palace.[1116]

He and Elaine were to leave England on 29 July and return home by way of the Continent, Palestine and Hong Kong.[1117] All the information readily available is that they visited the German Baptist Seminary in Hamburg and Baptist work among refugees in Hong Kong. In the latter place they were looked after by Rev Frank Marsh, the Principal's predecessor as President-General of Australian Baptists. They reached Sydney on 17 August, a week earlier than originally intended, so that two days later the President-General could be in Melbourne to chair the annual meetings of the Boards and Council of the Baptist Union of Australia.[1118]

On 31 August a service was held to commemorate the 20th Anniversary of Rev WA (Albert) Purdy's ministry at the Hornsby Church, George Morling's early pastorate. Though he had no part to play in the service it was noted as a pleasant surprise that he was in attendance.[1119]

When at the NSW Assembly meetings seven men were ordained on 11 September he was the preacher. An account of his address was published[1120],[tt] under the heading 'The Minister's Authority is from Christ'. In it he presented many of his ruling convictions concerning 'a balanced ministry'. He appeared in the Assembly program as Chair of the Baptist Historical Committee[1121], and was elected to the Executive Committee.[1122]

It was a tense Assembly for there was open criticism of Principal E Roberts-Thomson.[1123] Assembly had a notice of motion moved by Mr RE Walker, Chairman of the College Council, that a Principal not be appointed. George Morling again revealed his powers of leadership by his ability to sway the Assembly. He moved, and Dr John Hercus seconded, that the appointment be deferred to the 1964 Assembly, with

---

[tt] The printed program gives the title as 'The Necessity of Balance in an Effective Ministry.

Roberts-Thomson to continue in office meanwhile.[1124] He spoke warmly and strongly in defense of his successor, suggested that a Consultative Committee be appointed to assist the Principal, and proceeded to nominate such a committee from the floor of the house.[1125] Walker's motion was withdrawn.[1126] One of his former students subsequently wrote to him, 'Ever since the Assembly it has been my intention to write and say how much I respected your stand, realising how much personal disturbance you must have suffered in so doing'.

Some years later a friend recalled the scene – 'I know you and your tactful methods very well. I have seen them in various churches in the denomination, the college, in times of strife and stress and strain. I remember how kindly, tactfully, yet with determination you sat … Mr Porter down in the chair on the platform at Central, after he had stumped half way up the aisle to speak against Roberts-Thomson. Nobody except yourself could have sat him down just as he was about to speak against the Principal of the College, because he was a determined, trained man with a great mind. But you did it! And saved the situation, when the church was full of hostile, rebellious students. I can see the scene as I write. It would have ended in a fight - that meeting - had Mr Porter spoken'.

In the second week of October he was involved in the Assembly meetings of the Baptist Union of South Australia[1127] speaking on three occasions. One of these was a devotional session when he spoke on 'Prayer'. It brought a delightful letter of appreciation from Adeline Wesley-Smith, widow of a prominent Baptist minister. His address on Union Sunday at Brighton church was broadcast over the National radio station.[1128]

Not being able to be present at Granville's 75th Anniversary on 12 October he had sent a greeting to be read.[1129] On Sunday 13 October he was in Melbourne, preaching in the morning at Canterbury and in the evening at a service for the boys of Carey Baptist Grammar at Melbourne Town Hall.[1127]

Letters came in response to both services. The Canterbury secretary, having indicated many expressions of how meaningful and helpful the addresses had been, concluded, 'For some time now we have been endeavouring to find a means of having you in our pulpit and now, having done so, we shall be looking forward with pleasurable anticipation of doing so again'.

The other letter was also warmly appreciative but it had a sting in the tail, 'I think you left many thoughts with them (the boys) to ponder (even they thought it a bit long!)'.

He returned at once to South Australia for ministry in several of the churches, beginning on 16 October with an address to the South-West District Baptist Association in the Brighton Church. Among other commitments there was a time of retreat in the Adelaide hills with the Cheltenham Church. Later a tape of a talk by the Principal was sent to the church and the pastor wrote, 'Several remarked to me afterwards that they could shut their eyes and see you, sitting back in that old arm chair up in the hills, talking to us of the things of the Lord'. A report[1130] said, 'Rev GH Morling, OBE, MA, is still with us ... He has won the hearts of all who have heard him. He is an excellent ambassador to all Baptists in our southern State. ... At the moment he is meeting groups of ministers and addressing District Associations ... He leaves us all in his debt'.

On 24 October he was in the northern town of Whyalla taking the midweek Bible study.[1131] Not long after he must have returned to Sydney for there is a report of him inducting Rev Doug Vaughan to the Lakemba pastorate on 3 November[1132]. He conducted another such service on 24 November when Rev Neville Abrahams began a ministry at the North Sydney Church, taking as the subject of his address, 'The Commissioning of the Man of God'. The next weekend he travelled to Mudgee and preached at services opening an enlarged sanctuary and new hall.[1133] In the morning service he conducted a 'Dedication Service' as Rev and Mrs John Strugnell presented their son before the Lord.

At Punchbowl Church on 5 December he preached at a Commissioning Service for several of his former students who were proceeding to missionary service in New Guinea.[1134]

Somewhere towards the close of the year he paid a week-long visit to Tamworth where he had his first pastoral experience. The Mayor of Tamworth extended a civic reception to him as the President-General of the Baptist Union of Australia. In replying to a speech of welcome by the Mayor he said that his visit was 'in the nature of a jubilee celebration' as it was just 50 years since he first came to Tamworth.

A letter from Subodh Sahu dated 14 December indicated his great thoughtfulness for it was acknowledging the Principal's gift to Subodh's boys of pictures of Australian natives and also of local flora and fauna. 'We are extremely grateful to you,' he wrote, 'that you even remember us, and the small details of the conversations of my sons'.

On 22 December he preached at Strathfield-Homebush church – 'the service was taped and sent to missionaries in New Guinea'.[1135]

The Christmas-New Year season saw him back on the convention circuit for from 26 December to 1 January he was one of the speakers at the Mt Tamborine Convention in Queensland.[1136] The Queensland Secretary of the China Inland Mission in a subsequent letter spoke of the 'happy memory of fellowship with you at Mt Tamborine' and assured him that his ministry had been a blessing not only to many but to the writer personally.

1964
On 22 January he conducted the funeral of Rev LM Thompson at Burton Street Tabernacle.[1137]

Over the Australia Day Holiday week-end, 25-27 January, he was featured in another convention, this time at Tallangatta in northern Victoria. It was organised by the Baptist Association of North-East Victoria.

There was an entry in his diary on 14 February – 'Spent time in concentrated prayer until 9.30 reading Philippians and meditating. Felt a real sense of Presence and an awakening of aspiration. From 10 until 11 special intercession for the Retreat in March, Guidance for the studies on the Holy Spirit and the response of the ministers, especially the younger ones. Ask for ability to pray in dependence on the Holy Spirit; so quietly without nervous strain and in faith. Then read Philippians – Paul's aspiration after Christ. Until 12 o'clock prayer about the college situation'.

The reference to the 'Retreat' was to the Baptist ministers' School of Theology to be held in a few weeks time. There was fairly widespread concern about certain aspects of the teaching about the Holy Spirit that were being stressed. The ministers were looking to George Morling to set the teaching in true perspective. 'The College situation' referred to the pressure that Principal Roberts-Thomson was under to resign.

On 16 February he preached at the Induction Service of Rev Ian Spencer as he became the pioneer pastor of a new work at Green Valley, a Housing Commission area near Liverpool.[1138]

The following weekend he was in Victoria to preach at three services in connection with the Centenary Celebrations of the Warrnambool Church. The pastor, Rev PN Simmons, trained under him.

Then about a week later on 5 March he was the preacher at the Queensland College Commencement Service.

He had to return at once to NSW to induct Rev BGW Moore into the Punchbowl pastorate on 8 March.[1139] Then he was the main speaker for the Ministers' School of Theology at Katoomba 9-13 March.[1140] A letter of appreciation from the Secretary of the Fraternal concluded, 'So many have spoken of a new work of God's grace in their lives - all were enriched'. The Baptist Union of NSW was preparing to celebrate its centenary in 1968 and had set up a 'Centenary Committee'. The Centenary Crusade Director, Rev AC Prior, wrote, 'I have been asked to convey to you the very real appreciation of the Centenary Committee for the service which you gave in presenting the doctrine of the Holy Spirit at the recent Ministers' School of Theology. The members of the Committee believe that the leadership which you have given in this way will provide a basis upon which we can present this ... emphasis to our Diaconates and Churches'.

Apparently he went to Melbourne shortly after for a letter from the southern capital dated 6 April starts, 'Thank you for your note. We are glad you were happy here. We loved having you and have rated you the 'perfect guest'! - no trouble, most appreciative, good company and an inspiration to us'.

He inducted Rev Bruce Thornton into the pastorate of the Kogarah Central church.[1141]

On 20 March the Executive Committee of the NSW Baptist Union had before it the resignation of Rev Dr E Roberts-Thomson as Principal of the Theological College.[1142] This was a cause of sadness for the Principal-Emeritus both for friendship's sake and for the detrimental influence on the College. The Vice-Principal of the College, Rev BG Wright, was overseas on study leave. Under these circumstances George Morling accepted an invitation to lecture in theology at the College during the second and third terms.

However, for the immediate future he was off once more to Queensland to be the guest speaker at the Queensland Union's Half-Yearly Assembly Meetings at Warwick. His theme was 'Some Elements of the Faith and Life of the Baptists'. The reporter for the occasion said that he 'held the congregations almost spellbound as he expounded the Scriptures' and added, 'There is no doubt that Rev GH Morling is in a real sense God's gift to the Baptist Churches of Australia and his contributions to the thinking and the devotions of the Assembly added tremendously to the high spiritual tone that prevailed'.[1143]

Rev FJ Stone, General Secretary of the Queensland Union, in his letter of appreciation expressed the opinion that the visit of the President-General was also valuable in cementing relations between Australian Baptists, thus making for mutual understanding and co-operative effort. However, there was also a more personal note in the letter. The Secretary wrote, 'Now that you have been called to help in the work of the College in NSW I know that you will do this with complete reliance upon God and realising that as we emphasise the major issues of the Christian faith and experiences, the lesser issues often given more prominence, will fall into their place. I trust that you will now be able to have a period of complete rest and relaxation. We would also like to thank your daughter for her sacrifice in having you away for such a lengthy period'.

It may be commented that it was in fact many years before the College recovered from its hurtful experience. A further remark is that the letter contains the first official hint that all was not well with Elaine Morling. She was in fact already battling with a debilitating disease (cancer[1144]) that before a year was out claimed her life.

For the next few weeks it is possible that Principal Morling had some respite from the demands that were made upon him as President-General. Moreover, since a great many churches were involved in evangelistic missions conducted by preachers from Missouri, USA for several weeks, he probably had few requests to preach from Sydney churches. He presided over a welcome to the Missouri visitors on 16 April.[1145]

On 10 May[1146], 17 May[1147] and 24 May[1148], he preached at Central Baptist

Church. Rev Harry Rowe of that church had suffered a heart attack. GHM preached on the Holy Spirit. On 24 May, his title was 'The Holy Spirit as the Spirit of Christ'. On the following weekend he took a series of meetings at the Springwood Church.[1149]

Whatever break he may have had would have been taken up with lecture preparation for his renewed College responsibility.

Over the weekend of 20 and 21 June he shared in a Missionary Convention at Pennant Hills Church. Unable two days later to attend a function in Melbourne to mark the retirement of Chaplain-General A Brooke he sent a letter of greeting in which he spoke of Allen Brooke as 'one of his boys'.[1150]

About this time the health of his daughter, Elaine, took a distinct turn for the worse. A letter from Principal EC Burleigh of the South Australian College written on behalf of The Educational Board of the Baptist Union of Australia indicated this. It was dated 9 July and ran, 'We have heard of the serious illness and need of hospitalisation of your daughter, and of the shock that this must have brought to you. I write to convey our sympathy, and assure you of our prayerful remembrance. We trust that the operation has been completely successful and that your daughter's recovery will be speedy. We know something of the pressure on you during your term as President-General. Blessings on you as you visit and lead the Australian Baptists'.

The recovery did not occur and Principal Morling had to decline some invitations and meetings that otherwise he would have accepted. He did, however, speak at the sixth anniversary of Carlingford church[1151], and continued to lecture at the College. On 2 August he spoke at the commissioning of Rev GJ McArthur as first Principal of Christian Leaders' Training College in PNG, at Clemton Park church.[1152] At the College on 11 August, he shared in a service and unveiled a plaque to commemorate David Tuckwell, a former student, who had died of poliomyelitis. That same day Vice-Principal BG Wright arrived back from study overseas. On 22 August he spoke at the funeral of Rev EH Denning at Croydon church.[1153]

As the days went by George Morling began increasingly to commit himself. On 29 August he inducted Rev EE Dodge to the pastorate of Regents Park church.[1154] Early in September he confirmed his acceptance of an invitation to go to Hobart in the early part of the new year. On 5 September he inducted Rev DAC Taplin into the pastorate of the Merrylands Church in what was said to be a memorable service.

The President-General took but a small part in the NSW Assembly meetings. On 17 September he presented a report of the History Committee.[1155] When Rev BG Wright, MA, BD, was elected Principal of the College on 18 September[1156] he was one of those who not only congratulated his successor but seconded a vote of thanks to Rev JC Campbell who had been Acting Principal.[1157] Next day at a Men's Breakfast he brought a greeting as President-General. It was reported that he 'urged the value of a peculiarly Australian church life. He said Jowett had made the comment that because of the weather, British people lived behind closed doors and this was reflected in their attitudes. Mr Morling said that Americans on the other hand seemed to live out of doors and there was an almost too active church life. Australia should develop its own emphasis', he said. 'There was a growing similarity between the States where men were preaching the same gospel and sharing the same fellowship. There was an air of vitality which must be retained as part of our contribution to total church life'.[1158] He was re-elected to the BUNSW Executive Committee.[1159]

On 18 September his old friend Dr AT (Bert) Whale died and when the funeral was held on 21 September in the Stanmore Church he gave the tribute. 'A beautiful life,' he said, 'was crowned with a beautiful death. This was the final triumph of Christ'. The tribute began, 'Five weeks ago Dr Whale suffered a further occlusion and entered the Bankstown District Hospital. Increasing weariness ensued and it became evident to him that the time of his departure was close at hand. He sought permission to return home to be near his wife and, in his own words, to have her loving touch'.

'For two weeks, with mental powers unimpaired, he read his beloved Greek Testament up to the end - and in radiant peace he prepared for the end. Carefully with affectionate thought everything was brought into detailed order'.

'At two o'clock on the morning of Friday he wakened his wife, spoke to her in unbroken serenity of spirit, then, as strength waned, he told her again of his love for her and committed her to the unfailing care of the Heavenly Father. Thus he fell asleep'.

'It is no ordinary man that dies like that. AT Whale was not an ordinary man. I have thought of him as a simply believing, a simply loving; a simply trusting and a simply obeying man. Such simplicity is a mark of greatness, of greatness in the sight of the Lord which is the only true greatness'.[1161]

The body of the noble tribute that followed not only outlined the career, convictions and character of the man but was a revelation of the regard in which he was held by his long-time friend. Theirs was a rare and beautiful friendship.

At the Tasmanian Union Assembly in October it was decided to invite the President-General to visit Tasmania in the coming February. In supporting the resolution one minister said that the ministry of Principal Morling would be 'like the winds of God blowing through the Church'. And another, that he 'will come among our churches as a gracious benediction'.[1161]

The NSW College lecturing program came to an end late in October and the College Council wrote to express its appreciation to Principal-Emeritus George Morling. It was felt that quite apart from his lecturing his personal influence had helped immensely in the difficult College situation. The appreciation was even greater 'in view of your heavy commitments as President-General, your own health and your deep concern over your daughter's illness'.

The man thus thanked was off almost at once to New Zealand to be the guest preacher at the Baptist Union Assembly from 29 October to 4 November in Dunedin. He gave six addresses during the Assembly and then spent some time in New Zealand.

Back in Australia he took part in a function to honour Dr WL Jarvis held at Central Baptist church on 20 November.[1162] He opened the St Ives church hall on 21 November 1964.[1163] On 28 November he was in Canberra to officiate at the Opening and Dedication of the new Dickson Baptist Memorial Church.[1164] On 5 December he opened a new wing of 'Bethel', a convalescent hospital conducted by Ashfield church.[1165] On 8 December he spoke at a service farewelling Rev & Mrs Walter Schubert for their fourth term of service in Pakistan.[1166]

It had been a taxing year for the Principal with growing concern about his daughter Elaine. He still took the opportunity to express Christmas greetings to Australian Baptists.[1167] With the demands of the Christmas season over he came to the New Year very tired.

1965
On 13 January, 1965, he was in Melbourne to induct Rev W David Jackson into his office as Director of Christian Education and Publication for the Baptist Union of Australia. Of that service David Jackson wrote, 'There could not be a better start than the kind and helpful word you gave'.

The Australian Baptist carried two items relating to the Principal. The first was a contribution by him headed, 'GH Morling Advises Caution'.[1168] The issue of the paper presented several articles on the 'charismatic' or 'neopentecostal' movement. George Morling noted with thankfulness the new emphasis on the doctrine and experience of the Holy Spirit. However, with the judicious balance so characteristic of him he counselled caution concerning the interpretations of some of the advocates of the movement. 'He said that the phenomenon is too remarkable to be ignored but while being considered with caution should be recognised as a challenge to faith and devotion to Jesus Christ'.

A few pages further on there was an alarming if guarded announcement – 'Principal-Emeritus GH Morling has suffered a mild stroke, the extent of which has not as yet been fully diagnosed. It is requested that enquiries concerning Principal Morling be directed to the Union Office in view of the fact that Miss Elaine Morling, who has been unwell for some time, is at home'.[1169]

He had returned from Melbourne emotionally and physically overtaxed and almost at once was laid low. Other strokes followed[1170] and presently all hope that he would survive was abandoned. His son, Trevor, was told that he had completely collapsed and would not live through the weekend. One of his earlier students, Rev AC Prior, prepared his obituary for *The Australian Baptist*. Part of it may be quoted to show the almost reverential regard in which he was held. It described him as 'saint, mystic, scholar, teacher, expositor, preacher, evangelist, counsellor, mentor of students, pastor of pastors, beloved friend, father in God' and all of those descriptions could have been amply justified.

Moved to figurative eloquence Alan Prior wrote, 'For more than four decades he has been the most scintillating luminary in the Baptist sky in

New South Wales. Through all these years the sacrificial stardust of his life was scattered generously upon us, and in a special way upon the hundreds of men whom he guided and inspired in training for ministry. Something of that splendour will abide while there are those left in the churches who knew him. It lingers with us in rich luminosity now. In the writer's judgment the life and ministry of GH Morling has been the greatest single influence for the glory of God and the good of God's Kingdom in our denomination in New South Wales'.

The tribute went on to attempt an assessment of him in the richness and variety of his gifts and graces as evidenced in the ministry, in the College, in the denomination and in our hearts. It concluded, 'here was one who was and is greatly loved. He is <u>in Christ</u>. The doctrines which he taught so competently and lived so consistently are now experienced beatifically. By these he lived, in these he departed, in these he now lives fully, eternally. And it is thus we remember him : 'a man in Christ''.

'He said in reply, when the ministers honoured him in 1960, that his life had not been easy, but it had been a chain of the mercies of God. He affirmed that the deep truths for which his teaching had become known had arisen from his own need. He needed the doctrine of the Holy Spirit; he needed the truth of the soul's union with Christ'.

'Joshua Smith's portrait of GH Morling which hangs in the lounge at the College conveys much of what we would say of him. He sits in his chair, relaxed, revealing the rest and serenity which he sought and found in Jesus Christ. He wears his academic robes lightly, almost carelessly. His eyes and mouth betray more than a hint of the pain and hurt with which he turned from the evil and coarseness of the world. An aura of mysticism surrounds him. The copy of the Word of God in his hand is the focus of his attention and he meditates on what he has read there, and communes with the Divine Lord Who has come alive in his thoughts through its pages'.

'The last time the writer heard him preach was at the opening of the St Ives Church. His message centred on the text, 'Whom having not seen ye love'. Too much emphasis was being put on the Church in these days, he said: we ought to make more of Jesus Christ. And this he did in a characteristic expository sermon'.

'Many of us will make much more of Jesus Christ than otherwise we would have done, because of the life of George Henry Morling'.

As it turned out the anticipation of his passing was premature. On the critical weekend there was a remarkable concentration of prayer for him. Principal Gilbert Wright contacted ministers in strategic locations and got them to enlist the prayer support of surrounding churches. Baptists in other States joined in prayer for their President-General. In Brisbane Tabernacle there was a half-night of prayer. There is a record of intercession being made at a mid-day prayer gathering on the Yarra banks in Melbourne, while in Adelaide the Bible Institute had a time of special prayer for him. Those prayers were wonderfully answered.

However, just a few days later on 23 January as he clung to life his daughter, Elaine, died.[1171] Rev David Nicholas recalls a healing service in the Principal's study. Elaine was committed to God and her healing humbly, confidently requested. However those present especially remembered one prayer offered that afternoon, 'Lord, if it is Thy will to take Elaine to her heavenly home, let us not be selfish in holding her back'[1172]. Elaine was not healed physically but was taken to be with Christ which for her was far better. Her father's subsequent response was, 'The Heavenly Father may have a higher, better purpose than physical recovery. Heaven is higher than healing'.

The funeral service was held in the Ashfield Church on 26 January with Rev AH (Harry) Orr presiding. The address was given by Rev VJ Eldridge, pastor of the Carlingford Church where both father and daughter were in membership. In it he said, 'Principal Morling especially requested that it should be stated in this service that there is no sense in which it can be said that prayer has not been answered for Elaine. In the very early days of Elaine's illness, at the Principal' request a small group of men gathered at his home and committed Elaine into God's hands, praying that the Will of God might be done in her life. So many things have happened since that must be put down to the hand of God that the Principal is anxious to assure the hundreds whom he feels have been sharing in prayer that God has answered their prayers. He reminded me of the sudden change in plans little more than a year ago that enabled Elaine to join him in India, and share in his experiences there and elsewhere. No notion of what has since occurred was held then but in the light of subsequent events he considers this greatly appreciated experience together a gift from God ... Of course her father and Elaine were very close'. She had been director of the Sydney University Social Settlement in Camperdown, and children from there formed a guard of honour at her funeral.[1173]

'I gather this has been so from childhood but especially so in recent years when she has undertaken some of the responsibilities for so long exercised by her mother. She was devoted to him and he to her. Such a love and the love of the whole family and hers for them reaches beyond the incident of death and has the stamp of eternity on it. Even in this last week she was deeply worried, not about her health, but her father's, and she was relieved when he went to hospital because there he would get the attention he needed'.

Principal Morling had been taken to the Sanitarium Hospital at Wahroonga the day before Elaine died.[1171] It was some weeks before there was much change in his condition. Predictably a wave of concern swept over the whole Baptist constituency and many others besides. There followed an outpouring of love and sympathy as messages spoken and written flooded in.

One who described himself as one of Principal's 'old boys' wrote to the family, 'I do not know if Principal is able to receive messages, but if he is, you might assure him that he has a special place in our hearts that nothing else will fill ... All of us have been enriched by him, and we still pray that God may send him back to us for further service it if is His will'.

Letters came from friends, former students and denominational leaders near and far. Rev Frank Marsh, his predecessor as President-General, wrote to express deep concern and to offer to stand in for him at official functions in Victoria - though he himself was still recovering from a serious heart attack. Tasmanian Baptists with assurances of love and prayers for his recovery expressed the hope that it might be possible for him at some later time to make his necessarily postponed visit to that State.[1174] Not appreciating the full gravity of his illness the Western Australian Principal indicated that his friends in that State were praying for his rapid recovery and offered to cancel his visit there or to reduce the demands made on him. 'Your ministry', the letter concluded, 'always makes us hungry for more'.

One to whom he had ministered when her comparatively young husband had died was at Elaine's funeral and wrote later that day, 'You have been such a wonderful help and brought courage and strength to me and I know to many others, and it was no surprise to me when Mr Orr said this morning that you were 'serene'. My love and deep sympathy go to you and your family'.

By the day of the funeral service for his daughter the news of his illness had reached London and at the Chapel Service of the London Bible College Dr EF Kevan, the Principal, spoke of him as a 'valued friend' of all at the College and led the service in prayer for him. The man who informed him of this wrote, 'I have often said that it was worth going 12,000 miles to sit at your feet and learn from you the way of the Christian ministry as set out in the Word of God. Some have described you as a mystic, and that is a high compliment, but to me you are always a 'down-to-earth mystic', bringing the blessings of the spiritual into contact with everyday life'.

The Principal of the Christian Leaders' Training College in New Guinea included in his letter a grateful acknowledgment, 'That I have anything to give them (his students) of spiritual value is, 1 believe, on the human level, due to the ministry of your own life to mine. My beloved Principal, you opened the windows of heaven to my soul. You helped me to think magnificently about God and His Spirit. You introduced me in meaningful terms to the Holy Spirit'.

The South Australian correspondent of *The Australian Baptist* wrote, 'We have all been greatly concerned at the news of the illness of our beloved President, Principal-Emeritus GH Morling. He is truly beloved by Baptists in every State. His gracious personality, saintly counsel, his high spiritual concept of the ministry have all made their impact on ministers, members and churches throughout the land'.

Letter after letter gave assurance of prayer for his recovery.[1175, uu] These prayers were wonderfully answered and by the end of February he was able to sit up out of bed for brief periods. When the Commencement Service of the NSW College was held on 11 March a greeting from the Principal-Emeritus was read. It was described as 'a moving moment'.

Progress continued and a statement was issued on his behalf.[1176] 'I have come home from hospital after nine weeks' stay, a little earlier than had been anticipated because of a rapid improvement in my condition the last three weeks. There is, providentially, no deformity as a consequence of the cerebral thrombosis but there still remains considerable general weakness. The doctors have asked me to accept a further two months convalescence after which I may be able to resume limited duties'.

[uu] He had apparently suffered two strokes - *AB* 17 February 1965 page 7, 24 February page 7.

Even while still in hospital he had not been completely inactive. There is evidence of letters of advice and counsel being written and of his vital interest in denominational affairs. In particular he was concerned for the staffing of the NSW College and there were those who consulted him on that score. Rev BG Wright had become Principal. Rev Dr JA Thompson was leaving the College staff to take up a position with the Melbourne University. Despite his serious illness George Morling was the one whose advice was sought.

A message was published[1177] from the President-General headed 'To my Fellow Baptists Throughout Australia'. 'Now that 1 am steadily regaining strength I should like to make some acknowledgment, however inadequate, of the assurances of affectionate concern and prayer that came to me from State Unions, local churches, and individuals during the weeks of my recent illness. As I am reminded of a constant stream of personal inquiries and messages, and as with clearer mind again letters full of the spirit of love, I am both humbled and uplifted. The fellowship of Australian Baptists is certainly a reality. I should like to tell you that the urgent, importunate prayer that arose to the Throne on my behalf has been the main factor in my recovery. The doctors did not expect that I would live; the nursing staff used freely the word 'miracle' in respect to my case'

'I rejoice in God's goodness and thank all who prayed for me. I know you will continue to pray for a return to fullness of health so that I may fulfil any ministry which God still has for me'.

Later, speaking of his experience, he said, 'I had to fight my way back to health. There was a point of crisis when almost continuous hiccoughs added distress to an already weakened body and a poisoned brain. I had a reaction which had in it a touch of indigestion though there seems humour in it. 'Lord', I cried in semi-consciousness, 'I have preached that the indwelling Spirit gives the strength of God, and here I am in the power of hiccoughs. Is the might of Christ going to fail before hiccoughs?' Then, as strength slowly returned, 1 deliberately sought health and told myself that a stream of healing was flowing through my body. I think that, with the help of God, robustness was infused into my whole life'.

Certainly in the following years there was ample evidence that God had given him a new lease of life. He was back at church for the first time, attending the service at Carlingford on 25 April (or 9 May?[1178])

A letter from Rev LJ Gomm, President of the South Australian Baptist Union, on 5 May, expressed joy at hearing 'of your steadily increasing activity and of the possibility that after all you will be with us here for the Triennial Assembly'. *The Australian Baptist*[1179] carried a tribute by the Principal to his friend, Mr HG Lindstrom. The tribute awaited Principal's recovery for Mr Lindstrom had in fact died on 9 March. In part he wrote, 'The Apostle Paul uses the illuminating phrase, 'the simplicity that is towards Christ'. I have thought that such simplicity was the dominating feature of the life of Mr Harry Lindstrom ... When I met Mr Lindstrom first in their home at Bar Beach, Newcastle, where Mrs Lindstrom and he entertained a constant succession of the servants of Christ, that was the distinct impression I received. Here was a man whose whole life was unified by a complete devotion to Jesus Christ, and as, over the years, our acquaintance ripened into warm friendship, that impression was confirmed. It was that simplicity towards Christ that created a singularly sweet and lovable character ... And in the last phase of his life it was that which sustained him in much physical weakness and distress. I pay my tribute to a dear friend who, above all else, was a simple lover of Christ'.

The late Mr Lindstrom's niece, Mrs Joy Tinsley, wrote to Principal on 18 May. In her letter she thanked him for his 'Beautifully and truthfully expressed tribute to my uncle, which we all appreciated'. However, the main interest of the letter is the revelation it gives of the affection in which the Principal was held by Joy and Allan Tinsley, both of them children of his dear friends. The letter came from Adelaide where Rev Allan Tinsley was pastor of the Unley Park Church. In part it said, 'If you knew how thrilled we were to hear of your expected visit in August, you would be coming earlier. Your little room awaits you; so do our hearts'.

'When you were ill, Allan, in prayer, refused to let you go beseeching the Lord constantly, yet subjecting his humble request to the Lord's overruling. When word came through that you were on the mend, he hurried to me from the study ... smiling broadly and with tears in his voice he cried. 'The Prof's getting better. I'm so happy'.

A letter from a friend later in the month indicated that George Morling was contemplating doing some writing. For the time being at least his writing was confined to letters and many were surprised and delighted to receive a letter from him as their replies testified.

Beginning on 31 May he made a brief series of entries in a diary.

31 May - There is a new sense of the intimacy of the Heavenly Father in sharing with me the adjustments which are demanded of me in the light of the severe illness from January and also in the light of Elaine's death. The elimination of all traces of self-regard is a central objective.

1 June - The clear fact is that life in the Presence according to Hebrews 10 is dependent on willingness to draw near into the Holiest of all and for this there needs to be inner strength.

3 June - Psalm 37:11 impresses. 'The meek ... shall delight themselves in the abundance of peace'. Rush - inner excitement - : all aspects of self-regard rob one of this abundance, self-consciousness more especially. Isaiah 32:17 'The work of righteousness shall be peace; the effect of righteousness quietness and assurance for ever'.

4 June - Psalm 37:18 'The Lord knoweth the days of the upright', i.e. each fraction of the lives of those who are devoted to Him. There is an increased sense of the fruit of intimacy with God. Telling Him in a simple way everything. Knowing means loving sympathetic notice and attention.

5 June - Thankful that my health is better this morning. How much more work shall I be able to do? How much more shall I be able to be? The habit of looking to God instead of to self and thus obviating self-consciousness is growing.

On 3 June a function was held to mark the eightieth birthday of Rev SA McDonald. George Morling, a friend of long standing, attended and paid a tribute to the octogenarian. It was commented that he 'was looking remarkably well after his recent illness'.[1180]

In mid-July he was sufficiently recovered to travel to Melbourne to attend the Executive Committee of the Baptist Union of Australia. There were expressions of delight that his medical advisers had consented to him attending the Triennial Assembly though with restricted participation.[1181] It was planned that he should address the opening rally and take a series of Bible studies. Later it was decided to relieve him of the opening address, as the state of his health was uncertain.[1182]

Perhaps as a preparation for his Adelaide responsibilities he returned to the pulpit, preaching in the Epping Church on 25 July and at Eastwood on 15 August[1183]. At about this time it was decided that he should live permanently with his daughter, Dorothy, and her husband, Colin Goodman. GHM 'has advised that he has moved from his previous address to 158 Victoria Road, West Pennant Hills'[1184].

At the Triennial Assembly Meetings in Adelaide at the beginning of September tribute was paid to him. His visits to overseas and home churches had been a benediction.[1185] Missionaries were unanimous in their acknowledgement of the spiritual refreshment he had brought to them.[1186]

"It's all so beautifully, supernaturally natural and so restful!' This comment of Principal-Emeritus GH Morling's on the life of holiness could well be taken to describe his Bible Studies each morning of the Assembly. The minds of delegates were kept at full stretch as they faced the challenge of his high view of God expressed with a depth of scholarship and a warmth of devotion which seem to be so typical of him. 'The Holy Spirit is God, in His final self-giving, within, mediating Christ'. Using John 14 as his foundation Principal Morling unfolded the treasures of this declaration in such a way that each delegate was made aware of not only the greatness of God's provision but also his own spiritual poverty'.

Another commented, 'What a privilege and a benediction to sit at the feet of this great man in the closing days of his triennium as President-General. And how grateful we felt towards God for His gracious upholding of His servant'.

At the NSW Assembly he participated in the induction of Rev GS Parish as President of BUNSW.[1187] Next day he presented a report from the Historical Committee,[1188] which led to the publication of '*Some Fell on Good Ground*'. Mr FJ Church, Chairman of the Baptist Homes Trust, announced that as a tribute to the outstanding life and work of George Morling the Trust's new home for the aged in Canberra was to be called Morling Lodge.[1189] For the first time in many years, he was not a candidate for the Executive Committee.[1190]

During the Assembly on 24 September Mrs Nancy Andersen, wife of Rev NP Andersen, Dean of the NSW Baptist College, died.[1191] At the funeral service in the Epping Church Principal Morling gave the main address, paying tribute to a fine Christian woman.[1192]

On 5 November he left for Tasmania in order to fulfil an earlier undertaking to minister in a number of churches. He moved about for more than a fortnight, returning to Sydney on 23 November.[1193]

As a keepsake Bert Whale Jnr sent the Principal, from his late father's library, a copy of the first edition of the first book written by Charles Haddon Spurgeon, *The Saint and His Saviour*. The letter of acknowledgment dated 10 December gives interesting insight into the Principal and his relationship with his young friend [vv]. 'My dear Bert, I do appreciate the gift from your father's Spurgeon library. I do not accept the first edition lightly. It will have dear associations with your father whose memory I cherish and with yourself. I so often think about you and always with warm regard and understanding. I find much deep satisfaction in your maturing life and in the obvious depth of your character. I said to myself on Thursday night as I sat opposite you. There was so much in your face that was plainly indicative of quality ... I do respond so warmly to your affection. It is all very moving - and is of grace not desert. Thank you for your prayers during this difficult year'.

As 1965 came to a close he had his term as President-General behind him and health was steadily improving. Consequently the spotlight was not so constantly on him and detailed reports of his activities became fewer. It is clear, from such reports as there are that he was far from inactive.

1966
In January there was a return to his beloved Blackheath and he was the preacher at the church's 78th Anniversary.[1194]

Early in the year Morling Lodge was in the news. *The Australian Baptist*[1195] reported a 'huge subsidy for Morling Lodge' from the Federal Government. Baptists in the Capital Territory were showing imagination in raising funds for the Lodge. With decimal currency day coming up on 14 February they appealed to Australian Baptists to give their first dollar to the Morling Lodge fund. An editorial said 'We can imagine that this project will receive a lot of support especially as the elderly

---

[vv] The volume is now in Morling College Library.

people's home will honour one of the best loved and best known of Australian Baptists, Principal-Emeritus Rev GH Morling'.[1196]

At the end of January he went to Tasmania for ministry in the Ulverstone[1197], Burnie and Launceston churches. He returned to Sydney on 9 February and just over a fortnight later left for Western Australia. On 1 March he preached at the Commencement Service of the Western Australian Baptist College[1198] and then spent three weeks preaching around the churches.

On his return from the West there was a happy reunion with friends of former years. Mrs Le Quesne was in Australia to visit a son and a reception was held for her in the home of Mr and Mrs AS White.[1199] It was a great time of reminiscing for the Principal.

He had a couple of weeks to catch his breath and then travelled to Canberra. There he took the Easter Services at the Kingston Church and continued on through April with a teaching mission taking as his theme 'The Great Salvation'. The 'gifted teacher and preacher' completed his Canberra ministry speaking at a Men's Dinner on Tuesday 26 April.[1200]

On 6 June he gave the address at the funeral of Mrs Margaret Hercus at Chatswood church.[1201] On 10 July he preached for his old friend, Rev William Gibbins, at the 106th Anniversary of the Newtown Church.[1202]

On 28 June a diary entry gives a further glimpse of the Principal's spiritual sensitivity, 'Have been convicted of self-love especially in the light of Paul's word in Ephesians 1 – 'to the praise of His glory'. Determined to spend the rest of the week getting to the place of accepting death ever more deeply'.

1966 was the Jubilee year of the NSW Baptist College. In connection with it several functions were held. One was The Graduates' Jubilee Celebration Dinner at the College on 1 July. Graduates gathered to relive earlier experiences and to their delight their beloved Principal-Emeritus conducted the devotions that concluded a memorable evening.

On 10 July the Kew Church in Victoria began its Winter Bible Studies. These were held each Wednesday night, using as the basis for instruction and discussion notes on the First Epistle of John prepared by the

Principal.[1203] The pastor, Rev Arthur Wilkins, was one of his men.

One of his contemporaries, the notable missionary, Rev Victor White, died early in the month. At a memorial service held in the Parramatta Church on 17 July George Morling preached and paid a glowing and well-deserved tribute to his friend.[1204]

His former pastor at Ashfield, Rev AH (Harry) Orr, began a ministry at French's Forest Church on 24 July. The Principal conducted the service[1205] and gave the charge to church and pastor. And on 7 August he was the preacher at Chatswood's 47th Anniversary.[1206]

The next public event in connection with the College Jubilee was a Thanksgiving Service in the Ashfield Church on 12 August. It was altogether appropriate that Principal-Emeritus GH Morling, OBE, MA, should be the speaker.[1207] Moreover it was predictable that it should be felt that he 'worthily expressed for us all the sentiments and thanks of our hearts' as God's blessings on the life and work of the College over 50 years were remembered.

On the following day the enthronement of Marcus L Loane as (Anglican) Archbishop of Sydney took place in St Andrew's Cathedral. The Baptist Union asked George Morling to represent the President of the Union at the service.[1208] A letter written by the Archbishop said, 'It was extremely kind of you to write in the manner in which you have done and I greatly appreciated your letter. I could not wish for anyone whom I would rather have to represent the Baptist Union at the service in the Cathedral and I am delighted that you have been invited to do so. It has always been a great joy to share your ministry at various conventions and to enjoy your fellowship and I do trust that the Lord will continue to cheer and encourage you right on to the journey's end'.

He travelled a great many miles before his pilgrimage was through. On 23 August he left Sydney to preach and teach at Cairns, Rockhampton and Townsville Churches in North Queensland.[1209] Before leaving he wrote a guest editorial for the Epping Church paper. The Church had just lost its pastor and, among other things, the Principal spoke to that situation:

'Your church now has the serious responsibility of calling a minister. The way a Church goes about such a weighty business is a test of its spirituality and wisdom. Most certainly there must be a clear recognition that Jesus Christ is the Head of the Church from whom its life is derived and its direction given; and that the Holy Spirit is its Divine Administrator who makes known what is the mind and the will of the Exalted Head. This recognition should be humble, deliberate and wholly sincere. One feels increasingly that we may use words which are no more than an outward form without a corresponding inner reality. If every member of the Church made an 'act of faith' in deep reverence accepting the Lord Jesus as the Sovereign Head and the Holy Spirit the Divine Administrator of the Epping Baptist Church at this very time as it sets about the choice of a Pastor, that would put it in the way of a right decision. If that is accompanied by careful personal adjustment of the whole life to God and by corporate prayer then assuredly within the fellowship thus prepared will come the guidance of the Holy Spirit - the Divine plus to human deliberation. May it be so at this important juncture of the Church's history'.

On 29 August Mr TB Lumb died. He was a longstanding friend of the Principal and had done much building for the College while it was at Ashfield, including Principal's new cottage.[1210]

The man who thus counselled the church arrived back from North Queensland in time to give equally relevant counsel to the thirteen men who were ordained on 18 September during the NSW Assembly Meetings.[1211]

Early October saw the seemingly now indefatigable Principal off to South Australia to fulfil a variety of commitments, principally a denominational teaching mission held in the Flinders Street Church. The theme was the Holy Spirit and the teaching was designed as a corrective to certain emphases then current. He preached at Unley Park and Gumeracha, both pastored by former students, took a preaching mission at Cheltenham[1212] for yet another of his boys and even conducted a series of Bible studies at Port Lincoln.[1213]

The South Australian correspondent of *The Australian Baptist* wrote 'NSW might be his home state but in a deep and affectionate sense he belongs to Australia. The teaching mission he conducted at Flinders Street Church on 'The Ministry of the Holy Spirit' was an unqualified success. Attendances grew each night, the aggregate being in the vicinity of 2575. It was over four nights. In these days when the danger of overexaggerating facets of the faith cannot be denied, the fair and balanced and Scriptural summation as given by the Principal was satisfying both to the heart and the mind'.

By 9 November he was home again and on 13 November he commenced a three Sundays series of addresses at the Kogarah Central Church on 'The Person and Work of the Holy Spirit'.[1214] People everywhere were eager for his teaching on that area of doctrine.

Just after his return he shared in the funeral service of Miss Hilda Pennick in the Ashfield Church. Miss Pennick had been on the domestic staff of the College for sixteen years during Principal's long term of office.[1215]

He was teaching others much about the Holy Spirit but at the same time he was seeking to live what he taught. On 26 November he wrote, 'I today receive <u>for myself</u> the Holy Spirit, a dear, intimate, warm, inner Presence. I receive, welcome, consult, obey and worship Him. I expect Him to do a mighty, quiet, deep work within'.

The next day there was this further note - The Holy Spirit thus consciously (received) yesterday did give me a good day, yesterday. The heat caused some tiredness today but I held to my act of faith? and now recollect and trust the inner dear Presence'.

It was probably the following day that he added, 'It is again hot today. I commit myself to Christ through the Holy Spirit - the heart of God within. Help given in Philippians exegesis. 10.45 - Prayer for M(elbourne) B(ible) College Jubilee address'.

The reference to Philippians had to do with preparation for a stint of teaching he was to undertake at the New Zealand Bible Training Institute for three months from the coming February.[1216]

He was able to report on 29 November, 'A good morning. Philippians going well. A patch of nervous uncontrol this afternoon. Back to Thomas Kelly [ww].

. Then on 1 December, 'Tonight the MB College Jubilee. Still need help for the address which will have an effect upon the NZ visit. Seek, not to

---

[ww] Probably a reference to Thomas Kelly's *Testament of Devotion*.

desire vain glory (self) and for a quiet day. I pray to speak to the glory of God, in the name of Christ, in the power of the Spirit'.

Back from Melbourne he preached for three successive Sundays at Eastwood Church, 11, 18 December and on Christmas Day.

1967

On 7 February, he left Sydney for three months ministry in New Zealand. His major commitment was to teach in the New Zealand Bible Training Institute where Rev David G Stewart, one of his 'boys', was the Principal[1217] in succession to yet another, the late Rev John H Deane. During the period he was much in demand for preaching in the churches and for Convention ministry at Ngaruawahia.[1218]

He returned home on 1 May and that day shared in the marriage service of Rev SA McDonald, a friend of many years, in the Concord Church. Four days later at Carlingford he took part in the wedding of Miss Marion Bridgland to Rev NP Andersen, a former student and currently Dean of the NSW College.[1219]

The Australian Baptist[1220] reported that work on Morling Lodge in the Capital Territory had begun.

He was a life deacon of the Ashfield Church and on 21 May he preached at the induction of Rev John S Curtis to the Pastorate of the church. In the course of his address he shared some of his convictions about the church and its ministry. 'The essential of the church', he said, 'is 'Togetherness' - first vertical, joined with Christ, and then horizontal, sharing Christ together, having all things common. The ministry is the whole church ministering. Your minister is one of you, but leading you because of your calling him, your minister has had a calling to preach the unsearchable riches of Christ. His desire is to serve Christ in the ministry of the Word. Let us all cherish such holy moments. Keep the flame steadily burning'.[1221]

For the whole of June he preached at the morning services of the Central Baptist Church, taking four studies on 'Christ in Philippians'.[1222]

July was a month of celebration. On 8 July he spoke at the Jubilee Dinner of Pymble Church and the next morning preached at a Jubilee Service.[1223] Later in the month he was one of the preachers at Manly's

Diamond Jubilee and at Glenbrook's 64th anniversary.[1224] Then on 29 July the Principal who had been its first pastor in 1916 officiated at opening of Bankstown's new church building. In his address he stressed that the building was not the church but the home of the church.[1225]

On 1 August he flew to New Guinea to spend six weeks conducting pastoral and devotional sessions in all the Baptist mission stations.[1226] This tour was 'made possible by a special gift from an interested person in South Australia'.[1227] He also lectured at the Christian Leaders' Training College in Banz, where one of his students, Rev Gilbert McArthur was the Principal. There was also ministry in the Boroko Church of Port Moresby. While at Telefolmin he attended the first baptisms in the Mianmin Valley and brought the greeting of Australian Baptists at the formation of the church.[1228] An interesting feature of the baptisms was that an expatriate, Sister Marjory Taylor of the Boram Base Hospital, was one of the candidates. It was arranged for her to be interviewed by the Principal and he commended her for baptism. She was flown to the Mianmin Valley via Telefolmin by the same MAF plane that shuttled Principal Morling and the missionaries to the site of the baptisms. Letters from missionaries revealed that his visit had been an inspiration to them.

The seemingly tireless Principal arrived back in Sydney on 18 September. On 21 September he preached at the Missionary Rally of the Assembly Meetings.[1223-1229] Scots Church was packed for the occasion. He spoke on the 'Spirit of Missions' and designated it as a spirit of constraining love, of deep concern and of high adventure.[1230] Assembly was given an announcement - 'NSW Baptists have approved in principle the establishment of a multi-purpose chapel building in the grounds of the Baptist Theological College'. The chapel was to be named The GH Morling Chapel and a fund with that name was opened. At once the NSW Baptist Ministers' Fraternal handed over to the College Council an initial gift of $1125.[1231] It was more than five years before the Chapel was completed and opened but a significant start had been made.

Over the October long weekend he spoke at all the sessions of a convention at the Ingleburn Church.[1232] During that weekend Andrew Goldsworthy, a young medical student, for whom the Principal had a high regard, suddenly died of a virulent infection. On 4 October in the Epping Church Principal Morling brought a remarkable message to the grieving family and friends who crowded the church. In introducing his address he made three brief points:

1. 'One of the most notable of pulpit utterances came from the life of the Rev AJ Gossip, who became one of Scotland's greatest scholar preachers. It was preached when he returned to his ministerial duties after the death of his young wife who, without any warning, had died before his eyes. The sermon bore the title, 'When Life Tumbles in - What then?' The stricken husband and father gave the answer in one great blessed word - God. When life tumbles in, what then? God'.

2. 'At a time such as that and such as this, at any time indeed, there is no alternative to faith. Either we believe in God and despite our loss having Him have all; or we have nothing'.

3. We have God this day, God in Christ, God in Christ clothed with His gospel. We have God. It is enough, because He is enough'.

The tribute and message that followed was a noble and inspiring utterance.

Towards the end of October Principal Morling departed to Tasmania for a month's ministry in the island state. At Burnie he conducted a teaching mission on the work and ministry of the Holy Spirit.[1233] As so often happened, the messages were taped and so were shared by a wider circle. Services were conducted in several centres including the capital, Hobart on 19 November.[1234] He experienced encouragement in his Tasmanian ministry.

On 3rd December life deacon George Morling was back at Ashfield sharing in the services.[1235]

A little before Christmas a letter came to him from one of the men who had earlier left the ministry under unhappy circumstances. There had been regular contact by letter between them over the years and the Principal's prayers and faith had been vindicated. This letter as others from the same source revealed a man deeply devoted to Jesus Christ and one humbly grateful to God for George Morling.

1968

The Christmas/New Year season found him ministering first at Katoomba Convention[1236] and then moving on to the Belgrave Heights Convention in Victoria.[1237] His friend, Rev John Ridley, shared in the latter meetings and wrote soon after, 'Just a brief note to tell you how much we appreciated your loving fellowship at Belgrave Heights. To me personally your presence was a precious 'extra' from the Lord; a kind of pillar of support during the ministry of those 'Jubilee' days'.

'We may never be so close again in person during the few final miles of our earthly pilgrimage; hence, I want you to know how I shall value the memory of our unity and love during those days of service and sacred friendship'.

'Yes, we have long been friends in our different avenues of ministry, and Belgrave Heights 1967-8, has, in a manner, sealed our God-given bond of brotherhood'.

During seventeen years of George Morling's period as Principal Miss Grace Hannah was in charge of domestic arrangements in the College. She died on 14 January and at Dulwich Hill Church he gave the tribute. In it he emphasised that though she never married she was 'a mother to many', both to theological students and later to young men in the Groves Lodge at Dulwich Hill.[1238]

On Friday 9 February, the Sydney Town Hall was jammed with more than 2,500 Baptists and their guests as in the presence of His Excellency, the Governor of New South Wales, Sir Roden Cutler, Lady Cutler and other civic and ecclesiastical dignitaries, they celebrated the Centenary of the Baptist Union of New South Wales. The program included two major addresses, the first of them by George Morling.[1239] Of that address the report said[1240], 'Another hymn and Principal-Emeritus Morling paced to the pulpit, clasped his hands, peered into the congregation, clasped his hands behind him, then grasped his robe in his well-known gestures, and began to speak'.

What the reporter could not know was something that the Principal subsequently revealed. In a later address he said that as he had moved from his chair to the pulpit he had had as never before a sense of the presence of God.

It was his responsibility to remind his fellow Baptists, particularly, of their past heritage. The report said, 'It was all there, the quiet eloquence - the clear, distinctive inflection - the occasional memorable phrase - the emphatic gesture - the eloquent flow of language - the trembling, but understated, passion. Here was the authentic voice of a generation'.

As the Israelites were constantly called to remember all the way that the Lord their God had led them so the Principal summoned NSW Baptists. They 'needed to remember the problems of the past, the never-failing supplies of God and also His loving rebukes'. They needed also to remember past leaders and guides. Movingly he called to memory some of the great men of earlier days and their compelling personalities became vividly alive.

With deep feeling he declared, 'I call you back to the passion of your earlier ministry, as though it was my last message to you. I call you to follow the great hearts of the church who are our example. I call you to the cross of Calvary, red with the blood of sacrifice'.

From remembrance he turned to reaffirmation. He cherished the fact that as one joined to Christ he belonged to the whole Church, the mystical body of Christ. But each denomination had its own distinctives and held them dear. He called on his fellow Baptists to reaffirm their acknowledgment of the rights of the Redeemer, the competency of the individual soul to enter into direct relations with God and the concept of the church as the gathered community of God's people with Christ in the midst.

'History', the report concluded, 'had crowded close around the congregation' and as the Principal resumed his seat 'noble phrases still rang in its ears'.

On 3 March he was the ever-welcome guest preacher of the Epping Church when he inducted the Rev DAC Taplin into its pastorate.[1241]

Beginning on 13 March he made a series of brief entries in his diary.
'Have been helped by hymns on union with Christ as an aid to devotion. They write of 'moments beautiful and rare' but they are an incentive to aspiration'.

14 'See the need to 'use' the Holy Spirit to show me the love of Christ as in hymn 308. My Beloved's mine etc. He too must take away self-love that dims the love of Christ - always through union and the cleansing blood. I should live and work (1) for Christ (2) with Christ (3) in Christ'.
15 'Still seeking and, in part, realising the consciousness of Christ's love and Christ's glory. Going to Canberra today - ask for the quiet and rest of Christ and helpfulness in contacts. May the visit glorify God'.

16 'The opening of the Lodge at Canberra: moved by the function attended by Mr Gorton the Prime Minister. The memorial to Gladys in the garden court given by Gordon (Morling) pleased greatly'.

Morling Lodge was to be opened by Mrs Gorton[1242], but she was ill, and Mr Gorton declared the home open.[1243] In a report of the occasion George Morling was quoted as saying that he was deeply moved and humbled by the honour shown him. Referring to the memorial to his wife he said he rejoiced for she had greatly enriched his ministry.

17 'Preached at Chester Hill on Romans 6. 'The Way of Release". (It was a favourite topic.)
18 'Need to regain spiritual poise after the excitement of the opening of the Lodge. Can always regain (it) by an act of faith.
19 'Much greater quietness this morning. Am attempting three half-hours (of) 'pure' prayer today, like Andrew Bonar, in view of Brighton Mission.
21 'The practice of joyousness to release tension and inner tiredness. Saw the force of Doddridge's hymn '0 Happy Day' - a baptismal vow'.

In mid-April he departed for South Australia. Leighton Ford had conducted a Crusade in Adelaide and as a follow-up the Principal led a teaching mission in the Brighton Church. In the Flinders Street Church he took a series of studies on Ephesians and on 16 May he inducted Rev Ivan Kilvert to the pastorate of the Cheltenham Church.[1244] He preached at Gumeracha church on 'A Robe of Healing'.[1245]

On the way home he ministered for about three weeks in Victoria and was back in NSW by the middle of June.[1246]

On his arrival he would have been greatly encouraged by a letter from a former student who shared with him that he had had a new experience of Christ that had completely changed him and his ministry.

His first Sunday home, 16 June, found Ashfield's life-deacon sharing in the services of that church.[1247]

In South Australia Rev GB Ball was appointed Principal of the Baptist Theological College in succession to Principal EC Burleigh.[1248] Principal Morling accepted an invitation to give the occasional address at Principal Ball's induction during the South Australian Assembly meetings. On 2 July Gerald Ball sent him a letter saying, 'I am writing to tell you how delighted I am that you have been able to accept the invitation. I am sure that Mr Webb (the Secretary of the Union) would have told you that, when he asked me to suggest a speaker, you were the one I asked the Union to invite. I wanted that the speaker should be someone experienced in the field of theological education, and there is no one in this category whom I would rather have than you. I count it an honour that you will be serving as special preacher at this service, which, as you will readily appreciate, is tremendously important as far as I am concerned'.

At the end of the month he had a week-long teaching mission for the Beverly Hills Church. Then he was off to Brisbane to induct Rev Neville Abrahams as the pastor of the City Tabernacle on 4 August.[1249] It was a brief visit for he had to be back in Sydney for a family celebration on 6 August.[1250] His Brisbane hostess wrote expressing a desire for another visit from him, adding 'We did miss your happiness around the place'. It is remarkable in view of problems and concerns that he could dispense so much happiness to others.

Moreover he constantly made himself available to those who sought his help and counsel. This is instanced by a letter early in September from a South Australian minister who made a 'whirlwind' visit to Sydney to be interviewed by a suburban church. He wrote, 'I was very grateful indeed for the opportunity to speak with you at quite short notice, and glad indeed of the advice which you gave'.

As promised he attended the South Australian Assembly Meetings to induct Rev Gerald Ball as Principal-Elect of the Baptist Theological College.[1251] On 26 September Rev Ken Webb, the Union Secretary, wrote, 'You were right when you said you thought we had adopted you. We really have. So we have been delighted to have you in our midst these few days. We have felt the presence of God in your presence. Your address and your participation in the Induction Service for Gerald will long be remembered for we were all moved in the face of a man being asked to accept such responsibility on behalf of us all. As a father in God I am sure you helped Gerald feel that a mantle of God's enabling was his, as it has been yours over the years'.

The man most concerned in the service wrote to the preacher, 'I want to thank you once again for your ministry to me personally and to our Assembly, on the occasion of my Induction as Principal-Elect of the College. Now that lectures have concluded I have been able to sit down and listen again to the tape recording of the service. It was a most moving service and I am grateful to you for your part in it. The charge you delivered was all that I prayed it might be. You will be interested to know that people are still talking (more than a month later) about that service and the theme you took 'Evangelicalism - Forthright, Balanced and Devoted' has, to a considerable degree, become part of our planning in these exciting days in Baptist work in SA. I valued your personal ministry, but you can be assured that you struck a note that was most timely and which has been echoed a number of times in recent weeks in Union circles'.

The Australian Baptist correspondent Rev H Law-Davis echoed much that has been said but his verdict is noteworthy, 'Give God the praise! We must. We heard Principal- Emeritus GH Morling at his most thrilling, masterly best', and 'It was great preaching on a great theme'.[1252]

At the Assembly Rev Allan Tinsley, one of Principal's *protégés*, much to his delight, was appointed General Superintendent of the Union.

The Principal was a great encourager of all worthwhile ventures. When Rev Rowan Gill, a young Victorian minister, launched *Anvil* as a Baptist Quarterly[1253] he was quick to send a gracious letter of encouragement commending it as a 'positive approach to dedicated Christian thought among our Baptist people'.

It was doubtless a source of pleasure and justifiable pride for him when early in December his son Trevor was appointed a Queen's Counsel.[1254]

Hon. Trevor Rees Morling QC.

1969
After fulfilling Christmas and New Year responsibilities he left Sydney on 4 January, 1969, for what was planned to be an almost five months visit to New Zealand. In the main he was to take lectures on Luke's Gospel at the New Zealand Bible Training Institute where Rev David G Stewart, who had trained under him, was the Principal. However, he was also to undertake a wide range of other ministries.[1255]

These plans, however, were interrupted. He had just completed an extensive tour mainly of the South island when news reached him that his daughter Dorothy was seriously ill (with cancer[1256]). He flew home to Sydney at once.[1257] On 11 February he wrote in his diary, 'Today set myself to make adjustments in the light of Dorothy's illness which threatens to be fatal - 3 to 6 months is the medical opinion about the duration of her life. What does God ask of me in the way of this adjustment?

1. Certainly and mainly the elimination from my life of all elements of a life of self-centredness such as love of praise - anything that weakens the effectiveness of prayer.
2. I ask God to speak to me this week concerning the pattern of prayer for Dorothy who seems so selfless in her care of mother, Elaine and me. It would be all wrong not to do all in my power to have God's best done for her and hers.
3. This fact comes to me with new force, Hudson Taylor's word, 'The one great circumstance is God' - not the cancer but God. '0 God, I believe. Help Thou mine unbelief'. It seems I have strength enough to acquiesce to the will of God but not for positiveness in following, by asking, seeking and knocking. Luke 11:10'.

There were further entries on three consecutive days.

11 February – 'The advance so far is the clear thought that in the strength of Christ I must accept this situation positively as God's opportunity for me to minister to Him for His glory and to minister to others, especially my own family. I was tired last night and this morning : but after rest I can again receive the love of Christ. Today I seek to reach the point where I come into the Presence, look into the 'one dear Face' for Dorothy's healing. At the end of the morning it is quite clear that I have to learn much more of the art of effective praying'.

12 February - 'There is a clearer and stronger sense of Presence and of power definitely to take Dorothy into that Presence and to pray for her as Jesus would pray for her - which is praying <u>in the name</u> - as also a deeper examination for hindrances to prayer in myself'.

13 February – 'I am learning to overcome uncertainty in the prayer of petition.
1. I can ask the Father <u>definitely</u> for Dorothy's restoration. He feels cancer more than I do. He loves Dorothy more than I do. He gave Jesus to die for her. There is individual prayer in the Heavenly

Sanctuary for her. 1 am helping God in praying for her
2. I can pray confidently if I fulfil the conditions of prevailing prayer. I must consider more definitely what these are'.

There is little recorded of his activities for the next few months. He attended the Commencement Service of the NSW Theological College on 11 March.[1258] On 19 April, he officiated and preached at the opening of the East Lindfield Baptist Church building.[1259] One of his 'boys' Rev Norris Brook was the pastor.

Principal's daughter, Dorothy, was away in New Guinea with her husband, Colin Goodman. Despite her deteriorating condition they had decided to go to New Guinea and visit some of the places where Colin had served during World War II and also some of the mission stations. On the day of the East Lindfield Church opening she wrote to her father from Mount Hagen assuring him that they had had a wonderful trip and that she was thoroughly enjoying herself.

On 19 June, 1919, six ladies had met in a cottage in Gordon to form the Women's Guild of the Pymble Baptist Church. Presiding over their meeting was their pastor, Rev GH Morling. Just 50 years later 100 ladies met to celebrate a half-century of service. There to bring a greeting was their beloved former pastor.

About this same time he travelled to Goulburn and preached for the Baptist Church which was without a pastor. When on 13 July the John H Deane Memorial Lecture Block of the Theological College was opened by Mrs Deane, widow of the former Vice-Principal, Principal-Emeritus Morling led the gathering in a prayer of dedication.[1260]

In a letter dated 25 July a former student wrote, 'It is Friday evening and I am linked in prayer with you all. I am happy to hear of the calm, the strength and, most of all, the lack of pain concerning Dorothy'.

The significance of the reference to Friday evening was that every Friday evening a group of her fellow church members, family and friends met with Principal Morling to pray for Dorothy's healing. It is recorded that after discussion they determined to pray after this fashion, 'Lord, we ask for Dorothy's complete healing, but if that is not Thy holy and loving will, we shall not be offended'.

Already Dorothy had lived longer than her doctor had thought but her insidious enemy was steadily eating her life away. It was a sore trial to her loving father. On 29 July one very close to him wrote, 'It was on my heart to write you, when your dear letter of exquisite patience and trust arrived ... I long to be able to look after you all and to relieve Dorothy's mind as she looses her moorings a little ahead of the rest of us'. Death was thought to be imminent but the end was not for several months.

On 17-August Principal Morling spoke at the Annual Rally of the Ryde-Gosford District Baptist Association in the North Epping Church.[1261] As he had opportunity he was eager to minister to others, although preoccupied with thoughts of his daughter.

On 23 August he wrote a long note in his diary, heading it 'A reappraisal of the situation in which I find myself because of Dorothy's illness.

1. Experience shows 1 must through the Holy Spirit and in union with Christ enter into quiet, descend into the rehabilitating silences.
2. I must look up for the Spirit through Christ, understand that He is with me because in me, and I must be with Him, welcome Him, cherish Him.
3. It is good then to contemplate each Person of the Godhead: The Father - my Father, my own dear Father; The Lord Jesus - Saviour – 'that best dear name'; The Holy Spirit - the Inner Helper – Consultant with whom I can commune.
4. Then gather all into the contemplation of God as God, as in Psalm 73:25-26. Looking, loving, listening.
5. When time allows I must meditate, contemplate, adore.

In respect to Dorothy -
1. I keep on renewing my straight out prayer for full healing.
2. To make this prayer effective I must always pray in the Spirit and accept His aid. Romans 8:26-27. He strengthens my purpose to pray. Ephesians 3:16. He gives the filial consciousness. Romans 8:15-16. He inspires faith. 1 Cor 12:9 - For this I specially pray. He enables me to fulfil the conditions of prayer, in the name, abiding, fellowship.

My attitude about Dorothy in this.
1. I continue to ask, seek, knock, submission being the undertone.
2. I seek to pray for the gift of faith seeking earnestly. 1 John 5:16a.
3. I strongly expect God to heal.

4. I shall not be offended if the Father's will is otherwise.
5. Today the Lord Jesus might come. Today He is doing something for Dorothy, healing in body, certainly healing in mind and spirit - and in Colin'.

Meanwhile life went on and other demands had to be met. Rev Doug Mill was leading a drive for funds to build the GH Morling Chapel on the Theological campus.[1262] For Saturday, 27 September, he had organised a Walkathon with hundreds of participants. The walkers converged on the College from as far as twenty miles. When they arrived George Morling was there to welcome them and a little later he gave a short message of congratulations and appreciation.

Almost immediately he had to leave for Western Australia, because months before he had agreed to be the speaker at the Assembly Meetings of the Baptist Union beginning on 30 September.[1263] He was kept busy and perhaps that was as well. The Union Secretary wrote, 'It was a refreshing experience to sit under the ministry of Principal Morling ... Great themes of the gospel were dealt with at the three evening meetings. In addiction, the charge to the ordinands on Sunday afternoon was great preaching. Sessions with the College students, a word to the Ministers' Fraternal and another to the ministers and their wives failed to tire out this grand man of God. We thank God for his visit'.

By the time he returned to Sydney Dorothy was failing rapidly. After three final days of severe suffering she died on 25 October. It had not been the Father's will to restore her and in this there was acquiescence. The funeral was conducted by Rev Denis Johnston in the Carlingford Baptist Church. His tribute dwelt much on her self-effacing love as she quietly served the interests of others.

To the many who assured the family of their condolences and remembrance the bereaved father sent the message 'Throughout the whole course of Dorothy's long illness your understanding sympathy, sustained prayer and many gifts have ministered to her need and to ours. We thank you. Your deep loyal friendship has enriched and strengthened us. We who knew her in the revealing intimacy of home life, pay our affectionate tribute. Dorothy's was a life warmly devoted, quite selfless, strong, wise, ever radiating happiness and help. It was a life firmly rooted in a Christ-centred faith, a faith which was simple, committed, unwavering, unquestioning. As wife, mother, daughter, sister, friend,

Dorothy Goodman was a choice example of Christian womanhood. We should like those who shared in an inner circle of prayer to know that Dorothy went home amid clear, even remarkable, evidences of the Heavenly Father's providential care. At the last, as before, there was great peace, great courage and a great testimony'.

Despite his sad loss George Morling travelled to Tamworth the following weekend and from 31 October to 2 November was the special speaker at Tamworth as he shared in the 80th Anniversary of the church where he began his ministry.[1264]

Late in the month one of his men about to leave NSW for an interstate pastorate in the course of a letter wrote, 'It was my intention to call personally and see you before I leave. I wish to thank you most sincerely for your kind interest and prayerful concern over one of your 'lesser' students. I will always be grateful to God for your contribution to my life and will continue to cherish your prayers for my ministry. It is an honour to belong to the great band of fellows who, over the years, have sat at your feet'.

In November he headed the 66th Anniversary celebrations of Hornsby, another of his early churches. On two successive Sundays and on the intervening Wednesday and Saturday evenings he gave five 'memorable addresses', centred on the Person of Christ and of His Spirit. The messages were tape-recorded.[1265, xx]

In the course of a week he took part in the funeral of the widows of two of his dear friends. In the Strathfield-Homebush Church on 12 December he gave a tribute to Mrs HS Pickup.[1266] Then on 17 December he conducted the funeral of Mrs Mildred R Tinsley[1267], widow of Rev Dr CJ Tinsley, at Stanmore Baptist Church.[1268]

1970
Early in 1970 there was another change of location for George Morling. He moved to Longueville to make his home with his youngest son, Trevor, his wife Ruth, and their family.[1269] It was about this time that one of his grandchildren wrote to him, 'Thank you for the Bible. It's something I can keep and treasure. I'd also like to thank you for the influence you've had on my life and I hope in time I'll be able to experience the peace I can see in your face'.

[xx] Hornsby church records do not give the precise dates.

On 2 February Miss Myrtle Pickup, daughter of the recently deceased Mrs HS Pickup, died. GHM delivered the tribute at the funeral service in the Strathfield-Homebush church.[1270]

On 1 March he was in Canberra for the opening of the second wing of Morling Lodge. He offered the Prayer of Benediction and performed the official opening.[1271] This was most fitting for not only had he given his name to the Lodge but, appointed its life chaplain, he made it his business to visit every guest two or three times a year.

It was his joy to introduce an old friend[1272], writing, 'It is in my heart to commend to my fellow Baptists in NSW Rev Subodh Sahu, who will soon be coming among us. Some years ago I shared a ministry in India with Mr Sahu; travelled with him, spoke with him, lived with him. I count the fellowship of those days among the most enriching experiences of my life'. He proceeded to pay a glowing tribute to his friend as a man of God of rare spirituality and with outstanding gifts. It was a disappointment for him that he would not be present to greet this distinguished Indian Christian. He was off to South Australia for a three month ministry.[1273]

During that period he took meetings in fourteen city and country churches under the auspices of the Union's Church Extension Department. He delivered a series of lectures to the students of the South Australian Baptist College being the first to occupy the College's new flat for visitors. There was also a visit to the Adelaide Bible Institute to address its student body.[1274]

His South Australian visit was featured in *The Advertiser*, Adelaide's leading morning paper, on Saturday, 13 June, by the religious columnist, Elizabeth Johnson. Under the heading 'Spiritual Comfort amid City Rush' she wrote of the need in the heart of the city for churches to provide quiet places where 'frazzled businessmen and frantic shoppers can pause for a while'. Then she confessed, 'These suggestions from a suburban Bible study group led last week by a distinguished Baptist visitor, Rev Principal-Emeritus George Morling, now 78 years young, and still inspiring ideas among the mixed bag of ministry and laity who avidly followed him as he preached and taught in Adelaide during a crowded seven days.

Always on the move he begged his SA colleagues to give him 'something to do'. Paradoxically his chief concern was to bring peace into the lives of those with too much to do. The anxious men and women whose lives revolve around the city rush and the suburban struggle'.[1275]

While he was away there was encouragement for those leading the project to erect the GH Morling Chapel on the campus of the Theological College. A promised gift of $10,000 was received to swell the building fund.[1276]

Back home he wrote in his diary on 3 July, 'I am preparing for the Katoomba Retreat next week. I want to spend this day from hour to hour directed by the Holy Spirit'.

He was the main speaker at the Baptist Ministers' School of Theology (Retreat) held 7-10 July.[1277] He felt the need for the messenger to be prepared as well as his messages. Those messages were on a favourite subject 'The Culture of the Soul'. In them he insisted on the necessity both of a worthy, full-orbed conception of God in His transcendence and immanence and an authentic experience of God within the life by His Spirit. One of the other speakers was the son of a ministerial friend of George Morling [yy]. The Principal subsequently wrote to him to tell him how well received his contribution had been. There came back a revealing response from which the following is taken.

'By far the most pleasant aspect of my time at the Retreat was my brief reunion with you. I am sure that you know how countless are the people who thank God upon every remembrance of you. But you may not be aware of the enormous debt which I owe you. As the years pass I find myself reflecting more carefully upon the many influences that have shaped me. Some of these are difficult to identify. But many are easily and joyfully noted. In my case you are very important among these'.

'I am not sure that increasing years bring me greater wisdom. I do know the many conclusions which once I would have accepted have been modified or abandoned. And I find this process a continuing one. And yet the central themes which I heard you enunciating during my childhood still remain memorably significant and meaningful to me and I am very much aware of the very obvious fact that you were practising what you had been preaching'.

[yy] Rogers does not name the speaker. JS thinks it was Mr Wilfred Jarvis.

'I know that some of my conclusions bewilder, dismay and disappoint many folk who may have remained more orthodox in their Baptist position than I have. And I have frequently been sorry about this; but I judged that it was not defensible to pretend that I was adopting positions that I could not genuinely support. However I have concluded that many of the most unpleasant disagreements which I have observed between Christians have been centred on issues which have not merited the attention they received or the discussion they created'.

'Your own emphasis on the love of God, and His unfailing compassion for failing mortals like myself means a great deal to me in everything I am attempting to do. I am unpleasantly aware that I fall distressingly short of the ideals which I would like to attain. And I surely know that when I am able to register some small achievements I am only expressing the contributions which have been made to me by many people, among whom you are certainly one of the most significant. I did again want to say an inadequate thanks to you'.

In August Life Deacon[1278] Morling took three addresses at his old church at Ashfield, again taking the theme, 'The Culture of the Soul'. A letter from a brother minister, himself engaged in theological teaching, told of personal blessing and of those who had been 'both moved and challenged' by his messages.

Towards the end of September he travelled to Ulverstone to be the guest preacher at the Tasmanian Baptist Assembly meetings held 28 September to 1 October.[1279] In the evenings he gave a series of addresses on the Holy Spirit, a subject with which he had come to be identified. While in Tasmania he ministered in other centres including Hobart.

Shortly after returning to Sydney his nephew, Mr AG (Tim) Lusted died. He had a great affection for his sister's son and it was fitting that he gave the tribute at the funeral service held 11 October.[1280] Subsequently Tim's sister, Joyce, wrote from her home in Queensland, 'To me, personally, it was a tremendous blessing to have you conduct the service so beautifully. It was very personal and special to me, and to our family'.

On 21 November there was a denominational garden party at the College to honour his birthday. There were stalls with goods for sale, the proceeds going to the GH Morling Chapel Fund. College students gave some items and the Principal himself brought a brief message.[1281]

On 22 November he led a meeting at Chatswood church to farewell Rev JG Leigh and Mrs Wedge.[1282]

At the College Graduation Service on 26 November the Principal-Emeritus was the speaker[1283], taking as his subject 'The Song of the Upward Look', a sermon based on Psalm 121.

On 20 December GHM opened and dedicated the new building of Carlingford church.[1284]

1971
An earlier visit to New Zealand had been curtailed because of the serious illness of his daughter, Dorothy. He set out once more for the sister dominion where he was to be a guest lecturer of the New Zealand Bible Training Institute for the whole of the first term.[1285]

The students took him to their hearts and before he left presented him with a song in his honour, set to the tune of 'Waltzing Matilda'. The lyrics were hardly classical but there could be no doubting the sincerity of the last line of the refrain, 'You're loved by the students at old BTI'.

One of the students, daughter of a ministerial student of his from earlier days wrote to express thanks for what his ministry had meant to her. 'As I look forward to future service on the mission field I'm sure your ministry has enriched my life'.

No sooner had he returned to Australia than he went north to Queensland to take a teaching mission in the South Brisbane Church and deliver the annual Queensland college lecture.[1286] Then he spent six weeks in northern NSW conducting teaching series in several churches, based at Alstonville[1287], and including Grafton, Murwillumbah, Lismore[1288] and Casino.[1289]

His return to Sydney was in time to share in a course for ministers' wives. His participation in such courses was always greatly appreciated. On 21 May, 'an evening with the Principal-Emeritus' was held at Ashfield church to raise funds for the GH Morling College Chapel.[1290]

Somewhat surprising was the response to his presence and teaching courses conducted by the House of the New World. The House of the New World was an outreach ministry to young people who, either with no church background or in reaction against their church background, were seeking an alternative lifestyle. It was doubtless an act of great daring or faith that led the organisers, Rev John Hirt and Rev Trevor Hulme, to invite the aged Principal to give lectures on theology to this diverse and revolutionary group. George Morling might well have been dismissed as a relic of a former generation, almost a being from another planet, but they responded to the genuine spirituality of the man and the profundity of his teaching in an overwhelming fashion. Despite the generation gap and his own other-worldliness he established rapport with his youthful auditors and communicated a sense of spiritual reality to them. He gave them a vital sense of God. Of this special ministry a friend wrote, 'At its weekly Bible study it is common to find up to 80 young people sitting on the floor of a room not much bigger than a normal lounge. The speakers are handsome young men and public figures whose status gives them great reputation, but the young people declare that one of the most popular speakers is Principal Morling. He commands attention for perhaps 40 minutes, discussing such lofty themes as the Holy Spirit and the Will of God. Some of that same group are members of Christian Surfboard Riders, an association of young men whose love of surf gives them unique opportunities to witness for Christ on the beaches. It is significant that Principal Morling, who is fond of bobbing about in the ocean but has probably not been on a surfboard in his life, has been enthusiastically elected as the Patron of the Christian Surfboard Riders'.

On 29 August the Baptist Homes Trust held a Service of Thanksgiving to mark the opening of its Willandra Village Centre. As the Trust's Chaplain George Morling was the special speaker and preached a memorable sermon on Psalm 23.[1291]

At the end of August the Triennial Assembly of the Baptist Union of Australia was held in Sydney and, as was inevitable, the former President-General shared in them. On 31 August he led the Assembly in a devotional session.[1292]

In an imaginative venture to raise funds for the Morling Chapel, Rev Doug Mill organised a concert in the Sydney Town Hall on 14 September.[1293] Rev Victor Eldridge, who had been both student and pastor of Principal Morling, was the compere. The Principal was present as the guest of honour.

On 19 September he wrote in his diary 'A new stage. There are clear indications that at this time of my life - I am nearly 80 - God wants me to do some writing. Preaching will be getting less. I ask for these things; (1) Inner strength to set myself to the ministry of writing. 'What thou seest write' - Rev 1:11. (2) I ask for a fresh anointing for the new task - Psalm 92:10. (3) This will need the strength of Ephes 3:16. (4) My writing must be an act of communion with God in Christ the Quickening Spirit - 1 Cor 15:45'.

It was probably with the same subject in mind that he wrote the next day 'Through Prayer (1) Frankly acknowledging my nothingness. (2) Thankfully accepting God's all. (3) Boldly asserting my competency in heart union with Christ - Phil 1:13'.

This was the last entry in his diary. It is sad to record that though there is abundant evidence in his papers that he attempted to address himself to the task of writing he seemed unable to concentrate his energies on it. At this stage he contemplated writing a sequel to his earlier book *The Quest for Serenity*. He proposed to call it 'The Quest for a Deeper Serenity'. Among his papers were several proposed outlines. What he intended to do was make a link with the earlier book. That book had been a record of an increasing discovery of serenity. However, since that book was written, factors in his personal life, in his family life and the life of the church had called for a yet deeper experience. In working with one of his former students who was putting together a 'memoir' of him he had reason to trace his spiritual pilgrimage. Now that he was '80 years young' he wanted to trace the final phase of that pilgrimage as an addendum to the earlier work.

Subsequently he abandoned the proposed title and thought instead of calling the book 'The Quest for the Spirit'. The change grew out of the conviction that the emphasis should not be on the experience of serenity but on the Spirit who makes real within the believer the life of God in all His fullness and so brings peace.

He spoke at the funeral of Mr RH Gordon in the Pymble church.[1294] Gordon died on 21 September; he had been a noted open air evangelist and leader in Sydney Christian circles.

Ashfield Church was packed when on Sunday, 14 November, a service was held to offer thanksgiving to God for the life and ministry of George

Morling who one week later was to celebrate his 80th birthday.[1295] There was a certain appropriateness in the timing of the service for in his boyhood days at Ashfield his birthday had mistakenly been celebrated a week earlier than it should have been. The Mayor of Ashfield and local State member were there to honour him and to share in the service. He, himself, was the preacher and took as his text, 'My times are in your hands' (Psalm 31:15). It was both a personal testimony and a challenge to his hearers. His father had put the date of his departure from England against this text in his Bible.

Among those who wrote to congratulate the octogenarian was Dr Geoffrey Blackburn of Victoria. In the course of his letter he wrote, 'It is wonderful how much you have been able to do and are still doing in the interests of the Kingdom. Wherever I go people speak in warm appreciation of your ministry. I know that it does not make you proud, but it must bring a warm glow to your heart to realise the wide-spread affection in which you are held. Even more important is the knowledge that your influence is being felt throughout the Commonwealth and overseas through the lives of the young men you trained for the ministry'.

On the actual day of his birthday in the presence of the Governor-General he preached at the 75th Anniversary of the North Sydney Church.[1296] He presented 'The Unchanging Christ' as the Church's eternal contemporary; the common ground for unification; and the only stable factor in a world of instability'.[1297]

Mrs Bessie Jarvis, wife of his friend Dr WL Jarvis, died on 9 December and he was asked to speak at the funeral. It was one of his bad days and he spoke at excessive length, to his own subsequent embarrassment. This was one of the signs that increasing years were taking their toll. However, for the most part he remained in control of his powers and continued to minister effectively.

After his death Alex Jamieson, a friend from the Chatswood Church, recalled an incident from a church picnic at Dee Why on Boxing Day 1971. 'He and I were in the surf together and he thoroughly enjoyed it. He said as he came up for breath as a wave broke over him 'How good God is to give us such a way of refreshment'. It was better than any sermon and I trust 1 have his faith enthusiasm if ever I pass the 80 mark'.

His friend and one of the great old Baptist ministers, Rev Joshua Robertson, died at Morling Lodge, Canberra in December.[1298, zz]

1972

George Morling was called to conduct a memorial service in the Kingston Church for Rev Joshua Robertson, and again on 6 February he preached at another memorial service in the Petersham Church, the scene of one of Joshua Robertson's notable ministries.[1299] He described his older friend as 'a man of outstanding personality, who would attract notice in any company, and impress himself deeply upon those who came within the range of his influence'. With a rich natural endowment he excelled in sport, captaining a Queensland State cricket team, and in studies, achieving a Master's degree in Arts and a diploma in Social Science. In temperament he was 'warm-hearted to a high degree ... the most loveable of men. Impulsive, forthright to the point of ruggedness but ever the loving, generous helper'. Of the last phase of his life he said 'he was very much the saintly patriarch who would pray with his friends of earlier days who visited him, then lay his hands upon their heads, and bless them in the name of Christ'.

It was typical of his unflagging interest in his men that when one of them, Rev LA (Tony) Cupit, was appointed Associate (Overseas) Secretary of the Australian Baptist Missionary Society, he should write to him expressing pleasure. His one reservation was that his young friend had left New Guinea to take up the appointment and he felt that the need there was very great. A reply from Tony Cupit on 10 February sought to give reassurance on that score.

In early February, 1972, he set off once more for NZ where for six weeks he lectured at the NZ Bible Training Institute.[1300] He had established a special niche for himself there and his ministry was eagerly awaited and greatly appreciated.

From 29 March to 9 April, he was principal speaker and gave five addresses at Chatswood church Easter 'Deeper Life Mission'.[1301]

On 18 April a series of studies by Principal Morling on the Holy Spirit was published in booklet form. Although only about thirty pages in

---

[zz] Various Baptist sources give three dates for Robertson's death - 14, 18 and 29 December. The 28th is confirmed by a funeral announcement in the Sydney Morning Herald.

length a great deal of his teaching on the Holy Spirit was compressed into it and it was warmly welcomed. The BUNSW was troubled about 'Neo-Pentecostalism'. The booklet was hastily 'printed and rushed to Katoomba' for the annual ministers' School of Theology.[1302] The contents of the booklet were published in instalments in *The Australian Baptist*.[1303]

The following day work began on the Morling Chapel at the College and it was hoped to open it during the Assembly Meetings of the Baptist Union in September.[1304] Because of building delays that was not to prove possible.[1305]

Happy in the knowledge that the dream of the Chapel was starting to become a reality George Morling went off to Canberra to visit Morling Lodge and to have three weeks' ministry in the ACT.[1306] From there he travelled on to South Australia for some weeks of teaching and preaching, including speaking at the Ministers' Retreat.[1307]

It was almost certainly at this time that he set himself to write *The Quest for the Spirit*. Attached to a Foreword for the book there was a puzzling page. It had the heading 'The Quest for the Spirit' and took the form of a brief letter seemingly intended for publication. The letter, certainly written from South Australia, but undated, read, 'My Dear Friends, Here is a beginning. I shall try to keep a steady stream of instalments. They work me quite hard over here but 1 am quite well. I shall still be at Allan Tinsley's, Snows Road, Stirling - after a week at Mt Gambier. In warm regards and thanks, As ever, GHM'.

Possibly the instalments were to appear first in some Christian publication but in all likelihood not even the first of them with its accompanying letter was sent. The Foreword, typed in duplicate, was still attached to the hand written letter.

For the insight it affords into its writer that foreword is reproduced in full.

THE QUEST FOR THE SPIRIT

FOREWORD

'These pages are the fruit of the reading, the thinking, and the seeking of a life time. By the grace of God the days of my years have been spent, in large part, within the walls of a Theological College. What I write here is the distillation of the teaching of the lecture room. It owes much to the fellowship of men upon whom God has placed the 'sacred crimson' of consecration to the ministry of the Gospel'.

'In the pulpit, in Bible Conventions, in University Students' Conferences, in Missionary Retreats overseas this teaching has been taken out into the wider life of the Church. There has been repeated request to set down in more permanent form what has been said'.

'I add a further introductory word. Some years ago I made pilgrimage to Canterbury Cathedral, ancient shrine of England. Clearly defined memories abide of an enriching experience. The impression of massiveness was inevitable. Here was solid masonry designed for endurance. A sense of magnificence was equally inescapable. Here was aesthetic harmony in which vastness and minuteness mingled. And all was touched with mystery. Seen through grey mist the great structure seemed to be a spirit that had come out of the centuries and, within, was the upreach of arched ceilings fading into insubstantial loftiness'.

'The experience of Canterbury has been before me as I have written these pages. In the doctrine of the Holy Spirit likewise I find massiveness, magnificence and mystery. I myself would not always have used the first two with any conviction. I should like to enter into a fellowship of study with those who read these pages and share my maturing thinking'.

'I recall another incident of the day spent in Canterbury. Our party was given into the care of a learned antiquary. As we entered the Cathedral which he obviously loved dearly, he suggested that we might be seated and compose ourselves before the inspection began. 'This is a place only for quiet minds and reverent spirits' he urged. Some such constraint should be upon us as we investigate the doctrine of the Holy Spirit for it is, in very truth, a most holy place'.

'The choice of the title, 'The Quest for the Spirit', is determined by the fact that an earlier book, *The Quest for Serenity*, has brought me a wide circle of friends who, I should like to believe, will regard this one as being of a piece with it in pointing the way to an ever-deepening serenity'.

Among his papers was a hand-written first draft of what was probably intended to be the next installment. It was headed, 'My Quest for the Spirit' with the sub-title 'Commencement and Direction'. No more than a very beginning it outlined his early spiritual experience leading up to his experience of assurance of acceptance in Christ when the Spirit bore witness with his spirit that he was indeed a child of God. The remainder of the fragment reads, 'That finding has brought two substantial gains. It has removed the difficulties of vagueness and elusiveness which so many encounter in regard to the Holy Spirit. If the Holy Spirit is known in Himself, as I am insisting He may be, that difficulties vanishes. And then, if we concentrate on knowing who the Spirit is we shall understand so much better what the Holy Spirit does'.

'In all this my main source of help and my constant point of reference has been the Lord's teaching recorded in the fourteenth chapter of John's Gospel, acknowledged to be the *locus classicus* of the biblical teaching on the sublime theme of the Spirit'.

'I invite you to share what, in this Paschal Discourse, has helped me in my quest for the Spirit'.

Though that particular exercise peters out at that point, happily the Principal left much in notes, and on tapes, to indicate the main drift of his teaching on the Holy Spirit. The major points of his exposition were: -

(1) The Holy Spirit is God.
(2) The Holy Spirit is God <u>in His Final Self-giving</u>.
(3) The Holy Spirit is God in His Final Self-giving <u>Within</u>.
(4) The Holy Spirit is God in His Final Self-giving Within, <u>ministering Christ</u>. But how that simple outline came alive as he opened it up.

Sympathy was expressed to him on the death at Ipswich, Queensland, of his sister, Ethel[1308], Mrs Lusted. He had been there bringing support and comfort to her and to the family. Some months later his niece Joyce wrote to him, 'You know, Uncle, I never think back on those weeks we spent finally with Mother at the hospital as harrowing or even distressing. I remember what a lovely patient she was and how willing she was to go to her Father. Then I cherish the lovely fellowship I was privileged to have with you – I often think of the things we spoke of".

Reports of his preaching by this time had become infrequent but he did maintain a preaching ministry despite advancing years. On 30 July, for example, he preached at the anniversary of the Dee Why Church[1309] - not far from his dear old friend Enos Coleman of Collaroy. Next day he led a day of prayer for Baptist ministers at Concord.[1310] On 20 August he preached at Blacktown church.[1311]

On 30 September he was one of the speakers at the opening of 'Ridgecrest' conference centre at Burrendong Dam in central NSW.[1312]

Later in the year his abiding interest in the church of his boyhood was manifest. There were internal tensions in the Ashfield Church concerning the appointment of a pastor to succeed Rev JS Curtis, who was leaving to become Director of Evangelism of the BUNSW. The nominee did not have the support of some church members.[1313] For three Sundays George Morling, the esteemed life-deacon poured oil on the troubled waters. A dear friend wrote on 30 October, 'Your three Sunday mornings, I feel, will have their sweetening effect on the church. Your addresses and confidential talks from the pulpit will bring their own fresh and serene atmosphere to the hearts of us all'. The outcome was the appointment of Rev KF Evans as interim pastor.[1314]

The Christmas season found him once more, and for the last time, in his beloved Blue Mountains.

1973
Letters that he kept indicate that he maintained a steady ministry of encouragement and counsel. Typical is one that came early in 1973 referring to his 'ever warm and gracious letter' and going on to say, 'Your comments and expressions have been read and re-read and I deeply appreciate all that you have said. Your words are always wise and challenging and to the point'. Another, also written in January, 1973, came from an ex-student who had been experiencing some turmoil. He wrote, 'I've worn myself out trying to gain what the great saints had'. He had at last given up the quest but felt a need to share his present condition with a wise spiritual director and mentor in the hope doubtless of receiving guidance and encouragement.

Sunday, 4 March, saw the culmination of the hopes and dreams of quite a few years. That day The GH Morling Chapel at the Baptist Theological College was officially opened by the President-General of the Baptist Union of Australia, Principal Morling's friend, the Rev Dr Geoffrey Blackburn[1315], in the presence of about 600 people. [1316.] For George Morling, for whom worship and preaching were essential elements of any vital Christian life and ministry, it was an occasion of great joy and thankfulness. A note in the program for the opening was most happily expressed. It said, 'Today, in the opening of our College Chapel, we honour Principal-Emeritus GH Morling - a scholar, teacher, preacher, colleague, friend. During the 40 years of his Principalship there were few projects, if any, dearer to his heart than a College Chapel. 'Holy, Holy, Holy, Lord God Almighty' were key words which unlocked the richness of his teaching ministry. The Chapel expresses the spiritual ideals of the Principal, ideals which he sought to impart to all who crossed the College threshold, called by God to be men of God'.[1317]. 'We thank God for the enriching past and pray with the Principal that future students may also be sensitive to the presence and power of the Holy Spirit, stand in awe of God's holiness, worship and serve Him who is the Way, the Truth and the Life'.

G.H.Morling Chapel

The pulpit, communion furniture and lectern in the Chapel are a tribute to the life of Gladys Morling by her husband (the Principal) and her family. All were built of solid cedar, the gift of Mr Evan Williams of Alstonville. A few days before the opening Rev AC (Bert) Maynard had written from Western Australia, -

'As one who was one of your students in the days when College classes were conducted in the Petersham school hall, and then one of the first resident students at Granville, your memory is enshrined in my heart and does not need any outward memorial. The impact of your life and teaching made possible my own ministry. As long as I live the memory of those days will be a blessing. But one realises that a generation has arisen which did not have the privilege of sharing those experiences and as time goes on the small number of those who did will become fewer and finally pass on to be with the Lord. So it is good to know that the chapel on the College campus will always stand to remind the students of you'. Maynard acknowledged Morling's contribution to the Western Australian Baptist cause through men trained by him and who exercised ministries in WA.[1008.]

Two days after the opening the Chapel was again packed for the College Commencement Service.[1313] It was just 50 years after George Morling had begun officially as Principal. Before that he had been Acting-Principal. Now he was the guest preacher and his subject, one he never tired of tackling in ever fresh ways, 'The Culture of the Soul'.[1318] Many treasure a tape recording of that address. It was widely distributed and years after was still being sought.

About this time he preached at Cronulla church during the pastor's holiday interstate.[1319]

It is significant that, despite his age, he still had an appeal to young people. A letter dated l2 March invited him to address a Youth Service at the Goulburn Church on 11 November. The writer acknowledged that the Youth Fellowship was 'adventuresome' in making the invitation but undertook to invite other groups in the area to share in the service. By November he would not be able - either to travel so far or to muster the energy to speak to people, young or old. It is interesting to note that thirteen years later the writer of the invitation, Gordon Deverell, entered Morling College to prepare for ordination.

Another who wrote to him expressing congratulations and good wishes on the opening of the Chapel was Miss Jean McDonald. In her letter she told him that her father, Rev SA McDonald, was seriously ill and had not long to live. 'l am sure', she wrote, 'a visit, a note from you would help him a lot at this very trying time'. On 27 March Rev Sydney Alexander McDonald, OBE, one of Australia's most widely known Baptist ministers died.[1320] Principal Morling's association with him had extended over more than 60 years and it naturally fell to him to give the tribute at the service in the Chatswood Church. 'The final impression one gained of our old friend', he said, 'is one of great kindliness of heart and practical helpfulness. He was the encourager and helper of many'.[1321]

However beyond the tribute there was a message for those who attended. One of his former students was constrained to write to say that his words 'meant much to me and I felt they must have meant much to many others also'. This man and his wife were in great distress because a dearly loved son was shortly to be tried on a serious charge and faced the prospect of a lengthy prison sentence. Later in the month, replying to a letter from the Principal he unburdened himself to one in whom he had complete trust. With the death of Syd McDonald few of George Morling's contemporaries were left.

Within a few days or so he was speaking at another funeral, this time in his home church at Ashfield. Mrs Sayer, one of the older members of the church, died and George Morling for old times sake spoke at the service making a deep impression upon members of the family and friends. So long as he was able he would refuse no opportunity to speak a good word for the Master.

Northbridge Baptist Church celebrated its 46th Anniversary on 6 May and he was the preacher.[1322] Doubtless he was reminded of an earlier experience when he went to preach at the same church. On that occasion he made his way to the local Presbyterian Church and it was some little time before the mistake was realised.

Back in the forties Ian Emmett and, for a short period, Nancy Mason, later to be his wife and share missionary service with him in East Bengal, had studied under Principal Morling at the Ashfield College. After a long and painful illness Nance Emmett died in Melbourne on 27 April.[1323] The Principal wrote at once to express his sympathy. A Service of Tribute was held in the Parramatta Church on 13th May and he was the main speaker.[1324]

Ivy, wife of another of his former students, David Grinham, died on 14 May and GHM took the funeral service in the Bexley Church.[1325] He paid tribute 'to the stirling qualities and spiritual attributes which endeared her to so many. Her unshakeable faith and deep love for her Lord had motivated her life and sustained her in every situation'.[1326]

When Avalon Church opened a beautiful new set of buildings on 26 May he preached[1327] and his subject was 'The Church and Its Essential Magnificence'.[1328]

Early in June he left for the north of the State where at Alstonville he was the guest of his friends Rev J C (Colin) Campbell and his wife, Eunice, for two months and conducted teaching sessions in various northern churches.[1329] On l0 June Winifred, widow of his dear English friend, Sydney Morris, in replying to one of his letters mused, 'It is Sunday evening and I wonder if you have been preaching today'. He had been and would be every Sunday for some weeks to come. Moreover he would be taking sessions during the week. For example, at the Armidale Church he took a series of studies on the Holy Spirit in home groups.

The subject of the Holy Spirit was creating much interest and as previously mentioned Principal Morling had recently put out a booklet on it. In June a missionary in New Guinea wrote, 'The study of your book has made us all truly seek the Holy Spirit and now He has filled us completely, and taken control. We are so full of praise for our Lord now and we are excited about what he will do here in the future'. Several years later in that area 'revival' broke out and swept the churches.

While in the north he conducted in July a Ministers' Retreat at Evans Head. His theme 'God. God in Himself'. His thinking, always theocentric, became increasingly so towards the end of his life. In the program he included a special session for the wives of the pastors. Such sessions were greatly appreciated.

For some time Rev David Nicholas, with much devotion, had been putting a memoir on Principal Morling for whom he had great admiration and affection. He had spent much time in personal conversation and in correspondence with him. By the middle of the year (when David Nicholas left South Australia to study in the United States[1330]) the work was almost complete and there was hope that it might be published by the end of the year. Events were to intervene and frustrate this purpose. Subsequently parts of the work appeared in the Billy Graham *Decision* magazine, and it eventually appeared in book form in 2003.[1331]

A letter written at this time from Adelaide indicated the affection the aged Principal drew out from others. One sentence ran, 'We love you dearly and can scarcely imagine our lives without your loving counsel and dear presence in our home'. Former fellow student, Stanley Dickson, wrote on 23 July, 'It has been a sheer delight to hear of your visitation to many of our churches … You appear to be the last of that wonderful band of stalwarts that once stalked through the land'.

He returned to Sydney early in August, and on 6 August led a denominational Prayer Retreat at the Concord Church. The Retreat grew out of a concern for the spiritual vitality of the Union and its constituent churches. No one was felt to be better qualified to be its spiritual director than 'our beloved Principal'.

On 18 and 19 August the Mortdale Church celebrated its 75th Anniversary and he was the speaker at all three sessions.[1332] In one of those sessions he indulged in a little reminiscing. Mortdale's earlier pastors has been his fellow students. Not a few of his own students had come from Mortdale and in turn others of his students had become pastors at Mortdale. Moreover, Mr RE Walker of Mortdale had been successively College Treasurer and College President. Some of Principal's closest friends were associated with that church and it was a most happy arrangement that he was the one to lead its Jubilee celebrations.

The following Sunday he preached in the Chapel that bore his name at the Theological College and it was a great day for him. At that time the College was advertising for a Superintendent of its Bible College.[1333] It says much for the regard in which he was held that an enquirer from another State wrote asking his candid opinion and wise counsel as to his suitability for the position. He had been Principal-Emeritus then for some thirteen years and was an old man but his advice was eagerly sought. When the Executive Council of the Baptist Union of Australia met at the end of August it sent a greeting to its former President-General. The letter from Rev JG Manning, the Secretary, mentioned a great deal of new and exciting movement in Union affairs but then added, 'everything we do today is built on the foundations which you and others did so much to lay in years gone by. Your colleagues remember you with respect'.

Up in Queensland the Baptist Union was relocating its Theological College and a complex of buildings was under construction on an extensive site. One of Morling's men, Dr EG Gibson, was the Principal. In mid-September an invitation came for the Principal-Emeritus to be the Guest Speaker at the opening of the new College early in March. It was an appointment that he was not able to keep.

At about this time it began to become apparent that his health was failing. He had planned a return visit to Armidale and Tamworth but had to cancel it because he was not well. Early in October he indicated to the Secretary of the Ministers' Fraternal that he had felt very tired during the two previous weeks.

However a letter from a dear friend, who was visiting Western Australia, mentioning the testimony of men there to his influence on their lives would have been an encouragement. Almost at the same time another came from Rev Harry Rowe, one of his men, who was pastoring a church in the United States. Harry Rowe had had a very effective ministry at Central Baptist and subsequently had been Professor of Homiletics at New Orleans Baptist Theological Seminary. He wrote 'I do want to tell you again how great I feel is my debt to you. Over the years I have been thankful to God that I was privileged to have my training for the ministry under your guidance. It has been the great blessing of my life, and I am very conscious of it. I know that such blessing and success (as) has attended my ministry over the years belongs, under God, to you'

A few days later on 28 October he attended a farewell function at Ashfield, his home church, extended to one of his boys, Rev JS Curtis, and paid tribute to his ministry. It pleased him that John was becoming the Director of Evangelism for the Baptist Union.[1334]

A letter written by his son, Bill, from America dated 8 November said, 'I'm very sad to learn that dad's health is failing. I know he doesn't want to go on with depleted mental power. I noticed on his second trip to New Zealand that he had gone downhill a little and we have noticed a greater tiredness in his letters during this year'.

His writing had deteriorated considerably. However in a letter dated 29 November either subsequently rewritten or never posted, he expressed the hope of visiting the north of the State later in the year and paying a call on old friends at Nambucca. For all that in a letter written probably the same day he said, 'I had another modified birthday party last week - the 82nd. I am feeling some wear and tear and I am having some mental confusion - a little more muddled than usual! But all is well. I am quite well as regards general health. I shall do less preaching and live more quietly'.

On 22 December he offered the prayer of thanksgiving at the wedding reception of Andrew Curtis and Rowena Nicholls.[1335]

Christmas was spent with his family at Longueville.

1974
In the second week in January he was taken for a drive and as he got out of the car he stumbled and sat down heavily on the pavement. The fall

caused damage to some of his vertebrae. He was taken to Royal North Shore Hospital and admitted in considerable pain. After about a fortnight of treatment he was transferred to Waldock, the geriatric hospital conducted by the Baptist Homes Trust. A good friend, Marj Bartlett, was the matron and he was very well looked after. Early reports said that he was improving daily yet suggested that visiting be restricted.[1336] It was very frustrating for him that he was not able to stand or walk without assistance. Former student, Principal David Stewart of the Bible College of New Zealand in writing referred to his inability to walk and went on to say, 'We are praying for you that you won't chafe under the limitations this will impose on you. Dorothy and I were thinking of how you loved to walk when you were here with us'. He also had periods of confusion and distress. As the days went by he was, as he confessed, impatient to be back home.

Friends far and near as they learned of his condition sent messages of encouragement, assuring him of their prayers. His former secretary, Miss Mary Kramer, from Adelaide, sent such a message in a beautiful card. Inside the card he wrote the outline of a sermon on one of his favourite texts Hebrews 7:25. In his sometimes confused state he imagined that he had appointments to preach. It was an indication of his continuing compulsion to proclaim God's word.

One of the first intake of Bible College students back in 1959 wrote from Victoria to cheer him. She wrote, in part, 'My recollections of you take the form of an inspired teacher searching out the depths of what it means to have the mind of Christ, coupled with a loving ministry. Perhaps in sending good wishes concerning your health, it is sufficient to wish for you those experiences which will best serve to glorify God, and thereby give you cause for personal rejoicing'.

A ministerial student from a much earlier time wrote 'Our dear and most valued friend, we were sorry to hear that you were 'cast down', but relieved to know that you are not 'destroyed'. I think you know what you mean to us, and although you are physically weak, your own splendid spirit is as vital as ever'.

The writer felt, moreover, that the Principal by his faithfulness had inspired and encouraged others to be more faithful too.

During the weeks of his final decline he was cheered by regular letters from his son, Bill, and daughter-in-law, Diana, in America. It must also have been encouraging to him that *The Australian Baptist* began to reprint a series of studies by him on The Epistle to the Hebrews.[1337]

As the days went by it became apparent that there was something seriously wrong with his left leg. On 14 March he was admitted to Sydney Hospital. A thrombosis had cut off the blood supply to his left leg and there were other complicating factors. A few days later it became necessary to amputate the leg. It was reported that he was convalescing well. Friends far and near sent assurances of their love and prayers for his recovery.[1338].

Diana and Bill, travelling in America and not knowing of the operation, wrote on successive days, 30 and 31 March, responding gladly to news they had received that he was making good progress. Before those letters, which included photographs of his little granddaughter, Sarah, arrived he was beyond receiving them. He went down hill rapidly and mercifully on 8 April death supervened. Not long before his death Rev Albert Dube, one of his men and latterly his pastor, read to him part of the fourteenth chapter of John's Gospel. When he came to the words, 'I will come again and take you to myself' the dying man said suddenly as with the full realisation for the first time of a familiar truth, 'The Lord Jesus Himself will come and receive me'. It was in that confidence that he died.

Mary Kramer, who at one time had been his secretary wrote to Trevor and Ruth Morling, 'If ever anyone was assured of a place in our Heavenly Father's mansions I know your dear Dad was. His life - and by that I mean his spiritual life – has been a challenge and encouragement to so many and I humbly include myself in that group'.

The funeral service was held on 10 April in the College Chapel named in his honour. The Chapel overflowed and many had to be content to listen to the service relayed to the College dining room.

They Loved Him

The President of the NSW Baptist Union, Rev Egerton Long, presided. He reminded the congregation that it was the time of the year when Christian thoughts centred on the Risen Christ who had 'abolished death and had brought life and immortality to light through the Gospel'. 'This basic fact which we call death', he said, 'God uses as a vehicle to transfer us into His immediate presence. Jesus, Who gave this truth, declared 'I am the Resurrection and the Life ... He that believeth in Me, though he were dead, yet shall he live, and he that believeth in Me shall never die'. He proved His claim by His own Resurrection, and became the firstfruits of them that sleep'.

'We are met to pay tribute to one of God's greatest saints'.[1339] 'GHM was God's gift to our churches. His ministry began at a time of great evangelism, at a time of our greatest numerical growth. God knew the need to teach and train these converts, and for a steady stream of pastors to minister as new churches were established. So God gave us GH Morling'.

'He held before our churches, our pastors and our people 'great thoughts of a great God'. 'We are in the evangelical stream today largely because of the Principal-Emeritus. The words of Paul concerning David, 'After he had served his own generation by the will of God, he fell on sleep', apply to him, and we wonder who will take his place'.

'In this denominational service we give praise and thanksgiving for his life and ministry, but there are those present who call him father and grandfather, and we would do nothing to overshadow this personal fact'. Mr Long conveyed to the family the deep love of the churches and the pastors – 'they loved him, your father - and our hearts go out to you today'.

Though it was a denominational service the President acknowledged that GH Morling belonged to the whole church in Australia.

He belonged to all

Bishop John Reid spoke on behalf of the wider constituency pointing to the Principal's extensive ministry beyond the borders of the Baptist churches and to his gracious Christ-like personality. He made reference to his close association with former Archbishop Dr HHK Mowll, Archdeacon RBS Hammond and Archbishop ML Loane. The latter, along with assistant Bishop, the Rt Rev AJ Dain, was in the congregation. 'Through his own expositions of Holy Scripture he had endeared himself to many people. They had been enriched by his public utterances and strengthened by his personal friendship', the Bishop said. 'He expounded the Scriptures with grace and strength'.

In particular he dwelt on the Principal's Bible teaching convention ministry which had enriched a great many people and endeared him to them. His teaching on the Holy Spirit, especially that drawn from John 14-16, was unparalleled. He particularly acknowledged his sensitive expositions on the work of the Holy Spirit, and testified he had never heard their equivalent, especially John chapters 14-16. 'It was also heard much more from the life of the man who had experienced what he had taught', Bishop Reid concluded.

Many apologies, expressions of sympathy and tributes had poured in from around the Commonwealth. Rev RH Nowlan was present in both a personal and representative capacity as President of the Queensland Union.

God's gift to us

Dr Geoffrey Blackburn, President-General of the Baptist Union of Australia, paid tribute on behalf of the wider Baptist constituency. 'It was a time of rejoicing', he said, 'that our beloved Principal-Emeritus has gone to be with the Lord. We thank God for his influence which is felt not only in this State, but all over the Commonwealth in the lives of men and women graduates of the NSW College - in our churches, on Baptist mission fields and in interdenominational missionary work'.

Referring to George Morling's time as President-General he said, 'there were times when the winsomeness of his personality shone through and in matters of intricate business his prayer had been considered more important in reaching a solution than the debate that had gone before. Few men were so universally loved and his serenity of spirit was a living example'.

Dr Blackburn also conveyed loving sympathy from the large number of NSW trained men serving in Victoria, and from the Victorian Union.

The funeral oration was delivered by Principal BG Wright. Its quality and presentation was not only a fitting tribute to GH Morling, but a reflection of Mr Wright himself, a man who had trained under and served with Principal Morling.

Many present that day felt that it was an inspired utterance, masterly in its delineation of its subject and moving in its eloquence. The report said of Gilbert Wright 'He spoke for all who knew and loved him (GHM) and spoke in a way that honoured God as well as His servant'[18]. The oration is reproduced as chapter 7 following.

Rev Doug Mill and Rev Colin Campbell assisted in the service. Graduates of the Theological College under Principal Morling, and other ministers, formed a Guard of Honour. Nearly ninety deeply-moved and thankful men lined the path in two ranks from the chapel to the roadway.

The cortege moved to the Northern Suburbs Lawn Cemetery where a short service was conducted by Rev Albert Dube and Rev Harry Orr, who had been the Principal's present and former pastors.[1340] Mr Dube recalled certain events during his recent illness and spoke of his gracious and Christ-like ministry. 'His was a victory over death, and eternal life because he trusted Christ', Mr Dube said.

Rev Harry Orr quoted from Archbishop Trench, 'He crossed over into the eternal land beside which he had lived all his days', and applied it to Principal Morling. 'His life is not over, his service not finished, his work still undone. There is the experience of that greater touch of God upon him' he said.

'In a sense he has gone on, but he still lives in my thoughts, still lives as a point of reference in my ministry, and any decisions yet to be made. His life had the characteristic of compulsion about it,' Mr Orr concluded, 'which brought many back to him again and again for counsel and advice, and will remain a continuing challenge to all who knew him'.

The last of his studies on Hebrews appeared in the issue of *The Australian Baptist* that reported his death along with the notation, 'He, being dead, yet speaketh'. He would continue to speak, for it was announced that in the following issue his series of studies on Ephesians would commence.[1341] The Ephesians studies appeared weekly till 21 August 1974, and were followed by his 'Upper Room Discourses' till 18 December 1974.

On 22 April a Memorial Service was held at the Balwyn Church in Melbourne. Rev JD Williams, the President of the Victorian Union, presided and brought a tribute. Two of the Principal's men, Rev Basil Brown and Rev Ian Emmett, also gave tributes and another, Rev Arthur Wilkins, delivered the eulogy.

During this period and for weeks to come messages of sympathy to the family and tributes to God's honoured servant poured in. These came from State and Federal Baptist Unions, Ministers' Fraternals, leaders in other denominations, interdenominational organisations, churches, former students, fellow ministers and friends.

A Victorian couple, quite unconnected with the NSW College, addressed their message of sympathy 'to the family of our beloved Principal'. That was the way in which he had come to be viewed by Baptists throughout Australia. The Queensland Baptist Ministers' Fraternal praised God 'for one of the most radiant and effective Christian leaders' He had ever given. Seldom was there felt to be more justification for the conviction that 'a prince and a great man had fallen in Israel'. Yet the dominant note was one of thankfulness to God because in the gift of George Morling He had so greatly enriched His people.

Many paid tribute to his teaching, especially on the Holy Spirit and on the 'Keswick' doctrine of holiness by faith. But even more prominent was the acknowledgment of the influence of what he was as 'a true saint of God' - which was how many saw him. In the sense they intended he would not have owned the title. However the whole record of his life shows that he was a man who thirsted for holiness, or, more accurately, for God. The word that particularly characterised his Christian pilgrimage could well be aspiration. What started as a quest for serenity and became a quest for a deeper serenity came at last to be seen as a quest for the Spirit. And that quest for the Spirit was to be seen as a quest for God in His final self-giving within the life of the believer effecting an experienced union with the Lord Jesus Christ.

That which he had long yearned for but had never fully experienced was at last his, not so much because his aspiration had been rewarded with attainment but because he was at last able to receive all that God in His grace offered him.

The Minute of Appreciation placed on record by the Executive Committee of the Baptist Union[1342] was largely taken up with details of his life and ministry, but also included material that pointed to the character of the man and his influence. From it the following is extracted. 'Baptists of NSW lost one of their outstanding leaders in the passing of Principal-Emeritus GH Morling, OBE, MA ... For more than fifty years the Principal expressed gifted personality and leadership through every channel of denominational life. ... His ministry as Principal of the Baptist Theological College of NSW extended for 40 years and today the great majority of ministers of the NSW churches are his graduates. Others serve in churches throughout Australia and New Zealand, on the Australian Baptist mission fields, and are scattered throughout the world in positions of leadership in the Christian Church'.

'It is of interest to note that of the five Baptist Theological Colleges in Australia, three Principals, two Vice-Principals and five members of their faculties were his students, as well as the Principal of the Bible College of New Zealand and the Principal of the Melbourne Bible Institute'.

'His principalship was marked by wise discipline, the highest expression of evangelical scholarship, unsurpassed lecturing in many fields, with a particular skill in exposition, and healthy emphasis upon the practical needs of the pastoral office. He was constantly in demand as a Convention speaker where his Bible readings were a feature which drew large crowds. He majored on the 'Keswick' teaching of holiness and the doctrine and work of the Holy Spirit'.[1343] When the statement was presented to the 1974 Annual Assembly, it was received by the Assembly standing in silent respect.[1344]

The College Council recorded the following Minute of Appreciation, 'With thanksgiving and praise this Council records the home going of Principal-Emeritus GH Morling in his 83rd year. For 40 years he moulded the traditions of the College. His Principalship was marked by high scholarship, careful biblical exegesis aglow with the evangelical emphasis, personal interest in all his students and his own deep experience of Christ'.

'The five present members of faculty were trained under him and the high spiritual and academic standards of the College today are directly attributable to his inspired leadership'.

'Many members of Council recall his wise counsel, his personal friendship, his fellowship in prayer, his life of faith and his fine biblical expositions. Above all he was one who inspired others to live for Christ. We record our gratitude to God for his life and ministry'.[1345]

JD Bollen, quoted by Eldridge, wrote 'Between the principalships of Gordon and Roberts-Thomson lay the peaceful 40 year term of GH Morling' ... (Eldridge states that he was 'essentially a man of peace who, if possible, avoided confrontation but to NSW Baptists he meant a great deal more than that.) A great deal of his contribution was in the spirituality of his life'.[1346]

'STIRRING EULOGY TO OUTSTANDING BAPTIST'

Principal B. Gilbert Wright,

CHAPTER 7 - 'STIRRING EULOGY T0 OUTSTANDING BAPTIST'

No finer tribute could have been paid to Principal-Emeritus GH Morling, OBE, MA, than that which was given by Principal BG Wright at his funeral service last Wednesday. It was a masterly and moving utterance, and those who heard it said that he had been inspired of God. Mr Wright, himself a student of the Principal, and Vice-Principal for the last ten years of his Principalship, swept us to the heights by his impassioned eulogy.

For the benefit of those who could not share in the inspiration, and indeed those who were blessed in its delivery, the funeral oration is reproduced verbatim, with a few minor deletions.

'My voice today must be, in some measure, however inadequate, the voice of the Baptists in New South Wales', Mr Wright said. 'It must also be the voice of hundreds of students in Australia and throughout the world who rise up to call Principal-Emeritus GH Morling blessed, and in a more general sense, the whole Christian world, with special reference to the many who know him through writings, his convention fellowship and messages at Katoomba, Upwey (now Belgrave Heights) and other centres in Australia and New Zealand, and the Inter-Varsity Fellowship of which he was at one time President - and the crowded Bible schools of the Ashfield College days. For almost two generations he has been God's gift to the Denomination, and to the Christian Church in Australia'. Principal Wright went on to say, 'In a more direct and intimate sense, I speak for and to those whom he loved, and who loved him dearly in return - the members of his own family circle.

Holy ideals

It is the stature of the Principal which makes it so difficult to paint his portrait or delineate his character. My brush is too short, my canvas too small, and I am unskilled in mixing such colours.

We must measure the sky before we can measure the man. The world of the Principal stretched from the last decade of the l9th Century to 1974. He was born at Ashfield on 21 November, 1891.

He came from a home, simple. austere, strong in the strict high ethic of the Baptist faith. His father, whom some of us knew, was a Bible class leader in the Ashfield Church.

How he loved to tell the story of the first supper at home after his ordination. His mother had it all set up in the front reception room. Slightly puzzled, he asked, 'Mother, why are we not having supper in the kitchen as usual?' His mother replied, 'George, you are a minister of the Gospel now'. He learned to magnify the office of the ministry and God's call. Its holy ideals became part of his life.

In 1913 he was accepted as a student for the Baptist Theological College of NSW but spent the first year at our Victorian College, before the NSW College was commenced in 1916. He would often speak of the academic successes of his contemporaries, who were especially gifted, but never of himself. We have in the College, historical records of the 1917 Calendar. In it the examiner in Biblical Theology said, 'Two papers, WH Bain's and GH Morling's were as nearly perfect as one could expect', in other subjects he was hard on the heels of the best student. In the preliminary year spent in Melbourne he obtained first place in subjects taken in the Presbyterian and Methodist Colleges in the Melbourne University.

In 1913 he graduated Bachelor of Arts at the University of Sydney and in 1925 received his Master's degree.

After serving at Dungog-Thalaba, Hornsby and Pymble, the Assembly of 1921 asked him to accept the position of Acting-Principal. Then in 1923 he became Principal. (Many said he was far too 'young'.)

In 1929-30 he served the Denomination as its President, and later, for three years 1960-63 as Ministerial Vice-President. In 1951 he represented the Baptists of Australia at the British Empire Baptist Congress and Conference of Principals, where he presented an address entitled 'The Baptist View of the Church and Sacraments'. From 1962 to 1965 he held the office of President-General of the Baptist Union of Australia. In the New Year's Honours of 1963 he was recognised by Her Majesty Queen Elizabeth II with the Order of the British Empire, and he journeyed to Buckingham Palace that year for it to be conferred.

What gigantic leaps the world has made since 1891. His world was that two great wars, of the awakening giants of nationalism, of nuclear physics, the conquest of space. No one was more sure or reiterated more carefully through all these years that God in Christ, as a Saviour from sin, could meet every real need of the human heart.

Those early years were not without romance, and God sent into his life a beautiful helpmeet, the lass from Wales, Gladys Rees. They were married in 1917. She stood by his side in his pastoral ministry and through the years of his Principalship with loving, loyal support, becoming the mother of their three sons and two daughters whom, when they were small, because they lived the same house and home as the student, she 'taught to cry softly'.

Dark night

He once described the wife of a missionary, whom he held in high regard, in words which I believe he would have used with even greater depth of feeling of his own wife, 'one who combined warmth and strength, tenderness and wisdom, spiritual idealism and robust common sense in a high degree'. The dedication of his book *The Quest for Serenity* was to her, in the simple and beautiful phrase, 'To whom I owe the blessing of a restful home'.

It was to be in his own family circle that he was to know his 'dark night of the soul'. God blessed him with deep sorrow, that holy experience of the Divine love that remains greatly dark to most of us who are ordinary selfish men, whom God has not broken to make anew.

Only those who have drunk deeply themselves of human suffering may hold the chalice of comfort to the quivering lips of others who suffer, and this the Principal was able to do on countless occasions, not only because he had suffered, but because he had found sufficient strength from One who said, 'The cup which my Father has given me, shall I not drink it?'

Towards the end of his Principalship it was given to him to stand helpless through long months of illness, while medical science and skills proved vain to bring healing to his life's partner. Then he himself was stricken down and for a long time his own life flickered feebly in the vast darkness of the valley of the shadow. In a remarkable way God saw fit to bring him back to full strength again, but during that time of illness he was to drink more deeply of sorrow, for Elaine, their younger daughter, had been stricken down with the most dread scourge of our western civilisation, and died while he himself was so ill. Then he found a home in the loving care of his elder daughter Dorothy, only to learn after a few short years that the same dread disease had become her lot.

As he stood for the third time in solemn loneliness, his faith never wavered nor his hope grew dim and the stigma of the Cross became more deeply stamped upon his life.

Let me speak briefly about his College ministry. That scholarly, pastoral, devotional impact he made on every student for more than 40 years, at Harris Street, then Petersham, at Granville and at Ashfield and finally at Eastwood. It was the central ministry of his life and he gave himself without reservation to 'The Training of the Twelve'.

What familiar titles given him by his students, crowd the mind while memory holds the door, 'GHM' 'Principal', 'Principal-Emeritus', but for most, if not all of us, and later, 'The Old Prof' became a name of great affection and will remain in our hearts with strong and tender memories so long as life shall last.

But it is the title 'Principal' which suits him best of all. While there is a touch of formality about it, he made radiant it with his own Christlike personality. He made it stand for unsurpassed lecturing, for wise discipline, for theological insights, for fellowship in the Gospel and changed its formality into rightful respect for office. Yet never did he substitute Christian piety for intellectual rigour. The dominant notes in the life of the College were worship, a robust faith, sane well-balanced evangelical fervour, the control of the life by the Holy Spirit, all concentrated in the overall theme of a passion for Christ. What he taught in the class room he preached in the pulpit (so did all his students) and lived in the home and in daily life.

His lectures were often inspired sermons, not in the generally accepted interpretation of that word (never just sermons!) but lectures compacted with pure doctrine and alight with a living faith - powerful, persuasive, never given impersonally and which at times left him exhausted. We would love to quote from his lectures on the Holy Spirit, or Ephesians, or the Song of Solomon, but it is not the time for that.

How he loved to talk about his own early pastoral ministry perhaps in classes on Pastoralia, or whenever he thought the season opportune.

And in the College, when he was at the height of his preaching power, he would say to his students, with a twinkle in his eye, 'I could preach in those days!'

Graciousness

Nothing was more marked than his gracious manner and approachableness. He made himself available to his students at all hours day or night. His door was always open. He was always patient with obtuse students and those who found their work difficult. Though it hurt his sensitive spirit, he often suffered fools gladly for the Gospel's sake.

He set himself to encourage men with ability to take academic honours. Today in our Australasian Colleges alone are five Principals, two Vice-Principals, five members of faculty, all his students.

What an infectious laugh! Who could tell a story like the old Prof? You may have heard it a score of times, but he made it come fresh minted from his overflowing bonhomie. You were immediately caught up with his boyish excitement of being alive. Sometimes you wanted to laugh and cry at the same time because what he said was so true to those poignant things of life that search our spirits.

When he preached, there were stories like the one about the little girl whose spirit was wounded because her brother trapped little birds and who prayed, 'Oh God, stop him!'. Then rose in triumph to say 'He can't catch them now'. Her mother replied, 'You must be very confident in your prayer, do you think you have enough faith'. To which she replied, 'Yes, yes, I am sure because I smashed all his traps'.

But that reflects the Principal's own understanding of faith as active, viable, using the gifts God has given us - and his was from the beginning a life of self-discipline and a triumph over handicaps - then trusting God to do the rest. With all the emphasis possible he would often say 'You can't trust God too much'.

Or Dr Mark Guy Pearce's story of the old fashioned Methodist Class meeting and the brother who prayed, 'Father, 1 have made an aberration from the alignment of rectitude'. 'Stop it', said the class leader, 'tell God you got drunk last night'. Again a reflection of his own direct, simple, unembarrassed speech and approach to life.

Positiveness

His love of positive preaching and thinking was often illustrated by his story (probably apocryphal) of a timid minister, who said, 'Unless you repent - as it were - and are converted - more or less - your souls will be lost – to some extent'.

Not only was he the prince of preachers and of story-tellers, but the prince of conversationalists with a mastery of English prose. That sensitivity for the right word that conveys the right meaning in the right place at the right time. Other men's conversation often descends to the lower levels, at best about mundane things. His conversation was about great themes, great men, great cathedrals, great preaching, the things of God.

How this Chapel delighted his heart! Immediately it became his favourite centre for prayer and preaching. All his Principalship he had longed for such a spiritual home in the life of the College because of that overwhelming sense of the majesty of God. 'Holy, holy, holy, Lord God Almighty' was his choice of hymn on so many occasions as he led us into the Holy of Holies in our devotions. He consistently organised little groups to join him in the vestries of neighbouring churches for quiet waiting upon God. The salvation of souls weighed heavily upon his heart.

Sensitivity

He nourished his soul on the great evangelical theologians of his day - Handley CG Moule, Peter Taylor Forsyth, HR Macintosh, Brooke Foss Westcott, RW Dale, James Denny and others. Men in whom brilliance of mind and a passion for Christ were finely balanced.

With this his sensitive spirit responded to the Christian mystics. How often he would quote from Julian of Norwich, Madame Guyon, St John of the Cross, Evelyn Underhill, William Law, Rufus Jones - the Quakers. But no one discerned more clearly than he that the source of all true mysticism lay in the Person of Christ, and only those whose minds were illuminated by the Holy Spirit came into this secret.

He loved to remind us as he spoke of Spurgeon and his characteristic preaching - how he would 'make a beeline for Christ'. So it was with the Principal. His language was the language of Zion and the atmosphere was filled with the bracing breezes of Galilee.

To use John Masefield's memorable phrase, his was 'the glory of the lighted mind'. And we add, a mind whose powers were heightened by the charisma of the Holy Spirit.

His Presidential address was entitled, 'The Church's Heritage of Power'. Of course the theme was the doctrine of the Holy Spirit as the needed power for work and witnessing in the Church. The doctrine of the Person and Work of the Holy Spirit was to become the dominant theme of his life's ministry. It illuminated everything he said and did.

To whom then shall we liken the Principal? To Greatheart? Yes! To a Prince in Israel? Yes! Yet there is another name which comes immediately to my mind which presses for acceptance. In Pilgrim's Progress, Good-Will says to Christian on that memorable journey as he approaches the Interpreter's House, 'He will show you excellent things'. In that story the Interpreter is meant to personify the Holy Spirit. There is a fascinating parallel between the ministry of Interpreter and the ministry of Principal GH Morling.

Strange, yet not so strange, that associated with the Interpreter's house is the healing of the Pilgrim's wounds.

A great deal of healing comes through knowledge and many of the wounds of the spirit and therefore of the body are closed and healed when a man gains clear views of God and guilt and forgiveness and life. This became the ministry of the Holy Spirit through the Principal. In the Conventions of later years he often took this as his theme.

In that story man lights a candle and Christian follows him. Scripture grows luminous on Principal's lips as the Interpreter teaches men with the coal from off the altar. Common facts and objects that belong to every day take on the highest spiritual meaning. In the midst of the day's mundane tasks they grow like Christ, who find Him there. This again was the ministry of the Holy Spirit through our Interpreter, the Principal.

He would often tell us, especially as he lectured through Ephesians, how easily the Spirit can be 'grieved' or 'quenched'. No figure in Bunyan's book is at once so awful and tender as this half seen and yet clearly sensed form of One like Christ, who had the secrets of eternity on his lips.

The Principal loved to ask us to sing - as he talked to us about the Holy Spirit – 'And His that gentle voice we hear. Soft as the breath of even; That checks each fault, that calms each fear, And speaks of heaven'.

There were many times when the Interpreter identified himself with George Morling, with the personality of this pilgrim, that others also might walk in newness of life with Christ.

And he wist not that the skin of his face shone and the mirror of his soul reflected the face of the Lord Jesus Christ.

Let me conclude with this thought: someone gently accused him quite recently of actually loving funerals. He agreed with reservation and interpretation, by reminding us of the Christian hope.

Gloriously alive

There was an oft repeated theme in the messages he gave at such times, and which he would give at the final communion service of the College year by year, when we would say goodbye to those graduating and would remember absent students, especially those who had passed into the presence of the Lord; greatly moved as he named them one by one he would say, 'It is impossible to estimate fully the significance of the communion of saints. At this moment we partake of a mystic fellowship which embraces not only those who are here present; but also a company which cannot be numbered ... We have spiritual nearness with countless Christians ... Is there not a fellowship of saints which also includes the spirits of the just made perfect?

Then, with voice vibrant with his own faith and hope and love, he would add ... 'our beloved friend and brother is now gloriously alive, because he has been taken up into the glowing life of the victorious Christ; who has abolished death and brought life and immortality to light through the Gospel'.

Today, he being dead yet speaketh. We sorrow not as those who have no hope. He rests from his labours. He has gone from one home to another ... blessed are the dead who die in the Lord, for their works do follow them. We will meet him again in the presence of the king. May the same Holy Spirit he loved and loved to speak about, comfort the hearts of his dear ones in the family circle and all our hearts, as we strive to reflect, as he did, the grace of God.

SELECTED TRIBUTES TO 'OUR BELOVED PRINCIPAL'

CHAPTER 8: SELECTED TRIBUTES TO 'OUR BELOVED PRINCIPAL'

Australian Baptist Missionary Society
'For our part we give thanks to God that the Principal exercised one of the greatest ministries in the course of Australian Baptist life. In particular he was instrumental in preparing successive generations of missionaries who have served in our mission fields and in the administration of the Mission. The remarkable blessing attending their service is in measure the fruit of his own ministry which, we believe, will continue for generations'.

Baptist Union of Queensland
'We acknowledge his tremendous ministry as Principal of the Baptist Theological College of NSW over many years and the value of this is seen in the men that now serve in every State of the Commonwealth'.

Baptist Theological College of Queensland
'We today join the large company who bless God for a man and brother in Christ whose life and testimony brought immeasurable inspiration and challenge. We thank God for a great leader and scholar whose contribution to the Australian Church will remain integral within its history'.

Queensland Baptist Ministers Fraternal
'At this time of denominational and personal loss we feel totally constrained to praise God humbly and whole-heartedly for one of the most radiant and effective Christian leaders God ever gave'.

Director, Church Extension Department - South Australian Baptist Union
'We thought him not only a true saint of God but a treasured and respected friend and father in the faith'.

Whitley College - Victorian Baptist Theological College
'Whitley College ... gives thanks for the life of Principal Morling'.

Hunter District Baptist Association Ministers' Fraternal
'We desire to express that we are deeply grateful to God for the long and useful life of our beloved Principal-Emeritus. Words would fail to adequately express the effect of his saintly life and influence as a teacher

of the Word of God. By this means he greatly enriched untold numbers of people, especially the many graduates of our Baptist Theological College of New South Wales'.

Scripture Union
'We greatly valued ... the contribution that he made in the fields of theology and Bible Study'.

Australian Evangelical Alliance
He 'was very wide in his sympathies and loved to have fellowship with evangelical Christians of all denominations. Thus it was not surprising that he took an active part in the Evangelical Alliance movement from its inception and was, for a time, President of the Evangelical Alliance of New South Wales. I (Rev Howard Knight) personally had the privilege of sharing the Convention platform with him on a number of occasions in Australia and New Zealand and it is my opinion that he was the most able exponent of what is termed the Keswick messages. This statement does not exclude overseas speakers'.

Aldermen of Ashfield Municipal Council
'A long lifetime was spent in untold (acts of) public service to the community in general and to the Baptist Church in particular, for which he was honoured by the Union. He was much loved and will be sadly mourned but his work will remain as a memorial to him'

NSW Baptist Homes Trust - Canberra Regional Board
His 'passing has concluded a great era in Baptist life and work in Australia. However, his influence will be felt for years to come. We in Canberra are grateful that our nursing home bears his name and will stand as a memorial to his work and service to his Lord and to humanity. The Board, staff and guests have been most appreciative of the many visits Mr Morling made to the Lodge. His counselling and compassion was most helpful and comforting to our guests'.

Bishop (later Archbishop) DWB Robinson
'My personal recollections of Principal Morling go back nearly 40 years, and my father enjoyed his friendship, and considered him highly as a Christian brother. I recall so many occasions when his teaching ministry - at Katoomba, at IVF and EU meetings, and elsewhere - made a deep impression on me for its reverent exposition and spirit of serious devotion. He was the creator of a wonderful unity and fellowship across denominational boundaries. There are very many of my generation at

University who owe him a debt of gratitude. As Chairman too, of the Evangelical Alliance of NSW I can speak of Mr Morling as one of our oldest members and most honoured councillors. His leadership and inspiration encouraged us all'.

Principal GN Vose of the Western Australian Baptist Theological College
'1 share with all NSW Baptists a deep sense of personal loss in the passing of the greatest Baptist Australia has yet produced. His life and ministry have left an indelible mark on us all'.

Dr JA Thompson
'It was for us a priceless privilege not only to know him but to work with him in the College. I still find myself turning to some of his perspectives in both theology and life. There was something penetrating and altogether gracious about so many of his utterances. We are the poorer for his going'.

Mr AI Oboohof, Secretary, Slavic Missionary Society
'A long time ago he taught many of us in the Christian Workers College and how he taught!!! How he loved the Word of God and the God of the Word. There was that other worldly atmosphere of heaven about him continually'.

Mr Arnold Dickenson - former Honorary Legal Adviser to the NSW Baptist Union
'I shall certainly miss his sincere friendship which I enjoyed over many years. He was a wonderful man and an example to others as a true Christian gentleman. The Baptist Union will certainly find that they have lost a man who is irreplaceable. I can clearly remember the first time I came into contact with him. I was only a lad at the time and he took the evening service in the Auburn Baptist Church replacing a preacher who was not able to take the service. (He) was a very young man and in my mind's eye I can see him now as I write the letter, a young man full of enthusiasm, with a personality that glowed impressively, a man to remember'.

From very many of his men
'I think it would be true to say that all who trained under him came to regard him more as a father than a principal. He loved us all, together with our wives and families, as individuals. I can remember many times

when he helped and encouraged me over hard places. His intense spirituality was balanced with a delightful sense of humour and an infectious laugh, and those were sufficient to help anyone who knew him. How patiently he bore sorrow and suffering! What an example to us in our lesser trials'.

A Students Tribute:.

> Not blossoms that tell of the springtime
> Nor growth in the bright summer sun
> But fruit, telling more of a harvest
> When cycle of seasons have run
>
> Not yours as for many a Christian
> The mem'ries of bitter regret
> Of life that has scattered the sheepfold
> Or thieves one was wont to abet
>
> Do things rise that you regret dearly
> As summer looks back over morn?
> We think not. You kept your course clearly
> And you'll hear Him say at the Dawn
>
> 'Well done, good servant and faithful!
> He only can praise you aright.
> Yet hear, sir, from hearts that are human
> 'You walked in the highways of light.'

James C. Wilson
Morling College, 1960-63.

REFERENCES

ABBREVIATIONS

BUNSW Baptist Union of New South Wales
EC Executive Committee
TB *The Baptist*, published prior to 1913
AB *The Australian Baptist*, published from 1913 to 1992

Copies of The Baptist and The Australian Baptist are available at the Archives of the Baptist Historical Society, Morling College, 120 Herring Road, Macquarie Park, NSW, 2113.

These volumes are in process of digntisation.

REFERENCES

1 Nicholas, David R.*'Because of Morling'* (now *'Journeys with God'*), BHS, 2003.
2 The *Australian Baptist* (AB) 17 April 1974 page 3.
3 AB 25 July 1939 page 1.
4 Nicholas *op cit* page 4.
5 AB 16 April 1935 page 3.
6 Baptist Archives collection. Ashfield and Burwood Baptist Churches membership rolls.
7 The Baptist (TB) 1 February 1910 page 3.
8 TB 1 September 1910 page 12.
9 Ashfield Membership Roll marginal comment.
10 Nicholas *op cit* page 10.

11 Home Mission Committee Minutes of 22 July 1913.
12 AB 17 August 1937 page 7.
13 AB 7 July 1914 page 16.
14 Nicholas *op cit*.
15 AB 18 October 1932 page 3.
16 AB 15 September 1914 page 2.
17 AB 20 October 1914 page 1.
18 AB 17 April 1974 pages 3, 5.
19 Nicholas *op cit* page 13.
20 AB 28 March 1916 page 16.

21 Eldridge, V. A history of Morling College, chapter 2 page 5. In preparation.
22 Eldridge *op cit* page 6.
23 AB 28 March 1916 page 16.
24 Baptist Archives Bankstown series 01 Minutes of Church Business Meetings page 10.
25 AB 15 January 1918 page 10.
26 BUNSW Executive Committee and Annual Assembly Minutes 1915-18 page 144 4 December 1917.
27 BUNSW Executive Committee and Annual Assembly Minutes 1915-18 page 147 18 December 1917.
28 AB 5 March 1918 page 2.
29 AB 19 March 1918 page 3.
30 AB 7 January 1919 page 10.

31 Sands Directory of Sydney 1920; Ashfield BC church roll 1884-1935 transfer of membership of Mr and Mrs CA Morling to Auburn August 1919.
32 AB 8 June 1920 page 5.
33 AB 24 August 1920 page 5. Rogers comments 'At that time, as often after a war, there was widespread interest in the possibility of communicating with the dead'.
34 BUNSW Executive Committee and Annual Assembly Minutes 1918-30 page page 10 of annual reports, inserted at page 140.
35 BUNSW Executive Committee and Annual Assembly Minutes 1918-30 page 164.

36 BUNSW Executive Committee and Annual Assembly Minutes 1918-30 pages 150, 159.
37 BUNSW Executive Committee and Annual Assembly Minutes 1918-30 page 161.
38 AB 19 July 1921 page 8.
39 AB 16 August 1921 page 6.
40 BUNSW Executive Committee and Annual Assembly Minutes 1918-30 page 220 21 September 1921.

41 BUNSW Executive Committee and Annual Assembly Minutes 1918-30 page 222 21 September 1921
42 AB 27 September 1921 page 4.
43 BUNSW Executive Committee and Annual Assembly Minutes 1918-30 page 235 23 September 1921
44 AB 13 December 1921 page 8.
45 AB 17 January 1922 page 4.
46 AB 19 January 1971 page 10 50th anniversary notice.
47 AB 7 February 1922 page 4.
48 AB 7 March 1922 page 10.
49 AB 10 January 1922 page 2.
50 AB 28 February 1922 page 4.

51 AB 14 March 1922 page 2.
52 AB 4 April 1922 page 3.
53 AB 25 April 1922 page 7.
54 The Australian Christian World 11 February 1921.
55 BUNSW Executive Committee and Annual Assembly Minutes 1918-30 page 258 26 April 1922.
56 AB 13 June 1922 page 10.
57 AB 27 June 1922 page 7.
58 AB 1 August 1922 page 4.
59 BUNSW Year Book 1922-23 page 63.
60 BUNSW Year Book 1922-23 page 65.

61 BUNSW Executive Committee and Annual Assembly Minutes 1918-30 page 293 22 September 1922.
62 AB 3 October 1922 page 4.
63 AB 24 October 1922 page 4.
64 AB 31 October 1922 page 9.
65 AB 26 December 1922 page 10.
66 BUNSW Executive Committee and Annual Assembly Minutes 1918-30 pages 311, 319, 7 November 1922, 6 February 1923.
67 BUNSW Executive Committee and Annual Assembly Minutes 1918-30 pages 331-332 3 April 1923.
68 AB 17 April 1923 page 3.
69 AB 28 August 1923 page 9.
70 BUNSW Year Book 1923-24 pages 68-69.

71 College Council Minutes 29 November 1923 page 6.
72 AB 4 December 1923 page 4 states this occurred on 28 October.

73 AB 8 January page 4.
74 College Council Minutes 24 January 1924 pages 9-10.
75 AB 29 January 1924 page 4.
76 AB 5 February 1924 page 4.
77 AB 18 March 1924 page 4.
78 AB 29 April 1924 page 2.
79 AB 15 April 1924 page 10.
80 College Council Minutes 27 May 1024 page 23.

81 AB 6 May 1924 page 3.
82 AB 17 June 1924 page 9.
83 College Council Minutes 22 July 1924 page 28.
84 AB 17 June 1924 page 10.
85 BUNSW Executive Committee and Annual Assembly Minutes 1918-30 page 405 3 June 1924.
86 BUNSW Executive Committee and Annual Assembly Minutes 1918-30 page 409 8 July 1924.
87 AB 15 July 1924 page 10.
88 AB 12 August 1924 page 9.
89 College Council Minutes 26 August 1924 page 32.
90 BUNSW Year Book 1924-25 pages 72-73.

91 BUNSW Year Book 1924-25 page 71.
92 BUNSW Executive Committee and Annual Assembly Minutes 1918-30 page 431 26 September 1924.
93 BUNSW Executive Committee and Annual Assembly Minutes 1918-30 page 419 24 September 1924.
94 AB 16 September 1924 page 4.
95 AB 30 September 1924 page 2.
96 AB 2 December 1924 page 4.
97 AB 2 December1924 page 10.
98 College Council Minutes 25 November 1924 pages 41-42.
99 College Council Minutes 30 December 1924 page 45.
100 College Council Minutes 24 February 1925 page 53.

101 AB 31 March 1925 page 2.
102 College Council Minutes 31 March 1925 page 60.
103 College Council Minutes 31 March 1925 page 59.
104 AB 21 April 1925 page 10.
105 BUNSW Executive Committee and Annual Assembly Minutes 1918-30 page 452, 453.
106 College Council Minutes 12 May 1925 page 62.
107 Eldridge *op cit* chapter 3 page 6.
108 7 July 1925 page 10.
109 AB 21 July 1925 page 10.
110 College Council Minutes 28 July 1925 pages 65-66.

111 AB 4 August 1925 page 9.
112 AB 25 August 1925 page 15.
113 AB 1 September 1925 page 10.

114 BUNSW Executive Committee and Annual Assembly Minutes 1918-30 page 484.
115 BUNSW Year Book 1925-26 page 75.
116 College Council Minutes 27 October 1925 page 72.
117 College Council Minutes 24 November 1925 page 75.
118 AB 22 December 1925 page 10.
119 AB 22 December 1925 page 4.
120 AB 5 January 1926 page 3.

121 AB 25 May 1926 page 2.
122 AB 29 December 1925 page 11.
123 AB 29 December 1925 page 4.
124 BUNSW Year Book 1926-27 page 71.
125 AB 2 February 1926 page 9.
126 AB 2 March 1926 page 2.
127 AB 6 April 1926 page 2.
128 BUNSW Executive Committee and Annual Assembly Minutes 1918-30 pages 498-499 9 February 1926.
129 BUNSW Executive Committee and Annual Assembly Minutes 1918-30 page 501.
130 College Council Minutes 18 March 1926 page 80.

131 AB 8 March 1916 page 3.
132 BUNSW Executive Committee and Annual Assembly Minutes 1918-30 page 508 13 April 1926.
133 College Council Minutes 22 April 1926 page 84.
134 BUNSW Executive Committee and Annual Assembly Minutes 1918-30 page 517
135 College Council Minutes 15 May 1926 page 85.
136 BUNSW Executive Committee and Annual Assembly Minutes 1918-30 page 519 18 May 1926.
137 AB 22 June 1926 pages 2-3.
138 AB 15 June 1926 page 3.
139 13 July 1926 page 9.
140 College Council Minutes 17 June 1926 pages 86-87.

141 AB 31 August 1926 pages 1-4.
142 AB 3 August 1926 page 1.
143 AB 7 September 1926 page 8.
144 BUNSW Year Book 1926-27 pages 72-72.
145 BUNSW Executive Committee and Annual Assembly Minutes 1918-30 page 539 3 September 1926.
146 BUNSW Executive Committee and Annual Assembly Minutes 1918-30 page 491 6 October 1925.
147 BUNSW Executive Committee and Annual Assembly Minutes 1918-30 page 551 14 December 1926.
148 AB 30 November 1926 page 2.
149 AB 21 December 1926 page 10.
150 AB 28 December 1926 page 4.

151 BUNSW Executive Committee and Annual Assembly Minutes 1918-30 pages 555-556 18 January 1927.
152 BUNSW Executive Committee and Annual Assembly Minutes 1918-30 page 557 22 February 1927.
153 AB 8 March 1927 page 3.
154 AB 3 May 1927 page 4.
155 AB 10 May 1927 page 4.
156 AB 24 May 1927 page 4.
157 AB 18 October 1927 page 13.
158 AB 17 May 1927 page 10, 31 May 1927 page 8, 21 June 1927 page 10.
159 College Council Minutes 7 June 1927 page 105.
160 College Council Minutes 5 July 1927 page 108.

161 College Council Minutes 9 August 1927 page 109.
162 College Council Minutes 25 October 1927 page 112.
163 BUNSW Year Book 1927-28 page 65.
164 AB 4 October 1927 page 4.
165 BUNSW Executive Committee and Annual Assembly Minutes 1918-30 page 600 22 November 1927.
166 AB 6 December 1927 page 4.
167 AB 13 March 1928 page 13.
168 The Brisbane Courier 23 May 1928 page 7.
169 AB 8 May 1928 page 13.
170 AB 29 May 1928 page 3.

171 BUNSW Executive Committee and Annual Assembly Minutes 1918-30 page 618 12 June 1928.
172 College Council Minutes 28 June 1928 page 116.
173 AB 26 June 1928 page 13.
174 Nicholas *op cit* page 104.
175 AB 17 July 1928 page 4.
176 AB 7 August 1928 page 13.
177 AB 25 September 1928 page 3 photo; BUNSW Executive Committee and Annual Assembly Minutes 1918-30 page 633 19 September 1928.
178 BUNSW Executive Committee and Annual Assembly Minutes 1918-30 pages 638-9 20 September 1928.
179 BUNSW Year Book 1928-29 pages 54-55.
180 College Council Minutes 7 November 1928 pages 120, 122.

181 AB 11 December 1928 page 7.
182 AB 11 December 1928 page 14.
183 College Council Minutes 5 March 1930 page 127.
184 AB 19 March 1929 page 4.
185 BUNSW Executive Committee and Annual Assembly Minutes 1918-30 page 680 21 May 1929.
186 BUNSW Executive Committee and Annual Assembly Minutes 1918-30 page 683 18 June 1929.
187 College Council Minutes 10 September 1929 page 132.
188 AB 1 October 1929 page 1.
189 AB 1 October 1929 page 2.

190 BUNSW Executive Committee and Annual Assembly Minutes 1918-30 page 708 September 1929.

191 AB 30 July 1929 page 2.
192 AB 22 October 1929 page 2; 29 October 1929 page 4.
193 Merrylands Baptist Church membership roll May 1930.
194 AB 19 November 1929 page 13.
195 College Council Minutes 5 November 1929 page 136.
196 AB 10 December 1929 page 4.
197 AB 24 December 1929 page 1.
198 AB 7 January 1930 page 15.
199 AB 7 January 1930 page 4.
200 AB 21 January 1930 pages 4, 13.

201 AB 4 February 1930 page 13.
202 AB 25 February 1930 page 9.
203 AB 18 March 1930 page 10.
204 AB 11 March 1930 page 9.
205 AB 29 April 1929 page 9.
206 AB 11 March 1930 page 3.
207 Eldridge *op cit* chapter 3 pages 9-10.
208 AB 18 March 1930 page 4.
209 AB 8 April 1930 page 11.
210 AB 25 March 1930 page 5.

211 Croydon Baptist Church leaflet 'Foundation Stone Setting Ceremony' Baptist Historical Society Archives collection Croydon Box 3 Series 13.
212 AB 8 April 1930 page 3.
213 AB 22 April 1930 page 2.
214 BUNSW Executive Committee and Annual Assembly Minutes 1918-30 page 730 29 April 1930.
215 AB 27 May 1930 page 10.
216 AB 17 June 1930 page 9.
217 AB 1 July page 9, 8 July 1930 pages 3, 9.
218 AB 8 July 1930. page 8
219 College Council Minutes 5 July 1930 page 143.
220 BUNSW Executive Committee and Annual Assembly Minutes 1930-39 page 4 of insert between pages 1-2 23 September 1930.

221 BUNSW Year Book 1930-31 pages 61-62.
222 AB 23 December 1930 page 4.
223 AB 23 December 1930 page 9.
224 AB 5 March 1952, page 7 - obituary Mrs J Newport.
225 AB 3 February 1931 page 10.
226 AB 3 February 1931 page 7.
227 AB 10 February 1931 page 2.
228 College Council Minutes 17 February 1931 pages 150-151.
229 BUNSW Year Book 1931-32 page 50.
230 AB 17 March 1931 page 3.

231 College Council Minutes 5 May 1931 page 154.
232 AB 30 June 1931 page 9; 16 June 1971 page 14 – 40th anniversary comment.
233 AB 30 June 1971 pages 5, 14.
234 College Council Minutes 5 July1931 pages 155-156.
235 College Council Minutes 28 July 1931 pages 157-158.
236 College Council Minutes 6 October 1931 page 161.
237 College Council Minutes 3 November 1931 pages 163-164.
238 College Council Minutes 3 December 1931 pages169-170.
239 AB 24 November 1931 page 3; 1 December 1931 pages 2-3.
240 College Council Minutes 2 February 1932 page 176.

241 AB 8 March 1932 page 3.
242 AB 22 March 1932 page 9.
243 College Council Minutes 3 May 1932 page 185.
244 College Council Minutes 5 July 1932 pages 189-191.
245 College Council Minutes 6 September 1932 pages 195-196.
246 AB 4 October 1932 page 10.
247 BUNSW Year Book 1932-33 page 45.
248 AB 18 October 1932 page 3.
249 College Council Minutes 6 December 1932 pages 200-201.
250 AB 13 December 1932 page 3.

251 Eldridge *op cit* chapter 4 page 7 quoting Stuart Braga.
252 AB 7 February 1933 page 6.
253 AB 11 April 1933 page 1.
254 AB 30 May 1933 page 9.
255 AB 8 August 1933 page 9.
256 AB 29 August 1933 page 4.
257 AB 19 September 1933 page 4.
258 AB 12 September 1933 page 3.
259 College Council Minutes 5 September 1933 page 220.
260 AB 26 September 1933 page 3.

261 AB 19 September 1933 page 3.
262 AB 26 September 1933 pages 3, 9.
263 AB 26 September 1933 page 9.
264 AB 26 September 1933 page 4.
265 College Council Minutes 3 October 1933 page 223.
266 College Council Minutes 9 October 1933 pages 223-4.
267 AB 17 October 1933 page 9.
268 College Council Minutes 7 November 1933 page 230.
269 College Council Minutes 7 December 1933 page 233.
270 AB 12 December 1933 page 9.

271 AB 6 March 1934 page 11.
272 AB 22 May 1934 page 9.
273 AB 8 May 1934 page 3.
274 AB 29 May 1934 page 4.
275 AB 26 June 1934 page 4.
276 College Council Minutes 5 June 1934 page 247.

277 College Council Minutes 4 September 1934 page 253.
278 AB 3 July 1934 page 10.
279 College Council Minutes 3 July 1934 pages 249-251.
280 Reproduced in TAB 28 August 1934 page 9.

281 AB 17 July 1934 page 11, 7 August page 10.
282 AB 17 July 1934 page 9, 28 August page 9.
283 AB 4 September 1934 page 11.
284 Granville Baptist Church membership roll in Baptist Archives NSW collection.
285 AB 25 September 1934 page 3.
286 BUNSW Executive Committee and Annual Assembly Minutes 1930-39 page 207 27 September 1934.
287 BUNSW Year Book 1934-35 page 59.
288 AB 9 October 1934 page 3.
289 AB 23 September 1959 page 7. Silver wedding notice.
290 AB 9 October 1934 page 9.

291 AB 6 November 1934 page 4.
292 AB 23 October 1934 page 3.
293 AB 30 October 1934 page 10.
294 AB 1 January 1935 page 10.
295 AB 11 December 1934 page 9.
296 AB 5 February 1935 page 10.
297 AB 26 February 1935 page 9.
298 AB 26 March 1935 page 3.
299 AB 2 April 1935 page 2.
300 AB 26 March 1935 page 9.

301 AB 12 March 1935 page 9.
302 AB 23 July 1935 page 9.
303 AB 16 April 1935 page 9.
304 AB 25 June 1935 page 4.
305 AB 23 July 1935 page 4.
306 AB 30 July 1935 page 4.
307 AB 6 August 1935 page 3.
308 AB 16 July 1935 page 10.
309 AB 30 July 1935 page 10.
310 AB 20 August 1935 page 6.

311 AB 1 October 1935 page 6.
312 BUNSW Year Book 1935-36 page 59.
313 AB 5 November 1935 page 11.
314 AB 22 October 1935 page 10.
315 AB 5 November 1935 page 7.
316 AB 5 November 1935 page 5.
317 AB 31 December 1935 page 7.
318 AB 21 January 1936 page 11.
319 AB 28 January 1936 page 10.
320 AB 18 February 1936 page 10.

321 AB 3 March 1936 page 9.
322 AB 17 March 1936 page 10.
323 AB 3 March 1936 page 3 full page advertisement.
324 AB 17 March 1936 page 9.
325 AB 21 April 1936 page 9.
326 AB 5 May 1936 page 9.
327 AB 23 June 1936 page 10, 30 June page11..
328 AB 23 June 1936 page 1.
329 AB 7 July 1926 page 9.
330 AB 8 September 1936 page 6.

331 AB 6 October 1936 page 7.
332 AB 29 September 1936 page 10.
333 AB 29 September 1936 page 3.
334 BUNSW Year Book 1936-37 page 88.
335 BUNSW Year Book 1936-37 page 84.
336 AB 27 October 1936 page 5.
337 AB 27 October 1936 page 10.
338 AB 17 November 1936 page 10.
339 AB 22 December 1936 page 10.
340 AB 16 February 1937 page 10.

341 AB 23 February 1937 page 5 advertisement; 16 March page 10.
342 AB 2 March 1937 page 10.
343 AB 20 April 1937 page 11; 25 March page 11.
344 AB 27 April 1937 page 11.
345 AB 10 August 1937 pages 10-11.
346 AB 24 August 1937 page 10.
347 AB 20 April 1937 page 4.
348 AB 21 September 1937 page 11.
349 AB 24 August 1937 page 4.
350 AB 14 September 1937 page 12.

351 AB 2 November 1937 page 10.
352 AB 3 August 1937 page 4.
353 AB 17 August 1937 page 7.
354 BUNSW Year Book 1937-38 page 73.
355 AB 19 October 1937 page 1.
356 AB 26 October 1937 page 4.
357 AB 19 October 1937 page 15.
358 AB 2 November 1937 page 4.
359 AB 26 October 1937 page 9.
360 AB 7 December 1937 page 10.

361 AB 21 December 1937 page 10.
362 AB 4 January 1938 page 4.
363 AB 25 January 1938 page 4.
364 AB 8 March 1938 page 11.
365 AB 22 March 1038 page 4.
366 AB 22 March1938 page 10.

367 AB 29 March 1938 page 3.
368 AB 29 March 1938 page 10.
369 AB 12 April 1938 page 3.
370 AB 24 May 1938 page 9.

371 AB 31 May 1938 page 4.
372 AB 31 May 1938 page 4.
373 AB 5 July 1938 page 11.
374 BUNSW Year Book 1938-39 pages 102-103.
375 BUNSW Year Book 1938-39 page 104.
376 AB 6 December 1938 page 10.
377 AB 3 January 1939 page 4.
378 AB 10 January 1939 page 10.
379 AB 7 March 1939 page 2.
380 AB 31 January 1939 page 6.

381 AB 21 February 1939 page 6.
382 AB 21 February 1939 page 12.
383 AB 7 March 1939 page 11.
384 AB 14 March 1939 page 10.
385 AB 28 February 1939 page 6.
386 AB 28 February 1939 page 6.
387 BUNSW Executive Committee and Annual Assembly Minutes 1930-39 page 563.
388 BUNSW Year Book 1939-40 page 81.
389 BUNSW Year Book 1939-40 page 83.
390 AB 14 March 1939 page 6.

391 AB 21 March 1939 page 7.
392 AB 11 April 1939 page11.
393 AB 4 April 1939 page 3.
394 AB 16 May 1939 page 10.
395 AB 18 April 1939 page 6.
396 AB 25 April 1030 page 7.
397 AB 2 May 1939 pages 11-12.
398 AB 16 May 1939 page 4.
399 AB 16 May 1939 page 7.
400 AB 30 May 1939 page 6.

401 AB 6 June 1939 page 11.
402 AB 27 June 1939 page 6.
403 AB 27 June 1939 page 10.
404 AB 4 July 1939 page 10.
405 AB 18 July 1939 page 10.
406 AB 1 August 1939 page 10.
407 AB 25 July 1939 pages 1, 2.
408 AB 25 July 1939 page 6, 1 August 1939 page 6.
409 AB 8 August 1939 page 11.
410 AB 15 August 1939 page 11.

411 AB 5 September 1939 page 6.
412 AB 5 September 1939 page 10.
413 AB 12 September 1939 page 6.
414 AB 3 October 1939 page 11.
415 AB 26 September 1939 page 4.
416 BUNSW Executive Committee and Assembly Minutes Box 4 1939-44 page 37 27 September 1939.
417 BUNSW Year Book 1939-40 page 81.
418 BUNSW Year Book 1939-40 page 83.
419 AB 7 November 1939 page 7.
420 14 November 1939 page 8.

421 AB 14 November 1939 page 7.
422 AB 31 October 1939 page 4.
423 AB 7 November 1939 page 2.
424 AB 16 January 1940 page 2.
425 AB 7 November 1939 page 4.
426 AB 19 December 1939 page 2.
427 Nicholas *op cit* page 26.
428 AB 2 January 1940 page 4.
429 AB 9 January 1940 page 7.
430 AB 23 January 1940 page 4.

431 AB 30 January 1040 page 7.
432 AB 27 February 1940 page 4.
433 AB 23 January 1940 pages 1, 3.
434 AB 27 February 1940 page 4.
435 AB 12 March 1940 page 4.
436 AB 19 March 1940 page 5.
437 AB 26 March 1940 page 4.
438 AB 9 April 1940 page 4.
439 AB 26 March 1940 page 5.
440 AB 19 March 1940 page 5.

441 AB 16 April 1940 page 3; also BUNSW BUNSW Executive Committee and Assembly Minutes Box 4 1939-44 27 September 1939 page 68.
442 AB 14 May 1940 page 2.
443 AB 14 May 1940 page 7.
444 AB 21 May 1940 pages 4, 7.
445 AB 4 June 1940 page 4.
446 AB 11 June 1940 page 4.
447 AB 25 June 1940 page 3.
448 AB 9 July 1940 page 3.
449 AB 2 July 1940 page 6, 9 July page 2.
450 AB 9 July 1940 page 2.

451 AB 9 July 1940 page 4.
452 AB 16 July 1940 page 7.
453 AB 27August 1940 page 7.
454 BUNSW Year Book 1940-41 page 95.

455 BUNSW Executive Committee and Assembly Minutes Box 4 1939-44 page 117 20 September 1940.
456 AB 1 October 1940 page 4.
457 AB 15 October 1940 pages 4, 5.
458 AB 8 October 1940 page 4 advertisement.
459 AB 29 October 1940 page 2.
460 AB 29 October 1940 page 1.

461 AB 24 December 1940 page 7.
462 AB 17 December 1940 page 4.
463 AB 14 January 1941 page 3.
464 AB 3 December 1940 page 4.
465 AB 7 January 1941 page 4.
466 AB 21 January 1941 page 4.
467 AB 25 March 1941 page 7.
468 AB 18 March 1941 page 4.
469 AB 25 March 1941 page 1.
470 AB 1 April 1941 page 3.

471 AB 22 April 1941 page 7.
472 AB TAB 25 March 1941 page 4.
473 AB 22 April 1941 page 4.
474 AB 6 May 1941 page 4.
475 AB 13 May 1941 page 7.
476 AB 13 May 1941 page4.
477 AB 27 May 1941 page 8.
478 AB 17 June 1941 page 8.
479 AB 24 June 1941 page 4, 1 July 1941 pages 1-2.
480 AB 1 July 1941 page 5.

481 AB 15 July 1941 page 3.
482 AB 8 July 1941 page 6.
483 AB 2 September pages 2,4.
484 BUNSW Year Book 1941-42 page 97.
485 BUNSW EC Minutes 1939-45 page 208.
486 AB 14 October page 7.
487 AB 4 November 1941 page 4.
488 AB 27 November 1934 page 7.
489 2 December 1941 page 4.
490 AB 2 December 1941 page 3 advertisement.

491 AB 18 November 1941 page 4.
492 AB 3 February 1942 page 7.
493 AB 13 January page 4; 10 February 1942 page 2.
494 AB 20 January 1942 page 4, 17 March 1942 page 4; Glyn Clatworthy, personal communication.
495 AB 24 February 1942 page 3 advertisement, 10 March page 4.
496 BUNSW EC Minutes 1939-45 page 239 17 March 1942.
497 BUNSW EC Minutes 1939-45 pages 240, 242 24-25 March 1942
498 AB 21 April 1942 page 4.

499 AB 12 May 1942 page 4.
500 AB 19 May 1942 page 4.

501 AB 9 June 1942 page 4.
502 AB 23 June 1942 page 8.
503 AB 28 July 1942 page 7.
504 AB 18 August 1942 page 4.
505 AB 8 September 1942 page 4.
506 AB 20 October 1942 page 7.
507 BUNSW EC Minutes 1939-45 page 278 14 September 1942.
508 AB 6 October 1942 page 2.
509 AB 22 September 1942 page 4.
510 AB 29 September 1942 page 4.

511 AB 22 September 1942 page 5,
512 BUNSW Year Book 1942-43 page 94.
513 BUNSW EC Minutes 1939-45 page 298 20 October 1942.
514 AB 21 July 1942 page 5 advertisement.
515 AB 24 November 1942 page 4.
516 AB 24 November 1942 pages 7-8.
517 AB 17 November 1942 page 4.
518 AB 1 December 1942 page 4.
519 AB 8 December 1942 page 4.
520 AB 15 December 1942 page 4.

521 AB 12 January 1943 page 4.
522 AB 19 January 1943 page 4.
523 AB 16 February 1043 page 4.
524 AB 23 March 1943 page 4.
525 AB 2 March 1943 page 2.
526 AB 2 March 1943 page 4.
527 AB 16 March 1943 page 2.
528 AB 23 March 1943 page 4.
529 AB 13 April 1943 page 4.
530 BUNSW EC Minutes 1939-44 page 334.

531 BUNSW Year Book 1943-44 page 52.
532 AB 18 May 1943 page 7.
533 AB 18 May 1943 page 4.
534 AB 8 June 1943 page 7.
535 AB 1 June page 4, 8 June page 4, 15 June 1943 page 3.
536 BUNSW EC Minutes 1939-44 page 351.
537 BUNSW EC Minutes 1939-44 page 355.
538 BUNSW EC Minutes 1939-44 page 511.
539 AB 17 August 1943 page 4.
540 AB 27 July 1943 page 7.

541 AB 10 August 1943 page 7.
542 AB 27 July 1943 page 4.
543 AB 17 August 1943 page 2.

544 AB 28 September 1943 page 7.
545 AB 5 October 1943 page 7.
546 AB 7 November 1973 page 11.
547 AB 9 November 1943 page 4.
548 AB 7 December 1943 page 8.
549 AB 13 November 1968 page 15 25th anniversary notice.
550 AB 30 November 1943 page 4.

551 AB 7 December 1943 page 5.
552 AB 30 November 1943 page 4
553 AB 11 January 1944 page 4.
554 AB 1 February 1944 page 4.
555 AB 15 February 1944 page 4.
556 AB 8 February 1944 page 4.
557 AB 8 February 1944 page 5.
558 AB 29 February 1944 page 4.
559 AB 4 April 1944 page 7.
560 AB 9 May 1944 page 4.

561 AB 13 June 1944 page 3.
562 AB 30 May 1944 page 7.
563 AB 23 May 1944 page 2.
564 AB 27 June 1944 page 4.
565 AB 4 July 1944 page 5.
566 AB 8 August 1944 page 1; 15 August 1944 page 1.
567 BUNSW Year Book 1944-45 page 51.
568 BUNSW Minutes 1939-45 page 472.
569 BUNSW Year Book 1944-45 page 52.
570 AB 7 November 1944 page 2.

571 AB 3 December 1944 page 7.
572 AB 28 November 1944 page 4, 12 December page 7.
573 AB 2 January 1945 page 4.
574 AB 16 January 1945 page 4.
575 AB 20 February 1945 page 7.
576 AB 27 February 1944 page 2.
577 AB 24 April 1945 page 3.
578 BUNSW EC Minutes 1939-45 page 525.
579 AB 17 April 1945 page 8.
580 BUNSW EC Minutes 1939-45 pages 533-534; TAB 24 April 1945 page 4.

581 AB 1 May 1945 page 4.
582 AB 3 July 1945 page 8.
583 AB 5 June 1945 page 4, advertisement page 5.
584 AB 19 June 1945 page 2.
585 BUNSW EC Minutes 1939-45 page 549.
586 BUNSW EC Minutes 1939-45 page 562.
587 AB 21 August 1945 page 4.
588 AB 28 August 1945 page 4.
589 AB 18 September 1945 page 7.

590 AB 4 September 1945 page 4.

591 AB 4 September 1945 page 2.
592 AB 31 July 1945 page 4; 2 October 1945 page 3.
593 AB 18 September 1945 page 4.
594 AB 2 October 1945 page 4.
595 AB 2 October 1945 page 8.
596 AB 27 November 1945 page 3.
597 AB 27 November 1945 page 4.
598 AB 25 December 1945 page 3.
599 AB 22 January 1046 page 5.
600 AB 15 January 1945 page 4.

601 AB 5 February 1946 page 3.
602 AB 5 February 1946 page 4.
603 AB 12 February 1946 page 8.
604 AB 26 February 1946 page 7.
605 AB 5 March 1946 page 4.
606 AB 5 March 1946 page 4.
607 AB 19 March 1946 page 4.
608 AB 23 April 1946 page 7.
609 AB 2 April 1946 page 4.
610 AB 16 April 1946 page 4.

611 AB 23 April 1946 page 5.
612 AB 30 April 1946 page 3.
613 AB 30 April 1946 page 4.
614 AB 7 May 1946 page 4.
615 AB 28 May 1946 page 2.
616 AB 30 July 1946 page 4.
617 AB 27 August 1946 page 2.
618 AB 1 October 1946 page 8.
619 AB 24 September 1946 page 1.
620 BUNSW Year Book 1946-47 page 58.

621 Minutes of EC & Assembly 1945-54 page 100.
622 AB 24 September 1946 page 5.
623 AB 1 October 1946 page 1.
624 AB 1 October 1946 page 4.
625 AB 15 October 1946 page 4.
626 AB 15 October 1946 page 2.
627 AB 12 November 1946 page 4.
628 AB 26 November 1946 page 4.
629 AB 7 January 1947 page 7.
630 AB 14 January 1947 page 2.

631 AB 14 January 1947 page 4.
632 AB 21 January 1947 page 7.
633 AB 11March 1947 page 7.
634 AB 11 February 1947 page 4.

635 AB 4 March 1947 page 4.
636 AB 1 April 1947 page 7.
637 AB 1 April 1947 page 3.
638 AB 15 April 1947 page 4.
639 AB 15 April 1947 page 2.
640 Minutes of EC & Assembly 1945-54 page 170.

641 Prior AC. *Some Fell on Good Ground.* BUNSW 1966, page 281.
642 AB 29 April 1947 page 4.
643 AB 6 May 1947 page 3.
644 AB 24 June 1947 page 3.
645 AB 3 June 1947 page 4.
646 AB 27 May 1947 page 4.
647 AB 24 June 1947 page 6.
648 AB 17 June 1947 advertisement page 3.
649 AB 26 August 1947 page 7.
650 AB 22 July 1947 pages 3, 4.

651 AB 22 July 1947 page 6.
652 AB 29 July 1947 page 3.
653 AB 29 July 1947 page 4.
654 AB 2 September 1947 page 7.
655 AB 9 September 1947 page 3.
656 AB 23 September 1947 page 3.
657 BUNSW Year Book 1947-48 page 100.
658 BUNSW Year Book 1947-48 page 23. The students were David Stewart and ER Rogers – JS –Rogers modestly did not name himself.
659 Minutes of EC & Assembly 1945-54 page 232.
660 AB 14 October 1947 page 3.

661 AB 7 October 1947 page 3 advertisement.
662 AB 11 November 1947 page 7.
663 AB 21 October 1947 page 6.
664 AB 11 November 1947 pages 2, 4.
665 AB 18 November 1947 page 6.
666 AB 2 December 1947 page 4.
667 AB 3 February 1947 page 3.
668 AB 28 October 1947 page 1.
669 AB 23 December 1947 page 4.
670 AB 13 January 1948 page 1.

671 AB 16 December 1947 page 8 advertisement.
672 AB 3 February 1948 page 7.
673 AB 13 January 1948 page 4.
674 AB 20 January 1948 page 6.
675 AB 27 January 1948 page 4.
676 AB 17 February 1948 page 7.
677 AB 24 February 1948 page 4.
678 AB 2 March 1948 page 4.
679 AB 2 March 1948 page 6.

680 AB 5 April 1948 page 3.

681 AB 2 March 1948 page 7 advertisement.
682 AB 23 March 1948 page 4.
683 AB 6 April 1948 page 4.
684 Minutes of EC & Assembly 1945-54 pages 285, 287.
685 AB 11 May 1948 page 3.
686 AB 4 May 1948 page 8.
687 AB 4 May 1948 page 7.
688 AB 11 May 1948 page 3 display advertisement.
689 AB 18 May 1948 page 4.
690 AB 22 June 1948 page 9.

691 AB 25 May 1948 page 2.
692 AB 22 June 1948 page 3.
693 AB 29 June 1948 page 4; 13 July page 4..
694 AB 31 August 1948 page 7.
695 AB 28 September 1948 page 2.
696 AB 28 September 1948 page 3.
697 BUNSW YearBook 1948-49 page 104.
698 AB 28 September 1948 page 4.
699 AB 5 October 1948 page 4.
700 AB 5 October 1948 page 4.

701 23 November 1948 pages 4, 6.
702 AB 30 November page 4, 7 December 1948 page 6.
703 AB 4 January 1949 page 2.
704 AB 18 January 1949 page 9.
705 AB 18 January 1949 page 8.
706 AB 1 March 1949 pages 8-9.
707 AB 15 February 1949 page 9 adveriusement.
708 AB 5 April 1949 page 15.
709 AB 29 March 1949 page 15.
710 AB 22 March 1949 page 9, also 29 March 1949 page 5.

711 AB 26 April 1949 page 16.
712 Minutes of EC & Assembly 1945-54 pages 379, 389.
713 Minutes of EC & Assembly 1945-54 page 394.
714 Minutes of EC & Assembly 1945-54 page 393.
715 Minutes of EC & Assembly 1945-54 page 397.
716 AB 10 May 1949 page 8.
717 AB 31 May 1949 page 3.
718 AB 31 May 1949 page 4.
719 AB 31 May 1949 pages 14-15.
720 AB 7 June 1949 page 8.

721 AB 21 June 1949 page 8.
722 Minutes of EC & Assembly 1945-54 page 414.
723 Minutes of EC & Assembly 1945-54 pages 419, 426.
724 Minutes of EC & Assembly 1945-54 page 416.

725 AB 30 August 1949 page 15.
726 AB 13 September 1949 pages 4-5.
727 AB 13 September 1949 page 5, Minutes of EC & Assembly 1945-54 21 September 1949 page 435.
728 AB 27 September 1949 page 12.
729 BUNSW Year Book 1949-50 pages 93-95.
730 BUNSW Year Book 1949-50 pages 92-93.

731 Summa Supremo 1.1 September 1949.
732 AB 11 October 1949 page 3.
733 AB 25 October 1949 page 9.
734 AB 8 November 1949 page 9.
735 AB 22 November 1949 page 6.
736 AB 29 November 1949 page 4.
737 AB 10 January page 5, 17 January 1950 pages 5, 15.
738 AB 24 January 1950 page 4.
739 AB 21 February 1950 page 3.
740 AB 21 February 1950 page 7.

741 AB 14 February 1950 page 6.
742 AB 28 February 1950 page 6.
743 AB 21 March 1950 page 9.
744 AB 4 April 1950 page 8.
745 AB 9 May 1950 page 11.
746 AB 30 May 1950 page 14.
747 Minutes BUNSW 1945-54 pages 550-551.
748 AB 13 June 1950 page 7.
749 Nicholas *op cit* page 111 says 1952, and again republished by Word in 1989.
750 Minutes BUNSW 1945-54 page 556.

751 AB 1 August 1950 page 14.
752 Minutes BUNSW 1945-54 page 568.
753 AB 25 July 1950 page 13.
754 AB 22 August 1950 page 14.
755 AB 12 September 1950 pages 14-15.
756 Minutes BUNSW 1945-54 page 584.
757 BUNSW Year Book 1950-51 pages 98-99.
758 Minutes BUNSW 1945-54 page 587.
759 Minutes BUNSW 1945-54 page 588.
760 AB 12 September 1950 page 3.

761 AB 5 September 1950 page 9.
762 *Summa Supremo*, September 1950 page 26.
763 *Summa Supremo,* September 1950 page 18.
764 Minutes BUNSW 1945-54 page 608.
765 Minutes BUNSW 1945-54 page 619.
766 AB 3 October 1950 page 9.
767 Minutes BUNSW 1945-54 pages 625-626.
768 Minutes BUNSW 1945-54 page 629.
769 AB 28 November 1950 page 14.

770 AB 14 November page 8, 21 November 1950 page 10.

771 Minutes BUNSW 1945-54 pages 631, 639.
772 Minutes BUNSW 1945-54 19 December 1950 page 641.
773 AB 9 January 1951 page 10.
774 AB 14 February 1951 page 11.
775 AB 28 February 1951 page 7.
776 AB 28 February 1951 pages 5-6.
777 AB 7 March 1951 page 15.
778 AB 28 March page 11, 18 April 1951 page 15.
779 Minutes BUNSW 1945-54 20 March 1951 page 657.
780 AB 25 April 1951 page 6.

781 Minutes BUNSW 1945-54 17 April 1951 page 663.
782 AB 11 April 1951 page 11.
783 AB 1 August 1951 pages 1, 5.
784 AB 8 August 1951 page 3.
785 The Baptist Times, as quoted in TAB 29 August 1951 page 3, and TAB 19 September 1951 page 2.
786 AB 8 August 1951 page 6 quotes him in slightly different words.
787 AB 25 July 1951 page 10.
788 AB 1 August 1951 pages 1, 5-6.
789 Minutes BUNSW 1945-54 19 September 1951 page 691.
790 BUNSW Year Book 1951-52 page 97.

791 BUNSW Year Book 1951-52 page 96.
792 *Summa Supremo*, March 1952 pages 6-9.
793 AB 19 December 1951 page 6.
794 AB 13 February 1952 page 7.
795 AB 5 March 1952 page 8.
796 AB 12 March 1952 page 1.
797 AB 5 March 1952 page 5 advertisement.
798 AB 26 March 1952 page 6.
799 AB 19 March 1952 pages 1, 5.
800 AB 9 April 1952 page 12.

801 Minutes BUNSW 1945-54 pages 774, 777.
802 AB 11 June pages 3, 6; 18 June 1952 pages 6-7.
803 AB 25 June 1952 page 7.
804 AB 11 June 1952 page 7.
805 AB 16 July 1952 page 24.
806 AB 18 June page 7, 25 June page 6; 9 July 1952 pages 3, 7.
807 AB 20 August 1952 page 23.
808 Minutes BUNSW 1945-54 page 792.
809 AB 6 August pages 1, 5; 13 August 1952 pages 1, 5.
810 AB 23 July 1952 page 6.

811 AB 13 August 1952 page 6.
812 Minutes BUNSW 1945-54 page 801.
813 AB 17 September 1952 pages 23-24.

814 AB 24 September 1952 page 16.
815 AB 8 October 1952 page 15.
816 Minutes BUNSW 1945-54 page 808.
817 BUNSW Year Book 1952-53 page 94.
818 AB 24 September 1952 page 6.
819 AB 1 October 1952 page 11.
820 AB 1 October 1952 page 7.

821 AB 15 October 1952 page 7.
822 AB 4 February 1953 page 16.
823 Baptist Historical Archives, Tamworth Baptist Church series 01 Members' meeting minutes 30 July 1952
824 AB 5 November 1952 page 16.
825 AB 5 November 1952 page 15.
826 Minutes BUNSW 1945-54 page 845.
827 Minutes BUNSW 1945-54 page 848.
828 AB 5 November 1952 pages 6-7.
829 AB 5 November 1952 page 6.
830 Minutes BUNSW 1945-54 page 860.

831 AB 26 November 1952 page 7.
832 AB 10 December 1952 page 3.
833 AB 19 November 1952 page 6 advertisement.
834 AB 17 December 1952 page 22 advertisement.
835 AB 14 January 1953 page 6.
836 AB 18 February 1953 page 6.
837 AB 4 March 1953 page 1.
838 AB 12 August 1953 pages 6-7.
839 AB 18 March 1953 page 18.
840 Minutes BUNSW 1945-54 pages 881-882.

841 AB 18 March page 1, 1 April page 6, 15 April 1953 page 7.
842 AB 15 April 1953 page 6.
843 AB 15 April 1953 page 23.
844 AB 22 April 1953 page 6.
845 AB 13 May 1953 page 6.
846 AB 27 May page 6, 3 June 1953 page 6.
847 AB 24 June 1953 pages 15-16.
848 Minutes BUNSW 1945-54 pages 895-896.
849 AB 15 July 1953 page 3.
850 AB 29 July 1953 page 2.

851 AB 5 August 1953 pages 2-3.
852 Minutes BUNSW 1945-54 page 908.
853 Minutes BUNSW 1945-54 page 911.
854 AB 29 July 1953 page 6.
855 AB 5 August 1953 pages 14-15.
856 AB 19 August 1953 page 7.
857 AB 30 September 1953 page 15.
858 AB 7 October 1953 page 15.

859 BUNSW Year Book 1953-54 pages 104-105.
860 AB 7 October 1953 page 2.

861 AB 21 October 1953 pages 14-15.
862 Minutes BUNSW 1945-54 page 977.
863 AB 28 October 1953 page 14 advertisement.
864 AB 13 January 1954 page 1.
865 AB 24 February 1954 page 15.
866 AB 3 March 1954 page 1.
867 AB 17 February 1954 page 6.
868 AB 3 March 1954 pages 1, 4.
869 AB 17 March page 1, 24 March 1954 page 7.
870 AB 21 April 1954 page 15.

871 AB 21 April 1954 page 4.
872 AB 28 April 1954 p.7.
873 AB 19 May 1954 p.6.
874 AB 25 August page 7, 1 September 1954 page 6.
875 AB 22 September 1954 page 2.
876 BUNSW Year Book 1954-55 page 93.
877 AB 6 October 1954 pages 1, 7.
878 AB 29 September 1954 page 9.
879 AB 27 October 1954 page 14.
880 AB 3 November 1954 page 15.

881 AB 1 December 1954 page 13.
882 AB 10 November 1954 page 7 advertisement.
883 AB 1 December 1954 page 6.
884 AB 15 December 1954 page 6.
885 AB 8 December 1954 pages 1, 3.
886 AB 15 December 1954 page 10 advertisement.
887 AB 2 March 1955 page 7.
888 AB 2 March 1955 page 3.
889 AB 16 March 1955 page 10.
890 AB 23 March 1955 page 8.

891 AB 30 March 1955 page 2.
892 AB 6 April 1955 page 7.
893 AB 23 February 1955 page 6.
894 AB 20 April 1955 page 14.
895 AB 1 June 1955 page 14.
896 AB 20 April page 7, 27 April 1955 page 3.
897 AB 11 May 1955 page 15.
898 AB 8 June page 15.
899 AB 11 May 1955 page 14.
900 AB 25 May 1955 page 14.

901 AB 25 May 1955 page 6.
902 AB 15 June 1955 pages 14-15.
903 AB 6 July 1955 page 15.

904 AB 7 September 1955 page 5.
905 AB 17 August 1955 page 5.
906 AB 17 August 1955 page 14.
907 Minutes BUNSW 1954-8 page 23.
908 BUNSW Year Book 1955-56 pages 99-100.
909 Minutes BUNSW 1954-58 page 120.
910 On 19 October – TAB 12 October 1955 page 7.

911 AB 16 November 1955 page 8.
912 AB 19 October 1955 page 6 advertisement.
913 AB 23 November 1955 page 6.
914 AB 25 January 1956 page 15.
915 AB 15 February 1956 page 5.
916 AB 22 February 1956 page 5.
917 AB 29 February 1956 pages 1, 10.
918 Continuation TAB 7 March 1956 page 3.
919 AB 29 February page 5, 8 March 1956 pages 1, 3.
920 AB 29 February 1956 page 7.

921 AB 29 February 1956 page 6 advertisement.
922 The College Chronicle March 1956.
923 AB 21 March page 7, 4 April 1956 pages 1, 9.
924 AB 2 May 1956 page 14.
925 AB 2 May 1956 page 7.
926 AB 30 May 1956 page 14.
927 AB 30 May 1956 page 7.
928 AB 30 May 1956 page 1.
929 AB 11 July 1956 page 8.
930 AB 25 July page 6, 1 August page 6, 8 August 1956 page 5.

931 AB 8 August 1956 page 9.
932 AB 5 September 1956 page 14.
933 BUNSW Minutes 1954-58 page 218, TAB 3 October 1956 page 7.
934 BUNSW Minutes 1954-58 page 205.
935 BUNSW Year Book 1956-57 pages 127-128.
936 BUNSW Minutes 1954-58 page 234, TAB 26 September 1956 page 67'Theological College'.
937 8UNSW Minutes 1954-58 page 245, TAB 14 November page 8, 21 November 1956 page 6.
938 AB 31 October 1956 page 7 advertisement.
939 BUNSW Minutes 1954-58 page 201, TAB 19 September 1956 page 8 'Ministry of Women'.
940 AB 3 October 1956 page 7 'Points from the President'.

941 AB 14 November 1956 page 8, 28 November 1956 page 7.
942 AB 14 November page 9, 21 November 1956 page 15 advertisements.
943 AB 16 January 1957 page 6.
944 AB 16 January 1957 page 7.
945 AB 30 January 1957 page 6.
946 AB 30 January page 5, 6 March 1957 page 7.

947 AB 20 February 1957 page 7.
948 AB 6 March 1957 page 12.
949 AB 6 March 1957 pages 1, 3.
950 AB 10 April 1957 page 11.

951 AB 13 March 1957 pages 1, 2, 11.
952 AB 20 March 1957 page 6.
953 Notes prepared for the EC 5 April 1957. Hurstville BC file in Baptist Historical Society Archives.
954 Pastor and Officers to members, Hurstville BC 17 March 1957; Minutes BUNSW 1954-58 page 270.
955 Minutes BUNSW 1954-58 page 271.
956 Minutes BUNSW 1954-58 page 276.
957 Minutes BUNSW 1954-58 page 282.
958 Minutes BUNSW 1954-58 page 354, TAB 9 October 1957 page 6.
959 AB 15 May 1957 page 15.
960 AB 5 June 1957 pages 14-15.

961 AB 5 June 1957 page 15.
962 AB 22 May 1957 page 8.
963 AB 10 July 1957 page 8.
964 AB 10 July 1957 page 1.
965 AB 7 August 1957 page 15.
966 AB 14 August 1957 page 15.
967 AB 21 August 1957 page 1.
968 Minutes BUNSW 1954-58 page 306.
969 AB 25 September 1957 page 7.
970 AB 2 October 1957 page 8.

971 Minutes BUNSW 1954-58 page 317.
972 Minutes BUNSW 1954-58 pages 318, 319.
973 AB 6 November 1957 page 16.
974 AB 27 Novmeber 1957 page 7.
975 AB 13 November 1957 page 6.
976 AB 20 November 1957 page 15.
977 AB 4 December 1957 page 1.
978 AB 18 December 1957 page 8.
979 Minutes BUNSW 1954-58 page 383.
980 AB 5 March 1958 page 8 advertusement.

981 AB 5 March 1958 pages 1, 7.
982 AB 30 April 1958 page 15.
983 Minutes BUNSW 1954-58 page 391.
984 Minutes BUNSW 1954-58 page 398.
985 AB 18 June 1958 page 15.
986 AB 16 July 1958 page 15.
987 AB August 1958 page 16.
988 AB 27 August 1958 page 6 advertisement.
989 AB 8 October 1958 page 10.
990 Minutes BUNSW 1958-63 page 5.

991 Minutes BUNSW 1958-63 page 37, TAB 1 October 1958 page 11.
992 BUNSW Year Book 1958-59 pages 125-126.
993 AB 12 November 1958 page 15.
994 AB 15 October page 6, 29 October 1958 page 6.
995 AB 5 November 1958 page 8.
996 AB 24 December 1958 page 7.
997 AB 14 January page 7, photo 21 January 1958 page 8.
998 AB 14 January 1958 page 6.
999 AB 21 January 1959 page 7.
1000 AB 25 February 1959 page 16.

1001 AB 18 March 1959 page 1.
1002 AB 29 April 1959 page 16.
1003 AB 29 April 1959 page 6.
1004 BUNSW Year Book 1960-61 page 230.
1005 Nicholas op cit page 61.
1006 AB 20 May 1959 pages 6, 7.
1007 AB 3 June 1 959 page 6.
1008 AB 2 May 1973 page 11.
1009 AB 22 July 1959 page 9.
1010 AB 30 September 1959 page 1, Minutes BUNSW 1958-63 pages 56, 81..

1011 AB 28 October 1959 page 15.
1012 AB 25 November 1959 page 8.
1013 AB 18 November page 7, 2 December 1959 page 9.
1014 AB 13 January 1960 pages 1, 12.
1015 AB 24 February page 6, 16 March page 6, 6 April 1960 page 9.
1016 AB 16 March 1960 page 9.
1017 AB 23 March 1960 page 9.
1018 AB 23 March 1960 pages 1, 2.
1019 AB 30 March 1960 pages 3, 14.
1020 AB 20 April 1960 pages 6, 9.

1021 AB 13 April 1960 page 6.
1022 AB 27 April 1960 page 9.
1023 AB 11 May 1960 page 9.
1024 Daily Light morning text 21 May.
1025 AB 20 April 1960 page 11.
1026 AB 25 May 1960 page 11.
1027 AB 8 June page 9, 22 June 1960 page 16.
1028 AB 15 June 1960 page 6.
1029 AB 14 September page 6; 23 November 1960 page 6.
1030 AB 10 August 1960 page 15.

1031 AB 12 October 1960 page 15.
1032 AB 24 August 1960 page 15.
1033 AB 17 August 1960 page 8.
1034 AB 24 August 1960 page 11.
1035 AB 24 August 1960 page 6, Minutes 1958-63 page 106.
1036 AB 14 September page 7, 21 September 1960 page 15.

1037 AB 21 September 1960 pages 3, 6.
1038 BUNSW Minutes of Annual Assembly 1958-63 page 106 attachment.
1039 AB 21 September 1960 page 6.
1040 BUNSW Year Book 1960-61 page 78.

1041 AB 28 September 1960 page 6.
1042 AB 26 October 1960 page 16.
1043 AB 12 October page 7, 26 October 1960 page 9.
1044 AB 12 October 1960 page 7 advertisement.
1045 AB 2 November pages 3, 10; 9 November 1960 page 3.
1046 AB 30 November 1960 page 9.
1047 AB 16 November 1960 page 7 advertisement.
1048 AB 30 November 1960 pages 1, 3.
1049 *Summa Supremo* November 1960.
1050 AB 7 December 1960 page 3.

1051 AB 7 December 1960 page 7.
1052 AB 25 January page 7, 8 February 1961 page 7.
1053 AB 1 February 1961 page 6.
1054 AB 1 March page 6, 15 March 1961 page 7.
1055 AB 22 February 1961 page 6 advertisement.
1056 AB 8 March 1961 page 5.
1057 BUNSW Minutes 1958-63 page 201.
1058 AB 10 May 1961 page 1.
1059 AB 10 May 1961 page 6.
1060 AB 10 May 1961 page 7.

1061 AB 5 April page 6, 17 May page 6, 31 May 1961 page 6.
1062 AB 7 June 1961 page 3.
1063 AB 7 June 1961 page 6.
1064 Baptist Historical Society Archives. HT Johnston personal file.
1065 AB 26 July 1961 page 3.
1066 AB 23 August 1961 page 15.
1067 AB 6 September 1961 page 3.
1068 13 September 1961 page 13.
1069 BUNSW Minutes 1958-63 page 219, TAB 20 September 1961 page 7.
1070 AB 11 October page 3, 18 October 1961 pages 3, 15.

1071 1 November 1961 pages 10-11.
1072 AB 6 December 1961 page 10.
1073 AB 17 January 1962 page 11.
1074 AB 28 February 1962 page 15.
1075 AB 13 June 1962 page 8.
1076 AB 7 March 1962 pages 1, 16.
1077 AB14 March 1962 page 7.
1078 AB 14 March page 8, 18 April page 7, 23 May 1962 pages 9, 11.
1079 AB 4 April 1962 page 14.
1080 AB 9 May 1962 page 15.

1081 AB 23 May 1962 page 9.
1082 AB 30 May page 7, 13 June page 7, 20 June 1962 page 7.
1083 BUNSW Year Book 1962-63 pages 43-44.
1084 AB 1 August 1962 page 19.
1085 AB 18 July 1962 page 15.
1086 AB 27 June 1962 page 7.
1087 AB 11 July 1962, pages 1, 10.
1088 AB 1 August 1962 page 18.
1089 AB 5 September 1962 page 14.
1090 AB 12 September 1962 page 14.

1091 AB 19 September 1962 page 15.
1092 AB 25 July 1962 page 7.
1093 AB 5 September 1962 page 7.
1094 AB 12 September 1962 page 6.
1095 AB 19 September 1962 page 10.
1096 AB 19 September page 7, 3 October 1962 page 14.
1097 AB 26 September 1962 page 7.
1098 AB 17 October 1962 pages 9-10.
1099 AB 31 October 1962 page 14.
1100 AB 7 November page 6, 28 November 1962 page 9.

1101 AB Full page advertisement 12 December 1962 page 8.
1102 AB 5 December 1962 page 5.
1103 AB 5 December 1962 page 7.
1104 AB 21 November page 8, 28 November page 11, 12 December page 7, 19 December 1962 page 7.
1105 AB 19 December 1962 page 7.
1106 AB 16 january 1963 page 1.
1107 AB 13 February 1963 page 7.
1108 AB 16 January 1963 pages 1, 5.
1109 AB 3 April 1963 page 9.
1110 AB 3 April 1963 page 11.

1111 AB 3 April 1963 page 8.
1112 AB 10 April 1963 page 5.
1113 AB 27 March 1963 page 6.
1114 AB 10 April 1963 page 11.
1115 AB 1 May page 8, 19 June page 8, 3 July 1963 pages 1, 3.
1116 AB 8 May 1963 page 11.
1117 AB 10 July 1963 page 10.
1118 AB 21 August 1963 pages 10-11.
1119 AB 11 September 1963 page 15.
1120 AB 18 September 1963 page 11; BUNSW Minutes 1958-63 page 447 insert.

1121 BUNSW Minutes 1958-63 page 417 insert page 12.
1122 BUNSW Minutes 1958-63 page 533.
1123 AB 4 September 1963 page 2 editorial 'NSW Assembly'.
1124 BUNSW Minutes page 481, ballot paper pasted on page 491.
1125 BUNSW Minutes pages 507, 509.

1126 BUNSW Minutes page page 507.
1127 AB 9 October 1963 page 10.
1128 AB 30 October 1963 pages 14-15.
1129 AB 23 October 1963 page 10.
1130 AB 23 October 1963 page 6.

1131 AB 20 November 1963 page 15.
1132 AB 13 November 1963 page 10.
1133 AB 5 February 1964 page 11.
1134 AB 13 November 1963 page 15.
1135 AB 29 January 1964 page 14.
1136 AB 18 December 1963 page 9.
1137 AB 29 January 1964 page 10.
1138 AB 5 February page 8, 26 February 1964 page 11.
1139 AB 18 March 1964 page 14.
1140 AB 5 February 1964 page 10, advertisement page 11.

1141 AB 25 March 1964 page 13.
1142 AB 25 March 1964 pages 10, 11.
1143 AB 22 April 1964 page 9.
1144 Nicholas *op cit* page 63.
1145 AB 15 April page 9, 22 April 1964 page 1.
1146 AB 6 May 1964 page 11.
1147 AB 13 May 1964 page 11.
1148 AB 20 May 1964 page 11.
1149 AB 24 June 1964 page 13.
1150 AB 1 July 1964 page 12.

1151 AB 12 August 1964 page 14.
1152 AB 26 August 1964 page 10.
1153 AB 2 September 1964 page 11.
1154 AB 16 September 1964 page 10.
1155 BUNSW Minutes 1964-68 Assembly booklet attached to page 1.
1156 BUNSW Minutes 1964-68 page 83.
1157 BUNSW Minutes 1964-68 page 87.
1158 AB 23 September 1964 page 11.
1159 BUNSW Minutes 1964-68 page 121.
1160 AB 14 October 1964 page 10.

1161 AB 28 October 1964 page 9.
1162 AB 2 December 1964 page 12.
1163 AB 11 November 1964 page 12.
1164 AB 18 November 1964 page 11.
1165 AB 18 November page 12, 25 November page 12, 2 December 1964 page 15.
1166 AB 23 December 1964 page 7.
1167 AB 16 December 1964 page 9.
1168 AB 20 January 1965 pages 3, 14.
1169 AB 20 January 1965 page 11.
1170 AB 17 February page 9, 3 March 1965 page 7.

1171 AB 27 January 1965 page 11.
1172 Nicholas *op cit* page 67.
1173 Nicholas *op cit* pages 66-7.
1174 AB 10 February 1965 page 13.
1175 AB 17 February 1965 page 9.
1176 AB 7 April 1965 page 11.
1177 AB 14 April 1965 page 9.
1178 AB 12 May 1965 page 14 implies the date was 9 May.
1179 AB 5 May 1965 page 11.
1180 AB 23 June 1965 page 15.

1181 **AB 21 July 1965 page 6.**
1182 AB 25 August 1965 page 4.
1183 AB 4 August 1965 page 5.
1184 AB 25 August 1965 page 5.
1185 AB 8 September 1965 page 3.
1186 AB 15 September 1965 page 3.
1187 BUNSW Minutes 1964-68 page 135, page 8 of inserted program.
1188 BUNSW Minutes 1964-68 page 135, page 9 of inserted program.
1189 AB 29 September 1965 page 4.
1190 BUNSW Minutes 1964-68 page 249, ballot paper pasted in.

1191 AB 29 September 1965 page 7.
1192 AB 13 October 1965 page 5.
1193 AB 10 November 1965 page 5.
1194 AB 16 March 1966 page 8.
1195 AB 19 January 1966 page 3.
1196 AB 19 January 1966 page 2.
1197 AB 30 March 1966 page 8.
1198 AB 9 February page 5, 16 February page 8, 2 March page 4, 16 March 1966 page 5.
1199 AB 30 March 1966 page 5.
1200 AB 30 March page 13, 13 April page 7, 18 May 1966 page 8.

1201 AB 15 June 1966 page 4.
1202 AB 13 Juky 1966 page 8.
1203 AB 27 July 1966 page 8.
1204 AB 6 July page 6, 13 July 1966 page 8.
1205 AB 6 July 1966 page 15.
1206 AB 31 August 1966 page 8.
1207 AB 13 July page 6, 28 September 1966 page 8.
1208 AB 17 August page 6, 24 August 1966 page 1 photo.
1209 AB 7 September 1966 page 6.
1210 AB 28 September 1966 page 6.

1211 AB 24 August page 7, 21 September 1966 page 7, BUNSW Minutes 1964-68 page 10 of program pasted to page 272, order of service pasted to page 333.
1212 AB 5 October 1966 page 6.
1213 AB 7 December 1966 page 8.
1214 AB 16 November 1966 page 5.

1215 AB 23 November 1966 page 4.
1216 AB 14 December 1966 page 6.
1217 Fab 14 December 1966 page 6, 1 February 1967 page 5.
1218 AB 1 March 1967 page 6.
1219 AB 10 May 1967 page 5.
1220 AB 10 May 1967 page 6.

1221 AB 31 May 1967 page 15.
1222 AB 31 May 1967 page 3.
1223 AB 3 May page 5, 21 June 1967 page 6.
1224 AB 9 August 1967 page 8.
1225 AB 16 August 1967 pages 1, 3.
1226 AB 19 July 1967 page 7.
1227 AB 1 May 1968 page 6.
1228 AB 2 August 1967 page 14.
1229 AB 30 August page 6, 13 September 1967 page 5, BUNSW Minutes page 387 & program attached to page 479.
1230 AB 4 October 1967 page 8.

1231 AB 4 October 1967 page 1.
1232 AB 20 September page 15, 27 September 1967 page 6.
1233 AB 13 December 1967 page 14.
1234 AB 20 October 1967 page 4.
1235 AB 31 January 1968 page 14.
1236 AB 20 September page 15, 29 November page 6, 6 December 1967 page 6.
1237 AB 16 August 1967 page 14.
1238 AB 21 February 1968 page 10.
1239 AB 18 October 1967 page 5, 17 January page 3, 7 February 1968 page 3.
1240 AB 14 February 1968 pages 1, 3.

1240 AB 21 February page 7, 28 February 1968 page 7.

1241 AB 28 February pages 5, 14; 6 March 1968 page 4.
1242 AB 20 March 1968 page 1.
1243 AB 10 April 1968 page 6.
1244 Nicholas *op cit* page 96.
1245 AB 19 June 1968 page 6.
1246 AB 10 July 1968 page 14.
1247 AB 22 May page 3, 5 June 1968 page 14.
1248 AB 17 July 1968 page 4.
1249 Was this the engagement of his granddaughter Jennifer Goodman?
1250 AB 25 September page 13, 2 October 1968 page 16.

1251 AB 11 September 1968 page 4.
1252 AB 9 October 1968 page 6.
1253 AB 21 August 1968 page 6.
1254 AB 4 December 1968 page 6.
1255 AB 18 December 1968 page 4.
1256 Nicholas *op cit* page 68.
1257 AB 19 February page 4.

1258 AB 16 April 1969 page 4.
1259 AB 12 March 1969 page 9.
1260 AB 6 August 1969 pages 1, 6.

1261 AB 13 August 1969 page 6.
1262 AB 13 August 1969 page 7, 8 October 1969 pages 1, 4.

1263 AB 3 September page 16, 24 September 1969 page 3.
1264 AB 15 October page 6, 10 December 1969 page 4.
1265 AB 14 January 1970 page 3.
1266 AB 24 December 1969 page 6.
1267 AB 24 December 1969 page 6
1268 AB 28 January 1970 page 4.
1269 AB 4 February 1970 page 6.
1270 AB 11 February 1970 page 6.

1271 AB 18 February page 6, 25 February 1970 page 11.
1272 AB 18 March 1970 page 4.
1273 AB 1 April 1970 page 6.
1274 AB 24 June 1970 page 2.
1275 AB 15 July 1970 page 3.
1276 AB 3 June 1970 page 3.
1277 AB 1 July page 2, 29 July 1970 page 3.
1278 AB 17 April 1968 page 14.
1279 AB 12 August 1970 page 16.
1280 AB 9 December 1970 page 14.

1281 AB 4 November page 13, Bertha Wright to Editor 11 November 1970 page 2.
1282 AB 18 November 1970 page 15.
1283 AB 11 November page 6, 18 November 1970 page 6.
1284 AB 10 February 1971 page 3.
1285 AB 27 January 1971 page 4.
1286 AB 15 June 1971 page 4.
1287 AB 12 May 1971 page 16.
1288 AB 7 July 1971 page 5.
1289 AB 21 July 1971 pages 5-6.
1290 AB 12 May page 10, 19 May page 10, 2 June 1971 page 4.

1291 AB 8 September 1971 page 3.
1292 AB 25 August 1971 page 4.
1293 AB 26 May 1971 page 4, and subsequent advertisements in many issues.
1294 AB 13 October 1971 page 15.
1295 AB 3 November page 4, 24 November 1971 page 14.
1296 AB 13 October 1971 page 15.
1297 AB 1 December 1971 page 3.
1298 AB 2 February 1972 page 14 '14' and '29' December. Peter Young in a paper 'Rev Joshua Robertson' read to the Baptist Historical Society of NSW states 29 December. The BUNSW Year Book 1972-73 page 29 states 28 December.
1299 AB 2 February 1972 page 14.
1300 AB 16 February 1972 page 4.

1301 AB 29 March 1972 page 14.
1302 AB 17 May 1972 pages 1, 3.
1303 AB 10 May pages 7-8 study 1, 17 May pages 9-11 study 2, 24 May pages 9-11 study 3 part 1, 31 May pages 10-11 study 3 part 2, 14 June pages 11-12 study 4, 21 June 1972 pages 9-11 study 5.
1304 AB 19 April page 3, 28 June page 6, 26 July 1972 page 14.
1305 AB 23 August 1972 page 14.
1306 AB 26 April 1972 page 4.
1307 AB 26 April 1972 page 16.
1308 AB 14 June 1972 page 15.
1309 AB 13 September 1972 page 6.
1310 AB 26 July page 4, 23 August 1972 page 5.

1311 AB 11 October 1972 page 5.
1312 AB 18 October 1972 page 1.
1313 Rev IB Thornton, personal communication to JS.
1314 BUNSW Year Book 1973-74 page 359.
1315 AB 18 October 1972 page 4, 2 May 1973 page 1.
1316 AB 28 November 1973 page 12.
1317 AB 14 March 1973 page 1.
1318 AB 14 March 1973 page 14.
1319 AB 4 April 1973 page 4.
1320 AB 4 April 1973 pages 14-15.

1321 AB 25 April 1973 page 15.
1322 AB 23 May 1973 page 4.
1323 AB 2 May page 14, 9 May 1973 page 8.
1324 AB 30 May 1973 pages 14-15.
1325 AB 23 May 1973 page 15.
1326 AB 13 June 1973 page 15.
1327 AB 16 May page 12, 23 May 1973 page 6.
1328 AB 13 June 1973 page 1.
1329 AB 6 June 1973 page 15.
1330 AB 9 May 1973 page 16.

1331 Nicholas *op cit* Foreword.
1332 AB 1 August 1973 page 5.
1333 AB 1 Auguist 1973 page 13 advertisement.
1334 AB 21 November 1973 page 14.
1335 AB 23 January 1974 page 10.
1336 AB 30 January 1974 page 10.
1337 AB 13 February page 8 and subsequent weekly instalments through 17 April 1974.
1338 AB 27 March 1974 page 14.
1339 AB 17 April 1974 pages 1, 3, 5 – much coverage including the speeches given at the service.
1340 AB 17 April 1974 page 3.

1341 AB 17 April 1974 page 8.
1342 BUNSW Executive Committee Minutes 18 June 1974.
1343 BUNSW Year Book 1974-75 pages 28-30.

1344 BUNSW Annual Assembly Minutes 1969-75 page 460.
1345 College Council Minutes 1969-75 page 363 23 April 1974.
1346 Eldridge *op cit* chapter 5 page 25.

SELECT BIBLIOGRAPHY

The following Bibliography is one Morling students recollection of some of the books used by or referred to by George Henry Morling in his teaching programme.

Select Bibliography

Andrews, CF, *'Christ in the Silence'*, Hodder and Stoughton, London, 1933
Baillie, John, *'Our Knowledge of God'*, Charles Scribner's Sons, 1939.
Barbour, GF, *'Life of Alexander Whyte'*, Hodder and Stoughton, London, 1925.
Barth, Karl, *'Dogmatics in Outline'*, SCM Press, 1949.
Barth, Karl, *'The Doctrine of the Word of God'*, T & T Clark, Edinburgh, 1936.
Bruce, AB, *'The Training of the Twelve'*, Kregel Publications, 1871
Buber, Martin, *'I and Thou'*, T & T Clark, Edinburgh, 1958
Bunyan, John, *'The Pilgrims Progress'*, Christian Classics Ethereal Library, Michigan
Cave, Sydney, *'The Christian Estimate of Man'*, Gerald Duckworth and Company, London, 1944
Cave, Sydney, *'The Doctrines of the Christian Faith'*, Independent Press, London 1952.
Denney, James, *'Studies in Theology'*, Hodder and Stoughton, London 1910.
Denney, James, *'The Death of Christ'*, Tyndale Press, London, 1952.
Dale, RW., *'Christian Doctrine, A Series of Discourses'*, Hodder and Stoughton, London, 1907.
Farrer, HW (Dean), *'Life of Christ'*, H.P.Dutton and Company, Broadway, 1874.
Ferre, Nels FS., *'Strengthening the Spiritual Life'*, Collins, London, 1956.
Foakes-Jackson, FJ., *'A History of the Christian Church to the Council of Chalcedon 451'*, J.Hall and Sons, London 1891.
Forsyth, Peter Taylor, *'The Person and Place of Jesus Christ, The Congregational Lecture for 1909'*, Hodder and Stoughton, 1909.
Fullerton, WY., *'FB Meyer - a Biography'*, Marshall, Morgan and Scott, London.
Fullerton WY., *'Charles Haddon Spurgeon - a Biography'*, Marshall Morgan and Scott, London.
Galloway, G.., *'The Philosophy of Religion'*, International Theological Library, T&T Clark, Edinburgh, 1945.
Geldenhuys, J. Norval., *'Commentary on the Gospel of Luke'*, The New London Commentary on the New Testament, Marshall, Morgan and Scott, London, Edinburgh 1950.
Gordon, AJ., *'The Ministry of the Spirit'*, Fleming H. Revell Company, New York, Chicago, Toronto, 1894.
Gordon SD., *'Quiet Talks on Power'*, Fleming H. Revell Company, New

York, Chicago, Toronto.
Gossip, AJ., *'The Secret Place of the Most High'*, Independent Press, 1950
Guyon, Madame, *'Life of Madame Guyon'*, Christian Classics, Grand Rapids, Michigan.
Horton, RF., *'The Open Secret. A manual of devotion, a book for the times, being a guide to the practice of prayer'*, National Council of Evangelical Free Churches 1904.
Jackson, Samuel, *'The Life and Character of Gerhard Tersteegen'*, William Allen, 1846.
Kelly, Thomas, *'Testament of Devotion'*, Harper, San Francisco, 1941.
Lawrence, Brother, *'The Practice of the Presence of God'*, Christian Classics Ethereal Library, Michigan.
Lindsay, TM., *'The Reformation'*, T & T Clark, Edinburgh, 1949.
Macintosh, Hugh Ross, *'The Doctrine of the Person of Jesus Christ'*, International Theological Library, T & T Clark, Edinburgh, 1912
Morgan, G. Campbell, *'The Acts of the Apostles'*, Pickering and Inglis, 1948
Moule, Handley CG, *'Ephesians Studies, Lessons in Faith and Walk'*, Pickering and Inglis, London
Moule, Handley GC., *'Philippian Studies: Lessons in Faith and Love from St. Paul's Epistle to the Philippians'*, Pickering and Inglis, London
Murray, Andrew, *'With Christ in the School of Prayer'*, Nisbet and Co, London,
Nygren, Anders, *'Commentary on Romans'*, Muhlenberg Press, Philadelphia 1949.
Prior, Rev Alan C., *'Some Fell on Good Ground'*, Baptist Union of NSW, 1962,
Rowley, HH., *'The Biblical Doctrine of Election'*, Lutterworth Press, London, 1964.
Spurgeon, CH., *'Treasury of the New Testament'*, Zondervan, 1950
Strong, AH., *'Systematic Theology'*, Judson Press, 1886
Taylor, Dr and Mrs Howard, *'Hudson Taylor in Early Years, The Growth of a Soul'*, The China Inland Mission, London, 1925.
Thomas, W.Griffith, *'The Holy Spirit of God'*, William B Erdmans Publishing, Grand Rapids, 1955
Orr, James, *'The Christian view of God and the World'*, Charles Scribner's Sons, London, 1907.
Robinson, H. Wheeler, *'The Christian Experience of the Holy Spirit'*, Library of Constructive Theology, Nisbet, London, 1928.
Sanday, W and Headlam, AC., International Critical Commentary, *'The Epistle to the Romans'*, T & T Clark, Edinburgh, 1902.

APPENDICES

Appendix 1- Morling College 471

Appendix 2- GH Morling Graduates who became Theological Educators 473

Appendix 3- Presidential Address 475

MORLING COLLEGE

To acknowledge the outstanding service rendered by Rev Principal G.H Morling, MA, OBE to the Baptist Union of NSW, its churches and the whole christian community and as permanent personal recognition the 1985 Annual Assembly of the Baptist Union of NSW passed the following resolution -

'that the Theological College be called Morling College'.

This was referred to the Honorary Legal Adviser.

At the 1986 Annual Assembly, pursuant of the Baptist Union Incorporation Act 1919, the By-Law of the Baptist Union (By-Law 8) relating to the Theological College was amended to read -

'C. The Theological College may be called either 'Baptist Theological College of NSW' or 'Morling College''.

G H MORLING GRADUATES WHO BECAME THEOLOGICAL EDUCATORS

Rev Neville Andersen (Dean and Lecturer, NSW Baptist Theological College; Principal Bible College of Victoria),
Rev Professor Dr Basil Brown (Professor of Church History – Whitley College, Melbourne),
Rev Allan Burrow, (Principal, Adelaide Bible Institute),
Rev Arthur Cundall (Vice Principal, London Bible College; Principal, Bible College of Victoria),
Rev John Deane (Vice Principal, NSW Baptist Theological College; Principal, New Zealand Bible Training Institute),
Rev Professor Dr John Drakeford (Professor, Southwestern Theological Seminary, USA),
Rev Dr Victor Eldridge (Lecturer, Vice-Principal and Principal, Morling College),
Rev Dr E.G. (Ted) Gibson (Principal, Perth Bible Institute; Lecturer, NSW Baptist Theological College, Vice-Principal, Burleigh College, S.A., Principal, Queensland Baptist Theological College),
Rev Dr John Helm (Lecturer and Lecturer in Charge, Burleigh College, S.A.),
Rev Dr Jim Kime (Supervisor, NSW Baptist Bible College, Lecturer, Morling College),
Rev Dr Gilbert McArthur (Founding Principal, Christian Leaders' Training College, Banz, PNG.),
Rev Professor Dr Ken Manley (Lecturer, Morling College; Principal, Whitley College, Melbourne),
Rev E. Ron Rogers (Lecturer, Vice-Principal and Principal, Morling College),
Rev Professor HJ (Harry) Rowe, (Professor of Peaching, New Orleans Baptist Seminary USA)
Rev Professor Dr Craig Skinner (Dean, Queensland Baptist Theological College, Professor, Talbot Graduate School of Theology, Professor of Preaching, Golden Gate Baptist Seminary, San Francisco, USA),
Rev Dr David Stewart (Principal, Bible College of New Zealand),
Rev Dr Darcy Taplin (Lecturer, Morling College),
Rev Dr G Noel Vose (Founding Principal, Baptist Theological College of Western Australia),
Rev B. Gilbert Wright (Vice-Principal, Baptist Theological College of N.S.W; Principal, Morling College).

BAPTIST UNION OF NEW SOUTH WALES

PRESIDENTIAL ADDRESS

1929

INCOMING PRESIDENT

REV G H MORLING MA

THE CHURCH'S HERITAGE OF POWER

Fathers and Brethren, in your grace and, I hope, in your wisdom you have elected me to the Presidency of the Union. The honour is not mine alone; others whose llives are closely bound with mine in the bundle of life, stand with me tonight in this position of dignity. The nurture of a saintly father and mother, the devotion of a loyal wife, and the love of little children, the teaching of faithful men and women of God, the influence of true-hearted friends, the fellowship of my students, all have contributed to the personality of one who is neither unmindful or unappreciative.

The theme of an address from the Presidential chair cannot be lightly chosen. Here, if anywhere, a man should utter the deepest thoughts of his heart. But it has not been difficult for me to choose my subject. Throughout the years of my ministry there has been an ever growing conviction that the Church's greatest need is spiritual power, and further that many of the problems which now baffle us would vanish like a morning mist if we properly understood the fact of the Holy Spirit.

This is the situation which I see. On the one hand the Church has an unprecedented clear vision of her task, of its responsibilities, its opportunities, its possibilities – but on the other hand along with this clear vision, there is painful embarrassment because of inadequate resources. This situation obtains in every department of the Church's activities. She has vision in regard to Evangelism, to Missions, to Social Service, but she lacks the power for effective action.

In view of this situation it is my purpose to set forth some aspects of our heritage in the Spirit, who is the source of the Church's power.

I

The doctrine of the Holy Spirit runs up into the doctrine of the Godhead. It is well that we should have this large perspective of our theme. There is incalculable loss to faith in eliminating the mysteries and immensities from our thinking. "Beware of untheological devotion;" says a wise saint.

The Deity is not a bare solitary unit, but Himself a fellowship within one Indivisible Personality. There are three personal distinctions, each necessary to the other, each with distinct functions, the three blended in a holy unity of Love. As Father, God is the source and origin of all – God above us. As Son, He is Revealer, Mediator and Saviour – God for us. As Spirit He is the "Formative and Glorifying Principle" in creation, in history, in the Incarnation, in Redemption, in the formation and development of the individual Christian and the Church, in the accomplishment of all divine designs for the whole world. As Father, God is love in its fount; as Son, love in its manifestation; as Spirit, love in its impartation.

Let us review this sublime doctrine in so far as it has to do with the power of the Church.

II

The Holy Spirit is the Executive of the Godhead. He is God in action. He is God personally present in life, working out His redemptive purposes. The doctrine asserts that God is immanent as well as transcendent, and further that the imminent God is actively engaged in the world's redemption. "My Father worketh hitherto and I work," said the Lord Jesus. The Holy Spirit still continues what Jesus only began to do and teach. Here is a first consideration concerning the Holy Spirit, rich in helpfulness. It yields three great boons. -

IT DIGNIFIES OUR SERVICE

There come times when we are burdened with the apparent insignificance of our work. In moods of depression the glory fades and all seems so paltry – our church, little and unlovely, our preaching, our teaching, our service of whatever kind, commonplace and ineffective. We all have our fainting fits. But let us once understand that God is at work, and we are delivered from such paralysis because we can place our work in the magnificent setting of the world wide and age long operations of the Holy Spirit. If we think only of the divine accomplishments through the organised Baptist Church in the three centuries of its history, even without taking into account the work of other great sections of the Christian Church, we are proud that we are making some contribution, however small, to the splendid movement. Consider that a little handful of brave pioneers meeting in a tiny room in 1611 have grown and spread until that company small in numbers but mighty in faith and principle have become a host of the Lord, numbering twelve millions, and possessing such influence that Dr Rushbrooke could approach a European Government and say, "You dare not continue to persecute the Baptists in your land, because you insult a people worshipping in 91 countries, respected and honoured throughout the world, who have given a Prime Minister to Great Britain and a President to the United States."

Am I not right in saying that once we attain to that large view paralysis will yield to pride. We will say with the Psalmist "Thou hast set my feet in a large room."

IT EASES THE BURDEN OF RESPONSIBILITY

The profoundest secrets of the spiritual life are all at heart very simple, and are often merely a change in point of view. If it is true that God is at work, then this also is true, that not only are we working for God, but also that we are working with God. In that supplemental point of view there is rest of heart. I would not pass this point lightly. Most of us labour under almost intolerable strain. We belong to the type of the set jaw and clenched fist, and it is wrong and unnecessary.

Burke said that "the nation is indeed a partnership, but a partnership not only between those who are living, but between those who are living and those who are dead, and those who are yet to be born." The Church is a partnership grander still, because there is also a Divine Partner. And there is rest when we recognise Him and have the bracing consciousness that He is at work, and that we are working with Him.

IT PREPARES US FOR DIVINE SURPRISES.

Isaiah spoke of God doing things "which we looked not for." Believing in this present and active Spirit, we can always expect divine surprises. There are tides of the Spirit, points of time when slow moving processes reach fruition and times of refreshing come from the presence of the Lord.

> "For while the tired waves, vainly breaking,
> Seem here no painful inch to gain,
> Far back, through creeks and inlets making,
> Comes silent, flooding in, the main."

The pessimistic Jeremiah was once bidden at springtime to raise his eyes and see nature bursting into glorious life. It was a parable of encouragement to the dejected prophet. The Lord assured Him, "I, too, am waking to my work to perform it."

I ask seriously, whether there are not evidences that this is also a spiritual springtime, whether this is not a time when we shall see a floodtide of the Spirit. Modern historians write of the strange resemblances between our age and the age in which the Church arose. They speak of the "modernness" of the early ages of Christianity. There was then the feverish rush for pleasure and wealth, the restlessness, and also behind all, the wistfulness of our own day. In that day the Holy Spirit was abroad. There are signs pointing to His presence in Power now.

And are there not evidences that God is waiting to perform His work in the Eastern World. The new nationalism and the new spirit of intellectual inquiry have brought a situation there almost parallel to that obtaining in the early Reformation days. The East, as never before, has opened its doors to Christian missionaries and its mind to the Gospel. Those in a position to know, assure us that proud Mohamedanism is weakening and that Hinduism is relaxing something of its cruel grasp on the millions of its devotees.

Can we not believe that this is a spiritual springtide. Some time ago a firm of engineering contractors, experienced much difficulty in raising some sunken irons from the bottom of a harbour. Finally they bethought themselves of the action of the tide. They constructed a huge pontoon, made necessary attachments at low tide, then, when the tide rose, the rails were lifted and removed. They succeeded when they recognised and cooperated with divine forces. Which incident is a self-evident parable.

III

Let us turn to another aspect of our heritage in the Spirit intimately associated with the Church's power. The Holy Spirit means for us a Living Christ who is vividly real in Christian experience. The Holy Spirit is Christ's other self. He is the Vicar of Christ. The first disciples were promised another Comforter who would replace a physical, localised and temporary Presence with a spiritual, universal and abiding Presence who would be equally personal and precious. The Holy Spirit was to have for them the value of Christ for he was to reveal Christ, not witnessing of Himself, but taking the things of Christ and revealing them. "The world seeth me no more, but ye see Me." said the departing Lord. And the disciples never lost the vision. Nothing is more obvious than the keen, vivid spiritual perception of the Pentecostal Christians. "If we compare their dullness in the early days before the Spirit was received with their alertness afterwards, we shall see that the difference is most marked." The Master Himself describes them as "slow of heart." Their perceptions are blunt. They are dull to catch the spiritual side of things. But now we find this powerful sense of the Divine presence. It is as though a man were sitting in the room with another man but was only dimly aware of his presence; but then there came a refinement of his senses, and he gained a perfect assurance and a vivid knowledge of the other's company.

The Holy Spirit, I repeat, means a Living Christ vividly real in personal experience. A church assured of that is rich in spiritual resources. Such a church has the power of an irrepressible and sustained passion.

When Christ is really seen a genuine passion is always awakened. Let a man apprehend Christ, or rather be apprehended of Christ like the apostle Paul, and there will be in him something of the zeal throbbing in Paul's expectation and hope 'that in nothing I shall be ashamed, but that with all boldness, as always, so also now, Christ shall be magnified in my body whether it be by life or by death."

And this passion is not spasmodic and ephemeral. A living Christ not only evokes it, but He sustains it because that Presence supplies every requirement of the soul. Does not Paul dare to say "My God shall supply all your need according to His riches in glory by Christ Jesus." I have been impressed with the fact that men who face real dangers for Christ's sake seem, above all others, to realise the resources of the presence. Livingstone met the dangers of the wilds of Africa fortified by his favourite text, "Lo, I am with you always." Hudson Taylor endured the hardships of pioneering in China with the prayer constantly on his lips –

> "Lord Jesus, wilt Thou be to me
> A living, bright reality,
> More present to faith's vision keen
> Than any earthly object seen,
> More dear, more intimately nigh
> Than e'en the closest earthly tie."

And John G. Paton, hazarding his life daily in the New Hebrides speaks of the compensations of that presence.

Once he was forced to take refuge in a tree and to remain there in his precarious retreat. This is his record of that night. "The hours I spent live all before me as if it were but yesterday. I heard the frequent discharging of muskets and the yells of the savages. Yet I sat there among the branches as safe in the arms of Jesus! Never, in all my sorrows, did my Lord draw nearer to me, and speak more soothingly to my soul, than when that moonlight flickered among those chestnut trees and the night air playing on my throbbing brow as I told all my soul to Jesus. Alone, yet not alone! If it be to glorify my God, I will not grudge to spend many nights alone in such a tree, to feel again my Saviour's spiritual presence, to enjoy his consoling fellowship."

A church which has a real Christ has the secret of irrepressible and sustained passion. And such a church is a mighty church. Further, a church with that vivid spiritual apprehension has

THE POWER OF EFFECTIVE APPEAL.

The age demands reality in religion, and is searching for it. The demand is proper, but the methods are often wrong. Reality will not be found by the adjustment of truth to limited human perception. There is a more excellent way – the way of the Spirit who illumines the perception so that the Divine revelation of truth becomes meaningful and satisfying. A Church possessing the Spirit has reality and can point the way to reality.

But I am thinking especially of the appeal to non-Christian people. Dr Stanley Jones records the pathetic fact that he went through India, bent on discovering those who had been successful in their persistent pursuit of the realisation of God. He inquired in all possible places, but found not one man in the whole of India who had found God through the non-Christian faiths. Even Ghandi could say no more than this "The more I empty myself the more I can discover God. The world is a well-ordered machine and we may discover God in obeying its laws – but no miracles are to be expected, and it may take ages."

Has not the Christian Church an appeal to people whose religion at the best is a "noble despair?" We can tell how God may be found. Dr Jones says, "After I walked home that morning, pondering his words, something else welled up in my inmost being. I remembered that twenty-five years before, when I gave my bankrupt soul to Christ, a miracle was performed, and it did not take ages either. God has been the supreme reality in my experience ever since. I told Ghandi of this the next day, and our eyes grew very moist, and our hearts warm and tender as we talked."

In the glowing confidence of men who can declare, "We have found Christ!" and who, being men of the Spirit, walk manifestly with sure tread amid the mysteries of the Kingdom, the Christian Church has an asset which must surely spell ultimate triumph over faiths which have many seekers but no finders.

Again, a church having such spiritual vividness has

THE POWER OF COMBATING INTELLECTUAL DOUBT

There is need today for a strong intellectual presentation of the Christian faith. It is true today as it was in the first days of the Church, that the Church can out-think those who oppose her faith. But the most potent means of defeating doubt is to confront it with a triumphant certainty of Christian experience. After all, doubt is not merely a matter of the intellect, it has its roots in the heart, and the strength of conviction of a spiritually illumined mind goes far to relieve it.

Dr Alexander Whyte's biographer says that the great Scottish preacher did not meet the difficulties of his young men and women as did some other teachers of the day. But he did something higher and rarer. He stood through all that he said and all that he was a living proof of the unquestionable reality and final importance of the spiritual life. "In face of all unresolved enigmas, we felt, he writes 'that the experiences of which Alexander Whyte spoke and the power which made him what he was, were no fantasies of the imagination, but must in the long run prove to be the unshakeable foundation of the deepest life and truest knowledge.'" Others might defend Christianity by the weapons of the intellect, but he did so by the evidence of an inspired personality – by vision, not by arguments. The final truth of the verity of the Christian faith is the experience of Christ in the human soul, imparted by the Holy Spirit. Uncle Tom, in Mrs. Beecher Stowe's immortal story meets the skepticism of St. Clare with repeated assertion concerning Christ. "Felt Him in my soul, Mas'r, feel Him now." There is nothing more to be said.

IV

The doctrine of the Holy Spirit contributes to the Church's power in still another way. Man is prepared to dwell in the Divine abode by a Holy Spirit's energies. These energies express themselves in conviction, in regeneration, and in sanctification. The Holy Spirit disturbs the life. He renews the life. He indwells the life. As related to the work of Christ, the work of the Holy Spirit is to effect in man what Christ has made actual. Further, He is the Divine Agent in the mystical union of the soul with Christ in death, burial and resurrection.

I am not at pains to give a minute setting forth of these holy mysteries, but I am concerned to point out how they minister to the Church's equipment. And this in two main ways.

1. Believing in the Holy Spirit's operations in conviction and regeneration, the Church can confront human nature even at its worst, and know with certainty that it can be transformed. Dr Jowett has told us that this sublime confidence in the possible enrichment and ennoblement of the most debased, has been characteristic of all great soul-winners. John Wesley, he said, appeared to take almost a pride in recounting and describing the appalling ruin and defilement of mankind, that he might then glory in the all-sufficient power of redeeming grace. And Spurgeon preached with such magnificent assurance words like these. "The blood of Christ (applied by the regenerating Spirit) can wash out blasphemy, adultery, fornication, lying, slander, perjury, theft, murder. Though thou hast raked in the very kennels of hell, yet if thou wilt come to Christ and ask mercy, He will absolve thee from all sin."

And then think what a contribution the Church can make, and actually in some degree has made, to the solution of the world's problems, because of her message of regeneration. It is a commonplace to say that the world's problems at their centre resolve themselves into the one problem of the heart of man. But that heart, with its seeds of selfishness, hate, cruelty, greed and lust, can be renewed! It stirs one's imagination to consider what a Church, working in the power of the regenerating Spirit could accomplish in the healing of international, industrial and social troubles.

2) And then there is this second phase. Because of the Holy Spirit's work of sanctification, the church can exercise the far-reaching influence of saintliness.

If the doctrine of the Holy Spirit means anything it means that the believing life may be a holy life, negatively that there may be conquest over besetting sin; positively that the life may be robed with the beautiful grace of God. The Holy Spirit makes of ordinary people men and women of radiant holiness.

The church which has members thus saintly has within it a power which is beyond calculation, for nothing is so attractive and contagious as true saintliness and nothing so influential.

Let us examine this. Nothing, I say, is so attractive and contagious. I know there is a spurious species of holiness. "Do you desire to become a Christian? said a sour-visaged person to Tom Hood. "Not if it means feeling like you look!" said the blunt poet, himself a Christian man. Look at the marks of true holiness as it is exemplified in the Apostolic Church: - Its perfect naturalness, when the Spirit indwells a life, love, joy, peace, and other graces appear in the life as naturally and inevitably as fruit appears on a healthy tree.

Its joyous exuberance. The life of the Spirit is as a joyous, bubbling spring, a well of water springing up into everlasting life. The Spirit provides for the soul the exhilaration which wine produces in the body. The Spirit's calm excess at Pentecost produced a certain effect of intoxication. Its complete robustness. Holiness is healthiness of soul. The New Testament presentation includes all the manlier virtues, strength, courage, persistence, enterprise. New Testament saints did not cease to be men, rather were their qualities of true manhood enhanced. Again, its spontaneity of propagation. The Spirit-filled Christians of the early Church simply could not help speaking of Christ. Some were arrested, scourged and commanded not to speak any more of that Name. The authorities might just as well have tried to stop the laughter of a healthy child or the song of a soaring lark. "We cannot but speak the things which we have seen and heard," said these splendid people. Is not such holiness attractive and contagious?

Again, nothing, I say, is so influential as true holiness. There is a delightful incident in the life of St. Bernard of Clairvaux. The Emperor Henry came to the saint's monastery at Clairvaux to seek his advice and help. The Emperor, however, was told to wait until Bernard had finished washing the dishes in the kitchen. The scene is a symbol. The statesman must always wait for the saint. The reforms of statesmanship are impossible without the influence of a saintly Church.

A famous Englishman has said that "England's greatest strength lies in her village churches." He is supported by another writer who says "there are multitudes of men and women in out-of-the-way places, in backwoods, towns, and uneventful farms, who are the salt of the earth, and the light of the world in their communities, because they have had experiences which reveal to them realities that their neighbours missed."

> The influence of holiness is set forth in the gracious promise. "He that believeth on me, as the Scripture has said, out of his belly shall flow rivers of living water." A Church has the won drous power of "Ministering the Spirit." It is a power beyond estimation.

V

The doctrine of the Holy Spirit has to do both with the constitution of the Church and with revelation and inspiration. It is in my heart to point out how the spiritual fellowship of the Church and the authoritative character of the Holy Scriptures minister to the Church's power. But there are limits to the patience even to this intelligent and theologically instructed Baptist Assembly. I turn then, to a last and consummating feature of this great doctrine.

THERE IS A SPECIFIC POWER OF THE HOLY SPIRIT FOR SERVICE

Our Lord commanded the disciples to tarry in Jerusalem until they were "endued with power from on high." That power has its explanation in part only on the things which I have spoken about. The enduement has distinctive elements. Let us notice some of the accompanying effects.

It is a sealing. The Heavenly Father so endows the fully trusting soul that is marked as God's own possession. Such sealed persons have divine authority. All hearing them have to confess, "Here, manifestly, are people of God."

It is an anointing. The enduement is an unction from the Holy One. Such anointed ones have vision and glow.

It is a filling. The life completely opened to God is so possessed by the Divine Spirit that the human personality is heightened and enriched. Such lives are radiant.

It is a baptism of fire. This fire is now a controlled warmth like that of the domestic hearth, and now the onrush of the great conflagration. Such lives are irresistible.

There is a tendency to regard the enduement of the Spirit as something elusive, and attainable only by the special few, but it is perfectly apparent that the Spirit-filled life was the normal life in New Testament times. It may be said with complete certainty that the Holy Spirit will equip every man for His service who recognises and obeys the laws of His working.

Let us notice some fundamental things: -

1) **The Holy Spirit comes in Power into Lives which are properly organised.**

   Let no one expect to have the power of the Spirit whose life is slovenly or lazy. The disciples had their Pentecost when their lives were spiritually strenuous. He comes only into such lives. Personally, it helps me as a minister to have the rebuke and stimulus of words such as these from the strong but tender pen of Alexander Whyte. "Prayer and Work. all great and true and eminently successful ministers from Paul's day downward bear the same testimony: Prayer and Work...Let us pray and work, my brethren, in what remains to us in our time on earth, with all our might. We have plenty of time for all our work, did we husband out time and horde it up aright...Did we work early in the morning and late at night and hard all the livelong day. Oh no! We cannot look seriously into one another's faces and sayit is want of time. It is want of method. It is want of motive. It is want of conscience. It is want of heart. It is want of anything and everything but time."

2. **The Holy Spirit endues Lives which are otherwise stripped bare.** They who would be clothed with the Spirit must be drastic with themselves. They must ruthlessly cast away many a cloak of self deception, and many a robe of pride, and come to the throne as suppliants, with this confession and petition. "Here is my life, naked and unlovely, full of incompetence, weakness, failure and worse. Here is my life, not as others know it, but as Thou knowest it, and as I now know it. Clothe me Thou Divine Beautifier and Empowerer, that I may serve Thee in the power of the Spirit."

3. **The Pentecostal Power is given for the Pentecostal Task.** A fundamental principle is expressed in our Lord's words. "Ye shall receive power after that the Holy Ghost is come upon you, and ye shall be witnesses unto Me." Power is given only for the purpose of witnessing for Christ, but conversely one may be sure that power will be granted when that holy task is properly undertaken. Let us then, those of us who deplore our lack of the Spirit's presence rise up bravely and resolutely and attempt the Pentecostal task. Let us go and busy ourselves in telling others of the Lord Jesus, and we shall find that the task undertaken in trembling will bring the fulfillment of the Divine promise.

I have attempted to show you our heritage of power in the Holy Spirit. That heritage is not for admiration, but for realisation.
Let us pray that this Assembly shall bring to us such a vision both of our imperfections of life and service, and of the gracious possibilities of the Divine Love that we shall return to our churches filled with the Spirit to apply our new possession of power to the work to which we have set our hands.

EPILOGUE

From *'The Quest for Serenity'*

EPILOGUE

LEAVE IT ALL QUIETLY TO GOD

In the Sixty Second Psalm occur words which sink softly into the heart when strain and stress threaten to disturb its poise. Moffat renders it: "Leave it all quietly to God, my soul"[.1] The Psalmist's counsel has been of such help to me in my quest for serenity that I want to share it with fellow seekers. Let the Psalmist guide us now in the practice of peace.

"Leave it all quietly to God, my soul". Obviously, there is possible danger in an exhortation like that. To wait "only on God", as the Authorized version has it, might encourage a quiet which is only quiescence, a quiet which sits with folded hands in supine ease. The Psalmist had no such intention. There is something of passivity in His attitude to God, but it is entirely consistent with, and indeed demands, proper human activity.

General Booth, strong man of action as he was, loved to tell of a little girl who was distressed that her small brother trapped birds. One night she added a petition to her usual bedtime prayer. "And please, dear Lord, don't let Willie catch the nice little birds." Then, rising to her feet, she said happily to her mother: "He won't be able to catch them now, Mummy." "You have great faith," answered Mother. "But he can't," said the child, "I smashed all his traps." Surely God approved of her adding such works to prayer.

Nevertheless, the Psalmist's faith is valid. It is an unquestionable fact that, God and man, being what they are, we are shut up to God. For God is God and not man. He is the "I am", and "I am that I am"[2] which is the "style not only of permanence, but of permanence self-contained. To the proud, godless world He says 'resistance to my will can only show forth all its power. I sit upon the throne not only supreme, but independent, not only victorious, but unassailable: self-contained, self-poised, and self sufficing'". This God has Sovereign Will which overrides or takes up into itself all lesser wills. That Will is finally irresistible. As Moody used to say, a man cannot really break the law of God: it will sooner or later break him. Also, that will is unchangeable. God may adapt Himself to man's waywardness just as a master chess player adapts his moves to his opponent's game; but God never alters His purposes. "I the Lord do not change".[3]

And man is man, not God. A Thomas Henley may cry "I am the master of my fate. I am the captain of my soul," but he convinces very few. A Swinburne may exclaim, in an excess of humanistic enthusiasm: "Glory to man in the highest", but most will write him down as an obscurantist and foolish for they know that all too often mankind descends to the lowest. People are people and not God, and in their hearts, they know that they are shut up to God. "Gentlemen", said Lincoln one day to his generals "I have often been driven to my knees by an overwhelming conviction that I had nowhere else to go."

Understanding all that, let us make the widest possible use of the Psalmist's words. Consider first that we may leave our sin quietly to God. Because Jesus died for our sins that is a glad possibility. But let us be sure to do it. Even some of the greatest saints do not seem to have known full evangelical peace. In this, humbly we must insist, they have fallen short of the New Testament ideal which is restful enjoyment of the fruits of Divine pardon. One of my revered spiritual masters, Alexander Whyte of Free St. George's, Edinburgh, known as the last of the Puritans, was deficient in this respect. His friend, Marcus Dodds, said how much Whyte mourned over the evil of his heart. Moreover, the deficiency revealed itself in his preaching. Once he chose as his text St. Paul's famous words, "where sin abounded, grace did much more abound."[4] He informed his hearers that he had been reading Martin Luther. "Let us summon up the spirit of Luther to our midst to hear what he has to say on this verse," he declared to his people. Opening the door which led to the pulpit, he beckoned the imaginary reformer to stand beside him. "Martin Luther," said Whyte solemnly, "what am I to say to this people on this text?"

"What does it say? 'Grace did abound.' Do you know anything, then about grace, Alexander Whyte?" "Not very much" was the slow reply. "Stand aside and let me speak to this people about grace", and forthwith Whyte began to read extracts from Luther's works on grace. Having completed these he turned to the imaginary figure and asked:

"What else should be said on this text, Martin Luther?"

"What more does the text say? 'Where sin abounded'. Do you know anything about sin, Alexander Whyte?".[5]

"Sin", replied the minister in his thunderous voice 'Sin! Martin Luther, you may take your leave'. Sin! I know all about sin and will speak to this people on that". And forthwith, Whyte spoke of the blackness of the human heart, as only he could.

One asks seriously whether the scriptural balance was preserved in such an utterance. "Where sin increased, grace increased all the more", wrote Paul. Should not, therefore, the emphasis, both in life and preaching, be rather on grace and the peace in which it so happily issues. Contained in the words of the 23rd Psalm, "You prepare a table before me in the presence of my enemies", is a beautiful picture of the spiritual rest and enjoyment which God wants us to have. They represent the speaker as a criminal fugitive who is being pursued by the avengers of blood. They are hot upon his trail when he reaches a shepherd's tent. By Eastern law such a fugitive would not only be protected with all the resources of the person to whose mercy he appeals, but he would also be given the best hospitality which the encampment could offer. Here then is the fugitive being regaled at the sheik's table while the pursuers on the other side of the threshold glare at him in impotent rage. In the Psalmist's thought the pursuers are the sins which have come from the evil past of a person who flees to God for mercy. In His keeping the person is entirely safe from the blood-guiltiness of sin. For those who finds refuge in a forgiving God, there is no pursuing vengeance, but a table prepared by God's bounty.

Festival living is still more typical of the New Testament. "Christ our Passover lamb is sacrificed; therefore let us keep festival", wrote Paul.[7] The atmosphere of the New Testament is one of radiant happiness begotten of an experience of sins forgiven, covered by the Saviour's blood and then left quietly to God.

Associated with our sin is the spectre of the "might have been". A careless action, an error of judgment, even a foolish word can change the course of a life and involve us in bitter regrets and self-chiding for the rest of our days. Thus it was with Lord Curzon, whose last years were clouded with dark regrets that he had accepted appointment as Viceroy of India. During his term of office his wife had died and, for the rest of his days, the distinguished statesmen rebuked himself for not having discerned that the climate would undermine her health. Far better to leave all such untoward things quietly to God. As God of nature, our Heavenly Father wondrously renews the face of bushland after it has been seared by fire. As God of our lives He will put forth similar recuperative powers and restore to us the years. We can well afford also to leave the spectre of the "might have been" quietly to Him.

The Psalmist's counsel has relevance not only to the sense of sin, put also to Perplexity. I have in mind particularly the perplexity which arises out of dark experiences. Few travellers on life's highway escape the challenge to faith that comes to them from some stark happening. At such an hour of crisis we can do one of three things. We can follow the way of stoicism which hurls defiance at fate "or whatever gods there be" and cries, "My head is bloody but unbowed". But not thus is the "deep thunder" of our "want and woe" silenced. Or as we may allow far too often, we may yield place to doubt. Let it be said quite frankly that, in such a reaction there is nothing but weakness and folly. It means either crumpling up or becoming cynical; and the strong are ashamed to crumple up whilst the wise avoid cynicism as they do all nasty things.

The difficulty created by the "giant agony of the world" has engaged the attention of the greatest minds of the ages, yet no complete answer of an intellectual kind has ever been given. But if intellectual theory does not provide an answer, the experience of life does: and, since life is larger than logic, the practical answer is of greater value. An answer that suffices the heart is worth more than one that does no more than inform and convince the mind. The fact is that we find the solution to life's problems only when the problems vanish. God has not given us the full explanation of the presence of evil in the world. We understand a good deal when we realise that this world in which there is so much pain is a "vale of soul making", but that takes us only part of the way to an explanation. But, we repeat, there is a solution that comes out of life. It is this; that when faith bravely, patiently, trustingly faces its personal problem, it finds that the problem disappears in an experience of God which dispels all doubts and resentments.

A fine story told of a professor of Harvard University effectively illustrates this higher mode of facing perplexity. The professor sought an interview with Phillips Brooks upon a certain problem. He spent a radiant hour with the great preacher and came out a changed man whose life was transfigured. But presently it dawned upon him that during the interview he had quite forgotten to ask Phillips Brooks about his problem. He says, however, "I did not care; I found out that what I needed was not the solution of a special problem, but the contagion of a triumphant spirit".

If the answer to the enigmas of life is to be found in an attitude rather than in an enquiry, what is that attitude?

As I read the stories of triumphant sufferers, I find that, by faith they do three things that enable them to rise superior to their pain. In faith they accept their trial. They do not exhaust their energies in futile questionings, nor do they become resentful. They take, instead, an attitude of positive acceptance. It is the positiveness that makes the difference. They go even beyond resignation in regarding their trouble as being in some way, they know not how, within the scope of God's plan and, as such, something to be accepted, not endured. In that brave attitude of faith the noble Dr.

Edward Wilson sank into his last sleep amid the snows of Antarctica. Before he died he wrote to his wife words which are a sublime expression of the faith which accepts positively its trial as from the hand of God. We read with reverence these two extracts from his last letters. "I shall simply fall and go to sleep in the snow, and I have your little books with me in my breast-pocket…Don't be unhappy – all is for the best. We are playing a good part in a great scheme arranged by God himself, and all is well…."

"I leave this life in absolute faith and happy belief that if God wishes you to wait long without me it will be to some good purpose. All is for the best to those that love God, and oh, my Ory, we have both loved Him with all our lives. All is well..."

I find, too, that triumphant sufferers find relief from their pain in making their experience minister to others. They convert their own loss into gain. The Positiveness of their faith leads on to creativeness.

Josephine Butler did that. Returning home one evening with her husband she was greeted by their little daughter who, in her excitement, leaned too far over the stair rail, fell to the hallway beneath and lay dying at their feet. After the first shock of her grief had passed, Mrs Butler, with her husband's blessing, opened her home to shelter fallen girls. As she put it, "I have now no daughter of my own so I shall be a mother to any girl who needs me." And, in saving others, she saved herself.

Faith accepts positively; acts creatively; then, as its crowning expression, acquiesces restfully. Having been active, it becomes passive and leaves its problem quietly to God. I have found that the noblest sufferers have been able to do this the more readily when it has been borne home to their hearts that God has also suffered and still suffers. Dr Carnegie Simpson has made this strong declaration. "If God is not One who stands apart from human suffering, even though holding the explanation of it in His hand, but One who comes into it and shares it; that is a thought of God upon which faith could stand in any anguish. That character in God, that passion in God would be faith's deliverance", God is such a God. If people suffer because of the wrong doing of others, so did He. Once they have seen that men and women of faith have been able to leave their perplexity quietly to God. Such men and women understand what the Lord Jesus meant when he said "In that day you shall ask me no questions".[8]

I suggest one other application of the Psalmist's admonition. It has relevance also to the foreboding that so often robs life of its sunshine. Foreboding, which is a secret fear of the future, may relate to our personal affairs, to our spiritual development, and to our life service. In respect to the first, foreboding has no place in the life that has learned to leave all quietly to God.

Paul speaks of a peace of God that "passes understanding",[9] by which he means that extends beyond the point of human "minding" or planning. Very properly we make provision for the future, financial and otherwise, but we cannot provide against every contingency, and, in any case, our "minding" is necessarily confined to time. God's "minding" for us, however, foresees everything and reaches into eternity, so that for those who live in the world of God there are no uncertainties.

We can live very restfully when we have left the future quietly to the Father Who knows all that will come to us and has already provided for it. Let us, however, be sure that we do this with real quietness. Some of us can make a great burden of casting our burdens on the Lord.

Likewise is there rest for the soul that, giving all proper attention to spiritual culture, leaves its growth in the care of the Father. How well I remember the encouragement that came to me at a time of depression when an older friend who was "Far Ben" (as the Scotch describe the mature saint) reminded me of Paul's reassuring word –"He who began a good work in you will carry it on to completion until the day of Christ Jesus".[10] The Lord Jesus spoke of what one has called the "law of the lily" which God arrays even though it neither labors or spins.[11] All that the flower does to cultivate its beauty is to respond to the divine forces amidst which it is set.[12] So also does God clothe with glory the life that quietly leaves its development to Him. There must always be a hungering and thirsting after righteousness. But let us always remember the "law of the lily".

There need be no anxious fear about the result of life's service. The servant of God who realises that not only does he work for God but also with Him can well afford to leave that also quietly to God.

I have often found encouragement in the story of the Italian painter who, in old age, had lost something of his former skill. One evening he sat dejectedly before a painting which he had just completed, conscious that he had not been able to impart the touch which used to cause his canvasses to glow with life. As he went off to bed he was heard to say sadly "I have failed, I have failed." Later his son who was also an artist came into the studio to examine his father's work. He too was aware of deficiency. Then taking palette and brush he worked on into the night, until under his younger hand the picture fulfilled the father's vision. In the morning not knowing what had been done the older man went into the studio and stood in delight before the transformed picture: "Why", he exclaimed, "I have wrought better than I knew."

With reverent caution may we not regard the story as a parable? When life's day is done will parents, teachers, and all who have faithfully worked with God discover that they wrought better than they knew? Did not the Psalmist encourage us to think so when he wrote "the Lord will fulfil his purpose for me?"[13]

Leave it all quietly to God, my soul. We shall have advanced a long way in the quest for serenity when we can intelligently and strongly speak in this way to ourselves.

References:
[1] Psalm 62:5 (Moffat), [2] Exodus 3:14, [3] Malachi 3:6, [4] Romans 5:20, [5] Romans 5:20, [6] Psalm 23, [7] 1 Corinthians 5:7, [8] John 16:23, [9] Philippians 4:7, [10] Philippians 1:6, [11] Matthew 6:28, [12] Luke 12:27, [13] Psalm 138:8.

INDEXES
Chronological
General

CHRONOLOGIAL INDEX
BY YEAR

1908 12
1909-10 12

1911	**1931** 96	**1951** 224	**1971** 389
1912 13	1932 99	1952	1972 393
	1933 103	1953 228	1973 397
1913 17	1934 110	1954 242	1974 403
1914 18	1935 125	1935 246	
1915 20	1936 135	1956 249	
1916 22	1937 143	1957 259	
1917 24	1938 148	1958 264	
1918 27	1939 153	1959 268	
1919 29	1940 161	1960 276	
1920 32			
	1941-167	**1961** 317	
1921 34	1942 172	1962 334	
1922 39	1943 177	1963 344	
1923 44	1944 182	1964 353	
1924 49	1945 185	1965 259	
1925 53	1946 190	1966	
1926 58	1947 194	1967 373	
1927 68	1948 200	1968 275	
1928 75	1949 205	1969 38	
1929 83	1950 215	1970	

GENERAL INDEX

NOTES

The name Morling, George Henry, its compounds, derivatives or abbreviations recurring frequently throughout this book are not listed in this index.

Where there is a church and college in the same disstrict (e.g. Ashfield) church references are indexed iunder 'Baptist Churches' - college references are indexed under e.g 'Ashfield College'.

A

Abrahams, Rev Dr NL (Neville) 379, 352, 379
Acting-Principal 40, 41, 42, 43
Acts of the Apostles 177, 178
Adelaide 401
Adelaide Bible Institute 319, 361, 386
Advisory and Credentials Committee 70
Advisory Board 70, 71, 72
Africa 274
Ainsworth, P (Percy) 315
Amos 193, 304
Amos, Mr 82
Andersen, Mrs M (Marion/Bridgland) 373
Andersen, Mrs N (Nancy) 367
Andersen, Rev NP (Neville) 159, 287, 297, 367, 373, 474
Anderson, Professor John 178
Anderson, Sir Francis 13
Andrews, CT 111
Andrews, E Rev and Mrs 205
Andrews, Mr FE 156
Andrews, FE Mr and Mrs. 167
Andrews, Miss E (Edna) 167
Andrews, Rev EF (Ernest) 167
Angeleri., K (Kenneth) 171
Angus, Professor Dr S (Samuel) 105, 113, 134
Annual Assembly 29, 80, 88, 95, 101, 105
Annual Day of Prayer 203
Applicants' Committee 194, 199, 215, 261
Ardill, Mr W (William) 81, 82, 146
Agerakis, Rev E (Emanuel) 172
Arnold of Rugby 91
'Around the College' 214
Ashfield College 124, 133, 135, 182, 183, 189, 193, 199, 215, 230, 249, 263, 274, 285, 303, 319, 370, 372, 391, 400, 415,
Ashfield property 117
Ashfield Public School 11
Assembly Pastoral Session 236
Auber, Harriet 292
Australian Baptist Bible School 159, 160, 164, 170, 185, 199, 218
Australian Baptist College 22
Australian Baptist Missionary Society 338, 347
Australian Baptist New Guinea Mission 228
Australian Baptist Publishing House 218
Australian Baptist Union 333
Australian Baptist Youth Conference 204
Australian Christian World 41
Australian Institute of Archaeology, 259
Australian Nurses Christian Movement 198

B

Baptist Churches
Alstonville 389, 400
Armidale 224, 237, 401, 402
Arncliffe 198, 249
Ashfield 9, 12, 23, 27, 105, 135, 142, 146, 152, 153, 155, 156 157, 173, 182, 185, 190, 191 195, 274, 323, 326, 373, 375, 378 388, 391, 397, 415, 418
Auburn 12, 31, 44, 54, 87, 92, 95, 98, 119, 129, 171, 180, 247, 334
Auckland (NZ) 102, 148, 159 235
Avalon 400
Bankstown 22, 24, 32, 57, 147, 171, 374
Bathurst 27, 154
Bathurst Street (Central) 41, 105, 136
Bedford Park (WA) 342
Beverly Hills 379

Bexley 44, 156, 173, 180, 184, 197, 220, 235, 400
Big Creek 29
Black Mountain 69, 237
Blackheath 49, 54, 91, 100, 103, 106, 125, 136, 137, 153, 155, 161, 169, 172, 174, 185, 190, 200, 201, 208, 247, 260, 261, 269, 273, 276, 297, 344
Blacktown 212, 286, 397
Bloomsbury Chapel, (UK) 230
Bowral 166, 199
Brighton (SA) 351
Brisbane City Tabernacle (Qld) 130, 132, 134, 149, 191, 197, 248, 379
Broken Hill 274
Burnie (Tas) 369, 375
Burton Street 11, 65, 78, 104, 105, 167, 245, 248
Burwood 12, 96, 113, 176, 181, 190
Campsie 18, 190, 207, 242
Canberra (ACT) 150, 216, 253, 369
Canterbury (Vic) 44, 230, 351
Carlingford 356, 361, 389
Carlton 70, 145
Casino 188, 340, 389
Central 3, 136, 140, 148, 149, 150, 154, 163, 166, 167, 168, 171, 172, 176, 182, 183, 190, 197, 199, 200, 201, 202, 205, 206, 216, 226, 227, 233, 240, 244, 247, 251, 256, 258, 261, 268, 276, 281, 285, 300, 305, 318, 355, 358, 373
Cessnock 74
Chatswood 35, 234, 262, 319, 389, 392, 393, 399
Cheltenham (SA) 371
Chester Hill 269, 378
Chullora 50, 58, 67
Clemton Park 341
Cobar 263, 274

Collins Street (Vic) 93, 157, 20, 228
Concord 12, 57, 9, 96, 104, 134, 155, 179, 187, 191, 247, 373, 397
Cronulla 245, 252, 399
Croydon 91, 124, 129, 194, 249, 356
Dee Why 168, 171, 182, 260, 397
Dixson (ACT) 358
Drummoyne 39, 44, 182
Dubbo 206
Dulwich Hill 57, 60, 96, 135, 146, 168, 188, 192, 205, 235, 245, 376
Dungog 26, 69, 156, 270, 300
Dungog-Thalaba 24, 25, 26, 29, 357, 339, 416
Earlwood 123, 193, 203
East Chatswood 150, 161, 188, 236
East Hills 17, 20, 22, 23, 24
East Lindfield 382
Eastwood 42, 45, 50, 54, 252, 334, 343, 367, 373
Epping 245, 262, 265, 319, 367, 370, 374, 377
Ettalong 242
Evans Head 330, 401
Flinders Street (SA) 157, 224, 340, 371, 378
Footscray (Vic) 234
Frenchs Forest 370
Gladesville 136, 150, 256
Glenbrook 374
Glen Innes 237
Gosford 237
Goulburn 163, 175, 244, 382, 399
Grafton 52, 221, 389
Granville 44, 70, 73, 76, 81, 82, 86, 90, 93, 106, 109, 114, 117, 123, 125, 133, 142, 145, 148, 157, 169, 171, 247, 248, 267, 273, 351,
Greenacre 195, 262
Gumeracha (SA) 371, 378
Haberfield 25, 44, 48, 98, 136, 153, 181, 321, 322
Hamilton 273
Harris Street 23, 34, 274, 348, 418

Hobart (Tas) 357
Hornsby 24, 30, 31, 32, 34, 39, 44, 48, 53, 55, 199, 241, 242 350, 385, 416
Hornsby-Pymble 28, 29, 30, 68
Hurlstone Park 18, 20, 22, 34, 39, 45, 47, 50, 65, 67, 114, 127, 180, 183, 192, 203, 205, 234, 262, 289, 318, 339
Hurstville 127, 163, 180
Ingleburn 334
Islington 69, 172, 177, 191, 236, 259, 333
Katoomba 102, 144, 170, 249
Kerang 210
Kew 194, 335, 369
Kingsgrove 173
Kingston (ACT) 369
Kogarah Central 123, 150, 354, 372
Lakemba 284, 333
Lakemba' 245
Leeton 78
Leichhardt 96, 262
Leura 268
Lidcombe 220
Lismore 188, 340, 389
Lithgow 178
Maclean 340
Maitland 89
Manildra 201
Manly 104, 153, 162, 315, 324, 373
Maroubra 202
Marrickville 91, 206
Mayfield 69
Merrylands 73, 76, 87, 339, 357
Millthorpe 340
Mimosa 68
Molong 206
Mortdale 65, 91, 138, 146, 165, 175, 286, 402
Mosman 139, 211, 247, 320
Murwillumbah 152, 188, 389
Nambucca 403
Newcastle 39, 46, 56, 60, 69, 86, 273
Newtown 130
North Auburn 173
North Canberra (ACT) 249, 270
North Epping 318
North Sydney 30, 197, 338
Parkes 206
Parramatta 76, 146 175, 226, 339, 370, 400
Pennant Hills 195, 270, 345, 356
Perth Central (WA) 195
Petersham 9, 27, 40, 61, 77, 97, 157 189, 202, 211, 245, 282, 393, 398, 418
Punchbowl 263, 265, 354
Pymble 31, 34, 35, 36, 39, 44, 58, 170, 173, 180, 197, 199, 221, 238, 260, 267, 289, 373, 382, 416
Raymond Terrace 300
Regents Park 164, 219, 232, 356
Ringwood East (Vic) 335, 341
Riverwood 262, 286
Rockhampton (Qld) 370
Ryde 273
Sans Souci 186
South Brisbane (Qld) 389
South Carlton 245
Springwood 336
St Ives 358
Stanmore 32, 46, 68, 100, 104, 137, 145, 162, 183, 190, 203, 237, 250, 262, 281, 316, 330, 385
Strathfield-Homebush 164, 166, 172, 318, 319, 385, 386
Stroud 69, 156
Tahmoor 199
Tamworth 17, 18, 69, 237, 385, 402
Taree 152, 262
Temora 68
Thalaba 27, 69
Townsville (Qld) 370
Ulverstone (Tas) 369, 388
Undercliffe 47, 241

Unley Park (SA) 138, 145, 242, 365, 371
Warrnambool (Vic) 354
Waverley 90, 174, 191
Wellington 60, 91, 206
Wentworthville 241, 267
West Maitland 169
West Ryde 54, 168, 186, 206, 244
Wollongong 146, 176, 248
Woollahra 234
Woonona, 179, 249
Yagoona 198
Yaralla (Concord West) 163, 164

==================

Babu, Bilu 348
Bachelor of Arts 13, 201, 416
Bachelor of Divinity 55, 96
Baillie, Rev J (John) 65, 91
Bain, Rev WH 30, 33, 40, 46, 416
Baiyer River 334, 337
Baker, Rev JH (James) 44, 77
Ball, Mr RJ (Richard) 148
Ball, Rev GB (Gerald) 378, 379
Bamber, Rev TM 206
Banderanaike, Mrs 346
Baptist Assembly Meetings 189
Baptist Choral Society 240
Baptist Efficiency Commission. 223
Baptist Homes Trust 404
Baptist Ministers' Fraternal 176
Baptist Ministers' Retreat 318
Baptist Missionary Society 278
Baptist Theological College of Queensland 427
Baptist Union of Australia 5, 7, 83, 87, 170, 188, 196, 198, 207, 220, 221, 254, 335, 366, 390
Baptist Union of NSW 47, 88, 99, 313
Baptist Union of Queensland 188
Baptist Union of Western Australia 341
Baptist University Church. 232
Baptist Varsity Gospel Team. 80
Baptist Women's Home Mission Auxiliary 149
Baptist World Alliance 155, 200, 220
Barbour, Mr GP 149
Barnard, Rev AJ (Arthur) 232
Barnard, Rev CV (Victor) 234
Barry, Mrs Walter 191
Barry, Rev W (Walter) 59, 156, 157, 159, 172, 179, 199, 241
Barth, Karl 128, 137, 183
Bartlett, Miss M (Marjorie) 404
Beecroft, Mr CK (Colin) 306
Belgium 231
Belgrave Heights Convention 238, 246, 264, 276, 336, 375, 376
Believers' Baptism 276
Bell, Rev W 166
Bengal, Eastern, 159
Bengal. 58
Bennett, Rev KH (Keith) 302
Berkeley Baptist Divinity School 200, 240
Bethel 358
Betteridge, Rev AH (Albin) 136, 195
Bible College of New Zealand 404
Bible College students 404
Bible School 150
Biblical Doctrine of Election 220
Billy Graham Crusade 269, 270
Binks, RevTH (Tom) 270, 272, 290, 333, 335, 342
Birisiri 348
Birmingham 232
Black, Rev W Cleugh (William) 18, 20, 23, 29, 30, 34, 57, 62, 65, 70, 71, 85, 98, 104, 114, 128, 129, 134, 135, 145, 156, 166, 167, 192, 204, 205
Blackburn, Rev Dr GH (Geoffrey) 392, 398, 407
Blackheath 144, 149, 177, 183, 194, 206, 216, 246
Blaiklock, Professor 283
Blankley, Rev JA (Jack) 334

Blatch, Mr W (Wallace) 166
Blue Mountains. 397
Boddington 195
Bollen, JD 411
Bonar, A (Andrew) 378
Boreham, Rev Dr FW (Frank) 93
Boroko 334, 338, 374
Brainwood, Rev EW (Ern) 156
Bridgland, Miss M (Marion) 373
Brisbane 206
British Empire Baptist Congress 416
Brook, Rev N (Norris) 263, 382
Brook, Rev SMF (Syd) 145
Brooke, Rev Chaplain-General A (Allan) 202, 356
Brooks, Rev JH (John) 302, 303, 319
Brown, Rev Professor Dr BS (Basil) 31, 152, 169, 185, 198, 204, 219, 223, 235, 236, 277, 282, 294, 307, 333, 408, 474
Bryant, Rev CT 173
Bryson, Rev SM 175
Buber, Martin 312
Buckingham, Mr W (William) 30, 106
Buckingham Palace 230, 345
Bullock, Mr Luke 60, 61, 62, 82, 117
Bullock, Mr and Mrs Luke 143
Bullock, Mrs 169
Bunyan, John 230
Burchett, Dr P and Mrs (Peter) 339
Burleigh, Principal EC (Eric) 299, 356, 378
Burnard, Mr I (Ian) 306
Burnet, Mr and Mrs JH 75
Burnet, Mr JH 162, 163
Burnet, Mrs JH 191
Burniston, Miss G. (Gwen) 182
Burns, Mr RE 148
Burrow, Rev AL (Allan) 474
Burton, JN Rev and Mrs (John) 251
Burton, Mr F. 28
Burwood Christian Endeavour 55

Butler, Rev A (Albert) 95, 124, 128, 129, 132, 134, 197

C

Cairns 370
Cairns, Dr 33
Cairns, Dr GH 32
Calcutta 59
Callan, Pastor WM (Walter) 96
Callan, Rev K (Ken) 337
Calvin, John 144
Cambridge 287, 305
Cambridge University 281
Campbell, Mrs E (Eunice) 400
Campbell, Rev JC (Colin) 286, 357, 400
Canterbury Cathedral 395
Cardwell, Rev TJ (Tom) 290
Carey 230
Carey Baptist Church 344
Carey Baptist Grammar 227, 351
Carey, W (William) 129, 132
Cartwright, Mrs 117, 118
Cartwright, Rev WM (Montague) 12, 77, 133
Centenary Committee 354
Central Cumberland District Baptist Association 253
Chalmers, T (Thomas) 283
Chambers, Oswald 310
Chapel, GH Morling 162, 374, 384, 387, 389, 398, 405, 420
Chapman, Rev S (Samuel) 3, 157
Chapman, Wilbur 324
China Inland Mission 12, 252, 342, 344, 353
Christ in the Silence 111
Christian Commonwealth Crusade 198, 199, 201, 202, 203, 206, 210, 211
Christian Endeavour 204
Christian Endeavour Union. 106
Christian Leaders' Training College 356, 374

Christian Surfboard Rides 390
Christian, Pastor JF 31, 32
Christian View of God and the World. 18
Christian Workers' Training College 190, 202, 206, 216
Church Extension Department 386
Church, Mr FJ (Fred) 367
Churches of Christ 334
CJ Tinsley Medical Centre 339
Clark, Rev H (Henry) 83
Clatworthy, Rev E (Edward) 172, 173, 185, 197, 215, 290
Clatworthy, Rev E and Mrs (Edward) 185
Claughton, Mrs N 162
Coard, Pastor and Mrs J (John) 249
Cole, Dr A (Alan) 344
Coleman Affair 76
Coleman, Rev E (Enos) 20, 25, 32, 39, 42, 45, 46, 52, 81, 95, 164, 324, 343, 397
Coleman, Herbert 191
Coleman, Mr 76, 81
Coleman, Mrs NJ (Nancy Jane) 191
Coleman, Rev TR 19, 102, 183
Collaroy 244, 324
College Chronicle 163, 236
College Commemoration Service 238
College Commencement Service 26, 27, 30, 46, 60, 83, 91, 96, 136, 145, 149, 154, 163, 168, 178, 190, 202, 206, 240, 247, 251, 265, 281 363, 399
College Convention 136
College Council 25, 31, 35, 43, 53, 54, 55, 56, 57, 58, 60, 61, 62 70, 71, 72, 77, 83, 84, 94, 95, 98, 100, 102, 106, 107, 110, 114, 154, 174, 177, 186, 193, 205, 211, 221, 226, 258, 260, 262, 274, 285
College Day 85
College Graduation 189, 199, 205, 245, 249, 285, 389

College housekeeping. 78
College Month Prayer Meeting 243
College Motto 62
College Speech Day 95, 102, 103, 124, 148, 160, 171, 176
College Treasurer 98
Comilla 59
Committees - ex-officio 44
Commonwealth and Empire Baptist Congress 223, 225
Concord Repatriation Hospital 293
Connor, Rev JS (John) 320
Constable, Mrs C, 276
Co-operative Budget 243
Corlette, Rev Walter 344
Cousin, Miss H (Helen) 299
Cowling, Rev WS 24, 47
Cox, Rev J (Jim) 340
Craike, Rev GA 33, 40, 46, 48, 49, 74, 86, 97
Crawford, Mr JM 179
Criswell, Dr WA 280
Crowhurst, Rev DF (Don) 284
Croydon Public School 11
Cubis, Rev H (Horace) 25, 32, 39
Cumberland Association 87
Cumberland District Baptist Assoc=iation 41
Cumming, Evangelist J 161
Cundall, Rev A (Arthur) 349, 474
Cupit, Rev L A (Tony) 393
Curtis, Rev Dr A. (Andrew) 403
Curtis, Rev JS (John) 373, 397, 403
Cutler, Lady 376
Cutler, Sir Roden 376

D

Daily Light 282, 284, 288
Dain, Mr J later Bishop (Jack) 346, 406
Dale, Dr RW 308, 420
Dani 338
Davis, Mr D (David) 234
Davis, Mrs ML 268
Deakin, Dr A (Arthur) 232

Deane, Mrs R (Ruby) 382
Deane, Rev JH (John) 71, 73, 82, 84, 86, 90, 93, 101, 105, 107, 115, 125, 128, 129, 135, 136, 141, 142, 143, 147, 150, 153, 154, 164, 173, 180, 181, 184, 186, 188, 189, 192, 198, 211, 216, 219, 222, 263, 276, 277, 291, 373, 474
Deane, John H Memorial Lecture Block 382
Decision magazine 401
Denney, Dr J (James) 250, 308, 420
Denning, Rev EH 356
Dennis, Rev MHF (Michael) 272
Denominational Farewell 305
Deverell, Rev G (Gordon) 399
Dickens, C (Charles) 230
Dickman, Rev GF (George) 268
Dickson, Rev SA (Stanley) 341, 401
Diffey, Miss 78, 99
Diffey, Miss, 79
Director of Christian Education and Publication 359
Discipleship Campaign 125
Discourses in the Upper Room 178
Dixson, Sir Hugh 106
Doctor of Divinity 138, 200
Doctor of Philosophy 281
Doddridge, Philip 378
Dodge, Rev EE (Eric) 356
Donaldson, Miss VJ (Velma /Thornton) 274
Donaldson, Rev AC and Mrs (Charles) 274
Donaldson, Rev LCM 148
Doull, Rev WG 90
Drakeford, Rev Professor Dr JW (John) 172, 244, 254, 474
Driver, Rev A, (Alfred) 135
Drummond, Professor Henry 283, 329, 330
Dube, Rev AG (Albert) 181, 245, 405, 408
Duck-Chong, Adjutant 153

Dunkley, Rev FJ 17, 18, 65, 65, 69, 87, 103, 105, 106, 130, 134
Dykes, Mr KD (Kenneth) 232

E

East Bengal 182, 184, 197
East Pakistan 241, 347
Eastern Baptist Theological Seminary 205
Eastern Suburbs District Baptist Association 247
Eastwood campus. 143
Eden, Anthony 231
Edgeworth, Sir David 13
Edinburgh 230
Education Committee 18, 26, 83
Educational Board 67, 356
Educational Entrance 211
Edwards, Mrs 78
Eerdmans Publishing Company 220, 295
Elder 93
Eldridge, Rev Dr VJ (Victor) 300, 302, 361, 390, 474
Elements of New Testament Greek 94
Ellis, AJ 51
Emery, MrS 234
Emmett, Rev I (Ian) 400, 408
Emmett, Nance 400
England 106, 204, 227
Ephesians 302, 408
Epistle to the Hebrews 312, 405
Evangelical Alliance of India. 345
Evangelical Mysticism 139
Evangelistic and Propaganda Committee 31, 32, 33, 35, 56, 174
Evangelistic Committee 181
Evans, Rev HE (Harold) 152, 259
Evans, Mrs 259
Evans, Pastor FW 201
Evans, Rev KF (Keith) 397

Executive Committee 26, 27, 41, 46, 50, 55, 57, 58, 60, 61, 62, 68, 85, 93, 172, 185, 186, 194, 205, 207, 226, 257, 274
Executive Minute of Appreciation 409

F

'Fairmount' 114, 122, 123
Faith and Life Commission 223, 242, 248, 257, 263
Farrer, Mr FH 185
Farrer, Rev R (Ray) 221
Federal Board of Education 66, 227, 240
Federal Theological College 85
Fellowship of the Baptist College of NSW 128
Ferguson, Mr W (William) 320
First Epistle of John 93
Fleming, Rev Dr S (Sandford), 113, 200, 203, 240
Foote, Rev E. (Ern) 271
Foreign Mission Committee 69
Foreign Mission Conference 66
Foreign Missions. 35
Forsyth, PT (Peter Taylor) 307, 308, 309, 420
Forward Movement 155
Fourth Baptist Congress 55
Fox, Rev AC 30, 40
Francis of Assisi, 17, 46
Fraser, Mr S (Stuart) 289
Fraser, Rev RB 193

G

Gallagher, Rev F (Frank) 242
Gardiner, Temple 118
Garrett, Rev J (John) 304
Geale, Rev JS 9
General Secretary 198
General Superintendent 380
Germany 231
GH Morling Chapel Fund. 388

GHM 418
Gibbins, Rev W (William) 46, 53, 198, 369
Gibson, Rev Dr EG (Edward) 182, 185, 191, 213, 270, 271, 272, 281, 282, 288, 302, 319, 402, 474
Giles, Rev JD (John) 302
Gill, Rev R (Rowan) 380
Glad Tidings 318
Goble, Rev JH 3
Godwin, Rev JR (Jesse) 179, 268, 273
Golden Weddings 128, 129, 248, 330
Goldsworthy, Mr A (Andrew) 374
Gomm, Rev LJ (Leslie) 140, 145, 210, 340, 365
Goodman Memorial Hall 170
Goodman, Mr C (Colin) 146, 171, 367, 382
Goodman, Mrs D (Dorothy/Morling) 316, 324, 367, 381, 382, 383, 384, 385, 389, 418
Goodman, Rev P (Percy) 339
Goodman, Rev R (Robert) 136, 142, 146, 149, 152, 153, 156, 171, 155
Gordon, Mr RH (Roy) 156, 391
Gordon, Rev A (Alexander) 4, 22, 23, 27, 30, 33, 41
Gorton, The Hon JG (John) 378
Gossip, Rev AJ, 375
Governor of New South Wales 376
Governor-General of Australia 343, 392
Graduation Service 193, 215, 258, 300
Graham, Dr Billy 251
Graham, Ruth 220
Grammar School. 13
Granville deacons 84
Granville library 97
Granville College 60, 61, 65, 66, 72, 84, 95, 96, 109, 124, 149, 167, 169, 190, 398, 418

Granville residence 107
Gray, Mrs W (Winifred) 292
Gray, Rev CH (Charles) 73, 124,
Grigg, Principal Rev AJ 202, 211, 221, 330
Grinham, Rev D (David) 400
Groves Hostel 376
Guildford, Mr W (Wally) 156
Guinness, Dr H (Harry) 126
Guyon, Madame 420

H

Haigh, JR (Jack Raymond) 225
Half-Yearly Assembly 28, 52, 91
Ham, Rev RN (Ron) 298
Hammond, Archdeacon RBS 406
Hammond, Canon TC, 160
Hammond, Rev MW (Mervyn) 340
Handel's 'Messiah' 231
Hannah, Miss Grace 376
Harper, Rev DC 203
Harris, Miss F. (Flo) 219
Harris Scholarship. 216
Harrison, Rev LS (Sale) 24, 30, 32, 33
Harrison, Mr S (Samuel) 133
Harvey, Rev AJ 41, 75, 96, 109
Haughan, Messrs 82
Havelock, General 346
Havergal, Frances Ridley 287
Hayes, Mrs (Hilda) 234
Hayes, Rev PJ (Philip) 234, 276
Hayman, Miss 78
Hazel., Miss Una (Watson) 199
Heather, Rev EF (Edmund) 206, 223
Hedges, Mr and Mrs T, 158
Helm, Rev Dr JE (John) 474
Henry, Dr 41
Hercus, Dr. J (John) 302, 350
Hercus, Mr 78
Hercus, Mrs M (Margaret) 369
Hercus, Rev HG 182
Herring Road 268

Hibberd, Frederick 133
Higlett, Rev W (William) 25, 33, 40, 46, 48, 74, 84, 94, 323
Hillman, Miss A (Annie) 9, 189
Himbury, Principal DM (Mervyn) 297, 334
Hirt, Rev J (John) 300
Hoad, Rev FA 183, 241
Hockey family 107
Hockey, Rev EG 104, 153, 255
Hodge, Rev A (Alexander) 159
Holdsworth, Principal 21, 87, 317
Holland, Matron 322
Home Mission Committee 28, 32, 35, 57
Home Mission Society 53
Home Mission Superintendent 69, 77, 98, 100, 134, 179, 206, 218, 223
Home Work Scheme The 242
Horn, Rev AN (Neville) 179, 256, 316
Horton, Mr RF, 48
Hosea 304
Hostels Baptist 172
Hotston, Rev S. 30
House of the New World 389
Housekeeping staff 218
Howard, Mr M (Max) 110, 113, 119
Howes, Rev J (John) 236
Hubbard, Mr M 162
Hubble, Rev G (Gwynneth) 232
Hughes, Rev HP (Hugh Price) 19
Hughes, Principal W (William) 232
Hughes, RevHEstcourt 164
Hulme, Rev T (Trevor) 300

Hunter district 86
Hunter, J (Joseph) 46
Hunter, Rev and Mrs J (James) 92, 190
Hunter, Rev J (James) 61
Hutton, Dr JA 302

511

I

Iliffe, Mr AT 128
India 58, 344
Indian Renaissance 59
Ingleburn 374
Inter-School Christian Fellowship 319
Inter-Varsity Fellowship 415
Interpreter 421
Intervarsity Fellowship of Evangelical Unions 5, 202, 306
Ison, Mr J (John/Jack) 152, 156
Ison, Rev D (Doug) 182, 290

J

Jackson, Rev WD (David) 93, 228, 230, 359
Jamieson, Mr A (Alex) 392
Jarvis, Mrs B (Bessie) 392
Jarvis, Mr W (Wilfred) 387
Jarvis, Rev Dr WL (Wilfred) 105, 130, 178, 201, 233, 239, 260, 290, 294, 358, 392
Jenkins, Mr EH 138
Jennaway, Mr AH (Allan) 302
Jeskie, Mr HF 156
Jesus and the Life of Prayer 194
John 304
John, Rev Drakeford 244
Johnson, Dr CO (Oscar) 255
Johnson, E (Elizabeth) 386
Johnson, Mrs 255
Johnston, Rev HT 68, 320
Johnston, Mrs 68, 320
Johnston, Rev DN (Denis) 384
Jolly, Rev A (Archibald) 35, 42, 45, 50, 158, 171, 201
Jones, Dr G (Gordon) 229
Jones, Mrs O (Owen) 104
Jones, Dr R (Rufus) 324, 420
Jones, ES (Stanley) 256
Jowett, JH 250
Joyce, Mr AC 284

Joyramkura 348
Julian of Norwich 420

K

Katoomba Christian Convention 125, 135, 152, 161, 176, 177, 178, 185, 258, 343, 375
Kelly, T (Thomas) 372
Keswick Convention 140, 157, 410
Kevan, Rev Dr EF (Ernest) 305, 363
Kierkegaard, S (Soren) 255
Kilvert, Rev IF (Ivan) 270, 378
Kime, Rev Dr JR (Jim) 474
King, Mr BA (Bruce) 295
Kitchen, Mr JH (Howard) 336
Kompiam 334, 338
Kramer, Miss M (Mary) 255, 404, 405
Kroenert, Rev AA (Albert) 195
Kuyper, A (Abraham) 297

L

Ladies Zenana Society 146
Lady Secretary 207
Lamb, Rev W (William) 167
Lapolama 334, 338
Launceston 210, 369
Law, W (William) 420
Law-Davis, Rev H (Harold) 380
Lawrence, Brother 297
Lawrenson, Mr RH 172
Lawrenson, Mrs RH 114
Lay Preachers' Society 67
Leckie, Rev RW (Randolph) 302
Lee, Miss D (Dorothy/McMaster) 199
Leeder, Mrs AL 204
Leeder, Rev AL (Leonard) 49, 170, 323, 329
Leghorn, Rev RM (Robert) 127
LeQuesne 229, 230, 231
LeQuesne, Mr and Mrs CT 229
LeQuesne, Mr L. (Laurence) 279
LeQuesne, Mr CT 245

LeQuesne, Mrs 279, 349, 369
Lewis, CS 254
Lewis, Elvet 322
Library of Constructive Theology The 318
Licentiate of Theology 77
Lincolne, Mr 179
Lindstrom, Miss E (Esma/Wedge)186
Lindstrom, Miss J (Joy/Tinsley) 186
Lindstrom, Mr HG (Harry) 365
Lindstroms 344
Ling, Rev M (Murray) 290
Lloyd-Jones., Dr M (Martyn) 278
Loane, Archbishop ML (Marcus) 225, 370, 406
Lockyer, Rev CF (Charles) 189
London Bible College. 305
London University. 185
Long, Mrs I (Ivy) 30
Long, Rev EC (Egerton) 405
Longueville 385
Lord's Return, the. 196
LTh diploma 83
Luke's gospel 214
Lumb, Mr TB (Tom) 233, 371
Lusted, Mrs E (Ethel) 396
Lusted, Mr G. (George) 13
Lusted, Miss J (Joyce/Blatch) 166
Lusted, Mr AG (Tim) 388
Luther, Martin 231

M

MA 48, 49, 51
MacCullum, M (Mungo) later, Professor Sir 13
Macintosh, HR (Hugh Ross)308, 420
Mackay, JG 255
Mackay, Mr JC (Clifford) 259
Maclaren, Dr A (Alexander) 139
Maidment, Rev R (Ralph) 77
Main, Principal AR 176
Malayan Evangelical Mission. 202
Manley, Rev Professor Dr K (Ken) 302, 349, 474

Manning, Rev JG (Jack) 402
Marks, Rev EV (Eric) 123
Marks, Miss R (Ruth) 338
Marsh, Rev F (Frank) 179, 334. 350 362
Marshall, Dr 232
Marshall, Mrs EJ 247
Martin 82
Martin, Rev JC 69
Martiniere College 346
Masefield, John 421
Mason, Nancy 400
Master of Arts 21, 45, 55
Master of Arts gown 160
Matthew Henry 59
Maundrell, Mrs Annie (Ridge) 9
Maynard, Rev AC (Albert) 72, 167, 271, 342, 398, 399
Mayor of Ashfield 392
McArthur, Rev GJ (Gilbert) 292, 298, 356, 374, 474
McClendon, RevJames 233
McCullough, Rev M (Malcolm) 119, 281, 290, 335, 341
McDonald, Miss J. (Jean) 399
McDonald, Mrs E 319
McDonald, Rev SA (Syd) 87, 114, 155, 366, 373, 399, 400
McDougall, Rev T 44
McGee, Mrs M (Mary) 11
McKay, Joyce (Morling) 184
McKittrick, Rev S (Samuel) 297
McMaster, Ref FP (Fred) 199
Maidment, Rev R (Ralph) 77
Mead, Dr S. (Silas) 3, 157
Melbourne 354
Melbourne Bible Institute 224, 342
Melbourne College of Divinity 83, 85, 159, 204
Melbourne University 364
Memorial Service 408
Men's' Morning Meeting 76, 146
Metropolitan Bishop of India 344
Mianmin Valley 374
Middlesex Baptist Association 228

Mill, Mrs E (Ethel) 263
Mill, Rev DC (Douglas) 35, 117, 168, 280, 291, 343, 384, 390
Mill, Rev JD 117, 169, 182
Milson, Rev ER (Ernest) 167, 171
Ministerial Applicants' Committee 147
Ministers' Fraternal 67, 315
Ministers' Fraternal Meeting 180, 233
Ministers' Retreat 155, 183, 187, 191
Ministers' School of Theology 202, 354
Ministers' Wives Union 203
Minute of Appreciation 410
Missouri 355
Mitchell, Rev DF (Donovan) 30, 42
Mogensen, Vera 299
Monod, T (Theodore) 256
Moore, Rev BGW (Bernard) 354
Moore, Rev C (Cyril) 152, 184
Moore, Mrs E (Edna) 184
Morgan, G. Campbell 322
Morley, Rev J (John) 269, 341
Morling, Miss A (Annie) 9
Morling, Mr CA (Charles) 12, 31, 130, 146, 164, 189
Morling, Mrs D (Diana) 405
Morling, Miss D (Dorothy/Goodman) 27, 123, 146, 171, 218, 270, 316, 381
Morling, Miss E (Elaine) 32, 270, 300, 316, 324, 349, 355, 359, 361, 366, 417
Morling, Mr GGR (Gordon), 34, 183, 200, 344
Morling, Joyce (McKay) 344
Morling Lodge 367, 368
Morling Lodge. 386
Morling, Mr and Mrs CA 125, 128
Morling, Mrs G (Gladys/Rees) 26, 29, 34, 74, 97, 107, 125, 134, 188, 192, 202, 225, 227 230, 242, 251, 264, 270, 278, 279, 280, 282, 286, 292, 293, 303, 316, 317, 318, 321, 322, 325, 326, 327, 328, 398
Morling, Principal and Mrs. 52
Morling, Ruth (White) 385, 405
Morling, Miss S. (Sarah) 405
Morling, Hon. TR (Trevor) 74, 200, 216, 224, 316, 359, 380, 385, 405
Morling WC (William -Bill) 56, 173, 183, 192, 206, 403, 405
Morling, William (brother) 25, 142
Morling., George and Gladys 123
Morris, Dr Leon 265, 266
Morris, Rev SG and Mrs 228
Morris, Sydney 229, 278, 279, 317, 320, 345, 348, 349, 401
Morris, Sydney and Winifred 321
Morris, Mrs W (Winifred) 278, 349, 401
Mortdale 402
Morton, Mr HJ (Harry) 36, 201
Morton, Mrs HJ 201
Morton, Rev F (Frank) 232
Moscow 348
Moule, HCG (Handley) 49, 54, 308, 420
Mount Hagen 382
Mowll, Archbishop Rev Dr HWK (Howard) 406
Mt Hermon School 349
Mymensingh 59

N

Napoleon 231
Netherlands New Guinea 334
Nettle, Flying Officer Maurice A 169
Neville, RevA Horn 238
New Delhi 346
New Guinea 274, 337, 374, 401
New Guinea. 339
New Life Week. 240
New Orleans Baptist Theological Seminary. 403
New South Wales Stewards' Company 274

514

New Zealand 202, 358, 380, 389
New Zealand Bible Training Institute 188, 372, 373, 380, 389
Newcastle and District Association 93
Newcastle and Northern Districts Baptist Associati 253
Newcastle coalfields 86
Newport, Rev RE (Rowland) 50, 95, 109
Ngaruawahia 373
Nicholas, Rev DR (David) 160, 300, 316, 340, 401
Nicholls, Miss R (Rowena/Curtis) 403
Nicol, Robertson 92
North Baliem Valley 341
North Sydney Church 167, 392
Northbridge 400
Northern Baptist Convention 203
Northern District Baptist Association 32
Northern Rivers 218
Northern Suburbs District Baptist Association 35
Northern Suburbs District Baptist Association. 34
Northern Tablelands 237
Nowlan, Rev RH 407
NSW Assembly 223, 230
NSW Assembly Meetings 42
NSW Baptist College 22
NSW Baptist College Jubilee 369
NSW Baptist Home Mission Auxiliary 114
NSW Baptist Union 71
NSW College, 77
NSW College Bible School 127
NSW College Jubilee 370
NSW Education Committee 22
NSW Women's Home Mission Auxiliary 215
Nunn, Mr F (Frank) 104
Nunn, Mrs L. (Lillian) 104
NZ Bible Training Institute 393

O

Ogdens. 116
old Prof 419
Open Secret, The 48
Orama 110, 111
Orange 206
Ordaining Council 67, 68
Order of the British Empire 343, 345, 416
Ordination Council 67, 105
Ordination Service 105, 176, 179, 237, 242
Orford, Mrs CG 149
Orford, Rev CG 100, 106, 125
Oronsay 232
Orr, AD (Alan Douglas) 206
Orr, Dr J (James) 18
Orr, Mrs L (Lois) 206
Orr, Rev AH (Harry) 98, 119, 130, 184, 190, 206, 242, 248, 274, 277, 291, 295, 323, 361, 370, 408
Osborne, Rev K (Ken) 290
Otranto 227
Our Beloved Principal 36
Overseas Christian Fellowship 284
Overton, Mr 76
Owen, Rev JC (John) 237, 247

P

Packer, Mr JA (Jabez) 3, 148, 170
Paisley, D (Dorothy) 189
Pakistan 344
Palmer, Dr G (Gordon) 205
Papua New Guinea 336
Parish, Rev GS (Geoffrey) 179, 367
Parker, Rev G (Gray) 199
Parsons, Mr H (Horace) 90
Paterson, Mr and Mrs A (Arthur): 337
Paton, Rev H (Hugh) 168
Patten, Mr G (Gideon) 117
Pearce, Dr MG (Mark Guy) 419
Peffer, Mr FE (Frank) 283
Pennick, Miss H (Hilda) 372
Pentecostalism 3, 234, 237, 238,

239
Perkins, Rev LP (Leslie) 195
Perth Bible Institute 213
Philippians 302, 304
Phillips, Mr EJ 51, 159, 226, 262
Phillips, Rev WP (Probert) 70, 71, 72, 145
Pickering, Rev C 56
Pickup, Miss M (Myrtle) 324, 386
Pickup, Mrs HS 385, 386
Pickup, Rev RS (Robert) 40, 43, 145, 190, 191, 293, 302, 329
Pierce Memorial Shield 79
Pilgrim's Progress, 421
Pitt, Mr R (Robert) 230, 349
Pitt-Corbett Prize 216
Poona and Indian Village Mission 347
Pope, Rev RF (Reginald) 340
Port Hacking Baptist Camp 142
Port Moresby 334
Porter, Rev Dr T (Thomas) 3, 157, 244
Potter, Mr GS 170
Potter, Rev R (Ron) 184
Potter, Rev SM 131
Powell, Rev I (Ivor) 245
Presbyterian 45
President of the College 85
President of the Union 80, 84, 86, 93
President-General 5, 138, 333, 416
Presidential Address 84
Presidential year 83
Principal 43, 71, 357, 418
Principal - Acting 35, 39
Principal Emeritus 328, 418
Principal's Report 66, 73, 80
Principal's Residence 223, 234
Prior, Rev AC (Alan) 119, 302, 354, 359
Pritchard, Rev J (John) 235
"Prof", the 155, 341, 365
'Prof', the old 418
Protestant Reformation 163
Public Bible School 155

Purdy, Rev WA (Albert)) 350
Pymble Women's Guild 382

Q

Quakers. 420
Queen Elizabeth II 240
Queen's Counsel 380
Queen's Square Baptist Church 9
Queensland 304, 389
Queensland Baptist College 166
Queensland Baptist Ministers' Fraternal 409
Queensland College 191
Queensland College Commencement Service. 354
Queensland State cricket team 393
Queensland Union Centenary Assembly 248
Quest for Serenity 215
Quintilian 250

R

Raven, CE 220
Redman, Rev RK (Keith) 177, 179, 334
Rees, Elizabeth 39
Rees, Ethel 25
Rees, Miss G Gladys/Morling) 25, 417
Rees, Kenneth 169
Rees, Mrs 184
Reeve, Rev NF (Norm) 123, 190, 221, 235, 237
Reid, Bishop J (John) 406
Rentoul, Professor 21
Rice, Lieutenant C (Clive) 183
Ridden, Rev J (John) 74, 95, 271
Ridden, John and Ruby 98
Ridge, Miss A (Annie/Maundrell) 9
Ridgecrest 397
Ridley, Rev JG (John) 41, 100, 119, 194, 211, 237, 238, 240, 260, 281, 287, 293, 375
Rixon, Pastor CJ 32

Robert Goodman Memorial Hall 170
Roberts-Thomson, Principal Rev Dr E (Edward) 232, 288, 295, 318, 319, 350, 354, 411
Robertson, Rev J (Joshua) 91, 96, 97, 98, 99, 393
Robinson, Archdeacon RB 307, 314
Robinson, Rev F (Frank) 187, 192, 249
Robinson, Mr JA (Armitage) 215
Rofe, Miss M (Marcia) 192
Rogers, Rev ER (Ron) 289, 307, 323, 474
Rogers, Rev EJ 135
Roman Catholic 144
Rowe, Rev HJ (Harry) 256, 356, 403
Rowley, HH 220
Royal North Shore Hospital 404
Ruggles, Mr GW 136, 137, 143, 208
Ruggles, Mrs I D 207
Ruggles Wing 137, 145
Ryde- Gosford District Baptist Association 383

S

Sahu, Rev S (Subodh) 345, 386
Sales, Mr H (Herbert) 196
Sales, Mrs J (Jean) 196
Sales, Pastor HV 196
Sanders., Mr JO (Oswald) 302
Sanitarium Hospital 362
Sargent, Sir M (Malcolm) 231
Sau Valley 338
Saville, Rev GR (Gordon) 186
Saville, Sister 322
Sayer, Mrs 400
Schaefer, Rev RG, (Ray) 242
Schleiermacher 183
Schubert, Rev W (Walter) 192
Schubert, Rev and Mrs W (Walter) 358
Scripture Union 306
Scroggie, Dr G (Graham) 110, 113, 125, 126

Searle, Mr and Mrs 26
Searle, Mr G (George) 42, 270
Second Coming Convention 245, 282
Second Coming of Christ 4, 41, 203, 253
Secretary of the Baptist Union 70, 99
Secretary of the College Council 101
Sellars, Dr JF (James F) 321
Selwood, Mr and Mrs EG 9
Selwood, Mrs 9
Selwood, Mrs AM 189
Senior Girls' Missionary Union 127
Serampore 59
Shakespeare 302
Shakespeare, Rev LH (Leslie) 53, 55, 57, 58
Sharp, Rev S (Stephen) 30, 32, 33, 46, 48, 55, 56, 66, 72, 96, 129, 142, 205
Silver Jubilee 163
Simmons, Rev PN (Philip) 354
Singapore 344
Singh, Bahkt 347
Skillicorn, Mr and Mrs S 346
Skinner, Rev Professor Dr CP (Craig) 474
Smith, Pastor CT 67
Smith, Mr J (Joshua) 273, 284, 285, 294, 307, 360
Smith, Rev EC (Clive) 167, 210, 290
Smith, Rev FG (Fred) 99, 260
Smith, Rev FT (Fred) 67, 164, 170, 180, 290, 295
Smith, Rev KA 210
Smith, Rev RC (Ron) 193
'Social Law in the Spiritual World'. 324
Social Questions Committee 187
Some Fell on Good Ground 367
Soper, Rev JA (Albert) 9

South African Baptist Theological College. 232
South Australia 371
South Western Baptist Association 193
Southern Baptist Association Meetings. 228
Southern Highlands Christian Convention 249
Southwestern Baptist Seminary 244
Special Diploma Courses 300, 318
Special Diploma students 330
Speech Day 83, 167
Spencer, Rev IL (Ian) 354
Spurgeon Centenary 114
Spurgeon, Rev CH (Charles) 9, 44, 110, 312, 421
Spurgeon's 232
Spurgeon's College 166, 220
Spurgeon's Tabernacle 229
Squire, Mr SC (Stan) 299, 307, 323
St John of the Cross 420
St Therese 310
Starr, Rev FH (Frank) 119, 192, 208, 211, 213
Steed, Rev D (David) 26, 30
Stevenson, Mr D. (Dave) 79
Stewart, Mrs D (Dorothy) 404
Stewart, Rev Dr D (David) 198, 206, 212, 349, 373, 380, 404, 474
Stone, Rev FJ (Frank) 355
Streeter, Canon BH 217
Strugnell, Rev JR (John) 302, 352
Student Convention 173
Students' Associatio 83
Students' Association 23, 285
Students' Association Convention 263
Students' Convention 164, 264
Studies in the Epistle of James 199
Studies in the Song of Solomon 203
Sudan United Mission 205
Sudan United Mission. 167
Summa Supremo 214, 301
Sunday School anniversaries. 33
Sunday School Department 36
Swan, Rev EH 46, 54, 70
Sydney Bible Training Institute 274
Sydney City Mission 150
Sydney Evangelistic Crusade 156
Sydney Missionary and Bible College 101
Sydney Town Hall 376, 390
Sydney University 2, 80, 154, 201 306, 361, 416

T

Tabernacle The 142
Taj Mahal 346
Taligha 111
Taplin, Rev Dr DAC (Darcy) 300, 357, 377, 474
'Taringa' 64
Tasmania 204, 368, 369, 375
Tasmanian Baptist Assembly 358, 388
Taylor, J.Hudson 283, 342
Taylor, Miss C 167
Taylor, Sister M (Marjory) 374
Telefolmin 334, 338, 374
Terry, Deacon 76
Terry, Mr 81, 86, 87
Tersteegen 255
The Advertiser 386
The Australian Baptist 29, 36, 54, 57, 59, 93, 96, 102, 103, 128, 130 137, 138, 139, 144, 147, 156, 157 160, 164, 172, 173, 177, 178, 183, 187, 200, 201, 206, 211, 16, 220, 222, 224, 234, 235, 237, 238, 240, 242, 243, 244, 246, 47, 278, 280, 287, 289, 297, 306, 318, 329, 334, 337, 338, 339, 340 343, 345, 348, 359, 363, 365, 368, 371, 373, 380, 405
The Church's Heritage of Power 421, 471
'The Culture of the Soul' 92
The Educational Board 356

518

The Practice of the Presence of God 297
The Quest for a Deeper Serenity 391
The Quest for Serenity 11, 18, 126, 206, 218, 219, 222, 218, 222, 265, 282, 296, 334, 391, 396, 417
The Quest for the Spirit 391, 395
The Rest of Faith 208
The Saint and His Saviour 368
The Secret of Serenity 328
The Training of the Twelve 418
The Treasury of the New Testament 110
Third Baptist Congress 42
Thomas, G and O (Grace and Owen) 286
Thomas, Mr H 48
Thomas, Mr J 248
Thompson, Mrs M (Marion) 259, 287
Thompson, Miss BE (Betty Evelyn) 169
Thompson, Mr FP 174, 261
Thompson, Rev Dr JA (John) 253, 257, 259, 261, 262, 263, 264, 265, 266, 281, 287, 305, 364
Thompson, Rev LM (Lyle) 161, 214, 353
Thornton, Rev IB (Bruce) 274, 354
Tilbury Docks. 228
Tinsley, Joy and Allan 365
Tinsley, Mrs J (Joy) 365
Tinsley, Mrs M (Mldred) 385
Tinsley, Rev Allan and Joy 227, 242
Tinsley, Rev AS (Allan) 168, 186, 190, 335, 380
Tinsley, Rev Dr CJ (James) 3, 22, 77, 83, 85, 89, 94, 101, 135, 140, 143, 154, 177, 178, 181, 190, 192, 200, 239, 245, 250, 251, 263, 281, 287, 385
Tinsley, Rev Dr CJ and Mrs 248
Tiom 338

"To Be Near Unto God' 297
Toowong Cemetery 197
Tributes
Ashfield Municipal Council 428
Australian Baptist Missionary Society 427
Australian Evangelical Alliance 428
Baptist Union of Queensland 427
Robinson, Bishop (later Archbishop) DWB 428
Church Extension Department - South Australian 427
Thompson, Dr JA 429
Hunter District Baptist Association Ministers' 427
Oboohof, Mr AI, Secretary, Slavic Missionary Soc 429
Dickenson, Mr A (Arnold) - former Honorary Legal Adviser 429
NSW Baptist Homes Trust - Canberra Regional Board 428
One from very many of his men 429
Vose, Principal GN Western Australian Baptist College 429
Queensland Baptist Ministers Fraternal 427
Scripture Union 428
Whitley College - Victorian Baptist Theological College 427
Wilson, Rev J. (James), A Students Tribute 430
========================
Trench, Archbishop 408
Triennial Assembly Meetings 132, 198, 220
Tuckwell, Mr D (David) 356
Turk, Mr PV 99

U

Uncle John 183
Underhill, Miss E (Evelyn) 283, 420
Union Secretary 94
Upper Room Discourses 180, 408
Upwey Christian Convention 102, 135, 143, 161, 194, 200, 205

V

Vaughan, Mr TH 11, 96
Vaughan, Rev DH (Doug), 233, 352
Vaughan, Rev Doug and Mrs Rosemary 337
Vice-Principal 79, 80, 207, 212
Victorian Baptist College 22, 53, 77, 164, 191, 235, 330, 333
Victorian Baptist Ministers' Fraternal 299
Vose, Rev Dr GN (Noel) 195, 214, 219, 224, 227, 270, 271, 272, 288, 334, 349, 474

W

W.A. Commencement Service 369
Waldock Hospital 404
Waldock, Mrs 204
Waldock, Mrs AJ 192
Waldock, Professor AJA 216
Waldock, Rev Dr AJ (Arthur) 19, 31, 35, 50, 192, 216, 319
Walker, Mr RE (Ron) 143, 150, 165, 167, 270, 286, 294, 302, 307, 350, 402
Wallace, Mrs V (Vera) 299
Wallis, Rev RH (Roy) 241
Warriner, Rev Principal TC (Tom) 191, 202, 211, 305
Watson, Dr EL 88
Watson, Rev Dr EH (Ernest) 119, 138, 173, 244, 258
Watson, Rev HK (Keith) 199, 333
Watts, Mr EW 267
Watts, M (Margery) 171
Waugh, Pastor G (Geoff) 318
Wearne, Pastor W. 20
Webb, Rev K (Ken) 379
Wedge, Rev JGL and Mrs 389
Wedge, Rev JGL (Leigh) 186
Weller, Rev JJ 105
Wells, Mr MA 195
Wesley-Smith, Adeline 351

West Papua (Irian Jaya) 338
West Pennant Hills 343
West, Rev H (Henry) 348
Westcott, Bishop BF (Brooke Foss) 308, 314, 420
Western Australia 204, 274, 384, 403
Western Australian Union 193
Western Baptist Association 90
Western District Baptist Association 162
Westminster Chapel 277
Whale Mr AA 137, 161
Whale, Miss AP (Anne Patricia) 225
Whale, Rev Dr AT (Albert) 17, 21, 50, 84, 93, 94, 137, 140, 164, 187, 215, 221, 282, 317, 325, 357, 358, 368
Whale, Miss C (Constance Marjorie) 181
Whale, Rev Dr and Mrs AT 214, 330
Whale, Fred 89
Whale, Mr RN 89, 90, 225
Whale, Mrs RN 187 225
White, Miss D (Dorothy) 107
White, Dr P (Paul) 194
White, Mr H (Hilton) 119
White, Miss J (Jean) 183
White, Rev JE (John) 187
White, Mr AS (Alfred) 36, 58, 60, 69, 107, 115, 226
White, Mr CA 99
White, Mr W (William) 68, 149, 162
White, Mr and Mrs AS 183, 369
White, Mrs J (Joan) 324, 305
White, Rev H (Hilton) 210
White, Rev VJ (Victor) 290, 370
White., Dr W (Weeks) 305
Whyte, Rev A (Alexander) 250
Wilkin, Rev Professor Dr FJ, 42, 85, 87, 161
Wilkins, Rev A (Arthur) 119, 336, 370, 408
Willandra Village 390

Williams, Mr A (Alan) 152
Williams, Mr E. (Evan) 398
Williams, Rev MC (Mel) 214
Williams, Rev JD (John) 336, 338, 408
Willis, Rev F (Frank) 302
Willis, Rev VN (Victor) 252
Wilson, B (Briton) 39
Wilson, Rev JC (Jim) 302
Wilson, Rev KW (Keith) 272
Wilson, Rev JB and Mrs (John) 185
Wilson, Sir LO (Leslie Orme), 131
Wilson, Rev JB (John) 200
Winchester 228
Windsor Castle 112
Wingfield, Rev WH (William) 183
Winn, Miss E (Edna) 162
Winn Mr FW 192, 269
Winn, Mr and Mrs FW 90, 162
Winn, Miss T (Thirza) 90
Wishart, Mr 112
Women's Home Mission Auxiliary 164
Wood, (later, Professor Sir) George A 13
Wood, Professor GA 46, 51
World Council of Churches 207, 211, 219, 319, 333
Wright, Miss I (Ivy) 214
Wright, Miss N 177
Wright, Rev BG (Gilbert) 3, 21, 182, 184, 212, 221, 222, 223 231, 242, 258, 262, 264, 265, 307, 308, 323, 354, 356, 357, 361, 364, 407, 408, 415, 474
Wykes, Mr A 241
Wykes, Rev EG (Eric) 172, 188, 220, 241, 318

Y

Yates, Mr 26
YMCA 195
Yoritomo 175
Young, Dr. D (Dinsdale) 110
Young Men's Missionary League, 11
Young, Mr JA 123, 128, 135
Young., JA Mr and Mrs 123
Young, Mr L (Leslie) 206

Z

Zenana Missionary Society 105
Zurich 231

www.ingramcontent.com/pod-product-compliance
Lightning Source LLC
Chambersburg PA
CBHW020300010526
44108CB00037B/167